William Henry Green

A Hebrew Chrestomathy

Lessons in Reading and Writing Hebrew

William Henry Green

A Hebrew Chrestomathy
Lessons in Reading and Writing Hebrew

ISBN/EAN: 9783337420116

Printed in Europe, USA, Canada, Australia, Japan

Cover: Foto ©Thomas Meinert / pixelio.de

More available books at **www.hansebooks.com**

A

HEBREW CHRESTOMATHY;

OR,

LESSONS

IN

READING AND WRITING HEBREW.

BY

WILLIAM HENRY GREEN,

PROFESSOR IN THE THEOLOGICAL SEMINARY AT PRINCETON, N. J.

NEW YORK:
JOHN WILEY & SON,
15 ASTOR PLACE.
1872.

PREFACE.

THE value of grammatical exercises and of selected courses of reading, carefully annotated to suit the wants of beginners, has long been recognized in the classic tongues. But the study of Hebrew, even in our best institutions, is prosecuted at comparative disadvantage for lack of such aids. The student plods laboriously through the Grammar, adding paradigm to paradigm and rules to rules, until his memory is overloaded with the confused and ill-digested mass. He is then set at translating, but is embarrassed in his use of the Lexicon by his imperfect familiarity with the letters, and especially by the difficulty of distinguishing the radical or primary forms of words in all the metamorphoses to which they are subjected from prefixes, suffixes and inflections; and what renders this process yet more vexatious and trying is, that words thus painfully sought for are forgotten almost as soon as they are learned, and must be looked for afresh perhaps in the very next sentence. He is next confronted by the idioms of the language in the arrangement of words, the structure of sentences, and the use of peculiar forms of expression. Unless these are pointed out, and the true key furnished for their explanation, the finer and more delicate sort will likely be unnoticed, while others will be passed over with a vague and imperfect understanding of their real nature.

Those methods may well be distrusted, which propose to impart knowledge without proportionate toil. No valuable result can ever be gained without effort. The acquisition of a language involves a familiar acquaintance with its grammatical forms, the meanings of its words, and the entire multitude of its idioms: and this cannot be secured without time and labour. The problem is not how these can be dispensed with, but how they can be expended in the most profitable manner and be made productive of the largest results. No doubt energy and pains may be successful in surmounting the obstructions which beset the most rugged path. But if the way were first carefully prepared, unnecessary obstacles removed, and a helping hand given in case of need, a wearisome toil might be converted into a pleasant occupation, and patient diligence would be crowned with an ampler reward.

The thorough mastery of the Hebrew, as of any other tongue, implies a facility both in translation and in composition. These are so distinct that exclusive occupation with one will not beget the other, and yet so related that neither can be perfect unless both are possessed. While, therefore, the former is the end principally aimed at, the latter may serve an important purpose as subsidiary to it. Accordingly the first part of this Chrestomathy is devoted to the work of analysis and translation; the second part to that of composition.

The first part begins with a series of exercises designed to accompany the original study of the Grammar. Those on page 1 are for the practice of the student in the orthographic rules contained in the sections there designated. Those on pages 2–8 illustrate the verbal paradigms. These are to be translated, and each form should at the same time be analyzed or divided into its significant elements, the meaning of each separately stated, and the law of their combination given. Thus, קְטַלְתֶּם *ye* (masc.) *have killed* consists of קְטַל, the ground form of the Kal pret. § 82. 1 and תֶּם abridged from 2 m. pl. pron. אַתֶּם § 85. 1. *a* (1), the former losing its pretonic Kamets in the combination § 85. 2. *a* (4). And יִקְטְלוּ *they* (masc.) *will kill* consists of יְ from 3 m. pron. הִיא § 85. 1. *a* (2), which before a vowelless letter becomes יִ § 85. 2. *a* (1), and קְטֹל const. inf. § 84. 2, the basis of the future § 84. 3, which loses its vowel § 85. 2. *a* (2) before וּ abridged from the plur. ending וּן § 85. 1. *a* (2).

In order to save beginners the needless labor, discouragement, and loss of time incident to using a dictionary, before they have learned to trace the forms, with which they meet, to their roots or stem-words, a special vocabulary has been prepared for the first passage selected from the Old Testament, Gen. i.–iii., explaining every word in connection with the verse in which it first occurs. The student who masters, as he should, each verse as he proceeds, and is careful to remember what he has acquired, will, at the end of these three chapters, be acquainted with 250 words, most of which are of frequent occurrence. And if he steadfastly pursues this method to the end of the Chrestomathy, continuing to hold all the ground that he has gained and keeping in memory the words which he has learned, he will find himself in possession of a considerable proportion of the entire stock of words contained in the Hebrew Bible, and will be able to read in almost any part of it with tolerable ease.

The passages selected for reading have been chosen with a view to their intrinsic interest, their progressive difficulty, and the variety of their style and character. The notes are at the outset chiefly grammatical and of the most elementary kind, directing the attention of the student to those matters of form and of construction, which he is expected thenceforward to investigate for himself. The aid thus given both by the suggestion of principles and by references to the Grammar, is gradually withdrawn as the presumed progress of the student renders it superfluous; and questions of criticism and interpretation are admitted to greater prominence, the knowledge of the language being thus applied, as it is gained, to its most important end, the exposition of the Holy Scriptures.

This Chrestomathy is not designed to supply a complete course of Hebrew reading for theological students. Its aim is not to supplant the more general study of the Old Testament in the original, but to prepare the way for it. It has long been, and still is, a favourite wish of the author that a knowledge of Hebrew might be required in order to admission into our theological seminaries. If students entered upon their theological course with such a measure of forwardness in Hebrew as is required in Greek, the two great departments of Biblical learning could be brought nearer to a level. The time now spent upon mere grammatical routine and elementary linguistic training might then be devoted to the more serious work of the interpreter. In view of the growing importance of Old Testament studies, which bid fair to be yet more than they have been the battle-ground of Christianity and unbelief, and in view of the

vastness and momentous character of subjects, which from the
limited time afforded are now of necessity utterly neglected or
but slightly touched, the suggestion is here earnestly made to my
brethren in theological instruction and in ecclesiastical supervi-
sion, whether that cannot be done in this country which the last
General Assembly of the Free Church of Scotland has recommended there.   Cannot the study of Hebrew be begun and some
satisfactory progress made in it in our colleges and academies?

It may be thought that this would be to crowd what belongs
purely to a single profession into institutions of a broader basis
and a more general character.   But why might it not be introduced as an optional study, as it is in the Prussian gymnasia, and
as the modern languages are in the most of our collegiate institutions?   Much might be said to vindicate for the Hebrew
another than a purely professional interest, and to challenge for
it the attention of the liberally educated generally, both as the
representative of a family of tongues strikingly different from
that with which we are most familiar, and as containing a litera-
ture venerable from its antiquity and sacred as the gift of inspi-
ration, with its products of exalted genius and its peculiarities
as remarkable as those of the people amongst whom it had its
origin.

If, however, this be aspiring to more than can be hoped for,
and the theological curriculum must remain as it is, this volume
is offered as a manual for the first year of Hebrew study.   Its
size has been graduated by the amount supposed possible for
that term, and it has been prepared with the definite design
throughout of fitting students to appreciate and profit by those
lectures in criticism and interpretation which form the more advanced parts of their course.   The text adopted is, with a few
slight corrections from other sources, that of Hahn, except in the
Psalms, where Baer's new and accurate edition has been followed.
In the preparation of the notes the best critical commentators
have been consulted; and though the pedantry of parading their
names in so elementary a work has been avoided, this opportunity is taken of acknowledging in the general the aid which has
been derived from these sources upon every page.

CONTENTS.

HEBREW CHRESTOMATHY.

PART FIRST.

ANALYSIS AND TRANSLATION.

SHIN AND HHOLEM § 12.

The sections referred to throughout these exercises are those of Green's Hebrew Grammar.

שְׁלֹשִׁים, יָשֹׁב, יְשֻׁבַּח, קְשֹׁא, נָשֹׂא, נִשָּׂא, גֹּשׁוּ, יְקְשֹׁוּן, בָּאֹשׁ, עָשֹׂה,
עָשֹׂה, קֹשֵׁט, שֹׂנְאִי, שֹׁבֵן.

THE VOWEL LETTERS § 13.   ALEPH OTIANT § 16. 1.

בְּאֵר, לַאדֹנָי, הָאסַפְסֻף, הָלְכִיא, אֱוִיל, אֵין, אֵיתָן, הֹנֶה, לֹו, יִישַּׁר,
יִיחַל, נָאוֶה, צָוֹן, שְׁדֹו, לַאמֹר, מַלְאָה, תֹּחֶד, פָּנַי, זוּ, הֹוי, אֵירְסַיְרָם,
מַלְאָה, מַלְאָה, אִנְחַר, צַוָּאר, יְרָאוּ, לֹוָא, צֵרֵא.

KAMETS AND KAMETS HHATUPH § 19. 2.

לָקָם, מְלָכִים, דִּבְקָה, לָח, פָּרֹשׁ, פָּקַדְנִי, נֶהֶרוּ, שֶׁכְנָת, שָׁפַה, יְבֹאוּם.

PERFECT VERBS.

1. PARADIGM OF קָטַל. KAL.

Analyze and translate the following forms. The figures annexed to certain forms denote the number of times that they may be found in the Paradigm.

קְטַלְתֶּם, קָטְלָה, קְטַלְּי, קָטַל, קָטַלְתְּ, קָטַלְתִּי, קָטַלְתֶּן, קָטַלְתְּ, קָטַלְתִּי,
יִקְטְלִי, תִּקְטֹל (2), נִקְטֹל, יִקְטֹל, תִּקְטֹלְנָה (2), אֶקְטֹל, תִּקְטְלוּ, תִּקְטְלִי,
קִטְלִי, קְטֹל (2), קָטֹל, קְטֹלְנָה, קָטוֹל, קְטוּל.

2. PARADIGM OF קָטַל. NIPHAL.

נִקְטַלְתָּ, נִקְטְלוּ, נִקְטַלְתִּי, נִקְטַלְתֶּן, נִקְטְלָה, נִקְטַלְתִּי, יִקָּטֵל,
נִקְטַלְתֶּם, נִקְטַל, הִקָּטֵל (2), הִקָּטְלְנָה, הִקָּטְלִי, הִקָּטֵל, תִּקָּטְלִי (2),
אֶקָּטֵל, יִקָּטֵל, תִּקָּטְלוּ, תִּקָּטְלִי, נִקָּטֵל, תִּקָּטַלְנָה (2).

3. PARADIGM OF קָטַל. PIEL AND PUAL.

קִטַּלְתִּי, קִטַּלְתִּי, קִטַּלְתְּ, קִטַּלְתְּ, קִטֵּל, קִטְּלוּ, קִטַּלְתֶּם, קִטְּלָה, קִטְּלוּ,
קִטַּלְתֶּן, קֻטַּל (2), קְטַלְתִּי, קֻטְּלָה, קֻטַּלְתְּ, קֻטְּלִי, קֻטַּלְתֶּן, קֻטַּלְתְּ,
קֻטַּלְתֶּם, קֻטַּל (2), מְקַטֵּל, קַטֵּל, קַטְּלוּ, קַטְּלָה, מְקֻטָּל, קֻטְּלִי, קֻטְּלִי,
יְקַטֵּל, תְּקַטֵּל (2), תְּקַטֵּלְנָה (2), אֲקַטֵּל, נְקַטֵּל, אֲקַטֵּל, תְּקַטְּלִי,
תְּקַטְּלוּ, נְקַטֵּל, תְּקַטֵּלְנָה (2), תְּקַטְּלִי (2), יְקַטֵּל, תְּקַטֵּל (2), יְקַטֵּל,
יְקַטְּלוּ, תְּקַטְּלוּ.

4. PARADIGM OF קָטַל. HIPHIL, HOPHAL AND HITHPAEL.

הָקְטַל (2), הִתְקַטֵּל (3), הֻקְטַל (2), הִקְטִיל, הִקְטַלְתֶּם, הִתְקַטַּלְתֶּם,
הִקְטַלְנִי, הָקְטְלָה, הִקְטַלְתְּ, הִקְטַלְתֶּן, הִתְקַטַּלְתִּי, הִתְקַטֵּלְנִי, הָקְטְלָה,
הָקְטַלְתֶּם, הָקְטַלְתְּ, הֻקְטְלוּ, הִתְקַטֵּל (2), הִקְטַלְתִּי, הִתְקַטַּלְתִּי, הִקְטַלְוֹ,
הִקְטַלְתִּי, הִקְטַלְתְּ, הִתְקַטֵּל, הִתְקַטֵּלְתְּ, הֻקְטְלָה, הִקְטִילוּ, הִקְטַלְתֶּן,
הִתְקַטַּלְתֶּן, הַקְטֵל, מַקְטֵל, מְקַטֵּל, מְקָטָּל, הֻקְטְלוּ, הִתְקַטְּלִי, מַקְטִיל,
הָקְטֵל, הָקְטַלְנָה, הִתְקַטֵּלְנָה, הִתְקַטֵּל, הֻקְטַל, הַקְטִילִי, הֻקְטְלָה, יַקְטִילוּ,
נִקְטְלוּ, יִתְקַטְּלוּ, תִּתְקַטֵּל (2), תַּקְטֵלְנָה (2), אַקְטִיל, נֻקְטַל, תְּקֻטַּלְנָה (2),

יַקְטִיל, תָּקְטֵל (2), אֶתְקַטֵּל, נִתְקַטֵּל, תִּתְקַטַּלְנָה (2), תַּקְטִילִי, יָקְטֵל,
יִתְקַטֵּל, תַּקְטִיל (2), תִּתְקַטְּלִי, תָּקְטְלִי, תַּקְטִילוּ, אַקְטֵל ,תָּקְטְלוּ, נַקְטִיל.

5. The entire Paradigm of קָטֵל.

Supply the vowels. The figures denote, as before, the number of places
in the paradigm represented by the preceding form.

קָטַלְתֶּן (3), תַּקְטִלִי (5), קְטָלֵנִי (2), נִקְטַלְתֶּם, הַקְטִילוּ (2), קָטַלְתָּ (2), הָקְטַלְתְּ (4),
יַקְטִיל, תִּתְקַטְּלוּ, הִתְקַטַּלְנָה, תִתְקַטַּלְתְּ (2), קָטוֹל (2), הָקְטַלְתָּ (2), אַקְטִיל,
הָקְטַלְתֶּם (2), הָקְטֵל (8), יִתְקַטֵּל, הִתְקַטֵּל (4), יַקְטִילוּ, הַקְטִילָה, הַקְטֵלִי,
תַּקְטַלְנָה (12), קְטָלֻנִי (3), הָקְטַל (10), קָטֵל (3), מַקְטִיל (3), הִקְטִילוּ (2), הִתְקַטֵּלָה,
נִקְטַל, תִּתְקַטֵּל (2), הִתְקַטֵּלוּ, מַקְטִיל, הַקְטִיל (2), נִקְטְלָה, קָטְלוּ (5),
אַקְטֵל (5), אֶתְקַטֵּל, תַּקְטִילִי, נִקְטַלְתְּ (2), הַקְטִילוּ (5), נִתְקַטֵּל, מִתְקַטֵּל,
תַּקְטִילוּ, הִתְקַטַּלְתֶּם, הַקְטִילֶנָּה (2), נִקְטָלוּ, קְטָלְתַנִי (3), יִקְטֹל (5), נַקְטֵל (7),
תִּתְקַטְּלֶנָּה (2), הִתְקַטֵּל (2), הִקְטַלְנוּ (2), הִקְטַלְתִּי (2), נִקְטַלְתִּי (2), קְטָלִי (2), נָקְטַלְתֶּן,
קָטַלְתְּ (6), יִקְטְלוּ (5), הַקְטִילִי, הָקְטַלְתֶּן (2), יִתְקַטְּלוּ, קָטַל (11),
קָטְלָה (3), נִקְטָלוּ, הִקְטַלְתִּי (2), קָטַלְתֶּם (3), יִתְקַטְּלוּ, הִתְקַטַּלְתִּי,
הִתְקַטְּלִי, תַּקְטִיל (2), הִתְקַטַּלְתֶּן, הִתְקַטְּלִי.

6. Additional Examples.

See the Vocabulary, pp. 57 ff. for the meanings of the verbs in this and
the following exercises.

1. The following long vowels, viz.: Hholem of the Kal infinitives § 87,
future § 88 and active participle § 90, Shurek of the Kal passive participle
§ 90, Hhirik of the ultimate of Hiphil § 94, Tsere of the Hiphil absolute infinitive § 94. b, and final Kamets of the Preterite masc. sing. § 86. b (2 m.), though
commonly written as in the paradigm, may be expressed with or without
their appropriate vowel letters, e. g., יְשֵׁב or יְשֵׁיב.

2. Kibbuts and Kamets Hhatuph are occasionally exchanged in the Pual
§ 93. a and Hophal § 95. a ; e. g., מָרְבָּק Ho. part. for מָרְבָּק.

3. When the final radical is נ or ת and the personal endings begin with
the same letter, they are united by Daghesh-forte § 86. b (2 m.), § 88 (2 and
3 f. p.); e. g., הִשְׁבַּתִּי for הִשְׁבַּתְתִּי.

נְסֹגַּר, הִבְדִּילוּ, דְּבַקְתֶּם, הִתְקַדֵּשׁ, יִמְשֹׁל, יִבְדַּל, שֻׁכַּן, תַּלְבִּישׁ, תַּשְׁלִילוּ,
יִשְׁרְצוּ, רֶמֶשׂ, הַשְׁבִּית, שָׁמֹר, הִדְבַּקְתִּי, מְקֻדָּשׁ, לָבוּשׁ, נִכְבָּשָׁה, אַמְטִיר,
תַּפְדִּתִי, תַּלְבִּשׁוּ, קֻדַּשְׁתִּי, הִבְדִּילָה, הִבְדַּלְתֶּם, מָרַדְתַנוּ, שָׁמַרְנוּ, מָרַדְתָּ, יְקַדְּשׁוּ, תִּלְבַּשְׁנָה,

הֻקְדָּשׁ, הַטֻּבֵּל, הִשָּׁמְרִי, שֻׁבַּנְתִּי, מֻשְׁלַחַת, תְּשֻׁלַּח, הִתְקַדַּשׁוּ, כֻּבַּשׁ,
תִּשְׁבַּחְנָה, סֻגְרוּ, הִסָגִיר, יֻבָּשׁ, יְתְקַדֵּשׁ, יִתְקַדָּשׁוּ, שָׁבְתָה, יֻקְדָּשׁ,
מַמְטִיר, חֻפַּלְתִּי, יֻבָּל, הֻשְׁבַּתֶּם, יֻקְדָּשׁ, אֻשְׁתַּמֵּר, הֻמְשַׁל, סֻגְרִי, אֻקְדַּשׁ,
שֻׁבַּל, נִשְׁבְּתִי, נִשְׁבֵּינוּ, סֻגַּרְתְּ, שֻׁמַר.

7. Forms modified by the Accents, Makkeph and Euphonic Letters.

1. The pause accents § 36. 2. *a*, lengthen short vowels, restore such as have been dropped in the course of inflection, convert simple Sh'va to Seghol, and compound Sh'va to the corresponding long vowel § 65.

2. The removal of the accent from a long mixed ultimate, whether by shifting it to the penult § 85. 1, or by Makkeph § 43, occasions the shortening of the vowel § 64. 1.

3. The original final Nun is sometimes retained in those verbal forms which end in *o*, viz., 2 and 3 m. pl. future § 88, and more rarely 3 pl. preterite § 86. *b*. Nun is also occasionally added to 2 f. s. future which ends in *i* § 88.

מְשָׁל, שָׁכֵן: שָׁבְתָה, דְּבָקִי, וְשָׁמְרוּ, לָבָשְׁתָּ: הֻקְדָּשְׁנוּ, שְׁמַרְתִּי:
הִתְקַדֵּשׁ, קֻדָּשׁ, מְשָׁל, יִשְׁמֹר, תִּמְשָׁלִי, אֶשְׁכֹּן, יִקְדָּשׁ, תִּדְבָּק,
תִּלְבָּשִׁי, יְדָבְּקִי: יִשְׁבְּתִי: יִסָגֵרוּ: יְקֻדַּשׁוּ: תִּדְבָּקִין, תִּשְׁמְרוּן, הִשָּׁמֵר.

8. Paragogic and Apocopated Future and Imperative, and Vav Conversive.

The signification of the tenses when preceded by Vav Conversive is not absolute but relative, being dependent upon the time denoted by the antecedent verb or expression. In this and the following exercises the preterite with Vav Conversive should be translated as though conditioned by a previous future or imperative; and the future with Vav Conversive as though conditioned by a previous preterite.

וְשָׁרַץ, יִכְבְּשׁוּ, וְהִבְדַּלְתָּ, וְקִדַּשְׁתָּי, וַיַּמְטֵר, וַיִּשְׁבֹּת, וַיְקַדְּשׁוּ, יִדְבָּק,
תִּשָּׁצֵל, אֶשְׁכְּנָה, נִסְגְּרָה, וָאֶשְׁתַּפְּרָה, שָׁמְרָה.

9. Paradigm of קָטַל with Suffixes.

קְטָלֵינוּ, קְטָלוֹ, קְטָלִי, קְטַלְתֶּם, קְטָלַתִּיהָ, קְטַלְתִּים (2) קְטָלָהּ, קְטָלְךָ,
קְטַלְתִּים, קְטַלְתָּ, קְטַלְתָּנִי, הִקְטִילַךָ, קְטָלוֹ, קְטָלֵנִי (2), יִקְטְלֶהָ,

יִקְטְלוּנִי, יִקְטְלֵם, יִקְטְלֵנִי (2), קְטָלַנִי, קְטָלֶם, קְטָלֶם, קְטָלָם, קְטַלְתּוּנוּ,
קְטַלְתָּה, קְטָלְתָּה, קְטָלְתֵּךְ, קְטָלֵז, יִקְטְלֵנִי, הִקְטִילְךָ, יִקְטְלֵם, קְטַלְתָּיו (2),
קְטָלָה, קְטָלְתָּה, קְטָלָה, קְטָלֶךָ, קְטַלְתָּיִךְ, קְטַלְתָּיהִי, קְטָלֵנִי, קְטַלְתָּיז (2),
יִקְטְלֵךְ, קְטָלֶחֶם, קְטָלֵךְ, קְטָלֵךְ, קְטָלְתָּיהָ, קְטַלְתָּיו, קְטָלִי, קְטַלְתָּנִי,
קְטָלוּהוּ, קְטָלֵים, קְטָלָם, קְטָלָה, קְטָלֵנִי (2), קְטָלֵנִי, יִקְטְלוּכֶם,
קְטַלְתָּיךָ.

10. Other Perfect Verbs with Suffixes.

1. Verbal forms ending in *î* or *û* often drop their final vowel letter before suffixes § 11. 1. *a*, § 104. *l*.

2. Kal Futures and Imperatives with *a*, retain it even before those suffixes which cause the rejection of *ô* § 105. *d*, § 125. 1.

שְׁמָרֵנִי, קִדַּשְׁתָּם, וְהִלְבַּשְׁתָּיו, יְסָגְרֶךָ, תַּסְגִּירֵנִי, אַסְגִּירֶךָ, תִּשְׁמְרֵם,
וַיִּלְבָּשׁוּם, כְּבָשָׁה, הִבְדִּילֵם, שָׁכְנֵי, וְקִדַּשְׁתּוֹ, הִמְשִׁילָם, וְהִשְׁבַּתִּיךְ,
סְגָרֵנִי, הִדְבִּיקֵהִי, וְאַלְבִּשֵׁךְ, יַסְגִּירֵנִי, לְבָשֵׁם, אֶזְמְרֶנָּה, הַקְדֵּשׁוֹ,
הַשְׁמִילָם, שְׁמַרְתָּיו, הִבְדַּלְתָּם, הִדְבִּיקָתָּיו, קַדְּשׁוֹ, קִדְּשׁוֹ, הִסְגִּירָם,
וַיִּלְבָּשֵׁהִי, שְׁמָרֵם, שְׁמָרֵם, הִסְגַּרְתָּנִי, תִּשְׁמְרֶךָ, תַּמְשִׁילֵהִי, הִשְׁבַּתִּים,
אֶלְבָּשֶׁנָּה, שְׁמָרֵנִי, קִדַּשְׁתִּי, יִשְׁמְרֶךָ, הִקְדַּשְׁתָּיו, יַסְגְּרֵנִי, שְׁמָרָה,
וְקִדַּשְׁתִּי, יַבְדִּילֵם.

IMPERFECT VERBS.

11. Pe Guttural Verbs.

Verbs with ר in the root are in these exercises classed with perfect verbs, unless ר is the second radical and the verb used in the Piel species.

1. The guttural sometimes has simple instead of compound Sh'va § 112. 5.

2. In the Hiphil preterite (2 m. s. and 1 c. s.) ִ becomes ָ when Vav Conversive is prefixed § 112. 3.

אֹכֵל, אֶשׁוֹב, וְעָמַדְתָּ, הֶפְלָה, תַּחְמֹד, נֹאכַל, נֶאֱמַר, וַיַּעַבְדֵם, אָמַרְתִּי,
וַיֶּעֱבֹד, עָבַד, שְׁמָרִי, שָׁוֹב, אֹכְלִי, חָמַדְתִּי, וָאֶעֱמִיד, יַהְפֹּךְ, עָזְבָה,
וְהַאֲכַלְתִּי, מֵהֲהָפֹךְ, הָאֹכֵל, עָבְדֵי, יַהְפֹךְ, נֶעֱזָב, נַעֲמֹד, אַלְבִּישׁ, הֲהָפֹךְ,
תֹּאכְלִי, וַתִּקְטְלֹדְנָה, יַהְהַפְכִי, וְנֹאכַל, וָאֹכַל, אֹכִיל, הֹפֵךְ, בֶּעֱזָבוּ, וַיַּעֲבֹד,
מָעֳצָה, עֲזַבְתֶּם, הֶעֱמַדְתָּה, וְהַעֲמַדְתָּ, תֵּאֹכֵלְנָה, וַיֹּאכַל, תִּתְהַפֵּךְ,

יִתְאַמְּרוּ, נַעֲמֹדִי, קָנֹב, וַאֹמַר, תַּעֲבֹדוּן, וְאֹבֵלוּן: עָזְבָה, וַתַּעֲמֹד־, אֶעֱשֶׂלָרָה, תֶּאֱלַל, חָמֹד.

12. PE GUTTURAL VERBS WITH SUFFIXES.

Vav Conversive prefixed to the preterite has the same variety of pointing with Vav Conjunctivo § 100. 1, § 234.

עֲזָבוּנִי, וַאֲכַלְתֶּם, אֶחְמֹדֵם, וַיַּחֲפָלְהוּ, נֶעֶבְּדֶךָ: עֲזַבְתִּהוּ, אֲמַרְכֶּם, הֶעֶבַדְתִּיהָ, וַאֲכַלְנִי, יֹאבְלֵהוּ, וַעֲזָבוּךָ, תַּעֲבְדֵם, וְהֶעֱמַדְתִּיהוּ, וַעֲזָבְנָה, אֹבְלֵנִי, עֲזָבְתֶּנִי: עֲבָדֵהוּ, הֶאֱמִירְךָ, אֲכָלֵהוּ, הֶעֱבַדְתָּנִי, הִפְלוּ, הַאֲכִילֶהוּ, נַעֲזָבָה, אֹבְלֵנוּ, אֶאֱבָלֵתִהוּ, עֲבָלָה, עֲזַבְתִּים, עֲמָדוּ.

13. AYIN GUTTURAL VERBS.

בְּעֲקָה, רֶאֹב, בַּרְכֵנִי, בָּעֲקָה, וַיִּגְאָלוּ, וַיִּחְפָרֵהוּ, גָּרֵשׁ, וַיְבָעֵר, וַיִּבְעֲקוּ, בֵּרְכִי, גָּרְשָׁה, תִּבְלַהְ, בָּעֲקִי, וּבֵרַכְתֶּם, וַיְגֹרֶשׁ, מִתְבָּרֵךְ, מְבֹעֵק, יִגְאָל, מְלֵאָה, גֹּרְשׁוּ, בָּרִהַּ, יַרְחַךְ, יִפְעֲלוּ, הִפָּרֵד, תֶּאֱהַלֹוּ, אֶבְרָכָה.

בֵּרְכֵנִי, גֵּרְשָׁתוּ, אֲהַבְתָּהְ, בְּרַכְנֵיכֶם, הִפְרִידֹוּ, יִגְרְשֹׁים, גְּאָלֵיהָ, בֵּרַכְבִּ, בֵּרַכְתִּיהָ, אֲהֲבֶם, אֶגְרְשֹׁנוּ, וַיֵּאֲחֲבֵהוּ, יִגְאָלֶהוּ, אֶגְאָלֵם, אֲהַבְתִּיהִ, גֵּרֵשֵׁנִי.

14. LAMEDH GUTTURAL VERBS.

וּזְרַעְתֶּם, שָׁלַחְתִּי, וַיִּצְמַח, תִּשְׁמַע, וַתִּפְקַהְנָה, פָּקְחָה, זֹרֵעַ, מְשַׁלֵּחַ, שִׁמְעֶנָה, וַתִּשְׁלְחִי, זֹרְעִי, אַצְמִיחַ, שֹׁמַעַתְּ, פָּקַח, תִּשְׁלַחְנָה, שַׁלַּה, שִׁמְעוּ, הִשְׁלִיחַ, אֶפְקַחַ, כִּשְׁלֹחַ, יִזְרַע, וַיֵּשָׁמַע, וַיִּשְׁמְעוּן, תִּשְׁמַעְנָה, וִשְׁלֹחָה, וְאַשְׁמִעָה.

שָׁלַחָה, שֹׁמַעַהְ, תִּשְׁמָעֵיהָ, שְׁלַחְתֹּו, וְהִצְמִיחָה, שְׁמָעֵנִי, אַשְׁמִיעָהּ, שְׁלָחֹו, אֶשְׁלָחֲךָ, הַשְׁמִיעֵינִי, הַשְׁמִיעֵנִי.

15. PE NUN VERBS.

לָקַח to take resembles Pe Nun verbs in the rejection or assimilation of its first radical § 132. 2.

וַיִּסַּח, אֶתֵּן, תֹּפֹלְנָה, תִּשְּׁעִי, וַיִּקַּח, יִגְּלִי, תֵּחַז, תִּקְחֶז, נַגִּישֵׁם, נֶגְשֹׁהֶם, הֻגַּד, נִגִּישׁוּ, וַתִּקַּח, הִפַּחְתֶּם, נַגִּיד, מִגַּשׁ, גְּשֶׁת, קָחִי, תֵּל, לָקְחוּ, יִגַּע,

וַיַּגֵּד, תִּגֹּשֶׁת, הַגִּישׁוּ, וְהִגַּדְתָּ, גַּע, לְקַחְתּוּ, נָתַתְּ, נֹגֵּל, תֵּת, הִתְנַצֵּל, וַיִּגְּעִי, יֻפַּח, וְטָשׁוּ, יֻתַּן.

וְהִפַּלְתִּיו, הִגִּירָה, וְנִאַצְתִּים, קָהֲתִי, יִטָּהֵרוּ, אֶתְּנֶה, אֶתְּהוּ, נַגִּידָּיו, וַתִּטְעֶהָ, יִקָּחוּם, קָחֶנּוּ, תַּצְּחוּ, תֵּלֵם, נָתַיהָ, הִפִּילֶלֶם, נְתַתָּנִי, וּנְתַתִּיהוּ.

16. Ayin Doubled Verbs.

1. The addition of suffixes causes the insertion of Daghesh-forte in a final contracted consonant; and the consequent shifting of the accent occasions the rejection of pretonic Kamets or Tsere, and the shortening of a long vowel before the doubled letter § 141. 3, § 61. 5.

2. In the Kal and Hiphil futures of these verbs, as well as of Pe Yodh, and Ayin Vav or Ayin Yodh verbs, the accent is drawn back by Vav Conversive from a mixed ultimate to a simple penult, and the vowel of the ultimate shortened in consequence § 99. 3. *a*, § 140. 1 and 5.

לַי, גַּזּוֹתִי, וְסַבֹּתֶם, תָּחֹן, אָאֹר, תְּסֻבֶּינָה, וַיִּקֹּד, אָרוּר, גַּל, הַחֵל, הַרְתִּי, הֲסַבֹּתָ, הָרַע, תָּחֵל, נֵסַב, וַתַּחְלִינָה, וְהֵסֵב, הוּחַל, סֹבִּי, יֵגַל, וְסַבִּי, אֹרְךָ, יָחֹן, יַסֹּבִּי, מִתְגֹּלֵל, הִתְחַנַּנְתִּי, הִתְמַהְמְהוּ, תְּסוֹבֵב, תָּסֹב, הַחֵלּוּ, נֵסֵב הִתְגֹּלֵל, אֶקֹּד, יָחֹן, חַסְבִּי, מִתְמַהְמֵהַּ, וַיָּסָב, וַיֵּגַל, וַתָּחֵל, נֵסַבָּה, יוּאַר:

חַנֵּנִי, וְלִנְצֻלָתֵיהוּ, סְבָבִים, סַבֵּנִי, הִתְחַנָּנוּ, הִתְמַהְמָהֶם, יְחָנְּנוּ, יְסָבֻּהוּ, תְּסוֹבְבֵנִי, חַזֵּנִי, חַנּוּנִי, יְחָנֵּךָ, תְּחָנֵּם, יְסוֹבְבָה, וַיְסֻבֵּנִי, וַיִּסְבֹּּוּ.

17. Pe Yodh Verbs.

Construct infinitives of the form שֶׁבֶת drop the Seghol of the ultimate before suffixes, and either retain the preceding Seghol or change it to Hhirik or Pattahh; thus שִׁבְתִּי, שַׁבְתִּי § 148. 2, § 221. 5.

יֵלַךְ, תֵּשְׁבִי, לֶכָה, וֵילֵךְ, הַדְלַקְתָּ, הֹשִׁיבוּ, יוּצַר, גֵּשָׁב, תֵּלַכְנָה, נוֹדַע, תֵּילֵד וְהִישַׁבְתֶּם, תִּישַׁן, לֶכָה, לֵרְעִי, אֵשֵׁב, הוֹלִיךְ, תֵּירַדְלִי, תֵּלַךְ, אוֹלִיד דֵּעִי, שֵׁב, מֵישִׁיב, לֶכֶת, יָשׁוֹן, תֵּרְדְּ, תֵּדְעֵיךָ, נֵלְכוּן: וַיֵּלֶךְ.

הוֹלִיכֶם, וְהוֹשַׁבְתִּיהוּ, יוֹרְדֵם, דָּעֵהוּ, וַתַּשְׁבִֵּנֹהוּ, יְצַרְתִּיהָ, יְדַעְתִּיו, שִׁבְתָּם, לֶכְתֶּךָ.

18. Ayin Vav and Ayin Yodh Verbs.

Suffixes and paragogic letters occasion the rejection of pretonic Kamets and Tsere § 157. 3, § 158. 2, § 160. 2 and 3.

קֻמוּ, רִיבוּ, נַחְתִּי, שָׁבָה, שַׂמְתֶּם, וְהֲבִיאוּ, הוּנַח, הֵמַתּוּ, יָבִיא,

הָאָרְחָה, תָּשִׁיב, אָמְרְתִּי, תְּמֹּתִי, תְּשִׁיאֶּינָה, וַיָּשִׁיתוּ, הָשֵׁב, הֲבִישֹׁתָ,
הֲשִׁיבֹנוּ, נָאֹר, שׁוּבִי, שִׁיתִי, קֹמָּה, יְשִׁים, נָשׁוּב, מֹּתָה, יוּמַת, מַשִּׁיב,
יָעֶֶץ, מְמֹתֵת, בָּא, שׁוֹבֵב, תְּשׁוּבֵין, וַלָּעַג, וַלָּקֶם.
תָּשִׁיאֵנוּ, שָׁתֵּיהָ, הֱמִיתָם, הֲבִיאֹתִיהִי, יְקִימֵהָ, הֲשִׁיבֵנוּ, וְמִיתֶם,
אֲתָתֹתִיהִי, הֲבִיאֹם, שָׁמֵנִי, הֲשֵׁבֹתִיהוּ, הֲבִיאֲָם, סוּבִי.

19. Lamedh Aleph Verbs.

נִבְרָאוּ, יָצָאתִי, הֶחְבָּאֵי, קָרָאתָ, תִּמְצָא, קֹרָא, נָשֹׁא, מָלֵא, יִתְחַבֵּא,
הֹוצְרָא, יְרֵאֹנִי, אֶקְרָא, בְּרֹא, נִמְצֵאת, תִּקְרָאנָה, תִּמָּצֵאוּ, תֵּצֵא,
נִמְצָא, מְצָא, צֵאִי, קֹרֵא, יְרֵאֹה, מִלֵּאתֶם, הֶחְבָּא, תְּדָשֵׁא, הוֹצֵאתִי,
חֹשֵׁאת, קֹרֵאן.
הֶחְבִּיאֵנִי, בְּרָאֹנוּ, מְצָאתֶם, וַיִּירָאֵנִי, קְרָאתִיהוּ, הֻשֵׁיאֵנִי, יִקְרָאֶהָ,
קְרָאֹהִי, הֹוצֵאתִיהוּ, תַּמְצָאוּ, קְרָאֻנִי.

20. Lamedh He Verbs.

בָּלוּ, כְּלִיתֶם, הֹלִינִי, הִרְבֵּיתָ, צִלִּיתִי, הִגְלָה, עָשִׂיתֶן, נָרְאוּ, גֶּחֱלָה,
תַּרְבֵּי, יִפְלָה, תִּשְׁקֶינָ, יִקְוּוּ, אֶרְאֶה, יְצַוֶּה, יֵרְדִי, נִחְיֶה, תָּהְלֹנִינָה,
וַיִּגְלֶה, רָאֶינָה, בְּנֹה, יֶהֱלֶה, וַיִּשְׁקֵה, יֵרָאֶה, פְּרֹה, הֶעֱלֵית, שָׂחֹה,
נִגְלֶה, וַיֵּבֶן, גָּל, הֶרֶב, וַתֵּרֶא, וִיחַל, וַיֵּרֶב.
עָשׂוֹה, צִוִּיתָה, הִגְלָם, רְאֵינִי, הֶעֱלִיתָנִי, נַשְׁקֵנוּ, וַיִּרְאֵנִי, יְצַוֵּהוּ, תְּכַלֶּה,
יִבְגֶם, נֵרָאֶה, הַשְׁקֵינִי, הִרְאֹנִי, תֵּצֶם, אַשְׁקֶה, הַגְלֹתִי, הֱיוֹתָם.

21. Promiscuous Examples.

יָלִיחַ, וַיָּשָׁב, יָשָׁב: יוֹשֵׁב, וַיֵּשֶׁב, הִשִׁיבִי, הֵשִׁיבוּ, וַשֵּׁבִי, שִׁבִי, שָׁבִי,
יִרֶב, יָרוּב, רִבִּיתָ, וְרָבִיתָ, בָּאָה, רָאָה, יֵשֵׁב, יָפֹל, צָּשׁ, לִי, צֵ,
קְחוּ, תְּלוּ, בְּלִי, פָּאֹנִי, בְּנֵי, תַּגִּידוּ, תֵּרְעִי, נָשָׁב, נָרַע, נָשָׂע, וְחֹז,
יִרְאָה, נָמֹתָה, הֵיֵמֵחַ, הֵיִשְׁבְתֶּם, יוּשַׁב. (2).

SELECTIONS FROM THE OLD TESTAMENT.

------◆◆◆------

I. The Creation and Fall. *Genesis* 1–3.

CHAPTER I. א

‏א‎ 2 בְּרֵאשִׁית בָּרָא אֱלֹהִים אֵת הַשָּׁמַיִם וְאֵת הָאָרֶץ: וְהָאָרֶץ הָיְתָה תֹהוּ

3 וָבֹהוּ וְחֹשֶׁךְ עַל־פְּנֵי תְהוֹם וְרוּחַ אֱלֹהִים מְרַחֶפֶת עַל־פְּנֵי הַמָּיִם: וַיֹּאמֶר

4 אֱלֹהִים יְהִי אוֹר וַיְהִי־אוֹר: וַיַּרְא אֱלֹהִים אֶת־הָאוֹר כִּי־טוֹב וַיַּבְדֵּל

ה 5 אֱלֹהִים בֵּין הָאוֹר וּבֵין הַחֹשֶׁךְ: וַיִּקְרָא אֱלֹהִים ׀ לָאוֹר יוֹם וְלַחֹשֶׁךְ קָרָא

6 לָיְלָה וַיְהִי־עֶרֶב וַיְהִי־בֹקֶר יוֹם אֶחָד: פ   וַיֹּאמֶר אֱלֹהִים יְהִי

7 רָקִיעַ בְּתוֹךְ הַמָּיִם וִיהִי מַבְדִּיל בֵּין מַיִם לָמָיִם: וַיַּעַשׂ אֱלֹהִים אֶת־הָרָקִיעַ

וַיַּבְדֵּל בֵּין הַמַּיִם אֲשֶׁר מִתַּחַת לָרָקִיעַ וּבֵין הַמַּיִם אֲשֶׁר מֵעַל לָרָקִיעַ

8 וַיְהִי־כֵן: וַיִּקְרָא אֱלֹהִים לָרָקִיעַ שָׁמָיִם וַיְהִי־עֶרֶב וַיְהִי־בֹקֶר יוֹם שֵׁנִי:

9 פ   וַיֹּאמֶר אֱלֹהִים יִקָּווּ הַמַּיִם מִתַּחַת הַשָּׁמַיִם אֶל־מָקוֹם אֶחָד

י 10 וְתֵרָאֶה הַיַּבָּשָׁה וַיְהִי־כֵן: וַיִּקְרָא אֱלֹהִים ׀ לַיַּבָּשָׁה אֶרֶץ וּלְמִקְוֵה הַמַּיִם

11 קָרָא יַמִּים וַיַּרְא אֱלֹהִים כִּי־טוֹב: וַיֹּאמֶר אֱלֹהִים תַּדְשֵׁא הָאָרֶץ

דֶּשֶׁא עֵשֶׂב מַזְרִיעַ זֶרַע עֵץ פְּרִי עֹשֶׂה פְּרִי לְמִינוֹ אֲשֶׁר זַרְעוֹ־בוֹ

12 עַל־הָאָרֶץ וַיְהִי־כֵן: וַתּוֹצֵא הָאָרֶץ דֶּשֶׁא עֵשֶׂב מַזְרִיעַ זֶרַע לְמִינֵהוּ

13 וְעֵץ עֹשֶׂה־פְּרִי אֲשֶׁר זַרְעוֹ־בוֹ לְמִינֵהוּ וַיַּרְא אֱלֹהִים כִּי־טוֹב: וַיְהִי־עֶרֶב

14 וַיְהִי־בֹקֶר יוֹם שְׁלִישִׁי: פ   וַיֹּאמֶר אֱלֹהִים יְהִי מְאֹרֹת בִּרְקִיעַ

הַשָּׁמַיִם לְהַבְדִּיל בֵּין הַיּוֹם וּבֵין הַלָּיְלָה וְהָיוּ לְאֹתֹת וּלְמוֹעֲדִים וּלְיָמִים

טו 15 וְשָׁנִים: וְהָיוּ לִמְאוֹרֹת בִּרְקִיעַ הַשָּׁמַיִם לְהָאִיר עַל־הָאָרֶץ וַיְהִי־כֵן:

16 וַיַּעַשׂ אֱלֹהִים אֶת־שְׁנֵי הַמְּאֹרֹת הַגְּדֹלִים אֶת־הַמָּאוֹר הַגָּדֹל לְמֶמְשֶׁלֶת

17 הַיּוֹם וְאֶת־הַמָּאוֹר הַקָּטֹן לְמֶמְשֶׁלֶת הַלַּיְלָה וְאֵת הַכּוֹכָבִים: וַיִּתֵּן

18 אֹתָם אֱלֹהִים בִּרְקִיעַ הַשָּׁמָיִם לְהָאִיר עַל־הָאָרֶץ: וְלִמְשֹׁל בַּיּוֹם וּבַלַּיְלָה

19 וּלֲהַבְדִּיל בֵּין הָאוֹר וּבֵין הַחֹשֶׁךְ וַיַּרְא אֱלֹהִים כִּי־טוֹב: וַיְהִי־עֶרֶב

כ 20 וַיְהִי־בֹקֶר יוֹם רְבִיעִי: פ   וַיֹּאמֶר אֱלֹהִים יִשְׁרְצוּ הַמַּיִם שֶׁרֶץ

21 נֶפֶשׁ חַיָּה וְעוֹף יְעוֹפֵף עַל־הָאָרֶץ עַל־פְּנֵי רְקִיעַ הַשָּׁמָיִם: וַיִּבְרָא

אֱלֹהִים אֶת־הַתַּנִּינִם הַגְּדֹלִים וְאֵת כָּל־נֶפֶשׁ הַחַיָּה ׀ הָרֹמֶשֶׂת אֲשֶׁר

שָׁרְצוּ הַמַּיִם לְמִינֵהֶם וְאֵת כָּל־עוֹף כָּנָף לְמִינֵהוּ וַיַּרְא אֱלֹהִים כִּי־טוֹב:

22 וַיְבָרֶךְ אֹתָם אֱלֹהִים לֵאמֹר פְּרוּ וּרְבוּ וּמִלְאוּ אֶת־הַמַּיִם בַּיַּמִּים

23
24 וַתְּהִי־עֶ֫רֶב וַיְהִי־בֹ֖קֶר י֥וֹם הַחֲמִישִֽׁי׃ פ וַיֹּ֣אמֶר וְהָיְתָ֤ה רֶ֫כֶב בָּאָ֑רֶץ

אֱלֹהִ֗ים תּוֹצֵ֤א הָאָ֙רֶץ֙ נֶ֣פֶשׁ חַיָּה֙ לְמִינָ֔הּ בְּהֵמָ֥ה וָרֶ֛מֶשׂ וְחַֽיְתוֹ־אֶ֖רֶץ
לְמִינָ֑הּ וַֽיְהִי־כֵֽן׃ וַיַּ֣עַשׂ אֱלֹהִים֩ אֶת־חַיַּ֨ת הָאָ֜רֶץ לְמִינָ֗הּ וְאֶת־הַבְּהֵמָה֙

26 לְמִינָ֔הּ וְאֵ֛ת כָּל־רֶ֥מֶשׂ הָֽאֲדָמָ֖ה לְמִינֵ֑הוּ וַיַּ֥רְא אֱלֹהִ֖ים כִּי־טֽוֹב׃ וַיֹּ֣אמֶר
אֱלֹהִ֔ים נַֽעֲשֶׂ֥ה אָדָ֛ם בְּצַלְמֵ֖נוּ כִּדְמוּתֵ֑נוּ וְיִרְדּוּ֩ בִדְגַ֨ת הַיָּ֜ם וּבְע֣וֹף
הַשָּׁמַ֗יִם וּבַבְּהֵמָה֙ וּבְכָל־הָאָ֔רֶץ וּבְכָל־הָרֶ֖מֶשׂ הָֽרֹמֵ֥שׂ עַל־הָאָֽרֶץ׃ וַיִּבְרָ֨א

27 אֱלֹהִ֤ים ׀ אֶת־הָֽאָדָם֙ בְּצַלְמ֔וֹ בְּצֶ֥לֶם אֱלֹהִ֖ים בָּרָ֣א אֹת֑וֹ זָכָ֥ר וּנְקֵבָ֖ה
בָּרָ֥א אֹתָֽם׃ וַיְבָ֣רֶךְ אֹתָם֮ אֱלֹהִים֒ וַיֹּ֨אמֶר לָהֶ֜ם אֱלֹהִ֗ים פְּר֣וּ וּרְב֥וּ

28 וּמִלְא֤וּ אֶת־הָאָ֙רֶץ֙ וְכִבְשֻׁ֔הָ וּרְד֞וּ בִּדְגַ֤ת הַיָּם֙ וּבְע֣וֹף הַשָּׁמַ֔יִם וּבְכָל־חַיָּ֖ה
הָֽרֹמֶ֥שֶׂת עַל־הָאָֽרֶץ׃ וַיֹּ֣אמֶר אֱלֹהִ֗ים הִנֵּה֩ נָתַ֨תִּי לָכֶ֜ם אֶת־כָּל־עֵ֣שֶׂב ׀

29 זֹרֵ֣עַ זֶ֗רַע אֲשֶׁר֙ עַל־פְּנֵ֣י כָל־הָאָ֔רֶץ וְאֶת־כָּל־הָעֵ֛ץ אֲשֶׁר־בּ֥וֹ פְרִי־עֵ֖ץ זֹרֵ֣עַ
זָ֑רַע לָכֶ֥ם יִֽהְיֶ֖ה לְאָכְלָֽה׃ וּֽלְכָל־חַיַּ֣ת הָ֠אָרֶץ וּלְכָל־ע֨וֹף הַשָּׁמַ֜יִם וּלְכֹ֣ל ׀

31 רוֹמֵ֣שׂ עַל־הָאָ֗רֶץ אֲשֶׁר־בּוֹ֙ נֶ֣פֶשׁ חַיָּ֔ה אֶת־כָּל־יֶ֥רֶק עֵ֖שֶׂב לְאָכְלָ֑ה וַֽיְהִי־כֵֽן׃
וַיַּ֤רְא אֱלֹהִים֙ אֶת־כָּל־אֲשֶׁ֣ר עָשָׂ֔ה וְהִנֵּה־ט֖וֹב מְאֹ֑ד וַֽיְהִי־עֶ֥רֶב וַֽיְהִי־
בֹ֖קֶר י֥וֹם הַשִּׁשִּֽׁי׃ פ

CHAPTER II. ב

2 א וַיְכֻלּ֛וּ הַשָּׁמַ֥יִם וְהָאָ֖רֶץ וְכָל־צְבָאָֽם׃ וַיְכַ֤ל אֱלֹהִים֙ בַּיּ֣וֹם הַשְּׁבִיעִ֔י
מְלַאכְתּ֖וֹ אֲשֶׁ֣ר עָשָׂ֑ה וַיִּשְׁבֹּת֙ בַּיּ֣וֹם הַשְּׁבִיעִ֔י מִכָּל־מְלַאכְתּ֖וֹ אֲשֶׁ֥ר עָשָֽׂה׃

3 וַיְבָ֤רֶךְ אֱלֹהִים֙ אֶת־י֣וֹם הַשְּׁבִיעִ֔י וַיְקַדֵּ֖שׁ אֹת֑וֹ כִּ֣י ב֤וֹ שָׁבַת֙ מִכָּל־
מְלַאכְתּ֔וֹ אֲשֶׁר־בָּרָ֥א אֱלֹהִ֖ים לַעֲשֽׂוֹת׃ פ אֵ֣לֶּה תֽוֹלְד֧וֹת הַשָּׁמַ֣יִם

4 וְהָאָ֖רֶץ בְּהִבָּֽרְאָ֑ם בְּי֗וֹם עֲשׂ֛וֹת יְהוָ֥ה אֱלֹהִ֖ים אֶ֥רֶץ וְשָׁמָֽיִם׃ וְכֹ֣ל ׀ שִׂ֣יחַ

5 הַשָּׂדֶ֗ה טֶ֚רֶם יִֽהְיֶ֣ה בָאָ֔רֶץ וְכָל־עֵ֥שֶׂב הַשָּׂדֶ֖ה טֶ֣רֶם יִצְמָ֑ח כִּי֩ לֹ֨א הִמְטִ֜יר
יְהוָ֤ה אֱלֹהִים֙ עַל־הָאָ֔רֶץ וְאָדָ֣ם אַ֔יִן לַֽעֲבֹ֖ד אֶת־הָֽאֲדָמָֽה׃ וְאֵ֖ד יַֽעֲלֶ֣ה

7 מִן־הָאָ֑רֶץ וְהִשְׁקָ֖ה אֶֽת־כָּל־פְּנֵֽי־הָֽאֲדָמָֽה׃ וַיִּ֩יצֶר֩ יְהוָ֨ה אֱלֹהִ֜ים אֶת־
הָֽאָדָ֗ם עָפָר֙ מִן־הָ֣אֲדָמָ֔ה וַיִּפַּ֥ח בְּאַפָּ֖יו נִשְׁמַ֣ת חַיִּ֑ים וַֽיְהִ֥י הָֽאָדָ֖ם

8 לְנֶ֥פֶשׁ חַיָּֽה׃ וַיִּטַּ֞ע יְהוָ֧ה אֱלֹהִ֛ים גַּן־בְּעֵ֖דֶן מִקֶּ֑דֶם וַיָּ֣שֶׂם שָׁ֔ם אֶת־

9 הָֽאָדָ֖ם אֲשֶׁ֥ר יָצָֽר׃ וַיַּצְמַ֞ח יְהוָ֤ה אֱלֹהִים֙ מִן־הָ֣אֲדָמָ֔ה כָּל־עֵ֛ץ נֶחְמָ֥ד
לְמַרְאֶ֖ה וְט֣וֹב לְמַאֲכָ֑ל וְעֵ֤ץ הַֽחַיִּים֙ בְּת֣וֹךְ הַגָּ֔ן וְעֵ֕ץ הַדַּ֖עַת ט֥וֹב וָרָֽע׃
וְנָהָר֙ יֹצֵ֣א מֵעֵ֔דֶן לְהַשְׁק֖וֹת אֶת־הַגָּ֑ן וּמִשָּׁם֙ יִפָּרֵ֔ד וְהָיָ֖ה לְאַרְבָּעָ֥ה ׀

11 רָאשִֽׁים׃ שֵׁ֥ם הָֽאֶחָ֖ד פִּישׁ֑וֹן ה֣וּא הַסֹּבֵ֗ב אֵ֚ת כָּל־אֶ֣רֶץ הַֽחֲוִילָ֔ה

12 אֲשֶׁר־שָׁ֖ם הַזָּהָֽב׃ וּֽזֲהַ֛ב הָאָ֥רֶץ הַהִ֖וא ט֑וֹב שָׁ֥ם הַבְּדֹ֖לַח וְאֶ֥בֶן הַשֹּֽׁהַם׃

‏וְשֵׁם־הַנָּהָר הַשֵּׁנִי גִּיחֹון הִוּא הַסֹּובֵב אֵת כָּל־אֶרֶץ כּוּשׁ: וְשֵׁם־הַנָּהָר‏ 13
‏הַשְּׁלִישִׁי חִדֶּקֶל הוּא הַהֹלֵךְ קִדְמַת אַשּׁוּר וְהַנָּהָר הָרְבִיעִי הוּא פְרָת:‏ 14
‏וַיִּקַּח יְהֹוָה אֱלֹהִים אֶת־הָאָדָם וַיַּנִּחֵהוּ בְגַן־עֵדֶן לְעָבְדָהּ וּלְשָׁמְרָהּ:‏ ‏טו‏
‏וַיְצַו יְהֹוָה אֱלֹהִים עַל־הָאָדָם לֵאמֹר מִכֹּל עֵץ־הַגָּן אָכֹל תֹּאכֵל: וּמֵעֵץ‏ 16
‏הַדַּעַת טֹוב וָרָע לֹא תֹאכַל מִמֶּנּוּ כִּי בְּיֹום אֲכָלְךָ מִמֶּנּוּ מֹות תָּמוּת:‏ 17
‏וַיֹּאמֶר יְהֹוָה אֱלֹהִים לֹא־טֹוב הֱיֹות הָאָדָם לְבַדֹּו אֶעֱשֶׂה־לֹּו עֵזֶר‏ 18
‏כְּנֶגְדֹּו: וַיִּצֶר יְהֹוָה אֱלֹהִים מִן־הָאֲדָמָה כָּל־חַיַּת הַשָּׂדֶה וְאֵת כָּל־עֹוף‏ 19
‏הַשָּׁמַיִם וַיָּבֵא אֶל־הָאָדָם לִרְאֹות מַה־יִּקְרָא־לֹו וְכֹל אֲשֶׁר יִקְרָא־לֹו הָאָדָם‏
‏נֶפֶשׁ חַיָּה הוּא שְׁמֹו: וַיִּקְרָא הָאָדָם שֵׁמֹות לְכָל־הַבְּהֵמָה וּלְעֹוף‏ ‏כ‏
‏הַשָּׁמַיִם וּלְכֹל חַיַּת הַשָּׂדֶה וּלְאָדָם לֹא־מָצָא עֵזֶר כְּנֶגְדֹּו: וַיַּפֵּל יְהֹוָה‏ 21
‏אֱלֹהִים ׀ תַּרְדֵּמָה עַל־הָאָדָם וַיִּישָׁן וַיִּקַּח אַחַת מִצַּלְעֹתָיו וַיִּסְגֹּר בָּשָׂר‏
‏תַּחְתֶּנָּה: וַיִּבֶן יְהֹוָה אֱלֹהִים ׀ אֶת־הַצֵּלָע אֲשֶׁר־לָקַח מִן־הָאָדָם לְאִשָּׁה‏ 22
‏וַיְבִאֶהָ אֶל־הָאָדָם: וַיֹּאמֶר הָאָדָם זֹאת הַפַּעַם עֶצֶם מֵעֲצָמַי וּבָשָׂר‏ 23
‏מִבְּשָׂרִי לְזֹאת יִקָּרֵא אִשָּׁה כִּי מֵאִישׁ לֻקֳחָה־זֹּאת: עַל־כֵּן יַעֲזָב־אִישׁ‏ 24
‏אֶת־אָבִיו וְאֶת־אִמֹּו וְדָבַק בְּאִשְׁתֹּו וְהָיוּ לְבָשָׂר אֶחָד: וַיִּהְיוּ שְׁנֵיהֶם‏ ‏כה‏
‏עֲרוּמִּים הָאָדָם וְאִשְׁתֹּו וְלֹא יִתְבֹּשָׁשׁוּ:‏

CHAPTER III. ‏ג‏

‏וְהַנָּחָשׁ הָיָה עָרוּם מִכֹּל חַיַּת הַשָּׂדֶה אֲשֶׁר עָשָׂה יְהֹוָה אֱלֹהִים וַיֹּאמֶר‏ ‏א‏
‏אֶל־הָאִשָּׁה אַף כִּי־אָמַר אֱלֹהִים לֹא תֹאכְלוּ מִכֹּל עֵץ הַגָּן: וַתֹּאמֶר‏ 2
‏הָאִשָּׁה אֶל־הַנָּחָשׁ מִפְּרִי עֵץ־הַגָּן נֹאכֵל: וּמִפְּרִי הָעֵץ אֲשֶׁר בְּתֹוךְ־הַגָּן‏ 3
‏אָמַר אֱלֹהִים לֹא תֹאכְלוּ מִמֶּנּוּ וְלֹא תִגְּעוּ בֹּו פֶּן־תְּמֻתוּן: וַיֹּאמֶר‏ 4
‏הַנָּחָשׁ אֶל־הָאִשָּׁה לֹא־מֹות תְּמֻתוּן: כִּי יֹדֵעַ אֱלֹהִים כִּי בְּיֹום אֲכָלְכֶם‏ ‏ה‏
‏מִמֶּנּוּ וְנִפְקְחוּ עֵינֵיכֶם וִהְיִיתֶם כֵּאלֹהִים יֹדְעֵי טֹוב וָרָע: וַתֵּרֶא הָאִשָּׁה‏ 6
‏כִּי טֹוב הָעֵץ לְמַאֲכָל וְכִי תַאֲוָה־הוּא לָעֵינַיִם וְנֶחְמָד הָעֵץ לְהַשְׂכִּיל‏
‏וַתִּקַּח מִפִּרְיֹו וַתֹּאכַל וַתִּתֵּן גַּם־לְאִישָׁהּ עִמָּהּ וַיֹּאכַל: וַתִּפָּקַחְנָה עֵינֵי‏ 7
‏שְׁנֵיהֶם וַיֵּדְעוּ כִּי עֵירֻמִּם הֵם וַיִּתְפְּרוּ עֲלֵה תְאֵנָה וַיַּעֲשׂוּ לָהֶם חֲגֹרֹת:‏
‏וַיִּשְׁמְעוּ אֶת־קֹול יְהֹוָה אֱלֹהִים מִתְהַלֵּךְ בַּגָּן לְרוּחַ הַיֹּום וַיִּתְחַבֵּא‏ 8
‏הָאָדָם וְאִשְׁתֹּו מִפְּנֵי יְהֹוָה אֱלֹהִים בְּתֹוךְ עֵץ הַגָּן: וַיִּקְרָא יְהֹוָה‏ 9
‏אֱלֹהִים אֶל־הָאָדָם וַיֹּאמֶר לֹו אַיֶּכָּה: וַיֹּאמֶר אֶת־קֹלְךָ שָׁמַעְתִּי בַגָּן‏ ‏י‏
‏וָאִירָא כִּי־עֵירֹם אָנֹכִי וָאֵחָבֵא: וַיֹּאמֶר מִי הִגִּיד לְךָ כִּי עֵירֹם אָתָּה‏ 11
‏הֲמִן־הָעֵץ אֲשֶׁר צִוִּיתִיךָ לְבִלְתִּי אֲכָל־מִמֶּנּוּ אָכָלְתָּ: וַיֹּאמֶר הָאָדָם‏ 12

13 וַיֹּאמֶר מִדְּהִתָּן בְּתַחְתִּי נָתְנָה־לִי הִוא עִמָּדִי נָתַתָּה אֲשֶׁר הָאִשָּׁה
הִשִּׁיאַנִי הַנָּחָשׁ הָאִשָּׁה יֹּאמֶר תַּעֲשִׂית מַה־זֹּאת לָאִשָּׁה אֱלֹהִים יְהֹוָה 14
אַתָּה אָרוּר זֹאת עָשִׂיתָ כִּי הַנָּחָשׁ אֶל־הַנָּחָשׁ אֱלֹהִים יְהֹוָה וַיֹּאמֶר ׀ וָאֹכֵל
כְּל־יְמֵי תֹאכַל וְעָפָר תֵלֵךְ עַל־גְּחֹנְךָ הַשָּׂדֶה חַיַּת וּמִכֹּל מִכָּל־הַבְּהֵמָה
זַרְעֲךָ טו וּבֵין זַרְעֲךָ וּבֵין הָאִשָּׁה וּבֵין בֵּינְךָ אָשִׁית ׀ וְאֵיבָה ׀ חַיֶּיךָ
אֶל־הָאִשָּׁה אָמַר ס עָקֵב תְּשׁוּפֶנּוּ וְאַתָּה רֹאשׁ יְשׁוּפְךָ הִיא 16
תְּשׁוּקָתֵךְ וְאֶל־אִישֵׁךְ בָּנִים תֵּלְדִי בְּעֶצֶב וְהֵרֹנֵךְ עִצְּבוֹנֵךְ אַרְבֶּה הַרְבָּה
וַתֹּאכַל אִשְׁתְּךָ לְקוֹל כִּי־שָׁמַעְתָּ אָמַר וּלְאָדָם ס בָּךְ יִמְשָׁל־וְהוּא 17
הָאֲדָמָה אֲרוּרָה מִמֶּנּוּ תֹאכַל לֹא לֵאמֹר צִוִּיתִיךָ אֲשֶׁר מִן־הָעֵץ
לָךְ תַּצְמִיחַ וְדַרְדַּר וְקוֹץ חַיֶּיךָ יְמֵי כֹּל תֹּאכְלֶנָּה בְּעִצָּבוֹן בַּעֲבוּרֶךָ 18
אֶל־ תָּשׁוּב עַד לֶחֶם תֹּאכַל אַפֶּיךָ בְּזֵעַת הַשָּׂדֶה אֶת־עֵשֶׂב וְאָכַלְתָּ 19
וַיִּקְרָא כ תָּשׁוּב וְאֶל־עָפָר אַתָּה כִּי־עָפָר לֻקַּחְתָּ מִמֶּנָּה כִּי הָאֲדָמָה
יְהֹוָה וַיַּעַשׂ כָּל־חָי אֵם הָיְתָה הִוא כִּי חַוָּה אִשְׁתּוֹ שֵׁם הָאָדָם 21
וַיֹּאמֶר ס וַיַּלְבִּשֵׁם עוֹר כָּתְנוֹת וּלְאִשְׁתּוֹ לְאָדָם אֱלֹהִים 22
וְעַתָּה וָרָע טוֹב לָדַעַת מִמֶּנּוּ כְּאַחַד הָיָה הָאָדָם הֵן אֱלֹהִים יְהֹוָה
וָחַי וְאָכַל הַחַיִּים מֵעֵץ גַּם וְלָקַח יָדוֹ פֶּן־יִשְׁלַח 23
וַיְגָרֶשׁ 24 מִשָּׁם לֻקַּח אֲשֶׁר אֶת־הָאֲדָמָה לַעֲבֹד מִגַּן־עֵדֶן אֱלֹהִים יְהֹוָה
הַחֶרֶב לַהַט וְאֵת אֶת־הַכְּרֻבִים לְגַן־עֵדֶן מִקֶּדֶם וַיַּשְׁכֵּן אֶת־הָאָדָם
הַחַיִּים עֵץ אֶת־דֶּרֶךְ לִשְׁמֹר הַמִּתְהַפֶּכֶת ׃

II. The Life of Joseph, *Genesis* 37, 39–46 : 7.

CHAPTER XXXVII. לז

2 א תֹלְדוֹת ׀ אֵלֶּה ׃ כְּנָעַן בְּאֶרֶץ אָבִיו מְגוּרֵי בְּאֶרֶץ יַעֲקֹב וַיֵּשֶׁב
אֶת־ נַעַר וְהוּא בַּצֹּאן אֶת־אֶחָיו רֹעֶה הָיָה שָׁנָה שְׁבַע־עֶשְׂרֵה בֶּן־ יוֹסֵף
רָעָה אֶת־דִּבָּתָם יוֹסֵף וַיָּבֵא אָבִיו נְשֵׁי זִלְפָּה וְאֶת־בְּנֵי בִלְהָה בְּנֵי
3 לוֹ הוּא כִּי־בֶן־זְקֻנִים מִכָּל־בָּנָיו אֶת־יוֹסֵף אָהַב וְיִשְׂרָאֵל אֶל־אֲבִיהֶם ׃
4 אֶחָיו וַיִּרְאוּ פַּסִּים ׃ כְּתֹנֶת לוֹ וְעָשָׂה מִכָּל־אֶחָיו אֹתוֹ אָהַב כִּי־אֹתוֹ
ה לְשָׁלֹם ׃ דַּבְּרוֹ יָכְלוּ וְלֹא אֹתוֹ וַיִּשְׂנְאוּ לְאֶחָיו וַיַּגֵּד חֲלוֹם יוֹסֵף וַיַּחֲלֹם
6 אֲשֶׁר הַזֶּה הַחֲלוֹם שִׁמְעוּ־נָא אֲלֵיהֶם וַיֹּאמֶר אֹתוֹ ׃ שְׂנֹא עוֹד וַיּוֹסִפוּ
7 קָמָה וְהִנֵּה הַשָּׂדֶה בְּתוֹךְ אֲלֻמִּים מְאַלְּמִים אֲנַחְנוּ וְהִנֵּה חָלָמְתִּי ׃
8 וַיֹּאמְרוּ לַאֲלֻמָּתִי ׃ וַתִּשְׁתַּחֲוֶיןָ אֲלֻמֹּתֵיכֶם תְסֻבֶּינָה וְהִנֵּה נִצָּבָה וְגַם־
וַיּוֹסִפוּ בָנוּ אִם־מָשׁוֹל תִּמְשֹׁל עָלֵינוּ הֲמָלֹךְ תִּמְלֹךְ עָלֵינוּ אֶחָיו לוֹ

9 עוֹד שְׂנֹא אֹתוֹ עַל־חֲלֹמֹתָיו וְעַל־דְּבָרָיו : וַיַּחֲלֹם עוֹד חֲלוֹם אַחֵר

וַיְסַפֵּר אֹתוֹ לְאֶחָיו וַיֹּאמֶר הִנֵּה חָלַמְתִּי חֲלוֹם עוֹד וְהִנֵּה הַשֶּׁמֶשׁ

10 וְהַיָּרֵחַ וְאַחַד עָשָׂר כּוֹכָבִים מִשְׁתַּחֲוִים לִי : וַיְסַפֵּר אֶל־אָבִיו וְאֶל־אֶחָיו

וַיִּגְעַר־בּוֹ אָבִיו וַיֹּאמֶר לוֹ מָה הַחֲלוֹם הַזֶּה אֲשֶׁר חָלָמְתָּ הֲבוֹא נָבוֹא

11 אֲנִי וְאִמְּךָ וְאַחֶיךָ לְהִשְׁתַּחֲוֹת לְךָ אָרְצָה : וַיְקַנְאוּ־בוֹ אֶחָיו וְאָבִיו

12 שָׁמַר אֶת־הַדָּבָר : וַיֵּלְכוּ אֶחָיו לִרְעוֹת אֶת־צֹאן אֲבִיהֶם בִּשְׁכֶם : וַיֹּאמֶר

13 יִשְׂרָאֵל אֶל־יוֹסֵף הֲלוֹא אַחֶיךָ רֹעִים בִּשְׁכֶם לְכָה וְאֶשְׁלָחֲךָ אֲלֵיהֶם

14 וַיֹּאמֶר לוֹ הִנֵּנִי : וַיֹּאמֶר לוֹ לֶךְ־נָא רְאֵה אֶת־שְׁלוֹם אַחֶיךָ וְאֶת־שְׁלוֹם

15 הַצֹּאן וַהֲשִׁבֵנִי דָּבָר וַיִּשְׁלָחֵהוּ מֵעֵמֶק חֶבְרוֹן וַיָּבֹא שְׁכֶמָה : וַיִּמְצָאֵהוּ

16 אִישׁ וְהִנֵּה תֹעֶה בַּשָּׂדֶה וַיִּשְׁאָלֵהוּ הָאִישׁ לֵאמֹר מַה־תְּבַקֵּשׁ : וַיֹּאמֶר

17 אֶת־אַחַי אָנֹכִי מְבַקֵּשׁ הַגִּידָה־נָּא לִי אֵיפֹה הֵם רֹעִים : וַיֹּאמֶר הָאִישׁ

נָסְעוּ מִזֶּה כִּי שָׁמַעְתִּי אֹמְרִים נֵלְכָה דֹּתָיְנָה וַיֵּלֶךְ יוֹסֵף אַחַר אֶחָיו

18 וַיִּמְצָאֵם בְּדֹתָן : וַיִּרְאוּ אֹתוֹ מֵרָחֹק וּבְטֶרֶם יִקְרַב אֲלֵיהֶם וַיִּתְנַכְּלוּ

19 אֹתוֹ לַהֲמִיתוֹ : וַיֹּאמְרוּ אִישׁ אֶל־אָחִיו הִנֵּה בַּעַל הַחֲלֹמוֹת הַלָּזֶה בָּא ׃

20 וְעַתָּה לְכוּ וְנַהַרְגֵהוּ וְנַשְׁלִכֵהוּ בְּאַחַד הַבֹּרוֹת וְאָמַרְנוּ חַיָּה רָעָה

21 אֲכָלָתְהוּ וְנִרְאֶה מַה־יִּהְיוּ חֲלֹמֹתָיו : וַיִּשְׁמַע רְאוּבֵן וַיַּצִּלֵהוּ מִיָּדָם

22 וַיֹּאמֶר לֹא נַכֶּנּוּ נָפֶשׁ : וַיֹּאמֶר אֲלֵהֶם רְאוּבֵן אַל־תִּשְׁפְּכוּ־דָם הַשְׁלִיכוּ

אֹתוֹ אֶל־הַבּוֹר הַזֶּה אֲשֶׁר בַּמִּדְבָּר וְיָד אַל־תִּשְׁלְחוּ־בוֹ לְמַעַן הַצִּיל

23 אֹתוֹ מִיָּדָם לַהֲשִׁיבוֹ אֶל־אָבִיו : וַיְהִי כַּאֲשֶׁר־בָּא יוֹסֵף אֶל־אֶחָיו

24 וַיַּפְשִׁיטוּ אֶת־יוֹסֵף אֶת־כֻּתָּנְתּוֹ אֶת־כְּתֹנֶת הַפַּסִּים אֲשֶׁר עָלָיו : וַיִּקָּחֻהוּ

25 וַיַּשְׁלִכוּ אֹתוֹ הַבֹּרָה וְהַבּוֹר רֵק אֵין בּוֹ מָיִם : וַיֵּשְׁבוּ לֶאֱכָל־לֶחֶם

וַיִּשְׂאוּ עֵינֵיהֶם וַיִּרְאוּ וְהִנֵּה אֹרְחַת יִשְׁמְעֵאלִים בָּאָה מִגִּלְעָד וּגְמַלֵּיהֶם

26 נֹשְׂאִים נְכֹאת וּצְרִי וָלֹט הוֹלְכִים לְהוֹרִיד מִצְרָיְמָה : וַיֹּאמֶר יְהוּדָה

27 אֶל־אֶחָיו מַה־בֶּצַע כִּי נַהֲרֹג אֶת־אָחִינוּ וְכִסִּינוּ אֶת־דָּמוֹ : לְכוּ וְנִמְכְּרֶנּוּ

לַיִּשְׁמְעֵאלִים וְיָדֵנוּ אַל־תְּהִי־בוֹ כִּי־אָחִינוּ בְשָׂרֵנוּ הוּא וַיִּשְׁמְעוּ אֶחָיו :

28 וַיַּעַבְרוּ אֲנָשִׁים מִדְיָנִים סֹחֲרִים וַיִּמְשְׁכוּ וַיַּעֲלוּ אֶת־יוֹסֵף מִן־הַבּוֹר

וַיִּמְכְּרוּ אֶת־יוֹסֵף לַיִּשְׁמְעֵאלִים בְּעֶשְׂרִים כָּסֶף וַיָּבִיאוּ אֶת־יוֹסֵף

29 מִצְרָיְמָה : וַיָּשָׁב רְאוּבֵן אֶל־הַבּוֹר וְהִנֵּה אֵין־יוֹסֵף בַּבּוֹר וַיִּקְרַע אֶת־

30 בְּגָדָיו : וַיָּשָׁב אֶל־אֶחָיו וַיֹּאמַר הַיֶּלֶד אֵינֶנּוּ וַאֲנִי אָנָה אֲנִי־בָא :

31 וַיִּקְחוּ אֶת־כְּתֹנֶת יוֹסֵף וַיִּשְׁחֲטוּ שְׂעִיר עִזִּים וַיִּטְבְּלוּ אֶת־הַכֻּתֹּנֶת בַּדָּם :

32 וַיְשַׁלְּחוּ אֶת־כְּתֹנֶת הַפַּסִּים וַיָּבִיאוּ אֶל־אֲבִיהֶם וַיֹּאמְרוּ זֹאת מָצָאנוּ

33 הַכֶּר־נָא הַכְּתֹנֶת בִּנְךָ הִוא אִם־לֹא : וַיַּכִּירָהּ וַיֹּאמֶר כְּתֹנֶת בְּנִי חַיָּה

34 רָעָה אֲכָלָתְהוּ טָרֹף טֹרַף יוֹסֵף׃ וַיִּקְרַע יַעֲקֹב שִׂמְלֹתָיו וַיָּשֶׂם שַׂק
35 בְּמָתְנָיו וַיִּתְאַבֵּל עַל־בְּנוֹ יָמִים רַבִּים׃ וַיָּקֻמוּ כָל־בָּנָיו וְכָל־בְּנֹתָיו
לְנַחֲמוֹ וַיְמָאֵן לְהִתְנַחֵם וַיֹּאמֶר כִּי־אֵרֵד אֶל־בְּנִי אָבֵל שְׁאֹלָה וַיֵּבְךְּ
36 אֹתוֹ אָבִיו׃ וְהַמְּדָנִים מָכְרוּ אֹתוֹ אֶל־מִצְרָיִם לְפוֹטִיפַר סְרִיס פַּרְעֹה
שַׂר הַטַּבָּחִים׃
פ

CHAPTER XXXIX. לט

1 וְיוֹסֵף הוּרַד מִצְרָיְמָה וַיִּקְנֵהוּ פּוֹטִיפַר סְרִיס פַּרְעֹה שַׂר הַטַּבָּחִים
2 אִישׁ מִצְרִי מִיַּד הַיִּשְׁמְעֵאלִים אֲשֶׁר הוֹרִדֻהוּ שָׁמָּה׃ וַיְהִי יְהוָֹה אֶת־
3 יוֹסֵף וַיְהִי אִישׁ מַצְלִיחַ וַיְהִי בְּבֵית אֲדֹנָיו הַמִּצְרִי׃ וַיַּרְא אֲדֹנָיו כִּי
4 יְהוָֹה אִתּוֹ וְכֹל אֲשֶׁר־הוּא עֹשֶׂה יְהוָֹה מַצְלִיחַ בְּיָדוֹ׃ וַיִּמְצָא יוֹסֵף
חֵן בְּעֵינָיו וַיְשָׁרֶת אֹתוֹ וַיַּפְקִדֵהוּ עַל־בֵּיתוֹ וְכָל־יֶשׁ־לוֹ נָתַן בְּיָדוֹ׃
5 וַיְהִי מֵאָז הִפְקִיד אֹתוֹ בְּבֵיתוֹ וְעַל כָּל־אֲשֶׁר יֶשׁ־לוֹ וַיְבָרֶךְ יְהוָֹה
אֶת־בֵּית הַמִּצְרִי בִּגְלַל יוֹסֵף וַיְהִי בִּרְכַּת יְהוָֹה בְּכָל־אֲשֶׁר יֶשׁ־לוֹ בַּבַּיִת
6 וּבַשָּׂדֶה׃ וַיַּעֲזֹב כָּל־אֲשֶׁר־לוֹ בְּיַד יוֹסֵף וְלֹא־יָדַע אִתּוֹ מְאוּמָה כִּי
7 אִם־הַלֶּחֶם אֲשֶׁר־הוּא אוֹכֵל וַיְהִי יוֹסֵף יְפֵה־תֹאַר וִיפֵה מַרְאֶה׃ וַיְהִי
8 אַחַר הַדְּבָרִים הָאֵלֶּה וַתִּשָּׂא אֵשֶׁת־אֲדֹנָיו אֶת־עֵינֶיהָ אֶל־יוֹסֵף וַתֹּאמֶר
שִׁכְבָה עִמִּי׃ וַיְמָאֵן וַיֹּאמֶר אֶל־אֵשֶׁת אֲדֹנָיו הֵן אֲדֹנִי לֹא־יָדַע אִתִּי
9 מַה־בַּבָּיִת וְכֹל אֲשֶׁר־יֶשׁ־לוֹ נָתַן בְּיָדִי׃ אֵינֶנּוּ גָדוֹל בַּבַּיִת הַזֶּה מִמֶּנִּי
וְלֹא־חָשַׂךְ מִמֶּנִּי מְאוּמָה כִּי אִם־אוֹתָךְ בַּאֲשֶׁר אַתְּ־אִשְׁתּוֹ וְאֵיךְ אֶעֱשֶׂה
הָרָעָה הַגְּדֹלָה הַזֹּאת וְחָטָאתִי לֵאלֹהִים׃ וַיְהִי כְּדַבְּרָהּ אֶל־יוֹסֵף יוֹם׀
11 יוֹם וְלֹא־שָׁמַע אֵלֶיהָ לִשְׁכַּב אֶצְלָהּ לִהְיוֹת עִמָּהּ׃ וַיְהִי כְּהַיּוֹם הַזֶּה
וַיָּבֹא הַבַּיְתָה לַעֲשׂוֹת מְלַאכְתּוֹ וְאֵין אִישׁ מֵאַנְשֵׁי הַבַּיִת שָׁם בַּבָּיִת׃
12 וַתִּתְפְּשֵׂהוּ בְּבִגְדוֹ לֵאמֹר שִׁכְבָה עִמִּי וַיַּעֲזֹב בִּגְדוֹ בְּיָדָהּ וַיָּנָס וַיֵּצֵא
13 הַחוּצָה׃ וַיְהִי כִּרְאוֹתָהּ כִּי־עָזַב בִּגְדוֹ בְּיָדָהּ וַיָּנָס הַחוּצָה׃ וַתִּקְרָא
14 לְאַנְשֵׁי בֵיתָהּ וַתֹּאמֶר לָהֶם לֵאמֹר רְאוּ הֵבִיא לָנוּ אִישׁ עִבְרִי לְצַחֶק
בָּנוּ בָּא אֵלַי לִשְׁכַּב עִמִּי וָאֶקְרָא בְּקוֹל גָּדוֹל׃ וַיְהִי כְשָׁמְעוֹ כִּי־הֲרִימֹתִי
16 קוֹלִי וָאֶקְרָא וַיַּעֲזֹב בִּגְדוֹ אֶצְלִי וַיָּנָס וַיֵּצֵא הַחוּצָה׃ וַתַּנַּח בִּגְדוֹ
17 אֶצְלָהּ עַד־בּוֹא אֲדֹנָיו אֶל־בֵּיתוֹ׃ וַתְּדַבֵּר אֵלָיו כַּדְּבָרִים הָאֵלֶּה לֵאמֹר
18 בָּא אֵלַי הָעֶבֶד הָעִבְרִי אֲשֶׁר־הֵבֵאתָ לָּנוּ לְצַחֶק בִּי׃ וַיְהִי כַּהֲרִימִי קוֹלִי
19 וָאֶקְרָא וַיַּעֲזֹב בִּגְדוֹ אֶצְלִי וַיָּנָס הַחוּצָה׃ וַיְהִי כִשְׁמֹעַ אֲדֹנָיו אֶת־
דִּבְרֵי אִשְׁתּוֹ אֲשֶׁר דִּבְּרָה אֵלָיו לֵאמֹר כַּדְּבָרִים הָאֵלֶּה עָשָׂה לִי עַבְדֶּךָ
20 וַיִּחַר אַפּוֹ׃ וַיִּקַּח אֲדֹנֵי יוֹסֵף אֹתוֹ וַיִּתְּנֵהוּ אֶל־בֵּית הַסֹּהַר מְקוֹם

21 אֲשֶׁר־אֲסוּרֵי הַמֶּלֶךְ אֲסוּרִים וַיְהִי־שָׁם בְּבֵית הַסֹּהַר: וַיְהִי יְהֹוָה אֶת־
22 יוֹסֵף וַיֵּט אֵלָיו חָסֶד וַיִּתֵּן חִנּוֹ בְּעֵינֵי שַׂר בֵּית־הַסֹּהַר: וַיִּתֵּן שַׂר בֵּית־
הַסֹּהַר בְּיַד־יוֹסֵף אֵת כָּל־הָאֲסוּרִם אֲשֶׁר בְּבֵית הַסֹּהַר וְאֵת כָּל־אֲשֶׁר
23 עֹשִׂים שָׁם הוּא הָיָה עֹשֶׂה: אֵין ׀ שַׂר בֵּית־הַסֹּהַר רֹאֶה אֶת־כָּל־
מְאוּמָה בְּיָדוֹ בַּאֲשֶׁר יְהֹוָה אִתּוֹ וַאֲשֶׁר־הוּא עֹשֶׂה יְהֹוָה מַצְלִיחַ: פ

CHAPTER XL. מ

א וַיְהִי אַחַר הַדְּבָרִים הָאֵלֶּה חָטְאוּ מַשְׁקֵה מֶלֶךְ־מִצְרַיִם וְהָאֹפֶה לַאֲדֹנֵיהֶם
2 לְמֶלֶךְ מִצְרָיִם: וַיִּקְצֹף פַּרְעֹה עַל שְׁנֵי סָרִיסָיו עַל שַׂר הַמַּשְׁקִים וְעַל
3 שַׂר הָאוֹפִים: וַיִּתֵּן אֹתָם בְּמִשְׁמַר בֵּית שַׂר הַטַּבָּחִים אֶל־בֵּית הַסֹּהַר
4 מְקוֹם אֲשֶׁר יוֹסֵף אָסוּר שָׁם: וַיִּפְקֹד שַׂר הַטַּבָּחִים אֶת־יוֹסֵף אִתָּם
5 וַיְשָׁרֶת אֹתָם וַיִּהְיוּ יָמִים בְּמִשְׁמָר: וַיַּחַלְמוּ חֲלוֹם שְׁנֵיהֶם אִישׁ
חֲלֹמוֹ בְּלַיְלָה אֶחָד אִישׁ כְּפִתְרוֹן חֲלֹמוֹ הַמַּשְׁקֶה וְהָאֹפֶה אֲשֶׁר לְמֶלֶךְ
6 מִצְרַיִם אֲשֶׁר אֲסוּרִים בְּבֵית הַסֹּהַר: וַיָּבֹא אֲלֵיהֶם יוֹסֵף בַּבֹּקֶר וַיַּרְא
7 אֹתָם וְהִנָּם זֹעֲפִים: וַיִּשְׁאַל אֶת־סְרִיסֵי פַרְעֹה אֲשֶׁר אִתּוֹ בְּמִשְׁמַר בֵּית
8 אֲדֹנָיו לֵאמֹר מַדּוּעַ פְּנֵיכֶם רָעִים הַיּוֹם: וַיֹּאמְרוּ אֵלָיו חֲלוֹם חָלַמְנוּ
וּפֹתֵר אֵין אֹתוֹ וַיֹּאמֶר אֲלֵהֶם יוֹסֵף הֲלוֹא לֵאלֹהִים פִּתְרֹנִים סַפְּרוּ־נָא
9 לִי: וַיְסַפֵּר שַׂר־הַמַּשְׁקִים אֶת־חֲלֹמוֹ לְיוֹסֵף וַיֹּאמֶר לוֹ בַּחֲלוֹמִי וְהִנֵּה־
10 גֶפֶן לְפָנָי: וּבַגֶּפֶן שְׁלֹשָׁה שָׂרִיגִם וְהִיא כְפֹרַחַת עָלְתָה נִצָּהּ הִבְשִׁילוּ
11 אַשְׁכְּלֹתֶיהָ עֲנָבִים: וְכוֹס פַּרְעֹה בְּיָדִי וָאֶקַּח אֶת־הָעֲנָבִים וָאֶשְׂחַט
12 אֹתָם אֶל־כּוֹס פַּרְעֹה וָאֶתֵּן אֶת־הַכּוֹס עַל־כַּף פַּרְעֹה: וַיֹּאמֶר לוֹ יוֹסֵף
13 זֶה פִּתְרֹנוֹ שְׁלֹשֶׁת הַשָּׂרִגִים שְׁלֹשֶׁת יָמִים הֵם: בְּעוֹד ׀ שְׁלֹשֶׁת יָמִים
יִשָּׂא פַרְעֹה אֶת־רֹאשֶׁךָ וַהֲשִׁיבְךָ עַל־כַּנֶּךָ וְנָתַתָּ כוֹס־פַּרְעֹה בְּיָדוֹ
14 כַּמִּשְׁפָּט הָרִאשׁוֹן אֲשֶׁר הָיִיתָ מַשְׁקֵהוּ: כִּי אִם־זְכַרְתַּנִי אִתְּךָ כַּאֲשֶׁר
יִיטַב לָךְ וְעָשִׂיתָ־נָּא עִמָּדִי חָסֶד וְהִזְכַּרְתַּנִי אֶל־פַּרְעֹה וְהוֹצֵאתַנִי מִן־
15 הַבַּיִת הַזֶּה: כִּי־גֻנֹּב גֻּנַּבְתִּי מֵאֶרֶץ הָעִבְרִים וְגַם־פֹּה לֹא־עָשִׂיתִי מְאוּמָה
16 כִּי־שָׂמוּ אֹתִי בַּבּוֹר: וַיַּרְא שַׂר־הָאֹפִים כִּי טוֹב פָּתָר וַיֹּאמֶר אֶל־יוֹסֵף
17 אַף־אֲנִי בַּחֲלוֹמִי וְהִנֵּה שְׁלֹשָׁה סַלֵּי חֹרִי עַל־רֹאשִׁי: וּבַסַּל הָעֶלְיוֹן מִכֹּל
מַאֲכַל פַּרְעֹה מַעֲשֵׂה אֹפֶה וְהָעוֹף אֹכֵל אֹתָם מִן־הַסַּל מֵעַל רֹאשִׁי:
18 וַיַּעַן יוֹסֵף וַיֹּאמֶר זֶה פִּתְרֹנוֹ שְׁלֹשֶׁת הַסַּלִּים שְׁלֹשֶׁת יָמִים הֵם:
19 בְּעוֹד ׀ שְׁלֹשֶׁת יָמִים יִשָּׂא פַרְעֹה אֶת־רֹאשְׁךָ מֵעָלֶיךָ וְתָלָה אוֹתְךָ
20 עַל־עֵץ וְאָכַל הָעוֹף אֶת־בְּשָׂרְךָ מֵעָלֶיךָ: וַיְהִי ׀ בַּיּוֹם הַשְּׁלִישִׁי יוֹם

הֻלֶּדֶת אֶת־פַּרְעֹה וַיַּעַשׂ מִשְׁתֶּה לְכָל־עֲבָדָיו וַיִּשָּׂא אֶת־רֹאשׁ ׀ שַׂר הַמַּשְׁקִים

21 וְאֶת־רֹאשׁ שַׂר הָאֹפִים בְּתוֹךְ עֲבָדָיו : וַיָּשֶׁב אֶת־שַׂר הַמַּשְׁקִים עַל־

22 מַשְׁקֵהוּ וַיִּתֵּן הַכּוֹס עַל־כַּף פַּרְעֹה : וְאֵת שַׂר הָאֹפִים תָּלָה כַּאֲשֶׁר

23 פָּתַר לָהֶם יוֹסֵף : וְלֹא־זָכַר שַׂר־הַמַּשְׁקִים אֶת־יוֹסֵף וַיִּשְׁכָּחֵהוּ :

CHAPTER XLI.   מא

2 וַיְהִי מִקֵּץ שְׁנָתַיִם יָמִים וּפַרְעֹה חֹלֵם וְהִנֵּה עֹמֵד עַל־הַיְאֹר : וְהִנֵּה

מִן־הַיְאֹר עֹלֹת שֶׁבַע פָּרוֹת יְפוֹת מַרְאֶה וּבְרִיאֹת בָּשָׂר וַתִּרְעֶינָה בָּאָחוּ :

3 וְהִנֵּה שֶׁבַע פָּרוֹת אֲחֵרוֹת עֹלוֹת אַחֲרֵיהֶן מִן־הַיְאֹר רָעוֹת מַרְאֶה

4 וְדַקּוֹת בָּשָׂר וַתַּעֲמֹדְנָה אֵצֶל הַפָּרוֹת עַל־שְׂפַת הַיְאֹר : וַתֹּאכַלְנָה

הַפָּרוֹת רָעוֹת הַמַּרְאֶה וְדַקֹּת הַבָּשָׂר אֵת שֶׁבַע הַפָּרוֹת יְפֹת הַמַּרְאֶה

5 וְהַבְּרִיאֹת וַיִּיקַץ פַּרְעֹה : וַיִּישָׁן וַיַּחֲלֹם שֵׁנִית וְהִנֵּה ׀ שֶׁבַע שִׁבֳּלִים

6 עֹלוֹת בְּקָנֶה אֶחָד בְּרִיאוֹת וְטֹבוֹת : וְהִנֵּה שֶׁבַע שִׁבֳּלִים דַּקּוֹת וּשְׁדוּפֹת

7 קָדִים צֹמְחוֹת אַחֲרֵיהֶן : וַתִּבְלַעְנָה הַשִּׁבֳּלִים הַדַּקּוֹת אֵת שֶׁבַע הַשִּׁבֳּלִים

8 הַבְּרִיאוֹת וְהַמְּלֵאוֹת וַיִּיקַץ פַּרְעֹה וְהִנֵּה חֲלוֹם : וַיְהִי בַבֹּקֶר וַתִּפָּעֶם

רוּחוֹ וַיִּשְׁלַח וַיִּקְרָא אֶת־כָּל־חַרְטֻמֵּי מִצְרַיִם וְאֶת־כָּל־חֲכָמֶיהָ וַיְסַפֵּר

9 פַּרְעֹה לָהֶם אֶת־חֲלֹמוֹ וְאֵין־פּוֹתֵר אוֹתָם לְפַרְעֹה : וַיְדַבֵּר שַׂר הַמַּשְׁקִים

אֶת־פַּרְעֹה לֵאמֹר אֶת־חֲטָאַי אֲנִי מַזְכִּיר הַיּוֹם : פַּרְעֹה קָצַף עַל־עֲבָדָיו

וַיִּתֵּן אֹתִי בְּמִשְׁמַר בֵּית שַׂר הַטַּבָּחִים אֹתִי וְאֵת שַׂר הָאֹפִים :

11 וַנַּחַלְמָה חֲלוֹם בְּלַיְלָה אֶחָד אֲנִי וָהוּא אִישׁ כְּפִתְרוֹן חֲלֹמוֹ חָלָמְנוּ :

12 וְשָׁם אִתָּנוּ נַעַר עִבְרִי עֶבֶד לְשַׂר הַטַּבָּחִים וַנְּסַפֶּר־לוֹ וַיִּפְתָּר־לָנוּ אֶת־

13 חֲלֹמֹתֵינוּ אִישׁ כַּחֲלֹמוֹ פָּתָר : וַיְהִי כַּאֲשֶׁר פָּתַר־לָנוּ כֵּן הָיָה אֹתִי

14 הֵשִׁיב עַל־כַּנִּי וְאֹתוֹ תָלָה : וַיִּשְׁלַח פַּרְעֹה וַיִּקְרָא אֶת־יוֹסֵף וַיְרִיצֻהוּ

15 מִן־הַבּוֹר וַיְגַלַּח וַיְחַלֵּף שִׂמְלֹתָיו וַיָּבֹא אֶל־פַּרְעֹה : וַיֹּאמֶר פַּרְעֹה לֵאמֹר

אֶל־יוֹסֵף חֲלוֹם חָלַמְתִּי וּפֹתֵר אֵין אֹתוֹ וַאֲנִי שָׁמַעְתִּי עָלֶיךָ לֵאמֹר

16 תִּשְׁמַע חֲלוֹם לִפְתֹּר אֹתוֹ : וַיַּעַן יוֹסֵף אֶת־פַּרְעֹה לֵאמֹר בִּלְעָדָי אֱלֹהִים

17 יַעֲנֶה אֶת־שְׁלוֹם פַּרְעֹה : וַיְדַבֵּר פַּרְעֹה אֶל־יוֹסֵף בַּחֲלֹמִי הִנְנִי עֹמֵד

18 עַל־שְׂפַת הַיְאֹר : וְהִנֵּה מִן־הַיְאֹר עֹלֹת שֶׁבַע פָּרוֹת בְּרִיאוֹת בָּשָׂר

19 וִיפֹת תֹּאַר וַתִּרְעֶינָה בָּאָחוּ : וְהִנֵּה שֶׁבַע־פָּרוֹת אֲחֵרוֹת עֹלוֹת אַחֲרֵיהֶן

דַּלּוֹת וְרָעוֹת תֹּאַר מְאֹד וְרַקּוֹת בָּשָׂר לֹא־רָאִיתִי כָהֵנָּה בְּכָל־אֶרֶץ

20 מִצְרַיִם לָרֹעַ : וַתֹּאכַלְנָה הַפָּרוֹת הָרַקּוֹת וְהָרָעוֹת אֵת שֶׁבַע הַפָּרוֹת

הָרִאשֹׁנוֹת הַבְּרִיאֹת : וַתָּבֹאנָה אֶל־קִרְבֶּנָה וְלֹא נוֹדַע כִּי־בָאוּ אֶל־

21 קִרְבֶּנָה וּמַרְאֵיהֶן רַע כַּאֲשֶׁר בַּתְּחִלָּה וָאִיקָץ : וָאֵרֶא בַּחֲלֹמִי וְהִנֵּה

23 שֶׁבַע שִׁבֳּלִים עֹלֹת בְּקָנֶה אֶחָד מְלֵאֹת וְטֹבֹת: וְהִנֵּה שֶׁבַע שִׁבֳּלִים

24 צְנֻמוֹת דַּקּוֹת שְׁדֻפוֹת קָדִים צֹמְחֹת אַחֲרֵיהֶם: וַתִּבְלַעְןָ הַשִּׁבֳּלִים
הַדַּקֹּת אֵת שֶׁבַע הַשִּׁבֳּלִים הַטֹּבוֹת וָאֹמַר אֶל־הַחַרְטֻמִּים וְאֵין מַגִּיד

25 לִי: וַיֹּאמֶר יוֹסֵף אֶל־פַּרְעֹה חֲלוֹם פַּרְעֹה אֶחָד הוּא אֵת אֲשֶׁר הָאֱלֹהִים

26 עֹשֶׂה הִגִּיד לְפַרְעֹה: שֶׁבַע פָּרֹת הַטֹּבֹת שֶׁבַע שָׁנִים הֵנָּה וְשֶׁבַע הַשִּׁבֳּלִים

27 הַטֹּבֹת שֶׁבַע שָׁנִים הֵנָּה חֲלוֹם אֶחָד הוּא: וְשֶׁבַע הַפָּרוֹת הָרַקּוֹת
וְהָרָעֹת הָעֹלֹת אַחֲרֵיהֶן שֶׁבַע שָׁנִים הֵנָּה וְשֶׁבַע הַשִּׁבֳּלִים הָרֵקוֹת

28 שְׁדֻפוֹת הַקָּדִים יִהְיוּ שֶׁבַע שְׁנֵי רָעָב: הוּא הַדָּבָר אֲשֶׁר דִּבַּרְתִּי אֶל־

29 פַּרְעֹה אֲשֶׁר הָאֱלֹהִים עֹשֶׂה הֶרְאָה אֶת־פַּרְעֹה: הִנֵּה שֶׁבַע שָׁנִים בָּאוֹת

ל שָׂבָע גָּדוֹל בְּכָל־אֶרֶץ מִצְרָיִם: וְקָמוּ שֶׁבַע שְׁנֵי רָעָב אַחֲרֵיהֶן וְנִשְׁכַּח כָּל־

31 הַשָּׂבָע בְּאֶרֶץ מִצְרָיִם וְכִלָּה הָרָעָב אֶת־הָאָרֶץ: וְלֹא־יִוָּדַע הַשָּׂבָע בָּאָרֶץ

32 מִפְּנֵי הָרָעָב הַהוּא אַחֲרֵי־כֵן כִּי־כָבֵד הוּא מְאֹד: וְעַל הִשָּׁנוֹת הַחֲלוֹם
אֶל־פַּרְעֹה פַּעֲמָיִם כִּי־נָכוֹן הַדָּבָר מֵעִם הָאֱלֹהִים וּמְמַהֵר הָאֱלֹהִים לַעֲשֹׂתוֹ:

33 וְעַתָּה יֵרֶא פַרְעֹה אִישׁ נָבוֹן וְחָכָם וִישִׁיתֵהוּ עַל־אֶרֶץ מִצְרָיִם: יַעֲשֶׂה
34 פַרְעֹה וְיַפְקֵד פְּקִדִים עַל־הָאָרֶץ וְחִמֵּשׁ אֶת־אֶרֶץ מִצְרַיִם בְּשֶׁבַע שְׁנֵי

לה הַשָּׂבָע: וְיִקְבְּצוּ אֶת־כָּל־אֹכֶל הַשָּׁנִים הַטֹּבֹת הַבָּאֹת הָאֵלֶּה וְיִצְבְּרוּ־בָר

36 תַּחַת יַד־פַּרְעֹה אֹכֶל בֶּעָרִים וְשָׁמָרוּ: וְהָיָה הָאֹכֶל לְפִקָּדוֹן לָאָרֶץ
לְשֶׁבַע שְׁנֵי הָרָעָב אֲשֶׁר תִּהְיֶיןָ בְּאֶרֶץ מִצְרָיִם וְלֹא־תִכָּרֵת הָאָרֶץ בָּרָעָב:

37 וַיִּיטַב הַדָּבָר בְּעֵינֵי פַרְעֹה וּבְעֵינֵי כָּל־עֲבָדָיו: וַיֹּאמֶר פַּרְעֹה אֶל־עֲבָדָיו
38
39 הֲנִמְצָא כָזֶה אִישׁ אֲשֶׁר רוּחַ אֱלֹהִים בּוֹ: וַיֹּאמֶר פַּרְעֹה אֶל־יוֹסֵף
מ אַחֲרֵי הוֹדִיעַ אֱלֹהִים אוֹתְךָ אֶת־כָּל־זֹאת אֵין־נָבוֹן וְחָכָם כָּמוֹךָ: אַתָּה

41 תִּהְיֶה עַל־בֵּיתִי וְעַל־פִּיךָ יִשַּׁק כָּל־עַמִּי רַק הַכִּסֵּא אֶגְדַּל מִמֶּךָּ: וַיֹּאמֶר

42 פַּרְעֹה אֶל־יוֹסֵף רְאֵה נָתַתִּי אֹתְךָ עַל כָּל־אֶרֶץ מִצְרָיִם: וַיָּסַר פַּרְעֹה
אֶת־טַבַּעְתּוֹ מֵעַל יָדוֹ וַיִּתֵּן אֹתָהּ עַל־יַד יוֹסֵף וַיַּלְבֵּשׁ אֹתוֹ בִּגְדֵי־שֵׁשׁ

43 וַיָּשֶׂם רְבִד הַזָּהָב עַל־צַוָּארוֹ: וַיַּרְכֵּב אֹתוֹ בְּמִרְכֶּבֶת הַמִּשְׁנֶה אֲשֶׁר־לוֹ

44 וַיִּקְרְאוּ לְפָנָיו אַבְרֵךְ וְנָתוֹן אֹתוֹ עַל כָּל־אֶרֶץ מִצְרָיִם: וַיֹּאמֶר פַּרְעֹה
אֶל־יוֹסֵף אֲנִי פַרְעֹה וּבִלְעָדֶיךָ לֹא־יָרִים אִישׁ אֶת־יָדוֹ וְאֶת־רַגְלוֹ בְּכָל־

מה אֶרֶץ מִצְרָיִם: וַיִּקְרָא פַרְעֹה שֵׁם־יוֹסֵף צָפְנַת פַּעְנֵחַ וַיִּתֶּן־לוֹ אֶת־אָסְנַת

46 בַּת־פּוֹטִי פֶרַע כֹּהֵן אֹן לְאִשָּׁה וַיֵּצֵא יוֹסֵף עַל־אֶרֶץ מִצְרָיִם: וְיוֹסֵף
בֶּן־שְׁלֹשִׁים שָׁנָה בְּעָמְדוֹ לִפְנֵי פַּרְעֹה מֶלֶךְ־מִצְרָיִם וַיֵּצֵא יוֹסֵף מִלִּפְנֵי

47 פַרְעֹה וַיַּעֲבֹר בְּכָל־אֶרֶץ מִצְרָיִם: וַתַּעַשׂ הָאָרֶץ בְּשֶׁבַע שְׁנֵי הַשָּׂבָע

48 לִקְמָצִים: וַיִּקְבֹּץ אֶת־כָּל־אֹכֶל , שֶׁבַע שָׁנִים אֲשֶׁר הָיוּ בְּאֶרֶץ מִצְרַיִם

49 וַיִּתֶּן־אֹכֶל בֶּעָרִים אֹכֶל שְׂדֵה־הָעִיר אֲשֶׁר סְבִיבֹתֶיהָ נָתַן בְּתוֹכָהּ: וַיִּצְבֹּר
יוֹסֵף בָּר כְּחוֹל הַיָּם הַרְבֵּה מְאֹד עַד כִּי־חָדַל לִסְפֹּר כִּי־אֵין מִסְפָּר:

2

וּלְיוֹסֵף יֻלַּד שְׁנֵי בָנִים בְּטֶרֶם תָּבוֹא שְׁנַת הָרָעָב אֲשֶׁר יָלְדָה־לּוֹ אָסְנַת :

בַּת־פּוֹטִי פֶרַע כֹּהֵן אֹן : וַיִּקְרָא יוֹסֵף אֶת־שֵׁם הַבְּכוֹר מְנַשֶּׁה כִּי־נַשַּׁנִי 51

אֱלֹהִים אֶת־כָּל־עֲמָלִי וְאֵת כָּל־בֵּית אָבִי : וְאֵת שֵׁם הַשֵּׁנִי קָרָא אֶפְרָיִם 52

כִּי־הִפְרַנִי אֱלֹהִים בְּאֶרֶץ עָנְיִי : וַתִּכְלֶינָה שֶׁבַע שְׁנֵי הַשָּׂבָע אֲשֶׁר הָיָה 53

בְּאֶרֶץ מִצְרָיִם : וַתְּחִלֶּינָה שֶׁבַע שְׁנֵי הָרָעָב לָבוֹא כַּאֲשֶׁר אָמַר יוֹסֵף וַיְהִי 54

רָעָב בְּכָל־הָאֲרָצֹת וּבְכָל־אֶרֶץ מִצְרַיִם הָיָה לָחֶם : וַתִּרְעַב כָּל־אֶרֶץ מִצְרַיִם נה

וַיִּצְעַק הָעָם אֶל־פַּרְעֹה לַלָּחֶם וַיֹּאמֶר פַּרְעֹה לְכָל־מִצְרַיִם לְכוּ אֶל־יוֹסֵף

אֲשֶׁר־יֹאמַר לָכֶם תַּעֲשׂוּ : וְהָרָעָב הָיָה עַל כָּל־פְּנֵי הָאָרֶץ וַיִּפְתַּח יוֹסֵף 56

אֶת־כָּל־אֲשֶׁר בָּהֶם וַיִּשְׁבֹּר לְמִצְרַיִם וַיֶּחֱזַק הָרָעָב בְּאֶרֶץ מִצְרָיִם : וְכָל־ 57

הָאָרֶץ בָּאוּ מִצְרַיְמָה לִשְׁבֹּר אֶל־יוֹסֵף כִּי־חָזַק הָרָעָב בְּכָל־הָאָרֶץ :

CHAPTER XLII.   מב

וַיַּרְא יַעֲקֹב כִּי יֶשׁ־שֶׁבֶר בְּמִצְרָיִם וַיֹּאמֶר יַעֲקֹב לְבָנָיו לָמָּה תִּתְרָאוּ : א

וַיֹּאמֶר הִנֵּה שָׁמַעְתִּי כִּי יֶשׁ־שֶׁבֶר בְּמִצְרָיִם רְדוּ־שָׁמָּה וְשִׁבְרוּ־לָנוּ מִשָּׁם 2

וְנִחְיֶה וְלֹא נָמוּת : וַיֵּרְדוּ אֲחֵי־יוֹסֵף עֲשָׂרָה לִשְׁבֹּר בָּר מִמִּצְרָיִם : 3

וְאֶת־בִּנְיָמִין אֲחִי יוֹסֵף לֹא־שָׁלַח יַעֲקֹב אֶת־אֶחָיו כִּי אָמַר פֶּן־יִקְרָאֶנּוּ 4

אָסוֹן : וַיָּבֹאוּ בְּנֵי יִשְׂרָאֵל לִשְׁבֹּר בְּתוֹךְ הַבָּאִים כִּי־הָיָה הָרָעָב בְּאֶרֶץ ה

כְּנָעַן : וְיוֹסֵף הוּא הַשַּׁלִּיט עַל־הָאָרֶץ הוּא הַמַּשְׁבִּיר לְכָל־עַם הָאָרֶץ 6

וַיָּבֹאוּ אֲחֵי יוֹסֵף וַיִּשְׁתַּחֲווּ־לוֹ אַפַּיִם אָרְצָה : וַיַּרְא יוֹסֵף אֶת־אֶחָיו 7

וַיַּכִּרֵם וַיִּתְנַכֵּר אֲלֵיהֶם וַיְדַבֵּר אִתָּם קָשׁוֹת וַיֹּאמֶר אֲלֵהֶם מֵאַיִן בָּאתֶם

וַיֹּאמְרוּ מֵאֶרֶץ כְּנַעַן לִשְׁבָּר־אֹכֶל : וַיַּכֵּר יוֹסֵף אֶת־אֶחָיו וְהֵם לֹא הִכִּרֻהוּ : 8

וַיִּזְכֹּר יוֹסֵף אֵת הַחֲלֹמוֹת אֲשֶׁר חָלַם לָהֶם וַיֹּאמֶר אֲלֵהֶם מְרַגְּלִים 9

אַתֶּם לִרְאוֹת אֶת־עֶרְוַת הָאָרֶץ בָּאתֶם : וַיֹּאמְרוּ אֵלָיו לֹא אֲדֹנִי וַעֲבָדֶיךָ י

בָּאוּ לִשְׁבָּר־אֹכֶל : כֻּלָּנוּ בְּנֵי אִישׁ־אֶחָד נָחְנוּ כֵּנִים אֲנַחְנוּ לֹא־הָיוּ 11

עֲבָדֶיךָ מְרַגְּלִים : וַיֹּאמֶר אֲלֵהֶם לֹא כִּי־עֶרְוַת הָאָרֶץ בָּאתֶם לִרְאוֹת : 12

וַיֹּאמְרוּ שְׁנֵים עָשָׂר עֲבָדֶיךָ אַחִים אֲנַחְנוּ בְּנֵי אִישׁ־אֶחָד בְּאֶרֶץ 13

כְּנָעַן וְהִנֵּה הַקָּטֹן אֶת־אָבִינוּ הַיּוֹם וְהָאֶחָד אֵינֶנּוּ : וַיֹּאמֶר אֲלֵהֶם 14

יוֹסֵף הוּא אֲשֶׁר דִּבַּרְתִּי אֲלֵכֶם לֵאמֹר מְרַגְּלִים אַתֶּם : בְּזֹאת תִּבָּחֵנוּ חֵי טו

פַרְעֹה אִם־תֵּצְאוּ מִזֶּה כִּי אִם־בְּבוֹא אֲחִיכֶם הַקָּטֹן הֵנָּה : שִׁלְחוּ מִכֶּם 16

אֶחָד וְיִקַּח אֶת־אֲחִיכֶם וְאַתֶּם הֵאָסְרוּ וְיִבָּחֲנוּ דִּבְרֵיכֶם הַאֱמֶת אִתְּכֶם

וְאִם־לֹא חֵי פַרְעֹה כִּי מְרַגְּלִים אַתֶּם : וַיֶּאֱסֹף אֹתָם אֶל־מִשְׁמָר שְׁלֹשֶׁת 17

יָמִים : וַיֹּאמֶר אֲלֵהֶם יוֹסֵף בַּיּוֹם הַשְּׁלִישִׁי זֹאת עֲשׂוּ וִחְיוּ אֶת־הָאֱלֹהִים 18

<hr>

v. 50.   לְמַד קְמֵצָה

19 אִם־כֵּנִים אַתֶּם אֲחִיכֶם אֶחָד יֵאָסֵר בְּבֵית מִשְׁמַרְכֶם וְאַתֶּם אָנִי יָרֵא:

כ לְכוּ הָבִיאוּ שֶׁבֶר רַעֲבוֹן בָּתֵּיכֶם: וְאֶת־אֲחִיכֶם הַקָּטֹן תָּבִיאוּ אֵלַי

21 וְיֵאָמְנוּ דִבְרֵיכֶם וְלֹא תָמוּתוּ וַיַּעֲשׂוּ־כֵן: וַיֹּאמְרוּ אִישׁ אֶל־אָחִיו אֲבָל אֲשֵׁמִים ׀ אֲנַחְנוּ עַל־אָחִינוּ אֲשֶׁר רָאִינוּ צָרַת נַפְשׁוֹ בְּהִתְחַנְנוֹ אֵלֵינוּ

22 וְלֹא שָׁמָעְנוּ עַל־כֵּן בָּאָה אֵלֵינוּ הַצָּרָה הַזֹּאת: וַיַּעַן רְאוּבֵן אֹתָם לֵאמֹר הֲלוֹא אָמַרְתִּי אֲלֵיכֶם ׀ לֵאמֹר אַל־תֶּחֶטְאוּ בַיֶּלֶד וְלֹא שְׁמַעְתֶּם

23 וְגַם־דָּמוֹ הִנֵּה נִדְרָשׁ: וְהֵם לֹא יָדְעוּ כִּי שֹׁמֵעַ יוֹסֵף כִּי הַמֵּלִיץ

24 בֵּינֹתָם: וַיִּסֹּב מֵעֲלֵיהֶם וַיֵּבְךְּ וַיָּשָׁב אֲלֵהֶם וַיְדַבֵּר אֲלֵהֶם וַיִּקַּח מֵאִתָּם

כה אֶת־שִׁמְעוֹן וַיֶּאֱסֹר אֹתוֹ לְעֵינֵיהֶם: וַיְצַו יוֹסֵף וַיְמַלְאוּ אֶת־כְּלֵיהֶם בָּר וּלְהָשִׁיב כַּסְפֵּיהֶם אִישׁ אֶל־שַׂקּוֹ וְלָתֵת לָהֶם צֵדָה לַדָּרֶךְ וַיַּעַשׂ לָהֶם

26 כֵּן: וַיִּשְׂאוּ אֶת־שִׁבְרָם עַל־חֲמֹרֵיהֶם וַיֵּלְכוּ מִשָּׁם: וַיִּפְתַּח הָאֶחָד אֶת־
27 שַׂקּוֹ לָתֵת מִסְפּוֹא לַחֲמֹרוֹ בַּמָּלוֹן וַיַּרְא אֶת־כַּסְפּוֹ וְהִנֵּה־הוּא בְּפִי

28 אַמְתַּחְתּוֹ: וַיֹּאמֶר אֶל־אֶחָיו הוּשַׁב כַּסְפִּי וְגַם הִנֵּה בְאַמְתַּחְתִּי וַיֵּצֵא

29 לִבָּם וַיֶּחֶרְדוּ אִישׁ אֶל־אָחִיו לֵאמֹר מַה־זֹּאת עָשָׂה אֱלֹהִים לָנוּ: וַיָּבֹאוּ אֶל־יַעֲקֹב אֲבִיהֶם אַרְצָה כְּנָעַן וַיַּגִּידוּ לוֹ אֵת כָּל־הַקֹּרֹת אֹתָם לֵאמֹר:

ל דִּבֶּר הָאִישׁ אֲדֹנֵי הָאָרֶץ אִתָּנוּ קָשׁוֹת וַיִּתֵּן אֹתָנוּ כִּמְרַגְּלִים אֶת־הָאָרֶץ:

31 וַנֹּאמֶר אֵלָיו כֵּנִים אֲנָחְנוּ לֹא הָיִינוּ מְרַגְּלִים: שְׁנֵים־עָשָׂר אֲנַחְנוּ אַחִים
32 בְּנֵי אָבִינוּ הָאֶחָד אֵינֶנּוּ וְהַקָּטֹן הַיּוֹם אֶת־אָבִינוּ בְּאֶרֶץ כְּנָעַן: וַיֹּאמֶר

33 אֵלֵינוּ הָאִישׁ אֲדֹנֵי הָאָרֶץ בְּזֹאת אֵדַע כִּי כֵנִים אַתֶּם אֲחִיכֶם הָאֶחָד

34 הַנִּיחוּ אִתִּי וְאֶת־רַעֲבוֹן בָּתֵּיכֶם קְחוּ וָלֵכוּ: וְהָבִיאוּ אֶת־אֲחִיכֶם הַקָּטֹן אֵלַי וְאֵדְעָה כִּי לֹא מְרַגְּלִים אַתֶּם כִּי כֵנִים אַתֶּם אֶת־אֲחִיכֶם אֶתֵּן

לה לָכֶם וְאֶת־הָאָרֶץ תִּסְחָרוּ: וַיְהִי הֵם מְרִיקִים שַׂקֵּיהֶם וְהִנֵּה־אִישׁ צְרוֹר־כַּסְפּוֹ בְּשַׂקּוֹ וַיִּרְאוּ אֶת־צְרֹרוֹת כַּסְפֵּיהֶם הֵמָּה וַאֲבִיהֶם וַיִּירָאוּ:

36 וַיֹּאמֶר אֲלֵהֶם יַעֲקֹב אֲבִיהֶם אֹתִי שִׁכַּלְתֶּם יוֹסֵף אֵינֶנּוּ וְשִׁמְעוֹן אֵינֶנּוּ

37 וְאֶת־בִּנְיָמִן תִּקָּחוּ עָלַי הָיוּ כֻלָּנָה: וַיֹּאמֶר רְאוּבֵן אֶל־אָבִיו לֵאמֹר אֶת־שְׁנֵי בָנַי תָּמִית אִם־לֹא אֲבִיאֶנּוּ אֵלֶיךָ תְּנָה אֹתוֹ עַל־יָדִי וַאֲנִי אֲשִׁיבֶנּוּ

38 אֵלֶיךָ: וַיֹּאמֶר לֹא־יֵרֵד בְּנִי עִמָּכֶם כִּי־אָחִיו מֵת וְהוּא לְבַדּוֹ נִשְׁאָר וּקְרָאָהוּ אָסוֹן בַּדֶּרֶךְ אֲשֶׁר תֵּלְכוּ־בָהּ וְהוֹרַדְתֶּם אֶת־שֵׂיבָתִי בְּיָגוֹן שְׁאוֹלָה:

CHAPTER XLIII. מג

א וְהָרָעָב כָּבֵד בָּאָרֶץ: וַיְהִי כַּאֲשֶׁר כִּלּוּ לֶאֱכֹל אֶת־הַשֶּׁבֶר אֲשֶׁר הֵבִיאוּ
ג מִמִּצְרָיִם וַיֹּאמֶר אֲלֵיהֶם אֲבִיהֶם שֻׁבוּ שִׁבְרוּ־לָנוּ מְעַט־אֹכֶל: וַיֹּאמֶר אֵלָיו יְהוּדָה לֵאמֹר הָעֵד הֵעִד בָּנוּ הָאִישׁ לֵאמֹר לֹא־תִרְאוּ פָנַי בִּלְתִּי

אֲחִיכֶם אִתְּכֶם : אִם־יֶשְׁךָ מְשַׁלֵּחַ אֶת־אָחִינוּ אִתָּנוּ נֵרְדָה וְנִשְׁבְּרָה לְךָ 4

אֹכֶל : וְאִם־אֵינְךָ מְשַׁלֵּחַ לֹא נֵרֵד כִּי־הָאִישׁ אָמַר אֵלֵינוּ לֹא־תִרְאוּ פָנַי ה

בִּלְתִּי אֲחִיכֶם אִתְּכֶם : וַיֹּאמֶר יִשְׂרָאֵל לָמָה הֲרֵעֹתֶם לִי לְהַגִּיד לָאִישׁ 6

הַעוֹד לָכֶם אָח : וַיֹּאמְרוּ שָׁאוֹל שָׁאַל־הָאִישׁ לָנוּ וּלְמוֹלַדְתֵּנוּ לֵאמֹר 7

הַעוֹד אֲבִיכֶם חַי הֲיֵשׁ לָכֶם אָח וַנַּגֶּד־לוֹ עַל־פִּי הַדְּבָרִים הָאֵלֶּה הֲיָדוֹעַ

נֵדַע כִּי יֹאמַר הוֹרִידוּ אֶת־אֲחִיכֶם : וַיֹּאמֶר יְהוּדָה אֶל־יִשְׂרָאֵל אָבִיו 8

שִׁלְחָה הַנַּעַר אִתִּי וְנָקוּמָה וְנֵלֵכָה וְנִחְיֶה וְלֹא נָמוּת גַּם־אֲנַחְנוּ גַם־אַתָּה

גַּם־טַפֵּנוּ : אָנֹכִי אֶעֶרְבֶנּוּ מִיָּדִי תְּבַקְשֶׁנּוּ אִם־לֹא הֲבִיאֹתִיו אֵלֶיךָ 9

וְהִצַּגְתִּיו לְפָנֶיךָ וְחָטָאתִי לְךָ כָּל־הַיָּמִים : כִּי לוּלֵא הִתְמַהְמָהְנוּ כִּי־ י

עַתָּה שַׁבְנוּ זֶה פַעֲמָיִם : וַיֹּאמֶר אֲלֵהֶם יִשְׂרָאֵל אֲבִיהֶם אִם־כֵּן אֵפוֹא 11

זֹאת עֲשׂוּ קְחוּ מִזִּמְרַת הָאָרֶץ בִּכְלֵיכֶם וְהוֹרִידוּ לָאִישׁ מִנְחָה מְעַט

צֳרִי וּמְעַט דְּבַשׁ נְכֹאת וָלֹט בָּטְנִים וּשְׁקֵדִים : וְכֶסֶף מִשְׁנֶה קְחוּ בְיֶדְכֶם 12

וְאֶת־הַכֶּסֶף הַמּוּשָׁב בְּפִי אַמְתְּחֹתֵיכֶם תָּשִׁיבוּ בְיֶדְכֶם אוּלַי מִשְׁגֶּה הוּא :

וְאֶת־אֲחִיכֶם קָחוּ וְקוּמוּ שׁוּבוּ אֶל־הָאִישׁ : וְאֵל שַׁדַּי יִתֵּן לָכֶם רַחֲמִים 13 14

לִפְנֵי הָאִישׁ וְשִׁלַּח לָכֶם אֶת־אֲחִיכֶם אַחֵר וְאֶת־בִּנְיָמִין וַאֲנִי כַּאֲשֶׁר

שָׁכֹלְתִּי שָׁכָלְתִּי : וַיִּקְחוּ הָאֲנָשִׁים אֶת־הַמִּנְחָה הַזֹּאת וּמִשְׁנֶה־כֶּסֶף לָקְחוּ טו

בְיָדָם וְאֶת־בִּנְיָמִן וַיָּקֻמוּ וַיֵּרְדוּ מִצְרַיִם וַיַּעַמְדוּ לִפְנֵי יוֹסֵף : וַיַּרְא יוֹסֵף 16

אִתָּם אֶת־בִּנְיָמִין וַיֹּאמֶר לַאֲשֶׁר עַל־בֵּיתוֹ הָבֵא אֶת־הָאֲנָשִׁים הַבָּיְתָה

וּטְבֹחַ טֶבַח וְהָכֵן כִּי אִתִּי יֹאכְלוּ הָאֲנָשִׁים בַּצָּהֳרָיִם : וַיַּעַשׂ הָאִישׁ כַּאֲשֶׁר 17

אָמַר יוֹסֵף וַיָּבֵא הָאִישׁ אֶת־הָאֲנָשִׁים בֵּיתָה יוֹסֵף : וַיִּירְאוּ הָאֲנָשִׁים כִּי 18

הוּבְאוּ בֵּית יוֹסֵף וַיֹּאמְרוּ עַל־דְּבַר הַכֶּסֶף הַשָּׁב בְּאַמְתְּחֹתֵינוּ בַּתְּחִלָּה

אֲנַחְנוּ מוּבָאִים לְהִתְגֹּלֵל עָלֵינוּ וּלְהִתְנַפֵּל עָלֵינוּ וְלָקַחַת אֹתָנוּ לַעֲבָדִים

וְאֶת־חֲמֹרֵינוּ : וַיִּגְּשׁוּ אֶל־הָאִישׁ אֲשֶׁר עַל־בֵּית יוֹסֵף וַיְדַבְּרוּ אֵלָיו פֶּתַח 19

הַבָּיִת : וַיֹּאמְרוּ בִּי אֲדֹנִי יָרֹד יָרַדְנוּ בַּתְּחִלָּה לִשְׁבָּר־אֹכֶל : וַיְהִי כִּי־ 21 ᵒ

בָאנוּ אֶל־הַמָּלוֹן וַנִּפְתְּחָה אֶת־אַמְתְּחֹתֵינוּ וְהִנֵּה כֶסֶף־אִישׁ בְּפִי אַמְתַּחְתּוֹ

כַּסְפֵּנוּ בְּמִשְׁקָלוֹ וַנָּשֶׁב אֹתוֹ בְּיָדֵנוּ : וְכֶסֶף אַחֵר הוֹרַדְנוּ בְיָדֵנוּ לִשְׁבָּר־ 22

אֹכֶל לֹא יָדַעְנוּ מִי־שָׂם כַּסְפֵּנוּ בְּאַמְתְּחֹתֵינוּ : וַיֹּאמֶר שָׁלוֹם לָכֶם אַל־ 23

תִּירָאוּ אֱלֹהֵיכֶם וֵאלֹהֵי אֲבִיכֶם נָתַן לָכֶם מַטְמוֹן בְּאַמְתְּחֹתֵיכֶם כַּסְפְּכֶם

בָּא אֵלָי וַיּוֹצֵא אֲלֵהֶם אֶת־שִׁמְעוֹן : וַיָּבֵא הָאִישׁ אֶת־הָאֲנָשִׁים בֵּיתָה 24

יוֹסֵף וַיִּתֶּן־מַיִם וַיִּרְחֲצוּ רַגְלֵיהֶם וַיִּתֵּן מִסְפּוֹא לַחֲמֹרֵיהֶם : וַיָּכִינוּ אֶת־ כה

הַמִּנְחָה עַד־בּוֹא יוֹסֵף בַּצָּהֳרָיִם כִּי שָׁמְעוּ כִּי־שָׁם יֹאכְלוּ לָחֶם : וַיָּבֹא 26

יוֹסֵף הַבַּיְתָה וַיָּבִיאוּ לוֹ אֶת־הַמִּנְחָה אֲשֶׁר־בְּיָדָם הַבָּיְתָה וַיִּשְׁתַּחֲווּ־לוֹ

אָרְצָה : וַיִּשְׁאַל לָהֶם לְשָׁלוֹם וַיֹּאמֶר הֲשָׁלוֹם אֲבִיכֶם הַזָּקֵן אֲשֶׁר 27

28 אֲמַרְתֶּם הַעוֹדֶנּוּ חָי : וַיֹּאמְרוּ שָׁלוֹם לְעַבְדְּךָ לְאָבִינוּ עוֹדֶנּוּ חָי וַיִּקְּדוּ
29 וַיִּשְׁתַּחֲו : וַיִּשָּׂא עֵינָיו וַיַּרְא אֶת־בִּנְיָמִין אָחִיו בֶּן־אִמּוֹ וַיֹּאמֶר הֲזֶה
ל אֲחִיכֶם הַקָּטֹן אֲשֶׁר אֲמַרְתֶּם אֵלָי וַיֹּאמַר אֱלֹהִים יָחְנְךָ בְּנִי : וַיְמַהֵר
יוֹסֵף כִּי־נִכְמְרוּ רַחֲמָיו אֶל־אָחִיו וַיְבַקֵּשׁ לִבְכּוֹת וַיָּבֹא הַחַדְרָה וַיֵּבְךְּ
31 שָׁמָּה : וַיִּרְחַץ פָּנָיו וַיֵּצֵא וַיִּתְאַפַּק וַיֹּאמֶר שִׂימוּ לָחֶם : וַיָּשִׂימוּ לוֹ
32 לְבַדּוֹ וְלָהֶם לְבַדָּם וְלַמִּצְרִים הָאֹכְלִים אִתּוֹ לְבַדָּם כִּי לֹא יוּכְלוּן
33 הַמִּצְרִים לֶאֱכֹל אֶת־הָעִבְרִים לֶחֶם כִּי־תוֹעֵבָה הִוא לְמִצְרָיִם : וַיֵּשְׁבוּ
לְפָנָיו הַבְּכֹר כִּבְכֹרָתוֹ וְהַצָּעִיר כִּצְעִרָתוֹ וַיִּתְמְהוּ הָאֲנָשִׁים אִישׁ אֶל־
34 רֵעֵהוּ : וַיִּשָּׂא מַשְׂאֹת מֵאֵת פָּנָיו אֲלֵהֶם וַתֵּרֶב מַשְׂאַת בִּנְיָמִן מִמַּשְׂאֹת
כֻּלָּם חָמֵשׁ יָדוֹת וַיִּשְׁתּוּ וַיִּשְׁכְּרוּ עִמּוֹ :

CHAPTER XLIV. מד

א וַיְצַו אֶת־אֲשֶׁר עַל־בֵּיתוֹ לֵאמֹר מַלֵּא אֶת־אַמְתְּחֹת הָאֲנָשִׁים אֹכֶל כַּאֲשֶׁר
2 יוּכְלוּן שְׂאֵת וְשִׂים כֶּסֶף־אִישׁ בְּפִי אַמְתַּחְתּוֹ : וְאֶת־גְּבִיעִי גְּבִיעַ הַכֶּסֶף
תָּשִׂים בְּפִי אַמְתַּחַת הַקָּטֹן וְאֵת כֶּסֶף שִׁבְרוֹ וַיַּעַשׂ כִּדְבַר יוֹסֵף אֲשֶׁר
3 4 דִּבֵּר : הַבֹּקֶר אוֹר וְהָאֲנָשִׁים שֻׁלְּחוּ הֵמָּה וַחֲמֹרֵיהֶם : הֵם יָצְאוּ אֶת־
הָעִיר לֹא הִרְחִיקוּ וְיוֹסֵף אָמַר לַאֲשֶׁר עַל־בֵּיתוֹ קוּם רְדֹף אַחֲרֵי הָאֲנָשִׁים
ה וְהִשַּׂגְתָּם וְאָמַרְתָּ אֲלֵהֶם לָמָּה שִׁלַּמְתֶּם רָעָה תַּחַת טוֹבָה : הֲלוֹא זֶה
אֲשֶׁר יִשְׁתֶּה אֲדֹנִי בּוֹ וְהוּא נַחֵשׁ יְנַחֵשׁ בּוֹ הֲרֵעֹתֶם אֲשֶׁר עֲשִׂיתֶם :
7 6 וַיַּשִּׂגֵם וַיְדַבֵּר אֲלֵהֶם אֶת־הַדְּבָרִים הָאֵלֶּה : וַיֹּאמְרוּ אֵלָיו לָמָּה יְדַבֵּר
8 אֲדֹנִי כַּדְּבָרִים הָאֵלֶּה חָלִילָה לַעֲבָדֶיךָ מֵעֲשׂוֹת כַּדָּבָר הַזֶּה : הֵן כֶּסֶף
אֲשֶׁר מָצָאנוּ בְּפִי אַמְתְּחֹתֵינוּ הֱשִׁיבֹנוּ אֵלֶיךָ מֵאֶרֶץ כְּנָעַן וְאֵיךְ נִגְנֹב
9 מִבֵּית אֲדֹנֶיךָ כֶּסֶף אוֹ זָהָב : אֲשֶׁר יִמָּצֵא אִתּוֹ מֵעֲבָדֶיךָ וָמֵת וְגַם־
י אֲנַחְנוּ נִהְיֶה לַאדֹנִי לַעֲבָדִים : וַיֹּאמֶר גַּם־עַתָּה כְדִבְרֵיכֶם כֶּן־הוּא אֲשֶׁר
11 יִמָּצֵא אִתּוֹ יִהְיֶה־לִּי עָבֶד וְאַתֶּם תִּהְיוּ נְקִיִּם : וַיְמַהֲרוּ וַיּוֹרִדוּ
12 אִישׁ אֶת־אַמְתַּחְתּוֹ אָרְצָה וַיִּפְתְּחוּ אִישׁ אַמְתַּחְתּוֹ : וַיְחַפֵּשׂ בַּגָּדוֹל הֵחֵל
13 וּבַקָּטֹן כִּלָּה וַיִּמָּצֵא הַגָּבִיעַ בְּאַמְתַּחַת בִּנְיָמִן : וַיִּקְרְעוּ שִׂמְלֹתָם וַיַּעֲמֹס
14 אִישׁ עַל־חֲמֹרוֹ וַיָּשֻׁבוּ הָעִירָה : וַיָּבֹא יְהוּדָה וְאֶחָיו בֵּיתָה יוֹסֵף וְהוּא
ט עוֹדֶנּוּ שָׁם וַיִּפְּלוּ לְפָנָיו אָרְצָה : וַיֹּאמֶר לָהֶם יוֹסֵף מָה־הַמַּעֲשֶׂה הַזֶּה
16 אֲשֶׁר עֲשִׂיתֶם הֲלוֹא יְדַעְתֶּם כִּי־נַחֵשׁ יְנַחֵשׁ אִישׁ אֲשֶׁר כָּמֹנִי : וַיֹּאמֶר
יְהוּדָה מַה־נֹּאמַר לַאדֹנִי מַה־נְּדַבֵּר וּמַה־נִּצְטַדָּק הָאֱלֹהִים מָצָא אֶת־
עֲוֹן עֲבָדֶיךָ הִנֶּנּוּ עֲבָדִים לַאדֹנִי גַּם־אֲנַחְנוּ גַּם אֲשֶׁר־נִמְצָא הַגָּבִיעַ בְּיָדוֹ :

17 וַיֹּאמֶר חָלִילָה לִּי מֵעֲשׂוֹת זֹאת הָאִישׁ אֲשֶׁר נִמְצָא הַגָּבִיעַ בְּיָדוֹ הוּא
יִהְיֶה־לִּי עָבֶד וְאַתֶּם עֲלוּ לְשָׁלוֹם אֶל־אֲבִיכֶם :

18 וַיִּגַּשׁ אֵלָיו יְהוּדָה וַיֹּאמֶר בִּי אֲדֹנִי יְדַבֶּר־נָא עַבְדְּךָ דָבָר בְּאָזְנֵי אֲדֹנִי

19 וְאַל־יִחַר אַפְּךָ בְּעַבְדֶּךָ כִּי כָמוֹךָ כְּפַרְעֹה : אֲדֹנִי שָׁאַל אֶת־עֲבָדָיו לֵאמֹר

20 הֲיֵשׁ־לָכֶם אָב אוֹ־אָח : וַנֹּאמֶר אֶל־אֲדֹנִי יֶשׁ־לָנוּ אָב זָקֵן וְיֶלֶד זְקֻנִים קָטָן

21 וְאָחִיו מֵת וַיִּוָּתֵר הוּא לְבַדּוֹ לְאִמּוֹ וְאָבִיו אֲהֵבוֹ : וַתֹּאמֶר אֶל־עֲבָדֶיךָ

22 הוֹרִדֻהוּ אֵלָי וְאָשִׂימָה עֵינִי עָלָיו : וַנֹּאמֶר אֶל־אֲדֹנִי לֹא־יוּכַל הַנַּעַר לַעֲזֹב

23 אֶת־אָבִיו וְעָזַב אֶת־אָבִיו וָמֵת : וַתֹּאמֶר אֶל־עֲבָדֶיךָ אִם־לֹא יֵרֵד אֲחִיכֶם

24 הַקָּטֹן אִתְּכֶם לֹא תֹסִפוּן לִרְאוֹת פָּנָי : וַיְהִי כִּי עָלִינוּ אֶל־עַבְדְּךָ אָבִי

כה וַנַּגֶּד־לּוֹ אֵת דִּבְרֵי אֲדֹנִי : וַיֹּאמֶר אָבִינוּ שֻׁבוּ שִׁבְרוּ־לָנוּ מְעַט־אֹכֶל :

26 וַנֹּאמֶר לֹא נוּכַל לָרֶדֶת אִם־יֵשׁ אָחִינוּ הַקָּטֹן אִתָּנוּ וְיָרַדְנוּ כִּי־לֹא נוּכַל

27 לִרְאוֹת פְּנֵי הָאִישׁ וְאָחִינוּ הַקָּטֹן אֵינֶנּוּ אִתָּנוּ : וַיֹּאמֶר עַבְדְּךָ אָבִי אֵלֵינוּ

28 אַתֶּם יְדַעְתֶּם כִּי שְׁנַיִם יָלְדָה־לִּי אִשְׁתִּי : וַיֵּצֵא הָאֶחָד מֵאִתִּי וָאֹמַר אַךְ

29 טָרֹף טֹרָף וְלֹא רְאִיתִיו עַד־הֵנָּה : וּלְקַחְתֶּם גַּם־אֶת־זֶה מֵעִם פָּנַי וְקָרָהוּ

ל אָסוֹן וְהוֹרַדְתֶּם אֶת־שֵׂיבָתִי בְּרָעָה שְׁאֹלָה : וְעַתָּה כְּבֹאִי אֶל־עַבְדְּךָ אָבִי

31 וְהַנַּעַר אֵינֶנּוּ אִתָּנוּ וְנַפְשׁוֹ קְשׁוּרָה בְנַפְשׁוֹ : וְהָיָה כִּרְאוֹתוֹ כִּי־אֵין הַנַּעַר

32 וָמֵת וְהוֹרִידוּ עֲבָדֶיךָ אֶת־שֵׂיבַת עַבְדְּךָ אָבִינוּ בְּיָגוֹן שְׁאֹלָה : כִּי עַבְדְּךָ

עָרַב אֶת־הַנַּעַר מֵעִם אָבִי לֵאמֹר אִם־לֹא אֲבִיאֶנּוּ אֵלֶיךָ וְחָטָאתִי לְאָבִי

33 כָּל־הַיָּמִים : וְעַתָּה יֵשֶׁב־נָא עַבְדְּךָ תַּחַת הַנַּעַר עֶבֶד לַאדֹנִי וְהַנַּעַר יַעַל

34 עִם־אֶחָיו : כִּי־אֵיךְ אֶעֱלֶה אֶל־אָבִי וְהַנַּעַר אֵינֶנּוּ אִתִּי פֶּן אֶרְאֶה בָרָע
אֲשֶׁר יִמְצָא אֶת־אָבִי :

CHAPTER XLV. מה

א וְלֹא־יָכֹל יוֹסֵף לְהִתְאַפֵּק לְכֹל הַנִּצָּבִים עָלָיו וַיִּקְרָא הוֹצִיאוּ כָל־אִישׁ מֵעָלָי

2 וְלֹא־עָמַד אִישׁ אִתּוֹ בְּהִתְוַדַּע יוֹסֵף אֶל־אֶחָיו : וַיִּתֵּן אֶת־קֹלוֹ בִּבְכִי וַיִּשְׁמְעוּ

3 מִצְרַיִם וַיִּשְׁמַע בֵּית פַּרְעֹה : וַיֹּאמֶר יוֹסֵף אֶל־אֶחָיו אֲנִי יוֹסֵף הַעוֹד אָבִי

4 חָי וְלֹא־יָכְלוּ אֶחָיו לַעֲנוֹת אֹתוֹ כִּי נִבְהֲלוּ מִפָּנָיו : וַיֹּאמֶר יוֹסֵף אֶל־אֶחָיו
גְּשׁוּ־נָא אֵלַי וַיִּגָּשׁוּ וַיֹּאמֶר אֲנִי יוֹסֵף אֲחִיכֶם אֲשֶׁר־מְכַרְתֶּם אֹתִי מִצְרָיְמָה :

ה וְעַתָּה אַל־תֵּעָצְבוּ וְאַל־יִחַר בְּעֵינֵיכֶם כִּי־מְכַרְתֶּם אֹתִי הֵנָּה כִּי לְמִחְיָה

6 שְׁלָחַנִי אֱלֹהִים לִפְנֵיכֶם : כִּי־זֶה שְׁנָתַיִם הָרָעָב בְּקֶרֶב הָאָרֶץ וְעוֹד חָמֵשׁ

7 שָׁנִים אֲשֶׁר אֵין־חָרִישׁ וְקָצִיר : וַיִּשְׁלָחֵנִי אֱלֹהִים לִפְנֵיכֶם לָשׂוּם לָכֶם

8 שְׁאֵרִית בָּאָרֶץ וּלְהַחֲיוֹת לָכֶם לִפְלֵיטָה גְדֹלָה : וְעַתָּה לֹא־אַתֶּם שְׁלַחְתֶּם

אֹתִי הֵנָּה כִּי הָאֱלֹהִים וַיְשִׂימֵנִי לְאָב לְפַרְעֹה וּלְאָדוֹן לְכָל־בֵּיתוֹ וּמֹשֵׁל

9 בְּכָל־אֶרֶץ מִצְרָיִם: מַהֲרוּ וַעֲלוּ אֶל־אָבִי וַאֲמַרְתֶּם אֵלָיו כֹּה אָמַר
בִּנְךָ יוֹסֵף שָׂמַנִי אֱלֹהִים לְאָדוֹן לְכָל־מִצְרָיִם רְדָה אֵלַי אַל־תַּעֲמֹד:

י וְיָשַׁבְתָּ בְאֶרֶץ־גֹּשֶׁן וְהָיִיתָ קָרוֹב אֵלַי אַתָּה וּבָנֶיךָ וּבְנֵי בָנֶיךָ וְצֹאנְךָ

11 וּבְקָרְךָ וְכָל־אֲשֶׁר־לָךְ: וְכִלְכַּלְתִּי אֹתְךָ שָׁם כִּי־עוֹד חָמֵשׁ שָׁנִים רָעָב

12 פֶּן־תִּוָּרֵשׁ אַתָּה וּבֵיתְךָ וְכָל־אֲשֶׁר־לָךְ: וְהִנֵּה עֵינֵיכֶם רֹאוֹת וְעֵינֵי

13 אָחִי בִנְיָמִין כִּי־פִי הַמְדַבֵּר אֲלֵיכֶם: וְהִגַּדְתֶּם לְאָבִי אֶת־כָּל־כְּבוֹדִי
בְּמִצְרַיִם וְאֵת כָּל־אֲשֶׁר רְאִיתֶם וּמִהַרְתֶּם וְהוֹרַדְתֶּם אֶת־אָבִי הֵנָּה:

14 וַיִּפֹּל עַל־צַוְּארֵי בִנְיָמִן־אָחִיו וַיֵּבְךְּ וּבִנְיָמִן בָּכָה עַל־צַוָּארָיו: וַיְנַשֵּׁק

16 לְכָל־אֶחָיו וַיֵּבְךְּ עֲלֵהֶם וְאַחֲרֵי כֵן דִּבְּרוּ אֶחָיו אִתּוֹ: וְהַקֹּל נִשְׁמַע
בֵּית פַּרְעֹה לֵאמֹר בָּאוּ אֲחֵי יוֹסֵף וַיִּיטַב בְּעֵינֵי פַרְעֹה וּבְעֵינֵי עֲבָדָיו:

17 וַיֹּאמֶר פַּרְעֹה אֶל־יוֹסֵף אֱמֹר אֶל־אַחֶיךָ זֹאת עֲשׂוּ טַעֲנוּ אֶת־בְּעִירְכֶם

18 וּלְכוּ־בֹאוּ אַרְצָה כְּנָעַן: וּקְחוּ אֶת־אֲבִיכֶם וְאֶת־בָּתֵּיכֶם וּבֹאוּ אֵלָי

19 וְאֶתְּנָה לָכֶם אֶת־טוּב אֶרֶץ מִצְרַיִם וְאִכְלוּ אֶת־חֵלֶב הָאָרֶץ: וְאַתָּה
צֻוֵּיתָה זֹאת עֲשׂוּ קְחוּ־לָכֶם מֵאֶרֶץ מִצְרַיִם עֲגָלוֹת לְטַפְּכֶם וְלִנְשֵׁיכֶם

כ וּנְשָׂאתֶם אֶת־אֲבִיכֶם וּבָאתֶם: וְעֵינְכֶם אַל־תָּחֹס עַל־כְּלֵיכֶם כִּי־טוּב כָּל־

21 אֶרֶץ מִצְרַיִם לָכֶם הוּא: וַיַּעֲשׂוּ־כֵן בְּנֵי יִשְׂרָאֵל וַיִּתֵּן לָהֶם יוֹסֵף

22 עֲגָלוֹת עַל־פִּי פַרְעֹה וַיִּתֵּן לָהֶם צֵדָה לַדָּרֶךְ: לְכֻלָּם נָתַן לָאִישׁ חֲלִפוֹת

23 שְׂמָלֹת וּלְבִנְיָמִן נָתַן שְׁלֹשׁ מֵאוֹת כֶּסֶף וְחָמֵשׁ חֲלִפֹת שְׂמָלֹת: וּלְאָבִיו
שָׁלַח כְּזֹאת עֲשָׂרָה חֲמֹרִים נֹשְׂאִים מִטּוּב מִצְרָיִם וְעֶשֶׂר אֲתֹנֹת נֹשְׂאֹת

24 בָּר וָלֶחֶם וּמָזוֹן לְאָבִיו לַדָּרֶךְ: וַיְשַׁלַּח אֶת־אֶחָיו וַיֵּלֵכוּ וַיֹּאמֶר אֲלֵהֶם

כה אַל־תִּרְגְּזוּ בַּדָּרֶךְ: וַיַּעֲלוּ מִמִּצְרָיִם וַיָּבֹאוּ אֶרֶץ כְּנַעַן אֶל־יַעֲקֹב אֲבִיהֶם:

26 וַיַּגִּדוּ לוֹ לֵאמֹר עוֹד יוֹסֵף חַי וְכִי־הוּא מֹשֵׁל בְּכָל־אֶרֶץ מִצְרָיִם וַיָּפָג

27 לִבּוֹ כִּי לֹא־הֶאֱמִין לָהֶם: וַיְדַבְּרוּ אֵלָיו אֵת כָּל־דִּבְרֵי יוֹסֵף אֲשֶׁר דִּבֶּר
אֲלֵהֶם וַיַּרְא אֶת־הָעֲגָלוֹת אֲשֶׁר־שָׁלַח יוֹסֵף לָשֵׂאת אֹתוֹ וַתְּחִי רוּחַ

28 יַעֲקֹב אֲבִיהֶם: וַיֹּאמֶר יִשְׂרָאֵל רַב עוֹד־יוֹסֵף בְּנִי חָי אֵלְכָה וְאֶרְאֶנּוּ
בְּטֶרֶם אָמוּת:

CHAPTER XLVI. ‎מו

א וַיִּסַּע יִשְׂרָאֵל וְכָל־אֲשֶׁר־לוֹ וַיָּבֹא בְּאֵרָה שָּׁבַע וַיִּזְבַּח זְבָחִים לֵאלֹהֵי

2 אָבִיו יִצְחָק: וַיֹּאמֶר אֱלֹהִים לְיִשְׂרָאֵל בְּמַרְאֹת הַלַּיְלָה וַיֹּאמֶר יַעֲקֹב יַעֲקֹב

3 וַיֹּאמֶר הִנֵּנִי: וַיֹּאמֶר אָנֹכִי הָאֵל אֱלֹהֵי אָבִיךָ אַל־תִּירָא מֵרְדָה

4 מִצְרַיְמָה כִּי־לְגוֹי גָּדוֹל אֲשִׂימְךָ שָׁם: אָנֹכִי אֵרֵד עִמְּךָ מִצְרַיְמָה

ה וְאָנֹכִי אַעַלְךָ גַם־עָלֹה וְיוֹסֵף יָשִׁית יָדוֹ עַל־עֵינֶיךָ׃ וַיָּקָם יַעֲקֹב מִבְּאֵר
שֶׁבַע וַיִּשְׂאוּ בְנֵי־יִשְׂרָאֵל אֶת־יַעֲקֹב אֲבִיהֶם וְאֶת־טַפָּם וְאֶת־נְשֵׁיהֶם
6 בָּעֲגָלוֹת אֲשֶׁר־שָׁלַח פַּרְעֹה לָשֵׂאת אֹתוֹ׃ וַיִּקְחוּ אֶת־מִקְנֵיהֶם וְאֶת־
רְכֻשָׁם אֲשֶׁר רָכְשׁוּ בְּאֶרֶץ כְּנַעַן וַיָּבֹאוּ מִצְרָיְמָה יַעֲקֹב וְכָל־זַרְעוֹ
7 אִתּוֹ׃ בָּנָיו וּבְנֵי בָנָיו אִתּוֹ בְּנֹתָיו וּבְנוֹת בָּנָיו וְכָל־זַרְעוֹ הֵבִיא אִתּוֹ
מִצְרָיְמָה׃   פ

III. The Ten Commandments, *Exodus* 20 : 1–21.

2 א אָנֹכִי   ס   וַיְדַבֵּר אֱלֹהִים אֵת כָּל־הַדְּבָרִים הָאֵלֶּה לֵאמֹר׃
3 לֹא־ יְהוָה אֱלֹהֶיךָ אֲשֶׁר הוֹצֵאתִיךָ מֵאֶרֶץ מִצְרַיִם מִבֵּית עֲבָדִים׃
4 וְכָל־תְּמוּנָה פֶסֶל לְךָ תַעֲשֶׂה־לֹא אֲחֵרִים אֱלֹהִים לְךָ יִהְיֶה
מִתַּחַת בַּמַּיִם וַאֲשֶׁר מִתַּחַת בָּאֶרֶץ וַאֲשֶׁר מִמַּעַל בַּשָּׁמַיִם אֲשֶׁר
5 אֵל אֱלֹהֶיךָ יְהוָה אָנֹכִי כִּי תָעָבְדֵם וְלֹא לָהֶם תִשְׁתַּחֲוֶה־לֹא לָאָרֶץ
6 וְעֹשֶׂה לְשֹׂנְאָי וְעַל־רִבֵּעִים עַל־שִׁלֵּשִׁים עַל־בָּנִים אָבֹת עֲוֹן פֹּקֵד קַנָּא
7 לֹא תִשָּׂא אֶת־שֵׁם־   ס   לְאֹהֲבַי וּלְשֹׁמְרֵי מִצְוֹתָי׃ לַאֲלָפִים חֶסֶד
אֶת־שְׁמוֹ אֲשֶׁר־יִשָּׂא אֵת יְהוָה יְנַקֶּה לֹא כִּי לַשָּׁוְא אֱלֹהֶיךָ יְהוָה
8 9 תַּעֲבֹד יָמִים שֵׁשֶׁת לְקַדְּשׁוֹ הַשַּׁבָּת אֶת־יוֹם זָכוֹר   פ   לַשָּׁוְא׃
10 תַעֲשֶׂה לֹא־ לֵאלֹהֶיךָ שַׁבָּת הַשְּׁבִיעִי וְיוֹם מְלַאכְתֶּךָ׃ כָּל־ וְעָשִׂיתָ
אֲשֶׁר וְגֵרְךָ וּבְהֶמְתֶּךָ וַאֲמָתְךָ עַבְדְּךָ וּבִנְךָ־וּבִתֶּךָ אַתָּה כָל־מְלָאכָה
11 אֶת־הַיָּם וְאֶת־הָאָרֶץ אֶת־הַשָּׁמַיִם יְהוָה עָשָׂה יָמִים כִּי שֵׁשֶׁת־ בִּשְׁעָרֶיךָ׃
הַשַּׁבָּת אֶת־יוֹם יְהוָה בֵּרַךְ עַל־כֵּן הַשְּׁבִיעִי בַּיּוֹם וַיָּנַח אֲשֶׁר־בָּם וְאֶת־כָּל־
12 יָמֶיךָ יַאֲרִכוּן לְמַעַן וְאֶת־אִמֶּךָ אֶת־אָבִיךָ כַּבֵּד   ס   וַיְקַדְּשֵׁהוּ׃
13 לֹא תִּרְצָח׃   ס   נֹתֵן לָךְ׃ אֲלֹהֶיךָ אֲשֶׁר־יְהוָה הָאֲדָמָה עַל
14   ס   לֹא תִגְנֹב׃   ס   לֹא תִּנְאָף׃   ס
טו טז
16   ס   לֹא תַחְמֹד בֵּית רֵעֶךָ   ס   לֹא־תַעֲנֶה בְרֵעֲךָ עֵד שָׁקֶר׃
17 לֹא־תַחְמֹד אֵשֶׁת רֵעֶךָ וְעַבְדּוֹ וַאֲמָתוֹ וְשׁוֹרוֹ וַחֲמֹרוֹ וְכֹל אֲשֶׁר לְרֵעֶךָ׃
18   ס   וְכָל־הָעָם רֹאִים אֶת־הַקּוֹלֹת וְאֶת־הַלַּפִּידִם וְאֵת קוֹל הַשֹּׁפָר
19 וְאֶת־הָהָר עָשֵׁן וַיַּרְא הָעָם וַיָּנֻעוּ וַיַּעַמְדוּ מֵרָחֹק׃ וַיֹּאמְרוּ אֶל־מֹשֶׁה
כ דַּבֵּר־אַתָּה עִמָּנוּ וְנִשְׁמָעָה וְאַל־יְדַבֵּר עִמָּנוּ אֱלֹהִים פֶּן־נָמוּת׃ וַיֹּאמֶר
מֹשֶׁה אֶל־הָעָם אַל־תִּירָאוּ כִּי לְבַעֲבוּר נַסּוֹת אֶתְכֶם בָּא הָאֱלֹהִים
21 וּבַעֲבוּר תִּהְיֶה יִרְאָתוֹ עַל־פְּנֵיכֶם לְבִלְתִּי תֶחֱטָאוּ׃ וַיַּעֲמֹד הָעָם מֵרָחֹק
וּמֹשֶׁה נִגַּשׁ אֶל־הָעֲרָפֶל אֲשֶׁר־שָׁם הָאֱלֹהִים׃

IV. The Life of Samson, *Judges* 13–16.

CHAPTER XIII. יג

א וַיֹּסִ֙פוּ֙ בְּנֵ֣י יִשְׂרָאֵ֔ל לַעֲשׂ֥וֹת הָרַ֖ע בְּעֵינֵ֣י יְהוָ֑ה וַיִּתְּנֵ֧ם יְהוָ֛ה בְּיַד־

2 פְּלִשְׁתִּ֖ים אַרְבָּעִ֥ים שָׁנָֽה׃   וַיְהִי֩ אִ֨ישׁ אֶחָ֜ד מִצָּרְעָ֛ה מִמִּשְׁפַּ֥חַת

3 הַדָּנִ֖י וּשְׁמ֣וֹ מָנ֑וֹחַ וְאִשְׁתּ֥וֹ עֲקָרָ֖ה וְלֹ֣א יָלָֽדָה׃ וַיֵּרָ֥א מַלְאַךְ־יְהוָ֖ה אֶל־

הָאִשָּׁ֑ה וַיֹּ֣אמֶר אֵלֶ֗יהָ הִנֵּה־נָ֤א אַתְּ־עֲקָרָה֙ וְלֹ֣א יָלַ֔דְתְּ וְהָרִ֖ית וְיָלַ֥דְתְּ בֵּֽן׃

4 ה וְעַתָּה֙ הִשָּׁ֣מְרִי נָ֔א וְאַל־תִּשְׁתִּ֖י יַ֣יִן וְשֵׁכָ֑ר וְאַל־תֹּאכְלִ֖י כָּל־טָמֵֽא׃ כִּ֣י

הִנָּ֣ךְ הָרָ֗ה וְיֹלַ֣דְתְּ בֵּ֔ן וּמוֹרָה֙ לֹא־יַעֲלֶ֣ה עַל־רֹאשׁ֔וֹ כִּֽי־נְזִ֧יר אֱלֹהִ֛ים יִהְיֶ֥ה

6 הַנַּ֖עַר מִן־הַבָּ֑טֶן וְה֗וּא יָחֵ֛ל לְהוֹשִׁ֥יעַ אֶת־יִשְׂרָאֵ֖ל מִיַּ֥ד פְּלִשְׁתִּֽים׃ וַתָּבֹ֣א

הָאִשָּׁ֗ה וַתֹּ֣אמֶר לְאִישָׁהּ֮ לֵאמֹר֒ אִ֤ישׁ הָאֱלֹהִים֙ בָּ֣א אֵלַ֔י וּמַרְאֵ֕הוּ כְּמַרְאֵ֛ה

מַלְאַ֥ךְ הָאֱלֹהִ֖ים נוֹרָ֣א מְאֹ֑ד וְלֹ֤א שְׁאִלְתִּ֙יהוּ֙ אֵֽי־מִזֶּ֣ה ה֔וּא וְאֶת־שְׁמ֖וֹ

7 לֹא־הִגִּ֥יד לִֽי׃ וַיֹּ֣אמֶר לִ֔י הִנָּ֥ךְ הָרָ֖ה וְיֹלַ֣דְתְּ בֵּ֑ן וְעַתָּ֞ה אַל־תִּשְׁתִּ֣י ׀ יַ֣יִן

וְשֵׁכָ֗ר וְאַל־תֹּֽאכְלִי֙ כָּל־טֻמְאָ֔ה כִּֽי־נְזִ֤יר אֱלֹהִים֙ יִהְיֶ֣ה הַנַּ֔עַר מִן־הַבֶּ֖טֶן

8 עַד־י֥וֹם מוֹת֖וֹ׃   וַיֶּעְתַּ֥ר מָנ֛וֹחַ אֶל־יְהוָ֖ה וַיֹּאמַ֑ר בִּ֣י אֲדוֹנָ֔י אִ֣ישׁ

הָאֱלֹהִ֞ים אֲשֶׁ֣ר שָׁלַ֗חְתָּ יָֽבוֹא־נָ֥א ע֙וֹד֙ אֵלֵ֔ינוּ וְיוֹרֵ֕נוּ מַֽה־נַּעֲשֶׂ֖ה לַנַּ֥עַר

9 הַיּוּלָּֽד׃ וַיִּשְׁמַ֥ע הָאֱלֹהִ֖ים בְּק֣וֹל מָנ֑וֹחַ וַיָּבֹ֣א מַלְאַ֣ךְ הָאֱלֹהִ֡ים ע֣וֹד אֶל־

הָֽאִשָּׁה֩ וְהִ֨יא יוֹשֶׁ֜בֶת בַּשָּׂדֶ֗ה וּמָנ֛וֹחַ אִישָׁ֖הּ אֵ֥ין עִמָּֽהּ׃ וַתְּמַהֵר֙ הָֽאִשָּׁ֔ה

וַתָּ֖רָץ וַתַּגֵּ֣ד לְאִישָׁ֑הּ וַתֹּ֣אמֶר אֵלָ֔יו הִנֵּ֨ה נִרְאָ֤ה אֵלַי֙ הָאִ֔ישׁ אֲשֶׁר־בָּ֥א

11 בַיּ֖וֹם אֵלָֽי׃ וַיָּ֛קָם וַיֵּ֥לֶךְ מָנ֖וֹחַ אַחֲרֵ֣י אִשְׁתּ֑וֹ וַיָּבֹא֙ אֶל־הָאִ֔ישׁ וַיֹּ֣אמֶר

12 ל֗וֹ הַאַתָּ֥ה הָאִ֛ישׁ אֲשֶׁר־דִּבַּ֥רְתָּ אֶל־הָאִשָּׁ֖ה וַיֹּ֥אמֶר אָֽנִי׃ וַיֹּ֣אמֶר מָנ֔וֹחַ

13 עַתָּ֖ה יָבֹ֣א דְבָרֶ֑יךָ מַה־יִּֽהְיֶ֥ה מִשְׁפַּט־הַנַּ֖עַר וּמַעֲשֵֽׂהוּ׃ וַיֹּ֛אמֶר מַלְאַ֥ךְ

14 יְהוָ֖ה אֶל־מָנ֑וֹחַ מִכֹּ֥ל אֲשֶׁר־אָמַ֛רְתִּי אֶל־הָאִשָּׁ֖ה תִּשָּׁמֵֽר׃ מִכֹּ֣ל אֲשֶׁר־יֵצֵא֩

מִגֶּ֨פֶן הַיַּ֜יִן לֹ֣א תֹאכַ֗ל וְיַ֤יִן וְשֵׁכָר֙ אַל־תֵּ֔שְׁתְּ וְכָל־טֻמְאָ֖ה אַל־תֹּאכַ֑ל כֹּ֥ל

ט אֲשֶׁר־צִוִּיתִ֖יהָ תִּשְׁמֹֽר׃ וַיֹּ֥אמֶר מָנ֖וֹחַ אֶל־מַלְאַ֣ךְ יְהוָ֑ה נַעְצְרָה־נָּ֣א אוֹתָ֔ךְ

16 וְנַעֲשֶׂ֥ה לְפָנֶ֖יךָ גְּדִ֥י עִזִּֽים׃ וַיֹּאמֶר֩ מַלְאַ֨ךְ יְהוָ֜ה אֶל־מָנ֗וֹחַ אִם־תַּעְצְרֵ֙נִי֙

לֹא־אֹכַ֣ל בְּלַחְמֶ֔ךָ וְאִם־תַּעֲשֶׂ֣ה עֹלָ֔ה לַיהוָ֖ה תַּעֲלֶ֑נָּה כִּ֚י לֹא־יָדַ֣ע מָנ֔וֹחַ

17 כִּֽי־מַלְאַ֥ךְ יְהוָ֖ה הֽוּא׃ וַיֹּ֧אמֶר מָנ֛וֹחַ אֶל־מַלְאַ֥ךְ יְהוָ֖ה מִ֣י שְׁמֶ֑ךָ כִּֽי־יָבֹ֥א

18 דְבָרְךָ֖ וְכִבַּדְנֽוּךָ׃ וַיֹּ֤אמֶר לוֹ֙ מַלְאַ֣ךְ יְהוָ֔ה לָ֥מָּה זֶּ֖ה תִּשְׁאַ֣ל לִשְׁמִ֑י

19 וְהוּא־פֶֽלִאי׃ וַיִּקַּ֨ח מָנ֜וֹחַ אֶת־גְּדִ֤י הָעִזִּים֙ וְאֶת־הַמִּנְחָ֔ה וַיַּ֥עַל עַל־

כ הַצּ֛וּר לַֽיהוָ֖ה וּמַפְלִ֣א לַעֲשׂ֑וֹת וּמָנ֥וֹחַ וְאִשְׁתּ֖וֹ רֹאִֽים׃ וַיְהִי֩ בַעֲל֨וֹת

הַלַּ֜הַב מֵעַ֤ל הַמִּזְבֵּ֙חַ֙ הַשָּׁמַ֔יְמָה וַיַּ֥עַל מַלְאַךְ־יְהוָ֖ה בְּלַ֣הַב הַמִּזְבֵּ֑חַ

21 וּמָנֹ֗וחַ וְאִשְׁתֹּ֜ו רֹאִ֑ים וַיִּפְּל֥וּ עַל־פְּנֵיהֶ֖ם אָ֑רְצָה ׃ וְלֹא־יָסַ֣ף עֹ֗וד מַלְאַ֣ךְ
יְהוָ֗ה לְהֵרָאֹה֙ אֶל־מָנֹ֣וחַ וְאֶל־אִשְׁתֹּ֑ו אָ֚ז יָדַ֣ע מָנֹ֔וחַ כִּֽי־מַלְאַ֥ךְ יְהוָ֖ה
22 הֽוּא ׃ וַיֹּ֧אמֶר מָנֹ֛וחַ אֶל־אִשְׁתֹּ֖ו מֹ֣ות נָמ֑וּת כִּ֥י אֱלֹהִ֖ים רָאִֽינוּ ׃ וַתֹּ֧אמֶר 23
לֹ֣ו אִשְׁתֹּ֗ו לוּ֩ חָפֵ֨ץ יְהוָ֤ה לַהֲמִיתֵ֙נוּ֙ לֹֽא־לָקַ֤ח מִיָּדֵ֙נוּ֙ עֹלָ֣ה וּמִנְחָ֔ה וְלֹ֥א
24 הֶרְאָ֖נוּ אֶת־כָּל־אֵ֑לֶּה וְכָעֵ֕ת לֹ֥א הִשְׁמִיעָ֖נוּ כָּזֹֽאת ׃ וַתֵּ֤לֶד הָֽאִשָּׁה֙ בֵּ֔ן
כה 25 וַתִּקְרָ֥א אֶת־שְׁמֹ֖ו שִׁמְשֹׁ֑ון וַיִּגְדַּ֤ל הַנַּ֙עַר֙ וַֽיְבָרֲכֵ֖הוּ יְהוָֽה ׃ וַתָּ֙חֶל֙ ר֣וּחַ
יְהוָ֔ה לְפַעֲמֹ֖ו בְּמַחֲנֵה־דָ֑ן בֵּ֥ין צָרְעָ֖ה וּבֵ֥ין אֶשְׁתָּאֹֽל ׃

CHAPTER XIV.   יד

2 א וַיֵּ֧רֶד שִׁמְשֹׁ֛ון תִּמְנָ֑תָה וַיַּ֥רְא אִשָּׁ֛ה בְּתִמְנָ֖תָה מִבְּנֹ֥ות פְּלִשְׁתִּֽים ׃ וַיַּ֗עַל
וַיַּגֵּ֤ד לְאָבִיו֙ וּלְאִמֹּ֔ו וַיֹּ֕אמֶר אִשָּׁ֛ה רָאִ֥יתִי בְתִמְנָ֖תָה מִבְּנֹ֣ות פְּלִשְׁתִּ֑ים
3 וְעַתָּ֕ה קְחֽוּ־אֹותָ֥הּ לִּ֖י לְאִשָּֽׁה ׃ וַיֹּ֨אמֶר לֹ֜ו אָבִ֣יו וְאִמֹּ֗ו הַאֵין֩ בִּבְנֹ֨ות
אַחֶ֜יךָ וּבְכָל־עַמִּ֣י אִשָּׁ֗ה כִּֽי־אַתָּ֤ה הֹולֵךְ֙ לָקַ֣חַת אִשָּׁ֔ה מִפְּלִשְׁתִּ֖ים הָעֲרֵלִ֑ים
4 וַיֹּ֨אמֶר שִׁמְשֹׁ֤ון אֶל־אָבִיו֙ אֹותָ֣הּ קַֽח־לִ֔י כִּֽי־הִ֖יא יָשְׁרָ֥ה בְעֵינָֽי ׃ וְאָבִ֨יו
וְאִמֹּ֜ו לֹ֣א יָֽדְע֗וּ כִּ֤י מֵיְהוָה֙ הִ֔יא כִּֽי־תֹאֲנָ֥ה הֽוּא־מְבַקֵּ֖שׁ מִפְּלִשְׁתִּ֑ים וּבָעֵ֣ת
הַהִ֔יא פְּלִשְׁתִּ֖ים מֹשְׁלִ֥ים בְּיִשְׂרָאֵֽל ׃   וַיֵּ֧רֶד שִׁמְשֹׁ֛ון וְאָבִ֥יו וְאִמֹּ֖ו תִּמְנָ֑תָה
ו 6 וַיָּבֹ֙אוּ֙ עַד־כַּרְמֵ֣י תִמְנָ֔תָה וְהִנֵּה֙ כְּפִ֣יר אֲרָיֹ֔ות שֹׁאֵ֖ג לִקְרָאתֹֽו ׃ וַתִּצְלַ֨ח
עָלָ֜יו ר֣וּחַ יְהוָ֗ה וַֽיְשַׁסְּעֵ֙הוּ֙ כְּשַׁסַּ֣ע הַגְּדִ֔י וּמְא֖וּמָה אֵ֣ין בְּיָדֹ֑ו וְלֹ֤א הִגִּיד֙
7 לְאָבִ֣יו וּלְאִמֹּ֔ו אֵ֖ת אֲשֶׁ֥ר עָשָֽׂה ׃ וַיֵּ֕רֶד וַיְדַבֵּ֖ר לָאִשָּׁ֑ה וַתִּישַׁ֖ר בְּעֵינֵ֥י
8 שִׁמְשֹֽׁון ׃ וַיָּ֤שָׁב מִיָּמִים֙ לְקַחְתָּ֔הּ וַיָּ֣סַר לִרְאֹ֔ות אֵ֖ת מַפֶּ֣לֶת הָאַרְיֵ֑ה וְהִנֵּ֞ה
9 עֲדַ֧ת דְּבֹורִ֛ים בִּגְוִיַּ֥ת הָאַרְיֵ֖ה וּדְבָֽשׁ ׃ וַיִּרְדֵּ֣הוּ אֶל־כַּפָּ֗יו וַיֵּ֤לֶךְ הָלֹוךְ֙
וְאָכֹ֔ל וַיֵּ֙לֶךְ֙ אֶל־אָבִ֣יו וְאֶל־אִמֹּ֔ו וַיִּתֵּ֥ן לָהֶ֖ם וַיֹּאכֵ֑לוּ וְלֹֽא־הִגִּ֣יד לָהֶ֔ם כִּ֛י
י מִגְּוִיַּ֥ת הָאַרְיֵ֖ה רָדָ֥ה הַדְּבָֽשׁ ׃ וַיֵּ֥רֶד אָבִ֖יהוּ אֶל־הָֽאִשָּׁ֑ה וַיַּ֨עַשׂ שָׁ֤ם
11 שִׁמְשֹׁון֙ מִשְׁתֶּ֔ה כִּ֛י כֵּ֥ן יַעֲשׂ֖וּ הַבַּֽחוּרִ֑ים ׃ וַיְהִ֖י כִּרְאֹותָ֣ם אֹותֹ֑ו וַיִּקְחוּ֙
12 שְׁלֹשִׁ֣ים מֵֽרֵעִ֔ים וַיִּהְי֖וּ אִתֹּֽו ׃ וַיֹּ֤אמֶר לָהֶם֙ שִׁמְשֹׁ֔ון אָחֽוּדָה־נָּ֥א לָכֶ֖ם
חִידָ֑ה אִם־הַגֵּ֣ד תַּגִּ֩ידוּ֩ אֹותָ֨הּ לִ֜י שִׁבְעַ֨ת יְמֵ֤י הַמִּשְׁתֶּה֙ וּמְצָאתֶ֔ם וְנָתַתִּ֤י
13 לָכֶם֙ שְׁלֹשִׁ֣ים סְדִינִ֔ים וּשְׁלֹשִׁ֖ים חֲלִפֹ֥ת בְּגָדִֽים ׃ וְאִם־לֹ֣א תוּכְלוּ֮ לְהַגִּ֣יד
לִי֒ וּנְתַתֶּ֨ם אַתֶּ֥ם לִי֙ שְׁלֹשִׁ֣ים סְדִינִ֔ים וּשְׁלֹשִׁ֖ים חֲלִיפֹ֣ות בְּגָדִ֑ים וַיֹּ֣אמְרוּ
14 לֹ֗ו ח֤וּדָה חִֽידָתְךָ֙ וְנִשְׁמָעֶֽנָּה ׃ וַיֹּ֣אמֶר לָהֶ֗ם מֵהָֽאֹכֵל֙ יָצָ֣א מַאֲכָ֔ל וּמֵעַ֖ז
טו יָצָ֣א מָתֹ֑וק וְלֹ֥א יָכְל֛וּ לְהַגִּ֥יד הַחִידָ֖ה שְׁלֹ֥שֶׁת יָמִֽים ׃ וַיְהִ֣י ׀ בַּיֹּ֣ום
הַשְּׁבִיעִ֗י וַיֹּאמְר֤וּ לְאֵֽשֶׁת־שִׁמְשֹׁון֙ פַּתִּ֣י אֶת־אִישֵׁ֗ךְ וְיַגֶּד־לָ֙נוּ֙ אֶת־הַ֣חִידָ֔ה
פֶּן־נִשְׂרֹ֥ף אֹותָ֛ךְ וְאֶת־בֵּ֥ית אָבִ֖יךְ בָּאֵ֑שׁ הַלְיָרְשֵׁ֙נוּ֙ קְרָאתֶ֥ם לָ֖נוּ הֲלֹֽא ׃

16 וַתֵּבְךְּ אֵשֶׁת שִׁמְשׁוֹן עָלָיו וַתֹּאמֶר רַק־שְׂנֵאתַנִי וְלֹא אֲהַבְתָּנִי הַחִידָה
חַדְתָּ לִבְנֵי עַמִּי וְלִי לֹא הִגַּדְתָּה וַיֹּאמֶר לָהּ הִנֵּה לְאָבִי וּלְאִמִּי לֹא
17 הִגַּדְתִּי וְלָךְ אַגִּיד: וַתֵּבְךְ עָלָיו שִׁבְעַת הַיָּמִים אֲשֶׁר־הָיָה לָהֶם הַמִּשְׁתֶּה
וַיְהִי ׀ בַּיּוֹם הַשְּׁבִיעִי וַיַּגֶּד־לָהּ כִּי הֱצִיקַתְהוּ וַתַּגֵּד הַחִידָה לִבְנֵי
18 עַמָּהּ: וַיֹּאמְרוּ לוֹ אַנְשֵׁי הָעִיר בַּיּוֹם הַשְּׁבִיעִי בְּטֶרֶם יָבֹא הַחַרְסָה
מַה־מָּתוֹק מִדְּבַשׁ וּמֶה עַז מֵאֲרִי וַיֹּאמֶר לָהֶם לוּלֵא חֲרַשְׁתֶּם בְּעֶגְלָתִי
19 לֹא מְצָאתֶם חִידָתִי: וַתִּצְלַח עָלָיו רוּחַ יְהוָה וַיֵּרֶד אַשְׁקְלוֹן וַיַּךְ
מֵהֶם ׀ שְׁלֹשִׁים אִישׁ וַיִּקַּח אֶת־חֲלִיצוֹתָם וַיִּתֵּן הַחֲלִיפוֹת לְמַגִּידֵי
כ הַחִידָה וַיִּחַר אַפּוֹ וַיַּעַל בֵּית אָבִיהוּ: וַתְּהִי אֵשֶׁת שִׁמְשׁוֹן לְמֵרֵעֵהוּ
אֲשֶׁר רֵעָה לוֹ:

CHAPTER XV.   טו

א וַיְהִי מִיָּמִים בִּימֵי קְצִיר־חִטִּים וַיִּפְקֹד שִׁמְשׁוֹן אֶת־אִשְׁתּוֹ בִּגְדִי עִזִּים
2 וַיֹּאמֶר אָבֹאָה אֶל־אִשְׁתִּי הֶחָדְרָה וְלֹא־נְתָנוֹ אָבִיהָ לָבוֹא: וַיֹּאמֶר
אָבִיהָ אָמֹר אָמַרְתִּי כִּי־שָׂנֹא שְׂנֵאתָהּ וָאֶתְּנֶנָּה לְמֵרֵעֶךָ הֲלֹא אֲחֹתָהּ
3 הַקְּטַנָּה טוֹבָה מִמֶּנָּה תְּהִי־נָא לְךָ תַּחְתֶּיהָ: וַיֹּאמֶר לָהֶם שִׁמְשׁוֹן
4 נִקֵּיתִי הַפַּעַם מִפְּלִשְׁתִּים כִּי־עֹשֶׂה אֲנִי עִמָּם רָעָה: וַיֵּלֶךְ שִׁמְשׁוֹן וַיִּלְכֹּד
שְׁלֹשׁ־מֵאוֹת שׁוּעָלִים וַיִּקַּח לַפִּדִים וַיֶּפֶן זָנָב אֶל־זָנָב וַיָּשֶׂם לַפִּיד
ה אֶחָד בֵּין־שְׁנֵי הַזְּנָבוֹת בַּתָּוֶךְ: וַיַּבְעֶר־אֵשׁ בַּלַּפִּידִים וַיְשַׁלַּח בְּקָמוֹת
6 פְּלִשְׁתִּים וַיַּבְעֵר מִגָּדִישׁ וְעַד־קָמָה וְעַד־כֶּרֶם זָיִת: וַיֹּאמְרוּ פְלִשְׁתִּים
מִי עָשָׂה זֹאת וַיֹּאמְרוּ שִׁמְשׁוֹן חֲתַן הַתִּמְנִי כִּי לָקַח אֶת־אִשְׁתּוֹ
וַיִּתְּנָהּ לְמֵרֵעֵהוּ וַיַּעֲלוּ פְלִשְׁתִּים וַיִּשְׂרְפוּ אוֹתָהּ וְאֶת־אָבִיהָ בָּאֵשׁ:
7 וַיֹּאמֶר לָהֶם שִׁמְשׁוֹן אִם־תַּעֲשׂוּן כָּזֹאת כִּי אִם־נִקַּמְתִּי בָכֶם וְאַחַר
8 אֶחְדָּל: וַיַּךְ אוֹתָם שׁוֹק עַל־יָרֵךְ מַכָּה גְדוֹלָה וַיֵּרֶד וַיֵּשֶׁב בִּסְעִיף סֶלַע
9 עֵיטָם: וַיַּעֲלוּ פְלִשְׁתִּים וַיַּחֲנוּ בִּיהוּדָה וַיִּנָּטְשׁוּ בַּלֶּחִי: וַיֹּאמְרוּ
אִישׁ יְהוּדָה לָמָה עֲלִיתֶם עָלֵינוּ וַיֹּאמְרוּ לֶאֱסוֹר אֶת־שִׁמְשׁוֹן עָלִינוּ
11 לַעֲשׂוֹת לוֹ כַּאֲשֶׁר עָשָׂה לָנוּ: וַיֵּרְדוּ שְׁלֹשֶׁת אֲלָפִים אִישׁ מִיהוּדָה אֶל־
סְעִיף סֶלַע עֵיטָם וַיֹּאמְרוּ לְשִׁמְשׁוֹן הֲלֹא יָדַעְתָּ כִּי־מֹשְׁלִים בָּנוּ פְּלִשְׁתִּים
וּמַה־זֹּאת עָשִׂיתָ לָּנוּ וַיֹּאמֶר לָהֶם כַּאֲשֶׁר עָשׂוּ לִי כֵּן עָשִׂיתִי לָהֶם:
12 וַיֹּאמְרוּ לוֹ לֶאֱסָרְךָ יָרַדְנוּ לְתִתְּךָ בְּיַד־פְּלִשְׁתִּים וַיֹּאמֶר לָהֶם שִׁמְשׁוֹן
13 הִשָּׁבְעוּ לִי פֶּן־תִּפְגְּעוּן בִּי אַתֶּם: וַיֹּאמְרוּ לוֹ לֵאמֹר לֹא כִּי־אָסֹר
נֶאֱסָרְךָ וּנְתַנּוּךָ בְיָדָם וְהָמֵת לֹא נְמִיתֶךָ וַיַּאַסְרֻהוּ בִּשְׁנַיִם עֲבֹתִים
14 חֲדָשִׁים וַיַּעֲלוּהוּ מִן־הַסָּלַע: הוּא־בָא עַד־לֶחִי וּפְלִשְׁתִּים הֵרִיעוּ לִקְרָאתוֹ

וַתִּצְלַח עָלָיו רוּחַ יְהוָה וַתִּהְיֶינָה הָעֲבֹתִים אֲשֶׁר־עַל־זְרוֹעוֹתָיו כַּפִּשְׁתִּים

אֲשֶׁר בָּעֲרוּ בָאֵשׁ וַיִּמַּסּוּ אֲסוּרָיו מֵעַל יָדָיו : וַיִּמְצָא לְחִי־חֲמוֹר טְרִיָּה ט׳

16 וַיִּשְׁלַח יָדוֹ וַיִּקָּחֶהָ וַיַּךְ־בָּהּ אֶלֶף אִישׁ : וַיֹּאמֶר שִׁמְשׁוֹן בִּלְחִי הַחֲמוֹר

17 חֲמוֹר חֲמֹרָתָיִם בִּלְחִי הַחֲמוֹר הִכֵּיתִי אֶלֶף אִישׁ : וַיְהִי כְּכַלֹּתוֹ לְדַבֵּר

18 וַיַּשְׁלֵךְ הַלְּחִי מִיָּדוֹ וַיִּקְרָא לַמָּקוֹם הַהוּא רָמַת לֶחִי : וַיִּצְמָא מְאֹד

וַיִּקְרָא אֶל־יְהוָה וַיֹּאמַר אַתָּה נָתַתָּ בְיַד־עַבְדְּךָ אֶת־הַתְּשׁוּעָה הַגְּדֹלָה

19 הַזֹּאת וְעַתָּה אָמוּת בַּצָּמָא וְנָפַלְתִּי בְּיַד הָעֲרֵלִים : וַיִּבְקַע אֱלֹהִים

אֶת־הַמַּכְתֵּשׁ אֲשֶׁר־בַּלֶּחִי וַיֵּצְאוּ מִמֶּנּוּ מַיִם וַיֵּשְׁתְּ וַתָּשָׁב רוּחוֹ וַיֶּחִי

20 עַל־כֵּן ׀ קָרָא שְׁמָהּ עֵין הַקּוֹרֵא אֲשֶׁר בַּלֶּחִי עַד הַיּוֹם הַזֶּה : וַיִּשְׁפֹּט

אֶת־יִשְׂרָאֵל בִּימֵי פְלִשְׁתִּים עֶשְׂרִים שָׁנָה :

CHAPTER XVI. יו

2 א וַיֵּלֶךְ שִׁמְשׁוֹן עַזָּתָה וַיַּרְא־שָׁם אִשָּׁה זוֹנָה וַיָּבֹא אֵלֶיהָ : לַעַזָּתִים ׀ לֵאמֹר

בָּא שִׁמְשׁוֹן הֵנָּה וַיָּסֹבּוּ וַיֶּאֶרְבוּ־לוֹ כָל־הַלַּיְלָה בְּשַׁעַר הָעִיר וַיִּתְחָרְשׁוּ

3 כָל־הַלַּיְלָה לֵאמֹר עַד־אוֹר הַבֹּקֶר וַהֲרַגְנֻהוּ : וַיִּשְׁכַּב שִׁמְשׁוֹן עַד־חֲצִי

הַלַּיְלָה וַיָּקָם ׀ בַּחֲצִי הַלַּיְלָה וַיֶּאֱחֹז בְּדַלְתוֹת שַׁעַר־הָעִיר וּבִשְׁתֵּי

הַמְּזוּזוֹת וַיִּסָּעֵם עִם־הַבְּרִיחַ וַיָּשֶׂם עַל־כְּתֵפָיו וַיַּעֲלֵם אֶל־רֹאשׁ הָהָר

4 אֲשֶׁר עַל־פְּנֵי חֶבְרוֹן : וַיְהִי אַחֲרֵי־כֵן וַיֶּאֱהַב אִשָּׁה בְּנַחַל שֹׂרֵק

ה וּשְׁמָהּ דְּלִילָה : וַיַּעֲלוּ אֵלֶיהָ סַרְנֵי פְלִשְׁתִּים וַיֹּאמְרוּ לָהּ פַּתִּי אוֹתוֹ

וּרְאִי בַּמֶּה כֹּחוֹ גָדוֹל וּבַמֶּה נוּכַל לוֹ וַאֲסַרְנֻהוּ לְעַנֹּתוֹ וַאֲנַחְנוּ

6 נִתַּן־לָךְ אִישׁ אֶלֶף וּמֵאָה כָּסֶף : וַתֹּאמֶר דְּלִילָה אֶל־שִׁמְשׁוֹן הַגִּידָה־נָּא

7 לִי בַּמֶּה כֹּחֲךָ גָדוֹל וּבַמֶּה תֵאָסֵר לְעַנּוֹתֶךָ : וַיֹּאמֶר אֵלֶיהָ שִׁמְשׁוֹן אִם־

יַאַסְרֻנִי בְּשִׁבְעָה יְתָרִים לַחִים אֲשֶׁר לֹא־חֹרָבוּ וְחָלִיתִי וְהָיִיתִי כְּאַחַד

8 הָאָדָם : וַיַּעֲלוּ־לָהּ סַרְנֵי פְלִשְׁתִּים שִׁבְעָה יְתָרִים לַחִים אֲשֶׁר לֹא־חֹרָבוּ

9 וַתַּאַסְרֵהוּ בָּהֶם : וְהָאֹרֵב יֹשֵׁב לָהּ בַּחֶדֶר וַתֹּאמֶר אֵלָיו פְּלִשְׁתִּים

עָלֶיךָ שִׁמְשׁוֹן וַיְנַתֵּק אֶת־הַיְתָרִים כַּאֲשֶׁר יִנָּתֵק פְּתִיל־הַנְּעֹרֶת בַּהֲרִיחוֹ

אֵשׁ וְלֹא נוֹדַע כֹּחוֹ : וַתֹּאמֶר דְּלִילָה אֶל־שִׁמְשׁוֹן הִנֵּה הֵתַלְתָּ בִּי

11 וַתְּדַבֵּר אֵלַי כְּזָבִים עַתָּה הַגִּידָה־נָּא לִי בַּמֶּה תֵּאָסֵר : וַיֹּאמֶר אֵלֶיהָ

אִם־אָסוֹר יַאַסְרוּנִי בַּעֲבֹתִים חֲדָשִׁים אֲשֶׁר לֹא־נַעֲשָׂה בָהֶם מְלָאכָה

12 וְחָלִיתִי וְהָיִיתִי כְּאַחַד הָאָדָם : וַתִּקַּח דְּלִילָה עֲבֹתִים חֲדָשִׁים וַתַּאַסְרֵהוּ

בָהֶם וַתֹּאמֶר אֵלָיו פְּלִשְׁתִּים עָלֶיךָ שִׁמְשׁוֹן וְהָאֹרֵב יֹשֵׁב בֶּחָדֶר וַיְנַתְּקֵם

13 מֵעַל זְרֹעֹתָיו כַּחוּט : וַתֹּאמֶר דְּלִילָה אֶל־שִׁמְשׁוֹן עַד־הֵנָּה הֵתַלְתָּ בִּי

וַיְדַבֶּר אֵלַי כְּזָבִים הִגִּידָה לִּי בַּמֶּה תֵאָסֵר וַיֹּאמֶר אֵלֶיהָ אִם־תֵּאַרְגִי

14 אֶת־שֶׁבַע מַחְלְפוֹת רֹאשִׁי עִם־הַמַּסָּכֶת: וַתִּתְקַע בַּיָּתֵד וַתֹּאמֶר אֵלָיו
פְּלִשְׁתִּים עָלֶיךָ שִׁמְשׁוֹן וַיִּיקַץ מִשְּׁנָתוֹ וַיִּסַּע אֶת־הַיְתַד הָאֶרֶג וְאֶת־

טו הַמַּסָּכֶת: וַתֹּאמֶר אֵלָיו אֵיךְ תֹּאמַר אֲהַבְתִּיךְ וְלִבְּךָ אֵין אִתִּי זֶה
16 שָׁלֹשׁ פְּעָמִים הֵתַלְתָּ בִּי וְלֹא־הִגַּדְתָּ לִּי בַּמֶּה כֹּחֲךָ גָדוֹל: וַיְהִי כִּי־
17 הֵצִיקָה לּוֹ בִדְבָרֶיהָ כָּל־הַיָּמִים וַתְּאַלֲצֵהוּ וַתִּקְצַר נַפְשׁוֹ לָמוּת: וַיַּגֶּד־
לָהּ אֶת־כָּל־לִבּוֹ וַיֹּאמֶר לָהּ מוֹרָה לֹא־עָלָה עַל־רֹאשִׁי כִּי־נְזִיר אֱלֹהִים
אֲנִי מִבֶּטֶן אִמִּי אִם־גֻּלַּחְתִּי וְסָר מִמֶּנִּי כֹחִי וְחָלִיתִי וְהָיִיתִי כְּכָל־
18 הָאָדָם: וַתֵּרֶא דְּלִילָה כִּי־הִגִּיד לָהּ אֶת־כָּל־לִבּוֹ וַתִּשְׁלַח וַתִּקְרָא לְסַרְנֵי
פְלִשְׁתִּים לֵאמֹר עֲלוּ הַפַּעַם כִּי־הִגִּיד לָהּ אֶת־כָּל־לִבּוֹ וְעָלוּ אֵלֶיהָ סַרְנֵי
19 פְלִשְׁתִּים וַיַּעֲלוּ הַכֶּסֶף בְּיָדָם: וַתְּיַשְּׁנֵהוּ עַל־בִּרְכֶּיהָ וַתִּקְרָא לָאִישׁ
וַתְּגַלַּח אֶת־שֶׁבַע מַחְלְפוֹת רֹאשׁוֹ וַתָּחֶל לְעַנּוֹתוֹ וַיָּסַר כֹּחוֹ מֵעָלָיו:
כ וַתֹּאמֶר פְּלִשְׁתִּים עָלֶיךָ שִׁמְשׁוֹן וַיִּיקַץ מִשְּׁנָתוֹ וַיֹּאמֶר אֵצֵא כְּפַעַם
21 בְּפַעַם וְאִנָּעֵר וְהוּא לֹא יָדַע כִּי יְהוָה סָר מֵעָלָיו: וַיֹּאחֲזוּהוּ פְלִשְׁתִּים
וַיְנַקְּרוּ אֶת־עֵינָיו וַיּוֹרִידוּ אוֹתוֹ עַזָּתָה וַיַּאַסְרוּהוּ בַּנְחֻשְׁתַּיִם וַיְהִי טוֹחֵן
22 בְּבֵית הָאֲסִירִים: וַיָּחֶל שְׂעַר־רֹאשׁוֹ לְצַמֵּחַ כַּאֲשֶׁר גֻּלָּח: וְסַרְנֵי
23 פְלִשְׁתִּים נֶאֶסְפוּ לִזְבֹּחַ זֶבַח־גָּדוֹל לְדָגוֹן אֱלֹהֵיהֶם וּלְשִׂמְחָה וַיֹּאמְרוּ
24 נָתַן אֱלֹהֵינוּ בְּיָדֵנוּ אֵת שִׁמְשׁוֹן אוֹיְבֵנוּ: וַיִּרְאוּ אֹתוֹ הָעָם וַיְהַלְלוּ
אֶת־אֱלֹהֵיהֶם כִּי אָמְרוּ נָתַן אֱלֹהֵינוּ בְיָדֵנוּ אֶת־אוֹיְבֵנוּ וְאֵת מַחֲרִיב
כה אַרְצֵנוּ וַאֲשֶׁר הִרְבָּה אֶת־חֲלָלֵינוּ: וַיְהִי כִּי־טוֹב לִבָּם וַיֹּאמְרוּ קִרְאוּ
לְשִׁמְשׁוֹן וִישַׂחֶק־לָנוּ וַיִּקְרְאוּ לְשִׁמְשׁוֹן מִבֵּית הָאֲסוּרִים וַיְצַחֵק לִפְנֵיהֶם
26 וַיַּעֲמִידוּ אוֹתוֹ בֵּין הָעַמּוּדִים: וַיֹּאמֶר שִׁמְשׁוֹן אֶל־הַנַּעַר הַמַּחֲזִיק
בְּיָדוֹ הַנִּיחָה אוֹתִי וַהֲמִישֵׁנִי אֶת־הָעַמֻּדִים אֲשֶׁר הַבַּיִת נָכוֹן עֲלֵיהֶם
27 וְאֶשָּׁעֵן עֲלֵיהֶם: וְהַבַּיִת מָלֵא הָאֲנָשִׁים וְהַנָּשִׁים וְשָׁמָּה כֹּל סַרְנֵי פְלִשְׁתִּים
וְעַל־הַגָּג כִּשְׁלֹשֶׁת אֲלָפִים אִישׁ וְאִשָּׁה הָרֹאִים בִּשְׂחוֹק שִׁמְשׁוֹן: וַיִּקְרָא
28 שִׁמְשׁוֹן אֶל־יְהוָה וַיֹּאמַר אֲדֹנָי יֱהוִֹה זָכְרֵנִי נָא וְחַזְּקֵנִי נָא אַךְ הַפַּעַם
הַזֶּה הָאֱלֹהִים וְאִנָּקְמָה נְקַם־אַחַת מִשְּׁתֵי עֵינַי מִפְּלִשְׁתִּים: וַיִּלְפֹּת
29 שִׁמְשׁוֹן אֶת־שְׁנֵי עַמּוּדֵי הַתָּוֶךְ אֲשֶׁר הַבַּיִת נָכוֹן עֲלֵיהֶם וַיִּסָּמֵךְ עֲלֵיהֶם
ל אֶחָד בִּימִינוֹ וְאֶחָד בִּשְׂמֹאלוֹ: וַיֹּאמֶר שִׁמְשׁוֹן תָּמוֹת נַפְשִׁי עִם־פְּלִשְׁתִּים
וַיֵּט בְּכֹחַ וַיִּפֹּל הַבַּיִת עַל־הַסְּרָנִים וְעַל־כָּל־הָעָם אֲשֶׁר־בּוֹ וַיִּהְיוּ הַמֵּתִים
31 אֲשֶׁר הֵמִית בְּמוֹתוֹ רַבִּים מֵאֲשֶׁר הֵמִית בְּחַיָּיו: וַיֵּרְדוּ אֶחָיו וְכָל־בֵּית
אָבִיהוּ וַיִּשְׂאוּ אֹתוֹ וַיַּעֲלוּ וַיִּקְבְּרוּ אוֹתוֹ בֵּין צָרְעָה וּבֵין אֶשְׁתָּאֹל
בְּקֶבֶר מָנוֹחַ אָבִיו וְהוּא שָׁפַט אֶת־יִשְׂרָאֵל עֶשְׂרִים שָׁנָה:

V. David and Goliath, 1 *Samuel* 17.

א וַיַּאַסְפ֧וּ פְלִשְׁתִּים אֶת־מַֽחֲנֵיהֶם לַמִּלְחָמָה וַיֵּאָֽסְפוּ שֹׂכֹה אֲשֶׁר לִֽיהוּדָה
2 וַֽיַּחֲנוּ בֵּֽין־שׂוֹכֹה וּבֵין־עֲזֵקָה בְּאֶפֶס דַּמִּים: וְשָׁאוּל וְאִֽישׁ־יִשְׂרָאֵל נֶֽאֶסְפוּ
3 וַֽיַּחֲנוּ בְּעֵמֶק הָֽאֵלָה וַיַּֽעַרְכוּ מִלְחָמָה לִקְרַאת פְּלִשְׁתִּים: וּפְלִשְׁתִּים
עֹמְדִים אֶל־הָהָר מִזֶּה וְיִשְׂרָאֵל עֹמְדִים אֶל־הָהָר מִזֶּה וְהַגַּיְא בֵּֽינֵיהֶם:
4 וַיֵּצֵא אִֽישׁ־הַבֵּנַ֫יִם מִמַּֽחֲנוֹת פְּלִשְׁתִּים גָּלְיָת שְׁמ֧וֹ מִגַּת גָּבְה֖וֹ שֵׁשׁ אַמּ֥וֹת
5 וָזָֽרֶת: וְכ֥וֹבַע נְחֹשֶׁת עַל־רֹאשׁ֖וֹ וְשִׁרְי֣וֹן קַשְׂקַשִּׂ֖ים ה֣וּא לָב֑וּשׁ וּמִשְׁקַל֙
הַשִּׁרְי֔וֹן חֲמֵֽשֶׁת־אֲלָפִ֥ים שְׁקָלִ֖ים נְחֹֽשֶׁת: וּמִצְחַ֥ת נְחֹ֖שֶׁת עַל־רַגְלָ֑יו
6 וְכִיד֥וֹן נְחֹ֖שֶׁת בֵּ֥ין כְּתֵפָֽיו: וְעֵ֣ץ חֲנִית֗וֹ כִּמְנוֹר֙ אֹֽרְגִ֔ים וְלַהֶ֣בֶת חֲנִית֔וֹ
7 שֵׁשׁ־מֵא֥וֹת שְׁקָלִ֖ים בַּרְזֶ֑ל וְנֹשֵׂ֥א הַצִּנָּ֖ה הֹלֵ֥ךְ לְפָנָֽיו: וַֽיַּעֲמֹ֗ד וַיִּקְרָא֙
8 אֶל־מַֽעַרְכֹ֣ת יִשְׂרָאֵ֔ל וַיֹּ֣אמֶר לָהֶ֔ם לָ֤מָּה תֵֽצְאוּ֙ לַֽעֲרֹ֣ךְ מִלְחָמָ֔ה הֲל֧וֹא
אָֽנֹכִי֙ הַפְּלִשְׁתִּ֔י וְאַתֶּ֖ם עֲבָדִ֣ים לְשָׁא֑וּל בְּרוּ־לָכֶ֥ם אִ֖ישׁ וְיֵרֵ֥ד אֵלָֽי: אִם־
9 יוּכַ֞ל לְהִלָּחֵ֤ם אִתִּי֙ וְהִכָּ֔נִי וְהָיִ֥ינוּ לָכֶ֖ם לַֽעֲבָדִ֑ים וְאִם־אֲנִ֤י אֽוּכַל־לוֹ֙
וְהִכִּיתִ֔יו וִֽהְיִ֧יתֶם לָ֛נוּ לַֽעֲבָדִ֖ים וַֽעֲבַדְתֶּ֥ם אֹתָֽנוּ: וַיֹּ֙אמֶר֙ הַפְּלִשְׁתִּ֔י אֲנִ֗י
10 חֵרַ֛פְתִּי אֶת־מַֽעַרְכ֥וֹת יִשְׂרָאֵ֖ל הַיּ֣וֹם הַזֶּ֑ה תְּנוּ־לִ֣י אִ֔ישׁ וְנִֽלָּחֲמָ֖ה יָֽחַד:
11 וַיִּשְׁמַ֤ע שָׁאוּל֙ וְכָל־יִשְׂרָאֵ֔ל אֶת־דִּבְרֵ֥י הַפְּלִשְׁתִּ֖י הָאֵ֑לֶּה וַיֵּחַ֥תּוּ וַיִּֽרְא֖וּ
12 מְאֹֽד: וְדָוִד֩ בֶּן־אִ֨ישׁ אֶפְרָתִ֜י הַזֶּ֗ה מִבֵּ֥ית לֶ֙חֶם֙ יְהוּדָ֔ה וּשְׁמ֣וֹ
יִשַׁ֔י וְל֖וֹ שְׁמֹנָ֣ה בָנִ֑ים וְהָאִישׁ֙ בִּימֵ֣י שָׁא֔וּל זָקֵ֖ן בָּ֥א בַֽאֲנָשִֽׁים: וַיֵּ֣לְכ֔וּ
13 שְׁלֹ֤שֶׁת בְּנֵֽי־יִשַׁי֙ הַגְּדֹלִ֔ים הָֽלְכ֥וּ אַֽחֲרֵֽי־שָׁא֖וּל לַמִּלְחָמָ֑ה וְשֵׁ֣ם ׀ שְׁלֹ֣שֶׁת
בָּנָ֗יו אֲשֶׁ֤ר הָֽלְכוּ֙ בַּמִּלְחָמָ֔ה אֱלִיאָ֣ב הַבְּכ֗וֹר וּמִשְׁנֵ֙הוּ֙ אֲבִ֣ינָדָ֔ב וְהַשְּׁלִשִׁ֖י
14 שַׁמָּֽה: וְדָוִ֖ד ה֣וּא הַקָּטָ֑ן וּשְׁלֹשָׁה֙ הַגְּדֹלִ֔ים הָֽלְכ֖וּ אַֽחֲרֵ֥י שָׁאֽוּל: וְדָוִ֞ד
16 הֹלֵ֧ךְ וָשָׁ֛ב מֵעַ֥ל שָׁא֖וּל לִרְע֥וֹת אֶת־צֹ֥אן אָבִ֖יו בֵּֽית־לָֽחֶם: וַיִּגַּ֥שׁ הַפְּלִשְׁתִּ֖י
17 הַשְׁכֵּ֣ם וְהַֽעֲרֵ֑ב וַיִּתְיַצֵּ֖ב אַרְבָּעִ֥ים יֽוֹם: וַיֹּ֙אמֶר יִשַׁ֜י לְדָוִ֣ד בְּנ֗וֹ קַח־נָ֤א
לְאַחֶ֙יךָ֙ אֵיפַ֤ת הַקָּלִיא֙ הַזֶּ֔ה וַֽעֲשָׂרָ֥ה לֶ֖חֶם הַזֶּ֑ה וְהָרֵ֥ץ הַֽמַּחֲנֶ֖ה לְאַחֶֽיךָ:
18 וְ֠אֵת עֲשֶׂ֜רֶת חֲרִצֵ֣י הֶֽחָלָ֗ב הָאֵ֙לֶּה֙ תָּבִ֔יא לְשַׂר־הָאָ֑לֶף וְאֶת־אַחֶ֙יךָ֙ תִּפְקֹ֣ד
19 לְשָׁל֔וֹם וְאֶת־עֲרֻֽבָּתָ֖ם תִּקָּֽח: וְשָׁא֤וּל וְהֵ֙מָּה֙ וְכָל־אִ֣ישׁ יִשְׂרָאֵ֔ל בְּעֵ֖מֶק
הָֽאֵלָ֑ה נִלְחָמִ֖ים עִם־פְּלִשְׁתִּֽים: וַיַּשְׁכֵּ֨ם דָּוִ֜ד בַּבֹּ֗קֶר וַיִּטֹּ֤שׁ אֶת־הַצֹּאן֙
עַל־שֹׁמֵ֔ר וַיִּשָּׂ֣א וַיֵּ֔לֶךְ כַּֽאֲשֶׁ֥ר צִוָּ֖הוּ יִשָׁ֑י וַיָּבֹא֙ הַמַּעְגָּ֔לָה וְהַחַ֙יִל֙ הַיֹּצֵ֣א
21 אֶל־הַמַּֽעֲרָכָ֔ה וְהֵרֵ֖עוּ בַּמִּלְחָמָֽה: וַתַּֽעֲרֹ֤ךְ יִשְׂרָאֵל֙ וּפְלִשְׁתִּ֔ים מַֽעֲרָכָ֖ה
22 לִקְרַ֥את מַֽעֲרָכָֽה: וַיִּטֹּשׁ֩ דָּוִ֨ד אֶת־הַכֵּלִ֜ים מֵֽעָלָ֗יו עַל־יַד֙ שׁוֹמֵ֣ר הַכֵּלִ֔ים
23 וַיָּ֖רָץ הַמַּֽעֲרָכָ֑ה וַיָּבֹ֕א וַיִּשְׁאַ֥ל לְאֶחָ֖יו לְשָׁלֽוֹם: וְה֣וּא ׀ מְדַבֵּ֣ר עִמָּ֗ם
וְהִנֵּ֣ה אִ֣ישׁ הַבֵּנַ֡יִם עוֹלֶ֞ה גָּלְיָת֩ הַפְּלִשְׁתִּ֨י שְׁמ֤וֹ מִגַּת֙ מִמַּֽעֲר֣וֹת פְּלִשְׁתִּ֔ים

24 וַיְדַבֵּר כַּדְּבָרִים הָאֵלֶּה וַיִּשְׁמַע דָּוִד ׃ וְכֹל אִישׁ יִשְׂרָאֵל בִּרְאוֹתָם
כה אֶת־הָאִישׁ וַיָּנֻסוּ מִפָּנָיו וַיִּירְאוּ מְאֹד ׃ וַיֹּאמֶר ׀ אִישׁ יִשְׂרָאֵל הַרְּאִיתֶם
הָאִישׁ הָעֹלֶה הַזֶּה פִּי לְחָרֵף אֶת־יִשְׂרָאֵל עֹלֶה וְהָיָה הָאִישׁ אֲשֶׁר־יַכֶּנּוּ
יַעְשְׁרֶנּוּ ׀ הַמֶּלֶךְ ׀ עֹשֶׁר גָּדוֹל וְאֶת־בִּתּוֹ יִתֶּן־לוֹ וְאֵת בֵּית אָבִיו יַעֲשֶׂה
26 חָפְשִׁי בְּיִשְׂרָאֵל ׃ וַיֹּאמֶר דָּוִד אֶל־הָאֲנָשִׁים הָעֹמְדִים עִמּוֹ לֵאמֹר
מַה־יֵּעָשֶׂה לָאִישׁ אֲשֶׁר יַכֶּה אֶת־הַפְּלִשְׁתִּי הַלָּז וְהֵסִיר חֶרְפָּה מֵעַל
יִשְׂרָאֵל כִּי מִי הַפְּלִשְׁתִּי הֶעָרֵל הַזֶּה כִּי חֵרֵף מַעַרְכוֹת אֱלֹהִים חַיִּים ׃
27 וַיֹּאמֶר לוֹ הָעָם כַּדָּבָר הַזֶּה לֵאמֹר כֹּה יֵעָשֶׂה לָאִישׁ אֲשֶׁר יַכֶּנּוּ ׃
28 וַיִּשְׁמַע אֱלִיאָב אָחִיו הַגָּדוֹל בְּדַבְּרוֹ אֶל־הָאֲנָשִׁים וַיִּחַר־אַף אֱלִיאָב
בְּדָוִד וַיֹּאמֶר ׀ לָמָּה־זֶּה יָרַדְתָּ וְעַל־מִי נָטַשְׁתָּ מְעַט הַצֹּאן הָהֵנָּה
בַּמִּדְבָּר אֲנִי יָדַעְתִּי אֶת־זְדֹנְךָ וְאֵת רֹעַ לְבָבֶךָ כִּי לְמַעַן רְאוֹת
29 הַמִּלְחָמָה יָרָדְתָּ ׃ וַיֹּאמֶר דָּוִד מֶה עָשִׂיתִי עָתָּה הֲלוֹא דָּבָר הוּא ׃
ל וַיִּסֹּב מֵאֶצְלוֹ אֶל־מוּל אַחֵר וַיֹּאמֶר כַּדָּבָר הַזֶּה וַיְשִׁבֻהוּ הָעָם דָּבָר
31 כַּדָּבָר הָרִאשׁוֹן ׃ וַיִּשָּׁמְעוּ הַדְּבָרִים אֲשֶׁר דִּבֶּר דָּוִד וַיַּגִּדוּ לִפְנֵי־שָׁאוּל
32 וַיִּקָּחֵהוּ ׃ וַיֹּאמֶר דָּוִד אֶל־שָׁאוּל אַל־יִפֹּל לֵב־אָדָם עָלָיו עַבְדְּךָ יֵלֵךְ
33 וְנִלְחַם עִם־הַפְּלִשְׁתִּי הַזֶּה ׃ וַיֹּאמֶר שָׁאוּל אֶל־דָּוִד לֹא תוּכַל לָלֶכֶת אֶל־
הַפְּלִשְׁתִּי הַזֶּה לְהִלָּחֵם עִמּוֹ כִּי־נַעַר אַתָּה וְהוּא אִישׁ מִלְחָמָה מִנְּעֻרָיו ׃
34 וַיֹּאמֶר דָּוִד אֶל־שָׁאוּל רֹעֶה הָיָה עַבְדְּךָ לְאָבִיו בַּצֹּאן וּבָא הָאֲרִי
לה וְאֶת־הַדּוֹב וְנָשָׂא שֶׂה מֵהָעֵדֶר ׃ וְיָצָאתִי אַחֲרָיו וְהִכִּתִיו וְהִצַּלְתִּי מִפִּיו
36 וַיָּקָם עָלַי וְהֶחֱזַקְתִּי בִּזְקָנוֹ וְהִכִּתִיו וַהֲמִיתִּיו ׃ גַּם אֶת־הָאֲרִי גַּם־
הַדּוֹב הִכָּה עַבְדֶּךָ וְהָיָה הַפְּלִשְׁתִּי הֶעָרֵל הַזֶּה כְּאַחַד מֵהֶם כִּי חֵרֵף
37 מַעַרְכֹת אֱלֹהִים חַיִּים ׃ וַיֹּאמֶר דָּוִד יְהֹוָה אֲשֶׁר הִצִּלַנִי מִיַּד
הָאֲרִי וּמִיַּד הַדֹּב הוּא יַצִּילֵנִי מִיַּד הַפְּלִשְׁתִּי הַזֶּה   ס   וַיֹּאמֶר
38 שָׁאוּל אֶל־דָּוִד לֵךְ וַיהֹוָה יִהְיֶה עִמָּךְ ׃ וַיַּלְבֵּשׁ שָׁאוּל אֶת־דָּוִד מַדָּיו
39 וְנָתַן קוֹבַע נְחֹשֶׁת עַל־רֹאשׁוֹ וַיַּלְבֵּשׁ אֹתוֹ שִׁרְיוֹן ׃ וַיַּחְגֹּר דָּוִד אֶת־
חַרְבּוֹ מֵעַל לְמַדָּיו וַיֹּאֶל לָלֶכֶת כִּי לֹא־נִסָּה וַיֹּאמֶר דָּוִד אֶל־שָׁאוּל
מ לֹא־אוּכַל לָלֶכֶת בָּאֵלֶּה כִּי לֹא נִסִּיתִי וַיְסִרֵם דָּוִד מֵעָלָיו ׃ וַיִּקַּח מַקְלוֹ
בְּיָדוֹ וַיִּבְחַר־לוֹ חֲמִשָּׁה חַלֻּקֵי אֲבָנִים ׀ מִן־הַנַּחַל וַיָּשֶׂם אֹתָם בִּכְלִי
41 הָרֹעִים אֲשֶׁר־לוֹ וּבַיַּלְקוּט וְקַלְעוֹ בְיָדוֹ וַיִּגַּשׁ אֶל־הַפְּלִשְׁתִּי ׃ וַיֵּלֶךְ
42 הַפְּלִשְׁתִּי הֹלֵךְ וְקָרֵב אֶל־דָּוִד וְהָאִישׁ נֹשֵׂא הַצִּנָּה לְפָנָיו ׃ וַיַּבֵּט
הַפְּלִשְׁתִּי וַיִּרְאֶה אֶת־דָּוִד וַיִּבְזֵהוּ כִּי־הָיָה נַעַר וְאַדְמֹנִי עִם־יְפֵה
43 מַרְאֶה ׃ וַיֹּאמֶר הַפְּלִשְׁתִּי אֶל־דָּוִד הֲכֶלֶב אָנֹכִי כִּי־אַתָּה בָא־אֵלַי
44 בַּמַּקְלוֹת וַיְקַלֵּל הַפְּלִשְׁתִּי אֶת־דָּוִד בֵּאלֹהָיו ׃ וַיֹּאמֶר הַפְּלִשְׁתִּי אֶל־

דֶּרֶךְ לְכָה אֵלַי וְאֶתְּנָה אֶת־בְּשָׂרְךָ לְעוֹף הַשָּׁמַיִם וּלְבֶהֱמַת הַשָּׂדֶה :

45 וַיֹּאמֶר דָּוִד אֶל־הַפְּלִשְׁתִּי אַתָּה בָּא אֵלַי בְּחֶרֶב וּבַחֲנִית וּבְכִידוֹן וְאָנֹכִי בָא־אֵלֶיךָ בְּשֵׁם יְהוָה צְבָאוֹת אֱלֹהֵי מַעַרְכוֹת יִשְׂרָאֵל אֲשֶׁר

46 חֵרַפְתָּ : הַיּוֹם הַזֶּה יְסַגֶּרְךָ יְהוָה בְּיָדִי וְהִכִּיתִךָ וַהֲסִרֹתִי אֶת־רֹאשְׁךָ מֵעָלֶיךָ וְנָתַתִּי פֶּגֶר מַחֲנֵה פְלִשְׁתִּים הַיּוֹם הַזֶּה לְעוֹף הַשָּׁמַיִם וּלְחַיַּת

47 הָאָרֶץ וְיֵדְעוּ כָּל־הָאָרֶץ כִּי יֵשׁ אֱלֹהִים לְיִשְׂרָאֵל : וְיֵדְעוּ כָּל־הַקָּהָל הַזֶּה כִּי־לֹא בְּחֶרֶב וּבַחֲנִית יְהוֹשִׁיעַ יְהוָה כִּי לַיהוָה הַמִּלְחָמָה וְנָתַן

48 אֶתְכֶם בְּיָדֵנוּ : וְהָיָה כִּי־קָם הַפְּלִשְׁתִּי וַיֵּלֶךְ וַיִּקְרַב לִקְרַאת דָּוִד

49 וַיְמַהֵר דָּוִד וַיָּרָץ הַמַּעֲרָכָה לִקְרַאת הַפְּלִשְׁתִּי : וַיִּשְׁלַח דָּוִד אֶת־יָדוֹ אֶל־הַכֶּלִי וַיִּקַּח מִשָּׁם אֶבֶן וַיְקַלַּע וַיַּךְ אֶת־הַפְּלִשְׁתִּי אֶל־מִצְחוֹ וַתִּטְבַּע הָאֶבֶן בְּמִצְחוֹ וַיִּפֹּל עַל־פָּנָיו אָרְצָה : וַיֶּחֱזַק דָּוִד מִן־הַפְּלִשְׁתִּי בַּקֶּלַע

51 וּבָאֶבֶן וַיַּךְ אֶת־הַפְּלִשְׁתִּי וַיְמִיתֵהוּ וְחֶרֶב אֵין בְּיַד־דָּוִד : וַיָּרָץ דָּוִד וַיַּעֲמֹד אֶל־הַפְּלִשְׁתִּי וַיִּקַּח אֶת־חַרְבּוֹ וַיִּשְׁלְפָהּ מִתַּעְרָהּ וַיְמֹתְתֵהוּ

52 וַיִּכְרָת־בָּהּ אֶת־רֹאשׁוֹ וַיִּרְאוּ הַפְּלִשְׁתִּים כִּי־מֵת גִּבּוֹרָם וַיָּנֻסוּ : וַיָּקֻמוּ אַנְשֵׁי יִשְׂרָאֵל וִיהוּדָה וַיָּרִעוּ וַיִּרְדְּפוּ אֶת־הַפְּלִשְׁתִּים עַד־בּוֹאֲךָ גַיְא וְעַד שַׁעֲרֵי עֶקְרוֹן וַיִּפְּלוּ חַלְלֵי פְלִשְׁתִּים בְּדֶרֶךְ שַׁעֲרַיִם וְעַד־גַּת וְעַד־

53 עֶקְרוֹן : וַיָּשֻׁבוּ בְּנֵי יִשְׂרָאֵל מִדְּלֹק אַחֲרֵי פְלִשְׁתִּים וַיָּשֹׁסּוּ אֶת־מַחֲנֵיהֶם :

54 וַיִּקַּח דָּוִד אֶת־רֹאשׁ הַפְּלִשְׁתִּי וַיְבִיאֵהוּ יְרוּשָׁלִָם וְאֶת־כֵּלָיו שָׂם בְּאָהֳלוֹ :

55 וְכִרְאוֹת שָׁאוּל אֶת־דָּוִד יֹצֵא לִקְרַאת הַפְּלִשְׁתִּי אָמַר אֶל־אַבְנֵר שַׂר הַצָּבָא בֶּן־מִי־זֶה הַנַּעַר אַבְנֵר וַיֹּאמֶר אַבְנֵר חֵי־נַפְשְׁךָ הַמֶּלֶךְ אִם־

56 יָדָעְתִּי : וַיֹּאמֶר הַמֶּלֶךְ שְׁאַל אַתָּה בֶּן־מִי־זֶה הָעָלֶם : וּכְשׁוּב דָּוִד
57 מֵהַכּוֹת אֶת־הַפְּלִשְׁתִּי וַיִּקַּח אֹתוֹ אַבְנֵר וַיְבִאֵהוּ לִפְנֵי שָׁאוּל וְרֹאשׁ

58 הַפְּלִשְׁתִּי בְּיָדוֹ : וַיֹּאמֶר אֵלָיו שָׁאוּל בֶּן־מִי אַתָּה הַנַּעַר וַיֹּאמֶר דָּוִד בֶּן־עַבְדְּךָ יִשַׁי בֵּית הַלַּחְמִי :

VI. The Prophet Elijah, 1 *Kings* 17–19.

CHAPTER XVII. יז

1 וַיֹּאמֶר אֵלִיָּהוּ הַתִּשְׁבִּי מִתּשָׁבֵי גִלְעָד אֶל־אַחְאָב חַי־יְהוָה אֱלֹהֵי יִשְׂרָאֵל אֲשֶׁר עָמַדְתִּי לְפָנָיו אִם־יִהְיֶה הַשָּׁנִים הָאֵלֶּה טַל וּמָטָר כִּי אִם־לְפִי

2 דְבָרִי : וַיְהִי דְבַר־יְהוָה אֵלָיו לֵאמֹר : 3 לֵךְ מִזֶּה וּפָנִיתָ לְךָ קֵדְמָה

4 וְנִסְתַּרְתָּ בְּנַחַל כְּרִית אֲשֶׁר עַל־פְּנֵי הַיַּרְדֵּן : וְהָיָה מֵהַנַּחַל תִּשְׁתֶּה וְאֶת־

5 הָעֹרְבִים צִוִּיתִי לְכַלְכֶּלְךָ שָׁם : וַיֵּלֶךְ וַיַּעַשׂ כִּדְבַר יְהוָה וַיֵּלֶךְ וַיֵּשֶׁב

6 בְּנַחַל כְּרִית אֲשֶׁר עַל־פְּנֵי הַיַּרְדֵּן ׃ וְהָעֹרְבִים מְבִיאִים לוֹ לֶחֶם וּבָשָׂר

7 בַּבֹּקֶר וְלֶחֶם וּבָשָׂר בָּעֶרֶב וּמִן־הַנַּחַל יִשְׁתֶּה ׃ וַיְהִי מִקֵּץ יָמִים וַיִּיבַשׁ

8 הַנָּחַל כִּי לֹא־הָיָה גֶשֶׁם בָּאָרֶץ ׃   וַיְהִי דְבַר־יְהֹוָה אֵלָיו לֵאמֹר ׃

9 קוּם לֵךְ צָרְפַתָה אֲשֶׁר לְצִידוֹן וְיָשַׁבְתָּ שָׁם הִנֵּה צִוִּיתִי שָׁם אִשָּׁה

י אַלְמָנָה לְכַלְכְּלֶךָ ׃ וַיָּקָם , וַיֵּלֶךְ צָרְפַתָה וַיָּבֹא אֶל־פֶּתַח הָעִיר וְהִנֵּה־שָׁם

אִשָּׁה אַלְמָנָה מְקֹשֶׁשֶׁת עֵצִים וַיִּקְרָא אֵלֶיהָ וַיֹּאמַר קְחִי־נָא לִי מְעַט־

11 מַיִם בַּכְּלִי וְאֶשְׁתֶּה ׃ וַתֵּלֶךְ לָקַחַת וַיִּקְרָא אֵלֶיהָ וַיֹּאמַר לִקְחִי־נָא לִי

12 פַת־לֶחֶם בְּיָדֵךְ ׃ וַתֹּאמֶר חַי־יְהֹוָה אֱלֹהֶיךָ אִם־יֶשׁ־לִי מָעוֹג כִּי אִם־

מְלֹא כַף־קֶמַח בַּכַּד וּמְעַט־שֶׁמֶן בַּצַּפָּחַת וְהִנְנִי מְקֹשֶׁשֶׁת שְׁנַיִם עֵצִים

13 וּבָאתִי וַעֲשִׂיתִיהוּ לִי וְלִבְנִי וַאֲכַלְנֻהוּ וָמָתְנוּ ׃ וַיֹּאמֶר אֵלֶיהָ

אֵלִיָּהוּ אַל־תִּירְאִי בֹּאִי עֲשִׂי כִדְבָרֵךְ אַךְ עֲשִׂי־לִי מִשָּׁם עֻגָה קְטַנָּה בָרִאשֹׁנָה

14 וְהוֹצֵאת לִי וְלָךְ וְלִבְנֵךְ תַּעֲשִׂי בָּאַחֲרֹנָה ׃ כִּי כֹה אָמַר יְהֹוָה אֱלֹהֵי

יִשְׂרָאֵל כַּד הַקֶּמַח לֹא תִכְלָה וְצַפַּחַת הַשֶּׁמֶן לֹא תֶחְסָר עַד יוֹם

טו תֵּת־יְהֹוָה גֶּשֶׁם עַל־פְּנֵי הָאֲדָמָה ׃ וַתֵּלֶךְ וַתַּעֲשֶׂה כִּדְבַר אֵלִיָּהוּ וַתֹּאכַל

16 הוּא־וָהִיא וּבֵיתָהּ יָמִים ׃ כַּד הַקֶּמַח לֹא כָלָתָה וְצַפַּחַת הַשֶּׁמֶן לֹא

17 חָסֵר כִּדְבַר יְהֹוָה אֲשֶׁר דִּבֶּר בְּיַד אֵלִיָּהוּ ׃   וַיְהִי אַחַר הַדְּבָרִים

הָאֵלֶּה חָלָה בֶּן־הָאִשָּׁה בַּעֲלַת הַבָּיִת וַיְהִי חָלְיוֹ חָזָק מְאֹד עַד אֲשֶׁר

18 לֹא־נוֹתְרָה־בּוֹ נְשָׁמָה ׃ וַתֹּאמֶר אֶל־אֵלִיָּהוּ מַה־לִּי וָלָךְ אִישׁ הָאֱלֹהִים

19 בָּאתָ אֵלַי לְהַזְכִּיר אֶת־עֲוֹנִי וּלְהָמִית אֶת־בְּנִי ׃ וַיֹּאמֶר אֵלֶיהָ תְּנִי־לִי

אֶת־בְּנֵךְ וַיִּקָּחֵהוּ מֵחֵיקָהּ וַיַּעֲלֵהוּ אֶל־הָעֲלִיָּה אֲשֶׁר־הוּא יֹשֵׁב שָׁם

כ וַיַּשְׁכִּבֵהוּ עַל־מִטָּתוֹ ׃ וַיִּקְרָא אֶל־יְהֹוָה וַיֹּאמַר יְהֹוָה אֱלֹהָי הֲגַם עַל־

21 הָאַלְמָנָה אֲשֶׁר־אֲנִי מִתְגּוֹרֵר עִמָּהּ הֲרֵעוֹתָ לְהָמִית אֶת־בְּנָהּ ׃ וַיִּתְמֹדֵד

עַל־הַיֶּלֶד שָׁלֹשׁ פְּעָמִים וַיִּקְרָא אֶל־יְהֹוָה וַיֹּאמַר יְהֹוָה אֱלֹהָי תָּשָׁב־נָא

22 נֶפֶשׁ־הַיֶּלֶד הַזֶּה עַל־קִרְבּוֹ ׃ וַיִּשְׁמַע יְהֹוָה בְּקוֹל אֵלִיָּהוּ וַתָּשָׁב נֶפֶשׁ־הַיֶּלֶד

23 עַל־קִרְבּוֹ וַיֶּחִי ׃ וַיִּקַּח אֵלִיָּהוּ אֶת־הַיֶּלֶד וַיֹּרִדֵהוּ מִן־הָעֲלִיָּה

הַבַּיְתָה וַיִּתְּנֵהוּ לְאִמּוֹ וַיֹּאמֶר אֵלִיָּהוּ רְאִי חַי בְּנֵךְ ׃ וַתֹּאמֶר הָאִשָּׁה אֶל־

24 אֵלִיָּהוּ עַתָּה זֶה יָדַעְתִּי כִּי אִישׁ אֱלֹהִים אָתָּה וּדְבַר־יְהֹוָה בְּפִיךָ אֱמֶת ׃

CHAPTER XVIII.   יח

א וַיְהִי יָמִים רַבִּים וּדְבַר יְהֹוָה הָיָה אֶל־אֵלִיָּהוּ בַּשָּׁנָה הַשְּׁלִישִׁית לֵאמֹר

2 לֵךְ הֵרָאֵה אֶל־אַחְאָב וְאֶתְּנָה מָטָר עַל־פְּנֵי הָאֲדָמָה ׃ וַיֵּלֶךְ אֵלִיָּהוּ

3 לְהֵרָאוֹת אֶל־אַחְאָב וְהָרָעָב חָזָק בְּשֹׁמְרוֹן ׃ וַיִּקְרָא אַחְאָב אֶל־עֹבַדְיָהוּ

v. 14.   v. 15. הִיא ק   ibid. וְהִיא ק   v. 20. קָמַץ בז"ק   v. 21. קָמַץ בו"ק
v. 1. הַפְטָרַת כִּי תִשָּׂא כְּמִנְהַג הָאַשְׁכְּנַזִּים

3

אֲשֶׁר עַל־הַבָּיִת וְעֹבַדְיָהוּ הָיָה יָרֵא אֶת־יְהוָֹה מְאֹד: וַיְהִי בְּהַכְרִית 4
אִיזֶבֶל אֵת נְבִיאֵי יְהוָֹה וַיִּקַּח עֹבַדְיָהוּ מֵאָה נְבִיאִים וַיַּחְבִּיאֵם
חֲמִשִּׁים אִישׁ בַּמְּעָרָה וְכִלְכְּלָם לֶחֶם וָמָיִם: וַיֹּאמֶר אַחְאָב אֶל־עֹבַדְיָהוּ 5
לֵךְ בָּאָרֶץ אֶל־כָּל־מַעְיְנֵי הַמַּיִם וְאֶל כָּל־הַנְּחָלִים אוּלַי , נִמְצָא חָצִיר
וּנְחַיֶּה סוּס וָפֶרֶד וְלוֹא נַכְרִית מֵהַבְּהֵמָה: וַיְּחַלְּקוּ לָהֶם אֶת־הָאָרֶץ 6
לַעֲבָר־בָּהּ אַחְאָב הָלַךְ בְּדֶרֶךְ אֶחָד לְבַדּוֹ וְעֹבַדְיָהוּ הָלַךְ בְּדֶרֶךְ־אֶחָד
לְבַדּוֹ: וַיְהִי עֹבַדְיָהוּ בַּדֶּרֶךְ וְהִנֵּה אֵלִיָּהוּ לִקְרָאתוֹ וַיַּכִּרֵהוּ וַיִּפֹּל 7
עַל־פָּנָיו וַיֹּאמֶר הַאַתָּה זֶה אֲדֹנִי אֵלִיָּהוּ: וַיֹּאמֶר לוֹ אָנִי לֵךְ אֱמֹר 8
לַאדֹנֶיךָ הִנֵּה אֵלִיָּהוּ: וַיֹּאמֶר מֶה חָטָאתִי כִּי־אַתָּה נֹתֵן אֶת־עַבְדְּךָ 9
בְּיַד אַחְאָב לַהֲמִיתֵנִי: חַי , יְהוָֹה אֱלֹהֶיךָ אִם־יֶשׁ־גּוֹי וּמַמְלָכָה אֲשֶׁר
לֹא־שָׁלַח אֲדֹנִי שָׁם לְבַקֶּשְׁךָ וְאָמְרוּ אָיִן וְהִשְׁבִּיעַ אֶת־הַמַּמְלָכָה וְאֶת־
הַגּוֹי כִּי לֹא יִמְצָאֶכָּה: וְעַתָּה אַתָּה אֹמֵר לֵךְ אֱמֹר לַאדֹנֶיךָ הִנֵּה 11
אֵלִיָּהוּ: וְהָיָה אֲנִי , אֵלֵךְ מֵאִתָּךְ וְרוּחַ יְהוָֹה , יִשָּׂאֲךָ עַל־אֲשֶׁר לֹא־אֵדָע 12
וּבָאתִי לְהַגִּיד לְאַחְאָב וְלֹא יִמְצָאֲךָ וַהֲרָגָנִי וְעַבְדְּךָ יָרֵא אֶת־יְהוָֹה
מִנְּעֻרָי: הֲלֹא־הֻגַּד לַאדֹנִי אֵת אֲשֶׁר־עָשִׂיתִי בַּהֲרֹג אִיזֶבֶל אֵת נְבִיאֵי 13
יְהוָֹה וָאַחְבִּא מִנְּבִיאֵי יְהוָֹה מֵאָה אִישׁ חֲמִשִּׁים חֲמִשִּׁים אִישׁ בַּמְּעָרָה
וָאֲכַלְכְּלֵם לֶחֶם וָמָיִם: וְעַתָּה אַתָּה אֹמֵר לֵךְ אֱמֹר לַאדֹנֶיךָ הִנֵּה 14
אֵלִיָּהוּ וַהֲרָגָנִי: וַיֹּאמֶר אֵלִיָּהוּ חַי יְהוָֹה צְבָאוֹת אֲשֶׁר עָמַדְתִּי לְפָנָיו
כִּי הַיּוֹם אֵרָאֶה אֵלָיו: וַיֵּלֶךְ עֹבַדְיָהוּ לִקְרַאת אַחְאָב וַיַּגֶּד־לוֹ וַיֵּלֶךְ 16
אַחְאָב לִקְרַאת אֵלִיָּהוּ: וַיְהִי כִּרְאוֹת אַחְאָב אֶת־אֵלִיָּהוּ וַיֹּאמֶר אַחְאָב 17
אֵלָיו הַאַתָּה זֶה עֹכֵר יִשְׂרָאֵל: וַיֹּאמֶר לֹא עָכַרְתִּי אֶת־יִשְׂרָאֵל כִּי אִם־ 18
אַתָּה וּבֵית אָבִיךָ בַּעֲזָבְכֶם אֶת־מִצְוֹת יְהוָֹה וַתֵּלֶךְ אַחֲרֵי הַבְּעָלִים:
וְעַתָּה שְׁלַח קְבֹץ אֵלַי אֶת־כָּל־יִשְׂרָאֵל אֶל־הַר הַכַּרְמֶל וְאֶת־נְבִיאֵי הַבַּעַל 19
אַרְבַּע מֵאוֹת וַחֲמִשִּׁים וּנְבִיאֵי הָאֲשֵׁרָה אַרְבַּע מֵאוֹת אֹכְלֵי שֻׁלְחַן אִיזֶבֶל:
וַיִּשְׁלַח אַחְאָב בְּכָל־בְּנֵי יִשְׂרָאֵל וַיִּקְבֹּץ אֶת־הַנְּבִיאִים אֶל־הַר הַכַּרְמֶל: 20
וַיִּגַּשׁ אֵלִיָּהוּ אֶל־כָּל־הָעָם וַיֹּאמֶר עַד־מָתַי אַתֶּם פֹּסְחִים עַל־שְׁתֵּי 21
הַסְּעִפִּים אִם־יְהוָֹה הָאֱלֹהִים לְכוּ אַחֲרָיו וְאִם־הַבַּעַל לְכוּ אַחֲרָיו וְלֹא־
עָנוּ הָעָם אֹתוֹ דָּבָר: וַיֹּאמֶר אֵלִיָּהוּ אֶל־הָעָם אֲנִי נוֹתַרְתִּי נָבִיא 22
לַיהוָֹה לְבַדִּי וּנְבִיאֵי הַבַּעַל אַרְבַּע־מֵאוֹת וַחֲמִשִּׁים אִישׁ: וְיִתְּנוּ־לָנוּ 23
שְׁנַיִם פָּרִים וְיִבְחֲרוּ לָהֶם הַפָּר הָאֶחָד וִינַתְּחֻהוּ וְיָשִׂימוּ עַל־הָעֵצִים
וְאֵשׁ לֹא יָשִׂימוּ וַאֲנִי , אֶעֱשֶׂה ׀ אֶת־הַפָּר הָאֶחָד וְנָתַתִּי עַל־הָעֵצִים וְאֵשׁ
לֹא אָשִׂים: וּקְרָאתֶם בְּשֵׁם אֱלֹהֵיכֶם וַאֲנִי , אֶקְרָא בְשֵׁם־יְהוָֹה וְהָיָה 24

הָאֱלֹהִים אֲשֶׁר־יַעֲנֶה בָאֵשׁ הוּא הָאֱלֹהִים וַיַּעַן כָּל־הָעָם וַיֹּאמְרוּ טוֹב

כה הַדָּבָר: וַיֹּאמֶר אֵלִיָּהוּ לִנְבִיאֵי הַבַּעַל בַּחֲרוּ לָכֶם הַפָּר הָאֶחָד וַעֲשׂוּ

רִאשֹׁנָה כִּי אַתֶּם הָרַבִּים וְקִרְאוּ בְּשֵׁם אֱלֹהֵיכֶם וְאֵשׁ לֹא תָשִׂימוּ:

26 וַיִּקְחוּ אֶת־הַפָּר אֲשֶׁר־נָתַן לָהֶם וַיַּעֲשׂוּ וַיִּקְרְאוּ בְשֵׁם־הַבַּעַל מֵהַבֹּקֶר

וְעַד־הַצָּהֳרַיִם לֵאמֹר הַבַּעַל עֲנֵנוּ וְאֵין קוֹל וְאֵין עֹנֶה וַיְפַסְּחוּ עַל־

27 הַמִּזְבֵּחַ אֲשֶׁר עָשָׂה: וַיְהִי בַצָּהֳרַיִם וַיְהַתֵּל בָּהֶם אֵלִיָּהוּ וַיֹּאמֶר

קִרְאוּ בְקוֹל־גָּדוֹל כִּי־אֱלֹהִים הוּא כִּי־שִׂיחַ וְכִי־שִׂיג לוֹ וְכִי־דֶרֶךְ לוֹ

28 אוּלַי יָשֵׁן הוּא וְיִקָץ: וַיִּקְרְאוּ בְּקוֹל גָּדוֹל וַיִּתְגֹּדְדוּ כְּמִשְׁפָּטָם בַּחֲרָבוֹת

29 וּבָרְמָחִים עַד־שְׁפָךְ־דָּם עֲלֵיהֶם: וַיְהִי כַּעֲבֹר הַצָּהֳרַיִם וַיִּתְנַבְּאוּ עַד

ל לַעֲלוֹת הַמִּנְחָה וְאֵין־קוֹל וְאֵין־עֹנֶה וְאֵין קָשֶׁב: וַיֹּאמֶר אֵלִיָּהוּ לְכָל־

הָעָם גְּשׁוּ אֵלַי וַיִּגְּשׁוּ כָל־הָעָם אֵלָיו וַיְרַפֵּא אֶת־מִזְבַּח יְהֹוָה הֶהָרוּס:

31 וַיִּקַּח אֵלִיָּהוּ שְׁתֵּים עֶשְׂרֵה אֲבָנִים כְּמִסְפַּר שִׁבְטֵי בְנֵי־יַעֲקֹב אֲשֶׁר הָיָה

32 דְבַר־יְהֹוָה אֵלָיו לֵאמֹר יִשְׂרָאֵל יִהְיֶה שְׁמֶךָ: וַיִּבְנֶה אֶת־הָאֲבָנִים מִזְבֵּחַ

33 בְּשֵׁם יְהֹוָה וַיַּעַשׂ תְּעָלָה כְּבֵית סָאתַיִם זֶרַע סָבִיב לַמִּזְבֵּחַ: וַיַּעֲרֹךְ

34 אֶת־הָעֵצִים וַיְנַתַּח אֶת־הַפָּר וַיָּשֶׂם עַל־הָעֵצִים: וַיֹּאמֶר מִלְאוּ אַרְבָּעָה

כַדִּים מַיִם וְיִצְקוּ עַל־הָעֹלָה וְעַל־הָעֵצִים וַיֹּאמֶר שְׁנוּ וַיִּשְׁנוּ וַיֹּאמֶר

לה שַׁלֵּשׁוּ וַיְשַׁלֵּשׁוּ: וַיֵּלְכוּ הַמַּיִם סָבִיב לַמִּזְבֵּחַ וְגַם אֶת־הַתְּעָלָה מִלֵּא

36 מָיִם: וַיְהִי בַּעֲלוֹת הַמִּנְחָה וַיִּגַּשׁ אֵלִיָּהוּ הַנָּבִיא וַיֹּאמַר יְהֹוָה אֱלֹהֵי

אַבְרָהָם יִצְחָק וְיִשְׂרָאֵל הַיּוֹם יִוָּדַע כִּי־אַתָּה אֱלֹהִים בְּיִשְׂרָאֵל וַאֲנִי

37 עַבְדֶּךָ וּבִדְבָרְךָ עָשִׂיתִי אֵת כָּל־הַדְּבָרִים הָאֵלֶּה: עֲנֵנִי יְהֹוָה עֲנֵנִי

וְיֵדְעוּ הָעָם הַזֶּה כִּי־אַתָּה יְהֹוָה הָאֱלֹהִים וְאַתָּה הֲסִבֹּתָ אֶת־לִבָּם

38 אֲחֹרַנִּית: וַתִּפֹּל אֵשׁ־יְהֹוָה וַתֹּאכַל אֶת־הָעֹלָה וְאֶת־הָעֵצִים וְאֶת־הָאֲבָנִים

39 וְאֶת־הֶעָפָר וְאֶת־הַמַּיִם אֲשֶׁר־בַּתְּעָלָה לִחֵכָה: וַיַּרְא כָּל־הָעָם וַיִּפְּלוּ

מ עַל־פְּנֵיהֶם וַיֹּאמְרוּ יְהֹוָה הוּא הָאֱלֹהִים יְהֹוָה הוּא הָאֱלֹהִים: וַיֹּאמֶר

אֵלִיָּהוּ לָהֶם תִּפְשׂוּ אֶת־נְבִיאֵי הַבַּעַל אִישׁ אַל־יִמָּלֵט מֵהֶם וַיִּתְפְּשׂוּם

41 וַיּוֹרִדֵם אֵלִיָּהוּ אֶל־נַחַל קִישׁוֹן וַיִּשְׁחָטֵם שָׁם: וַיֹּאמֶר אֵלִיָּהוּ לְאַחְאָב

42 עֲלֵה אֱכֹל וּשְׁתֵה כִּי־קוֹל הֲמוֹן הַגָּשֶׁם: וַיַּעֲלֶה אַחְאָב לֶאֱכֹל וְלִשְׁתּוֹת

וְאֵלִיָּהוּ עָלָה אֶל־רֹאשׁ הַכַּרְמֶל וַיִּגְהַר אַרְצָה וַיָּשֶׂם פָּנָיו בֵּין בִּרְכָּו:

43 וַיֹּאמֶר אֶל־נַעֲרוֹ עֲלֵה־נָא הַבֵּט דֶּרֶךְ־יָם וַיַּעַל וַיַּבֵּט וַיֹּאמֶר אֵין

44 מְאוּמָה וַיֹּאמֶר שֻׁב שֶׁבַע פְּעָמִים: וַיְהִי בַּשְּׁבִעִית וַיֹּאמֶר הִנֵּה־עָב

קְטַנָּה כְּכַף־אִישׁ עֹלָה מִיָּם וַיֹּאמֶר עֲלֵה אֱמֹר אֶל־אַחְאָב אֱסֹר וָרֵד

מה וְלֹא יַעַצָרְכָה הַגָּשֶׁם: וַיְהִי עַד־כֹּה וְעַד־כֹּה וְהַשָּׁמַיִם הִתְקַדְּרוּ עָבִים

וְיַד 46　　　וְרוּחַ וַיְהִי גֶּשֶׁם גָּדוֹל וַיִּרְכַּב אַחְאָב וַיֵּלֶךְ יִזְרְעֶאלָה:
יְהֹוָה הָיְתָה אֶל־אֵלִיָּהוּ וַיְשַׁנֵּס מָתְנָיו וַיָּרׇץ לִפְנֵי אַחְאָב עַד־בֹּאֲכָה
יִזְרְעֶאלָה:

CHAPTER XIX. יט

וַיַּגֵּד אַחְאָב לְאִיזֶבֶל אֵת כׇּל־אֲשֶׁר עָשָׂה אֵלִיָּהוּ וְאֵת כׇּל־אֲשֶׁר הָרַג א
אֶת־כׇּל־הַנְּבִיאִים בֶּחָרֶב: וַתִּשְׁלַח אִיזֶבֶל מַלְאָךְ אֶל־אֵלִיָּהוּ לֵאמֹר כֹּה־ 2
יַעֲשׂוּן אֱלֹהִים וְכֹה יוֹסִפוּן כִּי־כָעֵת מָחָר אָשִׂים אֶת־נַפְשְׁךָ כְּנֶפֶשׁ
אַחַד מֵהֶם: וַיַּרְא וַיָּקׇם וַיֵּלֶךְ אֶל־נַפְשׁוֹ וַיָּבֹא בְּאֵר שֶׁבַע אֲשֶׁר 3
לִיהוּדָה וַיַּנַּח אֶת־נַעֲרוֹ שָׁם: וְהוּא־הָלַךְ בַּמִּדְבָּר דֶּרֶךְ יוֹם וַיָּבֹא 4
וַיֵּשֶׁב תַּחַת רֹתֶם אֶחָד וַיִּשְׁאַל אֶת־נַפְשׁוֹ לָמוּת וַיֹּאמֶר ׀ רַב עַתָּה
יְהֹוָה קַח נַפְשִׁי כִּי־לֹא־טוֹב אָנֹכִי מֵאֲבֹתָי: וַיִּשְׁכַּב וַיִּישַׁן תַּחַת רֹתֶם ה
אֶחָד וְהִנֵּה־זֶה מַלְאָךְ נֹגֵעַ בּוֹ וַיֹּאמֶר לוֹ קוּם אֱכוֹל: וַיַּבֵּט וְהִנֵּה 6
מְרַאֲשֹׁתָיו עֻגַת רְצָפִים וְצַפַּחַת מָיִם וַיֹּאכַל וַיֵּשְׁתְּ וַיָּשׇׁב וַיִּשְׁכָּב:
וַיָּשׇׁב מַלְאַךְ יְהֹוָה ׀ שֵׁנִית וַיִּגַּע־בּוֹ וַיֹּאמֶר קוּם אֱכֹל כִּי רַב מִמְּךָ 7
הַדָּרֶךְ: וַיָּקׇם וַיֹּאכַל וַיִּשְׁתֶּה וַיֵּלֶךְ בְּכֹחַ ׀ הָאֲכִילָה הַהִיא אַרְבָּעִים 8
יוֹם וְאַרְבָּעִים לַיְלָה עַד הַר הָאֱלֹהִים חֹרֵב: וַיָּבֹא־שָׁם אֶל־הַמְּעָרָה 9
וַיָּלֶן שָׁם וְהִנֵּה דְבַר־יְהֹוָה אֵלָיו וַיֹּאמֶר לוֹ מַה־לְּךָ פֹה אֵלִיָּהוּ:
וַיֹּאמֶר קַנֹּא קִנֵּאתִי לַיהֹוָה ׀ אֱלֹהֵי צְבָאוֹת כִּי־עָזְבוּ בְרִיתְךָ בְּנֵי
יִשְׂרָאֵל אֶת־מִזְבְּחֹתֶיךָ הָרָסוּ וְאֶת־נְבִיאֶיךָ הָרְגוּ בֶחָרֶב וָאִוָּתֵר אֲנִי
לְבַדִּי וַיְבַקְשׁוּ אֶת־נַפְשִׁי לְקַחְתָּהּ: וַיֹּאמֶר צֵא וְעָמַדְתָּ בָהָר לִפְנֵי 11
יְהֹוָה וְהִנֵּה יְהֹוָה עֹבֵר וְרוּחַ גְּדוֹלָה וְחָזָק מְפָרֵק הָרִים וּמְשַׁבֵּר
סְלָעִים לִפְנֵי יְהֹוָה לֹא בָרוּחַ יְהֹוָה וְאַחַר הָרוּחַ רַעַשׁ לֹא בָרַעַשׁ
יְהֹוָה: וְאַחַר הָרַעַשׁ אֵשׁ לֹא בָאֵשׁ יְהֹוָה וְאַחַר הָאֵשׁ קוֹל דְּמָמָה 12
דַקָּה: וַיְהִי ׀ כִּשְׁמֹעַ אֵלִיָּהוּ וַיָּלֶט פָּנָיו בְּאַדַּרְתּוֹ וַיֵּצֵא וַיַּעֲמֹד פֶּתַח 13
הַמְּעָרָה וְהִנֵּה אֵלָיו קוֹל וַיֹּאמֶר מַה־לְּךָ פֹה אֵלִיָּהוּ: וַיֹּאמֶר קַנֹּא 14
קִנֵּאתִי לַיהֹוָה ׀ אֱלֹהֵי צְבָאוֹת כִּי־עָזְבוּ בְרִיתְךָ בְּנֵי יִשְׂרָאֵל אֶת־
מִזְבְּחֹתֶיךָ הָרָסוּ וְאֶת־נְבִיאֶיךָ הָרְגוּ בֶחָרֶב וָאִוָּתֵר אֲנִי לְבַדִּי וַיְבַקְשׁוּ
אֶת־נַפְשִׁי לְקַחְתָּהּ: וַיֹּאמֶר יְהֹוָה אֵלָיו לֵךְ שׁוּב לְדַרְכְּךָ מִדְבַּרָה טו
דַמָּשֶׂק וּבָאתָ וּמָשַׁחְתָּ אֶת־חֲזָאֵל לְמֶלֶךְ עַל־אֲרָם: וְאֵת יֵהוּא בֶן־נִמְשִׁי 16
תִּמְשַׁח לְמֶלֶךְ עַל־יִשְׂרָאֵל וְאֶת־אֱלִישָׁע בֶּן־שָׁפָט מֵאָבֵל מְחוֹלָה תִּמְשַׁח
לְנָבִיא תַּחְתֶּיךָ: וְהָיָה הַנִּמְלָט מֵחֶרֶב חֲזָאֵל יָמִית יֵהוּא וְהַנִּמְלָט 17
מֵחֶרֶב יֵהוּא יָמִית אֱלִישָׁע: וְהִשְׁאַרְתִּי בְיִשְׂרָאֵל שִׁבְעַת אֲלָפִים כׇּל־ 18

19 הָרַבִּים אֲשֶׁר לֹא־כָרִיתָ לֹא עֲזַבְתָּם בַּמִּדְבָּר אֶת־עַמּוּד הֶעָנָן לֹא־סָר מֵעֲלֵיהֶם בְּיוֹמָם לְהַנְחֹתָם בְּהַדֶּרֶךְ וְאֶת־עַמּוּד הָאֵשׁ בְּלַיְלָה לְהָאִיר לָהֶם וְאֶת־הַדֶּרֶךְ אֲשֶׁר יֵלְכוּ־בָהּ :

20 וְרוּחֲךָ הַטּוֹבָה נָתַתָּ לְהַשְׂכִּילָם וּמַנְךָ לֹא־מָנַעְתָּ מִפִּיהֶם וּמַיִם נָתַתָּה לָהֶם לִצְמָאָם :

21 וְאַרְבָּעִים שָׁנָה כִּלְכַּלְתָּם בַּמִּדְבָּר לֹא חָסֵרוּ שַׂלְמֹתֵיהֶם לֹא בָלוּ וְרַגְלֵיהֶם לֹא בָצֵקוּ :

VII. THE CONFESSION OF THE LEVITES, *Nehemiah 9.*

1 וּבְיוֹם עֶשְׂרִים וְאַרְבָּעָה לַחֹדֶשׁ הַזֶּה נֶאֶסְפוּ בְנֵי־יִשְׂרָאֵל בְּצוֹם וּבְשַׂקִּים וַאֲדָמָה עֲלֵיהֶם :

2 וַיִּבָּדְלוּ זֶרַע יִשְׂרָאֵל מִכֹּל בְּנֵי נֵכָר וַיַּעַמְדוּ וַיִּתְוַדּוּ עַל־חַטֹּאתֵיהֶם וַעֲוֹנוֹת אֲבֹתֵיהֶם :

3 וַיָּקוּמוּ עַל־עָמְדָם וַיִּקְרְאוּ בְּסֵפֶר תּוֹרַת יְהוָה אֱלֹהֵיהֶם רְבִעִית הַיּוֹם וּרְבִעִית מִתְוַדִּים וּמִשְׁתַּחֲוִים לַיהוָה אֱלֹהֵיהֶם :

4 וַיָּקָם עַל־מַעֲלֵה הַלְוִיִּם יֵשׁוּעַ וּבָנִי קַדְמִיאֵל שְׁבַנְיָה בֻּנִּי שֵׁרֵבְיָה בָּנִי כְנָנִי וַיִּזְעֲקוּ בְּקוֹל גָּדוֹל אֶל־יְהוָה אֱלֹהֵיהֶם :

5 וַיֹּאמְרוּ הַלְוִיִּם יֵשׁוּעַ וְקַדְמִיאֵל בָּנִי חֲשַׁבְנְיָה שֵׁרֵבְיָה הוֹדִיָּה שְׁבַנְיָה פְתַחְיָה קוּמוּ בָּרְכוּ אֶת־יְהוָה אֱלֹהֵיכֶם מִן־הָעוֹלָם עַד־הָעוֹלָם וִיבָרְכוּ שֵׁם כְּבוֹדֶךָ וּמְרוֹמַם עַל־כָּל־בְּרָכָה וּתְהִלָּה :

6 אַתָּה־הוּא יְהוָה לְבַדֶּךָ אַתָּ עָשִׂיתָ אֶת־הַשָּׁמַיִם שְׁמֵי הַשָּׁמַיִם וְכָל־צְבָאָם הָאָרֶץ וְכָל־אֲשֶׁר עָלֶיהָ הַיַּמִּים וְכָל־אֲשֶׁר בָּהֶם וְאַתָּה מְחַיֶּה אֶת־כֻּלָּם וּצְבָא הַשָּׁמַיִם לְךָ מִשְׁתַּחֲוִים :

7 אַתָּה הוּא יְהוָה הָאֱלֹהִים אֲשֶׁר בָּחַרְתָּ בְּאַבְרָם וְהוֹצֵאתוֹ מֵאוּר כַּשְׂדִּים וְשַׂמְתָּ שְּׁמוֹ אַבְרָהָם :

8 וּמָצָאתָ אֶת־לְבָבוֹ נֶאֱמָן לְפָנֶיךָ וְכָרוֹת עִמּוֹ הַבְּרִית לָתֵת אֶת־אֶרֶץ הַכְּנַעֲנִי הַחִתִּי הָאֱמֹרִי וְהַפְּרִזִּי וְהַיְבוּסִי וְהַגִּרְגָּשִׁי לָתֵת לְזַרְעוֹ וַתָּקֶם אֶת־דְּבָרֶיךָ כִּי צַדִּיק אָתָּה :

9 וַתֵּרֶא אֶת־עֳנִי אֲבֹתֵינוּ בְּמִצְרָיִם וְאֶת־זַעֲקָתָם שָׁמַעְתָּ עַל־יַם־סוּף :

10 וַתִּתֵּן אֹתֹת וּמֹפְתִים בְּפַרְעֹה וּבְכָל־עֲבָדָיו וּבְכָל־עַם אַרְצוֹ כִּי יָדַעְתָּ כִּי הֵזִידוּ עֲלֵיהֶם וַתַּעַשׂ־לְךָ שֵׁם כְּהַיּוֹם הַזֶּה :

11 וְהַיָּם בָּקַעְתָּ לִפְנֵיהֶם וַיַּעַבְרוּ בְתוֹךְ־הַיָּם בַּיַּבָּשָׁה וְאֶת־רֹדְפֵיהֶם הִשְׁלַכְתָּ בִמְצוֹלֹת כְּמוֹ־אֶבֶן בְּמַיִם עַזִּים :

12 וּבְעַמּוּד עָנָן הִנְחִיתָם יוֹמָם וּבְעַמּוּד אֵשׁ לַיְלָה לְהָאִיר לָהֶם אֶת־הַדֶּרֶךְ אֲשֶׁר יֵלְכוּ־בָהּ :

13 וְעַל הַר־סִינַי יָרַדְתָּ וְדַבֵּר עִמָּהֶם מִשָּׁמָיִם וַתִּתֵּן לָהֶם מִשְׁפָּטִים יְשָׁרִים וְתוֹרוֹת אֱמֶת חֻקִּים וּמִצְוֹת טוֹבִים :

14 וְאֶת־שַׁבַּת קָדְשְׁךָ הוֹדַעְתָּ לָהֶם וּמִצְוֹת וְחֻקִּים וְתוֹרָה צִוִּיתָ לָהֶם בְּיַד מֹשֶׁה עַבְדֶּךָ :

וְתוֹרָה צִוִּיתָ לָהֶם בְּיַד מֹשֶׁה עַבְדֶּךָ׃ וְלֶחֶם מִשָּׁמַיִם נָתַתָּה לָהֶם טו

לִרְעָבָם וּמַיִם מִסֶּלַע הוֹצֵאתָ לָהֶם לִצְמָאָם וַתֹּאמֶר לָהֶם לָבוֹא לָרֶשֶׁת

אֶת־הָאָרֶץ אֲשֶׁר־נָשָׂאתָ אֶת־יָדְךָ לָתֵת לָהֶם׃ וְהֵם וַאֲבֹתֵינוּ הֵזִידוּ 16

וַיַּקְשׁוּ אֶת־עָרְפָּם וְלֹא שָׁמְעוּ אֶל־מִצְוֺתֶיךָ׃ וַיְמָאֲנוּ לִשְׁמֹעַ וְלֹא־זָכְרוּ 17

נִפְלְאֹתֶיךָ אֲשֶׁר עָשִׂיתָ עִמָּהֶם וַיַּקְשׁוּ אֶת־עָרְפָּם וַיִּתְּנוּ־רֹאשׁ לָשׁוּב

לְעַבְדֻתָם בְּמִרְיָם וְאַתָּה אֱלוֹהַּ סְלִיחוֹת חַנּוּן וְרַחוּם אֶרֶךְ־אַפַּיִם וְרַב־

חֶסֶד וְלֹא עֲזַבְתָּם׃ אַף כִּי־עָשׂוּ לָהֶם עֵגֶל מַסֵּכָה וַיֹּאמְרוּ זֶה אֱלֹהֶיךָ 18

אֲשֶׁר הֶעֶלְךָ מִמִּצְרָיִם וַיַּעֲשׂוּ נֶאָצוֹת גְּדֹלוֹת׃ וְאַתָּה בְּרַחֲמֶיךָ הָרַבִּים 19

לֹא עֲזַבְתָּם בַּמִּדְבָּר אֶת־עַמּוּד הֶעָנָן לֹא־סָר מֵעֲלֵיהֶם בְּיוֹמָם לְהַנְחֹתָם

בְּהַדֶּרֶךְ וְאֶת־עַמּוּד הָאֵשׁ בְּלַיְלָה לְהָאִיר לָהֶם וְאֶת־הַדֶּרֶךְ אֲשֶׁר יֵלְכוּ־

בָהּ׃ וְרוּחֲךָ הַטּוֹבָה נָתַתָּ לְהַשְׂכִּילָם וּמַנְךָ לֹא־מָנַעְתָּ מִפִּיהֶם וּמַיִם כ

נָתַתָּה לָהֶם לִצְמָאָם׃ וְאַרְבָּעִים שָׁנָה כִּלְכַּלְתָּם בַּמִּדְבָּר לֹא חָסֵרוּ 21

שַׂלְמֹתֵיהֶם לֹא בָלוּ וְרַגְלֵיהֶם לֹא בָצֵקוּ׃ וַתִּתֵּן לָהֶם מַמְלָכוֹת וַעֲמָמִים 22

וַתַּחְלְקֵם לְפֵאָה וַיִּירְשׁוּ אֶת־אֶרֶץ סִיחוֹן וְאֶת־אֶרֶץ מֶלֶךְ חֶשְׁבּוֹן וְאֶת־

אֶרֶץ עוֹג מֶלֶךְ־הַבָּשָׁן׃ וּבְנֵיהֶם הִרְבִּיתָ כְּכֹכְבֵי הַשָּׁמָיִם וַתְּבִיאֵם אֶל־ 23

הָאָרֶץ אֲשֶׁר־אָמַרְתָּ לַאֲבֹתֵיהֶם לָבוֹא לָרֶשֶׁת׃ וַיָּבֹאוּ הַבָּנִים וַיִּירְשׁוּ

אֶת־הָאָרֶץ וַתַּכְנַע לִפְנֵיהֶם אֶת־יֹשְׁבֵי הָאָרֶץ הַכְּנַעֲנִים וַתִּתְּנֵם בְּיָדָם 24

וְאֶת־מַלְכֵיהֶם וְאֶת־עַמְמֵי הָאָרֶץ לַעֲשׂוֹת בָּהֶם כִּרְצוֹנָם׃ וַיִּלְכְּדוּ עָרִים כה

בְּצֻרוֹת וַאֲדָמָה שְׁמֵנָה וַיִּירְשׁוּ בָּתִּים מְלֵאִים־כָּל־טוּב בֹּרוֹת חֲצוּבִים

כְּרָמִים וְזֵיתִים וְעֵץ מַאֲכָל לָרֹב וַיֹּאכְלוּ וַיִּשְׂבְּעוּ וַיַּשְׁמִינוּ וַיִּתְעַדְּנוּ

בְּטוּבְךָ הַגָּדוֹל׃ וַיַּמְרוּ וַיִּמְרְדוּ בָּךְ וַיַּשְׁלִכוּ אֶת־תּוֹרָתְךָ אַחֲרֵי גַוָּם 26

וְאֶת־נְבִיאֶיךָ הָרָגוּ אֲשֶׁר־הֵעִידוּ בָם לַהֲשִׁיבָם אֵלֶיךָ וַיַּעֲשׂוּ נֶאָצוֹת

גְּדוֹלֹת׃ וַתִּתְּנֵם בְּיַד צָרֵיהֶם וַיָּצֵרוּ לָהֶם וּבְעֵת צָרָתָם יִצְעֲקוּ אֵלֶיךָ 27

וְאַתָּה מִשָּׁמַיִם תִּשְׁמָע וּכְרַחֲמֶיךָ הָרַבִּים תִּתֵּן לָהֶם מוֹשִׁיעִים וְיוֹשִׁיעוּם

מִיַּד צָרֵיהֶם׃ וּכְנוֹחַ לָהֶם יָשׁוּבוּ לַעֲשׂוֹת רַע לְפָנֶיךָ וַתַּעַזְבֵם בְּיַד 28

אֹיְבֵיהֶם וַיִּרְדּוּ בָהֶם וַיָּשׁוּבוּ וַיִּזְעָקוּךָ וְאַתָּה מִשָּׁמַיִם תִּשְׁמַע וְתַצִּילֵם

כְּרַחֲמֶיךָ רַבּוֹת עִתִּים׃ וַתָּעַד בָּהֶם לַהֲשִׁיבָם אֶל־תּוֹרָתֶךָ וְהֵמָּה הֵזִידוּ 29

וְלֹא־שָׁמְעוּ לְמִצְוֺתֶיךָ וּבְמִשְׁפָּטֶיךָ חָטְאוּ־בָם אֲשֶׁר־יַעֲשֶׂה אָדָם וְחָיָה

בָהֶם וַיִּתְּנוּ כָתֵף סוֹרֶרֶת וְעָרְפָּם הִקְשׁוּ וְלֹא שָׁמֵעוּ׃ וַתִּמְשֹׁךְ עֲלֵיהֶם ל

שָׁנִים רַבּוֹת וַתָּעַד בָּם בְּרוּחֲךָ בְּיַד־נְבִיאֶיךָ וְלֹא הֶאֱזִינוּ וַתִּתְּנֵם בְּיַד

עַמֵּי הָאֲרָצֹת׃ וּבְרַחֲמֶיךָ הָרַבִּים לֹא־עֲשִׂיתָם כָּלָה וְלֹא עֲזַבְתָּם כִּי אֵל־ 31

חַנּוּן וְרַחוּם אָתָּה׃ וְעַתָּה אֱלֹהֵינוּ הָאֵל הַגָּדוֹל הַגִּבּוֹר וְהַנּוֹרָא שׁוֹמֵר 32

---

v. 27. קָמֵץ בז"ק   v. 26. קָמֵץ בז"ק   v. 17. יתיר ו'

הַבְּרִית וְהֶחָסֵד אַל־יִמְעַט לְפָנֶיךָ אֵת כָּל־הַתְּלָאָה אֲשֶׁר־מְצָאַתְנוּ לִמְלָכֵינוּ
לְשָׂרֵינוּ וּלְכֹהֲנֵינוּ וְלִנְבִיאֵינוּ וְלַאֲבֹתֵינוּ וּלְכָל־עַמֶּךָ מִימֵי מַלְכֵי אַשּׁוּר

33 עַד הַיּוֹם הַזֶּה: וְאַתָּה צַדִּיק עַל כָּל־הַבָּא עָלֵינוּ כִּי־אֱמֶת עָשִׂיתָ

34 וַאֲנַחְנוּ הִרְשָׁעְנוּ: וְאֶת־מְלָכֵינוּ שָׂרֵינוּ כֹּהֲנֵינוּ וַאֲבֹתֵינוּ לֹא עָשׂוּ

לה תוֹרָתֶךָ וְלֹא הִקְשִׁיבוּ אֶל־מִצְוֺתֶיךָ וּלְעֵדְוֺתֶיךָ אֲשֶׁר הַעִידֹתָ בָּהֶם: וְהֵם
בְּמַלְכוּתָם וּבְטוּבְךָ הָרָב אֲשֶׁר־נָתַתָּ לָהֶם וּבְאֶרֶץ הָרְחָבָה וְהַשְּׁמֵנָה

36 אֲשֶׁר־נָתַתָּ לִפְנֵיהֶם לֹא עֲבָדוּךָ וְלֹא־שָׁבוּ מִמַּעַלְלֵיהֶם הָרָעִים: הִנֵּה
אֲנַחְנוּ הַיּוֹם עֲבָדִים וְהָאָרֶץ אֲשֶׁר־נָתַתָּ לַאֲבֹתֵינוּ לֶאֱכֹל אֶת־פִּרְיָהּ

37 וְאֶת־טוּבָהּ הִנֵּה אֲנַחְנוּ עֲבָדִים עָלֶיהָ: וּתְבוּאָתָהּ, מַרְבָּה לַמְּלָכִים
אֲשֶׁר־נָתַתָּ עָלֵינוּ בְּחַטֹּאותֵינוּ וְעַל־גְּוִיֹּתֵינוּ מֹשְׁלִים וּבִבְהֶמְתֵּנוּ כִּרְצוֹנָם
וּבְצָרָה גְדֹלָה אֲנָחְנוּ:

VIII. JUDAH COMFORTED, *Isaiah* 40—42.

CHAPTER XL. מ

ב נַחֲמוּ נַחֲמוּ עַמִּי יֹאמַר אֱלֹהֵיכֶם: דַּבְּרוּ עַל־לֵב יְרוּשָׁלַ͏ִם וְקִרְאוּ אֵלֶיהָ
כִּי מָלְאָה צְבָאָהּ כִּי נִרְצָה עֲוֺנָהּ כִּי לָקְחָה מִיַּד יְהֹוָה כִּפְלַיִם בְּכָל־

3 חַטֹּאתֶיהָ:   קוֹל קוֹרֵא בַּמִּדְבָּר פַּנּוּ דֶּרֶךְ יְהֹוָה יַשְּׁרוּ בָּעֲרָבָה

4 מְסִלָּה לֵאלֹהֵינוּ: כָּל־גֶּיא יִנָּשֵׂא וְכָל־הַר וְגִבְעָה יִשְׁפָּלוּ וְהָיָה הֶעָקֹב

ה לְמִישׁוֹר וְהָרְכָסִים לְבִקְעָה: וְנִגְלָה כְּבוֹד יְהֹוָה וְרָאוּ כָל־בָּשָׂר יַחְדָּו

6 כִּי פִּי יְהֹוָה דִּבֵּר: קוֹל אֹמֵר קְרָא וְאָמַר מָה אֶקְרָא כָּל־הַבָּשָׂר

7 חָצִיר וְכָל־חַסְדּוֹ כְּצִיץ הַשָּׂדֶה: יָבֵשׁ חָצִיר נָבֵל צִיץ כִּי רוּחַ יְהֹוָה

8 נָשְׁבָה בּוֹ אָכֵן חָצִיר הָעָם: יָבֵשׁ חָצִיר נָבֵל צִיץ וּדְבַר אֱלֹהֵינוּ יָקוּם

9 לְעוֹלָם: עַל הַר־גָּבֹהַּ עֲלִי־לָךְ מְבַשֶּׂרֶת צִיּוֹן הָרִימִי בַכֹּחַ קוֹלֵךְ
מְבַשֶּׂרֶת יְרוּשָׁלָ͏ִם הָרִימִי אַל־תִּירָאִי אִמְרִי לְעָרֵי יְהוּדָה הִנֵּה אֱלֹהֵיכֶם:

י הִנֵּה אֲדֹנָי יֱהֹוִה בְּחָזָק יָבוֹא וּזְרֹעוֹ מֹשְׁלָה לוֹ הִנֵּה שְׂכָרוֹ אִתּוֹ

11 וּפְעֻלָּתוֹ לְפָנָיו: כְּרֹעֶה עֶדְרוֹ יִרְעֶה בִּזְרֹעוֹ יְקַבֵּץ טְלָאִים וּבְחֵיקוֹ יִשָּׂא

12 עָלוֹת יְנַהֵל: מִי־מָדַד בְּשָׁעֳלוֹ מַיִם וְשָׁמַיִם בַּזֶּרֶת תִּכֵּן וְכָל

13 בַּשָּׁלִשׁ עֲפַר הָאָרֶץ וְשָׁקַל בַּפֶּלֶס הָרִים וּגְבָעוֹת בְּמֹאזְנָיִם: מִי־תִכֵּן

14 אֶת־רוּחַ יְהֹוָה וְאִישׁ עֲצָתוֹ יוֹדִיעֶנּוּ: אֶת־מִי נוֹעַץ וַיְבִינֵהוּ וַיְלַמְּדֵהוּ
טו בְּאֹרַח מִשְׁפָּט וַיְלַמְּדֵהוּ דַעַת וְדֶרֶךְ תְּבוּנוֹת יוֹדִיעֶנּוּ: הֵן גּוֹיִם כְּמַר

16 מִדְּלִי וּכְשַׁחַק מֹאזְנַיִם נֶחְשָׁבוּ הֵן אִיִּים כַּדַּק יִטּוֹל: וּלְבָנוֹן אֵין דֵּי

17 בָּעֵר וְחַיָּתוֹ אֵין דֵּי עוֹלָה: כָּל־הַגּוֹיִם כְּאַיִן נֶגְדּוֹ מֵאֶפֶס וָתֹהוּ

נֶחְשָׁבוּ־לוֹ : וְאֶל־מִי תְּדַמְּיוּן אֵל וּמַה־דְּמוּת תַּעַרְכוּ־לוֹ : הַפֶּסֶל נָסַךְ 18
19

חָרָשׁ וְצֹרֵף בַּזָּהָב יְרַקְּעֶנּוּ וּרְתֻקוֹת כֶּסֶף צוֹרֵף : הַמְסֻכָּן תְּרוּמָה עֵץ כ

לֹא־יִרְקַב יִבְחָר חָרָשׁ חָכָם יְבַקֶּשׁ־לוֹ לְהָכִין פֶּסֶל לֹא יִמּוֹט : הֲלוֹא 21

תֵדְעוּ הֲלוֹא תִשְׁמָעוּ הֲלוֹא הֻגַּד מֵרֹאשׁ לָכֶם הֲלוֹא הֲבִינוֹתֶם מוֹסְדוֹת

הָאָרֶץ : הַיֹּשֵׁב עַל־חוּג הָאָרֶץ וְיֹשְׁבֶיהָ כַּחֲגָבִים הַנּוֹטֶה כַדֹּק שָׁמַיִם 22

וַיִּמְתָּחֵם כָּאֹהֶל לָשָׁבֶת : הַנּוֹתֵן רוֹזְנִים לְאָיִן שֹׁפְטֵי אֶרֶץ כַּתֹּהוּ עָשָׂה : 23

אַף בַּל־נִטָּעוּ אַף בַּל־זֹרָעוּ אַף בַּל־שֹׁרֵשׁ בָּאָרֶץ גִּזְעָם וְגַם־נָשַׁף בָּהֶם 24

וַיִּבָשׁוּ וּסְעָרָה כַּקַּשׁ תִּשָּׂאֵם : וְאֶל־מִי תְדַמְּיוּנִי וְאֶשְׁוֶה יֹאמַר קָדוֹשׁ : כה

שְׂאוּ־מָרוֹם עֵינֵיכֶם וּרְאוּ מִי־בָרָא אֵלֶּה הַמּוֹצִיא בְמִסְפָּר צְבָאָם לְכֻלָּם 26

בְּשֵׁם יִקְרָא מֵרֹב אוֹנִים וְאַמִּיץ כֹּחַ אִישׁ לֹא נֶעְדָּר : לָמָּה 27

תֹאמַר יַעֲקֹב וּתְדַבֵּר יִשְׂרָאֵל נִסְתְּרָה דַרְכִּי מֵיְהֹוָה וּמֵאֱלֹהַי מִשְׁפָּטִי

יַעֲבוֹר : הֲלוֹא יָדַעְתָּ אִם־לֹא שָׁמַעְתָּ אֱלֹהֵי עוֹלָם יְהֹוָה בּוֹרֵא קְצוֹת 28

הָאָרֶץ לֹא יִיעַף וְלֹא יִיגָע אֵין חֵקֶר לִתְבוּנָתוֹ : נֹתֵן לַיָּעֵף כֹּחַ וּלְאֵין 29

אוֹנִים עָצְמָה יַרְבֶּה : וְיִעֲפוּ נְעָרִים וְיִגָעוּ וּבַחוּרִים כָּשׁוֹל יִכָּשֵׁלוּ : ל

וְקוֹיֵ יְהֹוָה יַחֲלִיפוּ כֹחַ יַעֲלוּ אֵבֶר כַּנְּשָׁרִים יָרוּצוּ וְלֹא יִיגָעוּ יֵלְכוּ 31

וְלֹא יִיעָפוּ :

CHAPTER XLI. מא

הַחֲרִישׁוּ אֵלַי אִיִּים וּלְאֻמִּים יַחֲלִיפוּ כֹחַ יִגְּשׁוּ אָז יְדַבֵּרוּ יַחְדָּו א

לַמִּשְׁפָּט נִקְרָבָה : מִי הֵעִיר מִמִּזְרָח צֶדֶק יִקְרָאֵהוּ לְרַגְלוֹ יִתֵּן לְפָנָיו 2

גּוֹיִם וּמְלָכִים יַרְדְּ יִתֵּן כֶּעָפָר חַרְבּוֹ כְּקַשׁ נִדָּף קַשְׁתּוֹ : יִרְדְּפֵם יַעֲבוֹר 3

שָׁלוֹם אֹרַח בְּרַגְלָיו לֹא יָבוֹא : מִי־פָעַל וְעָשָׂה קֹרֵא הַדֹּרוֹת מֵרֹאשׁ אֲנִי 4

יְהֹוָה רִאשׁוֹן וְאֶת־אַחֲרֹנִים אֲנִי־הוּא : רָאוּ אִיִּים וְיִירָאוּ קְצוֹת הָאָרֶץ ה

יֶחֱרָדוּ קָרְבוּ וַיֶּאֱתָיוּן : אִישׁ אֶת־רֵעֵהוּ יַעְזֹרוּ וּלְאָחִיו יֹאמַר חֲזָק : 6

וַיְחַזֵּק חָרָשׁ אֶת־צֹרֵף מַחֲלִיק פַּטִּישׁ אֶת־הוֹלֶם פָּעַם אֹמֵר לַדֶּבֶק טוֹב 7

הוּא וַיְחַזְּקֵהוּ בְמַסְמְרִים לֹא יִמּוֹט : וְאַתָּה יִשְׂרָאֵל עַבְדִּי 8

יַעֲקֹב אֲשֶׁר בְּחַרְתִּיךָ זֶרַע אַבְרָהָם אֹהֲבִי : אֲשֶׁר הֶחֱזַקְתִּיךָ מִקְצוֹת 9

הָאָרֶץ וּמֵאֲצִילֶיהָ קְרָאתִיךָ וָאֹמַר לְךָ עַבְדִּי־אַתָּה בְּחַרְתִּיךָ וְלֹא

מְאַסְתִּיךָ : אַל־תִּירָא כִּי עִמְּךָ אָנִי אַל־תִּשְׁתָּע כִּי־אֲנִי אֱלֹהֶיךָ אִמַּצְתִּיךָ י

אַף־עֲזַרְתִּיךָ אַף־תְּמַכְתִּיךָ בִּימִין צִדְקִי : הֵן יֵבֹשׁוּ וְיִכָּלְמוּ כֹּל הַנֶּחֱרִים 11

בָּךְ יִהְיוּ כְאַיִן וְיֹאבְדוּ אַנְשֵׁי רִיבֶךָ : תְּבַקְשֵׁם וְלֹא תִמְצָאֵם אַנְשֵׁי 12

מַצֻּתֶךָ יִהְיוּ כְאַיִן וּכְאֶפֶס אַנְשֵׁי מִלְחַמְתֶּךָ : כִּי אֲנִי יְהֹוָה אֱלֹהֶיךָ 13

‫14 מַחֲזִיק יְמִינֶךָ הָאֹמֵר לְךָ אַל־תִּירָא אֲנִי עֲזַרְתִּיךָ׃ אַל־תִּירְאִי‬
‫תוֹלַעַת יַעֲקֹב מְתֵי יִשְׂרָאֵל אֲנִי עֲזַרְתִּיךְ נְאֻם־יְהוָה וְגֹאֲלֵךְ קְדוֹשׁ‬
‫טו יִשְׂרָאֵל׃ הִנֵּה שַׂמְתִּיךְ לְמוֹרַג חָרוּץ חָדָשׁ בַּעַל פִּיפִיּוֹת תָּדוּשׁ הָרִים‬
‫16 וְתָדֹק וּגְבָעוֹת כַּמֹּץ תָּשִׂים׃ תִּזְרֵם וְרוּחַ תִּשָּׂאֵם וּסְעָרָה תָּפִיץ אֹתָם‬
‫17 וְאַתָּה תָּגִיל בַּיהוָה בִּקְדוֹשׁ יִשְׂרָאֵל תִּתְהַלָּל׃ הָעֲנִיִּים וְהָאֶבְיוֹנִים‬
‫מְבַקְשִׁים מַיִם וָאַיִן לְשׁוֹנָם בַּצָּמָא נָשָׁתָּה אֲנִי יְהוָה אֶעֱנֵם אֱלֹהֵי‬
‫18 יִשְׂרָאֵל לֹא אֶעֶזְבֵם׃ אֶפְתַּח עַל־שְׁפָיִים נְהָרוֹת וּבְתוֹךְ בְּקָעוֹת מַעְיָנוֹת‬
‫19 אָשִׂים מִדְבָּר לַאֲגַם־מַיִם וְאֶרֶץ צִיָּה לְמוֹצָאֵי מָיִם׃ אֶתֵּן בַּמִּדְבָּר אֶרֶז‬
‫שִׁטָּה וַהֲדַס וְעֵץ שָׁמֶן אָשִׂים בָּעֲרָבָה בְּרוֹשׁ תִּדְהָר וּתְאַשּׁוּר יַחְדָּו׃‬
‫כ לְמַעַן יִרְאוּ וְיֵדְעוּ וְיָשִׂימוּ וְיַשְׂכִּילוּ יַחְדָּו כִּי יַד־יְהוָה עָשְׂתָה זֹּאת‬
‫21 וּקְדוֹשׁ יִשְׂרָאֵל בְּרָאָהּ׃ קָרְבוּ רִיבְכֶם יֹאמַר יְהוָה הַגִּישׁוּ‬
‫22 עַצֻּמוֹתֵיכֶם יֹאמַר מֶלֶךְ יַעֲקֹב׃ יַגִּישׁוּ וְיַגִּידוּ לָנוּ אֵת אֲשֶׁר תִּקְרֶינָה‬
‫הָרִאשֹׁנוֹת מָה הֵנָּה הַגִּידוּ וְנָשִׂימָה לִבֵּנוּ וְנֵדְעָה אַחֲרִיתָן אוֹ הַבָּאוֹת‬
‫23 הַשְׁמִיעֻנוּ׃ הַגִּידוּ הָאֹתִיּוֹת לְאָחוֹר וְנֵדְעָה כִּי אֱלֹהִים אַתֶּם אַף־תֵּיטִיבוּ‬
‫24 וְתָרֵעוּ וְנִשְׁתָּעָה וְנֵרֶא יַחְדָּו׃ הֵן־אַתֶּם מֵאַיִן וּפָעָלְכֶם מֵאָפַע תּוֹעֵבָה‬
‫כה יִבְחַר בָּכֶם׃ הַעִירוֹתִי מִצָּפוֹן וַיַּאת מִמִּזְרַח־שֶׁמֶשׁ יִקְרָא בִשְׁמִי‬
‫26 וְיָבֹא סְגָנִים כְּמוֹ־חֹמֶר וּכְמוֹ יוֹצֵר יִרְמָס־טִיט׃ מִי־הִגִּיד מֵרֹאשׁ וְנֵדָעָה‬
‫וּמִלְּפָנִים וְנֹאמַר צַדִּיק אַף אֵין־מַגִּיד אַף אֵין מַשְׁמִיעַ אַף אֵין־שֹׁמֵעַ‬
‫27 אִמְרֵיכֶם׃ רִאשׁוֹן לְצִיּוֹן הִנֵּה הִנָּם וְלִירוּשָׁלַ͏ִם מְבַשֵּׂר אֶתֵּן׃ וְאֵרֶא‬
‫28‬
‫29 וְאֵין אִישׁ וּמֵאֵלֶּה וְאֵין יוֹעֵץ וְאֶשְׁאָלֵם וְיָשִׁיבוּ דָבָר׃ הֵן כֻּלָּם אָוֶן‬
‫אֶפֶס מַעֲשֵׂיהֶם רוּחַ וָתֹהוּ נִסְכֵּיהֶם׃‬

CHAPTER XLII. ‫מב‬

‫א הֵן עַבְדִּי אֶתְמָךְ־בּוֹ בְּחִירִי רָצְתָה נַפְשִׁי נָתַתִּי רוּחִי עָלָיו מִשְׁפָּט‬
‫2 3 לַגּוֹיִם יוֹצִיא׃ לֹא יִצְעַק וְלֹא יִשָּׂא וְלֹא־יַשְׁמִיעַ בַּחוּץ קוֹלוֹ׃ קָנֶה‬
‫4 רָצוּץ לֹא יִשְׁבּוֹר וּפִשְׁתָּה כֵהָה לֹא יְכַבֶּנָּה לֶאֱמֶת יוֹצִיא מִשְׁפָּט׃ לֹא‬
‫יִכְהֶה וְלֹא יָרוּץ עַד־יָשִׂים בָּאָרֶץ מִשְׁפָּט וּלְתוֹרָתוֹ אִיִּים יְיַחֵלוּ׃‬
‫ה כֹּה־אָמַר הָאֵל יְהוָה בּוֹרֵא הַשָּׁמַיִם וְנוֹטֵיהֶם רֹקַע הָאָרֶץ וְצֶאֱצָאֶיהָ‬
‫6 נֹתֵן נְשָׁמָה לָעָם עָלֶיהָ וְרוּחַ לַהֹלְכִים בָּהּ׃ אֲנִי יְהוָה קְרָאתִיךָ בְצֶדֶק‬
‫7 וְאַחְזֵק בְּיָדֶךָ וְאֶצָּרְךָ וְאֶתֶּנְךָ לִבְרִית עָם לְאוֹר גּוֹיִם׃ לִפְקֹחַ עֵינַיִם‬
‫8 עִוְרוֹת לְהוֹצִיא מִמַּסְגֵּר אַסִּיר מִבֵּית כֶּלֶא יֹשְׁבֵי חֹשֶׁךְ׃ אֲנִי יְהוָה‬
‫9 הוּא שְׁמִי וּכְבוֹדִי לְאַחֵר לֹא־אֶתֵּן וּתְהִלָּתִי לַפְּסִילִים׃ הָרִאשֹׁנוֹת הִנֵּה‬

שִׁירוּ ,   בָּאֵי וַחֲדָשׁוֹת אֲנִי מַגִּיד בְּטֶרֶם תִּצְמַחְנָה אַשְׁמִיעַ אֶתְכֶם :
לַיהֹוָה שִׁיר חָדָשׁ תְּהִלָּתוֹ מִקְצֵה הָאָרֶץ יוֹרְדֵי הַיָּם וּמְלֹאוֹ אִיִּים
11 וְיֹשְׁבֵיהֶם : יִשְׂאוּ מִדְבָּר וְעָרָיו חֲצֵרִים תֵּשֵׁב קֵדָר יָרֹנּוּ יֹשְׁבֵי סֶלַע
12 מֵרֹאשׁ הָרִים יִצְוָחוּ : יָשִׂימוּ לַיהֹוָה כָּבוֹד וּתְהִלָּתוֹ בָּאִיִּים יַגִּידוּ :
13 יְהֹוָה כַּגִּבּוֹר יֵצֵא כְּאִישׁ מִלְחָמוֹת יָעִיר קִנְאָה יָרִיעַ אַף־יַצְרִיחַ עַל־
14 אֹיְבָיו יִתְגַּבָּר :   הֶחֱשֵׁיתִי מֵעוֹלָם אַחֲרִישׁ אֶתְאַפָּק כַּיּוֹלֵדָה
טו אֶפְעֶה אֶשֹּׁם וְאֶשְׁאַף יָחַד : אַחֲרִיב הָרִים וּגְבָעוֹת וְכָל־עֶשְׂבָּם אוֹבִישׁ
16 וְשַׂמְתִּי נְהָרוֹת לָאִיִּים וַאֲגַמִּים אוֹבִישׁ : וְהוֹלַכְתִּי עִוְרִים בְּדֶרֶךְ לֹא
17 יָדָעוּ בִּנְתִיבוֹת לֹא־יָדְעוּ אַדְרִיכֵם אָשִׂים מַחְשָׁךְ לִפְנֵיהֶם לָאוֹר
וּמַעֲקַשִּׁים לְמִישׁוֹר אֵלֶּה הַדְּבָרִים עֲשִׂיתִם וְלֹא עֲזַבְתִּים : נָסֹגוּ אָחוֹר
יֵבֹשׁוּ בֹשֶׁת הַבֹּטְחִים בַּפָּסֶל הָאֹמְרִים לְמַסֵּכָה אַתֶּם אֱלֹהֵינוּ :
18 הַחֵרְשִׁים שְׁמָעוּ וְהַעִוְרִים הַבִּיטוּ לִרְאוֹת : מִי עִוֵּר כִּי אִם־עַבְדִּי
19
וְחֵרֵשׁ כְּמַלְאָכִי אֶשְׁלָח מִי עִוֵּר כִּמְשֻׁלָּם וְעִוֵּר כְּעֶבֶד יְהֹוָה : רָאוֹת
 כ
21 רַבּוֹת וְלֹא תִשְׁמֹר פָּקוֹחַ אָזְנַיִם וְלֹא יִשְׁמָע : יְהֹוָה חָפֵץ לְמַעַן צִדְקוֹ
22 יַגְדִּיל תּוֹרָה וְיַאְדִּיר : וְהוּא עַם־בָּזוּז וְשָׁסוּי הָפֵחַ בַּחוּרִים כֻּלָּם
וּבְבָתֵּי כְלָאִים הָחְבָּאוּ הָיוּ לָבַז וְאֵין מַצִּיל מְשִׁסָּה וְאֵין־אֹמֵר הָשַׁב :
23
24 מִי בָכֶם יַאֲזִין זֹאת יַקְשֵׁב וְיִשְׁמַע לְאָחוֹר : מִי־נָתַן לִמְשׁוֹסֶה יַעֲקֹב
וְיִשְׂרָאֵל לְבֹזְזִים הֲלוֹא יְהֹוָה זוּ חָטָאנוּ לוֹ וְלֹא־אָבוּ בִדְרָכָיו הָלוֹךְ
25 וְלֹא שָׁמְעוּ בְּתוֹרָתוֹ : וַיִּשְׁפֹּךְ עָלָיו חֵמָה אַפּוֹ וֶעֱזוּז מִלְחָמָה וַתְּלַהֲטֵהוּ
מִסָּבִיב וְלֹא יָדָע וַתִּבְעַר־בּוֹ וְלֹא־יָשִׂים עַל־לֵב :

IX. Messiah's Humiliation and Glory, *Isaiah* 53.

2 א מִי הֶאֱמִין לִשְׁמֻעָתֵנוּ וּזְרוֹעַ יְהֹוָה עַל־מִי נִגְלָתָה : וַיַּעַל כַּיּוֹנֵק לְפָנָיו
וְכַשֹּׁרֶשׁ מֵאֶרֶץ צִיָּה לֹא־תֹאַר לוֹ וְלֹא הָדָר וְנִרְאֵהוּ וְלֹא־מַרְאֶה
3 וְנֶחְמְדֵהוּ : נִבְזֶה וַחֲדַל אִישִׁים אִישׁ מַכְאֹבוֹת וִידוּעַ חֹלִי וּכְמַסְתֵּר
4 פָּנִים מִמֶּנּוּ נִבְזֶה וְלֹא חֲשַׁבְנֻהוּ : אָכֵן חֳלָיֵנוּ הוּא נָשָׂא וּמַכְאֹבֵינוּ
ה סְבָלָם וַאֲנַחְנוּ חֲשַׁבְנֻהוּ נָגוּעַ מֻכֵּה אֱלֹהִים וּמְעֻנֶּה : וְהוּא מְחֹלָל
מִפְּשָׁעֵנוּ מְדֻכָּא מֵעֲוֹנֹתֵינוּ מוּסַר שְׁלוֹמֵנוּ עָלָיו וּבַחֲבֻרָתוֹ נִרְפָּא־לָנוּ :
6 כֻּלָּנוּ כַּצֹּאן תָּעִינוּ אִישׁ לְדַרְכּוֹ פָּנִינוּ וַיהֹוָה הִפְגִּיעַ בּוֹ אֵת עֲוֹן כֻּלָּנוּ :
7 נִגַּשׂ וְהוּא נַעֲנֶה וְלֹא יִפְתַּח־פִּיו כַּשֶּׂה לַטֶּבַח יוּבָל וּכְרָחֵל לִפְנֵי גֹזְזֶיהָ
8 נֶאֱלָמָה וְלֹא יִפְתַּח פִּיו : מֵעֹצֶר וּמִמִּשְׁפָּט לֻקָּח וְאֶת־דּוֹרוֹ מִי יְשׂוֹחֵחַ

---

9 פַּר נִגְזַר מֵאֶרֶץ חַיִּים מִפֶּשַׁע עַמִּי נֶגַע לָמוֹ : וַיִּתֵּן אֶת־רְשָׁעִים קִבְרוֹ
י וְאֶת־עָשִׁיר בְּמֹתָיו עַל לֹא־חָמָס עָשָׂה וְלֹא מִרְמָה בְּפִיו : וַיהֹוָה חָפֵץ
דַּכְּאוֹ הֶחֱלִי אִם־תָּשִׂים אָשָׁם נַפְשׁוֹ יִרְאֶה זֶרַע יַאֲרִיךְ יָמִים וְחֵפֶץ
11 יְהֹוָה בְּיָדוֹ יִצְלָח : מֵעֲמַל נַפְשׁוֹ יִרְאֶה יִשְׂבָּע בְּדַעְתּוֹ יַצְדִּיק צַדִּיק
12 עַבְדִּי לָרַבִּים וַעֲוֺנֹתָם הוּא יִסְבֹּל : לָכֵן אֲחַלֶּק־לוֹ בָרַבִּים וְאֶת־עֲצוּמִים
יְחַלֵּק שָׁלָל תַּחַת אֲשֶׁר הֶעֱרָה לַמָּוֶת נַפְשׁוֹ וְאֶת־פֹּשְׁעִים נִמְנָה וְהוּא
חֵטְא־רַבִּים נָשָׂא וְלַפֹּשְׁעִים יַפְגִּיעַ :

X. The Restoration of Israel, *Ezekiel* 37.

א הָיְתָה עָלַי יַד־יְהֹוָה וַיּוֹצִיאֵנִי בְרוּחַ יְהֹוָה וַיְנִיחֵנִי בְּתוֹךְ הַבִּקְעָה
2 וְהִיא מְלֵאָה עֲצָמוֹת : וְהֶעֱבִירַנִי עֲלֵיהֶם סָבִיב ׀ סָבִיב וְהִנֵּה רַבּוֹת
3 מְאֹד עַל־פְּנֵי הַבִּקְעָה וְהִנֵּה יְבֵשׁוֹת מְאֹד : וַיֹּאמֶר אֵלַי בֶּן־אָדָם
4 הֲתִחְיֶינָה הָעֲצָמוֹת הָאֵלֶּה וָאֹמַר אֲדֹנָי יְהֹוִה אַתָּה יָדָעְתָּ : וַיֹּאמֶר
אֵלַי הִנָּבֵא עַל־הָעֲצָמוֹת הָאֵלֶּה וְאָמַרְתָּ אֲלֵיהֶם הָעֲצָמוֹת הַיְבֵשׁוֹת
5 שִׁמְעוּ דְּבַר־יְהֹוָה :   כֹּה אָמַר אֲדֹנָי יְהֹוִה לָעֲצָמוֹת הָאֵלֶּה הִנֵּה
6 אֲנִי מֵבִיא בָכֶם רוּחַ וִחְיִיתֶם : וְנָתַתִּי עֲלֵיכֶם גִּידִים וְהַעֲלֵתִי עֲלֵיכֶם
בָּשָׂר וְקָרַמְתִּי עֲלֵיכֶם עוֹר וְנָתַתִּי בָכֶם רוּחַ וִחְיִיתֶם וִידַעְתֶּם כִּי־אֲנִי
7 יְהֹוָה : וְנִבֵּאתִי כַּאֲשֶׁר צֻוֵּיתִי וַיְהִי־קוֹל כְּהִנָּבְאִי וְהִנֵּה־רַעַשׁ וַתִּקְרְבוּ
8 עֲצָמוֹת עֶצֶם אֶל־עַצְמוֹ : וְרָאִיתִי וְהִנֵּה עֲלֵיהֶם גִּדִים וּבָשָׂר עָלָה
9 וַיִּקְרַם עֲלֵיהֶם עוֹר מִלְמָעְלָה וְרוּחַ אֵין בָּהֶם : וַיֹּאמֶר אֵלַי הִנָּבֵא
אֶל־הָרוּחַ הִנָּבֵא בֶן־אָדָם וְאָמַרְתָּ אֶל־הָרוּחַ כֹּה־אָמַר ׀ אֲדֹנָי יְהֹוִה
י מֵאַרְבַּע רוּחוֹת בֹּאִי הָרוּחַ וּפְחִי בַּהֲרוּגִים הָאֵלֶּה וְיִחְיוּ : וְהִנַּבֵּאתִי
כַּאֲשֶׁר צִוָּנִי וַתָּבוֹא בָהֶם הָרוּחַ וַיִּחְיוּ וַיַּעַמְדוּ עַל־רַגְלֵיהֶם חַיִל גָּדוֹל
11 מְאֹד מְאֹד : וַיֹּאמֶר אֵלַי בֶּן־אָדָם הָעֲצָמוֹת הָאֵלֶּה כָּל־בֵּית יִשְׂרָאֵל
12 הֵמָּה הִנֵּה אֹמְרִים יָבְשׁוּ עַצְמוֹתֵינוּ וְאָבְדָה תִקְוָתֵנוּ נִגְזַרְנוּ לָנוּ : לָכֵן
הִנָּבֵא וְאָמַרְתָּ אֲלֵיהֶם כֹּה־אָמַר אֲדֹנָי יְהֹוִה הִנֵּה אֲנִי פֹתֵחַ אֶת־
קִבְרוֹתֵיכֶם וְהַעֲלֵיתִי אֶתְכֶם מִקִּבְרוֹתֵיכֶם עַמִּי וְהֵבֵאתִי אֶתְכֶם אֶל־אַדְמַת
13 יִשְׂרָאֵל : וִידַעְתֶּם כִּי־אֲנִי יְהֹוָה בְּפִתְחִי אֶת־קִבְרוֹתֵיכֶם וּבְהַעֲלוֹתִי אֶתְכֶם
14 מִקִּבְרוֹתֵיכֶם עַמִּי : וְנָתַתִּי רוּחִי בָכֶם וִחְיִיתֶם וְהִנַּחְתִּי אֶתְכֶם עַל־
אַדְמַתְכֶם וִידַעְתֶּם כִּי אֲנִי יְהֹוָה דִּבַּרְתִּי וְעָשִׂיתִי נְאֻם־יְהֹוָה :
16 וַיְהִי דְבַר־יְהֹוָה אֵלַי לֵאמֹר : וְאַתָּה בֶן־אָדָם קַח־לְךָ עֵץ אֶחָד וּכְתֹב

עָלָיו לִיהוּדָה וְלִבְנֵי יִשְׂרָאֵל חֲבֵרָו וּלְקַח עֵץ אֶחָד וּכְתֹב עָלָיו לְיוֹסֵף

17 עֵץ אֶפְרַיִם וְכָל־בֵּית יִשְׂרָאֵל חֲבֵרָו : וְקָרַב אֹתָם אֶחָד אֶל־אֶחָד לְךָ

18 לְעֵץ אֶחָד וְהָיוּ לַאֲחָדִים בְּיָדֶךָ : וְכַאֲשֶׁר יֹאמְרוּ אֵלֶיךָ בְּנֵי עַמְּךָ

19 לֵאמֹר הֲלוֹא־תַגִּיד לָנוּ מָה־אֵלֶּה לָּךְ : דַּבֵּר אֲלֵהֶם כֹּה־אָמַר אֲדֹנָי

יְהֹוָה הִנֵּה אֲנִי לֹקֵחַ אֶת־עֵץ יוֹסֵף אֲשֶׁר בְּיַד־אֶפְרַיִם וְשִׁבְטֵי יִשְׂרָאֵל

חֲבֵרָו וְנָתַתִּי אֹתָם עָלָיו אֶת־עֵץ יְהוּדָה וַעֲשִׂיתִם לְעֵץ אֶחָד וְהָיוּ אֶחָד

21 בְּיָדִי : וְהָיוּ הָעֵצִים אֲשֶׁר תִּכְתֹּב עֲלֵיהֶם בְּיָדְךָ לְעֵינֵיהֶם : וְדַבֵּר אֲלֵיהֶם

כֹּה־אָמַר אֲדֹנָי יְהֹוָה הִנֵּה אֲנִי לֹקֵחַ אֶת־בְּנֵי יִשְׂרָאֵל מִבֵּין הַגּוֹיִם אֲשֶׁר

22 הָלְכוּ־שָׁם וְקִבַּצְתִּי אֹתָם מִסָּבִיב וְהֵבֵאתִי אוֹתָם אֶל־אַדְמָתָם : וְעָשִׂיתִי

אֹתָם לְגוֹי אֶחָד בָּאָרֶץ בְּהָרֵי יִשְׂרָאֵל וּמֶלֶךְ אֶחָד יִהְיֶה לְכֻלָּם לְמֶלֶךְ

23 וְלֹא יִהְיֶה־עוֹד לִשְׁנֵי גוֹיִם וְלֹא יֵחָצוּ עוֹד לִשְׁתֵּי מַמְלָכוֹת עוֹד : וְלֹא

יִטַּמְּאוּ עוֹד בְּגִלּוּלֵיהֶם וּבְשִׁקּוּצֵיהֶם וּבְכֹל פִּשְׁעֵיהֶם וְהוֹשַׁעְתִּי אֹתָם

מִכֹּל מוֹשְׁבֹתֵיהֶם אֲשֶׁר חָטְאוּ בָהֶם וְטִהַרְתִּי אוֹתָם וְהָיוּ־לִי לְעָם וַאֲנִי

24 אֶהְיֶה לָהֶם לֵאלֹהִים : וְעַבְדִּי דָוִד מֶלֶךְ עֲלֵיהֶם וְרוֹעֶה אֶחָד יִהְיֶה

כה לְכֻלָּם וּבְמִשְׁפָּטַי יֵלֵכוּ וְחֻקֹּתַי יִשְׁמְרוּ וְעָשׂוּ אוֹתָם : וְיָשְׁבוּ עַל־הָאָרֶץ

אֲשֶׁר נָתַתִּי לְעַבְדִּי לְיַעֲקֹב אֲשֶׁר יָשְׁבוּ־בָהּ אֲבוֹתֵיכֶם וְיָשְׁבוּ עָלֶיהָ

הֵמָּה וּבְנֵיהֶם וּבְנֵי בְנֵיהֶם עַד־עוֹלָם וְדָוִד עַבְדִּי נָשִׂיא לָהֶם לְעוֹלָם :

26 וְכָרַתִּי לָהֶם בְּרִית שָׁלוֹם בְּרִית עוֹלָם יִהְיֶה אוֹתָם וּנְתַתִּים וְהִרְבֵּיתִי

27 אוֹתָם וְנָתַתִּי אֶת־מִקְדָּשִׁי בְּתוֹכָם לְעוֹלָם : וְהָיָה מִשְׁכָּנִי עֲלֵיהֶם וְהָיִיתִי

28 לָהֶם לֵאלֹהִים וְהֵמָּה יִהְיוּ־לִי לְעָם : וְיָדְעוּ הַגּוֹיִם כִּי אֲנִי יְהֹוָה

מְקַדֵּשׁ אֶת־יִשְׂרָאֵל בִּהְיוֹת מִקְדָּשִׁי בְּתוֹכָם לְעוֹלָם :

XI. The Prophecy of Obadiah.

א חֲזוֹן עֹבַדְיָה כֹּה־אָמַר אֲדֹנָי יְהֹוָה לֶאֱדוֹם שְׁמוּעָה שָׁמַעְנוּ מֵאֵת

2 יְהֹוָה וְצִיר בַּגּוֹיִם שֻׁלָּח קוּמוּ וְנָקוּמָה עָלֶיהָ לַמִּלְחָמָה : הִנֵּה קָטֹן

3 נְתַתִּיךָ בַּגּוֹיִם בָּזוּי אַתָּה מְאֹד : זְדוֹן לִבְּךָ הִשִּׁיאֶךָ שֹׁכְנִי בְחַגְוֵי־סֶלַע

4 מְרוֹם שִׁבְתּוֹ אֹמֵר בְּלִבּוֹ מִי יוֹרִדֵנִי אָרֶץ : אִם־תַּגְבִּיהַּ כַּנֶּשֶׁר וְאִם־

ה בֵּין כּוֹכָבִים שִׂים קִנֶּךָ מִשָּׁם אוֹרִידְךָ נְאֻם־יְהֹוָה : אִם־גַּנָּבִים בָּאוּ־לְךָ

אִם־שׁוֹדְדֵי לַיְלָה אֵיךְ נִדְמֵיתָה הֲלוֹא יִגְנְבוּ דַּיָּם אִם־בֹּצְרִים בָּאוּ לָךְ

7 6 הֲלוֹא יַשְׁאִירוּ עֹלֵלוֹת : אֵיךְ נֶחְפְּשׂוּ עֵשָׂו נִבְעוּ מַצְפֻּנָיו : עַד־הַגְּבוּל

v. 16. חביריו קרי id. חביריו קרי v. 19. חביריו קר v. 22. יהיו קרי

v. 28. כד כאן v. 1. חפטרת ושלח id. קמץ בז״ק

שֹׁלְחֶיךָ כָּל אַנְשֵׁי בְּרִיתֶךָ הִשִּׁיאֶיךָ יָכְלוּ לְךָ אַנְשֵׁי שְׁלֹמֶךָ לַחְמְךָ

8 יָשִׂימוּ מָזוֹר תַּחְתֶּיךָ אֵין תְּבוּנָה בּוֹ : הֲלוֹא בַּיּוֹם הַהוּא נְאֻם־יְהֹוָה

9 וְהַאֲבַדְתִּי חֲכָמִים מֵאֱדוֹם וּתְבוּנָה מֵהַר עֵשָׂו : וְחַתּוּ גִבּוֹרֶיךָ תֵימָן

י לְמַעַן יִכָּרֶת־אִישׁ מֵהַר עֵשָׂו מִקָּטֶל : מֵחֲמַס אָחִיךָ יַעֲקֹב תְּכַסְּךָ בוּשָׁה

11 וְנִכְרַתָּ לְעוֹלָם : בְּיוֹם עֲמָדְךָ מִנֶּגֶד בְּיוֹם שְׁבוֹת זָרִים חֵילוֹ וְנָכְרִים

12 בָּאוּ שְׁעָרָו וְעַל־יְרוּשָׁלַ͏ִם יַדּוּ גוֹרָל גַּם־אַתָּה כְּאַחַד מֵהֶם : וְאַל־תֵּרֶא

בְיוֹם־אָחִיךָ בְּיוֹם נָכְרוֹ וְאַל־תִּשְׂמַח לִבְנֵי־יְהוּדָה בְּיוֹם אָבְדָם וְאַל־

13 תַּגְדֵּל פִּיךָ בְּיוֹם צָרָה : אַל־תָּבוֹא בְשַׁעַר־עַמִּי בְּיוֹם אֵידָם אַל־תֵּרֶא

14 גַם־אַתָּה בְּרָעָתוֹ בְּיוֹם אֵידוֹ וְאַל־תִּשְׁלַחְנָה בְחֵילוֹ בְּיוֹם אֵידוֹ : וְאַל־

תַּעֲמֹד עַל־הַפֶּרֶק לְהַכְרִית אֶת־פְּלִיטָיו וְאַל־תַּסְגֵּר שְׂרִידָיו בְּיוֹם צָרָה :

טו כִּי־קָרוֹב יוֹם־יְהֹוָה עַל־כָּל־הַגּוֹיִם כַּאֲשֶׁר עָשִׂיתָ יֵעָשֶׂה לָּךְ גְּמֻלְךָ יָשׁוּב

16 בְּרֹאשֶׁךָ : כִּי כַּאֲשֶׁר שְׁתִיתֶם עַל־הַר קָדְשִׁי יִשְׁתּוּ כָל־הַגּוֹיִם תָּמִיד

17 וְשָׁתוּ וְלָעוּ וְהָיוּ כְּלוֹא הָיוּ : וּבְהַר צִיּוֹן תִּהְיֶה פְלֵיטָה וְהָיָה קֹדֶשׁ

18 וְיָרְשׁוּ בֵּית יַעֲקֹב אֵת מוֹרָשֵׁיהֶם : וְהָיָה בֵית־יַעֲקֹב אֵשׁ וּבֵית יוֹסֵף

לֶהָבָה וּבֵית עֵשָׂו לְקַשׁ וְדָלְקוּ בָהֶם וַאֲכָלוּם וְלֹא־יִהְיֶה שָׂרִיד לְבֵית

19 עֵשָׂו כִּי יְהֹוָה דִּבֵּר : וְיָרְשׁוּ הַנֶּגֶב אֶת־הַר עֵשָׂו וְהַשְּׁפֵלָה אֶת־פְּלִשְׁתִּים

וְיָרְשׁוּ אֶת־שְׂדֵה אֶפְרַיִם וְאֵת שְׂדֵה שֹׁמְרוֹן וּבִנְיָמִן אֶת־הַגִּלְעָד :

כ וְגָלֻת הַחֵל־הַזֶּה לִבְנֵי יִשְׂרָאֵל אֲשֶׁר־כְּנַעֲנִים עַד־צָרְפַת וְגָלֻת יְרוּשָׁלַ͏ִם

21 אֲשֶׁר בִּסְפָרַד יִרְשׁוּ אֵת עָרֵי הַנֶּגֶב : וְעָלוּ מוֹשִׁעִים בְּהַר צִיּוֹן לִשְׁפֹּט

אֶת־הַר עֵשָׂו וְהָיְתָה לַיהֹוָה הַמְּלוּכָה :

XII. THE PROPHECY OF NAHUM.

CHAPTER I. א

ב מַשָּׂא נִינְוֵה סֵפֶר חֲזוֹן נַחוּם הָאֶלְקֹשִׁי : אֵל קַנּוֹא וְנֹקֵם יְהֹוָה נֹקֵם

3 יְהֹוָה וּבַעַל חֵמָה נֹקֵם יְהֹוָה לְצָרָיו וְנוֹטֵר הוּא לְאֹיְבָיו : יְהֹוָה

אֶרֶךְ אַפַּיִם וּגְדָל־כֹּחַ וְנַקֵּה לֹא יְנַקֶּה יְהֹוָה בְּסוּפָה וּבִשְׂעָרָה דַּרְכּוֹ

4 וְעָנָן אֲבַק רַגְלָיו : גּוֹעֵר בַּיָּם וַיַּבְּשֵׁהוּ וְכָל־הַנְּהָרוֹת הֶחֱרִיב אֻמְלַל

ה בָּשָׁן וְכַרְמֶל וּפֶרַח לְבָנוֹן אֻמְלָל : הָרִים רָעֲשׁוּ מִמֶּנּוּ וְהַגְּבָעוֹת

6 הִתְמֹגָגוּ וַתִּשָּׂא הָאָרֶץ מִפָּנָיו וְתֵבֵל וְכָל־יֹשְׁבֵי בָהּ : לִפְנֵי זַעְמוֹ מִי

יַעֲמוֹד וּמִי יָקוּם בַּחֲרוֹן אַפּוֹ חֲמָתוֹ נִתְּכָה כָאֵשׁ וְהַצֻּרִים נִתְּצוּ

8 7 מִמֶּנּוּ : טוֹב יְהֹוָה לְמָעוֹז בְּיוֹם צָרָה וְיֹדֵעַ חֹסֵי בוֹ : וּבְשֶׁטֶף עֹבֵר

כָּלָה יַעֲשֶׂה מְקוֹמָהּ וְאֹיְבָיו יְרַדֶּף־חֹשֶׁךְ׃ מַה־תְּחַשְּׁבוּן אֶל־יְהֹוָה כָּלָה 9
הִיא עֹשֶׂה לֹא־תָקוּם פַּעֲמַיִם צָרָה׃ כִּי עַד־סִירִים סְבֻכִים וּכְסָבְאָם ו
סְבוּאִים אֻכְּלוּ כְּקַשׁ יָבֵשׁ מָלֵא׃ מִמֵּךְ יָצָא חֹשֵׁב עַל־יְהֹוָה רָעָה יֹעֵץ 11
בְּלִיָּעַל׃ כֹּה אָמַר יְהֹוָה אִם־שְׁלֵמִים וְכֵן רַבִּים וְכֵן נָגֹזּוּ וְעָבָר 12
וְעִנִּתֵךְ לֹא אֲעַנֵּךְ עוֹד׃ וְעַתָּה אֶשְׁבֹּר מֹטֵהוּ מֵעָלָיִךְ וּמוֹסְרֹתַיִךְ אֲנַתֵּק׃ 13
וְצִוָּה עָלֶיךָ יְהֹוָה לֹא־יִזָּרַע מִשִּׁמְךָ עוֹד מִבֵּית אֱלֹהֶיךָ אַכְרִית פֶּסֶל 14
וּמַסֵּכָה אָשִׂים קִבְרֶךָ כִּי קַלּוֹתָ׃

CHAPTER II. ב

הִנֵּה עַל־הֶהָרִים רַגְלֵי מְבַשֵּׂר מַשְׁמִיעַ שָׁלוֹם חָגִּי יְהוּדָה חַגַּיִךְ שַׁלְּמִי א
נְדָרָיִךְ כִּי לֹא יוֹסִיף עוֹד לַעֲבוֹר־בָּךְ בְּלִיַּעַל כֻּלֹּה נִכְרָת׃ עָלָה מֵפִיץ 2
עַל־פָּנַיִךְ נָצוֹר מְצוּרָה צַפֵּה־דֶרֶךְ חַזֵּק מָתְנַיִם אַמֵּץ כֹּחַ מְאֹד׃ כִּי 3
שָׁב יְהֹוָה אֶת־גְּאוֹן יַעֲקֹב כִּגְאוֹן יִשְׂרָאֵל כִּי בְקָקוּם בֹּקְקִים וּזְמֹרֵיהֶם
שִׁחֵתוּ׃ מָגֵן גִּבֹּרֵיהוּ מְאָדָּם אַנְשֵׁי־חַיִל מְתֻלָּעִים בְּאֵשׁ־פְּלָדֹת הָרֶכֶב 4
בְּיוֹם הֲכִינוֹ וְהַבְּרֹשִׁים הָרְעָלוּ׃ בַּחוּצוֹת יִתְהוֹלְלוּ הָרֶכֶב יִשְׁתַּקְשְׁקוּן ה
בָּרְחֹבוֹת מַרְאֵיהֶן כַּלַּפִּידִם כַּבְּרָקִים יְרוֹצֵצוּ׃ יִזְכֹּר אַדִּירָיו יִכָּשְׁלוּ ו
בַּהֲלִיכוֹתָם יְמַהֲרוּ חוֹמָתָהּ וְהֻכַן הַסֹּכֵךְ׃ שַׁעֲרֵי הַנְּהָרוֹת נִפְתָּחוּ ז
וְהַהֵיכָל נָמוֹג׃ וְהֻצַּב גֻּלְּתָה הֹעֲלָתָה וְאַמְהֹתֶיהָ מְנַהֲגוֹת כְּקוֹל יוֹנִים 8
מְתֹפְפֹת עַל־לִבְבֵהֶן׃ וְנִינְוֵה כִבְרֵכַת־מַיִם מִימֵי הִיא וְהֵמָּה נָסִים 9
עִמְדוּ עֲמֹדוּ וְאֵין מַפְנֶה׃ בֹּזּוּ כֶסֶף בֹּזּוּ זָהָב וְאֵין קֵצֶה לַתְּכוּנָה
כָּבֹד מִכֹּל כְּלִי חֶמְדָּה׃ בּוּקָה וּמְבוּקָה וּמְבֻלָּקָה וְלֵב נָמֵס וּפִק 11
בִּרְכַּיִם וְחַלְחָלָה בְּכָל־מָתְנַיִם וּפְנֵי כֻלָּם קִבְּצוּ פָארוּר׃ אַיֵּה מְעוֹן 12
אֲרָיוֹת וּמִרְעֶה הוּא לַכְּפִרִים אֲשֶׁר הָלַךְ אַרְיֵה לָבִיא שָׁם גּוּר אַרְיֵה
וְאֵין מַחֲרִיד׃ אַרְיֵה טֹרֵף בְּדֵי גֹרוֹתָיו וּמְחַנֵּק לְלִבְאֹתָיו וַיְמַלֵּא־טֶרֶף 13
חֹרָיו וּמְעֹנֹתָיו טְרֵפָה׃ הִנְנִי אֵלַיִךְ נְאֻם יְהֹוָה צְבָאוֹת וְהִבְעַרְתִּי 14
בֶעָשָׁן רִכְבָּהּ וּכְפִירַיִךְ תֹּאכַל חָרֶב וְהִכְרַתִּי מֵאֶרֶץ טַרְפֵּךְ וְלֹא־יִשָּׁמַע
עוֹד קוֹל מַלְאָכֵכֵה׃

CHAPTER III. ג

הוֹי עִיר דָּמִים כֻּלָּהּ כַּחַשׁ פֶּרֶק מְלֵאָה לֹא יָמִישׁ טָרֶף׃ קוֹל שׁוֹט א 2
וְקוֹל רַעַשׁ אוֹפָן וְסוּס דֹּהֵר וּמֶרְכָּבָה מְרַקֵּדָה׃ פָּרָשׁ מַעֲלֶה וְלַהַב 3
חֶרֶב וּבְרַק חֲנִית וְרֹב חָלָל וְכֹבֶד פָּגֶר וְאֵין קֵצֶה לַגְּוִיָּה וְכָשְׁלוּ

v. 3. יִשְׁבֹּל קרי   v. 6. יִתְהֹר ו   v. 1. יִתְהֹר ו

4 בְּנֵיכֶם ׃ מֵרֹב זְמִינֵי זוֹנָה טוֹבַת חֵן בַּעֲלַת בְּשָׁפִים כִּשָּׁפִים הַמֹּכֶרֶת גּוֹיִם

5 בִּזְנוּנֶיהָ וּמִשְׁפָּחוֹת בִּכְשָׁפֶיהָ ׃ הִנְנִי אֵלַיִךְ נְאֻם יְהֹוָה צְבָאוֹת וְגִלֵּיתִי

6 שׁוּלַיִךְ עַל־פָּנָיִךְ וְהַרְאֵיתִי גוֹיִם מַעְרֵךְ וּמַמְלָכוֹת קְלוֹנֵךְ ׃ וְהִשְׁלַכְתִּי

7 עָלַיִךְ שִׁקֻּצִים וְנִבַּלְתִּיךְ וְשַׂמְתִּיךְ כְּרֹאִי ׃ וְהָיָה כָל־רֹאַיִךְ יִדּוֹד מִמֵּךְ

8 וְאָמַר שֻׁדְּדָה נִינְוֵה מִי יָנוּד לָהּ מֵאַיִן אֲבַקֵּשׁ מְנַחֲמִים לָךְ ׃ הֲתֵיטְבִי

מִנֹּא אָמוֹן הַיֹּשְׁבָה בַּיְאֹרִים מַיִם סָבִיב לָהּ אֲשֶׁר־חֵיל יָם מִיָּם

9 חוֹמָתָהּ ׃ כּוּשׁ עָצְמָה וּמִצְרַיִם וְאֵין קֵצֶה פּוּט וְלוּבִים הָיוּ בְּעֶזְרָתֵךְ ׃

10 גַּם־הִיא לַגֹּלָה הָלְכָה בַשֶּׁבִי גַּם עֹלָלֶיהָ יְרֻטְּשׁוּ בְּרֹאשׁ כָּל־חוּצוֹת

11 וְעַל־נִכְבַּדֶּיהָ יַדּוּ גוֹרָל וְכָל־גְּדוֹלֶיהָ רֻתְּקוּ בַזִּקִּים ׃ גַּם־אַתְּ תִּשְׁכְּרִי

12 תְּהִי נַעֲלָמָה גַּם־אַתְּ תְּבַקְשִׁי מָעוֹז מֵאוֹיֵב ׃ כָּל־מִבְצָרַיִךְ תְּאֵנִים עִם־

13 בִּכּוּרִים אִם־יִנּוֹעוּ וְנָפְלוּ עַל־פִּי אוֹכֵל ׃ הִנֵּה עַמֵּךְ נָשִׁים בְּקִרְבֵּךְ לְאֹיְבַיִךְ

14 פָּתוֹחַ נִפְתְּחוּ שַׁעֲרֵי אַרְצֵךְ אָכְלָה אֵשׁ בְּרִיחָיִךְ ׃ מֵי מָצוֹר שַׁאֲבִי־לָךְ

15 חַזְּקִי מִבְצָרָיִךְ בֹּאִי בַטִּיט וְרִמְסִי בַחֹמֶר הַחֲזִיקִי מַלְבֵּן ׃ שָׁם תֹּאכְלֵךְ

אֵשׁ תַּכְרִיתֵךְ חֶרֶב תֹּאכְלֵךְ כַּיָּלֶק הִתְכַּבֵּד כַּיֶּלֶק הִתְכַּבְּדִי כָּאַרְבֶּה ׃

16 הִרְבֵּית רֹכְלַיִךְ מִכּוֹכְבֵי הַשָּׁמָיִם יֶלֶק פָּשַׁט וַיָּעֹף ׃ מִנְּזָרַיִךְ כָּאַרְבֶּה

17 וְטַפְסְרַיִךְ כְּגוֹב גֹּבָי הַחוֹנִים בַּגְּדֵרוֹת בְּיוֹם קָרָה שֶׁמֶשׁ זָרְחָה וְנוֹדַד

18 וְלֹא־נוֹדַע מְקוֹמוֹ אַיָּם ׃ נָמוּ רֹעֶיךָ מֶלֶךְ אַשּׁוּר יִשְׁכְּנוּ אַדִּירֶיךָ נָפֹשׁוּ

19 עַמְּךָ עַל־הֶהָרִים וְאֵין מְקַבֵּץ ׃ אֵין־כֵּהָה לְשִׁבְרֶךָ נַחְלָה מַכָּתֶךָ כֹּל ׀

שֹׁמְעֵי שִׁמְעֲךָ תָּקְעוּ כַף עָלֶיךָ כִּי עַל־מִי לֹא־עָבְרָה רָעָתְךָ תָּמִיד ׃

XIII. Twelve Selected Psalms.

PSALM I. א

1 אַשְׁרֵי הָאִישׁ אֲשֶׁר לֹא הָלַךְ בַּעֲצַת רְשָׁעִים וּבְדֶרֶךְ חַטָּאִים לֹא עָמָד

2 וּבְמוֹשַׁב לֵצִים לֹא יָשָׁב ׃ כִּי אִם־בְּתוֹרַת יְהֹוָה חֶפְצוֹ וּבְתוֹרָתוֹ לְהָגֶּה

3 יוֹמָם וָלָיְלָה ׃ וְהָיָה כְּעֵץ שָׁתוּל עַל־פַּלְגֵי מָיִם אֲשֶׁר פִּרְיוֹ ׀ יִתֵּן בְּעִתּוֹ

4 וְעָלֵהוּ לֹא־יִבּוֹל וְכֹל אֲשֶׁר־יַעֲשֶׂה יַצְלִיחַ ׃ לֹא־כֵן הָרְשָׁעִים כִּי אִם־כַּמֹּץ

5 אֲשֶׁר־תִּדְּפֶנּוּ רוּחַ ׃ עַל־כֵּן ׀ לֹא־יָקֻמוּ רְשָׁעִים בַּמִּשְׁפָּט וְחַטָּאִים בַּעֲדַת

6 צַדִּיקִים ׃ כִּי־יוֹדֵעַ יְהֹוָה דֶּרֶךְ צַדִּיקִים וְדֶרֶךְ רְשָׁעִים תֹּאבֵד ׃

PSALM II. ב

1 2 לָמָּה רָגְשׁוּ גוֹיִם וּלְאֻמִּים יֶהְגּוּ־רִיק ׃ יִתְיַצְּבוּ ׀ מַלְכֵי־אֶרֶץ וְרוֹזְנִים

3 נוֹסְדוּ־יָחַד עַל־יְהֹוָה וְעַל־מְשִׁיחוֹ ׃ נְנַתְּקָה אֶת־מוֹסְרוֹתֵימוֹ וְנַשְׁלִיכָה

4 5 מִמֶּנּוּ עֲבֹתֵימוֹ ׃ יוֹשֵׁב בַּשָּׁמַיִם יִשְׂחָק אֲדֹנָי יִלְעַג־לָמוֹ ׃ אָז יְדַבֵּר

אֵלֵימוֹ בְאַפּוֹ וּבַחֲרוֹנוֹ יְבַהֲלֵמוֹ: וַאֲנִי נָסַכְתִּי מַלְכִּי עַל־צִיּוֹן הַר־קָדְשִׁי: 6

אֲסַפְּרָה אֶל־חֹק יְהֹוָה אָמַר אֵלַי בְּנִי אַתָּה אֲנִי הַיּוֹם יְלִדְתִּיךָ: שְׁאַל 7 8

מִמֶּנִּי וְאֶתְּנָה גוֹיִם נַחֲלָתֶךָ וַאֲחֻזָּתְךָ אַפְסֵי־אָרֶץ: תְּרֹעֵם בְּשֵׁבֶט בַּרְזֶל 9

כִּכְלִי יוֹצֵר תְּנַפְּצֵם: וְעַתָּה מְלָכִים הַשְׂכִּילוּ הִוָּסְרוּ שֹׁפְטֵי אָרֶץ: עִבְדוּ 11

אֶת־יְהֹוָה בְּיִרְאָה וְגִילוּ בִּרְעָדָה: נַשְּׁקוּ־בַר פֶּן־יֶאֱנַף וְתֹאבְדוּ דֶרֶךְ 12

כִּי־יִבְעַר כִּמְעַט אַפּוֹ אַשְׁרֵי כָּל־חוֹסֵי בוֹ:

PSALM III. ג

מִזְמוֹר לְדָוִד בְּבָרְחוֹ מִפְּנֵי אַבְשָׁלוֹם בְּנוֹ: יְהֹוָה מָה־רַבּוּ צָרָי 2

רַבִּים קָמִים עָלָי: רַבִּים אֹמְרִים לְנַפְשִׁי אֵין יְשׁוּעָתָה לּוֹ בֵאלֹהִים 3

סֶלָה: וְאַתָּה יְהֹוָה מָגֵן בַּעֲדִי כְּבוֹדִי וּמֵרִים רֹאשִׁי: קוֹלִי אֶל־יְהֹוָה 4 5

אֶקְרָא וַיַּעֲנֵנִי מֵהַר קָדְשׁוֹ סֶלָה: אֲנִי שָׁכַבְתִּי וָאִישָׁנָה הֱקִיצוֹתִי כִּי יְהֹוָה 6

יִסְמְכֵנִי: לֹא־אִירָא מֵרִבְבוֹת עָם אֲשֶׁר סָבִיב שָׁתוּ עָלָי: קוּמָה יְהֹוָה 7 8

הוֹשִׁיעֵנִי אֱלֹהַי כִּי־הִכִּיתָ אֶת־כָּל־אֹיְבַי לֶחִי שִׁנֵּי רְשָׁעִים שִׁבַּרְתָּ: לַיהֹוָה 9

הַיְשׁוּעָה עַל־עַמְּךָ בִרְכָתֶךָ סֶּלָה:

PSALM IV. ד

לַמְנַצֵּחַ בִּנְגִינוֹת מִזְמוֹר לְדָוִד: בְּקָרְאִי עֲנֵנִי אֱלֹהֵי צִדְקִי בַּצָּר 2

הִרְחַבְתָּ לִּי חָנֵּנִי וּשְׁמַע תְּפִלָּתִי: בְּנֵי־אִישׁ עַד־מֶה כְבוֹדִי לִכְלִמָּה 3

תֶּאֱהָבוּן רִיק תְּבַקְשׁוּ כָזָב סֶלָה: וּדְעוּ כִּי־הִפְלָה יְהֹוָה חָסִיד לוֹ 4

יְהֹוָה יִשְׁמַע בְּקָרְאִי אֵלָיו: רִגְזוּ וְאַל־תֶּחֱטָאוּ אִמְרוּ בִלְבַבְכֶם עַל־ 5

מִשְׁכַּבְכֶם וְדֹמּוּ סֶלָה: זִבְחוּ זִבְחֵי־צֶדֶק וּבִטְחוּ אֶל־יְהֹוָה: רַבִּים 6 7

אֹמְרִים מִי־יַרְאֵנוּ טוֹב נְסָה־עָלֵינוּ אוֹר פָּנֶיךָ יְהֹוָה: נָתַתָּה שִׂמְחָה 8

בְלִבִּי מֵעֵת דְּגָנָם וְתִירוֹשָׁם רָבּוּ: בְּשָׁלוֹם יַחְדָּו אֶשְׁכְּבָה וְאִישָׁן 9

כִּי־אַתָּה יְהֹוָה לְבָדָד לָבֶטַח תּוֹשִׁיבֵנִי:

PSALM V. ה

לַמְנַצֵּחַ אֶל־הַנְּחִילוֹת מִזְמוֹר לְדָוִד: אֲמָרַי הַאֲזִינָה יְהֹוָה בִּינָה 2

הֲגִיגִי: הַקְשִׁיבָה לְקוֹל שַׁוְעִי מַלְכִּי וֵאלֹהָי כִּי־אֵלֶיךָ אֶתְפַּלָּל: יְהֹוָה 3 4

בֹּקֶר תִּשְׁמַע קוֹלִי בֹּקֶר אֶעֱרָךְ־לְךָ וַאֲצַפֶּה: כִּי לֹא אֵל חָפֵץ רֶשַׁע 5

אָתָּה לֹא יְגֻרְךָ רָע: לֹא־יִתְיַצְּבוּ הוֹלְלִים לְנֶגֶד עֵינֶיךָ שָׂנֵאתָ כָּל־ 6

פֹּעֲלֵי אָוֶן: תְּאַבֵּד דֹּבְרֵי כָזָב אִישׁ־דָּמִים וּמִרְמָה יְתָעֵב יְהֹוָה: 7

---

8 וַאֲנִי בְּרֹב חַסְדְּךָ אָבוֹא בֵיתֶךָ אֶשְׁתַּחֲוֶה אֶל־הֵיכַל קָדְשְׁךָ בְּיִרְאָתֶךָ׃

9 יְהוָה ׀ נְחֵנִי בְצִדְקָתֶךָ לְמַעַן שׁוֹרְרָי הַוְשַׁר לְפָנַי דַּרְכֶּךָ׃ כִּי אֵין בְּפִיהוּ

11 נְכוֹנָה קִרְבָּם הַוּוֹת קִבְרָם קָבֶר־פָּתוּחַ גְּרֹנָם לְשׁוֹנָם יַחֲלִיקוּן׃ הַאֲשִׁימֵם ׀

אֱלֹהִים יִפְּלוּ מִמֹּעֲצוֹתֵיהֶם בְּרֹב פִּשְׁעֵיהֶם הַדִּיחֵמוֹ כִּי מָרוּ בָךְ׃

12 וְיִשְׂמְחוּ כָל־חוֹסֵי בָךְ לְעוֹלָם יְרַנֵּנוּ וְתָסֵךְ עָלֵימוֹ וְיַעְלְצוּ בְךָ אֹהֲבֵי

13 שְׁמֶךָ׃ כִּי־אַתָּה תְּבָרֵךְ צַדִּיק יְהוָה כַּצִּנָּה רָצוֹן תַּעְטְרֶנּוּ׃

PSALM VI. ו

2 לַמְנַצֵּחַ בִּנְגִינוֹת עַל־הַשְּׁמִינִית מִזְמוֹר לְדָוִד׃ יְהוָה אַל־בְּאַפְּךָ

3 תוֹכִיחֵנִי וְאַל־בַּחֲמָתְךָ תְיַסְּרֵנִי׃ חָנֵּנִי יְהוָה כִּי אֻמְלַל אָנִי רְפָאֵנִי

4 יְהוָה כִּי נִבְהֲלוּ עֲצָמָי׃ וְנַפְשִׁי נִבְהֲלָה מְאֹד וְאַתָּ יְהוָה עַד־מָתָי׃

6 שׁוּבָה יְהוָה חַלְּצָה נַפְשִׁי הוֹשִׁיעֵנִי לְמַעַן חַסְדֶּךָ׃ כִּי אֵין בַּמָּוֶת זִכְרֶךָ

7 בִּשְׁאוֹל מִי יוֹדֶה־לָּךְ׃ יָגַעְתִּי ׀ בְּאַנְחָתִי אַשְׂחֶה בְכָל־לַיְלָה מִטָּתִי

8,9 בְּדִמְעָתִי עַרְשִׂי אַמְסֶה׃ עָשְׁשָׁה מִכַּעַס עֵינִי עָתְקָה בְּכָל־צוֹרְרָי׃ סוּרוּ

10 מִמֶּנִּי כָּל־פֹּעֲלֵי אָוֶן כִּי־שָׁמַע יְהוָה קוֹל בִּכְיִי׃ שָׁמַע יְהוָה תְּחִנָּתִי

11 יְהוָה תְּפִלָּתִי יִקָּח׃ יֵבֹשׁוּ ׀ וְיִבָּהֲלוּ מְאֹד כָּל־אֹיְבָי יָשֻׁבוּ יֵבֹשׁוּ רָגַע׃

PSALM VII. ז

2 שִׁגָּיוֹן לְדָוִד אֲשֶׁר־שָׁר לַיהוָה עַל־דִּבְרֵי־כוּשׁ בֶּן־יְמִינִי׃ יְהוָה אֱלֹהַי

3 בְּךָ חָסִיתִי הוֹשִׁיעֵנִי מִכָּל־רֹדְפַי וְהַצִּילֵנִי׃ פֶּן־יִטְרֹף כְּאַרְיֵה נַפְשִׁי פֹּרֵק

4,5 וְאֵין מַצִּיל׃ יְהוָה אֱלֹהַי אִם־עָשִׂיתִי זֹאת אִם־יֶשׁ־עָוֶל בְּכַפָּי׃ אִם־

6 גָּמַלְתִּי שׁוֹלְמִי רָע וָאֲחַלְּצָה צוֹרְרִי רֵיקָם׃ יִרַדֹּף אוֹיֵב ׀ נַפְשִׁי וְיַשֵּׂג

7 וְיִרְמֹס לָאָרֶץ חַיָּי וּכְבוֹדִי ׀ לֶעָפָר יַשְׁכֵּן סֶלָה׃ קוּמָה יְהוָה ׀ בְּאַפֶּךָ

8 הִנָּשֵׂא בְּעַבְרוֹת צוֹרְרָי וְעוּרָה אֵלַי מִשְׁפָּט צִוִּיתָ׃ וַעֲדַת לְאֻמִּים

9 תְּסוֹבְבֶךָ וְעָלֶיהָ לַמָּרוֹם שׁוּבָה׃ יְהוָה יָדִין עַמִּים שָׁפְטֵנִי יְהוָה

10 כְּצִדְקִי וּכְתֻמִּי עָלָי׃ יִגְמָר־נָא רַע ׀ רְשָׁעִים וּתְכוֹנֵן צַדִּיק וּבֹחֵן לִבּוֹת

11,12 וּכְלָיוֹת אֱלֹהִים צַדִּיק׃ מָגִנִּי עַל־אֱלֹהִים מוֹשִׁיעַ יִשְׁרֵי־לֵב׃ אֱלֹהִים

13 שׁוֹפֵט צַדִּיק וְאֵל זֹעֵם בְּכָל־יוֹם׃ אִם־לֹא יָשׁוּב חַרְבּוֹ יִלְטוֹשׁ קַשְׁתּוֹ

14 דָרַךְ וַיְכוֹנְנֶהָ׃ וְלוֹ הֵכִין כְּלֵי־מָוֶת חִצָּיו לְדֹלְקִים יִפְעָל׃ הִנֵּה יְחַבֶּל־

16 אָוֶן וְהָרָה עָמָל וְיָלַד שָׁקֶר׃ בּוֹר כָּרָה וַיַּחְפְּרֵהוּ וַיִּפֹּל בְּשַׁחַת

17 יִפְעָל׃ יָשׁוּב עֲמָלוֹ בְרֹאשׁוֹ וְעַל־קָדְקֳדוֹ חֲמָסוֹ יֵרֵד׃ אוֹדֶה יְהוָה

18 כְּצִדְקוֹ וַאֲזַמְּרָה שֵׁם־יְהוָה עֶלְיוֹן׃

PSALM VIII. ח

לַמְנַצֵּחַ עַל־הַגִּתִּית מִזְמוֹר לְדָוִד ׃ יְהֹוָה אֲדֹנֵינוּ מָה־אַדִּיר שִׁמְךָ 2 א

בְּכָל־הָאָרֶץ אֲשֶׁר־תְּנָה הוֹדְךָ עַל־הַשָּׁמָיִם ׃ מִפִּי עוֹלְלִים וְיֹנְקִים יִסַּדְתָּ 3

עֹז לְמַעַן צוֹרְרֶיךָ לְהַשְׁבִּית אוֹיֵב וּמִתְנַקֵּם ׃ כִּי־אֶרְאֶה שָׁמֶיךָ מַעֲשֵׂה 4

אֶצְבְּעֹתֶיךָ יָרֵחַ וְכוֹכָבִים אֲשֶׁר כּוֹנָנְתָּה ׃ מָה־אֱנוֹשׁ כִּי־תִזְכְּרֶנּוּ וּבֶן־ 5 ה

אָדָם כִּי תִפְקְדֶנּוּ ׃ וַתְּחַסְּרֵהוּ מְּעַט מֵאֱלֹהִים וְכָבוֹד וְהָדָר תְּעַטְּרֵהוּ ׃ 6

תַּמְשִׁילֵהוּ בְּמַעֲשֵׂי יָדֶיךָ כֹּל שַׁתָּה תַחַת־רַגְלָיו ׃ צֹנֶה וַאֲלָפִים כֻּלָּם 8 7

וְגַם בַּהֲמוֹת שָׂדָי ׃ צִפּוֹר שָׁמַיִם וּדְגֵי הַיָּם עֹבֵר אָרְחוֹת יַמִּים ׃ יְהֹוָה 9 י

אֲדֹנֵינוּ מָה־אַדִּיר שִׁמְךָ בְּכָל־הָאָרֶץ ׃

PSALM XXII. כב

לַמְנַצֵּחַ עַל־אַיֶּלֶת הַשַּׁחַר מִזְמוֹר לְדָוִד ׃ אֵלִי אֵלִי לָמָה עֲזַבְתָּנִי 2 א

רָחוֹק מִישׁוּעָתִי דִּבְרֵי שַׁאֲגָתִי ׃ אֱלֹהַי אֶקְרָא יוֹמָם וְלֹא תַעֲנֶה וְלַיְלָה 3

וְלֹא־דֻמִיָּה לִי ׃ וְאַתָּה קָדוֹשׁ יוֹשֵׁב תְּהִלּוֹת יִשְׂרָאֵל ׃ בְּךָ בָּטְחוּ 4 ה

אֲבֹתֵינוּ בָּטְחוּ וַתְּפַלְּטֵמוֹ ׃ אֵלֶיךָ זָעֲקוּ וְנִמְלָטוּ בְּךָ בָטְחוּ וְלֹא־בוֹשׁוּ ׃ 6

וְאָנֹכִי תוֹלַעַת וְלֹא־אִישׁ חֶרְפַּת אָדָם וּבְזוּי־עָם ׃ כָּל־רֹאַי יַלְעִגוּ לִי 8 7

יַפְטִירוּ בְשָׂפָה יָנִיעוּ רֹאשׁ ׃ גֹּל אֶל־יְהֹוָה יְפַלְּטֵהוּ יַצִּילֵהוּ כִּי חָפֵץ 9

בּוֹ ׃ כִּי־אַתָּה גֹחִי מִבָּטֶן מַבְטִיחִי עַל־שְׁדֵי אִמִּי ׃ עָלֶיךָ הָשְׁלַכְתִּי 11 י

מֵרָחֶם מִבֶּטֶן אִמִּי אֵלִי אָתָּה ׃ אַל־תִּרְחַק מִמֶּנִּי כִּי־צָרָה קְרוֹבָה כִּי אֵין 12

עוֹזֵר ׃ סְבָבוּנִי פָּרִים רַבִּים אַבִּירֵי בָשָׁן כִּתְּרוּנִי ׃ פָּצוּ עָלַי פִּיהֶם אַרְיֵה 13 14

טֹרֵף וְשֹׁאֵג ׃ כַּמַּיִם נִשְׁפַּכְתִּי וְהִתְפָּרְדוּ כָּל־עַצְמוֹתָי הָיָה לִבִּי כַּדּוֹנָג 15 טו

נָמֵס בְּתוֹךְ מֵעָי ׃ יָבֵשׁ כַּחֶרֶשׂ כֹּחִי וּלְשׁוֹנִי מֻדְבָּק מַלְקוֹחָי וְלַעֲפַר־ 16

מָוֶת תִּשְׁפְּתֵנִי ׃ כִּי־סְבָבוּנִי כְּלָבִים עֲדַת מְרֵעִים הִקִּיפוּנִי כָּאֲרִי יָדַי וְרַגְלָי ׃ 17

אֲסַפֵּר כָּל־עַצְמוֹתָי הֵמָּה יַבִּיטוּ יִרְאוּ־בִי ׃ יְחַלְּקוּ בְגָדַי לָהֶם וְעַל־ 18 19

לְבוּשִׁי יַפִּילוּ גוֹרָל ׃ וְאַתָּה יְהֹוָה אַל־תִּרְחָק אֱיָלוּתִי לְעֶזְרָתִי חוּשָׁה ׃ 20 כ

הַצִּילָה מֵחֶרֶב נַפְשִׁי מִיַּד־כֶּלֶב יְחִידָתִי ׃ הוֹשִׁיעֵנִי מִפִּי אַרְיֵה וּמִקַּרְנֵי 21 22

רֵמִים עֲנִיתָנִי ׃ אֲסַפְּרָה שִׁמְךָ לְאֶחָי בְּתוֹךְ קָהָל אֲהַלְלֶךָּ ׃ יִרְאֵי יְהֹוָה 23

הַלְלוּהוּ כָּל־זֶרַע יַעֲקֹב כַּבְּדוּהוּ וְגוּרוּ מִמֶּנּוּ כָּל־זֶרַע יִשְׂרָאֵל ׃ כִּי לֹא־ 24 כה

בָזָה וְלֹא שִׁקַּץ עֱנוּת עָנִי וְלֹא־הִסְתִּיר פָּנָיו מִמֶּנּוּ וּבְשַׁוְּעוֹ אֵלָיו 26

שָׁמֵעַ ׃ מֵאִתְּךָ תְהִלָּתִי בְּקָהָל רָב נְדָרַי אֲשַׁלֵּם נֶגֶד יְרֵאָיו ׃ יֹאכְלוּ 27

עֲנָוִים וְיִשְׂבָּעוּ יְהַלְלוּ יְהֹוָה דֹּרְשָׁיו יְחִי לְבַבְכֶם לָעַד ׃ יִזְכְּרוּ 28

וְיָשֻׁבוּ אֶל־יְהֹוָה כָּל־אַפְסֵי־אָרֶץ וְיִשְׁתַּחֲווּ לְפָנֶיךָ כָּל־מִשְׁפְּחוֹת גּוֹיִם ׃

כִּי לַיהֹוָה הַמְּלוּכָה וּמֹשֵׁל בַּגּוֹיִם ׃ אָכְלוּ וַיִּשְׁתַּחֲווּ כָּל־דִּשְׁנֵי־אֶרֶץ 29 ל

31 לְפָנָיו יִכְרְעוּ כָּל־יוֹרְדֵי עָפָר וְנַפְשׁוֹ לֹא חִיָּה : זֶרַע יַעַבְדֶנּוּ יְסֻפַּר

32 לַאדֹנָי לַדּוֹר : יָבֹאוּ וְיַגִּידוּ צִדְקָתוֹ לְעַם נוֹלָד כִּי עָשָׂה :

PSALM XLV. מה

2 א לַמְנַצֵּחַ עַל־שֹׁשַׁנִּים לִבְנֵי־קֹרַח מַשְׂכִּיל שִׁיר יְדִידֹת : רָחַשׁ לִבִּי , דָּבָר

3 טוֹב אֹמֵר אָנִי מַעֲשַׂי לְמֶלֶךְ לְשׁוֹנִי : עַם , סוֹפֵר מָהִיר : יָפְיָפִיתָ מִבְּנֵי

4 אָדָם הוּצַק חֵן בְּשְׂפְתוֹתֶיךָ עַל־כֵּן בֵּרַכְךָ אֱלֹהִים לְעוֹלָם : חֲגֹר חַרְבְּךָ

5 עַל־יָרֵךְ גִּבּוֹר הוֹדְךָ וַהֲדָרֶךָ : וַהֲדָרְךָ , צְלַח רְכַב עַל־דְּבַר־אֱמֶת

6 וְעַנְוָה־צֶּדֶק וְתוֹרְךָ נוֹרָאוֹת יְמִינֶךָ : חִצֶּיךָ שְׁנוּנִים עַמִּים תַּחְתֶּיךָ

7 יִפְּלוּ בְּלֵב אוֹיְבֵי הַמֶּלֶךְ : כִּסְאֲךָ אֱלֹהִים עוֹלָם וָעֶד שֵׁבֶט מִישֹׁר שֵׁבֶט

8 מַלְכוּתֶךָ : אָהַבְתָּ צֶּדֶק וַתִּשְׂנָא רֶשַׁע עַל־כֵּן , מְשָׁחֲךָ אֱלֹהִים אֱלֹהֶיךָ

9 שֶׁמֶן שָׂשׂוֹן מֵחֲבֵרֶךָ : מֹר וַאֲהָלוֹת קְצִיעוֹת כָּל־בִּגְדֹתֶיךָ מִן־הֵיכְלֵי

י שֵׁן מִנִּי שִׂמְּחוּךָ : בְּנוֹת מְלָכִים בִּיקְּרוֹתֶיךָ נִצְּבָה שֵׁגַל לִימִינְךָ בְּכֶתֶם

11 אוֹפִיר : שִׁמְעִי־בַת וּרְאִי וְהַטִּי אָזְנֵךְ וְשִׁכְחִי עַמֵּךְ וּבֵית אָבִיךְ :

12,13 וְיִתְאָו הַמֶּלֶךְ יָפְיֵךְ כִּי הוּא אֲדֹנַיִךְ וְהִשְׁתַּחֲוִי־לוֹ : וּבַת־צֹר , בְּמִנְחָה

14 פָּנַיִךְ יְחַלּוּ עֲשִׁירֵי עָם : כָּל־כְּבוּדָּה בַת־מֶלֶךְ פְּנִימָה מִמִּשְׁבְּצוֹת זָהָב

ט לְבוּשָׁהּ : לִרְקָמוֹת תּוּבַל לַמֶּלֶךְ בְּתוּלוֹת אַחֲרֶיהָ רֵעוֹתֶיהָ מוּבָאוֹת

16,17 לָךְ : תּוּבַלְנָה בִּשְׂמָחֹת וָגִיל תְּבֹאֶינָה בְּהֵיכַל מֶלֶךְ : תַּחַת אֲבֹתֶיךָ

18 יִהְיוּ בָנֶיךָ תְּשִׁיתֵמוֹ לְשָׂרִים בְּכָל־הָאָרֶץ : אַזְכִּירָה שִׁמְךָ בְּכָל־דֹּר וָדֹר

עַל־כֵּן עַמִּים יְהוֹדוּךָ לְעֹלָם וָעֶד :

PSALM LXXII. עב

2 א לִשְׁלֹמֹה , אֱלֹהִים מִשְׁפָּטֶיךָ לְמֶלֶךְ תֵּן וְצִדְקָתְךָ לְבֶן־מֶלֶךְ : יָדִין

3 עַמְּךָ בְצֶדֶק וַעֲנִיֶּיךָ בְמִשְׁפָּט : יִשְׂאוּ הָרִים שָׁלוֹם לָעָם וּגְבָעוֹת בִּצְדָקָה :

4 ד יִשְׁפֹּט , עֲנִיֵּי־עָם יוֹשִׁיעַ לִבְנֵי אֶבְיוֹן וִידַכֵּא עוֹשֵׁק : יִירָאוּךָ עִם־שָׁמֶשׁ

6 וְלִפְנֵי יָרֵחַ דּוֹר דּוֹרִים : יֵרֵד כְּמָטָר עַל־גֵּז כִּרְבִיבִים זַרְזִיף אָרֶץ :

7,8 יִפְרַח בְּיָמָיו צַדִּיק וְרֹב שָׁלוֹם עַד־בְּלִי יָרֵחַ : וְיֵרְדְּ מִיָּם עַד־יָם

9 וּמִנָּהָר עַד־אַפְסֵי־אָרֶץ : לְפָנָיו יִכְרְעוּ צִיִּים וְאֹיְבָיו עָפָר יְלַחֵכוּ :

י מַלְכֵי תַרְשִׁישׁ וְאִיִּים מִנְחָה יָשִׁיבוּ מַלְכֵי שְׁבָא וּסְבָא אֶשְׁכָּר יַקְרִיבוּ :

11,12 וְיִשְׁתַּחֲווּ־לוֹ כָל־מְלָכִים כָּל־גּוֹיִם יַעַבְדוּהוּ : כִּי־יַצִּיל אֶבְיוֹן מְשַׁוֵּעַ

13 וְעָנִי וְאֵין־עֹזֵר לוֹ : יָחֹס עַל־דַּל וְאֶבְיוֹן וְנַפְשׁוֹת אֶבְיוֹנִים יוֹשִׁיעַ :

14 ט מִתּוֹךְ וּמֵחָמָס יִגְאַל נַפְשָׁם וְיֵיקַר דָּמָם בְּעֵינָיו : וִיחִי וְיִתֶּן־לוֹ מִזְּהַב

16 שְׁבָא וְיִתְפַּלֵּל בַּעֲדוֹ תָמִיד כָּל־הַיּוֹם יְבָרֲכֶנְהוּ : יְהִי פִסַּת־בַּר , בָּאָרֶץ

17 בֵּרֹאשׁ חָרִים יִרְעָשׁ כַּלְּבָנוֹן פִּרְיוֹ וְיָצִיצוּ מֵעִיר כְּעֵשֶׂב הָאָרֶץ ׃ יְהִי
שְׁמוֹ ׀ לְעוֹלָם לִפְנֵי שֶׁמֶשׁ יָנִין שְׁמוֹ וְיִתְבָּרְכוּ בוֹ כָּל־גּוֹיִם יְאַשְּׁרֻהוּ ׃
18 בָּרוּךְ ׀ יְהֹוָה אֱלֹהִים אֱלֹהֵי יִשְׂרָאֵל עֹשֵׂה נִפְלָאוֹת לְבַדּוֹ ׃ וּבָרוּךְ ׀ שֵׁם
10
כְּבוֹדוֹ לְעוֹלָם וְיִמָּלֵא כְבוֹדוֹ אֶת־כָּל־הָאָרֶץ אָמֵן ׀ וְאָמֵן ׃ כָּלּוּ תְפִלּוֹת ב
דָּוִד בֶּן־יִשָׁי ׃

PSALM CX. קי

א לְדָוִד מִזְמוֹר נְאֻם יְהֹוָה ׀ לַאדֹנִי שֵׁב לִימִינִי עַד־אָשִׁית אֹיְבֶיךָ
2 הֲדֹם לְרַגְלֶיךָ ׃ מַטֵּה עֻזְּךָ יִשְׁלַח יְהֹוָה מִצִּיּוֹן רְדֵה בְּקֶרֶב אֹיְבֶיךָ ׃
3 עַמְּךָ נְדָבֹת בְּיוֹם חֵילֶךָ בְּהַדְרֵי־קֹדֶשׁ מֵרֶחֶם מִשְׁחָר לְךָ טַל יַלְדֻתֶיךָ ׃
4 נִשְׁבַּע יְהֹוָה ׀ וְלֹא יִנָּחֵם אַתָּה־כֹהֵן לְעוֹלָם עַל־דִּבְרָתִי מַלְכִּי־צֶדֶק ׃
5 אֲדֹנָי עַל־יְמִינְךָ מָחַץ בְּיוֹם־אַפּוֹ מְלָכִים ׃ יָדִין בַּגּוֹיִם מָלֵא גְוִיּוֹת ה 6
7 מָחַץ רֹאשׁ עַל־אֶרֶץ רַבָּה ׃ מִנַּחַל בַּדֶּרֶךְ יִשְׁתֶּה עַל־כֵּן יָרִים רֹאשׁ ׃

XIV. THE EXHORTATION OF WISDOM, *Proverbs* 8.

2 א הֲלֹא־חָכְמָה תִקְרָא וּתְבוּנָה תִּתֵּן קוֹלָהּ ׃ בְּרֹאשׁ־מְרֹמִים עֲלֵי־דָרֶךְ בֵּית
4 3 נְתִיבוֹת נִצָּבָה ׃ לְיַד־שְׁעָרִים לְפִי־קָרֶת מְבוֹא פְתָחִים תָּרֹנָּה ׃ אֲלֵיכֶם
ה אִישִׁים אֶקְרָא וְקוֹלִי אֶל־בְּנֵי אָדָם ׃ הָבִינוּ פְתָאִים עָרְמָה וּכְסִילִים
7 6 הָבִינוּ לֵב ׃ שִׁמְעוּ כִּי־נְגִידִים אֲדַבֵּר וּמִפְתַּח שְׂפָתַי מֵישָׁרִים ׃ כִּי־אֱמֶת
8 יֶהְגֶּה חִכִּי וְתוֹעֲבַת שְׂפָתַי רֶשַׁע ׃ בְּצֶדֶק כָּל־אִמְרֵי־פִי אֵין בָּהֶם נִפְתָּל
9 וְעִקֵּשׁ ׃ כֻּלָּם נְכֹחִים לַמֵּבִין וִישָׁרִים לְמֹצְאֵי דָעַת ׃ קְחוּ־מוּסָרִי וְאַל־
11 כֶּסֶף וְדַעַת מֵחָרוּץ נִבְחָר ׃ כִּי־טוֹבָה חָכְמָה מִפְּנִינִים וְכָל־חֲפָצִים לֹא
12 13 יִשְׁווּ־בָהּ ׃ אֲנִי חָכְמָה שָׁכַנְתִּי עָרְמָה וְדַעַת מְזִמּוֹת אֶמְצָא ׃ יִרְאַת
14 יְהֹוָה שְׂנֹאת רָע גֵּאָה וְגָאוֹן ׀ וְדֶרֶךְ רָע וּפִי תַהְפֻּכוֹת שָׂנֵאתִי ׃ לִי־
 טו עֵצָה וְתוּשִׁיָּה אֲנִי בִינָה לִי גְבוּרָה ׃ בִּי מְלָכִים יִמְלֹכוּ וְרֹזְנִים
16
17 יְחֹקְקוּ צֶדֶק ׃ בִּי שָׂרִים יָשֹׂרוּ וּנְדִיבִים כָּל־שֹׁפְטֵי אָרֶץ ׃ אֲנִי אֹהֲבֶיהָ
18 אֵהָב וּמְשַׁחֲרַי יִמְצָאֻנְנִי ׃ עֹשֶׁר־וְכָבוֹד אִתִּי הוֹן עָתֵק וּצְדָקָה ׃ טוֹב
19
פִּרְיִי מֵחָרוּץ וּמִפָּז וּתְבוּאָתִי מִכֶּסֶף נִבְחָר ׃ בְּאֹרַח־צְדָקָה אֲהַלֵּךְ בְּתוֹךְ
21 נְתִיבוֹת מִשְׁפָּט ׃ לְהַנְחִיל אֹהֲבַי יֵשׁ וְאֹצְרֹתֵיהֶם אֲמַלֵּא ׃ יָחֹד
22
23 יְהֹוָה קָנָנִי רֵאשִׁית דַּרְכּוֹ קֶדֶם מִפְעָלָיו מֵאָז ׃ מֵעוֹלָם נִסַּכְתִּי מֵרֹאשׁ מִקַּדְמֵי
24 כה אָרֶץ ׃ בְּאֵין־תְּהֹמוֹת חוֹלָלְתִּי בְּאֵין מַעְיָנוֹת נִכְבַּדֵּי־מָיִם ׃ בְּטֶרֶם הָרִים
26 הָטְבָּעוּ לִפְנֵי גְבָעוֹת חוֹלָלְתִּי ׃ עַד־לֹא עָשָׂה אֶרֶץ וְחוּצוֹת וְרֹאשׁ

---

27 עַפְרוֹת תֵּבֵל ׃ בַּהֲכִינוֹ שָׁמַיִם שָׁם אָנִי בְּחֻקּוֹ חוּג עַל־פְּנֵי תְהוֹם ׃

28 בְּאַמְּצוֹ שְׁחָקִים מִמָּעַל בַּעֲזוֹז עִינוֹת תְּהוֹם ׃ בְּשׂוּמוֹ לַיָּם ׀ חֻקּוֹ וּמַיִם
29 לֹא יַעַבְרוּ־פִיו בְּחוּקוֹ מוֹסְדֵי אָרֶץ ׃ וָאֶהְיֶה אֶצְלוֹ אָמוֹן וָאֶהְיֶה

30 שַׁעֲשֻׁעִים יוֹם ׀ יוֹם מְשַׂחֶקֶת לְפָנָיו בְּכָל־עֵת ׃ מְשַׂחֶקֶת בְּתֵבֵל אַרְצוֹ
31 וְשַׁעֲשֻׁעַי אֶת־בְּנֵי אָדָם ׃ וְעַתָּה בָנִים שִׁמְעוּ־לִי וְאַשְׁרֵי דְּרָכַי
32 יִשְׁמֹרוּ ׃ שִׁמְעוּ מוּסָר וַחֲכָמוּ וְאַל־תִּפְרָעוּ ׃ אַשְׁרֵי אָדָם שֹׁמֵעַ לִי
33
34 לִשְׁקֹד עַל־דַּלְתֹתַי יוֹם ׀ יוֹם לִשְׁמֹר מְזוּזֹת פְּתָחָי ׃ כִּי מֹצְאִי מָצָא
36 חַיִּים וַיָּפֶק רָצוֹן מֵיְהוָה ׃ וְחֹטְאִי חֹמֵס נַפְשׁוֹ כָּל־מְשַׂנְאַי אָהֲבוּ מָוֶת ׃

XV. JOB'S COMPLAINT AND TRIUMPH, *Job* 3. 19.

CHAPTER III. ג

2 אַחֲרֵי־כֵן פָּתַח אִיּוֹב אֶת־פִּיהוּ וַיְקַלֵּל אֶת־יוֹמוֹ ׃ וַיַּעַן אִיּוֹב
3 וַיֹּאמַר ׃ יֹאבַד יוֹם אִוָּלֶד בּוֹ וְהַלַּיְלָה אָמַר הֹרָה גָבֶר ׃ הַיּוֹם הַהוּא
4 יְהִי חֹשֶׁךְ אַל־יִדְרְשֵׁהוּ אֱלוֹהַּ מִמָּעַל וְאַל־תּוֹפַע עָלָיו נְהָרָה ׃ יִגְאָלֻהוּ
5 חֹשֶׁךְ וְצַלְמָוֶת תִּשְׁכָּן־עָלָיו עֲנָנָה יְבַעֲתֻהוּ כִּמְרִירֵי יוֹם ׃ הַלַּיְלָה הַהוּא
7 יִקָּחֵהוּ אֹפֶל אַל־יִחַדְּ בִּימֵי שָׁנָה בְּמִסְפַּר יְרָחִים אַל־יָבֹא ׃ הִנֵּה
8 הַלַּיְלָה הַהִיא יְהִי גַלְמוּד אַל־תָּבֹא רְנָנָה בוֹ ׃ יִקְּבֻהוּ אֹרְרֵי־יוֹם
9 הָעֲתִידִים עֹרֵר לִוְיָתָן ׃ יֶחְשְׁכוּ כּוֹכְבֵי נִשְׁפּוֹ יְקַו־לְאוֹר וָאַיִן וְאַל־
10 יִרְאֶה בְּעַפְעַפֵּי־שָׁחַר ׃ כִּי לֹא סָגַר דַּלְתֵי בִטְנִי וַיַּסְתֵּר עָמָל מֵעֵינָי ׃

11 לָמָּה לֹא מֵרֶחֶם אָמוּת מִבֶּטֶן יָצָאתִי וְאֶגְוָע ׃ מַדּוּעַ קִדְּמוּנִי בִרְכָּיִם
12
13 וּמַה־שָּׁדַיִם כִּי אִינָק ׃ כִּי־עַתָּה שָׁכַבְתִּי וְאֶשְׁקוֹט יָשַׁנְתִּי אָז ׀ יָנוּחַ לִי ׃
14 עִם־מְלָכִים וְיֹעֲצֵי אָרֶץ הַבֹּנִים חֳרָבוֹת לָמוֹ ׃ אוֹ עִם־שָׂרִים זָהָב לָהֶם
16 הַמְמַלְאִים בָּתֵּיהֶם כָּסֶף ׃ אוֹ כְנֵפֶל טָמוּן לֹא אֶהְיֶה כְּעֹלְלִים לֹא־רָאוּ
17 אוֹר ׃ שָׁם רְשָׁעִים חָדְלוּ רֹגֶז וְשָׁם יָנוּחוּ יְגִיעֵי כֹחַ ׃ יַחַד אֲסִירִים
18
19 שַׁאֲנַנּוּ לֹא שָׁמְעוּ קוֹל נֹגֵשׂ ׃ קָטֹן וְגָדוֹל שָׁם הוּא וְעֶבֶד חָפְשִׁי מֵאֲדֹנָיו ׃
20 לָמָּה יִתֵּן לְעָמֵל אוֹר וְחַיִּים לְמָרֵי נָפֶשׁ ׃ הַמְחַכִּים לַמָּוֶת וְאֵינֶנּוּ
21
22 וַיַּחְפְּרֻהוּ מִמַּטְמוֹנִים ׃ הַשְּׂמֵחִים אֱלֵי־גִיל יָשִׂישׂוּ כִּי יִמְצְאוּ־קָבֶר ׃
23 לְגֶבֶר אֲשֶׁר־דַּרְכּוֹ נִסְתָּרָה וַיָּסֶךְ אֱלוֹהַּ בַּעֲדוֹ ׃ כִּי־לִפְנֵי לַחְמִי אַנְחָתִי
24
25 תָבֹא וַיִּתְּכוּ כַמַּיִם שַׁאֲגֹתָי ׃ כִּי פַחַד פָּחַדְתִּי וַיֶּאֱתָיֵנִי וַאֲשֶׁר יָגֹרְתִּי
26 יָבֹא לִי ׃ לֹא שָׁלַוְתִּי וְלֹא־שָׁקַטְתִּי וְלֹא־נָחְתִּי וַיָּבֹא רֹגֶז ׃

'פתח בא v. 9.   יתיר ו v. 35.

CHAPTER XIX. יט

2 א : וַיַּעַן אִיּוֹב וַיֹּאמַר : עַד־אָנָה תּוֹגְיוּן נַפְשִׁי וּתְדַכְּאוּנַנִי בְמִלִּים

4 3 : זֶה עֶשֶׂר פְּעָמִים תַּכְלִימוּנִי לֹא־תֵבֹשׁוּ תַּהְכְּרוּ־לִי : וְאַף־אָמְנָם שָׁגִיתִי

ה : אִתִּי תָלִין מְשׁוּגָתִי : אִם־אָמְנָם עָלַי תַּגְדִּילוּ וְתוֹכִיחוּ עָלַי חֶרְפָּתִי

7 6 וְלֹא : דְּעוּ־אֵפוֹ כִּי־אֱלוֹהַּ עִוְּתָנִי וּמְצוּדוֹ עָלַי הִקִּיף : הֵן אֶצְעַק חָמָס

8 אֶעֱנֶה אֲשַׁוַּע וְאֵין מִשְׁפָּט : אָרְחִי גָדַר וְלֹא אֶעֱבוֹר וְעַל־נְתִיבוֹתַי

9 ו : חֹשֶׁךְ יָשִׂים : כְּבוֹדִי מֵעָלַי הִפְשִׁיט וַיָּסַר עֲטֶרֶת רֹאשִׁי : יִתְּצֵנִי סָבִיב

11 : וָאֵלַךְ וַיַּסַּע כָּעֵץ תִּקְוָתִי : וַיַּחַר עָלַי אַפּוֹ וַיַּחְשְׁבֵנִי לוֹ כְצָרָיו

13 12 : יַחַד יָבֹאוּ גְדוּדָיו וַיָּסֹלּוּ עָלַי דַּרְכָּם וַיַּחֲנוּ סָבִיב לְאָהֳלִי : אַחַי

14 : מֵעָלַי הִרְחִיק וְיֹדְעַי אַךְ־זָרוּ מִמֶּנִּי : חָדְלוּ קְרוֹבַי וּמְיֻדָּעַי שְׁכֵחוּנִי

טו 16 : גָּרֵי בֵיתִי וְאַמְהֹתַי לְזָר תַּחְשְׁבֻנִי נָכְרִי הָיִיתִי בְעֵינֵיהֶם : לְעַבְדִּי

17 : קָרָאתִי וְלֹא יַעֲנֶה בְּמוֹ־פִי אֶתְחַנֶּן־לוֹ : רוּחִי זָרָה לְאִשְׁתִּי וְחַנּוֹתִי

18 : לִבְנֵי בִטְנִי : גַּם־עֲוִילִים מָאֲסוּ בִי אָקוּמָה וַיְדַבְּרוּ־בִי : תִּעֲבוּנִי כָּל־

19 ו : מְתֵי סוֹדִי וְזֶה־אָהַבְתִּי נֶהְפְּכוּ־בִי : בְּעוֹרִי וּבִבְשָׂרִי דָּבְקָה עַצְמִי

21 : וָאֶתְמַלְּטָה בְּעוֹר שִׁנָּי : חָנֻּנִי חָנֻּנִי אַתֶּם רֵעָי כִּי יַד־אֱלוֹהַּ נָגְעָה

23 22 : בִּי : לָמָּה תִּרְדְּפֻנִי כְמוֹ־אֵל וּמִבְּשָׂרִי לֹא תִשְׂבָּעוּ : מִי־יִתֵּן אֵפוֹ

24 : וְיִכָּתְבוּן מִלָּי מִי־יִתֵּן בַּסֵּפֶר וְיֻחָקוּ : בְּעֵט־בַּרְזֶל וְעֹפָרֶת לָעַד בַּצּוּר

כה 26 : יֵחָצְבוּן : וַאֲנִי יָדַעְתִּי גֹּאֲלִי חָי וְאַחֲרוֹן עַל־עָפָר יָקוּם : וְאַחַר עוֹרִי

27 : נִקְּפוּ־זֹאת וּמִבְּשָׂרִי אֶחֱזֶה אֱלוֹהַּ : אֲשֶׁר אֲנִי אֶחֱזֶה־לִּי וְעֵינַי רָאוּ

28 : וְלֹא־זָר כָּלוּ כִלְיֹתַי בְּחֵקִי : כִּי תֹאמְרוּ מַה־נִּרְדָּף־לוֹ וְשֹׁרֶשׁ דָּבָר

29 : נִמְצָא־בִי : גּוּרוּ לָכֶם מִפְּנֵי־חֶרֶב כִּי־חֵמָה עֲוֹנוֹת חָרֶב לְמַעַן תֵּדְעוּן

שַׁדִּין :

XVI. The Love of the King and his Bride.

The Song of Solomon, 1, 2.

CHAPTER I. א

2 א : שִׁיר הַשִּׁירִים אֲשֶׁר לִשְׁלֹמֹה : יִשָּׁקֵנִי מִנְּשִׁיקוֹת פִּיהוּ כִּי־טוֹבִים דֹּדֶיךָ

3 : מִיָּיִן : לְרֵיחַ שְׁמָנֶיךָ טוֹבִים שֶׁמֶן תּוּרַק שְׁמֶךָ עַל־כֵּן עֲלָמוֹת אֲהֵבוּךָ

4 : מָשְׁכֵנִי אַחֲרֶיךָ נָּרוּצָה הֱבִיאַנִי הַמֶּלֶךְ חֲדָרָיו נָגִילָה וְנִשְׂמְחָה בָּךְ

ה : נַזְכִּירָה דֹדֶיךָ מִיַּיִן מֵישָׁרִים אֲהֵבוּךָ : שְׁחוֹרָה אֲנִי וְנָאוָה בְּנוֹת

6 : יְרוּשָׁלַ͏ִם כְּאָהֳלֵי קֵדָר כִּירִיעוֹת שְׁלֹמֹה : אַל־תִּרְאֻנִי שֶׁאֲנִי שְׁחַרְחֹרֶת

שֶׁשֱּׁזָפַתְנִי הַשָּׁמֶשׁ בְּנֵי אִמִּי נִחֲרוּ־בִי שָׂמֻנִי נֹטֵרָה אֶת־הַכְּרָמִים כַּרְמִי

7 שֶׁלִּי לֹא נְטָרְתִּי : הַגִּידָה שֶׁאָהֲבָה נַפְשִׁי אֵיכָה תִרְעֶה אֵיכָה
8 תַּרְבִּיץ בַּצָּהֳרַיִם שַׁלָּמָה אֶהְיֶה כְּעֹטְיָה עַל עֶדְרֵי חֲבֵרֶיךָ : אִם־לֹא
תֵדְעִי לָךְ הַיָּפָה בַּנָּשִׁים צְאִי־לָךְ בְּעִקְבֵי הַצֹּאן וּרְעִי אֶת־גְּדִיֹּתַיִךְ עַל
9 מִשְׁכְּנוֹת הָרֹעִים : לְסֻסָתִי בְּרִכְבֵי פַרְעֹה דִּמִּיתִיךְ רַעְיָתִי : נָאווּ לְחָיַיִךְ
11 בַּתֹּרִים צַוָּארֵךְ בַּחֲרוּזִים : תּוֹרֵי זָהָב נַעֲשֶׂה־לָּךְ עִם נְקֻדּוֹת הַכָּסֶף :
13 / 12 עַד־שֶׁהַמֶּלֶךְ בִּמְסִבּוֹ נִרְדִּי נָתַן רֵיחוֹ : צְרוֹר הַמֹּר ׀ דּוֹדִי לִי בֵּין שָׁדַי
14 יָלִין : אֶשְׁכֹּל הַכֹּפֶר ׀ דּוֹדִי לִי בְּכַרְמֵי עֵין גֶּדִי : הִנָּךְ יָפָה רַעְיָתִי
16 / ס׳ הִנָּךְ יָפָה עֵינַיִךְ יוֹנִים : הִנְּךָ יָפֶה דוֹדִי אַף נָעִים אַף־עַרְשֵׂנוּ רַעֲנָנָה :
17 קֹרוֹת בָּתֵּינוּ אֲרָזִים רַחִיטֵנוּ בְּרוֹתִים :

CHAPTER II. ב

2 / א אֲנִי חֲבַצֶּלֶת הַשָּׁרוֹן שׁוֹשַׁנַּת הָעֲמָקִים : כְּשׁוֹשַׁנָּה בֵּין הַחוֹחִים כֵּן רַעְיָתִי
3 בֵּין הַבָּנוֹת : כְּתַפּוּחַ בַּעֲצֵי הַיַּעַר כֵּן דּוֹדִי בֵּין הַבָּנִים בְּצִלּוֹ חִמַּדְתִּי
4 וְיָשַׁבְתִּי וּפִרְיוֹ מָתוֹק לְחִכִּי : הֱבִיאַנִי אֶל־בֵּית הַיָּיִן וְדִגְלוֹ עָלַי
5 / ה אַהֲבָה : סַמְּכוּנִי בָּאֲשִׁישׁוֹת רַפְּדוּנִי בַּתַּפּוּחִים כִּי־חוֹלַת אַהֲבָה אָנִי :
7 / 6 שְׂמֹאלוֹ תַּחַת לְרֹאשִׁי וִימִינוֹ תְּחַבְּקֵנִי : הִשְׁבַּעְתִּי אֶתְכֶם בְּנוֹת
יְרוּשָׁלַ͏ִם בִּצְבָאוֹת אוֹ בְּאַיְלוֹת הַשָּׂדֶה אִם־תָּעִירוּ ׀ וְאִם־תְּעוֹרְרוּ אֶת־
8 הָאַהֲבָה עַד שֶׁתֶּחְפָּץ : קוֹל דּוֹדִי הִנֵּה־זֶה בָּא מְדַלֵּג עַל־הֶהָרִים
9 מְקַפֵּץ עַל־הַגְּבָעוֹת : דּוֹמֶה דוֹדִי לִצְבִי אוֹ לְעֹפֶר הָאַיָּלִים הִנֵּה־זֶה
10 / י עוֹמֵד אַחַר כָּתְלֵנוּ מַשְׁגִּיחַ מִן־הַחַלֹּנוֹת מֵצִיץ מִן־הַחֲרַכִּים : עָנָה
11 דוֹדִי וְאָמַר לִי קוּמִי לָךְ רַעְיָתִי יָפָתִי וּלְכִי־לָךְ : כִּי־הִנֵּה הַסְּתָו עָבָר
12 הַגֶּשֶׁם חָלַף הָלַךְ לוֹ : הַנִּצָּנִים נִרְאוּ בָאָרֶץ עֵת הַזָּמִיר הִגִּיעַ וְקוֹל
13 הַתּוֹר נִשְׁמַע בְּאַרְצֵנוּ : הַתְּאֵנָה חָנְטָה פַגֶּיהָ וְהַגְּפָנִים סְמָדַר נָתְנוּ
14 רֵיחַ קוּמִי לָכְי רַעְיָתִי יָפָתִי וּלְכִי־לָךְ : יוֹנָתִי בְּחַגְוֵי הַסֶּלַע בְּסֵתֶר
הַמַּדְרֵגָה הַרְאִינִי אֶת־מַרְאַיִךְ הַשְׁמִיעִנִי אֶת־קוֹלֵךְ כִּי־קוֹלֵךְ עָרֵב
15 / ס׳ וּמַרְאֵיךְ נָאוֶה : אֶחֱזוּ־לָנוּ שֻׁעָלִים שֻׁעָלִים קְטַנִּים מְחַבְּלִים כְּרָמִים
16 וּכְרָמֵינוּ סְמָדַר : דּוֹדִי לִי וַאֲנִי לוֹ הָרֹעֶה בַּשּׁוֹשַׁנִּים : עַד שֶׁיָּפוּחַ
17 הַיּוֹם וְנָסוּ הַצְּלָלִים סֹב דְּמֵה־לְךָ דוֹדִי לִצְבִי אוֹ לְעֹפֶר הָאַיָּלִים
עַל־הָרֵי בָתֶר :

VOCABULARY.

The words in Gen. i-iii., proper names excepted, are here arranged in the order of their first occurrence. An alphabetical index follows, by the aid of which the student can readily find the place of any word in the Vocabulary. The verbs in these chapters, together with a few added at the end of the list, are also employed in the preliminary exercises, pp. 3–8.

The abbreviations readily explain themselves, the capitals being the initials of the verbal species, and the small letters of the parts of speech, genders, or numbers.

GENESIS. CHAP. I.

1. בְּ prep. *in, into.*

רֵאשִׁית n. f. *beginning.*

בָּרָא v. K. *to create.* N. *to be created.*

אֱלֹהִים n. m. *God.*

אֵת sign of the definite object.

הַ art. *the.*

שָׁמַיִם n. m. pl. *heaven.*

וְ conj. *and.*

אֶרֶץ n. m. f. (וֹת) *earth, land.*

2 הָיָה v. K. *to be.* N. *to become.*

תֹּהוּ n. m. *desolateness.*

בֹּהוּ n. m. *emptiness.*

חֹשֶׁךְ n. m. *darkness.*

עַל prep. *over, upon.*

פָּנֶה n. m. *face.*

תְּהוֹם n. m. f. (וֹת) *ocean, the deep.*

רוּחַ n. m. f. (וֹת) *breath, wind, spirit.*

רָחַף v. P. *to brood, hover over.*

מַיִם n. m. pl. *water.*

3. אָמַר v. K. *to say.* N. *to be said.* H. *to cause to say.* Hith. *to talk of one's self.*

אוֹר n. m. *light.*

4. רָאָה v. K. *to see.* N. Pu. *to be seen.* H. *to cause to see, show.* Ho. *to be shown.* Hith. *to look at one another.*

כִּי conj. *that, because, for.*

טוֹב adj. *good.*

בָּדַל v. H. *to separate, divide.* N. *to be separated.*

בֵּין prep. *between.*

5. קָרָא v. K. *to call.* N. Pu. *to be called.*

לְ prep. *to.*

יוֹם n. m. (יָמִים) *day.*

לַיִל n. m. (וֹת) *night.*

עֶרֶב n. m. f. (וֹת) *evening.*

בֹּקֶר n. m. *morning.*

אֶחָד num. *one.*

6. רָקִיעַ n. m. *firmament.*

תָּוֶךְ n. m. *midst.*

7. עָשָׂה v. K. *to do, make, pro-duce.* N. Pu. *to be done, made.*

אֲשֶׁר pr. *who, which;* conj. *that, because.*

מִן prep. *from.*

תַּחַת prep. *under, instead of.*

כֵּן adv. *so.*

8. שֵׁנִי num. *second.*

9. קָוָה v. N. *to be gathered to-gether.*

אֶל־ prep. *to, unto.*

מָקוֹם n. m. f. (וֹת) *place.*

יַבָּשָׁה adj. f. *dry* land.

10. מִקְוֶה n. m. *gathering together.*

יָם n. m. (יַמִּים) *sea.*

11. דָּשָׁא v. K. *to spring up,* said of grass. II. *to cause to spring up, bring forth* grass.

דֶּשֶׁא n. m. *grass.*

עֵשֶׂב n. m. (וֹת) *herb.*

זָרַע v. K. *to sow.* N. Pu. *to be sown.* II. *to produce seed.*

זֶרַע n. m. *seed.*

עֵץ n. m. *tree.*

פְּרִי n. m. *fruit.*

מִין n. m. *species, kind.*

12. יָצָא v. K. *to go forth.* II. *to cause to go forth, bring forth.* IIo. *to be brought forth.*

13. שְׁלִישִׁי num. *third.*

14. מָאוֹר n. m. (יִם & וֹת) *lumi-nary.*

אוֹת n. m. f. (וֹת) *sign.*

מוֹעֵד n. m. (יִם & וֹת) *season*

שָׁנָה n. f. (יִם & וֹת) *year.*

15. אוֹר v. K. N. *to shine.* H. *to cause to shine, give light.*

16. שְׁנַיִם num. *two.*

גָּדוֹל adj. *great.*

מֶמְשָׁלָה n. f. *dominion, rule.*

קָטֹן, קָטָן (קְטַנָּה) adj. *little, small.*

כּוֹכָב n. m. *star.*

17. נָתַן v. K. *to give, put.* N. Ho. *to be given.*

18. מָשַׁל v. K. *to rule.* H. *to cause to rule.*

19. רְבִיעִי num. *fourth.*

20. שָׁרַץ v. K. *to creep, teem with.*

שֶׁרֶץ n. m. *reptile.*

נֶפֶשׁ n. m. f. (יִם & וֹת) *soul.*

חַיָּה n. f. *life, living thing, beast.*

עוֹף n. m. *fowl, birds.*

עוּף v. K. P. *to fly.* Hith. *to fly away.*

21. תַּנִּין n. m. *sea-monster.*

כֹּל n. m. (כֻּלּוֹ) *all, whole.*

רָמַשׂ v. K. *to creep.*

כָּנָף n. f. *wing.*

22. בָּרַךְ v. K. P. *to bless.* N. Pu. *to be blessed.* H. *to cause to kneel.* Hith. *to bless one's self.*

פָּרָה v. K. *to be fruitful.* H. *to make fruitful.*

רָבָה v. K. *to be many, multi-ply,* intrans. P. H. *to make many, multiply,* trans.

מָלֵא v. K. *to fill* or *be full.* P. *to fill.* N. Pu. *to be filled.* Hith. *to complete each other.*

23. חֲמִישִׁי num. *fifth.*

24. בְּהֵמָה n. f. *beast, cattle.*

רֶמֶשׂ n. m. *reptile.*

25. אֲדָמָה n. f. *ground.*

26. אָדָם n. m. *man, Adam.*

צֶלֶם n. m. *image.*

דְּמוּת n. f. *likeness.*

רָדָה v. K. *to rule, have dominion.*

דָּגָה n. f. *fish.*

27. זָכָר n. m. *male.*

נְקֵבָה n. f. *female.*

28. כָּבַשׁ v. K. P. *to subdue.* N. *to be subdued.*

29. הִנֵּה , הֵן int. *lo! behold!*

אָכְלָה n. f. *food.*

30. יֶרֶק n. m. *greenness.*

31. מְאֹד adv. *mightily, very.*

שִׁשִּׁי num. *sixth.*

CHAPTER II.

1. כָּלָה v. K. *to come to an end.* P. *to finish.* Pu. *to be finished.*

צָבָא n. m. (ות & יִם) *host.*

2. שְׁבִיעִי num. *seventh.*

מְלָאכָה n. f. *work.*

שָׁבַת v. K. (fut. ō & a) *to rest.* H. *to cause to rest.* N. *to be caused to rest.*

3. קָדַשׁ v. K. (pret. ĕ in pause, fut. a) *to be holy.* P. H. *to make holy, sanctify.* N. Pu. *to be sanctified.* Hith. *to sanctify one's self.*

4. זֶה m. זֹאת f. אֵלֶּה pl. *this, these.*

תּוֹלֵדָה n. f. *generation.*

יְהוָֹה n. m. *Jehovah.*

5. שִׂיחַ n. m. *bush, shrub.*

שָׂדֶה n. m. (יִם . & ות) *field.*

טֶרֶם adv. *not yet, before.*

צָמַח v. K. P. *to sprout, shoot forth.* H. *to cause to sprout.*

לֹא adv. *not.*

מָטָר v. H. *to cause to rain.* N. *to be rained upon.*

אַיִן *nothing, there is not.*

עָבַד v. K. *to serve, work, till.* N. Pu. *to be served.* H. *to cause to serve.* Ho. *to be caused to serve.*

6. אֵד n. m. *mist, vapor.*

עָלָה v. K. *to go up.* H. *to cause to go up, bring up.* N. Ho. *to be brought up.* Hith. *to lift one's self up.*

שָׁקָה v. H. *to cause to drink, to water.* Pu. *to be watered.*

7. יָצַר v. K. (fut. וַיִּיצֶר) *to form.* N. Pu. Ho. *to be formed.*

עָפָר n. m. (ות) *dust.*

נָפַח v. K. H. *to breathe, blow.* Pu. *to be blown.*

אַף n. m. (אַפַּיִם) *nostril.*

נְשָׁמָה n. f. *breath.*

חַיִּים n. m. pl. *life.*

8. נָטַע v. K. *to plant.* N. *to be planted.*

גַּן n. m. f. (גַּנִּים) *garden.*

קֶדֶם n. m. *east.*

שׂוּם or שִׂים v. K. II. *to place.*
Ho. *to be placed.*

שָׁם adv. *there.*

9. חָמַד v. K. P. *to desire.* N. *to be desired.*

מַרְאֶה n. m. *sight, appearance.*

מַאֲכָל n. m. *food.*

יָדַע v. K. *to know.* N. *to be known.* II. *to cause to know, to make known.* Ho. *to be made known.* Hith. *to make one's self known.*

רַע adj. (רָעָה) *evil.*

10. נָהָר n. m. (וֹת & יִם) *river.*

פָּרַד v. K. P. II. *to separate, part.* N. Pu. *to be parted.* Hith. *to separate one's self.*

אַרְבָּעָה num. *four.*

רֹאשׁ n. m. (רָאשִׁים) *head, source.*

11. שֵׁם n. m. (וֹת) *name.*

הוּא m. הִיא, f. *he, she, that.*

סָבַב v. K. N. P. *to turn, surround.* II. *to cause to turn or surround.* Ho. *to be caused to turn.*

זָהָב n. m. *gold.*

12. בְּדֹלַח n. *bdellium.*

אֶבֶן n. m. f. *stone.*

שֹׁהַם n. m. *onyx.*

14. חָלַךְ or יָלַךְ § 151. 1. v. K. P. *to go.* II. *to cause to go.* Hith. *to go for one's self, walk about.*

קִדְמָה n. f. *east.*

15. לָקַח v. K. *to take.* N. Pu. Ho *to be taken.*

נוּחַ v. K. *to rest.* II. *to cause to rest, put, place.* Ho. *to be caused to rest.*

שָׁמַר v. K. *to keep.* N. Hith. *to keep one's self, take heed.*

16. צָוָה v. P. *to command.* Pu. *to be commanded.*

אָכַל v. K. *to eat, devour.* N. Pu. *to be eaten.* II. *to cause to eat.*

17. מוּת v. K. *to die.* P. H. *to cause to die, kill.* Ho. *to be killed, put to death.*

18. בַּד n. m. (בַּדִּים) *separation.*

עֵזֶר n. m. *help.*

כְּ prep. *according to, as.*

נֶגֶד prep. *before, over against.*

19. בּוֹא v. K. (fut. יָבוֹא) *to come.* II. *to cause to come, bring.* Ho. *to be brought.*

מַה pr. *what? whatever.*

20. מָצָא v. K. *to find.* N. *to be found.* II. *to cause to find.*

21. נָפַל v. K. *to fall.* II. *to cause to fall, throw down.* Hith. *to throw one's self down.*

תַּרְדֵּמָה n. f. *deep sleep.*

יָשֵׁן v. K. (fut. יִישַׁן) *to sleep* P. *to cause to sleep.* N. *to be old;* applied to grain which has long *slept* in its depository.

צֵלָע n. f. (con. צֶלַע, יִם & וֹת) *side, rib.*

סָגַר v. K. P. *to shut up, close.*
N. Pu. *to be shut up.* H. *to cause to shut up.*

בָּשָׂר n. m. *flesh.*

22. בָּנָה v. K. *to build.* N. *to be built.*

אִשָּׁה n. f. (con. אֵשֶׁת, pl. נָשִׁים) *woman, wife.*

23. פַּעַם n. m. f. (יִם & וֹת) *time.*

עֶצֶם n. m. f. (יִם & וֹת) *bone.*

אִישׁ n. m. (אֲנָשִׁים) *man, husband.*

24. עָזַב v. K. *to leave, forsake.* N. Pu. *to be forsaken.*

אָב n. m. (con. אֲבִי, pl. אָבוֹת) *father.*

אֵם n. f. (אִמּוֹת) *mother.*

דָּבַק v. K. (pret. ê in pause, fut. a) *to cleave, adhere.* H. *to cause to cleave.* Ho. *to be caused to cleave.*

25. עָרוֹם adj. (עֲרֻמָּה) *naked.*

בּוֹשׁ v. K. (fut. יֵבוֹשׁ), Hith. *to be ashamed.* H. *to make ashamed.*

CHAPTER III.

1. נָחָשׁ n. m. *serpent.*

עָרוּם adj. *cunning, subtle.*

אַף conj. *also, even.*

3. נָגַע v. K. *to touch.* P. *to touch with violence, smite.* N. Pu. *to be smitten.* H. *to cause to touch.*

פֶּן conj. *lest, that not.*

5. פָּקַח v. K. *to open.* N. *to be opened.*

עַיִן § 208. 3. c. n. f. *eye.*

6. תַּאֲוָה n. f. *desire.*

שָׂכַל v. K. *to be wise.* P. *to act wisely.* H. *to make wise, act wisely.*

גַּם conj. *also.*

עִם prep. *with.*

7. עֵירֹם n. m. *nakedness.*

תָּפַר v. K. P. *to sew.*

עָלֶה n. m. *leaf.*

תְּאֵנָה n. f. (יִם) *figtree.*

חֲגוֹרָה n. f. *apron.*

8. שָׁמַע v. K. *to hear.* N. *to be heard.* P. II. *to cause to hear.*

קוֹל n. m. (וֹת) *voice, sound.*

חָבָא v. H. *to hide.* Pu. Ho. *to be hid.* N. Hith. *to hide one's self.*

9. אֵי adv. *where?*

10. יָרֵא v. K. *to fear.* N. *to be feared.* P. *to cause to fear, terrify.*

אָנֹכִי pron. *I.*

11. מִי pron. *who? whoever.*

נָגַד v. H. *to tell.* Ho. *to be told.*

אַתָּה pron. *thou.*

הֲ sign of interrogation.

בִּלְתִּי adv. *not.*

13. נָשָׁא v. H. *to deceive.* N. *to be deceived.*

14. אָרַר v. K. P. *to curse.* N. Ho. *to be cursed.*

גָּחוֹן n. m. *belly.*

15. אֵיבָה n. f. *enmity.*

שִׁית v. K. *to put.* Ho. *to be put.*

שׁוּף v. K. *to bruise, crush.*

עָקֵב n. m. (con. עֲקֵב, ים, & ות) *heel.*

16. עִצָּבוֹן n. m. *pain, sorrow.*

הֵרָיוֹן n. m. *conception.*

עֶצֶב n. m. *pain, sorrow.*

יָלַד v. K. *to bear.* N. Pu. Ho. *to be born.* H. *to cause to be born.* Hith. *to represent one's self as born,* i. e. *have one's name recorded in genealogical lists.*

בֵּן n. m. (בָּנִים) *son.*

תְּשׁוּקָה n. f. *desire.*

17. בַּעֲבוּר prep. *on account of.*

18. קוֹץ n. m. *thorn.*

דַּרְדַּר n. m. *thistle.*

19. זֵעָה n. f. (זֵעַת) *sweat.*

לֶחֶם n. m. f. *food, bread.*

עַד prep. *unto, until.*

שׁוּב v. K. *to return.* P. H. *to cause to return, bring back.* Pu. Ho. *to be brought back.*

20. חַי adj. (חַיָּה) *living.*

21. כְּתֹנֶת, כֻּתֹּנֶת n. f. *coat, tunic.*

עוֹר n. m. (ות) *skin.*

לָבֵשׁ or לָבַשׁ K. (fut. a) *to put on, wear, be clothed with.* H. *to cause to put on, to clothe.* Pu. *to be clothed.*

22. עַתָּה adv. *now.*

שָׁלַח K. P. H. *to send, put forth.* N. Pu. *to be sent.*

יָד n. f. (יָדַיִם) *hand.*

חָיָה v. K. *to live.*

עוֹלָם n. m. *eternity.*

24. גָּרַשׁ v. K. P. *to drive out.* N. Pu. *to be driven out.*

שָׁכַן v. K. (pret. ē in pause) *to dwell.* P. H. *to cause to dwell, to station.*

כְּרוּב n. m. *cherub.*

לַהַט n. m. *flame.*

חֶרֶב n. f. (ות) *sword.*

הָפַךְ v. K. *to turn.* N. Ho. *to be turned.* Hith. *to turn one's self.*

דֶּרֶךְ n. m. f. *way.*

ADDITIONAL.

אָהֵב K. (pret. ē in pause), P. *to love.* N. *to be loved.*

צָעַק K. P. *to cry.* H. *to convoke by a crier* (prop. *to cause to cry*). N. *to be convoked.*

גָּלַל K. P. (גִּלְגֵּל) H. *to roll.* N. Pu. *to be rolled.* Hith. *to roll one's self.*

חָלַל II. *to begin.* Ho. *to be begun.*

חָנַן K. *to be gracious.* P. *to make gracious.* Ho. *to be treated graciously.* Hith. (הִתְחַנֵּן) *to make to be gracious to one's self, entreat.*

מָהַהּ Hith. (הִתְמַהְמַהּ) *to linger.*

קָדַד K. *to bow.*

רָעַע K. *to be evil.* II. *to do evil.*

GRAMMATICAL AND EXEGETICAL NOTES.

GENESIS, CHAPTER I.

Verse 1. בְּרֵאשִׁית composed of the inseparable preposition בּ § 231. 1, with Daghesh lene § 21. 1, and the noun רֵאשִׁית of class IV, derived from רֹאשׁ *head* by the addition of the vowel י, § 194 and the feminine ending ת § 196. § 198. *a* (4), and denoting 'that which belongs to the head' i. e. the *beginning*. The accent is on the ultimate for a double reason § 32. 1 and 2. The expression is indefinite § 248, comp. ἐν ἀρχῇ John 1 : 1, and equivalent to the adverbial phrase *at first*. See Alexander on Acts 11 : 15. It does not of itself designate a fixed and determinate point of time, but simply the order of occurrence. The particular time intended must be inferred from the subject spoken of. The absence of the article is thus sufficiently accounted for, and there is no necessity of assuming that the noun is definite without the article, and hence is in the construct state § 246. 3, § 256, before the following words, which must then form a relative clause with the relative אֲשֶׁר omitted § 255. 2. This needlessly complicates the simple and obvious construction by making ver. 2 a continuation of the sentence begun in ver. 1, "in the beginning when God created the heavens and the earth, then (וְ after a statement of time § 287. 3) the earth was etc.," or by a construction still more forced and unnatural ver. 2 is regarded as a parenthesis and ver. 3 as a continuation of ver. 1, "in the beginning, when God created etc. (and the earth was etc.) then God said etc." These constructions have been advocated by those who would have Moses teach the eternal and independent existence of matter, or at least that it existed prior to God's act of creation. But this conclusion would not follow even if the strained renderings which they propose were adopted. The circlet over בּ refers to the marginal note רַבָּתִי בּ (fem. of the adjective רַב with paragogic י, § 218) i. e. *large Beth*, the initial letter of the book being above the ordinary size § 4. *a.* The Rabbins profess to see in this a mystic allusion to the magnitude of the work of creation, as well as to the twofold product of creative power, 'the heavens and the earth,' inasmuch as the numerical value of ב is 2, § 2. See Buxtorf Comment. Masorethicus p. 154.

ברא, לא verb § 162. 2, in the preterite, which here expresses past time absolutely § 262. 1; it agrees in sense though not in form with its subject in the singular § 275. 3. Daghesh lene § 21. 1. The accent is on the ultimate § 32. 2. The verb precedes its subject, and this is followed by the object, which is the natural order in Hebrew § 270. *a.* *Created:* this verb does not necessarily or invariably denote production out of nothing, as is shown by its use ver. 27, comp. 2 : 7, to describe the formation of man from the dust of the ground, and Ps. 51 : 12 where an inward spiritual change is spoken of as the creation of a clean heart. It properly signifies the production of an effect, for which no natural antecedent existed before, and which can only be the result of immediate divine agency. It is hence used only of God in the Kal species, which is thus distinguished from the Piel, where it has the sense of *cutting* or *forming* § 78. 1. That the creation here described is *ex nihilo* is apparent, however, from the nature of the case. The original production of the heavens and the earth is attributed to the immediate and almighty agency of God. And as the earth, even in its rude, unformed and chaotic condition is still called 'the earth' ver. 2, the matter of which it is composed is thereby declared to owe its existence to his creative power. Creation is also described as a voluntary act, and as one which took place in time or at 'the beginning' of time; consequently matter can neither be eternal nor an emanation from the divine essence. The Mosaic account is, therefore, equally opposed to hylezoism and to pantheism; and the only alternative is creation *ex nihilo.* The word ברא is further used in this chapter only in ver. 21 upon the creation of fishes and birds, which was the first introduction of the entirely new principle of animal life, and in ver. 27 where it is thrice repeated to emphasize the creation of man, who is a being not only of a higher grade but of a different order from those which had preceded, not merely another animal made of the same constituents in a more sublimated form or more curiously compounded, but a person possessing elements of intellectual and spiritual life not before communicated.

אלהים a monosyllabic noun of class I. § 183, from the root אלה, which some have thought to be an equivalent of אול *to be strong,* hence the *Mighty One,* but which is better explained from the corresponding Arabic root *to fear, adore,* hence the object of reverence, or adoration. It

is in form a plural § 199, although only one Being is referred to, and
hence the verb agrees with it in the singular; when it is used in a
plural sense of false gods, words belonging to it are put in the plural
§ 275. 3. *a.* The singular is rarely used except in poetry, and particularly in the poetical chapters of the book of Job, where it occurs almost
to the exclusion of the more ordinary plural. The current use of the
plural form of this word is not, as some have fancied, a relic of polytheistic times, the term "gods" which then became the fixed designation of what was divine having been retained after the transition to
monotheism, for if the faith was changed the words which described it
would change also. Nor can it be an anticipation of the doctrine of the
Trinity, as is shown by its application to heathen deities and occasionally even to creatures of exalted dignity. It is a plural of majesty, and
expresses not numerical multiplicity, but rather the combination of many
in one, the concentration of whatever is adorable § 201. 2.   As a
proper noun it is without the article § 246. 1, though when used as a
common or appellative noun it may receive the article to designate the
true God in distinction from those which are not really gods, Deut.
32 : 21, but only falsely called so § 246. 1. *a.*   Accent on ultimate
§ 23, 1.

אֵת the sign of the definite object § 238. 2, § 270, very frequently
connected with the noun by Makkeph § 43, but here perhaps from the
emphasis of this opening sentence accented as a separate word.

הַשָּׁמַיִם the article § 229. 1, distinguishing the object before which it
stands as the only one of its class § 245. 4; and a plural noun from the
obsolete singular שָׁמֶה § 201. 1, class I. form 2, § 185. *d,* derived from
שָׁמָה *to be high,* and hence denoting the upper regions, i. e. *heaven,* the
plural designating not distinct heavens of various elevation, but rather
extent in all directions, and comprehending all the parts of the vast
expanse above us.   The accent on the penult is contrary to the analogy
of ordinary plurals, and appears to be an assimilation to the dual ending § 203. *c.*

וְאֵת the conjunction § 234, and the sign of the definite object § 238.
2, § 270.

הָאָרֶץ: the article § 229. 3, § 245. 4, and the segholate noun of
class I. אֶרֶץ § 183, the first vowel being assimilated to that of the article
§ 229. 4. *b,* or changed to Kamets by the pause accent § 65.   It is of
common gender though mostly feminine § 197. *b,* plural אֲרָצוֹת.   Accent
on the penult § 32. 3.   Soph Pasuk § 36. 1.

The verse is divided by the accents into two clauses or branches.
The first, embracing the verb and its subject, is limited by Athnahh

under אֱלֹהִים; and the second, containing the compound object, is limited by Silluk under the last word of the verse § 36. 1. Silluk is preceded by the conjunctive Merka under the closely related particle אֵת, and the disjunctive Tiphhha under the other term of the compound object הַשָּׁמָיִם, the Tiphhha being preceded by the conjunctive Merka under the particle אֵת § 38. 1. Athnahh is preceded by the conjunctive Munahh under בָּרָא, which is thus linked with its subject, and by the disjunctive Tiphhha under בְּרֵאשִׁית, which is not directly dependent on what follows, and not so closely related to it § 38. 2. The disjunctive accents indicate the pauses which a reader would naturally make or ought to make after the words to which they are affixed; these vary according to the strength or value of the accent, from such as are almost imperceptible to those of more considerable duration. Words marked with conjunctives admit no interval between themselves and those which succeed them.

Upon one view of this verse, it describes the initial act in the work of creation, viz. the original production of the matter composing the earth and the heavens, which it was the work of the six days either to organize or to reconstruct, according as the Mosaic narrative unfolds, directly from this point, or an interval is assumed between ver. 1 and 2 covering the geologic eras, the changes which took place upon this planet prior to its being fitted up for the habitation of man being then supposed to be passed over in silence, as not falling within the province of revelation to disclose. In favour of this it is urged that the next verse commences with *and*, implying that the narration does not begin there but is continued from the preceding. That the term 'earth' may denote the matter of the globe in a chaotic and unformed state, appears from ver. 2, where it is so employed. According to another view of ver. 1 it is a title or summary statement of the contents of the following section, 1 : 1—2 : 3, and connected with it by 'and,' as in Isa. 2 : 2, Hos. 1 : 2, Amos 1 : 2.

Upon either hypothesis the entire section is divided into seven parts by the seven days whose work or rest is recorded, viz. the first day vs. 1–5, the second day vs. 6–8, third vs. 9–13, fourth vs. 14–19, fifth vs. 20–23, sixth vs. 24–31, seventh 2 : 1–3.

2. וְהָאָרֶץ conjunction § 234, article § 229. 3, and noun, which stands emphatically before the verb § 270. *a*. This inversion of the customary order is frequent in descriptive clauses or sentences, occurring at the beginning or in the course of a narrative, e. g. 2 : 12, 3 : 1, 37 : 3, both because the attention is there more strongly drawn to the subject to be described, and because this collocation admits of a preterite instead of a

future with Vav conversive § 99. 1, § 265. The latter is proper only in statements which are a sequence from the preceding, and which directly continue a narrative previously begun. This form of the sentence is pressed by those who suppose that the inspired writer indicates by it that the state of things described in this verse was not the immediate sequence of the creative act, ver. 1.

הָיְתָה from לה verb הָיָה § 169. 1, with Methegh § 45. 2, which here distinguishes Kamets from Kamets Hhatuph § 19. 2. It is here used as a copula, *was*, § 258. 3, or it may be itself part of the predicate *existed*, and that in the condition stated in the succeeding words.

וָבֹהוּ תֹהוּ Segholate nouns from לה roots § 184. *b*, without Daghesh lene § 21. 1, the first with two accents § 30. 1. Abstracts used rather than adjectives § 254. 6. *a*, to express the idea in a stronger and more absolute manner, *wasteness and desolation ;* בֹהוּ occurs in but two other passages, Is. 34 : 11, Jer. 4 : 23, in both of which it is joined as here in assonance or paronomasia with תֹהוּ to add intensity to its meaning. Inasmuch as these words are used in other passages of the desolateness produced by devastation, some have supposed that they here contain the implication of a preceding catastrophe or convulsion by which the creation spoken of in ver. 1 was reduced to the chaotic waste here described.

וְחֹשֶׁךְ Hholem combined with the diacritical point § 12, Sh'va with final Kaph § 16. 1. Abstract nouns used in a general or universal sense, receive the article § 245. 5 ; but as חֹשֶׁךְ is not spoken of here in its totality, and does not mean all *darkness* but a certain portion or amount of it, the article is omitted. The subject is joined to its predicate without a copula § 258. 1.

עַל־ preposition *over* from the root עָלָה *to ascend*, which when contact is implied, as in this case, becomes *upon* § 237. 1, with Makkeph § 43.

פְּנֵי plur. noun I. 2. § 185. *d*, from the obsolete singular § 201. 1, פָּנֶה, לה root פָּנָה *to turn*, the parts *turned* towards any one, i. e. *the face or surface ;* in the construct § 214. 2, § 216. 1, here signifying possession § 254. 1, which does not admit the article § 246. 3, its definiteness being indicated sufficiently by that of the following noun.

תְהוֹם III. § 100. *b*, § 192. 2, הם root *to agitate*, hence an *agitated, raging mass*, elsewhere applied to the ocean, Gen. 7 : 11, Job 28 : 14, here to the vast expanse of water enveloping the earth prior to the formation or appearance of the dry land. Those who adopt the scientific hypothesis of La Place, suppose that the period here spoken of was prior to the separate existence of our planet, and that תְהוֹם denotes the agitated nebulous mass or ocean, in which all the matter of the solar system, our earth among the rest, was confusedly blended, although the inspired account speaks only of *the earth* as in this chaotic state because the formation of the earth is the principal thing to be described. The תְּחֹם is in the next clause spoken of as *waters;* but this, it is urged, may denote th ‘ ittenuated etherial fluid from which the terrestrial waters were sul ᵧᵢently condensed, as in ver. 7, ‘the waters above the firmament,’ a₁ vidently not to be understood of water in its condensed and liquid sta ₂. This noun is used almost exclusively in poetry with the exception of this passage and twice in the account of the flood, Gen. 7 : 11, 8 : 2. In the singular it never receives the article, perhaps because it partakes somewhat of the character of a proper noun § 246. 1. It is of common gender § 197. *b;* plural תְּחֹמוֹת § 200. *a.*

רוּחַ monosyllabic noun of class I. from עו root § 186. *c,* of common gender, though mostly feminine § 197. *b,* plur. רוּחוֹת, meaning *breath,* hence *wind,* hence also *spirit,* which resembles breath as an invisible agent and connected -with vitality. It cannot here signify ‘ wind,’ whether by ‘ the wind of God’ be understood a *divine,* i. e. a *powerful wind* upon the doubtful assumption that the name of God is used to make a mere superlative of greatness, or a *wind divinely sent;* it must signify *spirit,* since the action attributed to him could only be predicated of a living agent. It is definite without the article by being in the construct before a proper noun § 246. 3 ; this is here not the construct of apposition or designation merely § 254. 3, ‘the spirit viz. God’ or ‘God who is a spirit,’ but either that of possession § 254. 1, ‘the spirit belonging to God’ or of the source § 254. 7, ‘the spirit proceeding from God.’ That the spirit here spoken of is neither a periphrasis for God himself nor a mere influence issuing from him, but the third person of the Godhead, we learn from other passages of Scripture which ascribe the performance of divine works *ad extra* and particularly the work of creation to this sacred agent.

מְרַחֶפֶת Piel participle of the ע guttural verb רָחַף § 116. 4, § 121. 1, fem. § 205, without the article, since it is a predicate § 259. 2, which here follows its subject in a descriptive clause as in the preceding branches of this verse. It expresses continuous action § 266. 1, belonging to the time before spoken of § 266. 3 ; *brooding* or *hovering,* the word is applied Deut. 32 : 11 to the eagle cherishing its young.

הַמָּיִם : noun used only in the plural § 201. 1, § 203. *c,* Pattahh changed to Kamets by the pause accent § 65 ; *the water* viz. that of the deep or ocean previously spoken of § 245. 3.

The verse is divided by Athnahh under מְרַחֶפֶת § 36. 1 into two clauses

describing respectively the physical condition of the earth and the agency
of the divine Spirit. The first is subdivided by Zakeph Katon over
וָבֹהוּ, and again by R'bhia over וְהָאָרֶץ § 36. 2, the emphatically prefixed
subject being thus erected into a minor subdivision, as though it stood
absolutely and required a brief pause after it, 'as for the earth—it
was, etc.' Zakeph Katon is preceded by the disjunctive Pashta on the
other term of the compound predicate, and this by the conjunctive
Merka on the closely related verb or copula § 38. 4, comp. § 38. 1. a.
Athnahh is preceded by Munahh on the closely related construct, and
by Tiphhha which marks the opposition of the subject to the predicate
§ 38. 2. The Silluk clause is subdivided by Zakeph Katon on אֱלֹהִים
§ 36. 2, thus balancing the prefixed subject against the predicate.
Zakeph Katon is preceded by Munahh on the closely related construct
§ 38. 4; and Silluk by Merka on the construct and Tiphhha on the
participle whose relation to what follows is less intimate § 38. 1.

3. וַיֹּאמֶר Kal fut. of פא verb אָמַר to say § 110. 3, with Vav conversive
§ 99, which draws back the accent to the penult § 33. 4, § 99. 3. a,
and changes Pattahh of the ultimate to Seghol § 111. 2. a; this continues the narration begun by the preterite הָיְתָה ver. 2. § 265. All the
verbs of this verse precede their subjects § 270. a. Each creative act is
preceded by the going forth of the divine word; some have found or
fancied in this an obscure allusion to the second person of the Trinity,
called in the New Testament 'the Word,' John 1 : 1, and to his agency
in the work of creation. It may be remarked that the phrase 'and God
said' occurs ten times in this chapter, once before each of the eight
creative acts, a duplicate work being assigned to the third and sixth
days respectively, and twice, vs. 28, 29, after the creation of man.

יְהִי Kal apoc. fut. § 97. 2 of פה verb הָיָה § 171. 1, § 177. 1, with a
jussive sense; here not a copula, but the predicate be, i. e. exist. וַיְהִי—
Daghesh-forte omitted after Vav Conv. § 25, § 99. 3, with Methegh
§ 45. 2.

The verse is divided at אוֹר § 36. 1 into a command and its result.
Each verb is closely connected with its subject by the appropriate accents
in the first clause § 38. 2 and by Makkeph in the second § 43.

4. וַיַּרְא Kal fut. of פה verb רָאָה with Vav Conv. § 171. 1, § 172. 4;
א otiant § 16. 1. Some read beheld the light, i. e. looked upon it with
favour or approbation, because it was good. But this sense is forbidden,
1. by the parallel expressions in subsequent verses, particularly in ver.
31, where the form of statement is varied; and 2. by the fact that רָאָה
in this sense is followed not by the direct object but by the preposition
ב, intimating that the sight was not only directed to the object but was

fastened upon it or bound up in it. *Saw the light that* it was *good* asserts a vision of the object itself as well as of its quality, and thus there
is a recognizable shade of difference between this and the phrase, which
accords better with the English idiom, 'saw that the light was good,'
which merely asserts the perception of the quality; this latter form of
speech is used in Hebrew likewise, e. g. 3 : 6. הָאִיר the article before
an object previously mentioned § 245. 1. כִּי־טוֹב the subject omitted,
since it is sufficiently plain from the connection § 243. 1, predicate adjective without the article § 259. 2. וַיַּבְדֵּל Hiph. fut. of בָּדַל with Vav
Conv. § 99. 3. בֵּין...וּבֵין prep. § 237. 1, *between the light and between the
darkness* for *between the light and the darkness.* This idiom is transferred to the Greek of the New Testament in Rev. 5 : 6, ἐν μέσῳ τοῦ
θρόνου καὶ τῶν τεσσάρων ζώων, καὶ ἐν μέσῳ τῶν πρεσβυτέρων, i. e. *between
the throne etc., and the elders.* Sometimes the second member is preceded by לְ as in ver. 6. Vav with Shurek § 231. הָאוֹר...הַחֹשֶׁךְ the
article either because they had been mentioned before § 245. 1, *the light,
the darkness,* or possibly the words may be used in their universal sense,
in which case the English does not admit the article § 245. 5, *light,
darkness.*

5. וַיִּקְרָא Kal future of לא verb קָרָא *to call* § 162. 2. It governs the
name directly, and the person or thing to whom the name is given by
the preposition לְ; or the preposition may be omitted, when the person
or thing named is in a very few instances also made a direct object,
Num. 32 : 41, Isa 60 : 18, but more frequently the word שֵׁם *name* is
inserted, Gen. 3 : 20, 41 : 51, 52, *God called (to) the light, day etc.* i. e.
he made them to be what these names denote; he gave them the fixed
character and relations suggested by these terms The majestic significance of this divine naming is heightened by its restriction to those
grand objects in nature which were the work of the first three days,
light and darkness—the firmament, ver. 8—land and sea, ver. 10, and
to man the crown of the whole, 5 : 2. The inferior animals received
their names not from God but from Adam, 2 : 20, who thus recognized
and expressed the nature given them by their creator.

ı אֱלֹהִים P'sik § 30. 1, § 38. 1. *a.* לָאוֹר prep. לְ with the vowel of the
the article § 231. 5. יוֹם *day,* noun irregular in the plural יָמִים § 207. 1.
f. קָרָא, for the sake of varying the construction, לַחֹשֶׁךְ is placed before
the verb, which necessitates a return to the preterite § 265; the conjunctive accent is thrown back upon the penult by reason of the following disjunctive § 35. 1. לַיְלָה from לַיִל *night,* a Segholate noun from an
לי root § 184. *b,* with He paragogic § 61. 6, § 219, which no doubt
originally had the adverbial sense of *at night,* but in usage came to be

equivalent to the simple noun, which it has almost supplanted, לֵל only occurring once, Isa. 16 : 3 ; with a pause accent § 65 ; in the plural לֵילוֹת § 208. 3. c. עֶרֶב I. 1. *evening*, from עָרַב *to be dark*, dual עַרְבַּיִם. plural עֲרָבִים ; עֲרָבִים is used in a different sense, § 200. *d.* בֹּקֶר I. 1 *morning*, from בָּקַר *to break forth*, plur. בְּקָרִים. אֶחָד : numeral *one* § 223. 1, is placed after its noun, with which it agrees § 250. 1.

And it was evening and it was morning, one day. This is by many understood to mean that the evening followed by the morning constituted one day, the first of creation. This view has been thought to be recom- mended by its agreement with the usage prevalent among the Jews and several other nations of antiquity, of beginning the day with the evening, and also by Dan. 8 : 14, where בֹּקֶר עֶרֶב *evening-morning* occurs as an enigmatical equivalent of day. According to another and perhaps pref- erable opinion, the days of creation are to be reckoned from morning to morning. In favour of this it may be urged, 1. The statement is not that ' the evening and the morning were the first day.' This could not be so expressed in Hebrew. The separate verb before עֶרֶב and בֹּקֶר shows that we have here not a compound subject but a twofold state- ment, and הָיָה in the sense of *become* or *constitute* is commonly followed by לְ, see ver. 14, 15, so that if this were the meaning the proper phrase would be *were to* (or *for*) *one day.* 2. The evening of this as of the other days of creation is spoken of as coming on after the work of the day is over, the future with Vav conversive וַיְהִי implying a sequence, § 265. *a.* The day began when the light broke forth at God's com- mand; then followed the other acts of the day, the divine contemplation of the light, dividing the light from darkness, and giving names to each ; finally when all was finished it was evening. and this was suc- ceeded by morning. One day is now ended and another begins. 3. From evening to morning would be a night, but not a day, unless the terms are taken with a latitude of meaning which they do not properly possess and which they do not have elsewhere. עֶרֶב means simply *evening*, not the entire period of darkness, and בֹּקֶר *morning*, not the en- tire period of light. For these לַיְלָה *night* and יוֹם *day* had just been stated to be the proper words. Dan. 8 : 14 affords no justification of this extension of the evening and the morning over the whole day. The prophet merely says that there shall be so many evenings and mornings before the fulfilment of his prediction. He might have said with the same propriety the sun shall set and rise so many times. But it could not be inferred from this that sunset and sunrise covered the entire day. 4. If the first day began with the evening, this must have been the darkness which preceded the creation of light, but that darkness was eternal. So that the first day would upon this hypothesis consist of an evening of infinite duration followed by a finite morning, which involves an enormous disproportion not only in its own parts but between this and the succeeding days. 5. An additional confirmation may perhaps be found in the narrative of the deluge. It appears from a comparison of Gen. 7 : 11 and 8 : 3, 4 that time was then reckoned not by lunar but by solar months of thirty days each. When the beginning of the month was fixed by the appearance of the new moon, it was natural that the evening should be regarded as the commencement of the day, in order that it might be determined at the outset by the aspect of the moon to which month the ensuing day belonged. But if solar time is used in the account of the deluge, it seems not improbable that it is used in that of the creation likewise; and solar days are reckoned from sunrise to sunrise.

This view, if correct, is interesting from its incidentally proving how far the account of the creation is from containing anything distinctively Jewish. It has been said that the week of creation is modelled on the Jewish week: that its six days of work followed by a day of rest were invented to give sanctity to the Jewish Sabbath from the divine example. This suggestion is sufficiently confuted by the traces of a septenary division of time among other ancient nations, and by the coincidences in several remarkable particulars between the narrative of the creation and widespread traditions showing that Moses has given no invention of his own, but a trusty report of the primeval revelation. But apart from this, the calendar of creation is not Jewish at all, the very days, as it would appear, being reckoned by a different standard.

As to the duration of the days of creation, the first impression made upon the common reader doubtless is that they were days of ordinary length limited by the regular succession of light and darkness. It has unquestionably been so understood by the vast majority of students of the Scriptures from the beginning, and we are not prepared to affirm positively that this may not be the real meaning. The scientific difficulties which beset this hypothesis may be disposed of by two considerations. 1. Physical science has no knowledge of the origin of the world. It merely ascertains existing phenomena and existing laws, and from these concludes that *if* the laws and properties of matter have always been the same, the present condition of things might have been brought about in a particular way. But as to the mode in which these things actually did come into being, it can affirm nothing. If creation be miraculous, it transcends the limits of scientific inquiry. 2. If the specific purpose of Gen. 1 is not the complete history of this planet from the beginning, but the immediate preparation of it for the abode of man, how is science to demonstrate that after its geologic epochs were over, God did not in the exercise of his almighty power do in six natural days all that this chapter records?

And yet there are considerations deserving the attention of the careful student, which make it doubtful whether this was in fact the meaning of Moses, and still more so whether this was intended by the Spirit of God, whatever the meaning of Moses may have been.

(1) There is a measure of indefiniteness in the term 'day.' In this very verse it is used in two distinct senses. In the first clause it denotes the periods of light alternating with the darkness of the night, and exclusive of the latter. In the second clause, even on the strictest and most literal hypothesis, it denotes the entire diurnal period, embracing, along with the day proper, the night also. In 2 : 4 it has a wider meaning still, and is applied to the whole week of creation. And its frequent use throughout the Scriptures in the metaphorical sense of a period of indefinite duration shows what a latitude was allowed to it in the Hebrew idiom. Thus we read of the 'day of prosperity' and the 'day of adversity,' Eccl. 7 : 14, the 'day of trouble,' Ps. 20 : 1, the 'day of affliction,' Jer. 16 : 19, the 'day of evil,' Jer. 17 : 17, the 'day of vengeance,' Isa. 61 : 2, the 'day of salvation,' 2 Cor. 6 : 2, the 'day of temptation in the wilderness,' Ps. 95 : 10, which lasted for forty years, the day of human life succeeded by the night of death, John 9 : 4, the day of final glory which is to follow this night of darkness and sin, Rom. 13 : 12, that eternal day which no night shall limit, Rev. 21 : 25.

(2) The days of prophecy, it is universally acknowledged, denote not ordinary days of twenty-four hours, but periods of much longer duration, see Dan. 12 : 11, 12, Rev. 11 : 3, etc., etc. If this term may be used enigmatically in prophecy in order to conceal the absolute duration intended, at the same time that its proportions and relations are made known, the same might be the case here, if it was the design of God darkly to image forth more than was to be absolutely disclosed. If the Creator has indeed left traces of the progress of his work in the crust of the globe, which it was his design that man should in the course of time decipher, and if he has also given a written revelation of his creative work, not with the design of enabling men to anticipate these scientific discoveries or to decide in advance between rival scientific hypotheses, but such as should be in accurate accordance with the facts when they came to be known, and should impress all readers with the conviction that He inspired it who knew the end from the beginning, how could

this be accomplished better than by such an enigmatical use of words as could hold a latent signification unsuspected until the time should arrive for it to be brought to light? This is what the analogy of Scripture would lead us to expect, since its predictions of the future are usually so veiled that they cannot be thoroughly understood until the event explains them, though they then become so plain, oftentimes, that they cannot be mistaken.

(3) The apostle Peter tells us, 2 Pet. 3 : 8, 'that one day is with the Lord as a thousand years, and a thousand years as one day.' Comp. Ps. 90 : 4. This might make us hesitate about a rigorous application of our puny measures of time to the eternal God. The day is, in the language of our Lord, John 9 : 4, the period of work as opposed to the night when no work is done. Now though the same word may be applied to things human and things divine, it does not follow that they are upon a level. A day is man's working-time ; God's working-time is also a day, but it may have an inconceivably grander scale of duration, as the work wrought in it is one to which human work bears no proportion.

(4) The divine Sabbath, with which the work of creation concludes, may naturally be supposed to have been of the same character with the days which preceded it. But if this Sabbath was a day of twenty-four hours, God rested no more on the seventh day than he did on the eighth or ninth. That the Sabbath of creation in the intention of the Scriptures was not an ordinary day, but a long period, which still continues, may be inferred (a) From the circumstance that while the regular formula of 'the evening and the morning' occurs at the end of each of the six preceding days, it is wanting in the seventh. This has had no evening, and no fresh morning has since dawned. (b) The apostle appears to teach the same thing in Heb. 4. The works of God were finished from the foundation of the world, ver. 3. Creation was then complete : and into the divine rest then inaugurated men are still invited to enter. The human week and the human Sabbath are modelled after those of God, but so reduced in dimensions as to be adapted to our short-lived insignificance. For as the heavens are higher than the earth, so are God's ways higher than our ways. Isa. 55 : 9.

(5) An additional ground of doubt respecting the length of the days of creation might be suggested by the fact that they certainly were not all solar days. The sun was not created, or at least was not made the measurer of time for the earth until the fourth day.

(6) The surprising correspondence between the successive works of the six days and the order in which according to geological researches

animated beings would seem to have made their first appearance on the
earth, creates a strong presumption that the periods of geology and the
days of Moses are identical.

 ɛ The Pentateuch is divided by the Jews into 669 sections or paragraphs, the end of each being sometimes, as here, marked by the letter
ɛ, at others, as 3 : 15, 16, by ס. The former is the initial of פְּתוּחָה
opened, indicating that the rest of the line was to be left vacant in the
manuscript. The latter is the initial of סְתוּמָה *closed*, indicating that
after leaving a blank space the writer should recommence in the same
line. It is also divided into 54 larger sections or lessons for the public
reading of the synagogue. These are not noted in this chrestomathy;
but in ordinary Hebrew Bibles they are marked by ססס or פפפ as they
coincide at the beginning with one or the other sort of smaller sections.

 6. רָקִיעַ I. 2. § 185 from רָקַע *to spread out*, denoting *that which is
spread out, expanse*. As the root also means ‘to hammer out,’ some
have judged that this word involves the conception of the sky as a solid
arch, like the Greek στερέωμα and the Latin *firmamentum*. Even if
this were so, however, which is by no means certain, the sacred writers
cannot be held responsible for the etymology of the words which they
employ, any more than a modern astronomer, who should speak of the
‘ fixed stars,’ would be held to sanction the notion that they are fastened
to the celestial sphere. The Scriptures nowhere profess to give a physical description of the sky; the language employed respecting it is
purely phenomenal and figurative. Thus while in Job 37 : 18 it is
spoken of as firm and like a molten looking-glass, the Psalmist, 104 : 2,
compares it to a curtain, and Isaiah, 40 : 22, to a tent or veil of the
thinnest and most subtile texture (דֹּק).

 בְּתֹוךְ prep. § 231. 1, with the const. of תָּוֶךְ § 183. *b*, § 216. 1. *d*.
מַבְדִּיל Hiph. part. of בָּדַל § 84. 5, denoting continuous action § 266. 1,
and referred by the tense of the accompanying substantive verb to the
future § 266. 3. *a*. לַמַּיִם prep. with Kamets § 231. 4, *between waters to
waters*, the interval beginning with the first and having respect also to
the second : our idiom requires *and* instead of *to*.

 7. וַיַּעַשׂ Kal fut. of the פ guttural and לה verb עָשָׂה with Vav conv.
§ 109. 3, § 171. 1, § 172. 4, the accent on the penult § 32. 3. הָרָקִיעַ
the article before an object spoken of before § 245. 1, Methegh in its
regular place § 44. הַמַּיִם with the article because it is defined by the
accompanying words § 245. 2. מֵאַחַת two prepositions אַ § 232 and
מִן § 237. 2 (1). In computing direction the Hebrews measure from
the object spoken of toward themselves or toward the object to which it
has relation, which is then indicated by לְ *to*, or may stand without לְ,

ver. 9. Thus, instead of saying that one object lay *to* the right of another, they would say that it lay *from* the right with respect to it. So here a downward direction from the firmament or *beneath* it is expressed by the phrase 'from under to the firmament'; and an upward direction or *above* it by *from over to* it. בְּעַל composed of מִן and עַל מִן adverb § 235. 3 (4). The verse has three accentual clauses § 36. 1. In the subdivision of Zakeph Katon, Pashta is repeated § 39. 4.

The waters above the firmament were by some ancient interpreters understood to imply a literal ocean above the vault of heaven. And unbelieving expositors of modern times have sought to fasten this conception upon the sacred writer. But the figurative expression occurring in the account of the deluge, Gen. 7 : 14, "the windows of heaven were opened," does not warrant the conclusion that he imagined sluices to be really existing in the sky through which the supernal waters poured in time of rain, any more than Malachi, 3 : 10, and the Israelitish lord mentioned 2 Kin. 7 : 1 supposed a literal granary of provisions in the sky to be poured down through these imaginary apertures. That the Hebrews were well aware that the rain came from the clouds, and that the clouds were formed by evaporation, is plain from numerous passages in every part of the Bible. Those who adopt the hypothesis of Laplace find the waters of this verse in the nebulous fluid. The waters beneath the firmament formed this terraqueous globe, both the water and the land of ver. 9; the waters above the firmament formed the heavenly bodies. The ordinary interpretation makes the waters above the firmament to be the clouds, which might be so called as well as the birds can be said, ver. 20, to 'fly *over* the face of the firmament.'

8. שֵׁנִי: ordinal number § 227. 1, follows the noun with which it agrees § 252. 1, *a second day*. The several days of creation are spoken of indefinitely, the sixth alone, upon which the whole was completed, being distinguished by the article, ver. 31.

The words 'and God saw that it was good' occur with regard to the work of every day but the second. Whence some have conjectured that they have here been dropped from the text, or, as these words occur twice in the account of the third day, that they have by some accident been misplaced, or that the formula announcing the end of the second day has been transposed from the end of ver. 10, and properly belongs there. The true explanation of the omission appears to be, that the first part of the third day's work is really a continuation of that which was begun on the second, and the divine approbation is withheld until the division and segregation of the waters was complete. The insertion of this clause in ver. 8 by the LXX without authority affords a good illustra-

tion of the manner in which various readings have arisen from transcribers or translators paying too much regard to parallel passages.

9. יֵרָאֶה Niph. fut. of קָוָה § 169. 1. מָקוֹם III. from root קום *to
stand* § 190. *b*, signifying that in which one can stand, i. e. *place* § 191.
3, of common gender though mostly masculine § 197. *b*, plur. מְקֹמוֹת.
וְתֵרָאֶה Niph. fut. of רָאָה, a ε guttural § 109. 4 and הל verb § 168, with
Methegh § 44. The apocopated future rarely occurs in the Niphal, and
never in the strictly passive species, because it did not accord with
Hebrew conceptions to address a command to the object of the action
§ 97. 2, *b*. The future expresses simple futurity, leaving the fact of its
being spontaneous or constrained and every other modal quality, for
which occidental languages employ distinct forms, to be inferred from
the circumstances of the case § 263. 1. In both instances in this verse
it denotes not only what *will* occur, but what *must* and *shall* take place,
and is therefore virtually equivalent to a command. הַיַּבָּשָׁה adjective
II. § 187. 1, intensive from יָבֵשׁ *dry*, used only in the fem. יַבְּשָׁה § 207.
1, or יַבָּשָׁת § 205, with the generic article § 245.5.*a*, *the dry*, viz.
land.

10. אֶרֶץ *earth* here used in its strict sense of the dry land exclusively, but in ver. 1 the world, embracing land and water, so named from
its principal and most important part. וּלְמִקְוֵה conj. § 234, prep. § 231.
1, and noun III. root קָוָה § 190. *b*, that which is gathered, *collection*
§ 119. 5, in the const. § 215. 2, followed by the material of which it
consists § 254. 4, definite without the article § 246. 3. יַמִּים plur.
§ 207. 2 of יָם, I. from an obsolete עו root § 186. 2. *c*, *seas*, because
distributed into separate basins, though as these all communicate they
may be viewed in their totality as one מִקְוֶה.

11. תַּדְשֵׁא Hiph. apoc. fut. § 97. 2, § 264, of דָּשָׁא § 162. 2, governing
in its strictest sense its cognate noun דֶּשֶׁא § 271. 3, and with a wider
extent of meaning also עֵשֶׂב and עֵץ, which are not in apposition with
דֶּשֶׁא, as though the latter were a generic name for all vegetable products
and the former were its subdivisions, but they are co-ordinated with it,
and constitute together the three great branches of the vegetable kingdom, not according to a scientific classification, but a popular and obvious division, grasses, seed-bearing plants and trees. Methegh § 45.
2. עֵשֶׂב masc. noun with plur. in הֹ § 200. *a*, which occurs but once,
commonly as here a collective § 201. 1, from root עָשַׂב *to be green*, accent
Y'thibh § 30. 2, § 38. 4. מַזְרִיעַ Hiph. part. of ל guttural verb § 123. 3,
follows the noun to which it belongs § 249. 1, governs a cognate noun
§ 271. 3, expresses what is permanent and habitual § 266. 1. זֶרַע
masc. collective § 201. 1, only once found in the plural. עֵץ has both

an individual and a collective signification, *tree* and *trees*, pl. עֵצִים § 207.
1, probably abridged from עֵץ root עָצָה *to be firm, hard* § 185. *d*, in the
const. § 215. 1, with the following word, which denotes its quality
§ 254. 6. פְּרִי *fruit* collective I. 1, root פָּרָה *to bear* § 184. *b*, G'ra-
shayim § 38. 1. *a*. עֹשֶׂה Hholem preceding Sin § 12, Kal act. part. of
עָלָה verb § 168. The accent, which is not Y'thibh but Mahpakh, since
it stands before Pashta in the subdivision of Zakeph Katon § 30. 2,
§ 38. 4, is shifted to the penult by § 35. 1. The point in the first letter
of the next word is Daghesh-forte conjunctive § 24. *a*. לְמִינוֹ prep.
§ 231. 1, מִין I. from an obsolete מוּן root § 186. 2. *b*, and pronom. suffix
§ 220. 1. אֲשֶׁר זַרְעוֹ־בוֹ oblique case of the relative pronoun § 74, § 285.
1, formed by appending the suffix to the noun § 221. 5, which is the
governing word, *whose seed* is *in it*, or the relative might be connected
with the suffix of the preposition § 233 and governed by it, *in which* is
its seed. עַל־ not to be connected with עֹשֶׂה פְּרִי as descriptive of the
tree in distinction from shrubs and grass *producing fruit over* (or *above*)
the earth, but with תַּדְשֵׁא and referring alike to grass, shrubs and trees
which were all to be produced *upon* the earth.

12. וַתֵּצֵא Hiph. fut. of יָצָא § 144. 1, § 145. 2 and לא verb § 162. 2,
with Vav conv. § 99. 3, § 166. 4, the accent remaining on the ultimate
§ 147. 5, תֵּצֵא T'lisha Gh'dhola § 38. 8. לְמִינֵהוּ 3 pers. suf. with the
connecting vowel *e* § 22). 1. *b*, sing. in a distributive sense referring to
the preceding collective § 275. 6.

13. שְׁלִישִׁי ordinal number § 227. 1, § 252. 1.

14. יְהִי singular verb preceding a plural subject § 275. 1, or it may
be explained by supposing יְהִי to partake of the nature of an impersonal
verb, 'let there be,' comp. *es gebe, qu'il y ait* § 275. 1. *c*. מְאֹרֹת masc.
III. from אוֹר root אוֹר *to shine* § 190. *b*, signifies *a luminous body* § 191. *a*,
thus differing from the noun אוֹר ver. 3, which signifies the element of
light; plur. has either ־ים or ־וֹת § 200. *c*. Hholem written defectively
§ 11. 1. *a*, § 14. בִּרְקִיעַ const. of apposition or specification § 254. 3.
לְהַבְדִּיל prep. expresses design, *to, in order to,* and requires the construct
form of the infinitive § 267. *b*.

וְהָיוּ pret. with Vav conv. § 100. 1, § 265, continuing the command
begun with יְהִי, in the plural because it comes after its subject § 275.
1. *b*. לְאֹתֹת the noun אוֹת *sign* of common gender § 197. *b*, from אָוָה *to
mark*, with the fem. ending ת § 196, which is retained contrary to the
ordinary rule before the plural ending § 199. *d, for signs,* i. e. of whatever
the heavenly bodies serve to indicate that is not included in the following particulars, whether ordinarily or in extraordinary cases in which
they may become portents of momentous events, Matt. 2 : 2, or of divine

6

judgments, Joel 2 : 31, Mat. 24 : 29, Luke 21 : 25.   There is no need of assuming that *for signs and for seasons* is put by hendiadys for *signs of seasons*, ɪor of making the subsequent words dependent upon אֹתֹת *signs both in respect to seasons and in respect to days and years.* וּלְמֹֽועֲדִים from מֹועֵד III. י root יָעַד *to appoint* § 190. *b, appointed time, season,* plur. in ־ים, though once it has ־ות.   Munahh takes the place of Methegh § 39. 3. *b,* § 45. 5. : וּלְיָמִים fem. noun שָׁנָה I. 2 from שׁנה root שָׁנָה *to repeat,* hence *a year,* in which the sun and the seasons repeat their course; the fem. ending causes the suppression of the last vowel proper to the form § 185. *d,* § 209. 1, plur. both in ־ים and ־ות, the latter only in poetry § 200. *d.*

The works of the first three days have, as has often been remarked, a certain measure of correspondence with those of the last three.

1. Light.   4. Celestial luminaries.
2. Division of the waters by   5. Aquatic animals and birds.
   the firmament.
3. Dry land and plants.   6. Terrestrial animals and man.

15. לְהָאִיר Hiph. inf. const. of יּ verb אֹור § 153. 1, having Hholem in the Kal pret. § 82. 1. *a* (3), with the prep. § 267. *b.*

16. וַיַּעַשׂ see ver. 7. שְׁנֵי cardinal number § 223. 1, in the construct before its noun § 250. 2 (2), without the article § 251. 4, *the two great lights,* not *two of the great lights,* which would be expressed by omitting אֶת before the indefinite object § 270. and inserting the preposition מִן in its partitive sense after שְׁנֵי. הַגְּדֹלִים adj. I. 2. § 185, with the article after הַמְּאֹרֹת § 249. 1, which it qualifies and with which it agrees in gender, though the termination is different § 200. *e.*   The noun is definite because the objects are well known § 245. 3.   They are called ' the great lights,' not from their absolute but their apparent magnitude, or rather from the measure of their effulgence as compared with the stars. הַמָּאֹור . . . הַגָּדֹל absolute or emphatic use of the positive degree § 260. 2 (2). קָטֹן takes the form קְטֹן with the pause accents § 65. *a,* or when declined, e. g. קָטְנִי, קְטֹנִים, קְטֹנֹות § 207. 2. *b.* לְמֶמְשֶׁלֶת III. § 190, root מָשַׁל *to rule,* meaning *dominion, rule* § 191. 4, a segholate form in the construct § 214. 1. *b,* the following noun denoting the object § 254. 9. The preposition expresses design, *in order to, for.* : הַכֹּוכָבִים II. probably softened from כָּבַב § 57. 1, from the obsolete יּ root כָּבַב *to wrap up* § 187. 1. *e,* hence globule, *star.*   Methegh § 44.

17. וַיִּתֵּן from פֹּ verb נָתַן § 129. 1, *gave, put.* אֹתָם sign of the definite object with pron. suf. § 238. 2, § 270, which has less independence than a noun, and usually, as here, follows the verb immediately, instead of com ing after the subject § 270. *a;* see also ver. 22.

18. וְלִמְשֹׁל const. infin. with prep. § 267. *b*, followed by בּ , which is not here used in its temporal sense, *in* or *during*, but according to the Hebrew idiom links this verb to its object. The day and night (with the generic article § 245. 5) were the domain *in* which the sway was exercised. Our idiom requires *rule over*, which is based on a different conception, that of the elevation of the ruler above the ruled. וּלְהַבְדִּיל Methegh § 45. 2. *a.*

No functions are here assigned to the heavenly bodies but those which they perform in relation to the earth, because these were all that the sacred writer was concerned to state. But it does not follow of course that this was the sole aim of their creation. The work of the fourth day need not include the original formation of these bodies ; if ver. 1 describes the first act in creation the contrary is explicitly declared. But they then made their appearance in the sky, and their relation to the earth was definitely determined.

20. יִשְׁרְצוּ command expressed by the simple future § 263. 1, in a person which has no distinct apocopated form § 97. 2. *b*, governs its cognate שֶׁרֶץ , a collective I. 1. § 183. This is by many understood to mean that fish were made from the element in which they move ; which, though not explicitly asserted, is not improbable in itself, and has in its favour the analogy of terrestrial animals, which were made of earth, 2 : 19. נֶפֶשׁ I. 1. vital principle, *soul*, here put for the animated being, common gender though mostly fem. § 197. *b*, plur. commonly תֹות , once נ× § 200. *c*, in apposition with the preceding noun § 253. 1. חַיָּה might be the fem. adj. from חַי *living*, I. from עע root חָיָה *to live* § 186. *c*, but the fact that when joined with נֶפֶשׁ the former alone receives the article, ver. 21, and also that the compound expression is construed as a masculine, 2 : 19, shows that it is a noun, *life*, and נֶפֶשׁ is in the construct before its attribute § 254. 6. עוֹף collect. *fowl, birds* § 201. 1, not the object of יִשְׁרְצוּ, with the relative understood, *fowl, which shall fly* § 285. 3, a construction which has sometimes been distorted into a contradiction with 2 : 19, but the subject of יְעוֹפֵף Piel fut. of the cognate עוּף verb § 154. 2, to which it is emphatically prefixed § 270. *a.* עַל־פְּנֵי *over* or across the *face* of the firmament, i. e. the part turned toward us.

21. הַתַּנִּינִם plur. of תַּנִּין § 199. II. intensive from obsolete root תָּנַן *to stretch* § 187. 1, hence that which is greatly extended, the *monsters* of the sea, *whales*, etc., so called from their length, the article before that which is well known § 245. 3. Hhirik of the ultimate long § 19. 1. וְאֵת before an object made definite by construction § 270. *b.* הָרֹמֶשֶׂת fem. Kal act. part. § 205, § 217, with the article § 249. 1, which may be resolved into the relative with the verb *that creep* or *move.*

לְאֵילֶהֹם plur. noun with 3 masc. plur. suffix § 220. 2. *b* referring to nouns of different genders § 276. 3. רָאֵי before אֶל־ § 270. *c*, shortened from כֹּל by Makkeph § 43. כָּנָף I. 2, root כָּנַף, hence a covering, a *wing*, fem. as double organs usually are § 197. *a*, occurs in the dual § 203. 1, and plur. in ־ֵי § 217, which is used in a different sense § 203. *a*, expresses the quality of the preceding construct § 254. 6, *fowl of wing*. i. e. *winged fowl*.

22. וַיְבָרֶךְ Piel fut. of ך Gutt. verb § 116. 4, § 121. 1, with Vav conv § 99. 3. *a*, no Daghesh lene in ב since the preceding Sh'va is vocal § 25 primarily *to kneel*, thence *to bless*. לֵאמֹר prep. with Tsere § 231. 3. *c.* so as to say, i. e. *in saying*. פְּרוּ וּרְבוּ Kal imper. of פָּרָה, רָבָה § 169. 1. וְרֵב Kal apoc. fut. § 171 1, Hhirik short though accented § 19. 1, subject emphatically prefixed.

24. הָאֹתָהּ see ver. 12, לְאֵילֶהּ 3 fem. sing. suffix § 72, § 220. 1, Mappik § 26. בְּהֵמָה I. 2, with fem. ending, root בָּהַם *to be dumb*, applied chiefly to the larger quadrupeds, and especially to the domestic animals, *beast, cattle*, const. בֶּהֱמַת, plur. בְּהֵמוֹת, const. בַּהֲמוֹת. חָיְתוֹ I. 1, collective § 201. 1. וְחַיְתוֹ־אֶרֶץ construct of חַיָּה, I. § 186. *c*, with fem. ending § 207. 2, from חַי root חָיָה *to live*, hence *living thing, beast*, with ו paragogic § 218. The article is constantly omitted from אֶרֶץ when preceded by this archaic or poetic form, perhaps by § 247, though when the ordinary form is used, the phrase is חַיַּת הָאָרֶץ, see ver. 25, *beasts of the earth*, i. e. wild beasts. Methegh § 45. 2. Daghesh forte omitted, and no Daghesh lene in ת § 25.

25. הָאֲדָמָה I. 2, with fem. ending, root אָדַם *to be red*, hence *the ground*, so called from the colour of the soil.

26. נַעֲשֶׂה Kal fut. of עָשָׂה § 109, § 168, 1 pers. plural, which is not to be explained as a royal style of speech, nor as associating the angels with God, for they took no part in man's creation, nor a plural of majesty which has no application to verbs, but as one of those indications of the plurality in unity in the divine Being which are repeatedly met with in the Old Testament, and which must be regarded as foreshadowings of the doctrine of the Trinity § 275. 3. *a*. The future tense expresses the divine determination, *we will make* § 263. 1, or, as the paragogic future rarely has a distinct form in לה verbs § 172. 3, and may therefore be regarded as included under the simple future, it may have the cohortative sense, *let us make*. אָדָם generic name *man*, has no construct or plural § 201. 1. בְּצַלְמֵנוּ from צֶלֶם I. 1, § 183. root צָלַם *to be dark*, hence *shadow*, and, as this resembles the object by which it is cast, *image*, with 1 plur. suf. § 220. 1, § 221. 5, and prep. בְּ *in* § 231. 1, the model being conceived of as enclosing the copy, every line of which is

directed by and drawn in the corresponding line of the former.
כִּדְמוּתֵנוּ , I. 1, with fem. ending § 184. *b*, § 198. *a* (4), from לה root דמה
to be like, hence *likeness*, not here distinguishable in its sense from the
preceding word, to which it is added for the sake of emphasis, comp.
§ 280. 3. *a*. That there is no special significance in the change of prepositions appears from their being reversed in the same phrase, 5 : 3.
וְיִרְדּוּ from רָדָה § 169. 1, plural because referring to the collective אָדָם
§ 275. 2, followed by ב which indicates the territory *in* which the dominion is exercised. בִּדְגַת prep. § 231. 2, const. § 214. 1, § 216. 1, of the
fem. collective noun דָּגָה § 198, I. 2, § 185. *d*, from root דָּגָה *to increase*,
hence *fish*, from their rapid multiplication.

27. אֹתוֹ might be taken distributively in the sense of the plural
§ 275. 6, but more probably the singular pronoun contains an allusion to
the fact that Adam was first created alone, 2 : 20. אֹתָם pronoun referring to both genders put in the masculine § 276. 3.

28. וַיֹּאמֶר לָהֶם, אָמַר followed by ל or אֶל is *to speak to*, more rarely
to speak of or *in reference to*. וּכְבָשֻׁהָ conjunction § 234, Kal imper. of
כָּבַשׁ § 84. 4, and pronominal suffix § 101 ; *u* written defectively § 11. 1.
a, § 14.

29. נָתַתִּי from נָתַן § 130. 1, *I have given* for *I hereby give*, in conformity with a purpose already formed § 262. 1. *b*.   אֶת־כָּל־ § 270. *c*.
זֶרַע § 245. 2. אֲשֶׁר־בוֹ § 74, § 285. 1.   זֹרֵעַ singular referring formally
to the nearest collective subject § 276. 1, or taken distributively § 275.
6, with ל be *to* you, i. e. you shall have it, be *for* food, i. e. answer for,
become.

30. אֶת־כָּל־יֶרֶק § 270. *c*, supply נָתַתִּי.   יֶרֶק עֵשֶׂב const. of designation § 254. 3, *greenness of herb*, i. e. *green herb*.

31. עָשָׂה past in relation to another past, i. e. pluperfect § 262. 1.
מְאֹד primarily a noun, *might*, then with an adverbial sense, *mightily*,
very § 235. 3 (1), follows the word which it qualifies § 274. 1.   יוֹם
הַשִּׁשִּׁי article omitted before the noun § 249. 1. *c*.

CHAPTER II.

1. וַיְכֻלּוּ Pual fut. of כָּלָה § 169. 1, 3 m. pl. with a compound subject
§ 276. 1, Daghesh forte omitted from י, Sh'va remaining vocal § 25,
§ 99. 3. צְבָאָם I. 2, § 185. 1, m. and f., pl. in וֹת § 200. *a*, from צָבָא
to go forth to war, masc. pl. suf. referring to nouns of different gender
§ 276. 3.   The phrase 'host of heaven' occurs repeatedly both of
celestial beings 1 Kin. 22 : 19 and celestial bodies Deut. 4 : 19.   The
host of the earth, an expression occurring only in this one passage

prior to the derangement of the fall, denotes its inhabitants and all that it contains. They are called 'a host' from their vast numbers and orderly array, and possibly also because they are under God's command and fighting against the kingdom of evil.

2. וַיְכַל *ended*, i. e. by discontinuing, not by performing the concluding portion, so that there is no need either of supposing that part of the work of creation was performed on the seventh day, or of changing 'seventh' to 'sixth' to evade the fancied difficulty. הַשְּׁבִיעִי ordinal number § 227. 1, its position and agreement § 251. 1, § 249. 1. מְלַאכְתּוֹ from מְלָאכָה, III., root לְאַךְ *to send*, hence a service upon which one is sent, *work*, in const. מְלֶאכֶת § 214. 1. *b*, with suf. § 221. 2. *a.* עָשָׂה in the sense of the pluperfect § 262. 1.

3. וַיְבָרֶךְ *blessed*, i. e. conferred upon it special honour and distinction, and made it fruitful of blessing. אֶת־יוֹם הַשְּׁבִיעִי the article omitted from the noun in a definite phrase § 249. 1. *c*, or else the noun is in the construct before its adjective § 252. 2, § 254. 6. *b.* Comp. שְׁנַת הַשְּׁבִיעִית Ezr. 7 : 8. וַיְקַדֵּשׁ *sanctified*, i. e. made sacred, set apart to a sacred use. The natural interpretation of the language is that this was done at the time of creation, and not ages afterwards at the giving of the law upon Sinai. This too agrees with the traces of weeks, Gen. 7 : 4, 8 : 10, 17 : 12, 50 : 10, and the sacredness of the number seven in the patriarchal age, Gen. 21 : 28 etc., as well as among several ancient nations, with the observance of the Sabbath in Israel before they came to Sinai, Ex. 16 : 23, etc. and with the exhortation in the fourth commandment to *remember* the Sabbath day as though it were an institution with which they were already acquainted and not then introduced for the first time. אֹתוֹ sign of definite object with suf. § 238. 2, § 270. בָּרָא . . . לַעֲשׂוֹת *created* so as *to make*, i. e. created not in its elements only, but so as to give it its completed form and full accomplishment, or the first verb may qualify the second § 269. *a, made in a creative manner*, or by creation.

4. אֵלֶּה demonstrative § 73. 1, predicate § 259. 2, referring either to what precedes, Gen. 10 : 5, 20, 31, 32, or to what follows, Gen. 10 : 1. This verse may be regarded as a formal conclusion of the foregoing narrative of the creation. *these are the generations*, i. e. such was the origin of the heavens and the earth. But it seems better to adopt the Jewish division of the text, and make it the heading of the ensuing section, 2 : 4—4 : 26; for (1) A like phrase occurs eleven times in Genesis, and invariably as the heading of successive portions of the book, e. g. 5 : 1, 6 : 9, 10 : 1 etc. (2) These titles in every other instance introduce an account, not of the ancestry of the persons named in them. but of their descendants and family history; hence *the generations* (תּוֹלְדוֹת III. f. pl

const. from ‎ root ‎יָלַד‎ *to bring forth* § 190. *b*) *of the heavens and the earth* record not how they came into being, but the origin and history of man who sprang from them or was formed out of them. In strictness indeed it was from the earth alone that man was made, but the heavens and the earth form one whole, the common theatre of the history now to be unfolded. For that reason the creation of both was described together, 1 : 1 etc. and now follow their *generations* or the further developments upon the scene thus prepared. This first stage of human history embraces a more minute account of the creation and original state of man, 2 : 4—25, as preliminary to ch. 3, the fall, the sequel of which is ch. 4, the sundering of the race into two opposite branches, and the initiation of the struggle foreshadowed, 3 : 15, between the seed of the woman and the seed of the serpent.

‎בְּהִבָּֽרְאָם‎ prep. ‎בְּ‎ with Niph. inf. const. of ‎בָּרָא‎ § 267. *b*, and 3 m. pl. suf. § 106. *a*, § 276. 3, here representing the subject § 102. 3, *in their being created*, i. e. when they were created. The marginal note is ‎זְעִירָא ה‎ (fem. of the Chaldee adj. ‎זְעֵיר‎ § 196. *d*) *small He* § 4. *a*, which the Rabbins explain as a mystic reference to the future diminishing and passing away of the material creation, or as suggestive of the anagram ‎בְּאַבְרָהָם‎ *in Abraham*, for whom, together with his seed, the universe was created, and which some critics have doubtfully conjectured to indicate a reading with ‎ה‎ omitted § 91. *b* ‎בְּיוֹם‎ *in the day* indefinitely for *at the time of*, Lev. 14 : 57, 2 Sam. 23 : 20; there is no implication, as some have imagined, at variance with ch. 1, that the creation occupied but one day. This may be parallel to and explanatory of the preceding ‎הִבָּֽרְאָם‎, comp. Num. 3 : 1, or it may be the beginning of a new sentence which is continued in ver. 5, comp. 5 : 1. ‎עֲשׂוֹת‎ const. before its subject ‎יְהֹוָה אֱלֹהִים‎ and governing ‎אֶרֶץ וְשָׁמָיִם‎ as its object § 254. 9. *b*. ‎יְהֹוָה‎ *Jehovah* III. § 192. 1, with the vowels of ‎אֲדֹנָי‎ *Lord* § 47, from the root ‎הָוָה‎ = ‎הָיָה‎ *to be*, denoting not a future quality, *he who will become*, i. e. will unfold or reveal himself hereafter, or *he who will be*, i. e. who is to come, but, as proper names so formed invariably do, a permanent essential characteristic, *he who is*, who has existence in its fullest and highest sense, the self-existent and hence eternal and unchangeable, paraphrased Rev. 1 : 4, 8, 'which is and which was and which is to come,' whence the conclusion has sometimes been erroneously drawn that ‎יְהֹוָה‎ is compounded of the future ‎יִהְיֶה‎, the participle ‎הֹוֶה‎ and the preterite ‎הָיָה‎. Hitherto God has been called exclusively ‎אֱלֹהִים‎; from this verse to the end of ch. 3 he is prevailingly called ‎יְהֹוָה אֱלֹהִים‎, and in ch. 4 ‎יְהֹוָה‎. This interchange, which is too remarkable to be accidental, and which though less conspicuous is yet perceptible in the rest of Genesis, gave

rise to the critical hypothesis that the sections using different divine
names have proceeded from different authors, one being distinguished
by his preference for אֱלֹהִים and the other by his preference for יְהוָה.
But this hypothesis, notwithstanding the ingenuity with which it has
been constructed, fails to account for the very unusual combination
יְהוָה אֱלֹהִים, which is found in but one other passage in the Pentateuch,
Ex. 9 : 30, and but rarely in the rest of the Bible, and also for the
frequent occurrence of one divine name in the midst of a section characterized mainly by the other. This shows that the phenomenon in
question has not arisen from an unconscious peculiarity of style in different writers, but is due to the intelligent selection of the appropriate
word as determined by the thought and the connection. Although these
names are in a multitude of cases used indiscriminately, as 'God' and
'Lord' are in English, and it would be vain to seek a reason in every
case why one is employed rather than the other, there is a real distinction between them, which is sometimes observed. Thus in the opening
chapters of Genesis אֱלֹהִים, which is the more general name of God, is
employed in the account of the creation ; but in that of the fall, with its
promise of redemption, from which all the subsequent revelations of
mercy are unfolded, the covenant name יְהוָה is used, which specially
belongs to him as the God of revelation and of grace. In the first step
of the transition from one to the other both names are combined to indicate their identity ; יְהוָה is no other than אֱלֹהִים, the God of the covenant is the same with the God of creation. The exceptional use of
אֱלֹהִים in 3 : 1. 3. 5 is because the serpent is either speaking or ad
dressed, where the covenant name of God would be as inappropriate as
in language uttered by idolatrous Gentiles or directed to them, Jud. 3 :
20, comp. ver. 28, 1 Sam. 4 : 7. 8, 30 : 15, 1 Kin. 20 : 23, comp. ver.
28. Again, in 4 : 25 Eve speaks of אֱלֹהִים because she has respect
to God as working in nature, whereas in 4 : 1 it is יְהוָה, who had
granted her a pledge of the promised redemption.

אֶרֶץ וְשָׁמָיִם earth, named before heaven, as in but one other passage, Ps. 148 : 13, as some suppose, to indicate the order of their formation, 1 : 9—19, the earth on the third day and the heavenly bodies on
the fourth ; but more probably because the earth was chiefly concerned
in the following narration. This inversion of the accustomed order
imparts to the expression a sort of poetic character, whence the omission
of the article § 247.

5. וְכֹל שִׂיחַ. Three constructions are possible : (1) שִׂיחַ may be the
object of עָשָׂה in ver. 4, comp. Ex. 12 : 34 ; so the LXX, Vulg. and Eng.
Ver. (2) It may be the subject of יְהוָה and the beginning of a new

sentence, *and no* § 256. *c, shrub of the field was yet in the earth,* comp.
1 Sam. 3 : 3. 7.   (3) The sentence may begin with מַיִם and וְ simply
form the connection with this statement of time § 287. 3, comp. Gen.
19 : 4, *in the day* etc. *then no shrub* etc.   This last construction seems
to be the best.   תוֹלְדוֹת I. 2, from an obsolete לה root § 185. *d;* its repeated occurrence in ch. 2 and 3, and that even in combinations in
which אֶרֶץ is found in ch. 1, e. g. חַיַּת הַשָּׂדֶה 2 : 19. 20, 3 : 1. 14, has been
perverted into an argument for diversity of authorship.   The simple explanation is that אֶרֶץ denotes *earth* in contrast with *heaven,* and *land* in
contrast with *water.*   But throughout this section there is a tacit opposition
between the *garden,* or the space enclosed for man's primeval habitation,
and the open space without, or the *field.*   טֶרֶם followed by the future
referring to past time § 263. 1. *b,* accent Y'thibh § 30. 2.   כִּי *because*
assigns a double reason for the non-existence of vegetation at the time
spoken of, the lack of rain to prepare the ground for its production, as
well as of man for whose use it was designed.   The period referred to
is before the creation of plants and trees upon the third day, or, in the
judgment of others, a vegetation suited to the wants of terrestrial animals
may first have been brought into being on the sixth day, prior to their
creation and that of man.   It is next stated how these two requisites
were supplied in ver. 6 rain, in ver. 7 man.   Every thing to the end of
this chapter is in the strictest sense preliminary to the history of the
fall.   Details necessary to acquaint us with the situation, vs. 5–17, and
the actors, vs. 18–25, which, though falling within the period covered by
chap. 1, would have been unsuited to its majesty and would have marred
its symmetry, were reserved for this place.   הִמְטִיר in the sense of the
pluperfect § 262. 1.   אַיִן § 236, in the absolute state § 258. *b.*

6. וְאֵד conj. וְ, not adversative *but,* as though it introduced a substitute for the missing rain, but copulative *and,* proceeding to show how
it was actually supplied § 287. 1 ; אֵד I. 2, from an obsolete אד root § 186.
c, vapour, which rising from the earth was condensed into rain and
watered the ground.   יַעֲלֶה, ע guttural § 109, and לה verb § 168, future
denoting repetition § 263. 4 ; the following pret. with Vav conv. וְהִשְׁקָה
§ 100. 1, has a like sense § 265.

7. וַיִּיצֶר from יצר verb § 144. 2, with a double object § 273. 3.   Vav
conv. draws back the accent and changes Pattahh to Seghol § 147. 5 ;
the postpositive accent § 30. 1 is repeated in some editions.   In 1 : 27,
where the immediate exercise of divine power in the creation of man
was to be made prominent, בָּרָא was employed ; here the thought is
directed to the material of which he was made, and the proper word is
יָצַר *to form,* used of a potter moulding vessels of clay.   וַיִּיצֶר ־ס § 129. 1

and שׁ guttural § 123. 1. בְּאַפָּיו prep. and noun אַף I. 1. § 184. b ('ם
and לם roots) by contraction for אֲנַף § 54. 2 from אנף *to breathe*, hence
breather, *nose*, here in the dual *nostrils*, with Daghesh-forte § 207. 2,
and 3 m. s. suf. § 220. 2. נִשְׁמַת I. with fem. ending § 198. a (2), const.
before its quality § 254. 6, which is expressed by the abstract חַיִּים
(= חַיָּה) *life* § 201. 1. a. וַיְהִי ... לְ *was to* or *unto*, the preposition
implying a change of state or condition, hence *became*, see 1 : 14. 29.

8. וַיִּטַּע, נטע § 129. 1 and ע׳ guttural § 123. 1. It has been charged
that ch. 2 contradicts ch. 1 in making the creation of man prior to that
of plants. But (1) the plants and trees here spoken of are those of the
garden of Eden, not those of the earth generally. (2) The priority ac-
corded to man, even as respects this garden, lies in the order of thought
rather than in the succession of time. To prepare the way for an account of the garden of Eden, the writer, ver. 5, reverts to the time when
there were yet no plants in the earth. As these, and especially the
trees of Eden, which he has chiefly in mind, were for the sake of man,
he speaks, ver. 7, of his creation, then, ver. 8, of planting the garden
and putting man in it, then, ver. 9, in order to reach the idea that it
was not only an abode but a place of trial, of the trees which were made
to grow there, and finally, ver. 15, of man's being placed there to dress
and to keep it. That this narration, though linked throughout by futures
with Vav conversive, does not aim at strict chronological succession, is
obvious, since the act of placing man in the garden could not both have
preceded and followed the production of the trees. And if the succession is that of the association of ideas rather than of chronology, then
the circumstance that the formation of man is named before the planting
of the garden, does not prove that it preceded it in actual fact. It is
indeed much more natural to assume that the contrary was the real
order of occurrence. גַּן I. § 186. c, from גנן root גָּנַן *to protect*, hence a
place protected, securely fenced about, *a garden*. בְּעֵדֶן this orthography
is appropriated exclusively to Eden, the abode of our first parents. The
Eden of later times, 2 Kin. 19 : 12, is עֶדֶן. מִקֶּדֶם. As the Hebrews
estimated direction by measuring from the object spoken of and not
toward it, as we are accustomed to do, see on מִתַּחַת 1 : 7, their *from east*
is equivalent to our *eastward*, i. e. from the rest of the land of Eden,
and consequently in the eastern part of the land. וַיָּשֶׂם, עׁ׳ verb § 153. 5.
As קֶדֶם also has a temporal sense, *antiquity*, this verse gave rise to
the legend that paradise was older than the world, 2 Esdras 3 : 6.

9. וַיַּצְמַח Vav conv. compresses Hhirik in Hiph. fut. to Tsere § 99.
3, which in ע׳ gutt. verbs becomes Pattahh § 123. 2, § 126. 1. וְנֶחְמָד
with simple Sh'va § 112. 5, the participle expressing not only a constant

experience but a permanent quality, not merely *desired* but *desirable*
§ 266. 1. לְמַרְאֶה III. § 190, from רָאָה *to see*, hence that which is seen
§ 191. 5, *as to appearance*. לְמַאֲכָל III. from אָכַל *to eat, for food*. עֵץ as
this is often a collective, some have been of opinion that there was not only
one but many trees of life and trees of knowledge ; the pronoun referring
to the latter, however, is always in the singular, ver. 17, 3 : 3, etc. The
article is prefixed to the following word הַחַיִּים § 246. 3, § 256, to render
עֵץ definite. For the same reason הַדַּעַת Kal const. inf. of יָדַע § 144. 3,
§ 148. 2, and § gutt. verb § 123, receives the article contrary to the
general rule § 245. 5. b, comp. 1 Kin. 10 : 19. : טוֹב וָרָע are the direct
object of the verb, *the tree of knowing good and evil*. The rhetorical
character of the accents is exemplified in the pause made upon the name
of this fatal tree and the deliberate manner in which it is to be pronounced, עֵץ though in the close connection of the construct state having
Zakeph Gadhol, and הַדַּעַת having Tiphhha.

10. וְנָהָר I. 2. from נָהַר *to flow*, subject preceding the verb in a descriptive clause, see on הָאָרֶץ 1 : 2. יֹצֵא time of participle § 266. 3.
לְהַשְׁקוֹת, לְ § 168, prep. expressing the design or the result, *in order to*
or *so as to*. יִפָּרֵד fut. because consequent to the preceding ; the river
waters the garden and *will be divided*, i. e. is afterwards divided § 263.
5. a. וְהָיָה pret. with Vav conv. assimilated in sense to preceding
future § 265, with לְ *be unto*, i. e. become, ver. 7. לְאַרְבָּעָה cardinal § 223.
1, peculiarity of form § 223. 2, and construction § 250. 2, § 251. : רָאשִׁים
1. 1. § 207. 1. f.

11. שֵׁם I. 2. abbreviated from obsolete שָׁמָה root § 185. d. הָאֶחָד *the
one*, where we would use the ordinal number, because in a series or
enumeration *the first* is counted *one*. פִּישׁוֹן IV. § 193, from פּוּשׁ *to
overflow*, like most other objects in antediluvian geography of doubtful
if not impossible identification. הַסֹּבֵב *the one compassing* § 259. b, not
necessarily making a complete circuit of the land, but *going around* one
side of it, or *going about* tortuously through it. הַחֲוִילָה I. 2. with fem.
ending, perhaps from חוֹל *sand* (root חוּל *to whirl about*), *the sandy
region, Havilah*, with the article on account of its original appellative
sense § 246. 1. a. אֲשֶׁר־שָׁם § 74. הַזָּהָב *the* well known metal *gold*
§ 245. 5 (see note c) ; for the same reason in ver. 12 הַבְּדֹלַח § 195. 1 and
: הַשֹּׁהַם.

12. וּזֲהַב § 16. 3. b, § 234. a. הַהִוא remote demonstrative § 71. a
(3), § 73. 3, § 47, with the article § 249. 2. טוֹב predicate follows the
subject in a descriptive sentence § 259. a.

13. גִּיחוֹן IV. from גִּיחַ *to burst forth*. : כּוּשׁ *the land of Cush*, the
region settled by the descendants of Cush, the son of Ham, Gen. 10 : 6,

though it is uncertain which portion of that vast territory is here designated by this name.

14. חִדֶּקֶל notwithstanding its seeming diversity is really a modification of the name *Tigris* by interchanging smooth and middle mutes and
liquids (*dkl = tgr*) and prefixing a guttural. קִדְמַת § 208. 2. *a*, either
east of, when אַשּׁוּר *Assyria* must be restricted to Mesopotamia, or *in
front of*, i. e. between the region where Moses was and Assyria, which
will then denote the empire so called exclusive of Mesopotamia. קִדְמַת
may be used adverbially or may be the direct object of הֹלֵךְ § 271. 2.
הוּא copula § 258. 2.   :פְרָת *Euphrates*, which was too familiar to need
further description.

15. יִקַּח § 132. 2.   :וַיַּנִּחֵהוּ from נוּחַ § 160. 1, with 3 m. s. suf. § 101.
2.   וּלְשָׁמְרָהּ לְעָבְדָהּ Kal inf. const. with suf. § 101. 3, no Daghesh lene in
ר § 22. *a* (1), both the positive and the negative side of his task.

16. וַיְצַו Piel fut. of צָוָה § 171. 1, here followed by עַל, because the
command is regarded as something laid *upon* the man, elsewhere occasionally by אֶל or ל before the person *to* whom it is directed: more
frequently the person commanded is, as in English, the direct object of
the verb. The language of the command is introduced by לֵאמֹר *so as to
say*. אָמַר § 87, § 282.   :תֹּאכֵל § 110. 3, § 111. 2. *a*, the future permissive § 263. 1.

17. וְהָיָה, *and* stands, even in adversative clauses, where our idiom
requires *but* § 287. 1.   יָדַע § 233 (see note *a*) repeats for greater
clearness the idea of עֵץ § 281.   כִּי *for* assigns the reason.   אָכְלְךָ
§ 106. *a*, no Daghesh lene § 22. *a* (6).   :מוֹת תָּמוּת § 153. emphatic infin.
§ 282; the phrase for the penalty of death in the laws of Moses is
modelled after this, though as it was to be executed by man it is varied
by the substitution of the Hophal for the Kal, e. g. Ex. 19 : 12, מוֹת
יוּמָת *he shall be put to death*.

18. הֱיוֹת § 177. 1, const. before הָאָדָם and subject of sentence § 242.
b, with a masc. predicate adj. § 275. 1, or as infinitives even when they
have a fem. ending regularly take a masc. adj. it may be explained as
a substitute for the neuter § 196. *a*.   לְבַדּוֹ prep. ל *to*, which when motion
is not implied becomes *at* or *in*, as in Lat. *ad*, Gr. εἰς ; בַד I. from בד
root בדד *to separate* § 186. *c*, with suf. § 221. 6, *in his separation*, i. e.
alone.   וֹ Dag. conj. § 24. *a*.   עֵזֶר abstract for concrete, *help* for *helper*.
:כְּנֶגְדּוֹ his counterpart, corresponding to him, lit. *as over against him*.

19. וַיִּצֶר § 147. 1 and 4, see ver. 7. The alleged discrepancy between this account and ch. 1 in respect to the time and the occasion of
creating the inferior animals is purely imaginary. It is not here declared that they were created after man and for the purpose of providing

a help meet for him. To suppose them made for this purpose is to charge God with failure in his first attempts, which the writer surely cannot have intended to do. And the future with Vav conv. does not always imply strict succession of time, see on ver. 8, also Gen. 12 : 1, comp. 11 : 32. Especially where two such verbs are connected as here נַיָּצַר .... וַיִּבֶא, the progress not infrequently lies wholly in the second, to which the first is in fact, though not in form, subordinate, the phrase being really equivalent to ' he brought the animals which he had formed etc.' So Deut. 31 : 9, 'And Moses wrote this law and delivered it,' can only mean 'he delivered this law which he had written.' וַיִּבֵא § 160. 3, § 166. 4, object omitted because sufficiently plain from the connection, comp. § 243. 1. לִרְאָ֫ות § 168. מַה § 75. 1. יִקְרָא fut. relative to a preceding past, would call § 263. 1, government see on וַיִּקְרָא 1 : 5. לֹ sing. in distributive sense § 275. 6, masc. § 276. 3. נֶפֶשׁ in apposition with לֹו § 253. 1. הוּא copula, for which our idiom requires the substantive verb was § 258. 2.

20. וּלְאָדָם here a proper noun, and therefore without the article § 246. 1.

21. וַיַּפֵּל § 129. 1, § 99. 3, that which is divinely sent is represented as descending from above. תַּרְדֵּמָה III. § 192. a, from רָדַם to be in a deep sleep denotes a deep and in most instances a supernatural sleep. אַחַת § 223. 1. a. תַּחְתֶּנָּה 3 f. s. suf. with ן epenthetic, a form used mostly with verbs § 238. 1. b, § 101. 2, § 105. b, under, then in place of, instead of.

22. וַיִּבֶן § 171. 1. לְאִשָּׁה fem. of אִישׁ § 207. 2 (see note e), § 214. 1. b, root אָנַשׁ to be feeble, sickly, the proper terms for the male and female of the human species, while זָכָר and נְקֵבָה are common to them with other animals, and are therefore used, 1 : 27, when man is contemplated as the head of the animate creation. וַיְבִאֶהָ § 153. 1, § 157. 3, § 160. 3.

23. זֹאת demonstrative § 73. 1. הַפַּעַם § 245. 3. b, from פָּעַם to beat, transferred to marking time. עֶצֶם from עָצַם to be strong. מֵאִישׁ § 232, אִישׁ like vir, ἀνήρ, denotes a man as distinguished from a woman, or in the married relation a husband as opposed to the wife; אָדָם like homo, ἄνθρωπος, is the generic name embracing both sexes, and is used, particularly with the article, in a collective sense of mankind, or individually of Adam, the progenitor of the race. When contrasted with each other, אָדָם denotes an ordinary man, or one of low rank, while אִישׁ is a man par excellence, one distinguished by manly qualities or high position. Both may have the sense of indefinite pronouns, a man, i. e. some one, any one, each. לֻקֳחָה Methegh § 45. 2, compound Sh'va § 16. 3. b, Daghesh forte omitted § 25.

24. The language of Adam continued, or a remark of the writer עַל־כֵּן *upon*, or, since the effect rests upon its cause, *because of, on account of, so*, i. e. *therefore*. עַל־כֵּן Makkeph § 43, § 88 (3 m.). אָבִיו § 220. 1. c. וְדָבַק *cleave*, followed by בְּ *in* denoting combination, *in union with*, elsewhere by לְ or אֶל *to*, or in the sense of ardent pursuit by אַחֲרֵי *after*.

25. וַיִּהְיוּ § 276. 3. שְׁנֵיהֶם *they two* § 250. 2. *a*, not *two of them*, which would require the insertion of the prep. אֵן, comp. אַחַת מִצַּלְעֹתָיו ver. 21. עֲרוּמִּים pl. of עָרוֹם § 207. 2. c, by Gesenius derived from עָרַם, but as this verb has a different sense, it is perhaps better to regard it as a shortened form of עֵירֹם IV. from עוּר *to be naked* § 193. c. The marginal note is דָּגֵשׁ אַחַר שׁוּרֶק *Daghesh after Shurek*, which is here a short vowel § 14. *a*, § 19. 1. יִתְבֹּשָׁשׁוּ § 154. 2, § 96. *b*, fut. since it follows from the preceding, *were not ashamed in consequence* § 263. 5. *a*.

CHAPTER III.

1. וְהַנָּחָשׁ onomatopoetic root נָחַשׁ *to hiss*, article § 245. 3, subject stands first in a descriptive sentence. עָרוּם I. 2, from עָרַם *to be cunning*, predicate § 259. 2, superlative § 260. 2 (1). אַף כִּי *also that* as an exclamation, It is then true *also that God has said!* or as a question, though without the usual sign of interrogation § 284, Is it true *also that* etc.? The accession implied in אַף is to whatever would be naturally understood. In addition to everything else *has he also* or *even said?* אֱלֹהִים, see on יְהֹוָה אֱלֹהִים 2 : 4. לֹא ... מִכֹּל might be translated *not from any* § 256. c, as though the tempter purposely exaggerated the rigour of the prohibition; this is the usual sense when כֹּל is indefinite, but as it is here definite by construction it seems better to read *not from all*, i. e. from a part only, comp. Num. 23 : 13.

2. נֹאכֵל, the future is permissive § 263. 1.

3. וּמִפְּרִי dependent upon הֲלֹא and repeated in תֹּאכְלוּ; not upon אֲשֶׁר, as the Eng. Ver. might be understood. תִּגְּעוּ בּוֹ § 129. 1, commonly followed by בְּ (as are also other verbs of sense, e. g. smell, hearing, and sight, though verbs of sight are modified in meaning by this construction, see on 1 : 4), indicating the intimate conjunction of the sense with its object; or if the prep. be taken in the partitive sense which it likewise has, it will resemble the Greek construction of this same class of verbs with the partitive genitive, 'to touch *in* a thing,' i. e. somewhere within its entire extent as opposed to uniform contact throughout. The verb is also sometimes followed by אֶל *to*, עַד *unto*, עַל *upon*, or by the direct object § 272. 2. תְּמֻתוּן § 88 (2 and 3 m. pl.), paragogic Nun causing the rejection of Kamets § 157. 3.

4. לְבִלְתִּי‎ emphatic infin. § 282; the negative adverb is also rendered prominent by being prefixed to the whole phrase, instead of standing in its customary place between the infinitive and the finite verb.

5. כִּי‎ confirmatory, *for.* כִּי‎ declarative, *that.* וְנִפְקְחוּ‎, Vav connects with בְּיוֹם‎ § 287. 3, by which the action is referred to the future § 265. *b*, plural verb with dual subject § 278. כֵּאלֹהִים‎ § 231. 3. *a.* יֹדְעֵי‎ may agree with the preceding noun § 275. 3. *a*, or better perhaps with the subject of the sentence § 276. 3, const. before its object § 254. 9. *b.*

6. וַתֵּרֶא‎ § 172. 4. —תַּאֲוָה‎ III. f. from אָוָה‎ *to long for,* hence *a desire, delight.* הֶעֵץ‎, observe the article. לְהַשְׂכִּיל‎ Gesen. *to behold,* others, as Eng. Ver. *to make wise.* מַצְּפֵי‎ § 221. 5. *c.* וַתֹּאכַל‎ § 35. 2.

7. עֵירֻמִּם‎ IV. root עוּר‎ *to be naked* § 193. *c,* see on 2 : 25, *nakednesses,* abst. noun for adj *naked* § 254. 6. *a.* עָלֵה‎ 1. 2, root עָלָה‎ *to ascend, grow up.* תְּאֵנָה‎ *fig-tree,* from its spreading, root תָּאַן‎ *to extend.* לָהֶם‎, the simple pronoun used as a reflexive, *for themselves.* חֲגֹרֹת‎ :, root חָגַר‎ *to gird.*

8. וַיִּשְׁמְעוּ‎ *to hear,* followed by the direct object or by בְּ‎, see on וַתֵּשֶׁמַע‎ ver. 3; with לְ‎ or אֶל‎ it means *to hearken to.* קוֹל‎ the kindred verb is obsolete in Heb. though in use in Arabic, *to say,* here not *voice* but *sound,* since מִתְהַלֵּךְ‎ (*to go for one's self* § 80. 1 (2), hence *to walk about,* comp. Fr. *se promener*) being without the article is a predicate and not a qualifying participle § 259. 2. It was consequently the noise of the walking which was heard, not the voice of God as he was walking. The subject with its predicate is subordinated to שָׁמַע אֶת־קוֹל‎ comp. 1 Kin. 14 : 6, just as it might be to קוֹל‎ alone § 273. 4. לְרוּחַ‎ *at* (see on לָבֹא‎ 2 : 18) *the wind* or breeze *of the day,* i. e. toward evening. וַיִּתְחַבֵּא‎ § 276. 1. מִפְּנֵי‎ *from the face* or presence *of,* generally used before persons as מִן‎ before things.

9. אַיֶּכָּה‎ : § 236. 3, § 104. *b*, § 105. *b.*

10. אֶת־קֹלְךָ‎, object emphatically prefixed § 270. *a.* וָאֵחָבֵא‎ :, Niphal reflexive § 77. 2.

11. מִי‎ § 75. 1. הִגִּיד‎ § 129. 1, properly signifies 'to cause to be before (prep. נֶגֶד‎) any one,' i. e. *to show, tell,* followed by לְ‎ or less frequently the direct object of the person. אֲשֶׁר . . . מִמֶּנּוּ—‎ § 230. 1., relative governed by מִן‎ § 74, § 285. 1. צִוִּיתִיךָ‎ § 169. 2, commonly followed by the direct object of the person, more rarely by עַל‎ *upon,* אֶל‎ *unto,* or לְ‎ *to,* the command being conceived of as laid upon a person or directed to him. לְבִלְתִּי‎, negative adverb formed by adding paragogic י‎ § 61. 6. *a,* to the obsolete בֶּלֶת‎ from בָּלָה‎ *to waste away,* be reduced to nothing; this is always used instead of לֹא‎ before the infin. with לְ‎.

12. נָתַתָּה‎ § 130. 1, § 86. *b* (2 m. s.). עִמָּדִי = עִמִּי‎, this prolonged form

of the prep. עִם occurs only before 1 sing. suffix. חוּא § 71. *a* (3), § 281 וְיָאֵלֽב § 111. 2. *b*.

14. מִכָּל-, prep. מִן in its comparative sense § 260. 2 (1). גְּחֹנְךָ I. 2 root גָּחַן *to bend*, hence that which bends or curves, *belly*. תֵּלֵךְ § 151. 1. The posture to which the serpent is doomed and his eating dust, not as his proper food, comp. Ps. 102 : 10, but as an incidental consequence of his prostrate form, is a standing type of the humiliation and doom of Satan the real seducer. יְמֵי from יוֹם § 207. 1. *f*.

15. וְאֵיבָה I. f. from אָיַב *to be hostile*. זַרְעֲךָ *thy seed*, i. e. devils and wicked men, Mat. 13 : 38, John 8 : 44. זַרְעָהּ *her seed*, i. e. in its widest sense, mankind limited only by the opposition just suggested in the 'seed of the serpent,' the defection of those who attach themselves to the party of the enemy. The tempted, ruined race shall trample under foot its enemy and seducer. So the apostle Paul applies it, Rom. 16 : 20. At the same time this victory is really achieved by One from amongst mankind, the Messiah, and the expressions are so framed as to be specially applicable to him. His birth of a virgin makes him peculiarly the seed of the woman, while the singular pronoun הוּא and his being said to bruise or *crush* Satan himself יְשׁוּפְךָ rather than his seed, gives it the appearance of a personal and individual conflict. That זֶרַע may be used of an individual appears from 4 : 25. רֹאשׁ, a second object indicating the part affected § 271. 4, § 273. 2.

16. הַרְבָּה § 175. 2. עִצְּבוֹנֵךְ IV. from עָצַב *to be afflicted* § 193. 2, hence *toil, sorrow*. וְהֵרֹנֵךְ IV. from הָרָה *to conceive*, contracted from הֵרָיוֹן, as if for הֵרְיֹנֵךְ § 53. 3. *a*. It is not necessary to assume a hendiadys for *the sorrow of thy conception;* the meaning is *thy sorrow* and especially *thy conception* considered as a painful suffering condition. תֵּלְדִי § 144. 2. בָּנִים § 207. 1. *a*, root בָּנָה *to build* § 185. *d*, offspring considered as constituting their parent's house. תְּשׁוּקָתֵךְ III. f. § 192. 2. *a*, from שׁוּק *to run after, desire*. יִמְשָׁל-בָּךְ Makkeph § 43, § 88 (3 m.); for the construction with בְּ, see on 1 : 18.

17. וּלְאָדָם here, as 2 : 20, a proper name, and therefore without the article § 246. 1. בַּעֲבוּרֶךָ *on thy account*. The origin of this sense has been variously accounted for; perhaps the simplest explanation is the following, suggested by Ewald. עֲבוּר, from עָבַר *to pass*, denotes that which passes out of something else, its 'product' or 'consequence'; as a noun it is used of the *produce* of the earth; as a preposition, in which case it is always compounded with בְּ, it means *in consequence of, on account of;* pause accent § 65. (3). תֹּאכֲלֶנָּה compound Sh'va § 16. 3. *b*, Nun epenthetic § 101. 2, *eat it*, i. e. the fruit of it, comp. Isa. 1 : 7.

18. וְקוֹץ *thorn* from קוּץ *to cut*, on account of its pricking or cutting.

וְדַרְדַּר II. § 187. 1. *e*, from דָּרַר, perhaps in the sense of growing luxuriantly, hence *a thistle*. לָךְ, pausal form for לְךָ § 65. *a*. וְאָכַלְתָּ, accent shifted by Vav conversive § 33. 4, § 100. *a*, *eat the herb of the field*, in contrast with the trees of the garden.

19. בְּזֵעַת I. f. from פּ root יָזַע *to flow* § 184. *b*, Tsere retained in the const. § 216. 1. *b*; the prep. בְּ expresses the condition *in* which he should eat bread, a condition induced, as is implied, by the toil necessary to procure it; or it may be used, as it often is, to denote the price, the thing purchased being regarded as contained *in* that which is paid as its equivalent, *in* return for or *at* the cost of *the sweat*, etc. אַפֶּיךָ, primarily *nose*, then used, as here, for the whole *face*. תֵּאָכֵל § 35. 1. לֶחֶם I. 1. root לָחַם *to consume*. כִּי is confirmatory of the thought that man must *return* to the ground; the second כִּי is coordinate with the first, stating the same reason but with greater fulness.

20. וַיִּקְרָא, construction different from 2:20. חַוָּה *Eve*, II. f. from root חָוָה archaic form of חָיָה *to live*, hence *life*, abst. for concr. source or dispenser of life; כִּי assigns the reason, *because* through her, as appeared from ver. 16, the race was to be preserved from extinction.

21. כָּתְנוֹת § 216. 2. *b*. עוֹר *skin*, root עוּר *to be naked*. וַיַּלְבִּשֵׁם § 276. 3.

22. כְּאַחַד construct though followed by a prep. § 255. 1; not an ironical reference to the language of the tempter, ver. 5, but an assertion of its truth, though in a very different sense from that in which he designed it to be understood. מִמֶּנּוּ § 233, § 275. 3. *a*. גַּם, not only take, as he has done, of the forbidden tree, but *also* etc. § 39. 4. The concluding sentence of this verse is incomplete: it is broken off by an abrupt change from word to deed, and instead of a mere declaration of the divine purpose the actual expulsion of man from Eden follows.

23. מֵעֵדֶן . . . אֲשֶׁר § 74.

24. וַיְגָרֶשׁ § 99. 3. *a*. וַיַּשְׁכֵּן, from the same root comes שְׁכִינָה *Shekinah*, the name given by the later Jews to the symbol of the divine *residence* in the tabernacle and the temple. מִקֶּדֶם, see on 1 : 7, 2 : 8. לַהַט *flame*, i. e. the flashing blade, or with the sense of the adjective *flaming sword* § 254. 6. *a*, from לָהַט *to burn*. הַחֶרֶב *sword*, from חָרַב *to be waste* or *lay waste*. חֶרֶב const. § 254. 9. *a*.

CHAPTER XXXVII.

1. וַיֵּשֶׁב fut. with Vav conv. continues the narration § 99. 1, though the succession thus indicated is not always that of time or of actual occurrence, see on 2 : 8. 19. The writer here resumes the direct narrative

7

35 : 27, from which he had diverged to introduce Isaac's death, 35 : 28. 29, and what he thought it necessary to say about Esau's line, ch. 36. Having thus dismissed them from the history, he can now pursue unin· terruptedly his account of Jacob's family. In like manner the history of Isaac's family, 25 : 19, follows the record of Abraham's death, 25 : 7, and of Ishmael's line, 25 : 12; and Shem's descendants, 11 : 10, succeed those of Noah's other sons, 10 : 1. The statement of this verse accord· ingly, though not posterior in time to what immediately precedes, is so in the order of narration to which the writer steadfastly adheres through· out the book, the direct line of descent of the chosen seed being post· poned until the lateral branches have first been traced. בְּאֶרֶץ § 246. 3. אֲבִיו § 220. 1. *c.*

2. אֵלֶּה § 259. 2. תֹּלְדוֹת יַעֲקֹב, *the generations of Jacob,* i. e. an ac· count of his descendants. This is the uniform style of the titles pre· fixed to the different sections of Genesis, see on 2 : 4. It appears to have been selected on account of the prevailingly genealogical character of the history, the genealogies constituting, as it were, the frame work of which the narrative is the filling up. Jacob is henceforth contem· plated not as an individual but as a patriarch, the father and head of a family, whose fortunes are interwoven with his own. בֶּן § 215. 1. *b.* Terms of natural relationship are extensively employed in Hebrew to express various kinds of relation or dependence § 254. 6. *a.* Time is viewed as the parent of that which is produced within it, and a person or thing as the offspring of the time during which he or it has existed. The ordinary mode of stating the age is that here employed, *son of seventeen years,* i. e. *seventeen years old.* The chronological difficulty, which some have fancied here, is purely imaginary, and has arisen from neglecting to observe that though the writer in pursuance of his plan (see on ver. 1) has recorded the death of Isaac, 35 : 29, before proceeding to the history of Jacob's family, that event did not take place for several years after the occurrences now to be related. שָׁנָה, in the singular after *seventeen* § 251. 2. *a.* הָיָה § 265, § 266. 3. *a,* verb following its subject in a descriptive clause. רֹעֶה. This verb is often followed by אֵת, the sign of the direct object. If that is the case here it must be read *superintend· ing his brothers* (who were) *with the flock.* But as it would more naturally have צֹאן for its object, and it is sometimes elsewhere construed with בְּ, אֵת is doubtless the preposition *with,* and it is to be rendered *feeding* or *tending the flock with his brothers* אֶחָיו for אֶחָיו from אָח § 63. 1. *a,* § 207. 2. *b.* The preposition בְּ will then indicate the sphere *within* which the action of the verb was exercised, lit. *acting as shepherd in the flock.* בַּצֹּאן § 245. 3. וַיְהִי נַעַר *and he was a lad* § 258. 1. בְּנֵי

from בֵּן § 207. 1. *a*, § 216. 1. נְבִי from אָנָה § 207. 2. *e.* וַיָּבֵא, verb לו and לֹא § 160. 3. דִּבָּתָם רָעָה, the suffix denotes the object § 254. 9; the noun is consequently indefinite, and no article is required by רָעָה § 249. 1. *b*, *an evil report respecting them.* Comp. Num. 14 : 37.

3. בֶּן־זְקֻנִים § 260. 2. *a.* בֶּן־זְקֻנִים § 201. 1. *b, a son of old age,* not one possessed of the qualities which usually accompany age, as wisdom and the like, but one born when his father was old, comp. 21 : 2. 7, 44 : 20, and the similar expression *wife of thy youth,* Prov. 5 : 18. The expression is indefinite, and the construct relation paraphrased by the following לוֹ § 257, perhaps because he was not the only son born to him at that period of his life. וְעָשָׂה § 35. 1, § 265. *b.* כְּתֹנֶת פַּסִּים: LXX χιτῶνα ποικίλον, Vulg. *tunicam polymitam.* Eng. Ver. *coat of many colours.* This explanation is based on the assumption that פַּסִּים means *pieces:* a 'coat of pieces' might then mean one of patchwork, or of pieces of various colours stitched together, or perhaps one so embroidered as to present the appearance of being so composed. In 2 Sam. 13 : 18. 19, the only other passage in which the expression occurs, it is rendered by the LXX χιτὼν καρπωτός, and by the Vulgate *tunica talaris.* In conformity with this the latest and best authorities understand by פַּסִּים *extremities; a tunic* or undergarment *of extremities* is one reaching to the wrists and ankles in contrast with those in ordinary use, which were without sleeves and extended only to the knees.

4. אֹתוֹ § 238. 2. דַּבְּרוֹ, infin. not preceded by a prep. § 267. *b ;* דִּבֶּר is commonly followed by לְ, אֶל *to* or עִם, אֵת (prep.) *with,* but here and in Num. 26 : 3 by the direct object of the person addressed. לְשָׁלֹם *in peace, peaceably,* comp. on כְּבִי, 2 : 18, or *unto peace,* with a peaceable design.

5. חֲלוֹם § 271. 3. וַיַּגֵּד § 129. 1, object omitted, comp. 2 : 19. וַיּוֹסִפוּ § 145. 1, *added again to hate,* i. e. hated yet more § 269. *a.* It is characteristic of Hebrew narrative that upon the first mention of Joseph's dreams the result of his telling them to his brethren is stated, before a more detailed account is given of them ; after which the resulting hatred or jealousy of his brethren is mentioned again, vs. 8. 11. See an instance of the same sort, 2 : 8, comp. ver. 15. No critic, even of those most disposed to discredit the original unity of Genesis, has ventured to impute this repetition to an intermingling of different narratives, and to ascribe vs. 6–11 to a writer distinct from the author of ver. 5. And yet this would be as reasonable as the like charges based on similar repetitions occurring elsewhere.

7. מְאַלְּמִים § 200. *c.* קָמָה, pret., not part., as shown by the accent § 34, *rose up* in contrast with נִצָּבָה § 65 (2) *stood.* תְּסֻבֶּינָה, fut. because

subsequent to the preceding § 263. 5. *a, afterward encircled* it. It is
better to give this word its proper verbal force than to regard it as
simply qualifying the verb which follows, *prostrated themselves around.*
וַיִּתְחֲווּ § 82. 5, § 176. 1, § 88 (2 and 3 f. pl.).

8. מָלֹךְ, emphatic infin. § 282, followed, as is usual, by עַל *over,*
since the monarch is *over* his subjects or exalted above them; more
rarely by בְּ *in,* to define the sphere *in* which the sway is exercised, since
the local use of the prep. to designate the royal residence, e. g. *reign in
Jerusalem* etc., makes this ambiguous.   On the other hand מָשַׁל *to rule,*
is commonly followed by בְּ *in,* and rarely by עַל *over,* see on 1 : 18.
אִם . . . הֲ § 283. 2 *shalt thou reign* as king *or even rule* in any way?
חֲלֹמֹתָיו, plur. used indefinitely, *his dreams,* though only one had been
actually related, it being regarded by his envious brothers as a representative rather than an individual fact, comp. 8 : 4, 21 : 7, 46 : 2, Judg.
12 : 7, 1 Sam. 17 : 43, Neh. 6 : 2, also Mat. 2 : 20, 27 : 44, where an apparent discrepancy with Luke 23 : 39 is thus reconciled.

10. וַיְסַפֵּר, followed by אֶל or לְ *to* before the person, and commonly
the direct object of the thing narrated, though in rare instances this is
preceded by עַל *concerning* or אֶל *in reference to.* וַיִּגְּעוּ בְּ, rarely followed by the direct object, commonly as here like other verbs expressive
of hostility by בְּ, the hostility being conceived of as not only directed
towards its object, but reaching and penetrating it. It expresses more,
therefore, than our preposition *at,* which may be used in like connections,
e. g. 'to scold *at.*' וְאֶת־אָבִיךְ, Leah, or in the judgment of others, Bilhah
ver. 2, or Joseph's own mother, Rachel, who was already dead, 35 : 19,
but is here mentioned by Jacob for that very reason, to make the apparent absurdity of the dream more glaring. הֲבוֹא § 230. 1, § 282. נָבוֹא
§ 157. 3, § 276. 1. אַרְצָה: § 219. 1.

11. וַיְקַנְאוּ־בוֹ, commonly followed by בְּ, see on וַיְסַפֵּר, ver. 10, less
frequently by the direct object or by לְ *to,* i. e. envious in reference *to.*
וְאָבִיו, Vav in a disjunctive sense § 287. 1; the noun on account of this
implied contrast is put emphatically before the verb and receives a disjunctive accent.

12. אֶת־. The marginal note is נְקֻדּוֹת עַל אֶת *point over* א *and* ת. According to the Masora such extraordinary points, § 4. *a,* occur ten times
in the books of Moses, four times in the Prophets, and once in the Hagio-
grapha. The Rabbins explain it by saying that, though pretending to
feed their father's flocks, they were in reality feeding their own spleen
against their brother. It may possibly have been designed to call attention to the construction : אֶת and בְּ follow רָעָה here as in ver. 2, but
with a different sense.

13. לֶכָה § 151. 1. וְאֶשְׁלָחֶךָ § 123. 4. וַיֹּאמֶר, notwithstanding the repeated change of subject, it is omitted from this and the following verbs, because it can create no real embarrassment § 243. 1.

14. וַהֲשִׁבֵנִי, commonly with the direct object of the thing brought, and אֶל before the person *to* whom or place *to* which it is brought. Here the person is regarded as the remote object § 273. 3. a, *bring me back word*, instead of *to me*.

15. תְּבַקֵּשׁ fut. because the action though begun is not finished § 263. 2, *what art thou seeking ?*

17. כִּי gives confirmation. אֹמְרִים § 273. 4.

18. מֵרָחֹק *at a distance*, see on מִמֶּחַת, 1 : 7. וַיִּתְקְרַב § 263. 1. b. וַיִּתְנַכְּלוּ § 80. 1, made themselves subtile or deceitful, i. e. *acted deceitfully*, here with a direct object, elsewhere with בְ, see on ver. 10. לַהֲמִיתוֹ § 160. 4.

19. הַלָּזֶה § 73. 2. בָּא part. § 266. 2, the same form as pret. ver. 23.

20. בְּאַחַד § 248. a, בְ properly *in*, but after a verb of motion, *into*. וְנִרְאֶה § 100. 2. a (1). אֲכָלָתְהוּ § 101. 1.

21. מִיָּדָם *out of their hand*, i. e. from their power or threatened violence. It is on account of this derived sense of the phrase that the noun is singular with a plur. suf.; so יָדוֹ ver. 27. נַכֶּנּוּ § 129. 1, § 169. 3, § 101. 2, the verb followed by a double object § 271. 4, *we will not*, or *let us not smite him as to life*, i. e. kill him.

22. אַל־ with the apoc. fut., which here does not differ from its simple form § 97. 2. b, is equivalent to a negative imperative, *shed not*.

23. כַּאֲשֶׁר־ § 285. 2, *according to* the time *that*, i. e. *when*. וַיַּפְשִׁיטוּ § 287. 3, § 273. 2.

24. וַיִּקָּחֻהוּ § 132. 2, § 39. 3. b. אֵין § 258. b.

25. יִשְׁמְעֵאלִים § 57. 2 (3) a. בָּאָה § 34.

28. מִדְיָנִים. There is no inconsistency in speaking of the same caravan as Ishmaelites, ver. 25, as Midianites, and as Medanites, ver. 36; for though these were, strictly speaking, distinct tribes, yet from their close affinity in origin, 25 : 2. 12, and character, the names might in a general sense be used promiscuously. The fact appears to be that both here and Judg. 8 : 24, comp. vs. 22. 26, Ishmaelite is a generic term, embracing not only the proper descendants of Ishmael, but other Arab tribes, just as Hellenes was used to designate the Greeks generally, though properly denoting one subdivision of them. Or each of these three tribes may in actual fact have been represented in this company of travelling merchants. Upon this interchange of names, which is so readily explicable, certain critics have based the assertion that two contradictory narratives are here blended. One is represented in vs. 25–27 and in

ver. 28 from הַמִּדְיָנִים onward; the other in ver. 28, as far as חָמִיר, and in ver. 36. According to the first Joseph's brethren sold him to the Ishmaelites, who carried him down to Egypt. According to the second certain Midianite merchants, accidentally discovering him in the pit where his brethren had left him to perish, drew him out and sold him into Egypt. But, 1. This is founded on a false theory of the constitution of the Pentateuch, as though it were not one continuous composition, but made up of detached portions from different pens. 2. It gratuitously impugns its credibility, as though it were a record of conflicting traditions instead of a consistent and well accredited history. 3. It is merely an ingenious cross-reading, made out by dividing one sentence and dislocating others. 4. It is apparent that the writer, or, if the critics please, the compiler saw no inconsistency in the different parts of what he has presented as one connected narrative; neither was such an inconsistency suspected by any of his readers until very recently. The mention of Joseph's being taken down to Egypt both at the beginning and close of the paragraph, vs. 28. 36 (comp. on ver. 5), and again 39 : 1, where the subject is resumed after a digression (comp. 37 : 1 with 35 : 27) lends no countenance to this critical hypothesis.

וַיִּמְשְׁכוּ. The subject of this and the next two verbs is not the Midianites but the brethren of Joseph, 45 : 5, see on ver. 13. בְּעֶשְׂרִים, the prep. denotes the price, see on 3 : 19. שֶׁקֶל shekels, which was the current standard of value, is to be supplied § 251. 2. c, with which כֶּסֶף is in apposition § 253. 2; for the price, comp. Ex. 21 : 32, Lev. 27 : 5.

32. —חָפַר § 129. 1, § 94. d.　　הַבָּרָה § 24. b, § 230. 2. a, § 283. 2. בָּא § 221. 3. a.

33. וַיַּכִּירָהּ § 105. a.　כְּתֹנֶת בְּנִי my son's coat! the abrupt brevity of the exclamation is admirably suited to the occasion. טָרֹף § 282. a.

34. בְּמָתְנָיו. We would say upon his loins, and the Heb. might use עַל, Jer. 13 : 1, 48 : 37; but here it has בְּ in, denoting intimate conjunction, i. e. in contact with, see on 3 : 3. וַיִּתְאַבֵּל § 80. 1, used chiefly in prose, the Kal being more usual in poetry, followed by עַל over, since the common attitude of mourners is that of bending over the object of their grief, or the prep. may mean on account of, the effect being conceived as resting upon its cause, the grief resting upon its source, see 2 : 24. It sometimes takes אֶל in reference to.

35. וַיָּקֻמוּ § 277. a, § 276. 3. בְּנֹתָיו § 205. b, § 207. 1. a. לְנַחֲמוֹ § 101. 3, § 102. 3. לְהִתְנַחֵם § 80. a (2). כִּי might be explicative, that, which commonly introduces an indirect citation, but is occasionally used even before a direct citation; but it is better to regard it as confirmatory, for, referring

to the implied language of his refusal, ' I will not be comforted, *for*, etc.
or *but*, to which יִּכ is often equivalent after a negative clause. שְׁאֹלָה,
the continued and conscious existence of the dead is implied. וַיֵּבְךְּ
§ 172. 4, followed here by the direct object, elsewhere by עַל *over*, לְ or
אֶל *in reference to, for*.

CHAPTER XXXIX.

1. הוּרַד § 265, *was brought down*, not only because there was an
actual descent in leaving Palestine southward, but because of the moral
elevation attaching to it as the centre of religious hopes and aspirations.
Hence men are said to ' go up ' to Palestine and to Jerusalem from all
directions, Zech. 14 : 16—19, *et passim*.

2. יְהֹוָה. The name Jehovah occurs significantly here and in a like
connection in vs. 3. 5. 21. 23. God's favour to Joseph was not a mere
providential benefit to him, but belonged to Jehovah's plan of grace and
his merciful dealings with his covenant people. After this chapter
יְהֹוָה occurs but once in the rest of the book, Gen. 49 : 18. When Joseph
speaks to the wife of Potiphar, ver. 9, to the servants of Pharaoh, 40 : 8,
to Pharaoh himself, 41 : 16—32, or to his brethren or they to him
while they thought him an Egyptian, 42 : 18, 43 : 29, 44 : 16, or when
Pharaoh speaks, 41 : 38. 39, or the steward of Joseph's house, 43 : 23,
the more general name אֱלֹהִים is the appropriate one. So in other cases,
where the thought is principally of God as ruling in providence, 42 : 28,
or a contrast is implied between what *man* devised and *God* appointed,
45 : 5. See on 2 : 4. אֵת prep. *with*, implying fellowship and aid § 238.
2. בְּבֵית § 216. 1. *d*, § 208. 3. *c.* אֲדֹנָיו § 201. 2, § 249. 1, *his Egyptian master*.

4. וַיְשָׁרֶת differs from עָבַד, see Gesen. Lex. וַיַּפְקִדֵהוּ, change of subject
plain from the connection § 243. 1, see 37 : 13. 28 וְכָל־יֶשׁ־לוֹ, ellipsis
of the relative, comp. ver. 5; § 285. 3.

5. בְּבֵיתוֹ, prep. בְּ *in*, suggests the sphere of his authority, and עַל *over*,
his elevation above what was thus subjected to him. בְּכָל־ *in all*, this
was the seat of the blessing. וַיְהִי § 275. 1.

6. אִתּוֹ suf. refers not to Potiphar, *he knew not anything with him*,
i. e. which was in his own possession, but to Joseph, comp. ver. 8, and
is not dependent on מְאוּמָה § 195. 3, *anything with him*, i. e. which was
in Joseph's charge, but, as the order of the words requires, on יָדַע *did not
know with him*, i. e. Joseph had not only the entire charge but the exclusive knowledge of everything; his master shared with him only the
knowledge of what came upon his table. לֶחֶם § 254. 10.

7. שִׁבְכָּה § 98. 1, § 22. a (1).

9. אֵינֶנּוּ § 263. 4, *he*, i. e. my master, *is not ;* the rendering ' there
is none greater, etc.' would require אֵין without the suffix, comp. 40 : 8.
41 : 8. גָּדֹל § 260. 1. — כִּי אִם *for if*, which after a negative clause
(see on 37 : 35) is equivalent to *but if* or *but when*, i. e. *except.* בַּאֲשֶׁר *in
that.* i. e. *because*, the effect being regarded as involved in its cause.
לֵאלֹהִים‎ § 231. 3. *a, in respect to God*, the prep. indicating the direction
of the offence.

10. כְּדַבְּרָהּ 'according to her speaking,' i. e. *as she spake*, the particle
strictly expressing the resemblance or identity between the time of her
speaking and his not hearkening, and thus receiving the temporal sense
of *at* or *when*. יוֹם יוֹם ׀ יוֹם § 280. 1. — וְלֹא § 287. 3. לִשְׁכַּב § 87.

11. כְּהַיּוֹם § 231. 5. *a*, since the particle of comparison may express
not only identity but a resemblance more or less remote, it is applied to
measures of time, space or quantity, not only to indicate exactness *at*,
but. a more general correspondence *about*, comp. Gr. ὡς, ὡσεί. מֵאֶצְלָהּ
prep. partitive.

12. בְּבִגְדוֹ § 22. *b*, § 221. 5. *a*, the prep. may be taken in its original
local sense as designating the part immediately affected by the seizure,
in his garment, or, which is more natural in English, it may indicate
the means, *in* which the action is regarded as involved, since that alone
rendered it possible, *by his garment.*

14. לְצַחֶק § 35. 1, § 92. *d*, לְ properly indicating the design, see on
1 : 14, which is here inferred from the result, comp. Ex. 17 : 3, Lev. 20 :
3. בָּנוּ § 34, according to the turn given to the preceding verb the prep.
may, as after verbs of hostility, see on 37 : 10, indicate the object at
which the laughter is directed, and *in* which it rests, *mock at us*, or it
may denote conjunction, see on 3 : 3, 37 : 34, *sport with us.* בְּקֹלִי , the
prep. בְּ may denote the cause, means, or as here the instrument, since
anything may be regarded as residing *in* that, by, through or with which
it is effected.

15. הֲרִימֹתִי § 153. 4. וַיַּעֲזֹב § 287. 3.

16. וַתַּנַּח § 160. 1 and 3.

17. לְצַחֶק might be dependent on הֵבִיא § 160. 2, see ver. 14, but is
more probably to be connected with בָּא .

18. וְאֶקְרָא, construction begun with the infinitive and continued with
the future and Vav conversive § 282. *c*.

20. מְקוֹם § 255. 2. — אֲשֶׁר by ellipsis for the fuller form אֲשֶׁר ... שָׁם
where, comp. 40 : 3, or אֲשֶׁר ... בּ ... *in which* § 74. אֲסוּרֵי K'thibh § 46,
for which the K'ri substitutes אֲסִירֵי , the usual form of the noun, whereas
אָסוּר is commonly the participle.

21. וַיֵּט § 172. 4. 'אֵלָיו suf. denotes the object § 254. 9, *he gave* graciously wrought *favour toward him*, in the mind of the keeper. שַׂר־בֵּית־הַסֹּהַר ו, a subordinate entrusted with the immediate oversight of the prison, while Joseph's master, the captain of the guard, held the supreme direction of its affairs, comp. 40 : 4.

CHAPTER XL.

1. חָטְאוּ fut. with Vav conv. might have been used, comp. 39 : 7, § 287. 3, with prep. לְ, comp. 39 : 9.

2. וַיִּקְצֹף followed by עַל, the prep. in a hostile sense indicating *upon* whom the anger is directed; it might also have אֶל *in respect to ;* our idiom requires *at*. שָׁנֵי § 250. 2, see on 1 : 16. סָרִיסָיו § 60. 3. c, § 210. a.

3. מִשְׁמַר § 255. 2, comp. 39 : 20.

4. אִתָּם, not *set him over them*, as though the prep. were עַל, see 39 : 4, but *put him in charge with them*, associated him with them to have the care of their necessities, to wait upon them, as is immediately added. According to the analogy of oriental courts these were officers of high rank, and Potiphar assigns them his servant as their attendant. יָמִים § 274. 2. a.

5. כְּמִשְׁפָּט § 250. 2. a.

7. הֵיוֹם § 245. 3. b.

8. אֵין, the absolute form is only used when it is the last word in its clause § 258. b.

9. וְהִנֵּה־ § 287. 3.

10. בַּגֶּפֶן § 223. 2, § 250. 2. כְּפֹרַחַת § 205. a, the prep. may denote comparison, *as if it were blossoming*, i. e. it seemed to blossom, or time *it* was *about blossoming*, see on 39 : 10. 11. עָלְתָה, construed transitively with the result of the action, *went up*, i. e. grew, put forth *its flowers* § 271. 1. נִצָּהּ, used collectively § 198. b, whereas the fem. נִצָּה denotes a single flower. הִבְשִׁילוּ § 80. a (1), either *matured grapes*, or by a transitive construction with the result of the action, *ripened* into *grapes*. אַשְׁכְּלוֹתֶיהָ § 183. c, § 210. e, § 216. 1. c.   It has been objected to the truth and the antiquity of this narrative that, according to Herodotus, 2. 77, there were no vines in Egypt (οὐ γάρ σφί εἰσι ἐν τῇ χώρῃ ἄμπελοι), and according to Plutarch, De Is. et Osir. 6, wine was not in use there before the time of Psammetichus (ἤρξαντο δὲ πίνειν ἀπὸ Ψαμμητίχου, πρότερον δ᾽ οὐκ ἔπινον οἶνον).   But Herodotus is only speaking of the region which he denominates ' the grain country' (τὴν σπειρομένην Αἴγυπτον), and even in regard to this his language must be taken with some limita-

tions. See Rawlinson's Herodotus, II. p. 108. Plutarch is speaking of the free indulgence in wine by kings and priests as introduced by Psammetichus in place of the restricted use which prevailed before. The monuments of Egypt show incontestably that wine was used and the grape cultivated there in the earliest periods by their delineations of the vintage, the winepress, vessels for drinking and for holding wine, and even persons in a state of intoxication.

12. שִׁלֹּשֶׁת § 250. 2, § 251. 2 and 4. הֵן, copula § 258. 2.

13. נְשָׂאֵבִדָּה § 160. 2. כַּנֶּה § 221. 6. *a.* אֲשֶׁר, used adverbially of time, as in 39 : 20 of place, *when,* the time *in which.*

14. אֲפִי אִם־זְכַרְתַּנִי, see on 39 : 9, *but if thou hast remembered me,* etc. with the implication as I trust thou wilt have done וְעָשִׂיתָ־נָּא, *then do kindness with me, I pray thee* § 287. 2, or *if* may be equivalent to *O if,* and express a wish, *but if thou wouldst remember me,* etc. and *wouldst do,* etc. Literally, *wouldst have remembered,* the pret. § 262. 1, denoting a past in relation to the fut. וַיֵּשֶׁב § 35. 1 ; this tense is used here because the act of memory at that time implies that he had been remembered during the entire preceding period, comp. the use of *memini* as a present in Latin. The following verbs עָשִׂיתָ etc. as they follow the future יֵשֶׁב obtain a future sense from Vav conv. הֵכ § 65. *a.* זְכֵרַ, see on 3 : 12.

15. נָגַע § 93. *d,* § 282. *a.* יֵצֵא § 156. 4, the unusual position of the accent is remarked in the marginal note § 32.

16. טוֹב *well* not correctly, for this could not yet be known, but acceptably. עַל־רֹאשִׁי Herodotus, 2. 35, states it as one of the customs in which the Egyptians differ from the rest of the world, that the men carry burdens upon their heads and the women upon their shoulders.

20. הֻלֶּדֶת § 150. 5, *day of Pharaoh's being born,* the subject of the passive verb receiving אֵת , since it is really the object of the action § 271. *a.*

23. וַיִּשְׁכָּחֵהוּ, Vav in an adversative sense.

CHAPTER XLI.

1. מִקֵּץ *from,* denoting separation in point of time, i. e. *after the end of.* שְׁנָתַיִם יָמִים § 202, *two years of days,* the measure or quantity being in apposition with the material § 253. 2. עַל־ *over,* because a person standing on the bank is above the surface of the river ; the English idiom requires *by.* הַיְאֹר . The number of Egyptian words occurring in this chapter affords an incidental proof of its genuineness and truth.

2. עֹלֹת מִן § 223. 2 ; the cow was the instrument and symbol of

agriculture, and is here represented as coming up from the Nile, which was the source of Egypt's fertility. יְאֹר § 254. 10.

3. שָׂפָה *lip*, then *edge* or *brink* § 3. 1. *a.* רְצֹת § 216. 1. *a* (1).

4. הַבָּשָׂר ... הַמַּרְאֶה, the article is for the sake of making the preceding adjectives agree in definiteness with the noun to which they belong § 249. 1. *a ;* the adj. themselves could not receive the art., being in the const. § 256. שֶׁבַע § 251. 4. הַיְאֹר § 147. 5.

5. שֵׁנִית § 235. 3 (3). שִׁבֳּלִים § 207. 1. *d*, § 16. 3. *b.* בְּקָנֶה *in the stalk*, because forming part of it, in intimate union and conjunction with it, see on 3 : 3.

6. וּשְׁדוּפֹת § 254. 9. *b.* קָדִים, the southeast wind from the great desert. Observe that ם is a radical, not the plural ending.

8. וַתִּפָּעֶם § 99. 3. *a.* חַרְטֻמֵי IV. § 193. *c.* חֲכָמֶיהָ suf. refers to מִצְרַיִם § 197. *d.* אֹתָם, the plur. and the sing. (חֲלֹמוֹ) are used indifferently, according as the dream is contemplated as one or two.

9. אֶת־חֲטָאַי, the prep. *with.* חַטָּאָי § 208. 3. ׃הַיּוֹם § 245. 3. *b.*

10. עַל־קָצַף, see on 40 : 2.　　11. וַנַּחַלְמָה § 99. 3, § 109. 3. *a.*

12. כְּפֶד לְשַׁר § 257. 2. אִישׁ, 'each according to his dream,' i. e. *according to the dream of each.* The construction of אִישׁ, when used as an indefinite pronoun, and standing in a possessive relation to nouns, often follows the analogy of the relative אֲשֶׁר § 285. 1, comp. 9 : 5, 15 : 10, Num. 26 : 51 ; though it may also preserve its usual construction as a noun, comp. כְּפֶר־אִישׁ 43 : 21, but אִישׁ ... כַּסְפּוֹ 42 : 35.

13. בַּאֲשֶׁר *according to* that *which*, i. e. *as* § 285. 2. הֵשִׁיב § 153. 1 ; the subject is not Joseph, as though he were said to do what he predicted, but Pharaoh, who though addressed is reverentially spoken of in the third person, comp. ver. 10. Examples of a like change of subject abound, see on 37 : 13. 28.

14. וַיְרִיצֻהוּ 3 pl. indefinite § 243. 2. וַיְגַלַּח, where the Hithpael might have been expected, as in English we can say *he shaved*, for *he shaved himself.* Another correspondence with Egyptian customs, which are here the reverse of the Hebrew. The Egyptians were ordinarily shaven, only suffering their beards and hair to grow in token of grief, Herod. 2. 36, whereas to be shaven was a token of grief among the Hebrews, Isa. 15 : 2, Amos 8 : 10.

15. עָלֶיךָ *respecting thee*, lit. 'upon thee,' the discourse being founded *upon* the subject spoken of. לֵאמֹר § 22. *a* (5).

16. בִּלְעָדָי *not to me* belongs this faculty of interpreting dreams.

21. קִרְבֶּנָה 3 f. pl. suf. with appended vowel ה, § 220. 1. *b*, which occasions the change of the preceding Kamets to Seghol. Comp. § 63. 1. *b* and *c*, § 219. 1. *b.* וּמַרְאֵיהֶן, the noun is singular § 221. 7. *a*, as is

shown by the adj. יְ-; the suf. הֶן is occasionally though rarely attached
to singular nouns § 220. 1. b.

22. נָצְרָא § 172. 4.   23. אֲחֵרִיתָהּ׃ § 275. 5.

24. וַתִּבְהֲלוּ § 88 (2 and 3 f. pl.).

25. הוּא § 258. 2.   אֶת אֲשֶׁר § 285. 2.   הָאֱלֹהִים § 246. 1. a.

26. חֲשֻׁב § 249. 1. c.   חֲלוֹם אֶחָד § 250. 1, *it is one dream.*

28. חִי־אָה § 175. 1.

29. שָׁבָע . . . . . שָׁנִים *years* of *great plenty,* descriptive apposition
§ 253. 2.

31. מִפְּנֵי *from the face of,* or *from before,* i. e. *by reason of,* the effect being regarded as proceeding *from* the cause.

32. עַל *in respect to,* lit. *upon* the subject of, see on ver. 15.   כִּי־,
this was done *because* etc. בֵּין § 153. 3.

33. יֵרֶא § 171. 1, § 35. 2, some editions have Tsere in the ultimate,
consequent upon the shifting of the accent.   נָבוֹן § 158. 4.   וִישִׁיתֵהוּ
§ 157. 3, receives a jussive sense from its connection with יֵרֶא.

34. יְקַבֵּץ expresses not simple futurity, but desire § 264. *a,* as is
shown by its association with the preceding and following apoc. futures.
וְיַפְקֵד § 97. 2.   תִּצָּבַע § 256.

35. וְיִקְבְּצוּ *and they shall gather,* or *that they may gather* § 263. 1.
הָאֹכֶל § 249. 2.

38. הַנִּמְצָא § 230. 1, Kal fut. though the form might also be found
in the Niph. pret.   רוּחַ אֱלֹהִים from Pharaoh's polytheistic stand-point
אֱלֹהִים is not a proper but a common noun, and the expression is consequently indefinite, *a divine spirit,* lit. *a spirit of divinity.*

39. אַחֲרֵי retains its strict temporal sense, *after* God had taught him
this, he had a superiority to others which he did not possess before.
הוֹדִיעַ § 267. b, followed by a double object, § 273. 1.   כָּמוֹךָ § 233. a.

40. יִשַּׁק some render, *upon thy mouth shall all my people kiss,* in
token of fidelity and homage. But it is objected to this that the kiss
of fealty was upon the hand or the foot, not upon the mouth, and that
this verb meaning *to kiss* is never construed with עַל, but either with the
direct object or with לְ before the person *to* whom the kiss is given.
Consequently others translate, *according to thy bidding all my people
shall dispose themselves,* the primary notion of the verb being assumed
to be *to adjust* or *dispose,* from which both its other senses *to kiss* and
to arm are derived. The preposition עַל obtains the meaning *according
to* from the conception that when one thing lies in every part precisely
upon another, it is conformable to it. The *mouth,* as the organ of
speech, is here put, as it frequently is, for speech itself, or for *command,*
הַעַם § 271. 4.   אֶגְדַּל § 260. 2. a.   מִמֶּךָּ § 233. a.

42. וַיָּסַר § 160. 3. 'מֵעַל יָדוֹ, royal edicts were authenticated by the king's signet-ring, the possession of which gave authority to act in the name of the monarch, Esth. 3 : 10. 12, 8 : 2. 10. רְבִד הַזָּהָב § 256, *the chain of gold* customary as a mark of distinction § 245. 3.

43. בְּמִרְכֶּבֶת § 241. 1. b, § 216. 2. b. הַמִּשְׁנֶה § 256, *the chariot of the second order*, or *the second chariot*, i. e. the one immediately following that of the monarch in state processions. אַבְרֵךְ, properly an Egyptian word, though assimilated in its orthography to abs. inf. Hiph. of בָּרַךְ which has a kindred sense § 94. b, see Gesen. Lex. וְנָתוֹן properly expresses the abstract idea of the verb, but when it continues a narration it is modified in sense by the tense, number and person of the preceding principal verb, here by וַיִּרְכֵּב, *and he set him over*, etc. lit. 'there was a *setting him over*, etc.'

44. פַּרְעֹה *Pharaoh*, i. e. *the king*, as the word signifies in Coptic. לֹא־יָרִים וגו § 9. 1, *shall not raise his hand*, i. e. to perform any action, and (our idiom requires *or* § 287) *his foot*, i. e. to take a step. The expression is a proverbial one.

46. ־פְּנֵי, see on 37 : 2. שָׁלִּשִׁים § 225. 1, § 251. 1 and 2. בְּעָמְדוֹ § 22. a (1), § 101. 3, *in his standing*, i. e. when he stood. וַיֵּצֵא a resumption after the intervening mention of Joseph's age, of the statement at the close of the preceding verse with a view to continue the narrative, see on 37 : 5.

47. הַשָּׂבָע § 256. לִקְמָצִים § 101. 2. b, § 208. 3. b, *by handfuls*, the prep. properly signifies *according to*, see on לְמִינוֹ 1 : 11.

48. אֶת־כָּל־אֹכֶל § 270. c.   49. הַרְבֵּה § 175. 2. לִסְפֹּר § 22. a (5).

50. יֻלַּד § 275. 1, the marginal note לָמֶד קְמוּצָה *Kamets'd Lamedh* calls attention to the fact that the vowel of the ultimate is prolonged, though without a pause accent § 65. b, whence some have unnecessarily inferred that it is an abbreviated participle § 53. 2. a, § 93. e. תָּבוֹא § 157. 3, § 263. 1. b.

51. וַיְנַשֵּׁנִי § 169. 3, § 92. c, the form of the verb is assimilated to the noun, whose etymology is to be explained; the direct is substituted for the indirect quotation.

52. אֶפְרָיִם § 183. c, *double-fruitfulness* § 203. 5. בְּנִיִי § 221. 5. c, § 62. 2. b.

54. וַתְּחִלֶּינָה § 141. 2 (p. 174).

55. לְכוּ § 151. 1, § 197. d, § 275. 2. b.

56. אֲשֶׁר בָּהֶם § 285. 1, *all in which there was food.*

57. וְכָל־הָאָרֶץ § 275. 2. b, *all the earth*, as we might say, 'everybody came.' General terms are necessarily limited by their application and the connection in which they are found. People came from all

quarters, not from the whole earth in its widest sense, of course, but from the entire region which under such circumstances would naturally look to Egypt for supplies. So ver. 54, *all the lands*, must mean *the countries adjacent to Egypt*, and with which the Hebrews were most familiar.

CHAPTER XLII.

1. לָמָּה § 231. 4. *a.*   תִּתְרָאוּ § 80. 1 (3).

3. עֶבְרָה § 250. 2 (3), § 251. 4.

4. אֲחֵי § 215. 1. *e.*   יִקְרָאֻנּוּ § 179. 1. *a.*

6. אֵֽהֶם § 30. 2, § 258. 2.   וַיִּשְׁתַּחֲווּ § 82. 5, § 176. 1.   אֵפֹּם § 274. 2. *e.*

7. קָשׁוֹת fem. in sense of neuter § 196. *a.*

9. לָהֶם *in reference to, respecting them.*

10. וַיֵּדַרְכָּהּ Vav adversative § 287. 1.

11. נַחְנוּ § 71. *a* (1). The fact that they were all sons of one man was presumptive evidence that they were peaceful traders and not a band of adventurers or emissaries. לֹא־הָיוּ § 262. 2, *have not been* and are not now acting as spies § 266. 3. *a.*

12. כִּי־ *for* which after a negative is equivalent to *but*, 37 : 35, 39 : 9.

13. שְׁנֵים עָשָׂר § 224, *thy servants are twelve, we are brethren*, etc. הַקָּטֹן § 260. 2 (2), comp. *minimus natu.* הַיּוֹם § 245. 3. *b.* וְהָאֶחָד *the remaining one* § 245. 3.

15. בְּזֹאת *by this*, see on 39 : 12. 14. חֵי § 215. 1. *d*, uttered as an exclamation, *the life of Pharaoh!* a formula of swearing, which in our idiom would require the preposition 'by.' אִם־ *if*, which in an oath obtains a negative sense. The complete form of the oath would be, 'God do so to me and more also *if you shall go forth*,' i. e. I swear that you shall not, etc., 1 Sam. 3 : 17. כִּי אִם־ *except by the coming*, see on 39 : 9. הֵנָּה § 235. 3 (4).

16. מִכֶּם prep. in partitive sense. וְאַתֶּם pron. expressed on account of the emphasis of the contrast with אֶחָד § 243. 1. הֵאָסְרוּ § 109. 4. הֵאָמֵת § 230. 3, indirect question § 283. 1 ; § 205. *b.* כִּי *that*, depending on the preceding form of oath, as if it were, 'I swear *that*.'

17. וַיֶּאֱסֹף § 274. 2. *a.*

18. וַיְחִי § 287. 1. יְרֵא, a verbal derivative taking a direct object, like the verb from which it is derived. הָאֱלֹהִים *the true God* § 246. 1. *a.*

19. אָחִיד, the article is omitted purposely, because the expression, contrary to the ordinary rule § 246. 2, is here indefinite, *one of your*

brethren, lit. 'one your brother.' Comp. ver. 33 הָאֶחָד , after a selection had been made of the one to be left behind. שֶׁבֶר רְעָבוֹן const. of the object § 254. 9, *grain for the famine,* the latter being the object for which the former is provided. וּ בְּחַיֵּכֶם § 208. 3. *c.*

20. וַיַּעֲשׂוּ־כֵן , a summary statement in advance of what is, after a brief reference to another subject, related in detail from ver. 26 onward. See on 37 : 5.

21. אִישׁ , in distributive apposition with the subject of וַיֹּאמְרוּ . עַל־כֵּן אָחִינוּ *concerning,* lit. *upon* the subject of, see on 41 : 15. 32. צָרַת § 216. 1. *a* (1). בְּהִתְחַנְנוֹ § 80. 1 (2), § 137, § 25. בָּאָה § 34.

22. אֶל־ , see on 37 : 22. הֶחָטָאוּ § 109. 3. *a,* followed by בּ , indicating that wherein the sin is committed, *in* the matter of *the boy ;* or the prep. may be used, as elsewhere after verbs of hostility, to indicate the object reached, and as it were penetrated by it, *sin against the boy,* see on 37 : 10.

23. הַמֵּלִיץ *the interpreter,* usual and necessary in the intercourse of Egyptians with foreigners § 245. 3. בֵּינֹתָם § 238. 1, § 220. 2. *a ;* the singular form of this preposition is used with singular suffixes (except twice in the K'ri, Josh. 3 : 4, 8 : 11), and the plural form with plural suffixes, the fem. plural being mostly preferred when the suffix embraces both the objects the interval between which is spoken of, and the other forms when the objects are separately stated, and the preposition repeated before each. Comp. Gen. 26 : 28. Before nouns the singular form of the prep. is employed except in one passage, Ezek. 10 : 2. 6. 7.

24. מֵעֲלֵיהֶם *from over them,* with allusion to his position on an elevated seat above them ; or as one projects over that beside which he stands, the idea of superior elevation may be merged, as it often is, in that of contiguity, and the meaning be *from by* or *from beside them.* לְעֵינֵיהֶם *to,* when no motion is implied, becomes *at* or *in,* see on 2 : 18, hence *in their eyes* or *their sight.*

25. וַיְמַלְאוּ Raphe § 27, with an indefinite subject § 243. 2, and a double object § 271. 1, § 273. 3, *and they filled.* כְּלֵיהֶם § 208. 3. *d.* וּלְהָשִׁיב , dependent upon וַיְצַו *and* he commanded *to restore.* The change of construction may have arisen from this order being addressed to a different person from those who fulfilled the preceding : and this may be still further intimated by the change of number in וַיַּעַשׂ to the 3 sing. indef. § 243. 2. כַּסְפֵּיהֶם , the plur. denotes *pieces of silver.* אִישׁ , in distributive apposition to the preceding suffix, see on ver. 21, *their money,* viz. that of *each ;* or, after the analogy of the relative, it may be connected with the suffix in שַׂקּוֹ , *into the sack of each,* see on 41 : 12. וַיֵּלְכוּ § 131. 4.

27. הָאֶחָד *the one*, distinguished as such in an enumeration, is of course *the first*, so that the cardinal is here practically equivalent to an ordinal It is not here added that the others made the same discovery, but we learn from 43 : 21 that they did : and this is not inconsistent with ver. 35. בְּפִי § 215. 2. *b.*

28. וַיֶּחֶרְדוּ § 22. *a* (2), with אֶל *they trembled unto*, i. e. turned trem- blingly unto § 272. 3.

29. בְּמֶּן § 22. *b.* הַקֹּרֹת from קֹרָה, § 209. 1, § 196. *a.*

30. וַיִּתֵּן *he gave*, made, i. e. regarded and treated *us as*, etc.

33. הַנִּיחַ § 160. 1.   רַעֲבוֹן *take the famine of your houses*, as if we were to say, *take the need of your houses*, i. e. what is necessary to sup- ply it, comp. ver. 19.

34. כִּי בְּנִים, see on ver. 12.

35. אִישׁ § 271. 4. *b*, as *for each*, *his bundle of money* § 256, see on 41 : 12.

36. עָלַי *upon me* as a burden, implying grief and care.   אָרֶ'ּ § 220. 1. *b* (3 pers.).

37. תִּתֵּן § 132. 1.   38. לְבַנִּי, see on 2 : 18.

CHAPTER XLIII.

2. וַיֹּאמֶר § 287. 2.

3. הֵעִד § 282, § 94. *a* (3 m. s.), *testified against us*, i. e. solemnly warned us : for the use of בְּ see on 37 : 10, 42 : 22.

4. יֶשְׁךָ § 258. *b.*   6. לָמָּה § 231. 4. *a.*   הֲרֵעֹתֶם § 136. 2.

7. לְנוּ *in reference to, respecting*, see on 42 : 9.   עַל־פִּי *according to* (see on 41 : 40) *the sound* or tenor, lit. mouth ; or the distinct sense of פִּי as a noun may be lost, as it not infrequently is, and the phrase signify simply *according to*.   נֵדַע fut. relative to preceding pret. § 263. 1, *were we to know?* or, as the implied negative rests on the assumed impossibility, *could we know?*

9. הֲבִיאֹתִיו pret. in relation to the future, *if I shall not have brought him*, § 262. 1.   וְהִצַּגְתִּיו § 144. 2, § 150. 4.   וְחָטָאתִי § 287. 2, § 100. *a* (1), followed by לְ, see on 39 : 9.   הַיָּמִים § 245. 5.

10. כִּי depends on שִׁלְחָה ver. 8, assigning a reason why the request to send Benjamin should be granted.   לוּלֵא § 239. 2 (3).   הִתְמַהְמָהְנוּ § 137, § 141. 2 (p. 175), pret. in relation to a past § 262. 1.   כִּי־ de- pending on an ellipsis, 'the fact is *that*,' or 'I affirm *that*.'   שַׁבְנוּ modi- fied by the conditional particle לוּלֵא *we would have returned*.   זֶה, used adverbially § 235. 3 (4).

11. מִזִּמְרַת prep. in partitive sense, *of the song of the land*, that

which is made the theme of song, its most celebrated productions; others explain the word in this place from a different signification of the root, *that which is cut* or obtained *from the land*, its productions.

12. וְכֶסֶף מִשְׁנֶה § 254. 6, *money of duplication*, may either mean 'double money,' comp. Ex. 16 : 22, as כֶּסֶף מִשְׁנֶה unquestionably does in ver. 15, or 'a duplicate parcel of money,' when it will be equivalent to כֶּסֶף אַחֵר ver. 22. That the latter is the meaning here is apparent from the separate mention of the 'money which was brought back.' בְּיֶדְכֶם § 221. 1. *a;* the sing. form of the noun is due to the special significance of the phrase, which does not mean literally *in your hands,* but in your possession or along with you, see on 37 : 21. הָשִׁיבוּ § 153. 1.

14. אַחֵר § 249. 1. *b.* שָׁכֹלְתִּי § 65. *o,* pret. in relation to a future § 262. 1, *when* (lit. *according to* the time *that* § 285. 2) *I shall have been bereaved, I shall have been bereaved.* If this results in my bereavement, it must be so: there is no avoiding it. Comp. John 19 : 22.

15. וּמִשְׁנֶה־כֶּסֶף § 24. 4, apposition of the quantity with the material § 253. 2, comp. 41 : 1. מִצְרָיִם is here the direct object of וַיֵּרְדוּ § 271. 2; it might with equal correctness have been מִצְרַיְמָה with He directive, 46 : 3. 4.

16. לַאֲשֶׁר § 285. 2. וּטְבֹחַ, the only example of Hholem with a ט gutt. imper. § 125. 1. בַּצָּהֳרָיִם § 203. 5, *the* well-known period of *noon* § 245. 3.

17. בֵּיתָה § 256. *d.*   18. בֵּית § 273. 5. וְלָקַחַת § 132. 2.
19. פֶּתַח § 274. 2. *b.*   20. בִּי § 240. 2.

21. וַיְפַתֵּחַ § 99. 3, the apodosis may begin here or with וְהִנֵּה § 287.
2. בְּמִשְׁקָלוֹ, the precious metals were weighed, not coined.

26. וַיָּבִיאוּ, the marginal note דגש א *dagheshed Aleph* calls attention to the point in this letter, which is commonly explained as Mappik § 26. וַיִּשְׁתַּחֲווּ § 176. 1.

27. וַיִּשְׁאַל, followed by לְ both before the person *to* whom and the subject *to* which the question was directed. הֲשָׁלוֹם used absolutely to indicate condition, *in health* § 274. 2. *e;* there is no need of assuming it to be an adjective. הֲזָקֵן § 249. 1, *your old father.*

28. וַיִּקְּדוּ § 141. 1; וַיִּשְׁתַּחֲווּ § 46.   29. יָחְנְךָ § 61. 1, § 141. 3.

30. הַחַדְרָה *to the inner apartment,* or it may mean *to his chamber* § 245. 3. *a.* שָׁמָּה *thither* is used, when previous motion is implied, even though this is not expressed by the immediately preceding verb, *wept* on coming *thither,* where our idiom requires 'wept there.'

32. The laws of caste in Egypt forbade promiscuous intercourse with foreigners, Herod. 2. 41; and Joseph, who was allied to the priestly caste, ate separately from the other Egyptians. יוּכְלוּן § 88 (2 and 3

m. pl.), § 263. 3. תּוֹעֵבַת not merely offensive, but an object of religious abhorrence.

33. וַיִּתְמְהוּ, followed by אֶל § 272. 3, expressed their wonder *to* one another by looks or words.

34. יְחַיֵּב § 260. *a.* מַשְׂאֵת § 215. 1. *b.* יָדוֹת *handfuls*, hence equal parts, *five times;* יָדַיִם would mean *hands*, the fem. plur. is commonly used for the derived senses § 203. *a.* וַיִּשְׁכְּרוּ, drunk to satiety, as much as they wanted, not necessarily to intoxication, though the word is often so used, comp. Hag. 1 : 6.

CHAPTER XLIV.

1. שָׁלֵו § 271. 1, § 273. 1. שְׂאֵת § 131. 4, without לְ, but see לֶאֱכֹל 43 : 32, § 267. *b.*

2. גְּבִיעַ § 256. כֶּסֶף const. of object § 254. 9, *his money for grain*, comp. on 42 : 19. בְּדָבָר § 22. *a* (5). יֵצֶר § 92. *c.*

3. אוֹר § 82. 1. *a* (3), § 156. 2.

4. וְהִשַּׂגְתָּם § 100. 1. לָמָּה § 231. 4. *a.*

5. זֶה *this*, assuming the presence of the cup, and their knowledge of what he referred to. יִשְׁתֶּה § 263. 4, with בְּ, a person being said 'to drink *in* a cup,' because he drinks what is in it. נַחֵשׁ abs. infin. § 92. *d.* הֲרֵעֹתֶם § 141. 2 (p. 174).

7. יְדַבֵּר § 263. 2, *why will my lord speak*, the thought being directed not only to the fact that he has just spoken in this manner, but to his probable persistence in it. חָלִילָה § 219. 1. *a*, lit. it is *unto profane to thy servants from doing*, we esteem it utterly profane and detestable, so that we would not do. The idiomatic phrase may perhaps be best rendered in English, 'far be it from thy servants to do.' מֵעֲשׂוֹת, the prep. in its negative sense before an infin. *away from doing*, i. e. so as not to do.

8. בְּכָּף, indefinite § 248. נִּגְנֹב fut. to preceding pret. § 263. 1, *how should we* after that steal.

9. נָמֵת § 156. 2, § 287. 2. יִחְיֶה with לְ twice, comp. 1 : 29. לַאדֹנָי § 231. 3. *a.*

10. עֶבֶד § 65 (1), the marginal note is abbreviated for קֵרָין זָקֵף קָטֹן *Kamets with Zakeph Katon*, § 9. 1. וְאַתֶּם, emphatic contrast § 243. 1.

12. בַּגָּדוֹל § 260. 2 (2), *in* or *at the eldest*, comp. in Lat. *maximus natu.* הֻחַל § 140. 5.

13. שִׂמְלֹתָם § 220. 2. *a.*   14. וַיָּבֹא § 276. 1. עוֹדֶנּוּ § 236. 2.

16. מַה־ pron. used adverbially § 235. 3 (4)   נִצְטַדָּק § 82. 5, § 96. *b.* מָצָא § 236. 1. בְּיָדוֹ ... אֲשֶׁר § 285. 5.

17. לְשָׁלוֹם , *in peace*, comp. 2 : 18, 37 : 4.

18. בִּי § 240. 2. בַּעֲבָדֶּךָ prep. expressive of hostility, *against*, see on 37 : 10. כִּי assigns the reason why he deprecated Joseph's anger. כָּמוֹךָ כְּפַרְעֹה, strictly *like thee like Pharaoh*, thou art like Pharaoh in authority.

20. מֵת pret. or part. § 156. 2. : אֲהֵבוֹ § 262. 2, *has loved him*, with the implication that he still does so.

22. וְעָזַב, lit. *and he will leave his father and he will die.* It is put in the form of an affirmation that he would do so, and this result would follow, the implied condition being if the father's inability to part with his son were disregarded.

23. תֹסִפוּן § 150. 2, § 269. *a.*

27. אַתֶּם וִידַעְתֶּם § 262. 2, the pronoun emphatic § 243. 1, *you know yourselves.*

28. הָאֶחָד § 245. 3. טֹרֹף § 282. *a.*

29. וּלְקַחְתֶּם pret. with Vav conv. has its signification here determined by the immediately preceding הַיֹּם § 265. *b, and* now *ye are taking*, etc.

32. כִּי refers generally to what precedes, and assigns the reason why Judah in particular was so urgent in the matter. I speak as I do, *for*, etc. עָרַב *pledged the lad from with my father*, i. e. obtained him from my father by the pledge or security which I gave.

33. תַּחַת, primarily *under;* then, as one thing coming in under another removes it and takes its place, *in place of, instead of.*

34. פֶּן depends on the implied answer to the preceding question, I cannot go up *lest*, etc. אֶרְאֶה with בְּ, *gaze upon*, is stronger than with the direct object, when it means simply *see.* The prep. denotes that the sight not only falls upon the object, but remains fixed, rests *in* it, see on 1 : 4, 3 : 3.

CHAPTER XLV.

1. לְכָל *in reference to all*, he could not maintain a self-restraint such as had regard to bystanders. עָלָיו *by him*, see on 42 : 24. מֵעָלָי *from by me*, or עַל may retain something of its original force, *from upon me*, their presence being represented as burdensome and lying as an oppressive load *upon* him, comp. 42 : 36. בְּהִתְוַדֲּע § 150. 3.

2. וַיִּשְׁמְעוּ § 197. *d*, § 275. 2. *b.* 4. אֲשֶׁר . . . אֲחִי § 285. 1.

5. בְּעֵינֵיכֶם *let it not burn in your eyes*, i. e. let not anger be kindled there. Anger is here and 31 : 35 spoken of as manifesting itself in the eye.

6. זֶה, used adverbially § 235. 3 (4), see 43 : 10.　אָמַר, see on 39
20, 40 : 13.　חֲרִישׁ § 185. *a.*　וְקָצִיר׃, Vav used after a negative dis-
junctively, *or* § 287. 1.

7. וּלְהַחֲיוֹת׃ followed by לְ § 272. 2. *a, to preserve life to you.* לִפְלֵיטָה
§ 207. 1. *c,* the fem may be used as an abstract, *unto a great deliverance,*
or as a collective § 198, *unto a large escape,* so that not a mere fraction
but a numerous body might escape this peril.

8. אַתֶּם, pronoun expressed because of the contrast with the following
הָאֱלֹהִים § 243. 1.　כִּי, *for,* after a negative equivalent to *but,* see 42 : 12.
לָבֶם. Pharaoh had the highest regard for him, was guided entirely by
his counsels, and had entrusted the supreme management of everything
to him.　וַיְשִׂמֵנִי followed by לְ, see on 1 : 18.

9. הֲרֶד § 148. 3.　　　10. וְהָיִיתָ § 100. *a* (1), § 276. 1.

11. וְכִלְכַּלְתִּי § 154. 3.　שָׁנִים § 253. 2.

12. רֹאוֹת § 259. 2, § 278.　אֲחִי, כִּי § 220. 1. *c.*　הַמְדַבֵּר is the subject and פִּי the predicate, *the* mouth *speaking to you is my mouth.*

15. וַיְנַשֵּׁק with the direct object, or more commonly, as here, with לְ
§ 272. 2. *a, gave a kiss to, etc.*

16. בְּה § 274. 2. *b.*　　　18. וְאִכְלוּ eat ye ; the imper. is permissive.

19. צֻוֵּיתָה § 86. *b* (2 m. s.), § 262. 2, *thou art charged* to say to
them, *etc.*

20. וְטַפְּכֶם, see on 37 : 21 ; pity like other emotions expresses itself in
the eye, comp. ver. 5.　אֶל־ see on 37 : 22.　תָּחֹס § 153. 5, § 157. 3, *to
have compassion upon, spare,* followed by עַל, since the act proceeds from
a superior and reaches down *upon* an inferior.　חוּס׃ § 258. 2.

21. וַתְּעַשׂוּ־בֵן, preliminary statement of what is more fully described
in detail from ver. 25 onward, comp. 42 : 20.　וַיִּתֵּן continues the narration according to the succession of ideas in the mind of the writer,
though it is not subsequent in the order of time to the statement of the
preceding clause, see on 2 : 8. 19.　עַל־פִּי *according to the command of,*
see on 41 : 40.

22. לְאִישׁ in distributive apposition to לְכֻלָּם ; when אִישׁ is used in the
sense of an indefinite pronoun it rarely receives the article. Where it
does receive it, as here and 1 Sam. 26 : 23, 1 Kin. 8 : 39, Prov. 20 : 3. 17,
the article has its generic or universal force § 245. 5, ' a suit of clothes
to the man' throughout the entire company, i. e. to each person.　חֲלִפֹת
changes, i. e. a suit ; the plur. is used with reference to the different articles composing the dress, for each of which a change was furnished.
שְׂלַ § 251. 1. *a.*　מֵאוֹת, supply 'shekels,' as that was the most familiar
denomination § 251. 2. *c ;* so 'a million of money' would mean dollars
in America and pounds sterling in Great Britain.　כֶּסֶף § 253. 2.

23. צָאת. Some refer the pronoun to what precedes, *like this*, i. e. the same as he had given his brothers, and in addition ten asses, etc. As, however, there is no conjunction before כְּזֹאת, it is more natural to refer זֹאת to what comes after, as in vs. 17. 19, so that *like this* is equivalent to 'as follows.' מֵאֵשֶׁב prep. in partitive sense.

24. אַל־תִּרְגְּזוּ, see on 37 : 22, Ges. renders *tremble not, be ye not timid*, but the ordinary meaning of the word yields a more suitable sense, *be not angry*, do not get into angry altercation with each other as to the part which you respectively took in this crime against me as well as against my father.

25. וַיַּגִּדוּ § 271. 2.

26. וְכִי־ *and that* depends upon לֵאמֹר, and marks a transition from the direct to the indirect mode of citation. מָשַׁל with בּ, see ver. 8. וַיָּפָג § 153. 5, *was benumbed*, remained cold and without emotion, or perhaps stunned by the intelligence which he was unable to credit. הֶאֱמִין followed by לְ before the person or thing *to* which faith is given.

27. לְמֵאת § 131. 4.

28. יִשְׂרָאֵל. Although the names Jacob and Israel are often used interchangeably as simple equivalents, there appears to be a significance in putting this language in the mouth of prevailing *Israel*, 32 : 28. אָמְרוּ § 263. 1. *b*.

CHAPTER XLVI.

1. וַיִּבָּא § 276. 2. בְּאֵרָה § 256. *d*. יִצְחָק:, in memory of the divine covenant there made with Isaac, and probably upon the altar which Isaac had built, 26 : 23—25.

2. בַּמַּרְאֹת, indefinite plur. though one only is intended, see on 37 : 8.

3. מֵרְדָה § 144. 3, § 148. 2, the prep. מִן usual after verbs of fearing may be explained as indicating the source *from* which the fear proceeds, or that *from* which the fear would incite to flee. Upon the latter hypothesis מִן would here have a negative sense before the infin. *away from going down*, i. e. so as not to go down, see on 44 : 7.

4. אָנֹכִי emphatic § 243. 1. אַעַלְךָ § 169. 3. עָלֹה 282. *a*, the emphasis of the repetition is increased by the unusual position of the infin. which here stands after instead of before the finite verb, and by the particle גַּם which implies accession, *I will bring thee up, yea, bring thee up*. וְיוֹסֵף, the subject stands emphatically before the verb § 270. *a*. יָשִׁית יָדוֹ *shall put his hand upon thine eyes*, pay the last tribute of affection by closing the eyes in death.

5. אֹתוֹ: § 276. 2.

EXODUS. CHAPTER XX.

2. ס The sections of the Masoretic text were doubtless intended to distinguish the several commandments, though it is remarkable that the division thus indicated agrees neither with that of the ancient Jews represented by Josephus and Philo, nor with that which prevails among the modern Jews. The former, like the majority of the Christian fathers and the Reformed Churches of the present day, regarded the prohibition of idolatry, ver. 3, as the first commandment, that of image-worship, vs. 4–6, the second, and under the tenth they included the whole of ver. 17. The latter find the first commandment in ver. 2, though it has not the form of a command, combine the prohibition of idolatry and image-worship, vs. 3–6, as the second, and include the whole of ver. 17 in the tenth. The sections of the text, on the contrary, agree with the division of Augustine, which after him became current in the Latin church, and was retained likewise by Luther. According to this the first commandment, vs. 2–6, prohibits both idolatry and image-worship, no distinction being made between offences against the unity of God and against his spirituality; and two commandments are devoted to the sin of coveting, ver. 17, though this is attended with the inconvenience of creating a distinction in things fundamentally identical, and is moreover precluded by a variation in the order of the clauses in Deut. 5, where the decalogue is repeated.

The פ after ver. 7 indicates a wider separation than ס (see on Gen. 1 : 5), and is perhaps designed to mark the limit of the first table, a more equable division of the matter being attained thus than by dividing at any other point.

This passage is provided with a double system of accents, § 39. 4. a, one having relation to its division into verses and the other into commandments. Thus vs. 2–6 are accented both as separate verses and as forming together one paragraph: so also vs. 8–11. And the sixth, seventh, eighth, and ninth commandments (according to the ordinary reckoning), are accented both individually and as forming together a single verse; they are so numbered in Deut. 5, though the common enumeration in Ex. 20 makes them four distinct verses. Where the limits of the verse and of the commandment are identical, as in the third, ver. 7, and the fifth, ver. 12, the two systems of accents coincide and are reduced to one. In ver. 17 there is but a single series of accents, its first clause having no separate accentuation to distinguish it as a complete commandment; the ס in this verse is also omitted in many manuscripts and in a few printed editions.

When considered as one paragraph, vs. 2–6 are divided into three clauses, § 36. 1, the first ending at חָסֶד, ver. 5, and the second at לְשֹׂנְאָי, ver. 5. The Segholate clause is subdivided at פֶּסֶל, אֱלֹהִים, and תְּמוּנָה, ver. 4, פָּנָי, ver. 3, עֲבָדִים and אֱלֹהֶיךָ, ver. 2. In the second clause both the subdivisions and the immediate antecedents of Athnahh coincide with the accents before Silluk, which marks the last clause of ver. 5 taken by itself. The third or Silluk clause is subdivided at לְאֹהֲבַי. Returning to the two subdivisions of the first clause in ver. 2, the Zakeph Katon of the first is preceded by Munahh and Pashta, the R'bhia of the second by Munahh and Geresh, and this by Kadhma, T'lisha K'tanna and Munahh. This same verse, when accented separately, consists of two clauses, the first ending at אֱלֹהֶיךָ, which is preceded by Munahh and Tiphhha, while עֲבָדִים is preceded by Merka and Tiphhha, and this by Merka and T'bhir, and this by Darga. In most editions, though not in all, עֲבָדִים has an Athnahh additional to the two accents already explained. This indicates a paragraph of two clauses, of which the first is ver. 2, and the second ver. 3, and consequently represents the ordinary Reformed view of the length of the first commandment.

3. לֹא, this may either be joined by Makkeph to the following word and receive Methegh, or it may receive Munahh whether as the second conjunctive before T'bhir or as the fourth before Geresh. יִהְיֶה § 275. 1. עַל־פָּנָי § 39. 4. a, upon my face, i. e. before me, an act performed in the presence of another being said to be upon his face, just as we speak of anything adjacent in a lateral direction as ' upon one's side' or ' upon his right or his left hand.' Others give to face here the sense, which it sometimes has, of person or self ; עַל־פָּנַי will then mean either above me, or besides me, the preposition denoting something superadded.

4. תַעֲשֶׂה § 243. 2, may either be followed by Makkeph or have one of the conjunctives by which it is accompanied ; in the former case the following ל will have Daghesh forte conjunctive, in the latter it will remain without it, as is indicated by the Raphe § 27. וְכָל § 256. c, see on Gen. 45 : 6. אֵת is not a second object of תַעֲשֶׂה § 273. 3, make an image or any form of God (out of) that which is, etc. but has תְּמוּנָה for its antecedent. אֲשֶׁר, מִתַּחַת, see on 1 : 7.

5. חָסֶד § 111. 3. a. שִׁלֵּשִׁים § 207. 1. a, that the second generation, though not explicitly mentioned, is not to be excluded, is both obvious in itself and apparent from 34 : 7. לְשֹׂנְאָי § 102. 3, in reference to those hating me. This law of divine retribution holds in regard to God's enemies, who are regarded as perpetuating from generation to generation an organized opposition to the divine government, and thus

as justly liable for the sins of their predecessors which they justify and
increase by accessions of their own. The links of this fatal connection
can only be broken by leaving the ranks of those who ' hate ' God, and
becoming allied to those who ' love ' him.

6. לַאֲלָפִים *to thousands,* not contemporaneous individuals merely, but
counted down the line of descent, i. e. so many generations, as appears
both from the contrast with the preceding verse and from the parallel
expression in Deut. 7 : 9. וּלְשׂמְרֵי § 254. 9. *b.*

7. תִשָּׂא *thou shalt not lift up the name of Jehovah thy God to vanity*
or *falsehood,* i. e. bring it into connection with what is false, or as the
' lifting up ' intended is by means of the voice, the verb may be translated *thou shalt not utter.* לַשָּׁוְא § 16. 1, the article before an abstract
noun in a universal sense § 245. 5.

8 זָכוֹר § 268. 2. The trifling differences in the text of the commandments in Exodus and in Deuteronomy are no disparagement to
the accuracy of either book. Exodus gives us doubtless an exact
transcript of the tables of stone upon which they were engraved. Deuteronomy contains the law as reiterated and enforced by Moses in his
address to the people, in which case it is natural to expect less regard
to verbal precision than t> the substantial meaning. Accordingly in
Deut. 5 : 12 שָׁמוֹר *observe* is substituted for זָכוֹר *remember,* and this latter
word is reserved to introduce the special consideration which is there
urged for the observance of the Sabbath : " And remember that thou
we st a servant in the land of Egypt and that the Lord thy God brought
thee out thence through a mighty hand and by a stretched-out arm ;
therefore the Lord thy God commanded thee to keep the Sabbath-day."
This is not inconsistent with the appointment of the Sabbath to com-
memorate the rest of God after the work of creation. In conformity
with this grand ideal, man weekly finishes his toil and enters into rest,
the rest which God has appointed, a type and foretaste of the ultimate
release which God is preparing for him in communion with himself.
The release from Egyptian bondage was a preliminary realization of
this great sabbatic idea, and a fresh type and pledge of the final consummation. It affords a fresh reason, therefore, and one of peculiar
force to Israel, why the Sabbath should be faithfully kept. It is accordingly quite appropriate, in the address of the lawgiver to the people,
while the law itself as engraved on stone presents a motive more in accordance with its universal and perpetual obligation. The other
variations are still more unimportant, and consist of the insertion or
omission of the conjunction ו *and ;* the substitution of one word for another which is synonymous, as שָׁוְא for שֶׁקֶר *falsehood* in the ninth com-

mandment, תִּתְאַוֶּה for חָמֹד *desire* or *covet* in the tenth ; a rhetorical am
plification, as in both the injunction and the promise of the fifth, the insertion of ox and ass along with cattle, as well as of the clause 'that
thy man-servant and thy maid-servant may rest as well as thou' in the
fourth, and of field after house in the tenth ; and the alteration in the
order of the clauses of the tenth, the importance of which in the question
of the proper division of the commandments has been already adverted
to, see on ver. 2.

Considered as one paragraph, vs. 8–11 are divided into three clauses,
the first ending with מְלַאכְתֶּךָ ver. 9, and the second with וַיְקַדְּשֵׁהוּ ver. 11.
The first clause is subdivided at לְקַדְּשׁוֹ ver. 8.   The second at אֱלֹהֶיךָ,
וּבְהֶמְתֶּךָ, וּבִתֶּךָ, מְלָאכָה, בִּשְׁעָרֶיךָ, ver. 10, besides the subdivisions in ver.
11, in which the two systems of accentuation coincide.

9. יָמִים § 274. 2. *a.*   :מְלַאכְתֶּךָ § 214. 1. *b*, § 221. 2. *a.*

10. וְיוֹם, the article omitted before the noun, though retained before
the adjective § 249. 1. *c*, or more probably the noun is in the construct,
see on Gen. 2 : 3. לֵיהוָֹה § 231. 3. *a.*   תַעֲשֶׂה § 276. 1 and 3.   וּבְתֶּךָ
§ 221. 2. *a.*   וַאֲמָתְךָ § 211. *a.*   :בִּשְׁעָרֶיךָ, used not of private dwellings
but of the gates of public edifices or of cities : here of course the latter.

11. יָנַח § 157. 3.   12. יַאֲרִיכוּן § 79. 2, § 88 (2 and 3 m. pl.).

16. בָּרָצֹה, see on Gen. 37 : 10.

18. רֹאִים § 275. 2 *see* in the wide sense of *perceive*, used of objects
some of which addressed themselves to a different sense than that of
sight, comp. Gen. 2 : 19, 42 : 1.   עָם predicate § 273. 4.   וַיַּרְא § 275.
2. *a.*   :מֵרָחֹק, see on Gen. 1 : 7, 37 : 18.

20. לְבַעֲבוּר, when the infin. with בַּעֲבוּר takes ל, this may either
precede the particle, 2 Sam. 14 : 20, 17 : 14, or follow it, 1 Chron. 19 : 3.
נַסּוֹת to *try you*, i. e. as explained in the following clause, whether you
can thus be made to fear him and avoid sin.   עַל־פְּנֵיכֶם, see on ver. 3,
that *his fear* § 254. 9 *may be before you.* This may mean either that
the fear of God may be inspired by the spectacle transacted before you,
or that his fear may be the thing to which you look in all your conduct,
and by which you are guided, comp. Ps. 36 : 2.   לְבִלְתִּי, see on Gen. 3 :
11, commonly followed by the infin., only in a few instances, as here,
by the finite verb.   :תֶחֱטָאוּ § 112. 4.

21. וַיִּגַּשׁ § 80. *a* (3).   הָעֲרָפֶל § 193. *c.*

JUDGES. CHAPTER XIII.

1. וַיֹּסִיפוּ § 150. 2 (p. 181), § 269. *a.*   הָרַע generic article § 245. 5.
a, LXX τὸ πονηρόν. The recurrence of the same phrase at the beginning

of each section of this book, 2 : 11, 3 : 7. 12, 4 : 1, 6 : 1, 10 : 6, affords a strong incidental proof of unity of authorship.   בְּעֵינֵי   *in the eyes of,* that which was evil in his view, as judged of by him.   בְּיַד־   *into the hand of,* i. e. into their power. The noun is singular on account of its secondary sense in this phrase, see on Gen. 37 : 21. The prep. בְּ properly means *in ;* it retains this sense after a verb of motion, denoting that the thing spoken of not only comes *to* a particular place, but remains *in* it. פְּלִשְׁתִּים, commonly, as here, without the article, because *Philistim,* Gen. 10 : 14, is the proper name of the nation, like Israel, Edom, Amalek. It is in this plural form rarely used as a Gentile derivative, so as to receive the article § 245. 5. *a,* thus הַפְּלִשְׁתִּים, 2 Sam. 5 : 19, 2 Chron. 21 : 16, 26 : 6.   אֲרַבְּעִים § 251. 1 and 2.   שָׁנָה׃ § 274. 2. *a.* These forty years extend beyond the life of Samson to the decisive victory gained over the Philistines at Mizpeh by Samuel, 1 Sam. 7 : 13.

2. Marg. note נְפִּטְרַת הַ, *Haphtarah of* נְשֹׂא, i. e. here begins the Haphtarah or lesson from the prophets corresponding to or to be read in connection with the Parashah or lesson from the law beginning Num. 4 : 21, and ca'led נְשֹׂא, because this word occurs near the commencement of it. אֶחָד § 248. *a.* מִצְרָעָה, a town originally assigned to Judah, Josh. 15 : 33, but subsequently transferred to Dan, Josh. 19 : 41. צָרְעָה׃ The supernatural circumstances connected with the birth of Samson, as with that of Isaac, of Samuel, and of John the Baptist, make more conspicuous the fact that he was not a product of nature but a gift of divine grace, in this a type of the great deliverer whose birth was supernatural in a still higher sense.

3. מַלְאַךְ־יְהֹוָה § 246. 3, not *an angel,* but *the angel of Jehovah,* who repeatedly appears in the Old Testament as the messenger of Jehovah, and yet is expressly identified with Jehovah, ver. 22, Ex. 3 : 2. 4, 23 : 20. 21, Judg. 6 : 12. 14. וְהָרִית § 16. 1, the sense of the pret. with Vav conv. is determined by its being a sequence of the present indicated by הִנֵּה § 265. *b.*

5. וְיַלָּדְתְּ part. with the inflection of the pret. § 90 (2 f. s.). נְזִיר *consecrated to God,* const. before the object § 254. 9, and hence not necessarily definite § 249. 1. *b,* a *Nazarite unto God.* רֵחֶל § 135. 2. Samson only *began* what was reserved for Samuel, Saul and David to complete.

6. אִישׁ הָאֱלֹהִים, *the man of God,* the person of whom she speaks is clearly defined in her own mind, and in the vividness of her impressions she speaks as though he were also known to her husband.   נוֹרָא § 266. 1.   שְׁאִלְתִּיהוּ § 119. 2.   אֵי־מִזֶּה § 75. 2, *from what* place ? *whence ?*

אֹתוֹ, the indirect quotation, which in Hebrew is much less frequent than the direct.

8. אֱ־בִּי § 240. 2, see Gen. 43 : 20, 44 : 18.　אֲדוֹנָי § 199. c, § 201. 2 הַיּוּלָּד Pu. pret. § 93. b, signifying a past in relation to the preceding future § 262. 1, with the art. in the sense of the relative pron. § 245. 5. b, *who shall have been born.* Others explain it as an abbreviated Pu. part. for הַמְיֻלָּד § 93. e. Marg. note *the ל with Daghesh.*

9. וַיִּשְׁמַע with בְּ as other verbs of sense, see on Gen. 3 : 3, implying the intimate contact of the sense with its object.　אַיִן, see on Gen. 40 : 8.

10. בַּיּוֹם, not *to-day,* which would be הַיּוֹם without the prep. § 245. 3. b, but *in the* well known *day,* or as we should say, ' the other day.'

11. אֲנִי *I* am. As there is no word in Hebrew answering to ' yes,' an affirmative answer is mostly given by means of the personal pronoun, Gen. 27 : 24, 1 Kin. 18 : 8, or by repeating the verb contained in the question, 1 Sam. 23 : 11. 12.

12. יָבֹא § 97. 2. b, § 275. 1.　מִשְׁפַּט הַנַּעַר וּמַעֲשֵׂהוּ. Gesenius, Lex. under מִשְׁפָּט translates, *what will be the manner of the child* (i. e. what sort of a child will he be) *and what will he do?* But it is plain both from Manoah's prayer, ver. 8, and from the angel's answer, vs. 13, 14, that the question relates not to the appearance and actions of the child, but to the duty of the parents. The true rendering, therefore, is, *what is the judgment of the child,* const. of object § 254. 9, the law or requirement respecting him, *and the treatment of him,* suf. denoting the object, what must we do to him, or even before his birth in relation to him?

16. אֹכַל § 111. 2. b, with בְּ in a partitive sense, *eat in* or *into thy bread,* i. e. eat of it.　כִּי *for* is connected with ver. 15, and explains how Manoah came to make such a request.

17. מִי *who* § 75. 1 is used because the reference is to a person, though מָה *what* might have been expected and actually occurs elsewhere in the like connexion, Gen. 32 : 28, Prov. 30 : 4.　כִּי־ assigns the reason for asking after his name, which is presented not conditionally but in the form of an assertion, comp. Gen. 44 : 22, *for thy words shall come to pass and we will honour thee.*　דְבָרֶיךָ, marg. note ' Yodh superfluous, so that the K'ri is דְּבָרְךָ, agreeing in number with the verb § 48, while the K'thibh דְבָרֶיךָ does not § 275. 1, comp. ver. 12.

18. תִּשְׁאַל § 263. 2, with לְ of the subject respecting which the inquiry is made, see on Gen. 40 : 27, 43 : 7, *why is this that thou wilt ask in respect to my name?* The state of mind, from which the question proceeded, still continued, and it was liable to be asked, until it should

be answered, comp. Gen. 44:7. וְהִנֵּא , marg. note, abbreviated for נֻסְחָאוֹת אֲחֵרִינָן בְּמֵקָף , *other copies with Makkeph*, in some editions וְהִנֵּא instead of having a disjunctive accent is joined by Makkeph to the following word. : פְּלִאי , marg. א יַתִּיר *Aleph superfluous*, so that the K'ri is : פֶּלִי , the pausal form § 65 (3) of פֶּלִי I. 1. from לֹא root § 184. *b*, cognate and equivalent to the לֹא noun פֶּלֶא , comp. Is. 9:5. The K'thibh is פְּלִאי , an a lj. derive l from the preceding noun § 184.

19. מַפְלִא subject omitted § 243. 1, *making marvellous to act*, i. e. acting marvellously § 269. *a*, see on Gen. 2:3. : רֹאִים § 276. 3, in respect to the repetition in the following verse, see on Gen. 37:5.

20. הַצּוּרָה . As there is no mention of the construction of an altar, doubtless the rock, ver. 19, upon which the offering was made is so called. The sacrifice of Manoah has sometimes been represented as a violation of the laws of the Pentateuch regarding the priesthood and the sanctuary. It is so only in appearance, however, not in reality. It was prescribed, Lev. 17:3—7, Deut. 12:5—14, that sacrifices should be offered only at the sanctuary, because there God ordinarily manifested himself; and he could be acceptably approached only through the appointed intervention of the priesthood, Num. 3:10, 16:40. But if God in an extraordinary way manifested himself in any other place, that became for the time a sanctuary: and if he appeared to any man without the intervention of the priesthood, that constituted him for the time a priest, and was his warrant for paying his worship directly without the aid of those officially appointed for the purpose. This extraordinary investiture, however, lasted only while the cause to which it was owing continued. While it was no violation of the law for Manoah to act as he did under the circumstances, it would have been sinful for him to have arrogated to himself thenceforward the functions of the priesthood, or to have established a permanent worship at the altar thus signally honoured.

21. לְהֵרָאֹה § 172. 2, § 173. 2.

23. לָקַח pret. conditioned by the preceding clause, *he would have taken* § 262. 1. הֶרְאָנוּ § 175. 1. וְכָעֵת *at the time*, i. e. at this time § 245. 3, *b*, see on Gen. 39:10.

25. וַתָּחֶל § 140. 5. לְפַעֲמוֹ § 119. 3. בְּמַחֲנֵה־דָן , so named from the circumstance related 18:12, and which occurred in the early settlement of the land, 18:1, Josh 19:47, long before the time of Samson, so that there is no anachronism in the mention of this name here. This was in the vicinity of Samson's residence ver. 2, and of the place of his burial, 16:31. Marg. note abbreviated from עַד כָּאן lit. *until so*, i. e thus far. This marks the limit of the lesson beginning at ver. 2.

CHAPTER XIV.

1. תִּמְנָתָה § 196. *b*, § 219. 1.   He local remains even after the prep. בְּ § 219. 1. *a*, and in ver. 5 after a noun in the const. בְּכַרְמֵי תִמְנָתָה *vineyards at Timnath*.   In Josh. 19 : 43 the vowel termination is added merely to prolong the name, without reference to its local or directive force § 61. 6. *a*.   It lay southwest of Zorah, in the direction of the plain of the sea-coast, and hence Samson 'went down' to Timnath, and 'went up' as he returned.

2. The marriage contract was usually made by the parents, Gen. 21 : 21, 24 : 3, etc., 34 : 4. 6. קְחוּ־ *take*, the verb which is commonly used in speaking of matrimonial alliances, *her to* (or *for*) *me to wife*, the prep. implying a transition from one state *to* another, comp. Gen. 1 : 29.

3. וַיֹּאמֶר § 276. 1.   אָבִי § 275. 6, the father and mother are represented as speaking separately.   לְקַחַת § 132. 2.   יָשְׁרָה § 262. 2, *she has been* and still is *right*, approved, pleasing.

5. וַיָּבֹא § 276. 2 and 3.   כְּפִיר אֲרָיוֹת § 208. 3. *d*, comp. גְּדִי עִזִּים 13 : 15. 19.

6. הַגְּדִי, generic article § 245. 5. *d*.

8. מִיָּמִים *from*, indicating separation in point of time, i. e. *after days*, an indefinite period, see on Gen. 41 : 1. בִּגְוִיַּת *in the body*, i. e. the skeleton, to which jackals and birds of prey would reduce it in a very short time.   The attempt has been made to fasten upon the sacred writer the notion once prevalent among the Greeks and Romans that bees were bred by a putrefying carcass, Virg. Georg. 4. 299, etc.   But his language suggests nothing of the kind.   A parallel more to the purpose is Herod. 5. 114, the swarm of bees which took possession of the skull of Onesilus and filled it with a honeycomb.

9. הָלוֹךְ וְאָכֹל § 282.   לָהֶם § 276. 3.

10. וַיַּעַשׂ § 263. 4.   הַבַּחוּרִים: § 210. *a*.

11. שְׁלֹשִׁים § 251. 2. *b*.   כִּרְאוֹתָם § 102. 3, *they*, the parents or friends of his wife, who are suggested by the context, though not expressly mentioned : for use of prep. see on Gen. 39 : 10.

12. שֶׁבַע § 251. 4, § 274. 2. *a*.

13. וּנְתַתֶּם § 287. 2.   אַתֶּם § 243. 1.

14. The lion which sought to devour Samson, the representative and champion of Israel, was slain, and out of his carcass came sweetness and food.   The riddle, like the incident which gave occasion to it, had a latent meaning for the Philistines and for every other foe, whether of the people of God or of the great captain of their salvation.

15. הַשְּׂבִיעִי.   The rise of various readings from supposed difficulties

is well illustrated by the fact that several ancient versions here substitute *fourth* הָרְבִיעִי for *seventh*, so the LXX, ἐν τῇ ἡμέρᾳ τῇ τετάρτῃ.
Doubtless they began their urgency as soon as they abandoned the hope
of discovering the solution for themselves, but on the seventh day they
enforced their request with the threat here mentioned. בָּאֵשׁ *with fire*
§ 245. 5, for the prep. see on Gen. 39 : 12. 14. הֲלָיָרְשֵׁנוּ Pi. inf.; some
editions omit Methegh converting into the Kal inf., though Yodh is
nowhere else retained in that form.

16. וַיַּגִּיד § 284.

17. שִׁבְעַת § 251. 4 *the seven days,* i. e. the rest of the seven days
from the time that the solicitation was first made of her, as in Josh. 4 :
14 ‘ all his life’ for ‘all the rest of his life.’

18. יָבֹא § 263. 1. *b ; to go in* applied to the sun is *to set,* as *to go
out* יָצָא is *to rise.* According to the Jewish reckoning the day ended
at sunset. הַחַרְסָה § 61. 6. *a,* § 196. *c.* מְתִיק § 260. 1. בְּעֶגְלָתִי, comp.
Gen. 39 : 14, *ploughed with my heifer,* performed the work by aid which
I furnished. מְצָאתֶם pret. modified by a previous condition § 262. 1.

19. אֲשֶׁקֳלוּן § 271. 2. וַיֵּן § 175. 3. מֵהֶם prep. partitive *of them,*
the inhabitants of the place, as is plainly enough implied, though they
had not been expressly mentioned. אִישׁ § 251. 2 and *a.* לְאֲנִיגָּרַי § 254.
9. *b.* בֵּיִת § 271. 2. אֲבִי־חוּר § 220. 1. *c.*

CHAPTER XV.

1. מִיָּמִים, see on 14 : 8. בִּגְדִי prep. expressing intimate conjunction,
see on Gen. 41 : 5, *with a kid,* taking a kid along with him.

2. הַנַּתְתִּי § 260. 2 (2). שִׂיב § 260. 1. תִּתְחַתֵּן, see on Gen. 44 : 33.

3. נִקֵּיתִי with אָז, which may be taken in a comparative sense
§ 260. *a,* or in its ordinary signification, *I am guiltless from the Philistines,* a parte Philistaeorum, i. e. as judged from their stand-point,
guiltless so far as they are concerned, comp. Num. 32 : 22 ; prop. *I have
been* and still am *guiltless* § 262. 2. הַמַּעַם § 245. 3. *b.* כִּי explains
in what he was guiltless, *that I am doing,* etc. ; part. expresses the
proximate future § 266. 2.

5. זַיִת כֶּרֶם. The ancient versions assume an ellipsis of the conjunction, *vineyards* and *olive trees,* comp. Deut. 24 : 17 ; according to
most modern interpreters כֶּרֶם is in the const. *olive-yards.*

6. וַיִּשְׂרְאוּ § 243. 2. וַיְהִי § 105. *a.* בָּאֵשׁ, see on 14 : 15.

7. תַּעֲשׂוּן § 263. 2, *if ye will do like this,* if you are going to act in
this manner, the action being regarded as not wholly past but as proceeding from a still existing state of mind, and therefore liable to be re-

peated, see on 13 : 18, Gen. 44 : 7. כִּי I declare *that*, see on Gen. 43 : 10, *if I shall have avenged myself* § 77. 2, § 262. 1, *of you*, בְּ expressing hostility, see on Gen. 37 : 10, *then* § 287. 2 *afterwards I will cease, but not before.*

8. שׁוֹק עַל־יָרֵךְ, a proverbial expression denoting the completeness or the dreadful character of the slaughter, but whose precise signification is obscure. According to some authorities *leg upon thigh*, the phrase standing absolutely § 274. 2. *e*, comp. Gen. 42 : 6, means that their mangled members were piled promiscuously in heaps, or it might refer to the confusion of the fray as they were huddled together in combat or in flight. According to others עַל *upon* here signifies *in addition to*, *he smote them in leg and thigh*, the phrase being directly governed by the verb, which will then have a triple object § 271. 4 utterly disabling them; with this the English phrase ' to have one on the hip' might be compared. שׁוֹק const. before the proper noun עֵיטָם : which consequently makes the whole phrase definite § 246. 3. A particular well-known cave is doubtless meant.

9. בְּיהוּדָה, the prep. may have its local sense *in*, or denote hostility *against.* בְּלֶחִי § 65 (3), § 246. 1. *a.*

11. אִישׁ § 251. 2. *a.* וַיֵּרְדוּ § 262. 2. מִצְלְחִים, see on Gen. 1 : 18, 45 : 8. 26.

12. לְהֵחַתְּךָ § 131. 4. תִּפְגְּעוּן with בְּ, see on Gen. 37 : 10. אַתֶּם § 243. 1.

13 כִּי־ *for*, after a negative *but.* וַיַּאַסְרֻהוּ § 130. 1, with בְּ, see on 13 : 1. בִּשְׁנָיִם prep. see on Gen. 39 : 12. 14.

14. חִיא § 243. 1. הָעֲבֹתִים, construed here as fem., but in ver. 13 as masc. § 200. *c.* בְּמַשְׁנֵיהֶם § 245. 5. *d.* בָּעֵר, the verb may be trans. with indef. subject § 243. 2, or intrans. and agree with אֲשֶׁר. בְּאֵשׁ, see 14 : 15, 15 : 6.

15. בָּהּ prep. in instrumental sense, comp. ver. 13.

16. חֲמוֹר *heap* § 280. *a*, this form of the word is selected instead of the more usual one חֹמֶר § 184. *a* (2), for the sake of the assonance or paronomasia, see on תֹּהוּ וָבֹהוּ, Gen. 1. 2. הִכֵּיתִי § 175. 1.

17. כְּכַלֹּתוֹ § 174. 3, see on Gen. 39 : 10. וַיִּקְרָא, construction, see on Gen. 1 : 5.

18. אַתָּה *thou*, not I myself § 243. 1. אָמוּת, declaratively, showing his expectation, *I shall die*, or interrogatively § 284. בַּצָּמָא § 245. 5, see on Gen. 39 : 12. 14.

19. אֱלֹהִים. The prayer was made to יהוה, it is answered by אֱלֹהִים; this may illustrate the facility with which these divine names are interchanged, and how slender a basis the employment of the one

or of the other affords for the critical hypotheses built upon it in respect
to the Pentateuch, see on Gen. 2 : 4. וַמַּכְתֵּשׁ *the socket,* a cavity in Lehi
(לֶחִי is here a proper noun), which received this name perhaps from
some fancied resemblance to the socket of a tooth. קָרָא 3 m. s. indefinite § 243. 2.

20. וַיִּשְׁפֹּט. The judges of Israel were not appointed for the purpose of deciding civil suits between man and man, nor were they simply
civil magistrates receiving this specific title, because in states where the
legislative, executive and judicial functions are combined in the same
hand, the administration of justice is one of the most important as well
as the most familiar attributes of sovereignty. But they were extraordinary officers divinely raised up and commissioned to *judge* Israel, i. e.
to do the chosen people justice against their oppressors by delivering the
former and punishing the latter, 2 : 16. 18, 10 : 1. 2. Several of them,
as occasion demanded, discharged civil functions likewise. But there is
no evidence of this in the case of all of them, none for example in the
case of Samson ; and at any rate this was not the main design of the
office. : שָׁנָה § 251. 2. and *a.* This preliminary statement of the length
of time that Samson judged Israel, which, after further details are given,
is repeated at the end of his life, 16 : 31, is quite in accordance with the
style of Hebrew history, see on Gen. 37 : 5. It, therefore, is no warrant
for the suspicion that the life of Samson originally ended here, and that
the following chapter was added subsequently, nor that this verse has by
some error been transposed from its true position at the close of ch. 16.

CHAPTER XVI.

2. לַעַזָּתִים, supply ' it was told,' comp. Isa. 5 : 9. עַד־, let us keep
quiet *until.* אוֹר may be in the inf. const. § 157. 1 or in the pret. § 156.
2, in the sense of the future perfect, being conditioned by the idea of
futurity involved in the preceding particle § 262. 1.

3. וַיֹּאחֵז, construed with direct object, or, as here, with בְּ, denoting
contact with the thing grasped, see on Gen. 3 : 3, as we say, ' to lay
hold on.' וּבִשְׁתֵּי § 251. 4. וַיִּסָּעֵם § 275. 5.

5. גָּדוֹל might be a qualifying adj. with the article omitted § 249. 1.
b, but it is more natural to regard it as the predicate § 259. *a, by what,*
see on Gen. 39 : 12. 14, *his strength* is or is made *great.* נוּכַל § 35. 1,
with לְ *prevail in respect to him,* i. e. over him. וַאֲנַחְנוּ, you do that *and
we* will do this § 243. 1. וְנִתַּן־ § 130. *b,* marg. *the Tav with Pattahh.*
אִישׁ, in distributive apposition. : כֶּסֶף. in apposition with 'shekels' § 253.
2, which is to be supplied § 251. 2. *c.*

7. כְּאַחַד הָאָדָם: *like an* ordinary *man,* see on Gen. 2 : 23, lit. *one of the* mass of *men* § 248. *a ;* in ver. 17 the expression is כְּכָל־הָאָדָם *like all* other *men.* הָאָדָם properly means *mankind, the human race* § 245. 5.

9. לָהּ *in reference to her,* for her, to aid her. עָלֶיךָ *upon thee,* indicating hostility and imminence of approach, already pouncing down upon their certain prey. יָדֶיךָ § 263. 3. פְתִיל־הַנְּעֹרֶת § 256, § 245. 5. *d.* בַּהֲרִיחוֹ § 102. 3, *in its smelling the fire ;* it cannot be rendered *when the fire smells it,* even if this yielded as good a sense, for the interposition of the suf. shows that the inf. is not in the const. before אֵשׁ § 256.

10. הֲתֵלְתָּ § 142. 3, § 141. 2 (p. 174), with בְּ denoting hostility.

11. בָּהֶם . . . אֲשֶׁר § 285. 1. נַעֲשָׂה § 111. 3. *b,* § 275. 1, the Niphal of this verb has Pattahh in all the forms which occur both of the preterite and participle, except 3 f. s. pret. נֶעֶשְׂתָה.

13. An illustration of the manner in which various readings arise under the influence of parallel passages is afforded by the LXX, which inserts after this verse, 'and fastenest it with the pin to the wall, then shall I be weak as another man. And it came to pass when he was asleep that Delilah took the seven locks of his head and wove them in the web.'

14. חָיִתִי § 246. 3. *a.*

15. אֲהֵבְתִּיךְ § 262. 2. זֶה § 235. 3 (4).

16. הֱצִיקָה § 272. 2. *a.* נַתְּאַלְצֵהוּ § 25, marg. *the Lamedh weak (Raphe),* i. e. without Daghesh forte § 27.

17. נָזִיר, see on 13 : 5. אִם־גֻּלַּחְתִּי may be translated, *if I had been shaven, then my strength would have departed,* with special reference to the period embraced in the preceding statement, or as a general truth, § 262. 3, *If I were shaven, my strength would depart.*

18. לָהּ the K'ri לוֹ substitutes the direct for the indirect quotation in the K'thibb לָהּ. וַיַּגֶּד § 265. *b.*

19. לָאִישׁ *the man* whose business it was, the barber § 245. 3.

20. בְּפַעַם בְּפַעַם § 280. 1, lit. *as time by time,* as at other times : the prep. בְּ denoting conjunction, see on Gen. 3 : 3, as though time were placed *by* or beside time in a continuous series.

21. הָאֲסִירִים, see on Gen. 39 : 20.

23. אֱלֹהֵיהֶם, referring to a single idol § 201. 2.

25. בִּיטוֹב K'thibb, for which the K'ri substitutes the infin. of the cognate verb כְּטוֹב § 179. 2. *a.* הָעַמּוּדִים § 245. 3.

26. הַמְּחֹזֵק with בְּ, comp. ver 3. וַהֲמִשֵׁנִי K'thibb § 150. 1 (p. 181), the K'ri has the וֹ form וַהֲמִשֵׁנִי.

9

27. מִלֵּא § 271. 1. הָאֲנָשִׁים § 245. 1, composing 'the people,' ver.
24. וַיֵּצֵא, see on Gen. 43:30. בְּלֶבֶד, see on Gen. 39:11. הָרֹאִים,
the part. with the art. may be resolved into the relative with the finite
verb, *the ones gazing at* i. e. *who gazed at;* on the construction of אֵת
with בְּ, see Gen. 1:4, 44:34; וְאִשָּׁה .... וַיֹּשֶׁם is parenthetic § 249. 1.

28. וַיֹּאמֶר § 35. 2. יָהֹוָה § 47. חַפֵּץ masc. here and 2 Sam. 23:
8 K'thibh § 197. *b.* הָאֱלֹהִים § 245. 2. וְיִנָּקְמָה § 91. *c*, § 271. 3, with
מִן before the thing *on account* of which vengeance is taken, considered
as the cause *from* which this effect proceeds : and also before the person
on whom vengeance is taken, this being regarded as a compensation for
past injuries exacted *from* them : in 15:7 it is followed by בְּ. נִקְמַת־אַחַת
vengeance of once § 235. 3 (3), § 254. 6 *b*, which shall at one time
avenge the entire wrong. Others make אַחַת refer to *eye*, and take the
following מִן in a partitive sense, *vengeance of* (or *for* § 254. 9) *one of
my two eyes*, supposing that he regards the vengeance, which he intends,
as but half a satisfaction for the injury inflicted upon him. The Rabbins
say that vengeance for the other was to be postponed to the retributions
of the world to come. מִשְּׁתֵּי § 22. *b*, § 223. 1. *a*.

29. וַיִּלְפֹּת agrees either with בַּיִת or with Samson : in either case it
is parenthetic, and the following clause must be connected with וַיֵּט.

30. נֶגַע § 172. 4. בְּכֹחַ the prep. denotes conjunction, *with might,*
see on Gen. 3:3.

1 SAMUEL, CHAPTER XVII.

3. אֶל־הָהָר *unto the mountain*, i. e. they extended to it and upon it
from the valley בַּעֵמֶק, ver. 2, in which the encampments were. מִזֶּה,
the Hebrews say *from this*, where our idiom requires 'in this direction'
or 'on this side,' see on Gen. 1:7; זֶה repeated is *this—that*, the finger
being supposed to point first in one direction and then in its opposite.
וְהַגַּיְא, this is the central ravine, while the valley עֵמֶק embraced the entire depression between the mountains, including the elevated plateaus
on which the rival armies lay. בֵּינֵיהֶם:, see on Gen. 42:23.

4. אִישׁ־הַבֵּנַיִם *the* well-known *champion* § 245. 3, from בֵּין. The
Vulg. *vir spurius* seems to derive it from בֵּן *a son.* וְגוֹ שֵׁשׁ. Herodotus, 1.
68, speaks of a skeleton seven cubits long. Pliny, Nat. Hist. 7. 16, speaks
of an Arabian of his own day who was nine feet nine inches high, and
two men in the reign of Augustus who were half a foot taller.

5. וְקַשְׂקַשֶּׂת § 216. 1. *e.* וְשִׁרְיוֹן § 273. 3. לְבוּשׁ § 90 (pass.). נְחֹשֶׁת:
§ 253. 2.

8. הַפְּלִשְׁתִּי § 245. 4, *the Philistine* par excellence, representing the
entire body.

9. יִחְיֶנִּי marg. abbreviated for קְמֵץ פְּזָקַף קָטוֹן.   אִיכַל־לוֹ, see on Judg. 16 : 5.   11. וַיֵּרְאָאוּ § 19. 1, § 147. 1.

12. הַזֶּה § 249. 2. c, *this Ephrathite*, Gen. 35 : 19, viz. the one spoken of 16 : 1, etc. וִיהוּדָה § 253. b. שְׁמֹנֶה, only seven are named, 1 Chron. 2 : 13—15, perhaps one may have died in early life or without issue. בָּא בַאֲנָשִׁים: , great age is elsewhere expressed by the words בָּא בַּיָּמִים *come into days* or *advanced in days*, Gen. 24 : 1, Josh. 13 : 1, 23 : 1 ; *advanced among men* is here used as an equivalent phrase.

13. שְׁלֹשֶׁת § 251. 4.   הַגְּדֹלִים § 260. 2 (2), repetition in ver. 14, see on Gen. 37 : 5.

14. הוּא § 258. 2.

15. מֵעַל *from beside Saul*, from being near him or with him, see on Gen 42 : 24, 45 : 1, although the original force of the prep. may possibly be preserved, *from waiting upon Saul;* as the servant stands while his lord sits, he may be said to be not only *by* him but *over* him. בֵּית־לָחֶם: may be the object of אֶל *to Bethlehem* § 271. 2, or stand absolutely, *at Bethlehem* § 274. 2. b.

17. לֶחֶם § 251. 2. c, § 253. 2.   וְהָרֵץ § 271. 2, § 273. 1.

18. לִשְׁלוֹם *in respect to health.* עֲרֻבָּתָם, pledge or token either of their welfare or of their receipt of the articles sent them.

20. עַל־שֹׁמֵר *upon a keeper*, in his charge, the care of them being devolved *upon* him, as though it were a burden to be carried. וְהֵחֵל , governed directly by וַיָּבֹא § 271. 2, and qualified by הַיֹּצֵא which cannot be a predicate since it has the article § 259. 2. יְהָרֵעוּ: § 160. 2.

21. וַתַּעֲרֹךְ agrees in form with מִלְחָמָה, which is in apposition with יִשְׂרָאֵל וּפְלִשְׁתִּים.

23. מַמְּעָרוֹת K'thibh *plains*, or it might be *caves*. מִמַּעַרְכֹת K'ri, *armies* or *ranks*. הָאֵלֶּה , viz. those above recited, vs. 8–10.

25. הַרְאִיתֶם § 24. b. יַעְשְׁרֶנּוּ § 104. h.

26. הַזֶּה § 73. 2. חַיִּים: § 275. 3. a.

29. הֲלֹא , either *was it not my father's command* by which he had been required to come, or better, perhaps, *was it not merely a word* which did not deserve such severe censure, Isa. 29 : 21.

32. עָלָיו suf. may refer to Goliath, who might readily be understood to be the subject of discourse, though he is not mentioned in the immediately preceding verses *because of him* the effect being regarded as resting *upon* its cause; or it may, after the analogy of like expressions occurring elsewhere, Ps. 42 : 5, 142 : 4, Hos. 11 : 8, *let no man's heart fall upon him*, sink down upon itself under the burden of its own emotions.

34. רֹעֶה with בְּ, see on Gen. 37 : 2. וּבָא § 265. b. הָאֲרִי § 245. 5

d, comp. *the wolf*, John 10 : 12. וְאֶת־הַדּוֹב § 271. *b.* חַי, K'thibh referring distributively to the lion and bear as subject of וּבָא, צָּר K'ri
object of the verb.

35. וְהֶחֱזַקְתִּי § 112. 3, with בְ connecting the verb with its object,
see on Judg. 16 : 3. 26, or denoting the means or instrument of seizure,
see on Gen. 39 : 12. 14. : וְהִכִּיתִיו § 14. *a*, § 61. 4. *a*, § 160. 2, marg.
the Tav with Daghesh.

36. הָיְתָה § 265. *b*, *has become*, see Gen. 3 : 22. בְּאַחַד § 255. 1.

37. Marg. פָּסוּק בְּאֶמְצַע בָּקָא *pause in the middle of a verse.*

39. מֵעַל, see on Gen. 1 : 7. וַיִּצֶּל § 150. 2 and 3 (p. 181).

40. חָזָק § 254. 2. וּבַיַּלְקוּט § 245. 3, as the two objects connected
by וְ are identical, it must be translated *even*, comp. 28 : 3.

41. וְקָרֵב § 185. *b*, § 282. *c.*   42. וַיִּרְאֶה § 172. 4.

43. בְּמַקְלוֹת indefinite plur. though only one is meant, see on Gen.
37 : 8. : בֵּאלֹהָיו, the use of the prep. בְ after verbs of cursing and swearing is by some derived from its signification of conjunction or nearness,
cursed by his gods, uttering in their immediate presence the imprecation
which they were expected to fulfil, and by others from its instrumental
sense, comp. the Latin *per*, *by his gods*, as the instruments or agents in
fulfilling his imprecation.

45. בְּשֵׁם *in the name of*, by the authority and as the representative
of; or *with the name*, etc., as what he brought to oppose the weapons of
the Philistine, the name of God, as that by which he is known, being
equivalent to God himself as revealed. יְהוָה § 253. *b.* : חֵרַפְתָּ § 65. *a*,
marg. abbreviated for פָּסוּק סוֹף בְּסוֹף פַּתָּח *Pattahh with Soph Pasuk*, i. e.
with Silluk § 36. 1.

46. וְיֵדְעוּ § 275. 2. *b.* : לְיִשְׂרָאֵל *there is a God to Israel*, Israel has
a God, or *God is for Israel*, on his side.

47. יְהוֹשִׁיעַ § 150. 2 (p. 181).   48. וְהָיָה § 265. *b.*

50. וַיִּתֵּן § 260. *a.*

51. אֶל־ *unto* after a verb of rest where previous motion is implied :
ran and stood unto the Philistine is equivalent to *ran unto the Philistine
and stood*, comp. עָמַד, Gen. 43 : 30. וַיִּתְיַצֵּב § 105. *a.*

52. וְיִשְׂרָאֵל וִיהוּדָה.   The schism in the time of Rehoboam only
deepened and perpetuated a distinction, which had in various ways and
for various causes been created long before between the powerful tribe
of *Judah*, to whom Jacob had promised the sovereignty, Gen. 49 : 10,
and the rest of *Israel*, comp. Josh. 11 : 21. פְּנֵיהֶם 2 m. s. indef.
§ 243. 2.

54. יְרוּשָׁלַםִ § 47, although the citadel was not taken until the reign
of David, 2 Sam. 5 : 7, part of the city was held by the Israelites from

the time of Joshua, Josh. 15 : 63, Judg. 1 : 8. 21. מֵאֹהֶל used here
not in the strict sense of *tent*, as David was not connected with the
army, but in the wider one of *habitation, dwelling,* compare 13 : 2, 1 Kin.
8 : 66. David now took Goliath's armour home with him as his lawful
spoils, though he must subsequently have deposited Goliath's sword in
the tabernacle, 21 : 9.

55. יֵצֵא § 273. 4. עַד § 249. 2. *a.* It has been thought strange
that Saul should make these inquiries about one who had played the
harp before him and been his armour-bearer, 16 : 21, etc. But we do
not know what interval had elapsed, nor how much David had altered.
Besides, the question concerns his parentage, which Saul had now a
special reason for wishing to know, ver. 25, but which he might easily
have forgotten, even if he recollected his person. הַעֶלֶם § 245. 2. —אִם ,
see on Gen. 42 : 15.

58. בֵּית הַלַּחְמִי : § 246. 3. *b.*

1 KINGS, CHAPTER XVII.

3. מִנַּחַל § 254. 3, prep. denoting close conjunction, *by the brook,*
or as נַחַל includes in its signification the *valley* with the brook, it may
have its primary sense *in.* עַל־פְּנֵי , as the brook cannot be certainly
identified, it is doubtful whether this means *before* or *east of.*

6. וַיִּשְׁתְּ § 263. 4.   7. יָבֵשׁ , see on Gen. 41 : 1.

11. לִקְחִי־ § 132. 2.

14. תֵּכְלֶה § 177. 3, § 179. 1. *a.* תֶּחְסָר K'thibh § 132. 1, תַּם K'ri.

15. הוּא־וְהִיא K'thibh, הִיא־וְהוּא K'ri.   16. חָסֵר § 277.

18. מַה־לִּי , declaratively or interrogatively § 284.

20. Marg. see 1 Sam. 17 : 9.

22. וַיְשָׁבׇ with בְּ , see on Judg. 13 : 9.

24. זֶה *this I know,* or adv. *this* time § 235. 3 (4).

CHAPTER XVIII.

1. וַיְהִי § 275. 1, see on Gen. 1 : 14. הַשְּׁלִישִׁית , reckoned not from
the beginning of the drought, but from Elijah's arrival at Zarephath,
Luke 4 : 25, James 5 : 17. Marg. *Haphtarah of* כִּי תִשָּׂא , i. e. here begins the lesson in the prophets corresponding to the lesson of the law,
Ex. 30 : 11 etc. so called from its opening words, *according to the
custom of the German Jews.*

3. הַבַּיִת *the royal house,* the palace § 245. 4. אֲשֶׁר , derivatives of
transitive verbs are often followed by a direct object.

4. בַּמְּעָרָה *in the cave,* i. e. in each cave, comp. לְאִישׁ, Gen. 45:22. בֶּהֶם § 273. 3.

5. נְבַעֵר *destroy,* be forced to kill them on account of our inability to feed them; others suppose it to mean simply *suffer to perish.* מֵהֶבְהֵמָה prep. partitive; marg. *other editions* have מִן בְּהֵמָה *K'thibh,* מֵהַבְּהֵמָה *K'ri.*

7. הַאַתָּה זֶה, as in English, *is this you?*

8. אָי, see on Judg. 13:11.

10. יִמְצָאֵנְךָ *will not,* because unable to do so, hence equivalent to *cannot,* or, as conditioned by the preceding preterite, *could not find thee.*

13. אֶת אֱמָר § 271. *a.* חַיִּים § 280. 1.

15. פֶּן, see on Gen. 42:16.

18. הַבְּעָלִים plur. because of the various epithets he bore, descriptive of the different characters under which he was worshipped, as Baal-berith Judg. 8:33, Baal-zebub, 2 Kin. 1:6, etc.

19. אֹכְלֵי § 254. 1, *eating at the table,* prop. eaters belonging to the table.

20. Marg. *Haphtarah of* כִּי תִשָּׂא *according to the custom of the Spanish Jews.*

21. פֹּסְחִים *limping upon two opinions* instead of treading firmly upon one. The LXX has *upon both knees,* ἰγνύαις, in which it is followed by a few modern interpreters. הַפֹּעֵל § 246. 1. *a.* סְעִף § 273. 2.

22. As the prophets of Astarte, ver. 19, are not separately mentioned here, or in vs. 25, 40, some have supposed that they were not present, but as the false prophets generally were gathered, ver. 20, and all of them were slain, 19:1, it is probable that the prophets of Baal only were named, since they were the most prominent and principal actors.

23. וַיִּתְּנוּ § 243. 2.

24. בְּשֵׁם prep. instrumental, *call with the name,* i. e. loudly utter the name § 272. 2. *b,* here by way of invocation; sometimes its proclamation is intended. הוּא § 258. 2. וַעֲנָה § 273. 2. *a.*

25. רָאשׁוֹן § 235. 3 (3). הָרַבִּים § 260. 2 (2).

26. וַיְפַסְּחוּ *and they limped beside* (see on Gen. 42:24, 45:1) *the altar,* contemptuously said of the dancing which formed part of their idolatrous service. עָשָׂה § 243. 2.

30. מִזְבֵּחַ § 215. 1. *b.* This, like other altars which had been similarly destroyed in different parts of the land, 19:10, was doubtless erected by the true worshippers of Jehovah after the time of the schism, when they were prohibited from going up to the temple at Jerusalem. In this period of defection, as in the corresponding period in the days of Samuel, the prophets were invested with extraordinary powers adapted

to the emergency, and, as the immediate messengers and representatives of God, assumed the functions and prerogatives of the priesthood, who had either abdicated their office or had been excluded from it.

31. שְׁמֶךָ *thy name*, and therefore of the entire people, not of a part merely, to which it had then been unlawfully restricted.

32. מִזְבֵּחַ § 273. 3. בְּמַ, see on 1 Sam. 17 : 45. סָאתַיִם § 203. 3, § 57. 2 (3), as two seahs or three pecks seem too small for the capacity of a trench surrounding the altar, some have thought that it occupied as much ground as would suffice for sowing two seahs of seed. But this on the other hand would make it too enormous. The suggestion is here offered whether the meaning may not be that its dimensions, viz. its width and depth, were those of a two-seah-measure בֵּית סָאתַיִם זֶרַע. Such a measure, which may have been a familiar one, would contain something less than a cubic foot; the trench would consequently be about a foot wide by a foot deep.

33. The order of procedure and even the terms employed are borrowed from the Mosaic law of sacrifice, Lev. 1 : 6—8.

34. מַיִם § 273. 3. וַיְמַלְאוּ 3 pl. fut., some editions are without Methegh, when it will be 2 pl. imper. וַיִּשְׁנוּ § 19. 1, § 147. 1.

36. וּבִדְבָרֶיךָ prep. indicates either the cause, see on Gen. 39 : 14, or the rule, as Gen. 1 : 26 ; marg. see on Judg. 13 : 17.

37. יִחְיֶה הָאֱלֹהִים § 246. 1. *a*, according to the accents יִחְיֶה is connected with אַתָּה, the subject, and separated from הָאֱלֹהִים the predicate. הֲסִבֹּתָ conditioned by the previous fut. יָדְעוּ, and expressing not what is already past at the moment of speaking, but what *will have* occurred, when they shall know it to be the case § 262. 1. אֲחֹרַנִּית back again to the faith and worship of their fathers, the patriarchs just recited.

39. הוּא § 258. 2. Marg. see on Judg. 13 : 25.

41. הֲמוֹן either *noise* or *abundance*.

43. עַד־נָא § 254. 9. *a*.

45. עַד־כֹּה וְעַד־כֹּה *until so and until so*, i. e. a very short time. This phrase is by some supposed to have been originally accompanied by a gesture of the hand, *until* one can do *so* and then *so*. Or the repeated adverb *so and so* may have an indefinite sense, whence *until so and so* means after an indefinite but brief period, as in English, ' by and by.'

46. Marg. Here begins *the Haphtarah* of פִּינְחָס, Num. 25 : 10, etc.

CHAPTER XIX.

1. אֲשֶׁר, used adverbially, ' the way in *which*,' *how*.

2. כִּי, as the formula of the oath precedes, equivalent to ' I swear *that*,' Gen. 42 : 16. כָּכָה § 245. 3. *b*. אַחֵר § 255. 1.

3. ‫אֶל‬‎ *in reference to*, for the sake of.

4. ‫אֲחַת‬‎ K'thibh, ‫אֶחָד‬‎ K'ri, as ver. 5, § 248. *a.* ‫וַיִּשְׁאַל‬‎ *asked his sou.* or himself *to die*, i. e. that himself might die. ‫בֵּי‬‎, comp. Gen. 45 : 28.

5. ‫הַי‬‎, § 235. 3 (4). ‫בָּצַע‬‎ with ‫בְּ‬‎ Gen. 3 : 3. 6. ‫וַיָּשָׁב‬‎ § 269. *a.*

7. ‫רַב‬‎ § 260. *b.* 9. ‫הַמְצֵרָה‬‎ § 245. 3. 11. ‫יִחְדָּו‬‎ § 275. 1. *c.*

13. ‫פֶּתַח‬‎ § 274. 2. *b.* 15. ‫מִדְבָּרָה‬‎ § 256. *d.* 16. ‫חָדְשָׁה‬‎ § 265.

18. ‫וְהִשְׁאַרְתִּי‬‎ § 100. 2, *I will leave*, preserve from slaughter. ‫פָּצָה‬‎, comp. on Gen. 41 : 40 ; marg. § 32.

19. ‫דִּשְׁנַיִם חֶזְקָר‬‎ § 227. 2, § 251. 4. *a.*

20. ‫אֲשָׁמָה‬‎ marg. *the Shin with Hhateph Kamets*.

21. ‫חַדְּשׁוֹר‬‎ § 271. 4. Marg. see on Judg. 13 : 25.

NEHEMIAH, CHAPTER IX.

1. ‫עֶשְׂרִים‬‎ § 225. 2, § 252. 2. 2. ‫וַיִּחְתַּוּ‬‎ § 150. 3 (p. 182).

3. ‫רְבִיעִית‬‎ § 227. 3.

5. ‫וּמֵרִים‬‎ § 161. 4, § 255. 1, *even* (1 Sam. 17 :40) a name *exalted.* Marg. abbrev. for ‫כֵּן צָרִיךְ לִהְיוֹת‬‎, *so it ought to be*, designed to certify the reader that the Pattahh under Mem is not an error for Kamets.

7. ‫בָּחַרְתָּ‬‎ with ‫בְּ‬‎, because the choice penetrates and rests in its object. ‫מָאוּר‬‎ § 253. *b.*

8. ‫וְכָרוֹת‬‎ § 268. 1. 11. ‫כְּמוֹ‬‎ § 233. *a.* 13. ‫טוֹבִים‬‎ § 276. 3.

17. ‫וְחָסֶד‬‎ marg. see Judg. 13 : 17.

18. ‫אַף כִּי‬‎, implying a fresh particular and one of greater magnitude, 'it was *also* (or *even*) true *that*, etc.' ‫נְאָצוֹת‬‎ II. § 187. 1 for ‫נָאָצוֹת‬‎ § 63. 1. *a.*

19. ‫אֶת־עַמּוּד‬‎ § 271. *b.*

22. ‫לְפֵאָה‬‎ *in respect to a corner*, or collectively *corners*, so that they occupied every corner of these subjugated kingdoms, or that the distribution of the land was made with fixed corners and boundaries between the several tribes. ‫וְאֶת־אֶרֶץ מֶלֶךְ‬‎, comp. ver. 5. Sihon was king of Heshbon, Deut. 1 : 4.

24. ‫ו . . . ו‬‎ *both—and*, as in Lat. *e —et.*

25. ‫מְלֵאִים‬‎ § 271. 1, comp. on 1 Kin. 18 : 3.

26. ‫חֲזֵרֵי‬‎ with ‫בְּ‬‎, Gen. 43 : 3. 27. ‫יַעֲקֹ‬‎ § 263. 4.

29. ‫בָּם‬‎ repeats the noun ‫אֶ‬‎ § 281.

32. ‫אֶת־כָּל‬‎ § 271. *a.* ‫מְצָאַתְנוּ‬‎; this verb may either govern the direct object or be construed with ‫לְ‬‎ § 272. 2. *a;* one construction is adopted with the pronoun, the other with the nouns in apposition with it, *happened us*, viz. *to our kings*, etc.

34. ‫וְאֶת‬‎ § 271. *b.* 35. ‫וּבְאֶרֶץ‬‎ § 249. 1. *c.*

37. ‫וּבִבְהֶמְתֵּנוּ‬‎ prep. *in* or *because of*, see on Gen. 39 : 14.

ISAIAH. CHAPTER XL.

The last twenty-seven chapters of this book form one connected prophecy, of which the foresight of the Babylonish captivity, 39 : 6, 7, was the starting-point and the historical occasion, and which was designed to remove the despondency produced by the prospect and especially the experience of this great calamity. The prophet is enabled to look out over the entire future of God's scheme of mercy, and he aims to comfort the people by shewing them that they had a grand mission to fulfil and a glorious destiny which should be accomplished notwithstanding all present and future evils.

The work of consolation is begun in this chapter by the assurance

(1) vs. 1–11, the Lord who seemed to have forsaken Jerusalem is about to return and achieve her salvation.

(2) vs. 12–26, the possibility of what appears so incredible is confirmed by an appeal to God's incomparable greatness.

(3) vs. 27–31, the despondency of the people is therefore groundless.

The theme of the whole prophecy is contained in ver. 1, 2, which not only characterize it in the general as consolatory, but even foreshadow its triple division, with the special topic of each.

1. נַחֲמוּ, the repetition is emphatic. The persons addressed are not specifically the priests (LXX), prophets (Targ.), elders, nor certain inquirers supposed to have consulted Isaiah respecting the future fortunes of the people, but all who hear the summons. The imperative form is unessential and does not belong to the main idea to be expressed. The thing insisted upon is not so much the duty and obligation of the work of consolation as the certainty that God's people were to be consoled. It was of no consequence who should administer the comfort; that is accordingly left indefinite. The point of real interest was that there was ground for comfort and that the people would receive it עַמִּי , not a vocative (Vulg.) but object of verb : this expression contains already the seeds of consolation, since it is a recognition of the relation as still existing between God and the people, which the latter might be tempted in their dejection to imagine had been broken off. יֹאמַר saith or is saying § 263. 2, for the utterance, though begun, is not completed; not will say, as though God would at some future time direct that comfort should be given to his people. For though it largely respects an emergency which had not yet arisen, 39 : 8, the comfort is not postponed to another time, but is given in this prophecy. And the same phrase is frequently used throughout Isaiah, and always in a present sense. אָמַר to say, introduces the very words of a speaker, while דִּבֶּר to speak, in-

volves no citation of the exact language. Marg. *Haphtarah of* נָאֶחָמוּ
i. e. corresponding to the Parashah or lesson of the law, beginning Deut
3 : 23.

2. עַל־לֵב *according to*, Gen. 41 : 40, *the heart*, in a manner agreeable to the heart or feelings ; or the strict local sense of the prep. may
be retained, *speak* not to the ears merely, but so as to reach down to and
remain *upon the heart.* לֵב denotes the whole interior nature of man,
including both the understanding, 1 Kin. 3 : 9, and the affections, Deut.
30 : 6. The meaning here is, speak so as to affect the feelings ; the
words themselves do not determine in what way, whether joyously or
the reverse, but usage confines it to the former. יְרוּשָׁלִַם § 47, the city
considered as the centre and capital of God's earthly kingdom, put for
that kingdom itself or for the people who compose it (as Rome for the
Roman empire), and hence equivalent to עַמִּי of ver. 1. Those critics,
who deny the genuineness of this prophecy and refer it to some imaginary writer at or near the close of the captivity, are compelled to understand by ' Jerusalem ' the desolated city itself, or its inhabitants in exile,
though it is hard to see why these should be thus singled out from the
rest of the exiles as the recipients of special comfort. וְקִרְאוּ *proclaim,*
cry in a loud tone, thus differing from זָצַק . The proclamation embraces
the three things which now follow. צְבָאָהּ , usually masc. here fem. means
both *a host* or *army*, and *military service.* In Num. 4 : 23 it is applied
to the Levitical ministrations in the sanctuary as a *militia sacra*, an
orderly and well appointed service by a special body organized and devoted to that particular function. It here denotes Jerusalem's period of
suffering, comp. Heb. 10 : 32, conceived of as a toilsome service, and
for a definite term. This is now *full*, i. e. completed. נִרְצָה , some
render *pardoned*, a sense which the word does not have ; Gesen. translates *is satisfied* or discharged by the infliction of the merited penalty ;
others *her punishment is accepted* as sufficient, but this gives an unproved meaning to רָצָה ; the verb properly means *to be accepted*, and is
technically used of the acceptance of sacrifices, whence the most probable
opinion is that רָצָה is here used as חַטָּאת ' sin,' so often is for ' a sin-
offering,' *an atonement for her iniquity is accepted.*

כִּי is most naturally taken in the same sense with the two that precede it, *that*, introducing the third particular of the comfort to be proclaimed. If rendered *for*, it assigns the reason of the preceding ; she is
released from further suffering, *for*, etc. לָקְחָה , the preterites of this
verse are prophetic § 262. 4. כִּפְלַיִם *double*, not in a strict numerical
sense ' two things,' whether, as some old writers explained it, justification and sanctification, or the two particulars before mentioned, but in-

definitely to denote the abundance or largeness of the blessings to be received, comp. 61 : 7. Those who render the preceding כִּי *for*, must refer 'double' not to blessings but to punishment or sufferings, as Jer. 16 . 18, Rev. 18 : 6, not as though she had suffered twice as much as her sins had deserved, or as God had intended to inflict, but amply for the purposes of punishment; their punishment was 'double,' not so as to exceed but to be commensurate with the vastness of their sins. בְּכָל־חַטֹּאתֶיהָ : the prep. may have its local sense *in all her sins*, in the midst of them, and by implication in spite of them ; or it may denote the price, comp. Gen. 3 : 19, 37 : 28, *for all her sins*, by a gracious recompense of good for evil.

The rest of the book may be divided into three principal sections, of nine chapters each, indicated by the refrain, 48 : 22, 57 : 21, and answering in a general way to the three topics of consolation just announced. The prominent though not the exclusive subject of

(1) ch. 40–48 is the overthrow of Babylon and Israel's deliverance from exile, culminating in ch. 45. This is a pledge and a preliminary fulfilment of the declaration that 'her warfare is accomplished.'

(2) ch. 49–57, the sufferings and reward of the Messiah, culminating in ch. 53: ' her sin-offering is accepted.'

(3) ch. 58–66, the future glory of Israel, culminating in ch. 60 ; 'she hath received of the Lord's hand double for all her sins.'

The remainder of the first division of this chapter consists of three stanzas of three verses each :

(1) vs. 3–5. In confirmation of what has just been announced, and as the method by which it is to be effected, it is declared that God will return to his long-forsaken people.

(2) vs. 6–8. This is indubitably certain : for it does not depend on frail and feeble man, but is secured by the unfailing word of God.

(3) vs. 9–11. It is represented as actually taking place before their eyes; God is seen returning to his people.

3. קוֹל , not a continuation of the command, vs. 1. 2, with יְהִי understood, 'let there be a voice,' but an exclamation, *a voice !* equivalent to ' 'hark !' or ' I hear a voice ;' const. as in LXX, Eng. Ver. ' voice of one crying,' or apposition, ' a voice crying.' קוֹרֵא alludes to קְרָא, ver. 2, following the injunction to cry, this voice is heard crying. The voice itself is undefined, only the quarter is recognized from which it comes, בַּמִּדְבָּר *in the wilderness*. This may be connected with what precedes and designate the locality where the voice is heard, or with what follows and show where the way is to be prepared. The parallelism of the last clause is urged in favour of connecting it with what follows : but the

different collocation of the words in the two clauses, together with the fact that one of its most remarkable fulfilments, as testified by all four of the evangelists, Mat. 3 : 3, Mark 1 : 3, Luke 3 : 4, John 1 : 23, was in John the Baptist, who came preaching in the wilderness of Judea, favours the other view. At the same time, while strictly belonging to what precedes, it will naturally be understood also with what follows ; the road was to be prepared where the voice was heard. מִדְבָּר is properly *a wilderness*, a waste, uncultivated region, producing a scanty herbage, fit only for pasturage ; עֲרָבָה is *a desert*, a sterile, arid region, totally destitute of products. Those interpreters who see no allusion in this prophecy to anything except the Babylonish exile and the restoration from it, understand by 'the wilderness' and 'the desert' the region between Babylon and Palestine, through which God here promises a safe and easy passage to his people returning from exile. But not a word is here said about the return of the people from captivity. The road is not for the people to march over, but for God himself. The figure is not even that of God marching at the head of his people, and leading them from bondage, as when he brought them out of Egypt. But it is God returning to his people who had alienated him by their sins and in consequence fallen into their present extremity. They are now exhorted to prepare the way for his return to accomplish their salvation. It has further been made a question whether 'the wilderness' is to be understood literally or figuratively, and accordingly whether it denotes the wilderness of Judea, where John preached repentance in fulfilment of this prediction, or a place of destitution, privation and trial, and represents the condition of sin and suffering in which the people were. But in point of fact these two meanings do not exclude each other. John's preaching in the wilderness, like his dress and his ascetic life, was itself symbolical of the spiritual and moral waste which Judah then presented, and which it was his mission to endeavour to reclaim. His appearance in a locality conformed to the literal terms of the prophecy was an index pointing him out as its subject, and one by whom it was fulfilled in its higher spiritual sense. A like mingling of the literal and the figurative is frequent in the prophecies, comp. Zech. 9 : 9, Ps. 22 : 18. It may be remarked, in addition, that this is a generic prophecy, and was fulfilled in the entire series of instruments and messengers from Isaiah onward, by which God wrought reformations among his people at various periods, and thus prepared the way for his more or less conspicuous return to them. In this class of predictions it is not unusual for the prophets to employ terms, which are in a general sense applicable to all the particulars included within the scope of the fulfilment, but which are in a more special and strict sense descriptive of some one of marked prominence, comp. Gen. 3 : 15, 2 Sam. 7 : 12–16. So here, while all God's messengers to the people preached repentance in a moral and spiritual waste, John the Baptist did so in a literal wilderness likewise.

פַּנּוּ, cause to turn away, *clear*, prepare by the removal of obstacles, as of sin by a timely repentance. דֶּרֶךְ § 254. 9. *a*, the way which Jehovah will use and over which he will come ; this is a general term under which מְסִלָּה is embraced as a particular kind of road, *highway*, or causeway raised above the ordinary surface. יַשְּׁרוּ, if the reference be to linear obliquity, *make straight*, if to superficial inequality, *make level ;* the next verse shows that the latter idea is here prominent.

4. An amplification of the preceding idea. The meaning is of course not that the valleys shall be converted into mountains and *vice versâ*, but that the one shall be raised and the other depressed, so as to form a smooth and level course. יִנָּשֵׂא, declarative, *shall be raised*, or perhaps mandatory, as this is included among the senses of the future, and might here be suggested by the preceding command, *let it be raised*. גַּיְא, also גֵּיְא and גֵּא, a steep narrow *valley*, comp. on 1 Sam. 17 : 3, while בִּקְעָה means *a* valley that is broad and open, or even one that is expanded to a plain. הֶעָקֹב, according to the Eng. Ver. which here follows the LXX, *crooked*, in contrast with מִישׁוֹר, *straightness :* but as the latter, comp. יַשְּׁרוּ, ver. 3, may refer to superficial equality, *evenness*, the former may denote *an eminence*, or as an adj. *uneven*, broken into numerous hillocks. וְהָרְכָסִים *difficult passes*, narrow gorges should be opened out to wide valleys or plains, or according to Dr. Alexander, *ridges.*

5. וְנִגְלָה *and* as a result of the preceding preparations *shall be revealed*. This is to be preferred to the indirect subjunctive rendering *that the glory of the Lord may be revealed*. The former is more forcible, as it certainly assures of this result, which the latter only does by implication.   * יְיָ כְּבוֹד, applied to any manifestation of Jehovah's presence or display of his perfections : used also of that symbolical brightness which often accompanied God's revelation of himself, as at the dedication of the temple, 1 Kin. 8 : 11. When the way was prepared for him by the penitence of his people, God himself would come and display his glorious perfections in the salvation of his people. This was true of their deliverance from exile, and other tokens of his presence, but especially of his personal coming in the flesh, of which the apostle John says, in language borrowed perhaps from this passage, 1 : 14, we beheld his glory, the glory as of the only begotten of the Father. כָּל־בָּשָׂר *all*

---

* A common abbreviation for יְהוָֹה.

flesh, in its widest sense, Gen. 7 : 21, all living animals ; here, as often elsewhere, all mankind. The glory displayed by the coming of God to his people should be so conspicuous that all mankind (not the chosen people only) should behold it. This was more conspicuously true of Christ's advent than of the deliverance from Babylon. יַחְדָּו *together*, may qualify the verb and denote identity of time, shall see it *immediately* on its being displayed, or qualify the noun, *all flesh together*. כִּי might be the object of וְרָאוּ *shall see that*, etc. : but it is better to make ' see ' govern an object understood, 'the glory of God,' and translate כִּי *for ;* this is its meaning wherever else the phrase occurs. It then confirms what precedes, *the mouth of Jehovah*, not man, *hath spoken* it.

6. It has just been announced on the authority of God that his glory would be revealed in the salvation of his people. The next stanza, vs. 6–8, declares how reliable and unfailing that word is. קוֹל אֹמֵר, as in ver. 3, an exclamation, either const. *voice of one saying* or, app. *a voice saying*. Some make the voice that of God, and the person addressed the prophet, a view of the case which has led in a few MSS. to pointing the next verb וָאֹמַר, and to the rendering in the LXX εἶπα, and in the Vulgate *dixi*. But there is no necessity of defining who the speaker is. וְאָמַר, a second voice, the person addressed by the first speaker here replies. Junius and Tremellius (quoted by Dr. Alexander) assume but a single voice and make קוֹל the subject, ' a voice says cry, and says or tells me what I shall cry.' כָּל־הַבָּשָׂר, as in the previous verse used of mankind : perhaps that may account for the use of the article, *all the flesh* just spoken of : this is not necessary, however, as the article may be used in its generic sense § 245. 5. חָצִיר *grass*, a comparison frequent in the Scriptures, the point of resemblance, as is plain from parallel passages and from this connexion, being that of evanescent frailty. The respect in which human frailty is here asserted will depend upon the meaning given to חַסְדּוֹ. Its primary signification is that of *kindness* or *benevolent regard*. It is used (1) of God's favour to men, (2) of men's love to God, or piety, (3) of men's benignity or kindness to one another. On the assumption that the precise thing here asserted is the vanity of human greatness and power, some interpreters assume that the word must have the sense of *beauty ;* comp. חֵן, and the English *grace*, which mean both favour and beauty. So Eng. Ver. *goodliness*, LXX δόξα, retained 1 Pet. 1 : 24. The adoption of this rendering by the apostle does not prove its accuracy as a verbal translation, but only that the sentiment expressed is true, and that it was sufficiently accurate for the purpose which he had in view in quoting it. But as the word occurs nowhere else in this sense, and as its meanings in other places yield a good sense here, there

is no need of departing from them. It may mean *favour* shewn to men—human favour is precarious and feeble; we cannot build much therefore on human promises, but this is the word of God. Or love to God, *piety :* it is used in this sense by Hosea 6 : 4, " your goodness is as a morning cloud." The meaning then is, human goodness is too feeble and frail to merit such an interposition as is here predicted. But the prediction is not based on any expectation of human merit, it rests solely on the gracious word of God. צִיץ הַשָּׂדֶה׃ *flower of the field,* i. e. ' wild flower,' as ' beast of the field ' denotes *wild beast.* It is not probable that any stress is to be laid here upon the distinction between wild and cultivated flowers, the former being less cared for, and especially liable to be trodden upon or cut down. The individualizing is due to the vividness of poetic conception, or it may have been suggested by association with the grass previously mentioned. The preceding clause contains a metaphor, here a particle of comparison is introduced. Those who insist on a literal understanding of our Lord's words 'this is my body,' should here believe, on the basis of this passage, that *all flesh* is, not by a figure but in its actual substance, *grass.*

7. The comparison suggested before is here developed, and the point of comparison stated. Man resembles grass because it dries up, and a flower since it fades or wilts. יָבֵשׁ § 262. 3. נָבֵל § 35. 1, § 42. *a,* editions vary in giving Merka or Methegh to the ultimate syllable. כִּי *for ;* some render *when,* a sense which the particle sometimes has, but it is best to adhere to the ordinary meaning when practicable. רוּחַ *Spirit,* since God's infinite Spirit conducts and presides over all operations of nature, great or minute; or, *the breath of Jehovah has blown upon it;* or, which amounts to the same thing though it is less poetical, *the wind of Jehovah,* i. e. sent by him, see on Gen. 1 : 2. אָכֵן, not a particle of inference, *therefore,* but of asseveration, *yea,* or *surely.* הָעָם. Some suppose without reason that the Chaldeans are meant ; yes, this powerful oppressing people is grass which his breath can wither. This word, when standing absolutely, often means *the people* by way of eminence, i. e. God's chosen people, Israel, as on the other hand גּוֹי stands for heathen nations; some so understand it here, yes, even Israel is grass, their goodness fleeting and void of all merit. But there is no need of restricting it in either of these ways ; it is better to take it, as in 42 : 5, for *people* generally, *mankind,* equivalent to " all flesh,' vs. 5. 6. Subject with article, predicate without, as commonly in Greek, though not a universal rule.

· 8. An emphatic repetition for the sake of making plainer the contrast to be presented. וּדְבַר *and,* where we must employ the adversative *but* § 287. 1.   *Word* in its wide sense, not limited to *promise* or *prophecy*, much less to the specific utterance which precedes, though that is of course included : nor to the *gospel* to which it is applied by Peter. קוּם stand, i. e. *be valid, firm*, opposed to fail of accomplishment. According to the meaning of יָקוּם, the sense will be, (1) No lack of goodness on the part of man can prevent God's word of grace from taking effect.   (2) The feebleness and frailty of man is no argument against the completion of so glorious a salvation, since God's word assures it. Or (3) the fleeting favour of man only heightens by contrast the endless favour of God and the certainty of his word.

The omission from צִיץ ver. 7, to צִיץ ver. 8, in the LXX, shows how various readings may arise from the proximity of clauses or paragraphs of like ending.

9. In the confidence of faith God is actually seen coming to Zion, and the capital city is directed to announce the fact to the rest of the land.   הַר־גָּבֹהַ, ascend a high mountain, that the voice may be heard more widely: some suppose an allusion to the mountains on which Jerusalem was built and by which it was surrounded.   עֲלִי־לָךְ, pleonastic use of the pronoun, *for thee, for thyself*.   מְבַשֶּׂרֶת *announcing glad tidings*, LXX εὐαγγελιζόμενος ; it thus differs from מַלְאָךְ which simply denotes a messenger, irrespective of the character of his message.   It may govern the following word, "bearing glad tidings to Zion ; " then fem. because it was the custom for women to celebrate victories with songs and dances, or as a term of office, comp. קֹהֶלֶת § 198, or as a collective = מְבַשְּׂרִים.   It is simpler, however, to regard it as in apposition with Zion ; Zion herself is to announce the glad message to inferior cities.   בַּכֹּחַ, announce it *in a loud tone*, without faltering or hesitation, for it is certainly true.   הָרִימִי, not *thyself*, but *thy voice*.   תִּירָאִי, have no fear to make the announcement, as though there were danger of being disappointed in the issue.   הִנֵּה *behold* him or *here he is*, either visibly coming or actually arrived, already in the midst of Jerusalem.

10. אֲדֹנָי יְהוִה § 47, the combination of divine names adds to the impressiveness.   בְּחָזָק, not *in strength*, for חָזָק is not an abstract, nor *against a strong one*, nor *with a strong one*, in conjunction with the Messiah as his agent and coadjutor, but *in* the capacity or character of *a strong one*.   לוֹ, not *over him*, as the object of מָשַׁל which is commonly followed by בְּ, but *for him ;* he shall come as a sovereign.   שְׂכָרוֹ *his reward*, that which he bestows, or possibly that which he receives, has merited or acquired, viz. his people, whom he saves, or the salvation which he bestows.   אִתּוֹ *with him*, i. e. in his possession.   וּפְעֻלָּתוֹ *work*, hence the *wages* which are its equivalent.

11. בְּרֹעֶה. God is often compared to a shepherd from the days of the patriarchs, Gen. 49: 24, and David, Ps. 23 : 1 ; the figure is adopted by our Lord in the parable of the good shepherd, John 10. The possible constructions are *as a shepherd* who *feeds his flock, as a shepherd his flock*, he, Jehovah, *will feed, as a shepherd he will feed his flock.* יִרְעֶה. not only *feed*, but the whole work of a shepherd. בִּזְרֹעוֹ, will gather *with* his arm, i. e. take up in his arms. עָלוֹת § 153. 1, not *pregnant*, but *giving suck.* יְנַהֵל, *lead ;* others render *sustain.*

Vs. 12–26. God's incomparable greatness is presented as a ground for trusting him to accomplish what in itself might seem incredible.

12. מִי־מָדַד. The true answer to this question is not simply 'no one,' as though it were designed to exalt the vastness of the material creation, which man could never compass with his puny measures. It is rather implied that this which no one has done or can do, God has done. He has determined with the utmost nicety the measure and weight of all the constituents and parts of the world, Job 28 : 25 ; he has balanced its masses and forces with a precision, which the investigations of science serve but to disclose more and more : so that the main idea is not the vastness of the universe, nor merely the harmony of its parts, but the infinite superiority of him by whom these vast masses were apportioned with the utmost ease and nicety. He measures and regulates without difficulty material nature, though in itself so vast as to be incomprehensible by us. And hence the measures spoken of in the verse are ordinary and diminutive ones : if the intention had been to enhance the magnitude of the world, measures of large capacity would have been employed, but God can measure the universe by the inch and the ounce. בְּשָׁעֳלוֹ, elsewhere *handful*, here the *hollow of his hand*, distinguished from כַּף the *palm* and יָד the *hand*. מַיִם indef., *water* as an element in the constitution of the world. Some have sought to explain the order in which the parts of the universe are mentioned from Gen. 1, water, then heaven or the firmament, then the earth. תִּכֵּן § 50. 1, to straighten, as the beam of a balance in weighing, thence extended to measurements of length as well as weight. כָּל not כָּל־ *köl, all*, as LXX, but pret. of כּוּל § 215. 1. *c.* שָׁלִשׁ a *third* part, probably of an ephah, comp. the English measures *quart, tierce.* עֲפַר not merely superficial *dust*, but the mass of the earth itself. Note the climax : *measure the earth*, or if not this, *weigh mountains* (indefinite), or even *hills.* בְּפֶלֶס *a balance*, probably an instrument like a steelyard, and so distinguished from מֹאזְנָיִם, whose dual form implies the double dish or scales.

13. A fresh climax ; none can measure God's works, still less can any measure their maker, fathom his spirit, and understand his plans,

or what is yet more incredible, outdo him in wisdom and suggest plans to him. This unbelief would do, fancying that he has overlooked, ver. 27, what he should have attended to. תֵּן, not *directed*, but as in the preceding verse *measured*. אִישׁ עֲצָתוֹ *his man of counsel*, or counsellor, so Ps. 119 : 24. This is better than to govern עֲצָתוֹ by the verb, *who, a man, will cause him to know his counsel*. The combination of the pre-terite and the future in the verse embraces all time § 263. 5. *a ;* who has done this or who will do it?

14. Expands the last clause of the preceding verse. וַיְבִינֵהוּ, not *that he might instruct him*, expressing the design of the consultation, but *and he instructed him*, its actual result. The subject of the preceding verb is the object of this. בְּאֹרַח prep. has its local sense, taught, i. e. guided *in* the path. מִשְׁפָּט *rectitude*, not merely in a moral sense, but the right way to accomplish a desired end, or *judgment*, the proper course for him as the universal judge, the ruler and arbiter of all things. תְּבוּנוֹת, signifi-cation heightened by the plural form § 201. 1. *c.* The future and the preterite employed in different clauses of the verse.

15. To the exhibition of God's infinite superiority to any individual creature now follows his infinite superiority to whole nations, vs. 15–17, and even to all nations combined. הֵן *lo !* It is impossible for God to be beholden to individuals, for *see !* whole *nations are reckoned as a drop*. מְּרִי occurs nowhere else, but without doubt means *drop*. מִדְּלִי, to have compared nations to a bucket of water would have implied their insignificance, but it is rather to a *drop from a bucket* which, when taken out, leaves no appreciable difference in the mass left behind, its abstraction is not noticeable ; the contrast thus suggested giving a stronger impression of littleness than simply to have said a drop of water. It does not mean *a drop* hanging *from a bucket*. כְּשַׁחַק, prima-rily *a cloud*, which might be intended here as an imponderable body ; but it is better to take it in its derived sense 'cloud of dust,' then *dust*, the fine particles left on scales after weighing substances, which have no appreciable effect in disturbing its balance. LXX ῥοπὴ ζυγοῦ and Vulg. *momentum stateræ*, the turning of the scales, that small quantity which is sufficient to decide the balance. But the figure denotes rather that which is wholly inappreciable. The English Version needlessly supplies the substantive verb in the first clause, 'nations are as a drop, etc. ;' גּוֹיִם is properly the subject of יֵחָשֵׁבוּ § 262. 3. אִיִּים from אִי, habitable lands as opposed to water, especially of islands, maritime regions, and territories beyond the sea which are distant and little known. (1) *Islands* are reckoned *as an atom which he*, any one, or *it*, the wind, *taketh up* יִשָּׂא from נָשָׂא. (2) *which is cast away*, יֻצָּר Ni. of

שׂוּ. (3) *He will*, if he chooses, i. e. *he can take up islands like an atom.*

16. *As for Lebanon there is no sufficiency for burning :* דַּי § 215. 1. *d*, followed by that for which anything is not sufficient. The meaning is not that the vastest sacrifice would be an inadequate expiation for human sin ; nor is it an assertion of the inefficiency of the Old Testament ritual offerings ; but such is God's infinite superiority that the grandest offerings on the most magnificent scale are unworthy of his acceptance. This is stated not as an abstract proposition, but is exhibited in a striking example. הַלְּבָנוֹן, the lofty double range separating Palestine from Syria, the highest mountains with which Israel was familiar, from לָבָן *white*, so called by reason of the snow resting upon its peaks, or the whitish colour of its limestone rock. וְחַיָּתוֹ collective.

17. A still stronger assertion of the truth in ver. 15, not merely *nations* but *all the nations* combined are not a *drop* which, however insignificant, still has existence and a certain magnitude, but מֵאַיִן *as nothing :* the prep. qualifies the expression, they are not absolutely nonexistent, but *as if* they were nothing. נֶגְדּוֹ *before him*, not merely in his judgment or esteem, but confronting him or compared with him. מֵאֶפֶס *end*, cessation of being, annihilation, while אַיִן is absolute negation of being, *nonexistence :* the former is here strengthened by וָתֹהוּ *emptiness.* The prep. is comparative, *less than nothing*, lit. *more of nothing than nothing* itself. Others make it partitive, *of nothing*, or indicative of the material or source, consisting *of nothing.* נֶחְשְׁבוּ belongs to both clauses. לוֹ, not *by him*, but *in respect to him*, or compared with him.

18. Sums up the preceding argument. וְאֶל־מִי *and now*, these things being so, *to whom*, etc. תְּדַמְּיוּן poetic form § 172. 1. אֵל, the mighty *God*, derived from אוּל *to be strong.* מַה־דְּמוּת, what similar thing *will ye compare* to him, or what similitude *will ye institute* in respect to him.

19. The question of ver. 18 suggests the likenesses which men in their folly have dared to make as representations of the infinite God. The puerile absurdity of idolatry is brought out by dwelling on the details of the process of *making a god*, its materials being selected and put together by human toil. הַפֶּסֶל may be the direct object of נָסַךְ, or the answer to the previous question with the relative supplied, *the image* which a workman has wrought! this would better account for the article and for the order of the words. It properly denotes *a graven image ;* some suppose that it here describes the wooden interior over which the metallic surface is cast. But the metallic plating follows : it must therefore be used in a wide sense for *idol*, irrespective of the mode of its

formation. נָתַךְ *to pour out* in the process of casting. בַּזָּהָב, with *the gold*, that allotted for the purpose. וְיְרַקְּעֵם, to beat into thin plates, then to cover with such plates. רְתֻקוֹת, silver *chains*, for ornament, or support. (1) צֹרֵף, noun as before and repeat verb of preceding clause, a *goldsmith* is beating out or preparing *silver chains*. (2) צֹרֵף, participle, *melting* or casting *chains*, or, as chains are not made by casting, *soldering* the chains, melting them so as to make them adhere to the image. The change of tenses represents the image as in process of manufacture; part is completed, part is yet to be performed § 263. 5. *a.*

20. הַמְסֻכָּן *one poor as to oblation*, who cannot afford to offer gold and silver to his god, must make his idol of something less precious. Or *impoverished by oblation*, but still persisting in his poor way in what has already beggared him. Or תְּרוּמָה may be in apposition with עֵץ, *chooses as an oblation a tree*, etc. עֵץ not *wood* but *tree*, he selects it while growing in the forest. יִרְקַב, as the god cannot preserve itself from rotting, he must be particular as to the quality of the wood. חָכָם *skilful* in his business or profession. לוֹ, *for himself;* others *for it,* i. e. the idol. הָכִין *to prepare, make,* or *to erect, set up,* so firmly that it cannot move.

21. This description is broken off abruptly by an indignant question and a renewed description of God's infinite superiority, vs. 21–24. הֲלוֹא תֵדְעוּ *will ye not know?* Is this ignorance and stupidity to continue? are you never going to know? הֲגֻד, some distinguish this from the following clause and suppose an allusion here to the revelation of God in his word as there in his works. מֵרֹאשׁ, not vaguely *of old,* but *from the beginning,* which has been variously explained of the origin of their lives, the origin of Israel as a nation, and the beginning of the world. The last is the most natural and agrees best with the parallel expression which follows. מוֹסְדוֹת *foundations,* not an actual material basis on which the world was imagined to be built, but concrete for abstract, *the founding* or original construction *of the earth,* which is here compared to an edifice. It is the object of the verb הֲבִינֹתֶם.

22. הַיֹּשֵׁב may be connected with the preceding and governed by הֲבִינֹתֶם or with what follows, in apposition with the suffix in תְּרִימֵנִי, ver. 25, which is however too remote; or the substantive verb may be supplied, as in Eng. Ver. 'It is he that sitteth.' Perhaps it may best be regarded as an abrupt and unconnected exclamation. The presence of the article shows that it is to be understood substantively, and is not a substitute for a finite tense, 'he sitteth.' It may mean *dwell,* or better, *sit* as a monarch, enthroned. חוּג occurs in two other passages, Prov. 8: 27, Job 22: 14, in which it denotes the hemispherical arch of the

heavens. The 'circle of the earth' is by some supposed to denote the arch which appears to rest upon the earth, and by others the earth itself, *orbis terrarum.* על will in the one case mean *upon* and in the other *over.* הַיֹּשֵׁב stands with designed allusion to יָשַׁב, he who sits or dwells above the earth being contrasted with those who dwell in or inhabit it. כַּחֲגָבִים *as locusts,* comp. Num. 13 :33, puny, insignificant; the prep. probably has the article, as is usual in comparisons § 245. 5. *d,* though the pointing does not determine. כַּדֹּק thin fine material (comp. דַּק, ver. 15) variously explained as a *veil, awning* or *curtain.* הַנּוֹטֶה, this part. as the preceding denotes present time, or rather expresses the agent irrespective of time § 266, 'the spreader out' who has done, does, and shall continue to do it. The continuous agency of God in preserving and upholding the universe is implied. The expression shows that the Hebrews did not conceive the vault of heaven as a solid sphere, see on Gen. 1 : 6. It is compared to the thinnest possible material; and even this is not a physical but poetical description. וַיִּמְתָּחֵם, a construction begun with a participle or infinitive often passes over into a preterite or future, since these are the fundamental tenses and embrace all the divisions of time § 282. *c.* : לָשֶׁבֶת, not connected with the preceding verb, *spreads them out to dwell in* whether for himself, for celestial beings, or for men who dwell under this spacious roof; but with אֹהֶל *tent for dwelling in.*

23. הָרוֹזְנִים. Nations had been described as nothing, so were their rulers. לְאָיִן, not the territory over which he places them, *gives them to* rule over *nothing,* but the condition to which they are themselves reduced. שֹׁפְטֵי poetic equiv. of רוֹזְנִים, denoting their official function as this their weight and influence, properly *judge,* but as this was one of the functions of sovereignty, used in the wider sense of *rulers.* : עָשָׂה, change of construction from participle to preterite § 282. *e.*

24. אַף בַּל *also not.* The first clause of this verse may be regarded as a sequel of the preceding, or as introductory to what follows. If the former, the annihilation is so complete that it appears as though *they had not even been planted.* No vestige remains to show that this had ever been the case; others understand it to mean that they have not been replanted, nor even a seed remaining been sown. If the latter, 'they were not even planted, and he blew upon them,' he can destroy them at any antecedent stage of their power as well as when they have arrived at the height of it. בָּהֶם, ease and completeness of their destruction, with the additional idea of worthlessness. If the figure were to be pressed, earthly rulers are as chaff which serves an important purpose during the maturing of the grain, but when the end for which they were brought into existence is answered, they are blown away as worth-

less chaff. The oriental method of winnowing was by casting the grain and chaff together up to the wind, that the former might be separated and the latter blown away. וּכְמֹץ, not ordinary wind, but violent storm, *whirlwind.* : תִּשָּׂאֵם, change of tense; the process is begun but not ended. They have withered and shall be blown away. The verb means either *to take up* or *to carry away.*

25. Substantial repetition of the question of ver. 18, but God is here the speaker. וְאֶשְׁוֶה, no need of the subjunctive rendering, *that I may be equal.* יֹאמַר *saith,* though some insist on future sense, God will continue by his word and works to say, see on 40 : 1. : קָדוֹשׁ, no article, as it assumes somewhat the character of a proper name. The primary idea is that of separation. As applied to things, e. g. the temple, its vessels, etc., it denotes separation from those of ordinary character and uses, setting apart, consecration. As applied to persons, it implies separation in a moral sense likewise, spiritual purity. Used of God, it denotes his separation from his creatures both in exaltation, which is chiefly dwelt upon in the context, and in his moral purity and excellence.

26. An appeal to the stars, and what they declare of the greatness of him who made and controls them, still further to exhibit God's infinite superiority. He who brings forth his heavenly host, calls all by name, and loses none, will not overlook the concerns of his people. שְׂאוּ, absolutely, *see,* viz. the heavens, not joined to what follows, *see who hath created,* etc. אֵלֶּה, evidently referring to stars, though they have not been expressly mentioned. הַמּוֹצִיא, not the answer to the preceding question, but a continuation of it, ʻWho is the one bringing out, etc.ʼ As יָצָא is used of the rising of the sun and stars, some render *causing them to rise.* But it is rather a military figure, *leading forth an army.* בְּמִסְפָּר (1) *by number,* denoting orderly arrangement. (2) *in full number,* completely; or (3) *in great number,* numerously. צְבָאָם, see on Gen. 2 : 1. אִישׁ may be used as an indef. pron. in relation to things, but is here perhaps suggested by the figure of a host, ʻnot *a man* is missing.ʼ Marg. see on Judg. 13 : 25, 1 Kin. 18 : 39.

27. The third and last division of the chapter begins here, shewing the unreasonableness of Israel's dejection and distrust. לָמָּה. The demand for a reason implies that there was none. הֹאמַר not merely *dost thou say,* but *wilt thou say,* why *continue to say* or *persist in saying.* יַעֲקֹב. The original name of the patriarch, never used of his descendants except in poetry. יִשְׂרָאֵל is distinguished from עִבְרִי *Hebrew* as the theocratic or sacred from the secular or gentile name. At the time of the schism the ten tribes composing the mass of the people usurped the name

of *Israel* for themselves, leaving the other kingdom to be called *Judah*, from the dominant tribe. "Israel" is here used in its sacred or theo-cratic sense, as describing the chosen people, and that although the kingdom of Judah is alone referred to. The ten tribes were apostate, and had been virtually exscinded by their overthrow and captivity. Judah was the true Israel in whom the continuity was preserved in spite of the rejection of the unbelieving mass. נִסְתְּרָה *hidden, out of sight,* whether unknown and forgotten or unattended to. דַּרְכִּי *way,* sometimes figuratively denoting *course of conduct,* but here *condition.* מִשְׁפָּטִי *my cause,* in its forensic sense, or *my right.* יַעֲבוֹר *shall pass away,* either my cause shall be neglected, the controversy with my enemies not com-ing up before God for trial, or being dismissed unsettled; or my right shall pass away, my rightful claim to protection against the injustice of my foes shall fail to be secured. Marg. Haphtarah of לֶךְ־לְךָ, Gen. 12 : 1.

28. The unreasonableness of this distrust is apparent from what they knew or ought to know. The infinite greatness of God is urged by sceptics as an argument against the salvation of the gospel. He who created and watches over the vast universe would not bestow such extra-ordinary attention on this speck of earth as the gospel supposes. But the objection is guilty of the very depreciation of God which it depre-cates. If this earth is as nothing, is the rest of the universe any greater in comparison with him? To the prophet God's infinite great-ness is an invincible ground of trust; no vastness of cares can so distract him that he shall be unable to do all that is needful for the feeblest and the least. הַאִם—אָ § 283. 2. *Hast thou not known, or hast thou not* at least *heard?* אֱלֹהֵי, in apposition with the following divine names which are here emphatically accumulated; others make יְהוָה the subject and אֱלֹהֵי עוֹלָם predicate, *Jehovah is the God of eternity* § 254. 6. קְצוֹת *extremities,* including all that is between them, the entire earth from one extremity to another. יִיעַף *faintness,* primarily arising from running, יִיגָע *weariness* from toil; they are here combined as equivalents to intensify the idea; fut. because this never will occur, involving of course a denial that it ever has occurred or is possible. חֵקֶר, the words might mean 'there is no searching to his understanding,' his knowledge is in-tuitive, not discursive, is not gained by investigation. Their meaning here is, it is impossible for man to investigate the divine understanding, it is limitless. As he cannot desert Israel for lack of power or through exhaustion, neither can he from want of knowledge whether of their wants or of the methods of supplying them.

29. He is not only the possessor of strength but the source of it. He not only never wearies himself but recuperates those who do. נֹתֵן

§ 259. 2. וּלְאֵין אוֹנִים, not only to the *weary* but to the *powerless*. יַרְבֶּה‎, he not only *gives* but *multiplies*, gives abundantly. Who among the powerless shall be thus succoured, is explained in what follows.

30. Human strength, even the most vigorous and active, is inadequate. What has been denied of God is here affirmed of the stoutest men and those in the prime of life. וּבַחוּרִים‎, the part. בָּחוּר‎ has plur. בְּחוּרִים‎, but in the special sense of choice young men, selected for their fitness for military duty, it has for distinction בַּחוּרִים‎ § 210. *a*. כָּשׁוֹל § 282. *a*.

31. קֹוֵי § 254. 9. *b*, *wait for*, expect him with faith and patience, which is also the sense of ' wait upon' in the Eng. Ver., though this phrase in modern English rather suggests the idea of personal attendance. This verb may be construed with the direct object or with לְ and אֶל. יַחֲלִיפוּ‎ *exchange*, especially for the better, improve, renew. יַעֲלוּ‎, not *shall go up* into *feathers*, i. e. put forth feathers, comp. Ps. 103 : 5, nor *mount up* with *wings*, but *shall raise the pinion*. יָעֵף and יָגַע‎, again as in ver. 28 : they who trust in God shall no more faint than God himself.

CHAPTER XLI.

In the preceding chapter the incomparable greatness of Jehovah had been asserted as a ground for Israel's trust in the salvation he had promised. Here the questions of 40 : 18. 25. are as it were resumed, and his supremacy demonstrated against all opposers. This is presented under the figure of a majestic trial, to which Jehovah, as the one party, summons all the nations and the gods whose claims they put forth or defend, challenging them to exhibit proofs of deity compared with his. The chapter consists of two unequal parts, viz. :

1. vs. 1–24, the trial in detail, with its result ;
2. vs. 25–29, a brief recapitulation.

The process of the trial is subdivided into :

(1) The setting forth of the evidences of Jehovah's power and foreknowledge, as these would be conspicuously displayed in what he was about to achieve :

a. The raising up of Cyrus, vs. 2–7.

b. Making Israel victorious over all foes, vs. 8–20.

(2) The futility of all other claims to divinity. The claimants can neither foretell anything nor bring anything to pass, vs. 21–24.

1. The summons of the nations and their gods to trial, to vindicate their claim to divinity in comparison with Jehovah. הַחֲרִישׁוּ § 272. 3, *be silent unto me*, i. e. be silent and turn to me. Some understand

this of conversion, cease your raging hostility and turn quietly and sub-
missively to me, and thus you shall gain the new strength promised,
40 : 31.   Others, be reduced to silence, as the result of the trial which
follows, this being already anticipated at the outset.   It would then be
a summons to be silenced by entering into trial with God, and finding
themselves unable to make out their claims.   It is better to regard it as
a call to attention ; listen silently to me, and then with your utmost
vigour maintain your cause.   God is the speaker throughout this chapter.   אִיִּים, see on 40 : 15.   The summons to the most distant nations
implies that those nearer at hand are likewise challenged.   יַחֲלִיפוּ כֹּחַ,
allusion to 40 : 31, where this is asserted of those waiting for Jehovah.
Let the nations, who will not wait on him, renew it for themselves,
summon all their strength, and, if possible, redouble it.   Change of
person § 279.   The future has an imperative sense, as is shown by the
preceding imperative and the cohortative at the end of the verse.   יִגָּשׁוּ
approach not one another but God, and this not as worshippers but as
adversaries.   יְדַבֵּרוּ, after the preliminary silence during the presentation
of God's claims to divinity, they may set forth their own or those of
the idols which they worship.   יַחְדָּו *together*, God and his adversaries.
לַמִּשְׁפָּט (1) judgment or trial. (2) judgment seat, place of trial.

2. The first proof of God's power and foreknowledge adduced is
the annunciation of his purpose to raise up Cyrus, whose appearance and
correspondence with what is here predicted of him would give evidence
both that God controlled human history, and that he foreknew whatever comes to pass.   Cyrus is described as, in prophetic vision, already
raised up (הֵעִיר) and pursuing his career of conquest (other verbs future).
That הֵעִיר is a prophetic preterite § 262. 4, and Cyrus, though ideally
present, belongs to the distant future, is apparent from the fact that the
announcement of his coming proves God's divinity against the idols.
God foretold the coming of Cyrus and brought it to pass, while the idols
could do nothing of the kind.   He is here spoken of in general terms,
simply as a great conqueror from the East, or, as this is supplemented
by ver. 25, from the North and East, i. e. Persia, which lay in this direction from Palestine.   In the progress of the prophecy he is more fully
described, and his very name announced.   צֶדֶק.   Some suppose Abraham,
and others Christ, to be referred to, and make צֶדֶק the object of הֵעִיר,
and abstract for concrete = צַדִּיק *righteous man*, so Eng. Ver.   But the object of הֵעִיר is not expressed, and the relative is to be supplied § 285. 3,
raised up him whom not *victory meets at every step*, which gives to צֶדֶק
an unauthorized sense, but *righteousness calls to its foot* as its servant
and follower.   He is raised up as an instrument of God's righteousness.

יִתֵּן, the subject is צֶדֶק, not *God*, nor *he*, the conqueror, drives nations before himself, nor עָם. יִתֵּן כֶּעָפָר חַרְבּוֹ (1) *will make his*, the conqueror's, swords (collective) *as dust*, i. e. numerous, *and his bows* fleet *as chaff;* but this figure is more appropriate to the subdued than the subjugator. (2) suf. collect. referring to kings, *make their sword as dust.* (3) חַרְבּוֹ may best be regarded as an absolute expression of the manner or instrument § 274. 2, *e, make* nations and kings *as dust by his sword*, i. e. that of Cyrus.

3. אֹרַח בְּרַגְלָיו § 274. 2. *e.* אֹרַח (1) *a way that he had not gone with his feet*, or previously passed over: this violates the tense of the verb. (2) *a way that with his feet he shall not come*, he shall not be compelled to retrace his steps. (3) *the way at his feet*, i. e. after him *one shall not come*, no one shall pursue him. (4) *a way he shall not go with his feet*, such shall be his speed that he shall rather fly than walk. The last is the best rendering.

4. The question of ver. 2, 3 is resumed. קָרָא (1) an answer to the question *he calling the generations from the beginning* has done it, he who is the universal controller of providence and history has controlled it in this instance. (2) continues the question and agrees with מִי: this is favoured by the absence of the article. *Calling* may mean calling into existence, or proclaiming, heralding, announcing beforehand. Who has exhibited this evidence of power and foreknowledge by raising up Cyrus? The answer is—*I the Lord; first and with the last*—before all and not survived by any. הוּא (1) I am *the same*, unchangeable; this gives a supposititious sense to the pronoun; (2) I am *he*, the one in question who has done this; (3) I *am* first and with the last § 258. 2.

Vs. 5-7 express the terror of the nations, their endeavours to nerve each other, and to put their gods in the best condition to render effectual help. The sarcasm lies in the fact that idols needing the services of ordinary workmen should be looked to in opposition to the infinite God. The immediate occasion of their terror may be Cyrus, whom God has raised up for the judgment of the nations, or this evidence of divine power and foreknowledge accomplishes their discomfiture in the grand trial which is represented as proceeding, and fills them with dismay. Yet instead of abandoning the contest and renouncing their follies for God's service, they but confirm one another in error and fly more frantically to their senseless idols, that these may establish by counter proofs their equality or superiority.

5. קָרְבוּ, *they drew near* to one another for mutual consultation and assistance, or to God, taking up the challenge or summons of ver. 1, and engaging in the unequal trial.

6. עָזָרוּ, they seek to relieve one another's fears by mutual exhortation to courage and persistence; fut. because descriptive of what is passing. The prophet places himself in the midst of the action; a part is performed and a part to come § 263. 5. *a.*

7. All who have had to do with making the idol encourage one another, each striving to remove the fears of the rest, and pronouncing his part of the work upon the idol good, or repairing what is yet weak or lacking, so that there may be no failure in this contest from its imperfect manufacture. לַדֶּבֶק, *respecting the soldering, it is good,* see on Gen. 1 : 28, not *it is good* i. e. ready for *soldering.*

8. The second proof of the divine omnipotence and foreknowledge is Israel's deliverance from all his foes, and their utter discomfiture and destruction, notwithstanding the weakness of the former and the power of the latter. This, when effected, as it certainly would be, would afford a grand proof of the divinity of Jehovah. As this is addressed to Israel's despondency, it is largely dwelt upon, and presented first in literal terms, vs. 8–13, then under two distinct figures, a worm threshing the mountains, vs. 14–16, and a supernatural flow of waters for those perishing with thirst, vs. 17–20. Israel is addressed and characterized, vs. 8. 9, his relation to God stated as a ground of confidence in what follows. God could not and would not desert to his foes, those for whom he had done so much, and whom he had destined to so great an end. יִשְׂרָאֵל, the substantive verb is not to be supplied, *Thou art Israel,* or *thou Israel art my servant.* The people are again addressed by the two names of their ancestor, used as poetic equivalents; the sacred name, however, is put first and gives its colour to the other, as the relation to God is prominent in his thoughts. In 40 : 27, where the sinful weakness of the people is prominent, the order is the reverse. עַבְדִּי *servant,* one employed to do a certain work. Moses is called God's servant, Deut. 34 : 5, Nebuchadnezzar, Jer. 25 : 9, the material creation, Ps. 119 : 91; here Israel. בְּחַרְתִּיךָ, not only engaged in God's service but appointed of God himself to be so, selected from others and rather than others for this special purpose. זֶרַע אַבְרָהָם *seed of Abraham,* whom God had promised to bless, and to make a blessing to all nations. אֹהֲבִי § 102. 3, *my lover* or *who loved me,* implying of course reciprocal affection.

9. God designated them as his and brought them from remote parts for his service the pains bestowed upon them making it more sure that he will not desert them now. מִקְצוֹת הָאָרֶץ, some refer to Abraham's call from Mesopotamia, others to bringing the people out of Egypt. אֲצִילֶיהָ, in Ex. 24 : 11 *nobles,* here *sides* or *joints,* parallel to קְצוֹת. אָמַרְתִּי, not only made him his servant, but announced to him that he stood

in that relation : 'thou art my servant' *par excellence*, as no other is,
Israel, including the Messiah, who was of the seed of Abraham, as are
also all his true people, is God's servant in a peculiar and the highest
sense, the one who above all others is appointed by him to do his work
in this world. ‏וְלֹא מְאַסְתִּיךָ‎, not *I will not reject thee*, which violates
the tenses, but *I have not rejected thee ;* this choice has never been re-
voked, implying, though not directly stating, that it never will be.

10. ‏אַל־תִּירָא‎. This is the exhortation addressed to the person described in the two preceding verses. It refers not to the victories of
Cyrus which, ver. 5, alarmed other nations, but need occasion no fear to
them ; but to perils foreseen or calamities experienced at any time and
from any quarter. ‏כִּי‎, the ground of exhorted fearlessness is God's
presence, which implies his protection. ‏אַל־תִּשְׁתָּע‎, not *be dismayed*, but *look
around* with anxiety and perplexity for help. ‏אִמַּצְתִּיךָ‎, not *I will
strengthen thee*, which violates the tense, but *I have strengthened thee*,
either their past experiences of God's protection are appealed to as an
argument of confidence for the future, or, I have already provided thee
with strength adequate for these future emergencies, as shall be manifested when the trial comes. ‏אַף‎, cumulative, though no climax is
traceable in the sense of the verbs, yet heaping together equivalent forms
of expression gives intensity or emphasis to the thought. ‏בִּימִין צִדְקִי‎
my right hand of righteousness § 254. 6, not *right hand of my righteousness*, the attribute personified and a right hand attributed to it. The
right hand is an instrument of action and a symbol of strength.

11. ‏הֵן‎ *Behold! see!* pointing as if to an object of sight. ‏יֵבֹשׁוּ וְיִכָּלְמוּ‎,
the accumulation of synonymous words makes the statement more emphatic. *Shame* denotes the frustration of plans and disappointed expectations. ‏בָּאֵשׁ‎, see on 40 : 17. ‏אַנְשֵׁי רִיבֶךָ‎ *thy men of strife* § 256, men
striving with thee.

12. Expansion and repetition of the last clause of the preceding verse.
‏הַמַּצֻּתֶךָ‎, an expression often used to denote total disappearance. They
shall vanish not only to a careless inspection, but the most earnest
scrutiny shall detect no trace of their existence. ‏כְּאַיִן וּכְאֶפֶס‎. see on
40 : 17.

13. The reason of Israel's safety and of the destruction of their foes.
‏מַחֲזִיק‎ (1) causative, *making strong*. This yields a good sense, but is
not the usual meaning of the word in Hiphil, and is not its meaning in
ver. 9 above. (2) *holding fast*, or firmly; the idea is not so much that
of guidance out of perplexity and danger, as of preservation from falling
or sinking. Not *will hold*, E. V. but *am holding* or *the holder of* for all
time § 266. ‏הָאֹמֵר‎, not (1) for finite tense *I am saying*, but (2) *I am*

the one *saying to thee*, or (3) *I the* one *saying to thee*, etc. *ha𝑒e helped thee*. According to (3) the thing said is simply אַל תִּירָא‎; according to (2) the whole to the end of the verse. According to (3) *I who say to thee fear not have* actually *helped thee*, and in this given a pledge that you have no occasion to fear ; according to (2) *I the Lord am the* one *saying* this, therefore it is no vain word but efficacious, truthful and strength imparting. עֲזַרְתִּיךָ‎, *have helped thee* in former times, as a pledge of present and future protection, or, have already granted the aid which you require in this case. The rendering *I will help* violates the tense.

14. The literal is, as is frequently the case in Isaiah, succeeded by a figurative statement. The first figure, vs. 14–16, is a worm, helpless and despicable, in danger of being crushed by the foot of every passer by, converted into a mighty engine which pulverizes the mountains and scatters them to the winds. The accomplishment of such a result by such an instrument is a clear proof of the omnipotence of God and his control of human history. אַל־תִּירְאִי‎, the frequent repetition of the exhortation not to fear, implies the strong temptation they were under to do so ; fem. to agree with תּוֹלַעַת‎ § 253. 1. or § 254. 3. This verse is a repetition and expansion of the divine voice at the close of ver. 13, the first clause dwelling upon the person addressed, the second on the person of the speaker. נְאֻם‎ § 90. (*pass.*) the only form of the word which occurs, except the future, which is found in combination with it, Jer. 23 : 31. It is used of a divine utterance, almost always in connection with the name of God, more rarely of an inspired man. וְגֹאֲלֵךְ‎, fem. suf. refers to תּוֹלַעַת‎, properly to purchase from the power of another by the payment of a ransom. It is used repeatedly of God's delivering Israel from the bondage of Egypt and the power of other foes, as the converse מָכַר‎ *to sell* is constantly used of his subjecting them to the bondage of their foes, though no price was paid in either case, so that it may simply mean *deliverer*. But in the typical institutions of the law this word was used to express one, who as a near kinsman of one impoverished or slain, redeemed his property and restored it to him, or avenged his death. How far גֹּאֵל‎, as applied to God, have been associated with that type, or how much it may have retained of the radical signification of the word, we cannot tell. But that type teaches what is more fully unfolded in the New Testament, that God is the redeemer of his people from present and eternal evil by the payment of an equivalent, even the life of the Son of God, who is the manifested Jehovah of the Old Testament, though this distinction of persons in the godhead was not clearly revealed to the consciousness of the saints of that economy. קְדוֹשׁ‎, see on 40 : 25, in-

cludes the ideas of infinitely exalted and perfectly pure, the holy God who is the God of Israel.

15. שַׂמְתִּיךְ, see on ver. 11.   שַׂמְתִּיךְ לְ *I have placed thee for,* converted thee into. This is what God has already made them, as will be shown in due time. לְמוֹרַג *threshing instrument, sharp, new,* not worn and dulled, *possessed of edges or blades.* פִּיפִיּוֹת, the reduplicated form is by some supposed to express number, many blades, strictly *mouths:* the 'edge' of a sword or sharp instrument is called its 'mouth.' תָּדוּשׁ, *thou shalt thresh mountains,* comp. Mic. 4 : 13 Dan. 2 : 34. 35. הָרִים, not specifically a symbol of kingdoms, but belonging to the imagery of the figure, which is that of a worm reducing mountains to powder.

16. The figure is continued; after the threshing comes the winnowing, which was performed by casting up to the wind; they shall be dispersed and driven away as completely as chaff from the threshing floor. וְאַתָּה, the pronoun is used to indicate the opposition of Israel to the enemies just spoken of § 243. 1. ו may be conjunctive, *and* thou shalt rejoice in consequence of the destruction of foes, or adversative, *and* on other hand, i. e. *but,* while they perish thou shalt have cause to rejoice. בַּיהוָֹה *in Jehovah,* in virtue of your relation to him, as to rejoice in wealth is in the possession of it or in the advantage it brings. :תִּתְהַלָּל *boast, glory:* He shall be the ground of triumphant confidence. Marg. see on 40 : 26.

17. Another figure; water is given in overflowing abundance to those perishing with thirst, when and where it could be least expected. This similitude is often used by Isaiah, suggested probably by the experience of Israel in the wilderness when coming up from Egypt. First the necessity is described. It is not the literal thirst of the exiles returning from Babylon which is intended, for (1) the language would then be hyperbolical and fanatical; no such miraculous gift of water occurred on their return; (2) this is a fresh image of what had been set forth under a different emblem in the preceding verses. There is no more reason for regarding this as literal description than the worm pulverizing mountains. Thirst is a figure for misery and destitution, for which an abundant and unexpected supply shall be provided. It is not to be confined to the suffering of the Babylonish exile, though that is of course included, comp. Amos 8 : 11–13. נָשַׁתָּה, the form appears to be from נָשַׁת, and so some take it. But as that word has the sense of *placing,* not of parching or drying up, which the context requires, it is probably from נָצָה with Daghesh-forte emphatic § 24. c. Secondly, the plentiful supply, *a.* its source, then *b.* in the next verse the supply itself. אֶעֱנֵם, *hear* prayer favourably, *answer* them; no prayer had been mentioned, but it was implied in the wretched-

ness above described; first affirmatively, then negatively, as is usual with Isaiah, *I will not desert them.*

18. שְׁפָיִים, not merely high places, but bare, *naked cliffs* or hills. מְקֹרוֹת, water shall abound everywhere, in hills and valleys. This is not a description of physical changes which shall be wrought, but figures of abundant blessing. The interpreter must not particularize cliff, valley, desert, and make each a symbol of some distinct individual thing, but take the whole image together as forming one picture of welcome and overflowing supply.

19. The wilderness, מִדְבָּר, containing only scanty vegetation, and even the desert, עֲרָבָה, absolutely destitute of verdure, comp. on 40 : 3, shall be made to produce stately trees. This is not a new figure, but a carrying out of that already employed. The trees are not designed to suggest shade and shelter from the heat, nor to delight the eye by beautiful groves, but to evidence the thoroughness of the change produced by this miraculous abundance of water; that is made fruitful which was sterile before.

20. לְמַעַן expresses the design, 'in order that *they* may see,' either 3 pl. indef. § 243. 2. *b, it may be seen,* or, the nations opposed to God in this strife. וְיָדְעוּ, ellipsis of עַל לֵב. בְּרָאָהּ, not only produced it but *created it,* implying something altogether new and above the operation of natural causes, see on Gen. 1 : 1.

21. The idols and their worshippers are addressed and challenged to exhibit like proofs of divinity. קָרְבוּ רִיבְכֶם *produce your cause,* i. e. your side in this great contest. עֲצֻמוֹתֵיכֶם *your strengths* or *strong ones,* those on which you rely. Some make it 'your champions,' i. e. idols. The Eng. Ver. better, 'your strong reasons.' מֶלֶךְ *the king,* both the ruler and defender *of Jacob.*

22. יַגִּישׁוּ וְיַגִּידוּ § 279; both verbs have the same subject and object, though some translate *let them bring near* their idols, *and let them,* the idols, *announce to us,* etc. הָרִאשֹׁנוֹת...הַבָּאוֹת. The contrast has been differently understood; either the proximate and the remoter future, or more probably *the former things* are past predictions already uttered and accomplished, while *the coming things* are predictions now to be made of what is yet future. אַחֲרִיתָן *the end of them,* their issue, whether they are fulfilled or not. *We,* i. e. God and his people on one side; *they,* i. e. idols and their followers on the other.

23. Change of person § 279. כִּי אֱלֹהִים, this was the thing to be decided. תֵּיטִיבוּ וְתָרֵעוּ, either *reward* your friends and *punish* your foes, or *do* some thing either *good or bad,* comp. Jer. 10 : 5, Zeph. 1 : 12. וְנִשְׁתָּעָה § 172. 3. וְנֵרֶא § 97. 2. *a.* נַחְדָּו, some connect with the subject *we,* both par-

ties *together ;* others with the verbs, *look about and see together,* or at the same time; others still with the object, see the *good and evil* ye have done *together.*

24. As they are unable to accept the challenge, and to adduce evidence to sustain them in their claim of divinity, sentence is given against them; they are proved worthless and condemned as such. מֵאַיִן *of nothing,* composed of it and equal to it, or *less than nothing,* see on 40 : 17. פָּעָלְכֶם *your work,* your idols which are of human workmanship, or which is better suited to the connection, *your deed,* what you, the idols, have done. תּוֹעֵבָה, abomination, an object of religious abhorrence, comp. Gen. 43 : 32. מֵאָפַע according to some = מֵאֶפַע *worse than a viper,* but the parallel expressions show it to be equivalent to, if not an orthographic variation for אֶפֶס.

25. The trial is recapitulated: the two great arguments of Jehovah's deity are repeated, with the failure of the idols to exhibit similar proofs, whereupon sentence is pronounced again. 1st proof: the raising up of Cyrus, ver. 25, the idols neither did it nor predicted it, ver. 26; 2nd proof: foretelling and accomplishing Israel's deliverance, ver. 27, the inability of the idols is manifested again, ver. 28, they are worthless, ver. 29. הַצְעִירֹתִי, similarity of expressions to ver. 2: the preterite here, as there, is shown to refer not to what is actually past, by being adduced as a proof of divine foreknowledge. מִמִּזְרָח . As the Babylonians invaded Palestine from the north, and Chaldea is called the north country, whereas this conqueror is said, ver. 2, to be raised up from the East, some refer the first clause to God's raising up Babylon to be a scourge to Israel, and the next to Cyrus' march to overthrow it. But this assumes a change of subject not intimated in the text. Others combine the North of this clause with the East of the following, and apply it to Cyrus as from both North and East, i. e. the North-East. There may perhaps be an allusion to his twofold origin, as he was descended from both the royal house of Media in the North and that of Persia in the East. יִקְרָא בִשְׁמִי, either *he shall call by,* i. e. upon *my name,* or *he shall call with,* i. e. proclaim *my name,* see on 1 Kin. 18 : 24; for the fulfilment in either case see his edict, Ezra 1 : 2. סְגָנִים § 271. 2, this word is specially applied to Babylonish nobles. הֹמֶר, trample them down, as something utterly worthless and vile, indicating the completeness of the subjugation and their inability to make resistance.

26. מֵרֹאשׁ *from the beginning,* not as 40 : 21 from the creation, but either indefinitely of old, or in contrast with מִלְּפָנִים, which means 'after the end of,' Gen. 41 : 1, מֵרֹאשׁ may mean '*before* the beginning of.' The question will then be, who announced Cyrus' coming before his appearance?

צֶדֶק, may be *right*, *true*, or the more exact meaning of the word may be retained, *righteous*. He in whose favour the judge pronounces is justified in his case, be it what it may ; so in this case, give decision in favour of the idols if they have foretold anything, pronounce them on that ground righteous in the claim which they are putting forth to divinity.

27. רֹאשׁוֹן, not as Eng. Ver. *the first* shall say, but *I first;* either supply ' say,' or introduce *give* from the last clause, i. e. give them the opportunity and privilege of saying *behold them.*

28. The incapacity of the idols. מֵאֵלֶּה prep. partitive, I saw *of these*, i. e. the idols. יוֹעֵץ, giving advice or information respecting the future. וְאֶשְׁאָלֵם דָּבָר, declarative *and they will* perhaps *return an answer,* subjunctive *that they may*, etc., or interrogative, *will they return*, etc.

29. As they have failed to make out their claim to divinity, sentence is given against them. כֻּלָּם, (1) *all of them are vanity, their works* or *deeds* are *nought*, but this violates the accents; (2) as for *all of them, their works* are *vanity, nought.*

CHAPTER XLII.

Chap. 40 promised to Israel deliverance and salvation, confirming the certainty of it by an appeal to God's incomparable greatness. In chap. 41 the sole divinity of Jehovah is demonstrated to the confusion of idols and their worshippers by his protection and exaltation of Israel. The idols can neither do good nor do evil, neither be the authors of any salvation to the people nor retard the salvation God has promised. In this chapter the divinely appointed destiny of Israel, which God's power is pledged to accomplish, and which the idols cannot prevent, is more fully unfolded, and seeming difficulties in the present and past aspect of things are removed.

The chapter consists of 3 parts, viz. :

1. vs. 1–9. Israel is God's chosen servant to extend his kingdom over the earth, and to enlighten and save the nations.

2. vs. 10–17. God's apparent apathy and inaction in the past presents a seeming improbability in the way of the accomplishment of this destiny: but this is to be exchanged for an activity which shall effect the most stupendous results.

3. vs. 18–25. The character and condition of the people add a fresh improbability : but their sins shall not obstruct what God does for his own righteousness' sake and the magnifying of his law : and their sufferings, so far from proving God's inability to protect and bless them, were sent for just reasons by God's own hand.

11

1. עַבְדִּי. The most important question connected with this entire prophecy is who is the servant of Jehovah, comp. 41 : 8, who so frequently recurs in it. He cannot be Cyrus, who was not commissioned to spread the true religion, nor Isaiah, or the prophets as a class, who were not sent to the Gentiles, nor Israel in its purely national character, whose sufferings were not vicarious, and from whom he is expressly distinguished, 49 : 6. It is plain from the attributes and works ascribed to him, that the Messiah is prominently referred to: this further appears from frequent applications to Christ, in the New Testament, of language employed respecting this servant here and elsewhere. Yet he is not exclusively intended, for (1) imperfection and sin are attributed to the servant of the Lord, 42 : 19. (2) The servant is repeatedly called Israel or addressed as Israel, 41 : 8, 44 : 1, 49 : 3. (3) The connection here demands not the introduction of a fresh subject, but a statement of what was designed for Israel. (4) What is here said of God's servant is applicable to the people as a whole in its measure. (5) Some of the expressions used respecting the servant of Jehovah are applied to the people of God, Jer. 11 : 19, Acts 13 : 47, 2 Cor. 6 : 2. The proper view seems to be that God's servant is Israel considered as embracing the Messiah, who was to spring from the midst of them, and by whom mainly the task of the world's salvation committed to this people, comp. John 4 : 22, was to be achieved : as we might attribute to France what was performed by Napoleon. This is precisely the sense of 'the seed of Abraham,' and may be further confirmed by the scriptural doctrine of the unity of Christ and his people, comp. 1 Cor. 12 : 12. אֶתְמָךְ־ *I will uphold him* or *will hold him fast*, retain him. There is no necessity for supplying the relative. This is applied to Christ, Mat. 12 : 18, etc., and twice by a voice from heaven, Mat. 3 : 17, 17 : 5, where the changes in the form of expression are for the sake of explanation or more exactly designating the person intended. בְּחִירִי, not merely *choice* or *excellent*, but actually *chosen*. עָלָיו *upon him* rather than *in him*, to denote descent from heaven. מִשְׁפָּט *judgment*, either the function of a judge, the administration of justice, not here the mere blessings of good government in a worldly sense, but his empire, his spiritual reign, or that which is just and right, his righteous laws, true religion. Israel, instead of being longer lorded over by the nations, shall give law to them in the person of his great representative and ruler. לַגּוֹיִם *to the nations*, i. e. mankind. יוֹצִיא׃ *cause to go forth*, i. e. from Jerusalem, the centre and seat of this empire, comp. 2 : 3, the facts of the new dispensation being presented under the emblems of the old.

2. This empire was not to be extended by such means as are em-

ployed in worldly conquests, not by noise and clamour, ver. 2, nor by violence, ver. 3, but by the truth. אִשָּׂא *lift up*, not himself, nor faces פָּנִים, i. e. accept persons, but *his voice ;* the true object is contained in the last word of the verse.

3. Figures of gentleness, and so applied by the evangelist Matthew 12 : 20, not merely as descriptive of the personal characteristics of the Redeemer, but of the method of extending his kingdom. כֵהָה, shown by the accompanying adjective *dim* and verb *extinguish* to mean *wick ;* its primary sense is *flax*. לֶאֱמֶת stands opposed to the methods of extending his empire previously described. The prep. admits of various explanations : (1) *according to truth, truly*, in a true and proper manner ; (2) *in reference to truth*, i. e. by means of truth ; (3) *belonging to truth*, i. e. in its service, acting as its embodiment and representative ; (4) *unto truth*, so as to secure its triumph and establishment. The rendering *in perpetuity* gives an unauthorized sense to the noun.

4. יִכְהֶה, allusion to כֵהָה, ver. 3, he shall neither use violence nor suffer it from others, he shall not fail in the performance of his task. יָרוּץ, some derive from רוּץ *run*, (1) shall neither be dim nor *run*, i. e. be precipitate, not too slow nor too hasty ; (2) *run away*, flee, be driven from the successful accomplishment of his work. It is more probably from רָצַץ § 140. 1, with allusion to רָצוּץ, ver. 3, *be broken*, defeated. אִיִּים *isles*, remote lands, see on 40 : 15. יְיַחֵלוּ *shall wait for his law*, may mean that they must remain deprived of the blessings of his kingdom until his reign comes to be extended over them, or that after their submission to him they shall wait for the utterances of the law from his mouth with a ready disposition to obey them.

5. The accumulation of titles heightens the sense of God's greatness and omnipotence, and thus gives confidence in his ability to effect what is promised in the following verses. וְנֹטֵיהֶם § 221. 7. *a*. לָעָם, mankind, not the Jews in contrast with the Gentiles, see on 40 : 7. Marg. Haphtarah of בְּרֵאשִׁית, Gen. 1 : 1.

6. קְרָאתִיךָ, summoned thee to this task, *called thee* to be my servant. בְּצֶדֶק *in the exercise of righteousness :* this is shown both in faithfulness toward his servant, fulfilling all rightful claims to assistance and support, and in the nature of the work itself to which he is called, a work illustrative of and determined by God's righteousness. וְאַחְזֵק § 97. 2. *a*, *hold thy hand*, sustain, uphold. לִבְרִית עָם, not *a covenant people* or mediating people, though this might describe Israel's function, but *a covenant of the people*, the mediator of a covenant with them, as light in the following clause means a dispenser of light. עָם may denote the Jewish

people in contrast with בְּנֵי, the Gentiles, or more probably is equivalent to it, denoting, as in ver. 5, *mankind.*

7. Figures of the removal of sin and suffering, which Israel especially through its great representative was appointed to accomplish.

8. Jehovah claims to himself the honour of this glorious result in contrast with graven images whose powerlessness has been previously exhibited.

9. The fulfilment of previous predictions (or, as some say, those of the nearer future, i. e. about Cyrus, when they come to pass) pledges and assures the fulfilment of others made respecting events before they *sprout* or spring up. How completely the glorious future here heralded was yet buried in the soil and had not even sprouted, appears from what follows. Two great sources of the improbability of what has been announced are considered, (1) God's seeming apathy and inaction; (2) Israel's character and fortunes, so opposite from those described or presupposed. These the prophet now proceeds to dispose of: but first he proclaims a universal jubilee and summons all the world to rejoice.

10. חָדָשׁ *new* song, indicating a fresh occasion of praise. מִקְצֵה, the remotest parts of the earth are to utter their joyful thanksgivings at the salvation of the world from sin and misery to be effected by Israel. וּמְלֹאוֹ, object of יוֹרְדֵי, 'going down to the sea and all that it contains,' or parallel to יוֹרְדֵי, and summoned to join in the praise, whether it denotes marine animals or inhabitants of lands in the bosom of the sea.

11. יִשְׂאוּ, see ver. 2. יָרֹנּוּ § 197. *d*, § 275. 2. *b.*

13. Jehovah will stir up his zeal on behalf of his people, lay aside the seeming inaction of the past, and accomplish the most stupendous results. יֵצֵא, military phrase for going forth to battle. קִנְאָה (1) zeal, excited feeling, (2) jealousy for his own name, or on his people's behalf. יָרִיעַ, the battle-cry or shout to rouse the warrior's ardour.

14. God's past apathy and inaction are contrasted with the new activity to be displayed on his people's behalf. אֶחֱרִישׁ, not interrogatively, but expressive of the determination formed during this period of seeming inaction, 'saying, *I will be silent.*' כַּיּוֹלֵדָה, the comparison has sometimes been referred to the subject, God, as one bringing forth, travailing in birth with Israel, effecting their regeneration and salvation, but it is better and more usual to connect the comparison with the actions described. אֶפְעֶה, in the two other places in which it occurs, is a noun, *viper;* here it is a verb. אֶשֹּׁם, not from שָׁמֵם *destroy*, but נָשַׁם *blow*, breathe hard. וְאֶשְׁאַף, not *devour*, but *pant.*

15. The effects produced by this zeal and activity of God metaphorically expressed. They are described as most surprising and stupendous,

implying the exercise of almighty power, and of a character precisely the reverse of those in 41 : 18. They represent mighty judgments on the foes of the people to accomplish the deliverance and welfare of the latter.

16. The result will be the safe guidance of those who could no more see a way of escape from perplexity than the blind. אָשִׂים, convert darkness into light, see 41 : 15. וּמַעֲקַשִּׁים crooked or uneven, as opposed to מִישׁוֹר, lineal or superficial straightness, see on 40 : 4. עֲשִׂיתִם I have done them these things, or for them, the people § 102. 2, § 273. 3. a.

17. נָסֹגוּ, driven back from the execution of their designs. While God's people should be thus favoured and blessed, the worshippers of idols would be utterly discomfited and disappointed, unable to accomplish Israel's destruction. The great temptation of the people was to distrust God's power and grace, and transfer their confidence to the idols whose worshippers had proved so much stronger than they. This is met here and repeatedly in this prophecy. אָתֶּם, i. e. both the graven and molten image.

18. The improbability arising from Israel's character and condition : these shall not obstruct his achieving this high destiny on his own behalf and that of the world. הַחֵרְשִׁים § 245. 2, the heathen may be addressed as especially characterized by moral deafness and blindness ; or perhaps the deaf and blind as a class, the deaf might be expected to hear and the blind to see these evidences of the folly of idolatry.

19. And yet Israel neither hears nor sees them, or acts as if he did not. מִי עִוֵּר, the question implies that his blindness is such that no other deserves the name; all other blindness disappears beside it. This shows that the servant of the Lord here spoken of is not the Messiah exclusively, for this can have no relation to him. מְשֻׁלָּם has been variously explained, (1) friend of God, (2) perfect, (3) devoted to God, (4) provided with שָׁלוֹם peace or welfare.

20. רָאִיתָ K'thibh 2 m. s. pret., K'ri const. inf. רְאוֹת. Israel is addressed in the first clause, and spoken of in the second § 279, thou hast seen many things, i. e. evidences of divine power and grace, but wilt pay no heed to them. פָּקוֹחַ, inf. for finite verb § 268. 1, God has opened his, Israel's, ears by his prophets, etc., or better, comp. ver. 7, it describes the destiny of Israel, set to open ears, and he will not hear himself, whether from indisposition or inability, or both.

21. This guilty incapacity and apparent gross unfitness of the people for their destined task shall not defeat it. God will accomplish this salvation for his own sake, not for theirs. צִדְקוֹ, some refer suf. to Israel, in order to his, Israel's, righteousness ; others to Messiah, on account of

his, Christ's, righteousness. It must refer to God, *on account of his own righteousness*. צֶדֶק cannot mean exactly *grace* or *mercy*. It may here denote faithfulness to his promises and engagements, which is one phase of the divine righteousness, or his righteousness in its ordinary sense, which the plan of salvation was designed to illustrate and display by putting away sin and diffusing holiness. יַגְדִּיל תּוֹרָה, not *magnify law* by inflicting judgment on those who had violated it, which is inappropriate in this connection : nor *give a great and glorious law*, but *illustrate and honour the law*, i. e. the Old Testament dispensation, that system of things which God had ordained to issue in the salvation of the world, and which should so issue in spite of Israel's unfaithfulness. תּוֹרָה from הוֹרָה *to instruct*, not mere advice but authoritative guidance, *law*.

22. The condition of Israel presented as great an apparent obstacle to his achieving this salvation as his character. Can a people who could not save themselves, and whom their God did not rescue, be the saviours of the world? This anomaly is here explained. הָפֵחַ בַּחוּרִים. Some derive the noun from בָּחוּר, then according as the verb is from פּוּחַ or from פָּחַח it may be rendered, there is *a snaring of young men, all of them*, all their young men are captured as birds in a snare, or *they all are the puffing derision of young men*. But it is better to regard בְּ as a prep. *a snaring them all in holes*, they are caught like wild beasts, or *panting in holes*, i. e. dungeons וּבְבָתֵּי כְלָאִים, both members of the compound expression are put in the plural. The terms of this verse are figurative, and describe not merely the Babylonish exile, but the suffering and oppressed condition of the people through a considerable portion of its history. מִשְׁסֶּה, לָבַז, allude to יְשַׁסֵּהוּ וַיִּצַּם of the first clause, and are resumed in מְשִׁיסִים, לְבֹזְזִים of ver. 24. הֵשִׁיב for הֵשַׁב § 65. *a*, *restore*, bring back, whether to their own land or to their former condition of prosperity.

23. The question implies the prophet's earnest desire that they should give ear, and at the same time his apprehension that few would do so. זֹאת does not refer to תּוֹרָה, ver. 21, which is too remote, nor to the preceding verse, but to the verse following, containing the solution of this anomaly, which is the main thing to be attended to. לְאָחוֹר, not hearken *to the past* but *hear for the future*, either describing the time of hearing, *in time to come*, or the object of it, hear with reference to the time to come.

24. Their sufferings do not prove that Jehovah is unable to deliver his people, for he gave them into their enemies' hand, and that for a sufficient cause. חָטָאנוּ, זוּ § 279.

25. אֶשְׁפֹּךְ, Vav conv. intimates a close connection or dependence, *and so he poured* § 99. 1. חֵמָה אַף § 253, *fury*, viz. *his anger*, or *his anger as fury*. וַתְּלַהֲטֵהוּ, the subject is אֶשְׁפֹּךְ or rather חֵמָה. וְלֹא יָדַע. not *unawares*, unexpectedly, but expressive of stupid unconcern, as is shown by the parallel expression, *he will not lay it to heart*. The change of tense is significant, and is designed to embrace both periods of time § 263. 5. *a*. Marg. see on Gen. 44 : 10. 17.

CHAPTER LIII.

That the Messiah is the subject of this chapter is evident from the following considerations:

1. Its terms are exclusively applicable to Christ. A spectacle is presented of extraordinary humiliation and suffering, terminating in a violent death. They, who first beheld it, mistook its real meaning and design, and despised what they should have honoured. This suffering and death were vicarious, due to no personal ill desert of the victim, and to no arbitrary infliction of God, but endured for the sins of others, and procuring for them justification and peace. The sufferer was himself righteous, vs. 9. 11; not in a comparative sense merely, but absolutely so, since what he endured was not on his own account, but wholly for the sake of others. These sufferings were, moreover, voluntarily assumed and borne without complaint, and they were to issue in a glorious reward. This is all strictly true of Christ, but of no other.

2. The subject is expressly stated to be the servant of the LORD, ver. 11, 52 : 13. To this servant Isaiah ascribes all that work which Israel, including the Messiah, was raised up and appointed to do for the glory of God and the salvation of man; see on 42 : 1. In some passages the language employed is applicable both to the people as a whole and to their great descendant. In others it is so framed as to refer only to one or the other of the constituents of this complex person. The imperfections charged upon this servant, 42 : 19, belong to the people alone. In the present chapter the Messiah is alone regarded. In proof of this it may be urged, (1) that what is here said of the servant of the Lord is true only of the Messiah, not of Israel as a people. Their sufferings were not vicarious, but as both Isaiah and other prophets testify, and as the facts declare, the just desert of their own sins. The church here possesses only a remote and distant resemblance to her head in so far as she takes part in the afflictions of Christ, and completes the destined

measure of that willing endurance for the good of others, which appertains to her as the body of a suffering head, Col. 1 : 24. (2) Here, as in 42 : 6, 49 : 5. 6, Israel is distinguished from the servant of the Lord. The speakers in the first part of the chapter are not gentile nations in contrast with Israel, with whom the prophet could not identify himself, and whom he could not thus introduce without explanation, but as in 59 : 9–12, 63 : 16—64 : 12, and as is distinctly intimated ver. 8, comp. ver. 4, the people of God. (3) The expressions imply that an individual person is intended. The singular is used throughout ; he is called " a man," ver. 3 ; his " soul" is spoken of, vs. 10. 11. 12, also his imprisonment and death, vs. 8. 9 ; he is contrasted with the " many," vs. 11. 12, whom he shall justify, and whose sins he bare. This is so convincing, that some of those who reject the Messianic interpretation, have sought to fix upon some other individual as the subject of the prophecy, some prophet, or king, or martyr, otherwise unknown. And the Ethiopian eunuch was led to ask whether the prophet spoke this ' of himself or of some other man.' Acts 8 : 34.

3. The analogy of prophecy. (1) Although the prophets dwell more upon the glory and blessedness of Messiah's reign than upon his antecedent humiliation, and although it is peculiar to this passage to unfold the vicarious nature of his sufferings, he is yet elsewhere predicted as a sufferer, in whom the acme of human endurance should be reached, and who should rise thence to proportionate exaltation and glory. This is already intimated in the primal promise, Gen. 3 : 15, and more distinctly set forth in the typical Psalms, e. g. Ps. 22, 69, and in the later prophets, e. g. Daniel 9 : 26, Zechariah 9 : 9, 12 : 10, 13 : 7. (2) This chapter stands in the relation of climax to others of like character in this same prophecy, see on 40 : 2, and must refer to the same subject. The declaration, 42 : 4, ' he shall not fail nor be discouraged,' implies that the servant of the Lord would meet with opposition and obstacles. He is spoken of, 49 : 4, as ' one whom man despiseth and whom the nation abhorreth ;' 50 : 6, he gave his back to the smiters and his cheeks to them that plucked off the hair. (3) The ' tender plant' and ' root out of a dry ground,' ver. 2, strongly resemble expressions which are used to characterize the Messiah elsewhere. These terms are doubtless identical in meaning with the rod out of the stem of Jesse and the branch growing out of his roots, 11 : 1, and ' my servant, the Branch,' Zech. 3 : 8.

4. The authority of the New Testament, which bears testimony to the Messianic character of this passage almost verse by verse ; 52 : 15 is quoted and applied to Christ, Rom. 15 : 21 ; so 53 : 1 in John 12 : 38,

Rom. 10:16; ver. 4 in Matt. 8:17, and with the following verses in 1 Pet. 2:22–25; vs. 7. 8 in Acts 8:32. 33; ver. 12 in Mark 15:28. Luke 22:37. As a suffering Saviour is more clearly and fully set forth in this chapter than in any other prophecy of the Old Testament, it must be prominently referred to in such general statements as Mark 9:12, 'it is written of the Son of Man that he must suffer many things and be set at nought,' and Luke 24:25–27, 44–46, Christ ought, agreeably to the prophets, to have suffered these things and to enter into his glory. The terms employed by the writers of the New Testament in stating the doctrine of vicarious atonement are also frequently borrowed from this chapter or contain manifest allusions to it. Thus Rom. 4:25, 'who was delivered for our offences,' alludes to ver. 5; the 'Lamb' 1 Pet. 1:19, the 'Lamb slain' Rev. 5:6; the 'blood of the Lamb' Rev. 7:14 to ver. 7; 'the Lamb of God which taketh away (ὁ αἴρων) the sin of the world,' John 1:29. 36 to vs. 7. 11; 1 John 3:5, comp. vs. 9. 11; 1 Cor. 15:3. 4, 2 Cor. 5:21, comp. vs. 8–11.

5. This is the most ancient and the almost universally received interpretation. The oldest Jewish authorities refer it to the Messiah, notwithstanding its contrariety to the carnal expectations of that people. And it was only to escape the necessity of confessing the signal fulfilment of this prophecy in Jesus of Nazareth that the Jews of later times abandoned this traditional explanation. In the Christian church this continued to be the unanimous interpretation for seventeen centuries, unless Grotius be regarded as an exception, who explained it in its primary sense of Jeremiah, but in its fullest and highest sense of Christ. It was not until the prevalence of rationalism, with its bold denials of the reality or possibility of prophetic foresight, that any other subject than the Messiah was imagined or suspected.

6. No other satisfactory explanation ever has been or can be suggested. The perfect righteousness of the subject and his vicarious sufferings are wholly inapplicable to the Jewish people as a whole, to the sacred order of the priesthood, or the collective body of the prophets, as well as to Hezekiah, Josiah, Isaiah, Jeremiah, or any other individual, actual or supposable, but Christ alone.

The chapter may be divided as follows, viz.:

1. vs. 1–9 describe the sufferings of Messiah.

2. vs. 10–12 his consequent reward.

The former of these sections may be subdivided into three stanzas or three verses each:

(1) vs. 1–3, his lowly and suffering condition led to his contemptuous rejection.

(2) vs. 4–6, these sufferings, so grossly misunderstood, were vicarious

(3) vs. 7–9, he dies by a judicial sentence, uncomplainingly, though innocent, for the sins of others.

1. ־ָ, While the Gentiles who ‘had not heard,’ 52 : 15, shall pay heed to Messiah's claims, the mass of the chosen people will reject him. The question does not necessarily imply that the unbelief was absolutely universal; the few who believed are overlooked beside the vast numbers who did not. לִשְׁמֻעָתֵנוּ suf. may denote the source § 254. 7, *the* thing *heard from us* prophets, our report, so Eng. ver.; or the subject § 254. 8, *the* thing *heard by us* the people of God; the latter explanation has the advantage of assuming the same speaker here as in the following verses. The prophetic teachings regarding the Messiah are intended in either case. זְרוֹעַ *the arm of Jehovah*, i. e. his presence and power, which, though manifested in Christ, were discovered by few. עַל־מִי, not simply *to whom*, as if the prep. were לְ or אֶל, but *over whom*, the figure being that of a celestial exhibition.

2. The reason why the Messiah was not recognized in his true character is found in his humble and unattractive exterior. וַיַּעַל § 262. 4, the ideal position of the prophet is between Christ's humiliation and his glory, so that what relates to the former is mostly spoken of as past, and what relates to the latter as still future. כַיּוֹנֵק § 245. 5. *d*, elsewhere *a suckling*, here in the sense of יוֹנֶקֶת *a sucker, sprout*. לְפָנָיו, some refer the suffix to God, *before him*, an object of divine attention and care, comp. Gen. 17 : 18, others to the people, i. e. in their esteem. The objection that this involves a gratuitous change of person, since the people are the speakers throughout the first part of the chapter, may be relieved by understanding it distributively, § 275. 6, in connection with the implied answer to the preceding question, ‘Almost every one disbelieved since Messiah *grew up before him*,’ etc. וְכַשֹּׁרֶשׁ *root*, or more probably a *shoot* attached to and springing from it, in which the root as it were reveals itself. צִיָּה מֵאֶרֶץ, and hence puny and insignificant: the explanations of the *dry land*, as Galilee, or as the Virgin Mary, show what extravagance results from giving a separate significance to every particular in a figurative or symbolical description. נִרְאֵהוּ is by some interpreters connected with what precedes, and rendered *that we should behold him* in the sense of looking upon him with pleasure; this is recommended by the like construction of the following וְנֶחְמְדֵהוּ. It is forbidden, however, by the accents, as well as by the fact that רָאָה has this sense only when followed by בְּ, see on Gen. 1 : 4. The prophet may here forsake his ideal stand-point, and speak of that as future which is actually so, or the future may be used relatively to the preceding וַיַּעַל, § 263. 5. *a*, because

the act described is subsequent to and consequent upon it, *and we saw him.*

3. נִבְזֶה, either in a passive sense, *forsaken of men,* or an active, *ceasing* to be *of men,* so disfigured by suffering as to be no longer counted a man, comp. Ps. 22 : 7. אִישִׁים § 207. 2. *e.* וִידוּעַ חֹלִי, not *known by* but *acquainted with sickness,* which may be used here as 1 Kin. 22 : 34 of the physical effect of wounds, but most probably stands by a poetic individualization for every form of suffering. וּכְמַסְתֵּר has been explained as an anomalous Hiph. part. *like* one *causing to hide the face from him,* or as the sense of the Hiph. in this verb is simply *to hide, like* one *hiding the face from us* in grief, 2 Sam. 15 : 30, or shame, Mic. 3 : 7, as the lepers, Lev. 13 : 45. As, however, such a form of the participle would be almost unexampled, § 94. *e,* it seems better to regard it as a noun, § 191. 4, when מַסְתֵּר, § 333, may be 1 pl. with the same sense as before, or 3 m. s. with the relative omitted, § 283. 3, *like* one *from whom* there is a *hiding of face,* whether the meaning be that we or men generally averted our faces to avoid the sight of so shocking a spectacle, or that he resembled one from whom God had hidden his face in anger, comp. 59 : 2, where פָּנִים stands as here without any qualifying expression, also 54 : 8, 64 : 6, Ps. 22 : 25. נִבְזֶה, not 1 pl. fut., but as at the beginning of the verse, Niph. part.

4. These sufferings were not in punishment of any sins of his own, nor were they mere calamities or arbitrary divine inflictions. The true explanation is given in the first clause. הוּא, as subsequently אֲנַחְנוּ, expressed on account of the emphatic contrast, § 243. 1. נָשָׂא, not simply *took away* but *bore,* as it was only by bearing our sufferings that he could have removed them ; this appears further from the parallel expression סְבָלָם, about whose meaning there can be no question, from the preceding verse where Messiah is characterized by the sickness and griefs which are here identified as 'ours,' and from the usage of this verb נָשָׂא in the phrase to which there is manifest allusion here, comp. ver. 11, 'to bear iniquity,' Ezek. 18 : 19. 20, Num. 9 : 13, i. e. to suffer its penalty. Matthew, 8 : 17, quotes these words as fulfilled in our Lord's miracles of healing ;—for, though they did not exhaust the meaning of the prophecy, they were types and incipient fruits of the salvation wrought by his vicarious sufferings. וּמַכְאֹבֵינוּ § 200. *c.* סְבָלָם suf. repeats the noun, § 281. נָגַע, this verb and its cognate noun נֶגַע are used of any plague divinely sent, and particularly of the leprosy, 2 Kin. 15 : 5, Lev. 13 : 1, whence the Jewish notion that Messiah was to be a leper. מֻכֶּה § 254. 9. *b.*

5. מְחֹלָל מִ rep. indicates the ground or reason, *on account of.*

אלשלומנו מוסר, not *instruction for our welfare*, § 254. 9, since the reference in the context is not to Christ as a teacher but as an atoning sacrifice, and the prep. עליו *upon him* suggests the idea of bearing suffering, as in ver. 4 ; but *chastisement* or punishment *of our peace*, that by which our peace or welfare is s cured.

6. The language of the people of God is still continued. כגאן § 245. 5. *d*, figure of sin and the helpless misery resulting from it.

7. נגש, not 1 pl. fut. Kal, *we shall oppress* him, but Niph. pret., and not impersonally, *it was exacted*, viz., the penalty due to our sin, but *he was oppressed*. נענה pron. expressed because the participle follows, which does not of itself indicate the person. נענה may be taken passively, *afflicted*, a synonymous expression added to strengthen the preceding statement, or reflexively, § 77. 2, *humbling himself*, suggesting the idea that he voluntarily submitted to this affliction. יפתח־ fut. relative to the foregoing verbs, § 263. 5. *a* ; in the vividness of the description the scene appears to be transacting before the prophet's eyes, and hence he uses successively the preterite, the participle, and the future to set it forth in its successive stages as in part past, in part present, and in part yet to come, *he has been oppressed, and he is being afflicted, and he will not open his mouth*. יפתח § 285. 3. Marg. see on Gen. 44 : 10. יפתח agrees not with רחל which is fem., nor with עם which is too remote, but with Messiah, who is the principal subject.

8. מעצר prep. may have its instrumental sense, as Eng. Ver. marg., *by oppression and by judgment*, i. e. a judicial sentence, or its local sense, *from confinement and from judgment*, i. e. the tribunal or judgment-seat. לקח has been referred to his being-taken to execution, as Prov. 24 : 11, or taken out of life, as Ezek. 33 : 4. 6, or his assumption to heaven, as Gen. 5 : 24, 2 Kin. 2 : 9, 10. Of the numerous interpretations proposed for the next clause there are but two which are consistent with the true sense and usage of the words. The first, which has the authority of the early versions in its favor, makes דורו the object of the following verb, *who shall speak* (or *think*) *his generation*, i. e. who can in word or thought recount their multitude? The 'generation' of the Messiah will then mean those who belong to the same class with him, who are assimilated to him in spirit and in life, as in the phrases 'generation of the righteous,' Ps. 14 : 5, 'generation of thy children,' Ps. 73 : 15, 'generation of the upright,' Ps. 112 : 2. It is thus in fact, though not in form, equivalent to his posterity or spiritual seed, זרע, spoken of ver. 10. The verb שיח, though commonly followed by the prep. ב, may nevertheless take a direct object, as is shown by Ps. 145 : 5. This rendering assumes that a preliminary glimpse is here afforded of Messiah's

exaltation and the reward of his voluntary endurance, while the cr..ire context relates to his sufferings and the full and proper consideration of their reward does not begin until ver. 10. According to the other view of the clause, וׁתֹ־חיִי stands absolutely in apposition with the subject of the verb § 271. 4. *b, as for his generation*, i. e. his contemporaries, *who shall think* (or *say*) *that*, etc., none of them, or comparatively few, shall recognize the fact that his sufferings are vicarious. נִגְזַר, most usually and naturally employed of a violent death. עַמִּי, Jehovah may be the speaker, as in vs. 11. 12, or the prophet, or as in the preceding verses the people of God, the singular being employed distributively § 275. 6, as 1 Sam. 5 : 10, Zech. 8 : 21. : לָמוֹ, not an unusual form for 3 m. s. *smiting* was *to him*, but 3 m. pl. and paragogic Vav § 104. *f*, § 233, with the ellipsis of the relative § 285. 3, *to whom smiting* belonged or was due, or the abstract נֶגַע for the concrete, *as a smiting*, one smitten, comp. Lev. 13 : 4, etc., *for them*. The word נֶגַע alludes to נָגוּעַ ver. 4 ; his contemporaries would think him stricken, but not that the stroke which he bore was one which had been deserved by themselves.

9. וַיִּתֵּן indef. § 243. 2 *and one gave*, put, appointed, equivalent to *it was given*. רְשָׁעִים *wicked*, distinguished as such by an ignominious burial, hence criminals, malefactors. With this is contrasted in the next clause the honourable burial of the rich. The servant of the Lord was destined to both, of course successively and by different parties. This enigmatical statement finds its explanation in the event. They who crucified Christ with malefactors, marked him out for a malefactor's grave ; but God by his providence ordered it otherwise. He was laid, as Matthew 27 : 57–60 expressly informs us, with special allusion doubtless to this prophecy, in a rich man's tomb. The exactness of the fulfilment has given great trouble to unbelieving interpreters, who have ineffectually tried by every expedient to get rid of the plain sense of the passage. The text has been altered without the slightest warrant of external authority ; עָשִׁיר has been declared, in defiance of invariable usage, to mean *wicked*, and finally it has been said that 'rich' is here equivalent to 'wicked,' inasmuch as riches lead to pride and impiety. It is, however, not the rich man's life, but his burial which is here spoken of, and that manifestly presents not a parallel but a contrast to the grave of the malefactor. Christ had his grave with malefactors in the intention of his murderers, with a rich man in the purpose of God and in actual fact. בְּמֹתָיו, not in the act of dying but in the state of death, equivalent to *after his death*, comp. 1 Kin. 13 : 31. The plural form has been supposed to express intensity § 201. 2, a death so dreadful that it seemed

like many deaths combined in one, or to be purely poetic, as Ezek. 28
8. 10, or to be such only in appearance, the suffix after מּׁ following the
analogy of those appended to fem. plur. nouns, comp. Ezek. 6 : 8, 16 ·
31, § 173. 2. There is no necessity, therefore, of assuming either that
the suffix refers to a collective person, or that the word is the plur. of
בָּמָה in the sense of *a sepulchral mound* or *tumulus*, a meaning which
this word never has; this would besides require an arbitrary change of
the points to בְּמֹתָיו, and it would after all leave the plural form unexplained. עַל prep. governing the following clause and hence equivalent
to the conj. עַל אֲשֶׁר, which may mean *because*, when his innocence will
be stated as the reason why his grave was finally assigned him with the
rich rather than with the wicked; or *although*, as in Job 16 : 17, a particular being added of a tenor contrary to the preceding, when the reference will be chiefly to the first clause, his grave was appointed him with
the wicked, though he had committed no crime in deed or word.

10. Introduces the second portion of the chapter, descriptive of Messiah's reward. This was the reason why Jehovah permitted his servant
to be thus afflicted, nay, why he himself imposed these afflictions upon
him. הֶחֱלִי § 175. 1 is by some thought to govern and qualify the preceding verb § 269. a, *was pleased, crushed him grievously* by § 269 for
was pleased to crush, etc., comp. Mic. 6 : 13, but it is better to preserve
its separate verbal force. אִם־ in its proper conditional sense, *if*. תָּשִׂים
put or *place*, i. e. make, not 2 m. s. referring to Jehovah who is spoken
of still in the third person, but 3 f. s. and the subject is נַפְשׁוֹ. This is
not a mere periphrasis for the pronoun *he*, but has the emphatic sense of
his soul, his life, which is represented as making the offering, because it
was the life which was sacrificed. אָשָׁם, the legal designation of the
trespass-offering, Lev. 5 : 15, 16, a modification of the sin-offering, in
which there was not only an expiation for the sin by the shedding of
blood, but a pecuniary compensation or amends for the injury committed.
An expiation for the forfeited life of the sinner and a full satisfaction to
the law and justice of God are combined in the sacrifice of Christ. The
mention of the condition is followed by that of the blessings suspended
upon it, viz., a numerous posterity, long life, and a successful prosecution
of the task which God had been pleased to commit to him. Like blessings were often promised and granted to the righteous, Job 5 : 23–26;
they are here pledged to the servant of God in their highest spiritual
meaning. בְּיָדוֹ *in* or *by his hand*, i. e. by his instrumentality, Lev. 8 : 36.

11. מֵעֲמַל prep. causal, *on account of*, not partitive, as though he
should see some but not all of the results of his toil. יִרְאֶה, the object
implied though not expressed is an ample reward, such as had been

promised in the preceding verse. בְּדַעְתּוֹ, not by the knowledge which he possesses, for Messiah is here spoken of as an atoning sacrifice and not as a teacher, but the suf. expresses the object § 254. 9, *by the knowledge of him* on the part of others, that practical knowledge and right apprehension of him which implies faith in him and reliance upon him. יַצְדִּיק, not *to make* inwardly *righteous,* a sense which the verb has, if at all, only in one passage, Dan. 12 : 3, but in the forensic sense *to justify* § 272. 2. *a.* צַדִּיק adj. contrary to the ordinary rule § 249. 1. *a,* stands emphatically before its noun and in a significant proximity to its cognate verb. In such cases the article is omitted, the new prominence which the adjective assumes conferring upon it a measure of independence and perhaps something of the character of a proper name, comp. Jer. 3 : 7. 10. יְהֹוָה, Jehovah is the speaker in this and the following verse.

12. Some render the first clause, *I will divide* (or *apportion,* comp. Job 39 : 17) *to him the many, and he shall divide strong ones as spoil,* i. e. his spiritual conquests shall embrace vast multitudes, and even the most powerful shall own him their victor. Others prefer to translate, *I will divide to him among the many, and he shall divide spoil with the strong,* comp. Prov. 16 : 19 ; he shall have the success which elsewhere attends multitudes and strength. He, like other great conquerors, shall have abundant spoil and reap large fruits from his victories. That his conquests are of a very different description from theirs, however, appears from the method by which they were gained as detailed in the remainder of the verse. הֶעֱרָה, either *poured out* or *bared,* exposed. יִמָּנֶה fut. because not confined to the period of his humiliation, but still performed in his state of exaltation.

EZEKIEL, CHAPTER XXXVII.

This chapter contains,

1. A symbolical vision, vs. 1–10, with its explanation, vs. 11–14.

2. A symbolical action, vs. 15–17, with its explanation, vs. 18–28.

The former, which is a real vision, and not merely an allegory in that form, is not designed to set forth the corporeal resurrection of Israel's dead, as has sometimes been inferred from vs. 12. 13, but as is plain from ver. 11 a glorious change to be wrought in Israel's condition, a change which to human view was as hopeless as that dry bones should be raised to life.

If we could presume that the doctrine of a future resurrection was understood and was a part of the popular faith at the time of the prophet,

it would be natural to suppose an allusion to it here. God, who shall
hereafter raise the dead, will restore Israel to a new life. Perhaps, however, it may better be conceived to be preparatory to the doctrine than
built upon it, an obscure hint of what was afterwards to be more fully
disclosed than an evidence that it was already familiarly known. Such
premonitory intimations occur with frequency in the Old Testament. A
method often employed for this purpose, and it is singularly adapted to
the end, is the use of figures, which, beside their obvious figurative interpretation, shall also have accomplishment as literal verities, see on Isa. 40 :
3. This view of the case is confirmed by the fact that the principle here
asserted is the very one upon which the doctrine of the resurrection of
the righteous rests. Israel's relation to God as his people gave assurance that though dead he must rise again. If this was true of the people
as a whole, it was applicable likewise to the individuals composing it so
far as they personally sustained this vital and vivifying relation to God.
If it was true of the death and ruin which had overtaken Israel as a
body, it was also applicable to the corporeal death of individual believers.
Death cannot annihilate or destroy those who belong to God. This is
in fact the point of view from which the Old Testament chiefly developes
the doctrine of the future state and of the corporeal resurrection. And
this is urged by our Lord against the Sadducees as underlying even the
earliest periods of divine revelation, Luke 20 : 37. 38.

1. יַד the hand, as the organ chiefly employed in action, is used as
a symbol of power, and here denotes that mighty spiritual influence,
by which the prophet's ordinary consciousness was suppressed and the
condition of ecstasy produced, comp. 1 : 3, 8 : 1, 40 : 1. בְרוּחַ in the
Spirit, i. e. intimately united with this divine agent and under his
control ; רוּחַ may be in const. before יְהֹוָה or as the accentuators seem to
have judged in the absolute, when it will be definite without the article,
as 8 : 3, § 246. 1, and יְהֹוָה will be the subject of the preceding verb.
מוֹצִאַת verbal adj. governing a direct object like the verb from which it is
derived § 271. 1, see on Gen. 42 : 18.

2. כְּבִים § 280. 3.

3. הֲתִחְיֶינָה expresses not possibility only, but futurity, shall they
live? אָלַי § 199. c.   יִחְיֶה § 47.

4. אֲלֵיהֶם § 275. 5 ; so יָדְעַתָּ, comp. ver. 5, etc.   הִנַּבֵּאתִי § 245. 2.

7. קוֹל ... רַעַשׁ, possibly thunder and earthquake, betokening the divine presence and agency, but more probably noise and shaking of the
bones. וַתִּקְרְבוּ § 88 (3 f. pl.)

8. עֵץ, see on Gen. 40 : 8.

11. לָנוּ, a pleonastic use of the dative of advantage, for ourselves,

so far as we are concerned, Eng. Ver. 'for our parts;' others render *to ourselves,* i. e. *cut off* from all hope or help and left *to ourselves.*

12. וְהֵבֵאתִי § 160. 2.   13. בְּצַרְתִּי § 106. *a.*

14. וְהִנַּחְתִּי § 160. 1 and 2.   בָּאֲ— § 90 (pass.). Marg. see on Judg. 13 : 25.

15. This spiritual resurrection is followed by a cessation of the schism between Judah and Israel, the type of all divisions among the people of God. Marg. *The Haphtarah of* וַיִּגַּשׁ Gen. 44 : 18, etc.

16. לִיהוּדָה § 257. 1. חֲבֵרָיו § 46, § 220. 2. *b,* such as attached themselves to Judah from the other tribes, 2 Chron. 11 : 12–17, 15 : 9, 30 : 11. 18. 25.

17. וְקַרְּב § 119. 1.   לְאֶחָדִים § 223. 1. *a.*

19. כִּי־אֶפְרָ͏יִם, Ephraim was the leader in the schism, and dominant among the revolted tribes. He had ambitiously grasped in his own hand as many tribes as he could bring beneath his own control; but all would be hereafter united in the hand of the Lord. עָלָיו suf. refers to Judah, and the following words are explanatory, *upon* or along with *him,* viz., *with the stick of Judah.* Others render, *I will put them,* the tribes of Israel, *together with him,* Ephraim, *with the stick of Judah.*

22. יְהְיֶ͏ה— § 86. *b* (3 pl.)   23. יִטַּמְּאוּ § 82. 5.

26. וְרָבֵיתִי § 86. *b* (2 m. s.).   אֹתָם § 238. 2. *a.*

28. מֶלֶךְ, predicate without the article § 259. 2. Marg. as ver. 14.

OBADIAH.

This prophecy is divisible into three parts, viz.:

(1) vs. 1–9, the utter destruction to which Edom is destined.

(2) vs. 10–16, the reason of it, viz.: Edom's unbrotherly conduct at the time of Jerusalem's calamity.

(3) vs. 17–21, the contrasted deliverance and enlargement of Jacob.

1. Marg. *The Haphtarah of* וַיִּשְׁלַח Gen. 32 : 4, etc. חֲזוֹן *vision,* not in the specific sense of an appearance beheld in an ecstatic state, but in the more general sense of a divine revelation or prophecy, affording an insight into the will and purposes of God. שָׁמַעְנוּ § 195. 3. After this brief title the nations are summoned to arise and make war upon Edom. כֹּה־אָמַר אֲדֹנָי. This introductory formula is elsewhere invariably followed by language in which God is himself the speaker; here, however, it is used to denote that what comes after is a communication from God, even though he does not throughout speak in the first person

12

This is simpler than to enclose the remainder of the verse in a parenthesis and connect this formula directly with ver. 2 ; or to assume an
anacoluthon, 'we have heard tidings from Jehovah,' when the construction with which the sentence began would have required instead, 'I,
Jehovah, have caused you to hear tidings ;' or, more violent still, to resort to the hypothesis of an interpolation, which is commonly a mere
cover of ignorance or unbelief, and is here peculiarly unfortunate, for if
the words 'Thus saith the Lord concerning Edom' be stricken from the
text, there will be nothing to intimate against whom war is to be prepared, nor who is addressed vs. 2–5, nor what is the subject of the
prophecy, until it is learned from ver. 6. It would be better to allow
the text to remain as it is, and confess the difficulty to be insoluble, than
to get rid of it in such an unwarrantable manner. The pret. אָמַר does
not here denote an action wholly past, as though the prophet were repeating what God had said at some former time, perhaps through the
medium of a preceding prophet, but in accordance with the constant
usage of this formula an action belonging to the present, already begun
but not yet finished, § 262. 2. And hence the fut. יֹאמַר may with equal
propriety be used in the same phrase, Isa. 40 : 1. לֶאֱדוֹם in respect to,
concerning Edom, or, if the remainder of the verse is parenthetic, to
Edom, see on Gen. 1 : 28. שָׁמַעְנוּ we, not the nations who are in the
next clause spoken of in the third person, but the people of God who
heard this in the prophet as their representative, or through him as their
medium of communication with the Lord ; the plural would then intimate that these tidings were received by the prophet not as an individual, but as a member and organ of the chosen people, and for the
sake of the whole. Or he may possibly speak in the name of the prophets, to others of whom like disclosures were made, comp. Isa. 53 : 1.
וְצִיר. This clause may be explanatory of the preceding, the tidings being
that a messenger had been sent, etc. Or if the tidings have a more
general relation to all that follows respecting Edom's overthrow, it may
be confirmatory, showing that measures were already taken to effect this
end. It does not form an opposition to the preceding clause, as though
the meaning were, We, the chosen people, have heard a summons (which
is not the sense of שְׁמוּעָה), and a messenger has also been despatched
among the heathen that both Jews and Gentiles might be united in the
war upon Edom. The messenger, if an ideal one sent by God to gather
the nations, simply expresses the thought that the Lord would certainly
bring about this result. The same idea is elsewhere conveyed under the
image of calling distant nations by a hiss or whistle, or setting up a
signal for them to congregate, Isa. 5 : 26, 7 : 18. Or the messenger

may be a real one, sent by one nation to solicit the aid of others. שְׁלַח,
Marg. see on Gen. 44 : 10.   קוּמוּ, the language of the messenger addressed to the nations, which is simpler than to regard it as the mutual
exhortations of the nations, roused by the messenger sent to them.   It
is quite unnatural, and contrary to the whole tenor of the following prediction, to suppose that the chosen people are in these words exhorting
one another to engage in a war to which the heathen had already been
divinely invited.   וְנָקוּמָה we, i. e. both the party represented by the
messenger and the nations addressed.   If he has been sent by God, then
by a bold figure God is represented as taking the initiative in the war
against Edom, and inviting the nations to coöperate with him.   Comp.
Isa. 13 : 4. 5, Joel 2 : 11.   עָלֶיהָ § 275. 2. b.

2. This gathering of the nations to war against Edom is in pursuance of the divine intention to reduce him to insignificance and to a
despicable condition.   נְתַתִּיךָ I have in purpose given, made thee small,
§ 262. 1. b ; the preterite is used because the purpose was already
formed, though not yet executed in actual fact.   It is not necessary,
therefore, to refer this to something wholly belonging to the past, to the
position which God originally assigned to Edom among the nations, as
though it were intended by its contrast with what follows to set his
arrogance in a more glaring light ; God had made him a small, despised
people, but his pride led him to fancy himself invincible.   אַתָּה, this result, divinely resolved upon, is spoken of as if it were already effected.

3. The confidence which he had entertained and still continued to
cherish in his inaccessible position, was a delusion.   זְדוֹן § 218, § 255. 1.
בְּחַגְוֵי־. This word is of rare occurrence, and interpreters are not agreed
as to its precise sense.   Gesenius renders it asylums: others clefts or
excavations, which is more aptly descriptive, has the ancient versions in
its favour, and admits of an equally satisfactory derivation.   מְרוֹם שִׁבְתּוֹ
§ 279, the lofty place of his inhabiting, i. e. which he inhabits ; this may
be in apposition to בְחַגְוֵי סֶלַע, from which the prep. בְּ is to be repeated,
or it may be governed immediately by שֹׁבְנִי, which sometimes takes a
direct object, inhabiting his lofty dwelling in the clefts of the rocks.
מִי, the question implies that no one could.

4. Though his habitations were more difficult of access than they
were, or than it was possible for them to be, God would dislodge him.
תַּגְבִּיהַּ may be taken absolutely, if thou shalt mount high as the eagle ;
or קֵן may be supplied from the next clause, if thou make thy nest high
as the eagle, in which case the infin. שִׂים will be assimilated to it in tense,
number, and person, § 268. 1, though others regard it as a passive participle, § 158. 3 ; or better still, תַּגְבִּיהַּ may govern שִׂים directly, if thou

make high the putting of thy nest, i. e. put thy nest high, § 269. *a,*
comp. Ps. 113:5, Job 5:7. עֵ֭ין בֵּ֣ין כּֽוֹכָבִ֑ים, not apparently, i. e. upon
summits so lofty that, viewed from beneath, they might seem to be
among the stars, but really.   This is of course an impossible supposition,
but its very absurdity only shows more clearly how inevitable was their
doom.   Comp. Amos 9 : 2, etc.

5. Transported in idea to the event which he was predicting, the
prophet exclaims at the completeness of the ruin and the pillage, such
as the ordinary causes and images of desolation were inadequate to effect
or to represent. גַּנָּבִים § 187. 1. *a, thieves* abstracting stealthily, שֹׁדְדֵי
§ 35. 1, *robbers* using violence to accomplish their purpose. *If thieves
came to thee,* etc., *would they not steal* (יִגְנְבוּ fut. because subsequent to
בָּאוּ § 263. 5. *a) enough for them,* as much as they wanted, could lay their
hands on, or were able to carry away ; still they would have left something, they could not have plundered thee of every thing. That it was
not ordinary thieves from whom Edom had suffered, but something far
worse, appeared from their having stripped him of all and ruined him
utterly, as is suggested by the interjected exclamation, *how hast thou
been destroyed!* § 86. *b* (2 m. s.), § 262. 4.   A similar sense may be
obtained by rendering אִם interrogatively in both clauses of the verse,
though this meaning of the particle is mostly confined to disjunctive
questions, § 283. 2 : *Have thieves come to thee,* etc.? it might seem as
if they had, and yet this would not account for such extreme desolation ;
do they not steal (fut. in habitual sense, § 263. 4) *enough for them?* they
do not despoil of every thing, as has been done in this case. Or אִם
both here and in ver. 6 may introduce an interrogation, though this is
less forcible than the exclamation: *If thieves had come to thee,* etc., *how
couldest thou have been destroyed* (pret. modified by the preceding condition, § 262. 1) as thou hast been?   The least satisfactory of all the interpretations which have been proposed, supposes that the prophet does
not contrast the 'thieves,' etc. with the actual plunderers of Edom, but
identifies them. *If thieves come to thee* (prop. *shall have come,* pret. in
relation to the following future, § 262. 1) as they certainly shall, etc.,
will they not steal their fill? the implication being not that they will
leave something, but that they will take every thing that they can get.
If grape gatherers, etc., *will they not leave* mere *gleanings,* i. e. the least
possible remnant?

6. בֹצְרִים agrees with עָלָיו as a collective noun, § 275. 2.   מַצְפֻּנָיו *secret places,* § 191. 3, or *hidden things,* concealed treasures, § 191. 5.

7. Edom's impregnable position could not protect him against this
unsparing pillage. His other grounds of dependence, the friendly dis-

position of allied nations and his own wisdom and valour would be
equally unavailing. From the description of this desolation the prophet
now reverts to the circumstances which preceded it. אַנְשֵׁי בְרִיתֶךָ *men of
thy covenant*, i. e. those in covenant with thee; and as the relations
spoken of are those of a nation, allied nations and not merely individuals must be intended. These have so far violated their engagements
and disappointed thy reasonable expectations, that they *have sent thee*
(pret. § 262. 4) *to the border*. When thou hast gone to them to obtain
the stipulated aid against invading foes, they have conducted thee, in
the person of thy representatives or ambassadors sent for this purpose,
to the borders of their territory, not in token of respect and honour,
as though the meaning were, they lavish every attention upon thee,
and make fair promises which they never fulfil; because upon this understanding of their act, the most essential thought, the non-fulfilment of
their promises, is not expressed. Their sending thee to the border is
simply equivalent to dismissing thee, refusing the solicited aid, and
sending thee out of the country. It has also with less probability been
understood to mean that they refuse to harbour the fugitives escaped
from the devastation before described; *they sent thee*, i. e. this fleeing
remnant which alone survived, *to the border;* or to denote active hostility, the border upon this hypothesis being not the limit of their own
territory, but that of Edom, *they sent thee to* thy *border*, i. e. expelled
thee to it and beyond it. This, however, would more naturally be attributed to the nations spoken of in ver. 1. The allies of Edom refuse
in his extremity to grant him aid; and what is yet more unexpected and
trying, אַנְשֵׁי שְׁלֹמֶךָ *the men of thy peace*, the nations at peace with thee,
and upon whose neutrality, at least, if not assistance, thou couldest
count, *have deceived thee, have prevailed with respect to thee*, i. e. over
thee. They have by open force, or secret treachery, taken the side of thy
foes to their advantage and thy hurt. And most astounding of all, לַחְמֶךָ,
either by a bold figure, or by an unusual ellipsis, although it is one
easily supplied from the preceding words, for *men of thy bread*, be-
friended by thee in their times of want, or deriving their subsistence
from thee, requite thy kindness with perfidy and injury. יָשִׂימוּ, fut. because the prophet speaks as if in the midst of what he is describing,
§ 263. 5. *a*. Edom has found himself disappointed in two classes, the
nations with whom he was in alliance, and those with whom he was at
peace; one class yet remains, those who had eaten his bread, and there
a similar disappointment awaits him. It may be observed here, that
these classes need not be exclusive of each other: the same nation might
perhaps belong to one or t another, according to the aspect under which

it is contemplated. But all, upon whom Edom could have reposed any reliance, failed to meet his natural and legitimate expectations. מְזוֹר, variously rendered *snare*, *falsehood*, and *wound*. The construction above proposed is on the one hand preferable to that which violates the accents by connecting לַחְמְךָ with the preceding clause, *the men of thy peace* and *of thy bread have*, etc. ; and on the other to that which governs לַחְמְךָ by יָשִׂימוּ *they*, indef., § 243. 2, *will make thy bread a snare under thee*, whether this be understood to mean that they treacherously entrap the fleeing remnant of Edom under pretence of affording them subsistence, or that they ungratefully replace or requite the bread which they have received from Edom by setting a snare for him. בּוֹ suf. refers not to מָזוֹר *snare*, *there is no perceiving it*, Edom does not perceive the snare set for him, which gives a wrong sense to תְּבוּנָה ; but it refers to Edom § 279, *there is no understanding in him*. This is not here stated as an explanation of the ill-usage just recited, as though he had brought it upon himself by his own folly ; nor as a deduction from it, as though his being so deceived and ensnared evidenced a lack of intelligence ; nor as a consequence of it, as though the perplexities resulting from the treachery of his supposed friends induced an entire confusion of counsels. It is rather a fresh particular in the hopelessness of his condition. Every resource fails him. He is not only deserted by others on whom he relied, but his own wisdom, in which he prided himself, and for which he was famed, Jer. 49 : 7, forsakes him.

8. This is not accidental or unexplained, but due to a special divine infliction. הֲלוֹא expects an affirmative answer. וְהַאֲבַדְתִּי § 112. 3, § 287. 3.

9. They should be deprived of courage as well as of sagacity. וְחַתּוּ § 100. 2. *a* (2). לְמַעַן expresses not simply the result, *so that*, but the design, *in order that*. Their bravery is taken from them with the view of giving them up to helpless slaughter. אִישׁ, used as an indefinite pronoun, *every one*. מִקָּטֶל, the sense of the prep. is not negative, *without a battle*, which does not give the noun its proper signification ; nor causal, *on account of slaughter*, thy slaughter of Jacob, for this was chargeable not upon Edom, but upon 'the strangers,' ver. 11 ; but instrumental, *by slaughter*. It violates the accents to connect this with the next verse, and read, *on account of the slaughter* and *on account of the violence*, etc.

10. The crime by which Edom has incurred so terrible a retribution. מֵחֲמַס, prep. causal, noun constr. before its object, § 254. 9. *a*, *on account of violence*, wrong, done to *thy brother*. תְּכַסְּךָ, not in allusion to blushes covering the countenance, nor to the disposition of those who

are ashamed to conceal or veil the face, but *shame shall cover*, overspread or overwhelm *thee*.   וְּכִסְּתָ alludes to ‎‑רָבְכָ: ver. 9.   Marg. see on Judg. 13 : 18 ; *other copies* accent ‎בְ, in which case the Vav must be regarded as simply conjunctive, or else the accent remains on the penult contrary to the ordinary rule after Vav Conversive, § 100. 2.

11. The time and circumstances of the commission of this crime. Esau's hostility toward Jacob was transmitted to his descendants, and revealed itself in the whole course of their history. It culminated at the overthrow of Jerusalem by the Chaldeans. In this hour of Judah's calamity, Edom, instead of burying his rancour, and showing the commiseration which might have been expected from a kindred people, displayed a malicious joy at the downfall of his ancient rival. He made common cause with the foreign invader, and added his insults and outrages to those of the merciless enemy, Ps. 137 : 7, Lam. 4 : 21. 22. Passing by all inferior manifestations of this long cherished animosity, the prophet singles out this most glaring and wanton exhibition of it, which he was enabled to foresee. בְּיוֹם connects not with what precedes, 'On account of the violence, etc. in the day ;' but with what follows, 'In the day, etc., thou too wast as one of them ;' indefinitely, as in Gen. 2 : 4. בְּעָמְדְךָ § 106. *a*. מִנֶּגֶד *over against, opposite*, whether as a spectator or as an enemy. בְּיוֹם, coördinate with the preceding בְּיוֹם. חֵילוֹ *forces, host*, as in ver. 20, or *wealth, substance*, as in ver. 13. בָּאוּ, change of construction from the infin. to the pret. § 282. *c*, with a direct object, § 271. 2, though it is commonly followed by the prep. בְּ *into*, or לְ, אֶל *to*. בְּשַׁעֲרוֹ § 255. 1, comp. on Gen. 3 : 22.

12. Instead of proceeding to describe the conduct of Edom at this time of Judah's sore distress, the prophet appears to be a witness of its atrocity, and in impassioned terms begs Edom not to commit the crimes which he is on the point or in the act of committing, viz., not to indulge in malicious joy at Judah's downfall, ver. 12, not to take part in the sack and plunder of Jerusalem, ver. 13, and not to slaughter or betray Judah's hapless fugitives, ver. 14. וְאַל‑תֵּרֶא § 264, § 171. 1, cannot mean, *thou shouldest not have looked*, but must be rendered *look not*. As it would be unnatural and contrary to analogy to dissuade from that which had already been committed, the conduct of Edom here complained of must have been still future, and hence the preterites of ver. 11 are prophetic like those of vs. 2. 6. 7. The prophecy must accordingly have been delivered prior to the destruction of Jerusalem by Nebuchadnezzar, and we thus have an incidental corroboration of its date as inferred from its position among the minor prophets after Amos and before Jonah and Micah. בְּיוֹם‑ may express the time of the action, in

which case נֵצֶר must stand absolutely without an object, *look not* at what may offer itself to your sight *in the day*, etc. ; or coördinating still the second בְּיוֹם of this clause with the first, בְּ may connect the verb with its object, denoting that the sight dwells upon it and rests in it with satisfaction, see on Gen. 44 : 34, Judg. 16 : 27, *look*, gaze *not at the day of thy brother*, i. e. the period of his calamity, comp. Ps. 137 : 7, *at the day of*, etc. ; or, which the regular structure of the following clauses seems to require, the first בְּיוֹם may express the object of the verb, and the second the time of the action, *gaze not at the day of thy brother in the day*, etc. נֵכְרוֹ, Ges., *his strange fate, calamity;* others, his being treated as a stranger, *his rejection.* תַּגְדֵּל פִּיךָ *enlarge thy mouth*, as a gesture of derision, Ps. 22 : 8, 35 : 21, Isa. 57 : 4, Lam. 2 : 16, or *make great thy mouth*, as the organ of speech, i. e. utter proud and insolent things, comp. Ezek. 35 : 13.

13. אַל־תַּשְׁלַחְנָה. This difficult form has been variously explained. Some make it 2 f. pl., the Edomites being addressed as women on account of the dastardly conduct ascribed to them, comp. Nah. 3 : 13 ; others 2 m. s. with נָה added for the particle of entreaty נָא, but this is never written as one word with the verb, never has ה in place of א, and when connected with a dissuasion its proper place is between אַל and the verb, comp. Gen. 18 : 3, the only exception is Judg. 19 : 23 ; others conceive נָה to be ן paragogic preceded by ה epenthetic, a combination which never occurs. Perhaps the simplest and best explanation, though it is not free from difficulties, is to regard תַּשְׁלַחְנָה as an unusual form for תִּשְׁלָחֶנָּה with 3 f. s. suffix and ן epenthetic, § 88 (3 f. pl.), *put it not forth*, viz., thy hand, which the prophet has in mind without distinctly naming it. Like instances of the employment of a suffix with reference to an object not mentioned in the context, but easily deducible from it, occur elsewhere, Isa. 1 : 6, 8 : 21, Ps. 18 : 15, 68 : 11. 15. Comp. 1 Sam. 24 : 11.

15. כִּי introduces the reason by which the preceding exhortations are enforced, *for* a time of recompense is coming shortly. יוֹם־יְהֹוָה *the day of Jehovah*, which belongs especially to him, inasmuch as he shall then manifest himself in his true character, particularly in his attributes of mercy and of justice. It shall be a day of gracious reward to his own people and of righteous retribution to his and their foes. In contrast with the day of Judah, ver. 12, the period of his humiliation and defeat, it is the period of Jehovah's exaltation and triumph, which his oppressed people shall share, but which shall bring ruin upon all who oppress them or oppose him. This day is further characterized by the words עַל־כָּל־הַגּוֹיִם, which are to be connected with יוֹם־יְהֹוָה, not with קָרוֹב, to denote the universality of the judgment then to be executed. By the

day of the Lord, of which the prophets speak, is manifestly meant not merely the final period of judgment to be executed simultaneously upon the whole word, from which the representation takes its form and colour ; but they likewise include under it the entire series of particular and partial judgments wrought successively on each of the nations in the course of God's providence. All spring from one source, and possess the same character. They form one work of divine retribution. The punishment of Edom is not viewed correctly, if it is regarded as an isolated fact. It is really a part of God's universal work of judgment, wrought in the course of human history, and consummated at its close. This day, which expands itself thus into a protracted period, is further said to be קָרוֹב *near*, because punishment would swiftly follow the offence which has been described. When that time arrives, to which the prophet has in idea been transported, and out of the midst of which he has been speaking, when Jerusalem shall fall and Edom shall insult over its ruins, his own doom shall not be long delayed. That portion of ' the day of the Lord upon all the nations,' to which Edom's punishment is assigned, shall then be near, at the very doors. נֶעֶשָׂה § 35. 1. גְּמֻלְךָ, divine punishment is not an arbitrary infliction, but simply the recoil of sin, the return of one's own deeds upon himself. בְּרֹאשֶׁךָ, prep., denotes conjunction or contact, see on Gen. 2 : 24, 3 : 3. The head, as the most prominent and important member, is the representative of the person. Hence the symbolical acts of crowning, Zech. 6 : 11, or anointing the head, Ps. 23 : 5, uncovering the head, Lev. 13 : 45, 21 : 10, casting dust on the head, Josh. 7 : 6, laying hands on the head, Lev. 1 : 4. Hence, too, the head is spoken of as bearing good, Isa. 35 : 10, Prov. 10 : 6 ; and evil, Jer. 23 : 19 ; guilt and punishment, Josh. 2 : 19, Joel 3 : 4. 7 ; this last is particularly appropriate when, as in the present instance, the offence is a capital one, and is to be capitally punished.

16. This verse confirms the statement of the preceding, that in the day of the Lord upon all nations an exact retribution shall be meted out to Edom. He has been guilty of drinking, indulging in festive carousals in his insolent exultation over Judah's calamity : and he shall be punished by having to drink, in common with other nations, a draught which shall cause his destruction. The sin of Edom is not, of course, the ground of the punishment of all nations, each of which is to suffer for its own crimes ; but it suggests the figure under which the doom of all is set forth. As the experience of pleasure or pain may be aptly represented by tasting or drinking what is agreeable, Ps. 36 : 9, or the reverse, Jer. 23 : 15, the endurance of divine wrath finds its appropriate emblem in a bitter and deadly draught which men are compelled to

swallow, Job 21 : 20, Ps. 75 : 9, Isa. 51 : 17. 22, Jer. 25 : 15, etc
אֱדוֹם, Edom is addressed as in the preceding verses. עַל־ *upon*, indi
cating the place of their revelry, which is more natural in the connection
than *over*, indicating its subject or occasion. הַר קָדְשִׁי § 254. 6, § 256,
my mountain of holiness, i. e. *my holy mountain*. תָּמִיד *continually*, not
of course that each nation should continue for ever drinking, for the
draughts are, as is immediately added, productive of speedy extinction ;
but they should drink in unending series until the entire number was
exhausted, comp. the phrase *continual burnt-offering*, Ex. 29 : 42, continual *shew-bread*, Ex. 25 : 30, 2 Chron. 2 : 3. Several manuscripts, and
a few of the early printed editions, substitute for this word סָבִיב *around*
or *in turn*, which, though preferred by some commentators, is doubtless
a gloss at first inserted in the margin by way of explanation, and subsequently transferred to the text. The common text has in its favour the
best and most accurate manuscripts and all the ancient versions. It is
an illustration of the tendency to substitute an easier reading in place
of one which involves a real or fancied difficulty. The rendering of this
phrase in the Septuagint may also serve to illustrate, on the one hand,
how errors may arise from the eye, transcribers or translators not seeing
accurately what is before them, and on the other, how even the errors
of a version may be turned to account by the critic, and afford him data
from which to conclude upon the true form of the original text. For
וְשָׁתוּ כָל־הַגּוֹיִם תָּמִיד the LXX. have πίονται πάντα τὰ ἔθνη οἶνον. It is
plain that the translator, misled by the similarity of the letters, has mis·
taken תמיר for חמיר = חֶמֶר *wine*. וְשָׁתוּ, emphatic repetition of the finite
form of the verb, § 282. *b*, *drink and drink*, i. e. continue drinking until
the whole is exhausted. וְלָעוּ § 100. 2. *a* (2). כְּלֹא § 285. 3, *as* those
who, etc. In the exposition of this verse already given, the word *drink*
is taken in its literal sense in the first clause, and figuratively in the
second. Other constructions have been proposed, which preserve the
same sense in both clauses. Thus literally in both : 1. *As ye* Edomites
have drunk upon my holy mountain, exulting over the ruin of Jerusalem,
all nations shall drink, exulting over your ruin. But *all* nations were
not to be combined against Edom., ver. 1 ; the essential thing in this interpretation, that the drinking of all the nations had relation to Edom,
or expressed their joy at his destruction, is not in the text, but must be
supplied ; and the kind of drinking intended is shown by its effect, *they
shall be as* those who *have not been*, who have never existed. Or, 2. *As
ye* Edomites *have drunk upon my holy mountain, all nations* shall do
the same, shall inflict similar injuries and insults, *shall drink* there and
perish in consequence, *be as* those who *have not been*. But this is inap·

propriate to the connection; the particle כִּי *for*, with which the verse begins, must be followed by a confirmation of the preceding statement that, as Edom has done it shall be done to him. The same objection may be made to those constructions in which *drink* is understood figuratively in both clauses, viz., 3. *As ye*, Edomites, *have drunk* the cup of divine wrath, the preterite prophetic § 262. 4, *on account of my holy mountain*, i. e. for your injurious treatment of God's people, *all nations shall drink* the same. And, 4. *As ye*, Jews (who are, however, nowhere addressed throughout the prophecy, and whom there is nothing in the context to suggest), *have drunk* of the divine wrath *upon my holy mountain, all nations shall drink* the same, but more copiously, and for a longer term. Thus understood, the verse would be parallel to Jer. 25 : 29, 49 : 12.

17. In contrast with the perdition of Edom and the nations, in contrast, too, with the injurious treatment that Judah shall experience at their hands, the concluding section of this prophecy dwells upon the ultimate salvation, victory, and enlargement of God's people. וּבְהַר § 254. 3. פְּלֵיטָה is by some regarded as an abstract, *escape, deliverance*, by others as a collective, *an escaped*, or *delivered* band, § 198. While the nations, who are enemies of God, are doomed to extinction, God's kingdom, of which Zion is the centre and seat, shall be preserved. It must pass through sore trials, such as that referred to vs. 11–14, and others beside, but there shall still be a remnant surviving them all, comp. Joel 3 : 5. קֹדֶשׁ may either be the subject, *and there shall be holiness*, viz. in mount Zion, or the predicate, *and it*, the body of those who have escaped, *shall be holiness*, or holy. This denotes not merely inward purity, but sacredness and inviolability. They belong to God, and are consequently under his special protection, comp. Joel 4 : 17, Jer. 2 : 3. בֵּית יַעֲקֹב, the entire covenant people. This expression is not to be restricted to Judah, either here or in the next verse. מוֹרָשֵׁיהֶם § 216. 1. a, *their own possessions*, from which they had previously been driven, see ver. 11; or it may mean the possessions of all the nations, ver. 16. The people of God shall not only be protected from further injury from other nations, but they shall conquer and possess the world, comp. ver. 21, Dan. 7 : 27. Upon the latter view of its meaning, the idea is here expressed in the general, of which an individual application is made in the following verses appropriate to the subject of this prophecy.

18. וּבֵית יוֹסֵף, *the house of Joseph* properly denotes the tribes of Ephraim and Manasseh, who were descended from him, Josh. 16 : 4, but is here applied to the kingdom of the ten tribes, which was under the

leadership of Ephraim, see on Ezek. 37 : 19. Although included in the house of Jacob already spoken of, they are separately mentioned to preclude all doubt as to their interest in what is here declared, and to give greater prominence to the reunion of the sundered tribes against the common enemy, comp. Isa. 11 : 13. 14. The figure employed suggests the idea of easy and complete destruction, comp. Isa. 5 : 24, 10 · 17.

19. The territorial enlargement of the covenant people in all directions. הַנֶּגֶב § 275. 2. *b.* The inhabitants of the southern part of Judah, contiguous to Edom, should remove southward and occupy this vacated territory. The dwellers in the vale, the low country in the west of Judah, should spread westward over the territory of the Philistines. וְיָרְשׁוּ. The subject is not expressed. Judah is evidently intended, as may readily be inferred from the previous mention of the south and the vale which were parts of that tribe. Judah shall expand not only southward and westward, but northward into the territory of Ephraim and Samaria, thus dispossessing Benjamin, who shall in turn occupy Gilead on the east of Jordan.

20. The ten tribes will thus be pushed northward into Phenicia. גֹּלָה *and the captivity of this host,* this captive host *of the children of Israel,* the ten tribes which, it is here presupposed, shall have been carried into captivity, shall possess *what Canaanites* do, the territory of the Canaanites or Phenicians, comp. Isa. 23 : 11, *unto Zarephath.* This yields a better sense than to make אֲשֶׁר־כְּנַעֲנִים descriptive of גֹּלָה, which must then be coördinated with the following גֹּלָה as the subject of יִרְשׁוּ in the last clause : *the captivity,* etc., *who are Canaanites,* etc., i. e. are captives in Phenicia and reside there, *and the captivity of Jerusalem,* etc., *shall possess,* etc. בִּסְפָרַד, some remote locality known only from this passage : it may perhaps be used in a general sense to denote a distant region. Some suppose it to be an appellative noun meaning *dispersion,* comp. root פָּרַד. Jerome identifies it with the Bosphorus, which may be a mere conjecture, from the sound of the name with the preposition prefixed. The rabbins give this name to Spain, Ἑσπερία, and make צָרְפַת to be France, though this latter is manifestly the town of Sarepta. הַנֶּגֶב׃, as the restored inhabitants of Jerusalem more than fill their former residence, they spread over the cities of the south vacated by the occupation of Edom, ver. 19.

21. מוֹשִׁעִים, an allusion to the judges whom God had at a former period raised up to deliver his people and punish their oppressors, comp. Judg. 2 : 16, Neh. 9 : 27. Such divinely commissioned champions should again ascend mount Zion, or perhaps, as the captivity is alluded to in the preceding verse, come up out of exile to mount Zion, see on Gen

39:1. The people restored from exile should be provided with deliverers and saviours, including and culminating in the great antitype of all. יָשַׁע § 22. a (5), see on Judg. 15:20. Marg. see on Judg. 13:25.

NAHUM. CHAPTER I.

This prophecy is appropriately divided into three chapters, of which Chap. i. announces the divine purpose to destroy Nineveh.

Chap. ii. describes its overthrow.

Chap. iii. assigns the reason for it, and declares its inevitable certainty.

1. The opening verse contains the title to the book, the first clause of which explains its subject, and the second names its author. Like the titles prefixed to other prophecies, it forms part of the original and authentic text, and is to be regarded as written by the prophet himself. מַשָּׂא is by some rendered *utterance, prophecy*, by others *burden*. In favour of the latter may be urged, (1) the uniform usage of the word when employed as it is here. It is not applied to prophecies indiscriminately, but only to such as are of a grievous and threatening import, which impose a burden of woe upon those who are the objects of them. (2) This is also its constant meaning, when not used in this technical sense; and it springs most directly from the radical signification of the verb נָשָׂא *to lift up, to bear: to lift up the voice* is a secondary application. The other meanings attributed to it by Gesenius, viz., *song*, in 1 Chron. 15:22. 27, and *proverb*, in Prov. 30:1, 31:1, are supposititious. See Hengstenberg's remarks on Zech. 9:1, in his Christology. (3) It never stands in the construct before the author of the prophecy, as it might be expected to do if it meant *the utterance of*, but (with the exception of Zech. 12:1, Mal. 1:1, where it is in the construct of apposition) only before its object, as here, *the burden of Nineveh*, the load which Nineveh must sustain. נַחוּם, see on Obad. ver. 1. הָאֶלְקֹשִׁי has been explained as a patronymic, *descended from Elkosh*, but more probably denotes the place of the prophet's birth or residence, § 194. 1.

The chapter consists of two parts, viz.:

vs. 2–8, a majestic description of Jehovah in those attributes which determine him to destroy Nineveh.

vs. 9–14, the completeness of the destruction which he has resolved to effect.

2. This is not a general account of the greatness and glory of the divine nature, but the prophecy is appropriately introduced by an exhibition of the basis upon which it rests. The overthrow of Nineveh is

grounded upon the immutable perfections of Jehovah, his jealousy and avenging wrath. אֵל from אול *to be strong* § 186. c (וּ root) in the usage of prose differs from אֱלֹהִים in never standing alone, but always associated with a qualifying adjective, or another divine name, or in the construct before a following noun. In poetry, on the contrary, this rule does not hold, and אֵל is often used without any adjunct, where the more prosaic אֱלֹהִים might have been expected. It is in prose never joined with suffixes, and in poetry only with that of the first pers. sing. The rule of poetry might here be applied, and אֵל taken separately as the subject, *God is jealous*. But the symmetry of the verse, which consists of three clauses with Jehovah as the subject, and a double attribute in in each, the collocation of the words, § 249. 1, and the comparison of the parallel passages, Ex. 20 : 5, 34 : 14, Deut. 4 : 24, 5 : 9, 6 : 15, Josh. 24 : 19, make it preferable to translate *Jehovah is a jealous and avenging God*, or *a jealous God and an avenger*. קַנּוֹא § 187. 1, as in Josh. 24 : 19, elsewhere קַנָּא *zealous*, denoting the energy of the divine nature, so that his love and hatred are not inoperative, as in the case of heathen deities, but active and efficient; and still more specifically *jealous*, indicating the actuating motive of this divine zeal and its twofold direction, as it springs from a regard to his own honour and worship, wherein he cannot endure a rival, Ex. 34 : 14, or from affection for his people, whom none may harm with impunity, Joel 2 : 18. Injuries suffered in either of these respects his jealousy leads him to *avenge*. נֹקֵם יְהוָֹה, the triple repetition of these words is not designed to suggest an allusion to the trinity, nor to three successive injuries inflicted by the Assyrians or to be inflicted upon them, but emphasizes and renders prominent the idea expressed, § 280. 3. *b*. The first clause deduces God's avenging or revenging from its primary source, the zeal or jealousy of the divine nature; the second reveals its ardour or intensity as attended by the *heat* of his wrath; the third indicates its objects, *his enemies*. בַּעַל חֵמָה, comp. Gen. 37 : 19; the divine wrath is not a transient fervour, but that settled indignation against evil and determination to punish it, which is inseparable from God's holiness. נוֹטֵר *keeping, retaining* wrath, which is easily supplied from חֵמָה in the preceding clause, though the same ellipsis occurs elsewhere, Ps. 103 : 9, Jer. 3 : 5. 12; others render *watching* with a view to punishment, comp. Job 10 : 14. The two verbs of this clause are likewise combined in Lev. 19 : 18.

3. This avenging jealousy is not discredited by the long delay of judgment, for it is associated, as the prophet adds, with the attribute of forbearance or long-suffering (אֶרֶךְ § 216. 1. *e*, § 254. 10), which is here particularly mentioned, as it had been so remarkably exhibited in

the case of Nineveh, Jon. 4 : 2. This, however, it is immediately de·
clared, involves neither weakness nor a relaxation of his purpose to punish. גְּדָל־כֹּחַ § 13. *u*, § 215. 1. *c*, Marg. see on Judg. 13 : 17 ; *power*,
in its ordinary sense, as exercised in the production of effects *ab extra*,
not power of endurance or self-restraint, as has needlessly been assumed
with the view of finding an exact parallel to the words immediately preceding. נַקֵּה § 92. *d*, § 174. 3. יְנַקֶּה § 172. 3, the phrase is drawn
from Ex. 34 : 7, Num. 14 : 18. יְהוָה, emphatically prefixed to its clause,
and repeated in the suffix at the end, § 281 ; the LXX connect it with
what precedes, but this violates the accents. This name occurs five
times in this and the foregoing verse, and ten times in the course of this
chapter. The recital of the attributes of Jehovah is followed by a sub-
lime description of his going forth in wrath to punish his enemies. This
is not the description of a thunder storm or of other natural phenomena,
which were conceived to indicate the presence of the deity. Nor is it a
prediction that the overthrow of Nineveh would be accompanied by
great catastrophes in the physical world. It is a poetical representation
of the wrath and power of Jehovah, whose vengeance is here denounced.
At the same time, the figures employed here and in other passages of a
similar nature, have not only a symbolical fitness, but, to a certain extent,
a real basis. Like phenomena have attended the manifestations of God's
presence, as the cloud, tempest, and earthquake of the descent on Sinai,
the drying up of the Red sea and of the Jordan, etc. ; and they shall in
vastly increased potency attend his final coming to judge the world.
These occasional and transient occurrences in the past and in the future
are manifestations of a permanent fact, which is valid for all time, the
infinite superiority of Jehovah, and his absolute control over all the
works of his hand, so that such majestic displays of his omnipotence are
imminent every where, and might at any time be exhibited if such were
his pleasure. The prophet consequently pictures to us the God who has
convulsed external nature by his presence and coming, who shall hereafter do so on a far grander scale, and who is able to do so to any extent
at all times. עָנָן, storm and cloud, as natural emblems of what is dark
and threatening, are fit accompaniments or symbols of the wrath of
God. The cloud, which envelopes or attends the advancing deity, is
beautifully likened to the dust raised by a warrior marching to battle.

4. The wrathful and avenging march of God spreads desolation and
terror. Grand and conspicuous objects of nature feel the weight of his
displeasure, or tremble in dread of it. גֹּעֵר, see on Gen. 37 : 10. The
vividness of the description is heightened by the use of the participle,
which denotes present time, § 266. 2, and places the action, as it were,

before the eyes, *He is rebuking.* The following future with Vav Con-versive is also to be rendered as a present, and denotes an action imme-diately consequent upon the preceding, § 265. *a.* The preterites that come after, announce in quick succession the further effects of this dis-play of wrath, as it seizes upon one object after another. וַיִּתְמֹגְגוּ § 150. 2 (p. 182). אֻמְלַל § 115. יָשֵׁב. The highlands of Bashan in the east, the promontory of Carmel in the west, and the lofty range of Lebanon in the north, were the most conspicuous objects in Palestine, and distin-guished for their fertility and verdure. They instantly wither at the rebuke of God. The mention of them here affords an incidental proof that the prophet was himself in the holy land, and not, as some have imagined, in exile in Assyria.

5. מִפָּנָיו, prep. in its causal sense, *on account of him, at him.* וַתִּשָּׂא, intrans., *lifted itself up, heaved,* as in an earthquake. This is better than the explanation, *raised itself,* i. e. went up in smoke, the figure being suggested by the melting of the hills before the fire of God's wrath, or the rendering *lifted up* its voice, cried out in terror. תֵּבֵל, from the root יָבַל *to come forth,* § 190. *b,* the productive or habitable earth, *the world.* It is used exclusively in poetry, and never occurs with the article, § 247. The repeated conjunction וְ — וְ, like the Latin *et — et,* signifies *both — and.* יֹשְׁבֵי § 35. 1, § 255. 1.

6. Such being the fearful consequences of his displeasure, none can resist it or stand before it. נִתְּכָה *poured out,* like fire rained down from heaven, perhaps with allusion to the judgment sent upon Sodom. הַצֻּרִים, singled out as a type of what is strongest and most enduring.

7. Another feature of the divine character, which, so far from being inconsistent with the preceding, is in reality but another side of the same essential attribute of righteousness. While to his enemies this be-tokens vengeance, it assures those who trust in him of love and protec-tion. The obverse side of this divine perfection is here presented, be-cause it contains an additional ground for the judgment upon Nineveh. יֹדֵעַ *know,* may be taken in an emphatic sense, involving acquaintance, intimacy, and friendship, comp. Ps. 144 : 3, Amos 3 : 2, Mat. 7 : 23; or it may be restricted to its ordinary meaning of simple intelligence, it being sufficient to assert that he knows who they are who trust in him; his blessing and favour follow from that as a matter of course.

8. וּבְשֶׁטֶף, the conjunction may be adversative, introducing a con-trast to what immediately precedes, *and* on the other hand, *but;* or it may be copulative, the destruction of Nineveh being a sequence of God's regard of his injured people, *and* consequently, etc. Isaiah, 8 : 8, had likened the Assyrian invasion of Judah to an inundation (שֹׁטֵף וְעָבָר).

Nahum declares that Nineveh herself shall be inundated; the figure is not to be restricted to an invading army, but includes the entire flood of evils by which she was to be visited and destroyed. Some commentators have supposed, that in addition to this figurative fulfilment, the words of the prophet were literally accomplished in an actual overflow of the Tigris, which, as Diodorus Siculus, ii. 27, narrates (he calls it the Euphrates), threw down twenty furlongs of the city wall, and thus gave entrance to the besiegers, in fulfilment of an ancient prophecy, that the city could never be taken till the river became its enemy. This would accord with the analogy of other prophecies, see on Isa. 40 : 3. The only doubt arises from the uncertainty as to the actual facts of the case. It has been made a question whether the narrative of Diodorus is entirely reliable; and if so, whether the overthrow which he describes was subsequent to the time of Nahum, and was the same that is here predicted. עֹבֵר might agree with Jehovah *passing with a flood*, but is more naturally connected with שֶׁטֶף *with an overrunning flood*, i. e. passing its bounds. מְקוֹמָהּ, the suffix refers not to כְּלָה, he will cause destruction in its place, i. e. in the place allotted to it, but to Nineveh, 1 : 1, which is prominent in the prophet's mind as the theme of his discourse. This is an additional proof that the title forms an original and integral part of the text of the prophecy, since otherwise the subject would be unexplained, and the reader left in doubt until 2 : 9. Interpreters have needlessly perplexed themselves about the form of expression here employed, as though the place of the city, or the soil on which it stood, was to be an object of destruction distinct from the city itself. If Nineveh were destroyed, of course its site would be made a desolation. It is unnecessary, therefore, to assume that Nineveh is personified as a queen, comp. Isa. 47 : 1, etc., and that *her place* or residence is the city itself. This passage affords an illustration of the manner in which various readings and wrong interpretations have arisen from a false view of the parallelism of clauses. Of the old Greek versions, Symmachus alone gives מְקוֹמָהּ its proper rendering; the rest, assuming that it should correspond in sense exactly with אֹיְבָיו of the following clause, translate, *of those rising up against him*, as if the reading were, or were equivalent to, מְקָמָיו. חֹשֶׁךְ *darkness*, a frequent figure of calamity; it may either be the subject of the verb, or stand absolutely after it to denote the place, *into darkness*, or instrument, *with darkness*, comp. on Isa. 41 : 2.

9. The second division of the chapter opens with a direct address to the Assyrians. מַה־תְּחַשְּׁבוּן § 88 (2 and 3 m.) *what will ye devise in reference to Jehovah?* his nature and purpose being what has just been described, how do you propose to resist him, or avert the destruction

which he is resolved to bring upon you? Or the reference may be to
offensive rather than defensive measures, as עַל חֹשֵׁב, ver. 11 ; *what are
ye devising in reference to, against Jehovah?* i. e. what new assault are
you meditating upon his people? You shall fail in your design ; you
shall not be allowed to afflict them again. Either of these explanations
is better than to suppose Judah addressed, *what think ye in reference to
Jehovah?* what do you imagine that he will do? צָרָה *affliction shall
not arise twice;* the allusion to ver. 7, where this same word is used of
the distress endured by God's people, determines this clause to mean,
that Judah has suffered the oppression of Nineveh, but shall never be
exposed to it again, see also 2 : 1. Another interpretation is, that God
would make such thorough work in his destruction of Nineveh, that he
would have no occasion to afflict it a second time, comp. 1 Sam. 26 : 8,
2 Sam. 20 : 10 ; another still, *the adversary* (צָרָה, as in 1 Sam. 1 : 6),
i. e. Nineveh *shall not arise twice,* shall not recover from this as from its
previous overthrow by Arbaces, comp. Jer. 51 : 64.

10. כִּי confirms the statement just made, that the Assyrians shall
never afflict Judah again ; the reason is, *for they shall have been* themselves *devoured,* consumed *as stubble,* a figure of easy, speedy, and total
destruction. אֻכָּלוּ, pret. relative to the future חָקִים § 262. 1. Its subject is qualified by the preceding participial clause, which has been variously understood according to the signification attributed to the figures
employed, and the sense put upon some of the terms. The simplest
view appears to be that which finds in these words the circumstances or
manner of their destruction. *Entangled unto* the extent of *thorns,* to
the degree that thorns are, like thorns, comp. 1 Chron. 4 : 27, i. e. joined
together in an inextricable mass, and thus affording the readier and
surer fuel to the flames, *and drunken as* by *their drink* (כְּסָבְאָם, absolutely
to denote the manner or instrument, § 274. 2. c), or, *according to their
drink,* with no other limitation than the amount of wine they have, that
is to say, either in a state of literal intoxication, as Diodorus Siculus records, or by a figure for the helplessness of drunken men, who are unable to resist or flee. Others resolve the participles into verbal forms, to
which they are often equivalent. Thus, if *being interwoven* be taken to
mean. *because they are interwoven,* etc., this clause will suggest the reason
why the Assyrians are to be destroyed, thorns, from their noxious character, being an emblem of wicked men, Ezek. 2 : 6, Mic. 7 : 4, and their
drunkenness being singled out as an evidence of their luxurious, abandoned lives. On the assumption that סִירִים has the sense of כִּירִית *stupe-
fied* (the senses *entangled* and confused) *by* flesh-pots might also be
referred to luxurious living. Or, if it mean, *although they are inter-*

woven, etc., it will represent their real or fancied security, which never
theless shall not protect them ; though their phalanx presents an im-
penetrable front, as firmly knit together as thorns, and though they have
all the confident security of merry drinkers, they are yet doomed to destruction.   Or the participles may be connected not directly with the
Assyrians but with סִירִים, and the clause describe the futility of resistance to their divinely ordained fate : *even to,* though they be like *thorns
woven together,* which defy all attempts to handle them, *and drenched as
their drink,* wet as wine itself, so that fire cannot burn them, *they shall*
nevertheless *be consumed,* etc.   : מָלֵא, not an adj. qualifying קַשׁ *full,*
mature and therefore burning more readily, but an adverb, § 235. 3 (3),
qualifying יֵשׁ, or more probably אֻכְּלוּ.

11.   This is confirmed by the example of Sennacherib, whose doom
foreshadowed that of Nineveh itself.   מִמֵּךְ, the suf. is by the majority
of interpreters referred to Nineveh, *out of thee proceeded* or *went forth.*
In the context, however, vs. 12. 13, 2 : 1, the 2 f. s. suffix (except in
כָּרַת 2 : 2) refers to Judah personified as a virgin, Isa. 37 : 22 ; in addressing Assyria the 2 masc. is used for the sake of distinction either in
the sing., ver. 14, or plur., ver. 9.   If this analogy be observed here,
Judah must be intended, *from thee has gone out,* or gone away, retreat-
ed.   יָצָא, Sennacherib, though it might also be taken collectively of all
the Assyrian monarchs who had oppressed or would oppress the people
of God, in which case יָצָא, like אֻכְּלוּ, ver. 10, must be under the influence of the preceding future.   : בְּלִיַּעַל § 195. 3, *worthlessness,* or as the
negation of what is morally good implies that which is morally bad,
wickedness, here used in its abstract sense ; among the later Jews it
came to be a name of Satan as the impersonation of wickedness, 2 Cor.
6 : 15.

12.   The completeness of his overthrow in the height of his power,
coupled with the assurance that Assyria should never be used to afflict
Judah again.   אִם־, the conditional clause, extends through כֵּן, the
apodosis beginning with וְעָבָר § 287. 2 ; *if* they, the Assyrian army
under Sennacherib, were *complete* in full strength and vigour, *and so
numerous,* as they are well known to have been, *and were so mown down,*
§ 140. 2, the figure perhaps suggested by the stubble, ver. 10 (others
render *shorn,* comp. Isa. 7 : 20), *and he,* Sennacherib, or the singular
may have a collective or distributive force, the whole, or every one of
them, *passed away,* perished, § 275. 6, *then,* by this be assured, *I have
afflicted thee,* O Judah, *and I will not afflict thee again.*   As certainly as
Sennacherib and his host were overthrown, so certainly shall Assyria be
humbled and prevented from trampling upon Judah again.   Or the

apodosis might begin with כֵּן גָּדֹלוּ *if*, even if, although, as Isa. 1 : 18, *they were complete*, etc., *yet so*, in the manner well known, or *thus*, in this condition of completeness and numbers, *were they mown down*, etc. Those who find no special allusion to the fall of Sennacherib, of which the terms are so aptly descriptive, understand this verse also collectively, and refer it to the future complete destruction of the Assyrian power, by placing these preterites, as well as that of ver. 11, under the influence of the preceding future. The suf. in וְעִנִּתִךְ is by some commentators referred to Nineveh, and the sense supposed to be, that such a blow should be struck as would not require to be repeated ; see on ver. 9.

13. יַעֲשֶׂה, what God was about to do *now*, contrasted with what he had already done to the host of Sennacherib. אֲשַׁבֵּר § 220. 1. *b* (3 pers.) *his yoke*, that of the Assyrians represented by Sennacherib ; the reference of the suffix is to חֹשֵׁב, ver. 11.

14. עָלֶיךָ, the oppressor spoken of in the immediately preceding verses is now addressed, § 279 ; the prep. indicates the subject of the command, *concerning thee*, see on Gen. 41 : 15, though it sometimes also denotes the person commanded, see on Gen. 2 : 16. מִשִּׁמְךָ, prep. in a partitive sense. The race shall be extinguished, not that of the monarch alone, but of the empire ; the Assyrian name shall cease to be perpetuated. אָשִׂים, the idols cannot even protect themselves, much less their worshippers. The Medes, who overturned Nineveh, and the Persians, with whom they were associated in the capture of Babylon, were the great iconoclasts of antiquity, comp. Isa. 21 : 9. קִבְרֶךָ § 65. *b*, *I will make thy grave*, i. e. cause thee to be slain and buried. Or שִׂים may, as it often does, govern a double object, *I will make* it, viz., the house of thy gods, *thy grave ;* this had a general fulfilment in a figurative sense, in so far as the idols of the Assyrians proved their ruin instead of their salvation, and a specific literal fulfilment in the murder of Sennacherib in an idol temple, Isa. 37 : 38. This event occurred several years after his invasion of Judah, and it is in this interval that the prophecy of Nahum was most probably uttered. Such a combination of the figurative and the literal is not unusual in the prophets, see on ver. 8. קַלּוֹתָ § 262. 2, *thou hast been* and art *light*, in a moral sense, equivalent to the sentence passed upon the Babylonish monarch, Dan. 5 : 27, ' weighed in the balances and found wanting.' Others render, *thou art become insignificant*, thy power is broken ; but this could not be a reason for the divine order just recited, except upon the forced assumption that ' I will make thy grave' means, thou shalt receive a dishonoured in place of a regal funeral.

CHAPTER II.

The divine purpose to destroy Nineveh has been announced, and traced to its source in God's immutable attributes. The actual execution of this purpose is now exhibited to view. This chapter, besides

an introduction, ver. 1, announcing the fall of the great oppressor, and

a conclusion, ver. 14, in which Jehovah pledges himself to effect it, is mainly devoted, vs. 2–13, to a vivid description of the overthrow of Nineveh. This may be further subdivided into,

(1) the preliminaries of the siege, by which the wrongs of Israel shall be avenged, vs. 2. 3.

(2) the assault, vs. 4. 5.

(3) the ineffectual defence, vs. 6. 7.

(4) the sack of the city, vs. 8–11.

(5) the resulting desolation, vs. 12. 13.

1. A messenger is seen coming in the distance with the tidings of Nineveh's fall. That this is the subject of his message rather than the disaster to Sennacherib, is evident, since it is the former and not the latter which is detailed in the following chapter, and is the principal theme of the prophecy, and Judah was once successfully invaded by Assyria after the time of Sennacherib, when king Manasseh was taken prisoner, 2 Chr. 33 : 11. This verse, which forms a kind of intermediate link between the first and second chapters, is attached to the former in the English and other modern versions, as a sequel to the divine purpose therein declared, but to the latter in the Hebrew and in the ancient versions, as preliminary to the more detailed account of its execution. The existing division of the sacred text into chapters and verses, it should be remembered, is altogether of recent origin, and is purely conventional. It is in the majority of instances, though not always, skillfully made ; yet, however valuable for purposes of convenience, it is never to be regarded as authoritative, and should not be suffered to destroy the sense of the unity of that which, as originally prepared, formed one continuous composition, with no breaks or pauses other than the subject itself suggests. הִנֵּה *lo !* as if pointing to an object of sight, and one that was unexpected and surprising. הֶהָרִים, the art. may be generic, § 245. 5, or it may specify the mountains in the direction of Nineveh, to which all eyes were directed. Mountains are spoken of, not as points from which a proclamation could be more extensively heard, as Isa. 40 : 9, but where a coming messenger could first be seen. רַגְלֵי, the feet are particularly mentioned,

as the organs used in running, comp. Acts 5 : 9. מְבַשֵּׂר, with the single exception of 1 Sam. 4 : 17, used only of a *bearer of good tidings*, see on Isa. 40 : 9. דָּגַ § 141. 1 (p. 174), § 271. 3. The meaning of this exhortation, which may be uttered either by the messenger or by the prophet, is not that the annual gatherings at Jerusalem, and the attendance upon the services of the temple, which had been interrupted by invasion or the fear of it, might now with safety be resumed. But this distinguished benefit on the part of God demands a new and strenuous devotion to his service, and calls especially for a celebration of the joyful festivals commemorative of deliverances which were themselves types for all future time (see on Ex. 20 : 8), and have now had a fresh fulfilment, and for a performance of the vows made in entreating relief from the recent oppression. יְהוּדָה § 275. 2. *b.* חֻגֶּיךָ § 269. *a.* —עֹבֵר לְ, marg. as 1 : 3. בָּךְ *in thee*, the land of Judah, for which, after the verb 'pass,' our idiom substitutes *through thee.* בְּלִיַּעַל, abstract for concrete, *wicked*, here used as a significant name of the monarch or empire of Assyria, comp. the enigmatical designations Jareb, Hos. 5 : 13, 10 : 6; Sheshach, Jer. 25 : 26, 51 : 41; Merathaim and Pekod, Jer. 50 : 21; Rahab, Isa. 51 : 9. This generic name shows that the person or object so designated is not viewed simply as an individual, but as the representative of a class or the embodiment of a principle. He is the type of the wicked foes of God and his people. It is in this character that he is cut off, and for reasons grounded in those attributes of God which determine him to destroy all such. The fall of Nineveh is, therefore, a typical fact. The principles of the divine administration, which it illustrates, as these are exhibited in this prophecy, secure the fall of every other power of wickedness, the complete and final deliverance of the true people of God, and the establishment of the reign of righteousness and peace. Nahum's prophecy, and that of Obadiah (see particularly ver. 21), may thus be said to be negatively predictive of the kingdom of the Messiah. The opening words of this verse are found again in Isa. 52 : 7, where they are used generically of the good things in store for the people of God, of which the deliverance from the Babylonish exile was a type and pledge. The apostle Paul, Rom. 10 : 15, repeats them in application to the glad tidings of the gospel. This triple repetition of the same language is not to be regarded as a casual and undesigned coincidence, nor an accommodation of what was originally spoken in reference to one subject to another wholly different. But the identity in expression directs attention to a real identity in subject. The destruction of Nineveh and the return from Babylon foreshadowed the salvation from sin, which is proclaimed in the gospel. נָלֹה § 220. 1. *b* (3 pers.), not from מָלֵא as the LXX seem to have explained it.

2. The advance of the invader, in view of which Nineveh is admonished to take every possible precaution. צָבָה, used technically of military expeditions, 1 Kin. 15 : 17, 20 : 22. מֵפִיץ may be a noun, as in Prov. 25 : 18, *hammer, maul*, but is more probably a part. *dispersing*, or, as others render, *dashing in pieces*. In either case it denotes the assailant of Nineveh, who is represented as already on his march against it, not the Messiah, though a name somewhat similar is applied to him Mic. 2 : 13, still less the Assyrians themselves, in their invasion of Judah. עַל־פָּנֶיךָ, not *against thy face*, the hardness of which, Ezek. 3 : 7–9, i. e. thy obstinacy this hammer shall break, but *before*, in front of *thee*, see on Ex. 20 : 3, with the implication of hostile intent. The 2 f. s. suf. refers not to Judah, as in the preceding verses, as though this verse were designed to encourage Jerusalem to hold out against Sennacherib, but to Nineveh. נָצוֹר מְצֻרָה according to the accents belongs to the first clause of the verse; the abs. inf. may, therefore, be modified by the preceding verb, § 268. 1, *he has besieged a siege*, מְצֻרָה as מָצוֹר, 3 : 14, or *the fortress;* the majority of interpreters, however, regard it as a substitute for the imperative, § 268. 2, and addressed to Nineveh. —צַפֵּה, this and the following verbs may either be imperatives, or abs. infin. used for the imper. If the former, as is more probable, the masc. is employed because the admonition is directed to the king or people, not to the city as such, as in צָבָה. A careful watch must be maintained upon the ways leading to the city, to guard against surprise. חַזֵּק *strengthen*, i. e. by means of the girdle, as Isa. 22 : 21. This is equivalent to a command to address himself or themselves to energetic action, inasmuch as girding up the loose oriental dress was a necessary preparation for activity.

3. כִּי introduces the reason why such formidable foes were gathering against Nineveh. It was because Jehovah had returned to his long-forsaken people, and was taking their part against their oppressors. גָּאוֹן, from the root גָּאָה *to be exalted*, § 193, denotes *exaltation*, and may be applied either to an inward feeling, *pride*, or to that which produces it, that of which one is proud, or by which he is exalted, *excellency, distinction;* 'the excellency of Jacob' would then mean the advantages of which this people was possessed, and which formed their chief boast and glory, Ps. 47 : 5, Am. 6 : 8; in Am. 8 : 7 this expression is applied to God himself. שָׁב, pret. or part. The transitive sense assigned to the Kal of this verb in this and some other places by lexicons and commentators is entirely supposititious, see Hengstenberg Beiträge, II. p. 104. It accordingly does not mean, *the Lord has turned away*, whether *the excellency of Jacob*, i. e. removed his privileges and advantages, or *the pride of Jacob*, if const. before the subject, § 254. 8, sufficiently hum-

bled his arrogance, the pride which he has himself indulged, if const. before the object, § 254. 9, is humbling the pride from which Jacob has
suffered, viz., that of Assyria.   Nor, for the same reason, does it mean,
Jehovah is restoring the excellency of Jacob, bringing back to him his
ancient privileges and prerogatives.   The only meaning which the
words can have, is, *Jehovah has returned* or *is returning to* § 271. 2 *the
exaltation* or *excellency of Jacob*, i. e. to Jacob himself, who is exalted or
possessed of eminent advantages, § 254. 2. *a*, comp. Ps. 5 : 8, 'the multitude of thy mercy' for 'thy abundant mercy.' יִשְׂרָאֵל, not the kingdom
of the ten tribes in distinction from Judah, who is then supposed to be
denoted by Jacob, as though the meaning were, God is returning in love
and grace to both branches of the covenant people, to one as well as to
the other.   This interpretation finds no warrant in the contrast between
Jacob and Joseph, Obad. ver. 18, as was shown in the exposition of that
verse.   Jacob was the ordinary name of the patriarch.   Israel was imposed by God himself, and was significant of his relation to God and his
prevalence with him.   Transferred to his descendants, the former describes them simply on their natural side as a nation sprung from a common ancestor, the latter describes them as in covenant with God, and
the objects of his favour and love, see on Isa. 40 : 27, 41 : 8. *Jehovah is
returning to the exaltation of Jacob as to the exaltation of Israel*, i. e.
He will deal with Jacob in the manner implied in the name of Israel,
his own chosen, peculiar people.   כִּי explains the reason ; God returned
to Jacob because his oppressors had reduced him to such a miserable condition, comp. Judg. 2 : 18. בְקָקוּם, indefinite. בְקָקוּם, suf. here and in
בְּזִמֹּרֵיהֶם refers not to the Ninevites, but to Israel; *their vine-branches*, not
in a literal sense simply, of the desolation of their vineyards, but figuratively ; Israel is a vine which has not merely been emptied or robbed of
its clusters, but mutilated and broken.   The specific explanation of vine-
branches as towns and cities, or as individual Israelites, is at fault only
in making too definite and precise what might better have a more general sense.

4. The attacking army and its fierce onset are described vs. 4. 5.
מָגֵן § 216. 1. *a* (3). גִּבֹּרֵיהוּ § 220. 2. *c* (3 pers.), suf. refers to מְצֻרָה,
ver. 2; some connect it with יְהוָֹה, ver. 3, comp. Isa. 13 : 3, Joel 2 : 11.
מְאָדָּם § 93. *a*, either because covered with leather or copper, or stained
with blood. בְּאֵשׁ־פְּלָדֹת *with fire*, flashing *of irons*, perhaps scythes with
which chariots were armed, although it has been remarked that none
have been found on the monuments of Nineveh.   Or it may denote their
polished armature or ornaments, or the weapons of those whom they
carried. הֲכִינוֹ § 102. 3 suf. not the object referring to רֶכֶב, but the sub

ject, and refers to the assailant of Nineveh ; *his preparing*, i. e. arranging them for battle. וְהַבְּרֹשִׁים *cypresses*, i. e. spears made of this wood.

5. בַּחֻצוֹת *fields*, the open country outside of the city walls. בָּרְחֹבוֹת *the broad ways* or spacious *areas* in the suburbs. מַרְאֵיהֶן, the suf. has been referred to רְחֹבוֹת and to פְּלָדוֹת ; but the simplest reference is to רֶכֶב, which is masc., but as it describes inanimate objects, the fem. suf. may have the sense of a neuter, § 196. *a*.

6. The measures of defence. יִזְכֹּר, the subject is the king or people of Nineveh, comp. ver. 2. אַדִּירָיו, some understand satraps commanding in the different provinces, who are summoned to the relief of the capital, but *stumble in their march* to it, being cut off by the invading army ; others, with greater probability, nobles within the walls, who stumble in their eager haste or from trepidation. בַּהֲלִיכֹתָם, K'thibh § 46, § 220. 2. *a*, for which the K'ri substitutes the sing. בַּהֲלִיכָתָם. חוֹמָתָהּ suf. refers to Nineveh, see on 1 : 8. הַסֹּכֵךְ, prop. *the covering*, though its precise sense as a military term is uncertain. Some understand by it the testudo or vinea, under shelter of which the besiegers approached to undermine or batter down the city wall. Others think it to be a structure erected for the protection of the besieged, or a body of men charged with the defence of the wall. Jerome renders it *umbraculum*, a roof by which the besieged were sheltered from the rays of the sun as well as from the darts of the enemy. The tense of the verb וְהֻכַן, which is not a preterite but a secondary future, § 265, appears to favour the opinion, that this like the preceding belongs to the measures of the besieged, not of the besiegers. But while they are thus actively engaged, the city, ver. 7, has already been attacked and carried in a different and unexpected quarter. The verbs of the next verse are accordingly preterites, while those in this are futures.

7. שַׁעֲרֵי הַנְּהָרוֹת. In addition to the Tigris and a small stream which still flows through the ruins, there were artificial moats and channels probably surrounding the city, some indications of which yet exist. The gates opening upon these may have been left open, as in the case of Babylon, Isa. 45 : 1, through negligence or treachery, or else they were forced. This is simpler than to explain *the gates of the rivers* to mean breaches in the walls made by an inundation of the river, see on 1 : 8, or the gates of the city through which the streams of its population or of invaders pour, or sluices by which the city might be flooded, and even the palace submerged (נָמוֹג) as a measure of defence, or in a metaphorical sense, sluices through which the streams of calamity were let in upon the devoted city. נָמוֹג *melted* or dissolved with terror, the palace being put for its occupants, the royal household.

8. Then follows the sack of the captured city; the captivity, ver. 8, or flight of its inhabitants, ver. 9, the plunder of its treasures, ver. 10, the terror which possesses all hearts, ver. 11. וְהֻצַּב, this word has greatly embarrassed interpreters, and has been very variously explained Gesenius derives it from נצב, and connects it with the last clause of the preceding verse literally understood, *the palace is dissolved and liquefied*, the unburnt bricks, of which it was built, crumbling by the action of the water. Others regard it as a proper name, whether of the queen of Nineveh or symbolically applied to Nineveh itself. It is best explained as the Hoph. of נצב taken impersonally, § 243. 3, *it is fixed, determined*, either it was so decreed of God or it is now decided by the event. גֻּלְּתָה, not *is led away captive*, which is the sense of the Hoph., but *is uncovered*, stripped of her clothing, comp. 3 : 5, Isa. 47 : 2. Nineveh is personified as a queen or lady of rank, fallen into the hands of her enemies and subjected to every indignity, amidst the impotent lamentations of her maids, which belong to the figure, and need not be too definitely explained, see on ver. 3, either as the women of the city or its dependent towns, comp. Num. 21: 25. 32. The tense of the verb should be preserved; the prophet describes the scene as if it had been transacted before his eyes. הֹעֲלָתָה § 60. 3. *b* (2), § 112. 2. וְאַמְהֹתֶיהָ § 211. *a*. מְנַהֲגוֹת, not *leading* but *moaning :* the part. expresses a time contemporaneous with the preceding preterites, § 266. 3. יוֹנִים, here referred to not merely as timid and helpless, but chiefly on account of their mournful note.

9. In the abundance of its wealth and the multitude of its inhabitants, Nineveh is compared to a pool of water, comp. Rev. 17 : 15, swelled by an influx from all quarters, which yet, when its banks are pierced or broken, speedily empties itself, and the outflow cannot be checked. הִיא מִימֵי § 220. 1. *a*, § 35. 1, *from her days*, or the relative may be supplied, § 255. 2, *from the days* that *she* has been, i. e. from her origin, during the entire period of her existence. וְהֵמָּה refers to מַיִם, or as the figurative are immediately exchanged for literal terms, to what these denote, the inhabitants laden with their wealth. עֲמֹדוּ, emphatic pausal form § 112. 4, not the language of the enemy, but of those who would reassure the frightened fugitives and rally them again for the defence of the city. מַפְנֶה *turning*, either intrans., pausing in his own flight, or trans., arresting the flight of others.

10. While upon one side is heard the ineffectual cry, *Stop! stop!* upon the other resound the loud cries of the victors inciting each other to the spoil. בֹּזּוּ, supply the substantive verb, there is *an abundance*, or it may be in apposition to the preceding noun, *to the store, the abundance*

of every precious article: the absence of the art. favours the former con
struction. אֲשֶׁר, the prep. indicates the material *from* which the abundance is derived, or of which it consists. Comp. אֲשֶׁר 3 : 8.

11. The absence of verbs converts the greater portion of this verse
into a series of exclamations, and the energy of the original will be marred if its form is changed in this particular by the supply even of the
substantive verb. בּוּקָה וּמְבוּקָה וּמְבֻלָּקָה, the paronomasia, see on Gen.
1 : 2 תֹּהוּ וָבֹהוּ, here extended to three terms of increasing length from
the same or kindred roots, may be feebly represented by *vacancy and
vacuity and evacuated!* נָמֵס § 140. 2, not pret. but part., *and melted
heart!* Like mental and physical effects are often ascribed to terror,
e. g. Josh. 2 : 11, 7 : 5, Isa. 13 : 7. 8, Ezek. 21 : 12. קִבְּצוּ פָארוּר, the old
interpretation, *blackness,* as of a pot, פָּארוּר, is quite superseded by the
derivation from פָּאַר § 187. 2. *c,* in the sense of *a glow, flush.* It may
then be rendered *gather a glow,* are flushed with excitement and agita-
tion ; or *gather in,* withdraw from the surface, lose *colour,* become pale,
comp. Joel 2 : 10, 4 : 15.

12. אַיֵּה, the question implies that it no longer exists. The figurative terms, by which its former power and conquests are described, imply
the justice of the retribution which has at length overtaken it. The rob-
ber city has itself been robbed. Nineveh, enriched with the spoils of
other nations, is compared to a den of lions filled with slaughtered prey.
This image is sufficiently distinct, without insisting upon a specific meaning for each of the details, as though the lion denoted the king, the lioness
the queen, and the young lions the nobles, citizens or soldiers, see on
2 : 3. 8.

13. Some supply אַיֵּה, or אֲשֶׁר־שָׁם from ver. 12, but this is unnecessary. טֶרֶף ... בֶּרֶף § 280. *a.*

14. The declaration of God, that he would destroy Nineveh, couched
partly in literal and partly in figurative terms. אֵלַיִךְ, commonly rendered *against thee,* as if it were עָלַיִךְ ; but the prep. properly indicates
motion *to, towards;* lo! *I unto thee,* i. e. am coming to thee. That this is
with a hostile intent is suggested not by the prep. but by the context ; so
also 3 : 5, Jer. 50 : 31 ; and hence the same phrase is used, where the design of the coming is gracious, Ezek. 36 : 9. Comp. ' I'll to Fife' for I
will go to Fife. יְהֹוָה צְבָאוֹת § 253. *b.* The entire universe is marshalled
under God's command, terrestrial persons and things and celestial beings
and bodies constitute his hosts, see on Gen. 2 : 1. This title is particularly appropriate to Jehovah as the God of battles and the author of Nineveh's destruction. בֶּעָשָׁן, the meaning is not that this should be done in
a conspicuous manner, in a fire emitting a great smoke, and consequently

visible at a great distance, but so that they should be converted into smoke, Ps. 37 : 20, and vanish away. רֶפֶשֶׁן §279. טֶרְפֵּ *thy prey*, treasures accumulated by extortion and conquest, or as a noun of action, *thy preying, plundering*, thou shalt not be allowed to prey upon the rest of the world any longer. : מַלְאָכֶֽכָה §220. 2. *c*, bearers of royal edicts, Esth. 3 : 13, or sent to denounce war and demand the submission of the nations, Isa. 37 : 9. The paraphrase of vs. 9–14, given by Josephus, Ant. IX. 11. 2, is interesting, as showing that he followed the Hebrew text rather than that of the Septuagint.

CHAPTER III.

This is not a second overthrow, distinct from that already described, as those have imagined who refer ch. ii. to the taking of Nineveh by Arbaces, and ch. iii. to its final capture by Cyaxares. But the prophet recurs to the same subject for the sake of exhibiting more distinctly the grounds of it, fortifying it by a striking example, and declaring its unfailing certainty.

    1. vs. 1–7, the crimes of Nineveh and their penalty.

    2. vs. 8–11, the fate of No-Ammon shall be hers.

    3. vs. 12–19, notwithstanding her strength and resources, her destruction shall be sudden, complete, and unlamented.

    1. The sin of Nineveh and its punishment are first stated in literal, vs. 1–3, and then in figurative terms, vs. 4–6. In her lust of dominion she scrupled not to extend it by every measure of fraud and violence. הוֹי is denunciatory, *Wo!* דָּמִים, plur. denotes drops of *blood*; hence blood as shed, and the guilt of shedding it. כַּחַשׁ, governed by מְלֵאָה, the adj. taking a direct object like the verb from which it is derived, §271. 1, see on Gen. 42 : 18 ; though others read, contrary to the accents, *all of it is deceit*, and *full of violence*. יָמִישׁ might be transitive, *it will not let go the prey*, restore it to its rightful owners ; some suppose a particular allusion to Israel retained in captivity. But as טֶרֶף is fem., and this form is mostly intrans., it is probably so here, *the prey departeth not*, or : טֶרֶף as a noun of action, 2 : 14, *plundering will not cease*.

    2. This and the following verse describe not the bustle of the great city and the crimes perpetrated there, but the onset of the attacking army and the resulting slaughter. The absence of verbs converts them into a series of abrupt exclamations, comp. 2 : 11. קוֹל *the sound of*, equivalent to *Hark!* see on Isa. 40 : 3. Some supply this throughout

the verse, and even in the first clause of ver. 3, but without necessity. שׁוֹא, collective.

3. מַעֲלֶה, the object of this participle is not the following nouns, as in the common version; nor is it to be rendered *lifting up himself,* i. e. mounting his horse, but *causing* his horse *to rear* or spring, making him bound along at a high speed. וְרֹב חָלָל, the number of the slain in the city is so great as to impede the advance of the assailants. The K'thibh is וְכֹבֶד, the future of this verb being supplied from the Niphal, since the Kal future is not in use, § 80. *a* (3).

4. Nineveh is figuratively charged with whoredom, which does not here denote idolatry and desertion of the true God, as when it is imputed to Israel, Hos. 1 : 2, but is tantamount to the deceit, violence and blood already charged upon her in literal terms, ver. 1. It refers, as in Isa. 23 : 17, Rev. 17 : 2, to promiscuous intercourse with other nations, whether in the way of trade or political alliances, which was of itself abhorrent to Jewish laws and usages, but became more offensive from the selfish ends pursued by means of these entanglements and artful solicitations. Under the pretence of love and friendship she was covertly but incessantly aiming at her own aggrandizement and the extension of her empire. To enhance her power and complete her conquests, this harlot relied not only upon her personal charms, the magnificence and attractiveness of Nineveh in the eyes of surrounding nations, but also upon sorceries. The allusion (comp. a like combination of זְנוּנִים and כְּשָׁפִים, 2 Kin. 9 : 22) is to the use of philters, love-potions, and magic incantations, to secure the attachment of lovers and gain control over them. The crafty, designing schemes of Nineveh, and the supernatural aid invoked in giving them effect, are doubtless intended by these occult arts. מֵרֹב, prep. causal, as in Isa. 53 : 5; the connection is not with what precedes but with the following verse, *on account of the multitude,* etc. *lo! I* am coming *to thee.* הַמֹּכֶרֶת *selling,* reducing to bondage to herself, as when God is said to sell his people into the hand of their enemies, Judg. 2 : 14, possibly with the accessory idea of a literal sale of captives into slavery to her own citizens or to other nations, comp. Joel 4 : 6. Some have, from an Arabic analogy, given to this word in this place the sense of *entangling, ensnaring;* but its constant meaning in Hebrew renders this alike unnecessary and inadmissible.

5. This shameless conduct shall be punished by a shameful exposure. She shall be stripped of her ornamental attire, and converted into a loathsome and revolting spectacle, to shock and disgust all beholders. From this and like figurative passages, e. g. Hos. 2 : 5. 12, Isa. 47 : 3, Jer. 13 : 26, Ezek. 16 : 37–39, it cannot be inferred that harlots were

actually punished in this way. עַל־פָּנֶיךָ, as 2 : 2 ; she shall be thus ignominiously treated to her face, seeing it, but unable to prevent it.' וְהִרְאֵיתִי § 112. 3, § 114.

6. שִׁקֻּצִים *abominable things*, not idols, to which this term is frequently applied, as if the meaning were, she shall be buried beneath the objects of her idolatrous worship, comp. 1 : 14, but whatever is filthy and offensive.

7. יֹאמַר agrees in form with כָּל־ § 277. *a*, or sing. with a distributive sense § 275. 6. וְאָמַר, the language of the spectators extends to כָּל. אֵלֶיךָ, Jehovah is again the speaker, or rather continues to be the speaker from ver. 5 to the close of this verse, for it is he who declares what all who behold her will say. The question implies that there would be none to pity or console her.

8. That the overthrow of so magnificent and powerful a city is not to be esteemed incredible, is shown by the fate of No-Ammon, or the Egyptian Thebes, one of the most famous cities of antiquity for its strength and resources. With our imperfect and fragmentary knowledge of its history, it is difficult to determine to what event the prophet here alludes. It is not improbable that Thebes may have been reduced by Sargon, king of Assyria, see Isa. ch. 20, though this is nowhere explicitly recorded. Another opinion is, that a capture by some other power, African or Asiatic, is intended ; and another, the least probable of any, that the event referred to had not yet taken place, but that its capture by Cambyses is here predicted. הֲתֵיטְבִי § 147. 4, § 260. *a*, *art thou better*, § 263. 2, not in moral character, but in condition, more impregnable or better defended, or *shalt thou be better* in the destiny that awaits thee. אָמוֹן, not as in Jer. 52 : 15, equivalent to הָמוֹן *multitude*, but as in Jer. 46 : 25, the name of an Egyptian deity ; whence נֹא אָמוֹן, in the LXX. μερίδα Ἀμμών, *part* or portion *of Ammon*, must have been a city sacred to that god. It is more exactly identified by the LXX., Ezek. 30 : 14. 16, as Διόσπολις, not of course the place of inferior magnitude so called in Lower Egypt, which would not have afforded a fitting parallel to Nineveh, but that which by way of distinction received the name of Diospolis the Great, or Thebes, the magnificent metropolis of Upper Egypt, whose splendour and greatness are not only attested by ancient writers, but by the magnitude of its ruins. יְאֹרִים, the Egyptian word for *river*, appropriated to the Nile and the artificial canals branching from it, constructed for irrigation or defence. אֲשֶׁר־חֵיל יָם, the rendering *whose wall* was *a rampart to sea from sea*, Mic. 7 : 12, i. e. extending to the Red sea from the Mediterranean, violates the accents ; *which* was *a fortress of the sea*, i. e. a place fortified by the sea, gives an

unproved meaning to חֵיל‎; the suf. is to be supplied to חֵיל‎ from : חֹמָתָהּ‎
in the next clause, comp. § 247. b, *whose rampart* was *a sea*, i. e. the
broad Nile, as in Isa. 19 : 5 ; the same term is applied to the Euphrates,
Isa. 21 : 1 ; comp. the language of Isocrates respecting Egypt, in Busiris
C. 6, ἀθανάτῳ δὲ τείχει τῷ Νείλῳ τετειχισμένην. מִיָּם‎, not extending *from
the sea* landward, nor rising *out of the sea*, but the prep. indicates the
material, consisting *of the sea ;* see a like use of the prep. 2 : 10, Ps.
16 : 4.

  9. This city, so strong in its natural position, was stoutly defended
by numerous and powerful auxiliaries. פּוּט וְלוּבִים‎. These may be different tribes inhabiting Libya; or *Lubim* may be the general name and
Phut a subordinate division. : בְּעֶזְרָתֵךְ‎ § 279, the prep. may be explained
as the *Beth essentiae, in* the character or capacity of *thy help,* comp. Ex.
18 : 4, Deut. 33 : 26, Prov. 3 : 26. See on Isa. 40 : 10 ; or it may be
read, *among thy help,* i. e. helpers, auxiliaries.

  10. ־גַם *even.* הָיְתָה‎ was *to,* became, see on Gen. 2 : 7, *exiles,* her
inhabitants were exiled ; or this word may be dependent on הָלְכָה *went
for exiles,* as exiles, *into captivity.* יְרֻטְּשׁוּ‎, fut. relative to and consequent upon the preceding pret. § 263. 5. *a.* יַדּוּ־גוֹרָל‎ § 207. 2. *b.*

  11. גַּם־אַתְּ‎, twice corresponding to the repeated גַם‎, ver. 10, *thou too.*
תִּשְׁכְּרִי‎, drink deeply of divine wrath, see Ob. ver. 16. תְּהִי נַעֲלָמָה‎ not in a
reflexive sense, *hiding thyself* for fear, but *hidden,* reduced to obscurity,
or completely destroyed. : מֵאוֹיֵב‎, to be connected, not with תְּבַקְשִׁי‎, as
though in her extremity she would be obliged to apply to her very enemies for protection, but with מָעוֹז *a defence from,* against *the enemy.*

  12. Against the fate thus foretold and illustrated every reliance
would be unavailing. מִבְצָרַיִךְ‎, either the fortifications of Nineveh itself
or other fortified places guarding the access to the capital. תְּאֵנִים‎, figure of easy capture, comp. Rev. 6 : 13. בִּכּוּרִים‎, the early ripe figs were
especially prized, Isa. 28 : 4. נָפְלוּ‎ § 287. 2.

  13. Her population, and especially her armies, should be destitute
of manly courage, comp. Homer, Il. 2. 235, Ἀχαιΐδες, οὐκέτ’ Ἀχαιοί, and
Virgil's imitation, Æn. 9. 617, Phrygiae, neque enim Phryges. לְאֹיְבַיִךְ‎
may be connected with what precedes, but better with what follows.
שְׁעָרֵי‎ § 282. *a.* אַרְצֵךְ‎, passages affording entrance to the land and egress
from it, comp. Jer. 15 : 7, Zech. 11 : 1 ; others understand the gates of
the various cities of the empire. : בְּרִיחָיִךְ‎ *bars* by which the gates were
fastened. This is a continuation of the figure of the preceding clause.
Every obstruction is removed to the advance of the enemy, who penetrates even to the capital. The change of the text to בְּרִיחָיִךְ‎ *thy fugitives* is without authority, and is of no advantage to the sense.

14. As the outposts have fallen, the people have shown unmanly weakness, and the passes opening free admission to the heart of the empire have been forced, the siege of the capital cannot be much longer delayed. Every preparation should therefore be made to meet it. נַצֵּב § 101. 3, the walls of Nineveh were chiefly of brick.

15. These efforts would be vain. שָׁם is never an adverb of time, *then*, though this sense has been attributed to it here and in a few other passages, but always of place, *there*, i. e. on the very spot where they are engaged in these defensive preparations. Others explain it demonstratively, as though the prophet was pointing to what he saw in prophetic vision, *there!* יֶלֶק, not the object, as though the allusion were to swarms of locusts checked by fires or combated with swords, but the subject, since locusts are more naturally and frequently contemplated as agents of destruction than as themselves liable to be destroyed. The devastation should resemble that effected by these devouring insects. The mention of locusts as an emblem of the invaders suggests the employment of the same emblem in the next clause, under another aspect, to represent the vast numbers of the Ninevites, and their sudden disappearance. יֶלֶק from יָלַק *to lick up, devour*, is a poetical name of the locust, while אַרְבֶּה from רָבָה *to be numerous*, is its ordinary name. הִתְכַּבְּדִי, addressed in the masc. to the people, and in the fem. to the city, see on 2 : 2.

16. פָּשַׁט *spreads itself*, or better, as in the text of the common version, *spoileth*. They commit their ravages and fly away; so the traders, and all the busy multitudes that frequented Nineveh, should suddenly take flight. There is no good ground for the opinion that יֶלֶק denotes the locust unwinged and not yet full grown, which must cast its skin before it attains its proper size and capacity of flight, and that the clause is to be translated, *larval locusts cast their skin and fly away*.

17. רֹבִי § 199. c, § 280. a. כְּיוֹם *day*, indefinitely for time, see Gen. 2 : 4. וְיִרְדֹּף § 142. 1. מְקוֹמָם אֵיָּם, one suf. agrees formally with יוֹם in the sing., the other logically in the plur. § 275. 2, *their place is not known, where they* were, no trace remains of their former presence ; or *where they* are, no one can tell whither they have gone ; or preserving more exactly the sense of the interrogative, *their place is not known ; where are they ?*

18. נָמוּ, not a figure for negligent security, but the sleep of death. רֹעֶיךָ, a frequent figure for rulers ; so Homer, ποιμένα λαῶν. יִשְׁכְּנוּ, mark the change of tense, *have fallen asleep, shall* continue to *lie.* נָפֹשׁוּ, as the shepherds have perished, the flock is scattered. Comp. 1 Kin. 22 : 17

19. תָּקְעוּ כָף, gesture of joy, Ps. 47 : 2.

PSALM I.

This Psalm may be divided into two parts, vs. 1–3 describing the blessedness of the righteous, and vs. 4–6 the misery of the wicked, or better, perhaps, into three parts, in which the righteous and the wicked are successively contrasted in character, vs. 1. 2 ; condition, vs. 3. 4 ; and destiny, vs. 5. 6.

1. אַשְׁרֵי § 201. 1, § 221. 5. *d*, an exclamation, *O the felicities of the man !* which is more natural as well as forcible than to supply the substantive verb, there are *felicities.* The person referred to is first described negatively, then in ver. 2 positively. He avoids all who are evil. *Walk, stand, sit,* " the three postures of a waking man express the whole course of life or conduct;" they also suggest a climax, or "successive stages of deterioration ; first, occasional conformity, then fixed association, then established residence." ALEXANDER. There may also be a progression in the three names of the wicked, *impii corde, peccatores opere, illusores ore.* עֵצָה *counsel,* not here in the sense of advice given to another, but plan or purpose which one forms for himself. כִּסֵּא § 156. 2. The verbs of this verse are in the preterite, those of ver. 2 in the future, but neither exclude the present ; combined they embrace all time, § 263. 5. *a.* It is first stated what he never has done, then what he designs and endeavours always to do ; evil is abandoned and past, that which is good alone remains before him in perpetual validity. In the freedom with which the conjunctive accents are used in the poetic consecution, § 40. 1, it will be sufficient to note the order of the disjunctives. This verse consists of three clauses, the first of which is limited at רְשָׁעִים by Merka-Mahpakh, the second at עָמָד by Athnahh, the third at יָשָׁב by Silluk. The first is subdivided by R'bhia over אִישׁ. Merka-Mahpakh is preceded by the disjunctive Zarka over הָלַךְ, Athnahh by Tiphhha initial under חַטָּאִים, and Silluk by R'bhia-Geresh over לֵצִים.

3. The happy estate, which was the subject of exclamation, ver. 1, is set forth by the expressive figure of a flourishing tree. שָׁתוּל, not wild, but *planted,* and that in a most favourable position. עַל *over,* overhanging, or *by,* see on Gen. 41 : 1. פַּלְגֵי § 42. 5, plur. does not express largeness or incessant flow, § 201. 2, nor intimate that מַיִם is collective, but artificial channels for irrigation are intended, and the same tree might overhang several. פִּרְיוֹ, not here a figure of good works, but belongs to the emblem of a prosperous, happy condition. נָתַן, the figure is exchanged for literal expressions. יַצְלִיחַ, intrans. *shall prosper,* or more probably trans. *he shall cause to prosper,* conduct to a successful termination.

14

4. In contrast with this vigorous growth, the wicked are compared to a lifeless vegetable product, not to a dead tree, which would be too exalted an image, but to chaff, which is utterly insignificant and worthless, and which therefore the wind is allowed to sweep away; an allusion to the oriental mode of winnowing, by casting the grain up to the wind. תִּדְּפֶנּוּ, fut. denoting customary action, § 263. 4. רוּחַ, indef. *a wind,* or art. omitted by poetic license, § 247.

5. עַל־כֵּן, see on Gen. 2 : 24 ; from this opposition of character and condition the Psalmist infers their opposite destiny. רְשָׁעִים, indef. because no longer spoken of as a class, but as individuals. It is not merely said that *the wicked* as a body *shall not stand,* endure the test, be vindicated, but no *wicked* men whatever shall do so. בַּמִּשְׁפָּט *the judgment,* not of men but of God, whether temporal or eternal, see on Obad. ver. 15. עֲדַת *congregation,* the body or class *of* the *righteous.* The term is commonly used of the congregation of Israel, the church. Sinners shall not remain forever mingled with it, undistinguished from its true and faithful members.

6. כִּי־. That such a distinction shall be made is proved by the divine omniscience. *God knows the way of righteous* men, i. e. either he is acquainted with the course of conduct which they pursue, it being implied, though not expressly stated, that he will deal with it as it deserves. Or *way* may, as in Isa. 40 : 27, Ps. 37 : 5, include the destiny as determined by the character and conduct ; the meaning will then be, God knows the issue of their course, and it shall be as he has declared it to be. תֹּאבֵד, the way *shall perish* with all who are upon it, i. e. it leads to destruction.

PSALM II.

The first Psalm exhibits it as a permanent fact in the moral government of God, in spite of contrary appearances and seeming contradictions, that the righteous are blessed and the wicked shall perish ; the one is as the flourishing and fruitful tree, the other as the dry and driven chaff. The same idea meets us again in the second Psalm, which is thus a sort of sequel or counterpart of the first. We find here the same contrast presented in the first place of two opposing characters and courses of conduct, viz. : resistance or submission to the authority and government of God, and in the second place of the issues that attend them, the perdition of the one, תֹּאבֵד, ver. 12, comp. 1 : 6, and the blessedness of the other, אַשְׁרֵי, ver. 12, comp. 1 : 1.

This common idea is, however, transferred to another sphere and exhibited upon a different theatre. 1. What was in Psalm 1 asserted of individuals is here declared of nations and their rulers. 2. What was there asserted as a general moral truth is here prophetically declared : the prophet foresees the mad resistance of the nations to the kingdom of the Messiah, and predicts its calamitous result. Three different views have been taken of the subject of this remarkable Psalm.

1. Naturalistic, that it describes the unsuccessful attempt at revolt on the part of certain subject nations.

2. Typical, that while primarily describing such a revolt from some one of the kings of Israel, it at the same time has a secondary relation to the kingdom of Messiah.

3. Messianic, that it is primarily and directly prophetic of Messiah's kingdom.

Of the naturalistic interpreters, some have referred the Psalm to one or other of the wars in the reign of David. Apart from other difficulties which press this view, however, none of his wars can be found which answer the requirements of the Psalm, even as interpreted by themselves. His wars with the Philistines, 2 Sam. 5 : 17–25, were before Zion could be called God's holy mountain, ver. 6. His wars, 2 Sam. 8, with Syrians, Edom, Moab, and others, were not against nations previously subdued, and who now threw off the yoke of Israel. His wars with Absalom and Ishbosheth were not against foreign but domestic enemies. Others refer it to a supposed revolt against Solomon, whereas, the history not only fails to record any such revolt, but expressly describes his reign as one of peace and quietness, 1 Chron. 22 : 9. Others, with still less probability, have referred it to later periods of the history, until the climax of absurdity was reached by Hitzig, who places it in the times of the Maccabees, and finds the occasion to be Alexander Jannaeus imposing circumcision on the Edomites.

The decisive objections to this view, however modified, are,

1. The universal and resistless sway of this prince, which belongs only to Messiah, and is always a characteristic of his reign among the prophets : this could be said of no actual monarch but by the grossest hyperbole.

2. The authority of the New Testament. In Acts 4 : 25. 26, it is quoted by the assembled apostles and applied to Herod and Pilate, the Gentiles and the Jews combining in the crucifixion of Jesus. In Acts 13 : 33 Paul quotes " Thou art my son," etc., in application to Christ; so in Heb. 1 : 5 ; so " thou shalt rule them with a rod of iron," in Rev. 2 : 27, 12 : 5, 19 : 15. This Psalm is also the basis of some of the characteristic names of Jesus, (1) the anointed, Messiah or Christ, only

found here and Dan 9 : 25, and (2) Son of God, used even by Nathanael, John 1 : 49, before he had been under Christ's instruction, so that it must have been prevalently adopted as a name of the coming Redeemer.

3. The history of interpretation : the ancient authorities among the Jews always explained it of the Messiah, the later Jews abandoning this view only to avoid the arguments thence drawn by Christians in favour of the claims of Jesus of Nazareth. This interpretation has always been the prevalent one among Christians.

The typical view may be presented under two different phases. The first supposes that the writer had primarily in mind some revolt of sub-jugated nations from the sway of an Israelitish king, but that his language was so framed, consciously or unconsciously, under the guidance of the Spirit, as to adapt it to the higher subject of Messiah's reign.

This would accord with the analogy of many of the Psalms which are typical in this sense; it would also be consistent with the authority of the New Testament, which, in applying this Psalm to Christ, does not necessarily deny its applicability also to a lower subject. It is, how-ever, forbidden, (1) by the terms of the Psalm, which cannot, without the most strained exaggeration, have been meant to apply to any actu-ally reigning king of Israel. Dominion over all nations was never claimed, much less exercised by any of them ; and the kings and na-tions of the whole earth were never combined against any of them. (2) The subjection demanded is not a political but a religious one. Re-bellion is directed against the Lord as much as against his anointed, and the thing demanded of the nations and rulers of the earth is, that they should serve the Lord as well as submit to his Son. It is on this ground that Hitzig has based his conceit that a religious war, backing the de-mand for the circumcision of the Edomites, is the one intended. His view may be accepted as a confession that no war for political freedom or subjugation meets the conditions of the case.

The second phase of the typical view supposes that the prerogatives and powers of the kingdom of Israel, as such, are here intended, and that no one historical event is particularly alluded to. The kingdom of Israel was divinely established and an object of divine protection ; its monarchs of the line of David stood in a filial relation to God, 2 Sam. 7 : 14, as the objects of his love and favour. This kingdom was destined ultimately to cover the earth, and he who is the Son of God in the high-est sense was to be also a son of David, and to sit upon his throne. This view supposes the kingdom here to be regarded as a whole, correspond-ing to its divine ideal, and the king to embrace all the monarchs of Da-vid's line, including the greatest and the last.

This would accord with the analogy of prophecy, e. g. with Deut. 18, which predicts the entire line of prophets, as well as Christ, the seal of the prophets, with the prediction 2 Sam. 7, of the kingdom of the son of David, etc. The objection to it is, that the terms of the Psalm suggest no other than the direct application to Messiah. Its language is all applicable to him, and to him alone, in its strict and proper sense, and seems to exclude all reference to any lower subject. Messiah is presented, indeed, as the ideal king of Israel, but the gaze of the seer is directed to him alone in whom the kingdom would find its consummation, not to him merely as one of a line of monarchs, who are all equally regarded. This Psalm is, therefore, not merely typical of Christ, but is directly and exclusively messianic.

The absence of a title deprives us of the usual means of settling authoritatively the date and author of this Psalm. This lack is supplied, however, by the New Testament, which in express language, Acts 4 : 25, refers it to David. It has been replied to this, that such a statement is merely a reproduction of the current belief of the time, and is not intended to vouch for its accuracy; just as we familiarly call the whole book the Psalms of David, though he did not write every individual Psalm. It would, however, be time enough to resort to such an explanation as this, if it could first be proved that the statement of the sacred writer is not strictly true in this case. But, on the other hand, all the probabilities are in favour of, not against its composition by David.

1. The other Psalms of the first book, Ps. 1–41, almost without exception, are in their titles referred to him, whence the probability that this is likewise his.

2. The impression made by the tone of the Psalm is, that it was written at a time when the kingdom was undivided, and was in its highest strength and glory. At such a time the devout mind would naturally pass, as is here done, from the type to the contemplation of its antitype.

3. The prophetic basis of this Psalm is found in a communication to David by the prophet Nathan, 2 Sam. 7 : 12–16, where the perpetuity of his kingdom is promised ; the very words of that promise are here alluded to, and the sonship promised applied to Messiah in its highest sense. David no doubt understood the promise to be, that Messiah should spring from his seed, and we have here the lyric reproduction of the revelations he received.

4. Its typical basis is found in the life of David, and in the kingdom as it was under his reign. He was a man of war, to whom God had granted victory over all his foes. It is under the figures of successful war and a throne established in Zion, that he describes Messiah's sway.

vs. 1–3, the vain rebellion of the nations and their rulers.

vs. 4–6, the Lord derides their impotent attempts.

vs. 7–9, the relation which this king bears to Jehovah, and the authority based upon it.

vs. 10–12, all rulers counselled to timely submission.

In each of these sections there is a different speaker: in the last verse of the first, the nations and their kings; in the last verse of the second, the Lord; throughout the third, the Messiah; in the fourth, the Psalmist himself gives the lessons of the prophetic scene which he has been surveying.

1. The Psalmist beholds the nations of the world in the tumult of actual revolt against the Lord, and expresses his astonishment and indignation at their wickedness and folly. לָמָּה *why*, for what reason? The question implies that no good reason exists. The question probably extends through the verse, though some confine it to the first clause, and others extend it to the second verse likewise. רָגְשׁוּ, applied to the noise of a tumultuous crowd; the verb, though used both in the Biblical and later Chaldee, occurs in Hebrew only in this place; the corresponding noun is found twice in the Psalms, meaning 'noise' or 'tumult.' The past tense shows that the Psalmist is describing a point of time after the revolt has begun, though, as the following futures show, it is not yet consummated. גוֹיִם *nations*, mostly foreign, gentile nations, though the application to the Gentiles and people of Israel, Acts 4 : 27, combined in the crucifixion of Christ, shows that it may include the nominal Israel when they have ceased to be God's true people, and put themselves on a par with heathen in their mad rebellion. This word, as well as its synonym לְאֻמִּים, is without the article. It is not yet brought to view that the revolt is absolutely universal, but only that it is one of vast dimensions, one of whole nations, not of petty neighbourhoods or individuals. The particular fact to which it is applied, Acts 4 : 27, though an instance of the hostility here referred to, does not exhaust it. יֶהְגּוּ, fut. why *will they* go on to *meditate*, i. e. plan or plot. רִיק *vain*, not in the conception of the plotters, of course, but in reality and actual fact.

2. יִתְיַצְּבוּ *are setting themselves*, taking their stand of hostility, comp 1 Sam. 17 : 16. מַלְכֵי־אֶרֶץ § 247, shows the universality of the rebellion, and at the same time, as they are merely earthly kings, prepares for the contrast to follow with 'him who sits in heaven.' The masses already seen in revolt have the countenance and aid of their legitimately constituted authorities. רוֹזְנִים stands absolutely, the qualification being understood from the parallel clause. נוֹסְדוּ from יָסַד *to lay a foundation*, to spread a bed as a base or foundation to rest upon; Niph. *to spread a*

bed for themselves, to lie down together upon a divan or oriental sofa, as was the custom for purposes of deliberation or consultation. The preterite is used because this mutual consultation has already taken place, and the resolve been formed. יְהֹוָה־עַל, even though in the intent of the actors (as in the crucifixion) only against Christ, it was still against the Lord. : מְשִׁיחוֹ, kings were anointed to symbolize the communication of spiritual gifts. Hence 'the Lord's anointed,' 2 Sam. 24 : 6, is synonymous with 'king.' The king of Israel, by way of eminence, receives the name Messiah, as anointed by the Spirit above measure.

3. The language of the nations and their rulers abruptly introduced. נְנַתְּקָה, paragogic form, § 97. 1, expresses strong resolve, *we will*, or mutual exhortation, *let us*. They will submit to this slavery no longer. עֲבֹתֵימוֹ § 221. 2. *c.*

4. While on the earth all is turmoil and confusion, in heaven the almighty object of this impotent hostility is perfectly serene, and derides these vain attempts. יוֹשֵׁב, the posture of a king on his throne, indicative of authority as well as of repose. יִשְׂחָק, § 51. 2 ; the LXX and Vulgate supply לָמוֹ from the next clause, *laughs at them*, which is possible, but not necessary. It may better be taken absolutely, the laughter indicating perfect security from threatened evil, comp. Job 5 : 22. —יִלְעַג *mocks* or *derides them ;* by a strong figure God is represented as employing insulting gestures to indicate the absurdity of their attempt, and the utter contempt in which he holds it and them.

5. אָז, not indefinitely, at some time, but *then ;* after he has first derided them, and allowed them for a while to make their impotent attempts, he will *then* speak. יְדַבֵּר, not in thunder, but the words that follow. : יְבַהֲלֵמוֹ *terrify*, throw into consternation and confusion, used of the rout of armies by a divinely inspired terror. The fright is produced by the announcement now to be made.

6. The words of God are introduced as abruptly as those of the nations and their rulers had previously been. וַאֲנִי *and*, connects with a thought suggested by what precedes ; 'You rebel against my anointed, *and I* have established him king ;' the pronoun is expressed on account of this implied opposition, § 243. 1. נָסַכְתִּי, not *anoint*, but *pour out* in casting metals ; hence *constitute, establis'*. מַלְכִּי *my king*, ruling in my name and by my authority. —עַל, not *over*, to indicate the territory ruled, but *upon*, as the seat of empire, its centre and capital : those who render the verb *anoint*, understand the place of anointing. צִיּוֹן Zion, the eminence in the southwest of Jerusalem, where the palace and stronghold of David were, and where the ark and tabernacle were placed during his reign ; the place of God's manifested presence, consequently

as well the residence of the earthly king. It is in later times, even
after the building of the temple, spoken of as the centre of the theocracy,
Moriah being regarded as a part of Zion, an additional summit of the
same mountain.   Old Testament language is here employed as usual in
describing New Testament things.   As Zion was the seat of the theocracy, and the residence of its kings, Christ, in whom this kingdom is
perpetuated, is said to be established on Zion, though he never locally
sat on a throne there.   We familiarly use "Zion" in like manner in religious language, without thinking of the locality so called.   : הַר־קָדְשִׁי
§ 256, *my mountain of holiness*, consecrated, hallowed by God's residence there.

7.   אֶל חֹק § 42. 5, not *in accordance with* nor *unto* a decree, so as to
become a fixed law, but *in reference to*.   חֹק is indefinite ; some connect it
with יְהוָה the *decree of Jehovah*, but the accents forbid.   בְּנִי, God calls
Israel his son because he was the author of his national existence, and
regarded him with tender love ; the kings of David's line were also sons
of God, 2 Sam. 7 ; so were the angels, Job 38 : 7.   But the expression
is here used in an emphatic sense, as appears from its being a ground
of universal empire, vs. 8, 9, and from the peculiar intimacy and relation to God shown in the words 'my king,' and in the rebellion being
directed alike against 'the Lord and his anointed.'   We learn from
Heb. 1 : 5 that it involves community of nature with God.   הַיּוֹם, the
point of time designated by this expression depends upon the date of
the decree referred to, and the determination of that will depend upon
the substance of the decree itself.   If 'I have begotten thee' denotes
the eternal generation of the son, then the decree must date back from
all eternity.   It seems more probable, however, that this phrase does
not denote the origin of the filial relation, but rather its solemn recognition, and is equivalent to 'I am thy father,' I this day declare myself
to be such.   If this be so, it belongs to some point of time at which this
relation was thus prominently manifested.   His resurrection is generally
assumed on the basis of Acts 13 : 33, Rom. 1 : 4, though the former passage may refer to his being raised up or brought into being as a man ;
this relation was also publicly recognized by a voice from heaven at the
baptism and the transfiguration of Christ.   Perhaps it is not necessary
to decide in favour of any one of these times and against the others, as
the point of time may be an ideal one, the coronation of Christ, his recognition as the divinely constituted king, which was accomplished with increasing distinctness at several different times.   : יְלִדְתִּיךָ § 150. 1 (p. 182).

8.   On the ground of this relation of sonship he had a right to
universal dominion.   נַחֲלָתֶךָ *thy inheritance*, thy portion as my son

אַפְסֵי־אָרֶץ *ends of the earth*, including all that is between them ; not the extreme limits of the land, a sense which the expression never has. This gift is suspended on his simply asking for it : that he had asked and obtained it, appears from his being in fact possessed of universal sway, against which the nations rebelled, and to which they are exhorted to submit.

9. His power to punish refractory subjects. תְּרֹעֵם from רָעַע *to break*, LXX as if תִּרְעֵם from רָעָה *to feed* or rule, ποιμανεῖς. בְּרָזֶל § 193. *c*, sceptre of *iron*, the hardest of metals, expressing his power and severity. כִּכְלִי יוֹצֵר, easily, utterly and remedilessly.

10. וְעַתָּה *and now*, in these circumstances, seeing these things are so. הַשְׂכִּילוּ *be wise*, prop. act wisely, § 79. 2. שֹׁפְטֵי § 35. 1, *judges*, parallel to kings, since judging was a regal function, and the Hebrew judges were supreme magistrates.

11. בְּיִרְאָה *with fear*, religious awe ; not merely political subjection. גִּילוּ *shout*, in acknowledgment of the sovereign, or *rejoice*, as you have reason with such a sovereign to rejoice and tremble too : not *quake*, a sense which Gesenius and others attribute to the word, but which it never has.

12. נַשְּׁקוּ־ *kiss*, an act of loyal homage, see on Gen. 41 : 40, comp. 1 Sam. 10 : 1 ; or of religious worship, 1 Kin. 19 : 18, Hos. 13 : 2, Job 31 : 27. בַּר § 51. 3, Aramaic for *son*, as in Simon *Bar*-Jonas. It occurs three times in Prov. 31 : 2. Forms common in the other dialects, but rare in Hebrew, are often used in poetry. An additional motive in this instance may have been to avoid the conjunction of like sounds, פֶּן and בַּר. This is the only rendering consistent with the connection. The LXX and Vulg. render *Embrace instruction ;* this gives false meanings to both verb and noun. Symmachus and Jerome render בַּר *purely*, and resolve the figure of the verb, *adorate pure*. Others take בַּר as an adjective, *kiss* the *pure* one, or the *chosen* one. יֶאֱנַף *he*, the son, *be angry ;* not Jehovah, which is more remote, and the son has the iron sceptre, to dash in pieces. וְתֹאבְדוּ דֶרֶךְ, not *perish on the way*, as they are marching against the anointed, without arriving at the capital; nor *lose the way*, wander from the right road of virtue and blessedness, but *perish as to the way*, comp. 1 : 6, find that your way leads to perdition, and you go to perdition in and with it. כִּמְעַט, not, when his wrath is kindled but a little, but *for his wrath will soon burn, is almost burning*, or hypothetically, *might easily burn.* חוֹסֵי בוֹ § 255. 1, *trust in him*, though it is sinful to trust in princes or in the son of man, a proof of his superhuman nature. Some refer the suffix to Jehovah ; but that is too remote, and only to be admitted, if Messiah could not properly be an object of religious trust, or if the Psalmist could not have contemplated him in that light.

PSALM III.

This Psalm is closely connected in subject with the preceding. Psalm 1 exhibits the contrast between the righteous and the wicked in their character and destiny. In Psalm 2 all nations are combined in vain rebellion against God's constituted king, the Messiah. In Psalm 3 we find the same struggle on a smaller scale and in a preliminary form, the wicked and causeless rebellion against David, the divinely appointed head of the theocracy, and his assurance of protection.

1. The titles of the Psalms are of different sorts, sometimes containing merely musical directions, sometimes, as here, a statement of the author and the occasion of the composition. These titles are doubtless entirely reliable, for (1) they are part of the text, and are to be ascribed to the authors of the several Psalms, there being the same external authority for their genuineness and correctness as that of the Psalms themselves. (2) Even if they were prefixed by others at a later time, their being admitted and suffered to remain could only be accounted for on the assumption of their correctness. (3) Nothing in the Psalms is inconsistent with these inscriptions. מִזְמוֹר § 191. 5, occurs only in the titles of the Psalms, and is prefixed to fifty-seven. The verb זָמַר is applied to instrumental music, or to vocal with an instrumental accompaniment, whence, like ψαλμός from ψάλλω, it denotes a composition designed for instrumental performance, as שִׁיר, which is also frequent in the titles of Psalms, means one designed to be sung. לְדָוִד § 257, *belonging to David*, as its author. The occasion stated is *when he fled from Absalom his son;* and the language of the Psalm is quite in accordance with the circumstances of that time. That the author was a monarch, may be inferred (1) from the vast numbers of his opposers, ver. 6; (2) from his pious prayer for the people as identified in fortunes with himself, ver. 8; and perhaps also (3) from his calling God 'his glory,' i. e. the source of his official elevation and distinction. Hence it cannot be the effusion of a godly man in a private station, surrounded by enemies. If then the author was a king, he must have been either David or Solomon, as these are the only two kings to whom Psalms are ever referred. It could not have been Solomon, for it does not agree with the characteristics of his reign, which was a peaceful one. If David was its author, it must, from its tone, have been at one of the most perilous crises of his life. Of these there were principally two, which might be thought of as furnishing an occasion for such a psalm, the persecution by Saul and the revolt of Absalom. That it could not be the former appears (1) from the reference to former trials and persecutions, ver. 7, from which he had

been delivered, which must include the hostility of Saul. (2) Zion was
not God's 'holy hill,' ver. 4, till David was king, and removed the ark
to that place; no other mountain ever received that name. It cannot
mean Sinai, for often as this expression occurs in Scripture, and especially in the Psalms, it always means Zion : and help is always sought
from the present dwelling-place of God, not from the scene of a past
revelation. Kimchi fixes the moment of the Psalm when David and the
people went weeping, barefoot, and with the head covered, up mount
Olivet, 2 Sam. 15 : 30. Hengstenberg refers it to the evening of that
day; but if it is possible to determine its time precisely, this may more
naturally be the next morning after he had safely slept through that first
night of most immediate peril, ver. 5, and in this protection found a
pledge of future deliverance. The Psalm describes his peril, vs. 2. 3 ;
protector, vs. 4. 5 ; confidence, vs. 6. 7 ; and prayer, vs. 8. 9.

2. מָה־, exclamation, *how*, the force of which may extend through
the verse, or only through the first clause. צָרַי might be from צוּר *as-
saulting me*, but is usually taken from צַר *my adversaries*. קָמִים עָלָי, a
general expression, equivalent to 'enemies,' Deut. 28 : 7 ; here it refers
to rebels, insurgents.

3. רַבִּים, these may be his enemies before spoken of, or false friends,
or disheartened followers. לְנַפְשִׁי, not a mere periphrasis of the pronoun
me, for this periphrasis, though frequent in Arabic, is always emphatically used in Hebrew, either where the life is in question, as Ps. 7 : 3,
'lest he rend my soul,' i. e. destroy my life. If it were so understood
here, the meaning would be—*say of my life, there is no help for it in
God;* but since נַפְשִׁי is fem. the following לוֹ must refer, not to it, but to
the person himself. Or where the feelings are concerned, *say* so as *to*
affect *his feelings* deeply, cut him to the heart; this is the sense here.
The preposition may be rendered *in reference to*, as Gen. 20 : 13, Isa.
41 : 7, or perhaps better *to*. Although this was not addressed to him,
as is shown by the use of the third person in the next clause, it is yet
said to his soul, goes to his heart. אֶרֶץ § 258. *b*. יְשׁוּעָתָה § 219. 2.
§ 196. *b*. If the ending have the sense of He directive, § 219. 1, *there
is not to salvation for him*, i. e., he cannot come to salvation. But as
this appears forced, it is better to regard the sense of the ending as
weakened or lost, as in לַיְלָה *by night*, also *night*. It is here used for
euphony, or at most as a poetic and emphatic form. בֵּאלֹהִים, God will
not help him because he is such a sinner, comp. 2 Sam. 16 : 7. 8, or
his condition is so desperate that even God cannot help him. Though
the former is doubtless to be included, yet the latter was also in his
mind, as is shown by the counter assertion of ver. 9, ' salvation be

longs tc God,' he is able to save, and does save. סֶלָה occurs in the Psalms seventy-one times, and three times in Habakkuk, chap. 3. It has been variously explained. (1.) It is accented as though it belonged to the preceding sentence: the Targum renders it לְעָלְמִין *for ever;* so Aquila, ἀεί; Symmachus, εἰς τὸν αἰῶνα. This is now universally abandoned. (2.) It is regarded as a musical term. *a.* Some make it an abbreviation, e. g. שׁ לְמַעְלָה הַשָּׁר *return above singer,* equivalent to *da capo.* But this leaves too much to conjecture, and there is no evidence of such abbreviations in Scripture. It is most probably derived either, *b.* from סָלָה *to be silent, rest,* denoting a pause in the singing to be filled up by the instruments, or *c.* from סָלָה = סָלַל *to lift up,* meaning *elevation, loud tone,* i. e. FORTE, and intended as a direction to the orchestra to play with new force while the singers are silent, or repeat the stanza just sung. In spite of the double derivation and opposite sense deduced, it amounts therefore to the same thing. As to the form of the word, some regard it as imp. Kal with ה paragog. in pause סֶלָה for סְלָה from סָלָה: others as a noun סֶלָה with ה parag. Though designed primarily for musical direction, it stands related to the sense of the passage, as the music was intended to conform to and express the sense. It occurs only after an important sentiment, which is thus emphasized, and commonly after some triumphant statement, which is thus celebrated and finds expression.

4. But though men considered his situation desperate, it was not so; he had a helper and one who regarded his prayers. וְאַתָּה *and thou,* in contrast with the conduct or the expectations of his enemies. מָגֵן *shield,* from גָּנַן *to protect,* a source of protection and defence, Gen. 15 : 1. בַּעֲדִי, not only *before* him, but *around* him; the primary sense of the preposition, according to Gesenius, is, *close to* me, on all sides of me; according to Hupfeld, *between* me and everything else. כְּבוֹדִי *my glory* or *honour,* i. e. the source and permanent ground of it, comp. Ps. 27 : 1, 'the Lord is my light and my salvation:' not merely the one who will now vindicate my honour by saving me from my enemies, but the original source of my honour, or regal dignity. As he has originally bestowed this royal authority, he will not suffer me to be thus violently despoiled of it. וּמֵרִים רֹאשִׁי, grief bows the head, deliverance from sorrow lifts it up again.

5. קוֹלִי, the immediate instrument of an action, instead of being preceded by a preposition, may be subordinated to the proper subject, either in apposition with it, " *my voice, viz.: I cry,*" or as an accusative, " *I as to my voice cry.*" This is no pleonasm, but is equivalent to *cry loudly.* אֶקְרָא, habitual action, § 263. 4, as the English present, *I cry.* וַיַּעֲנֵנִי,

Vav conversive after a future does not make a preterite, but indicates a consequent of the preceding verb, § 265. *b, and he hears me ;* the future in the same habitual sense as the preceding. Whenever I call, he hears me, or answers me, not merely in the sense of listening or speaking, but of granting the solicited and effectual aid.

6. God being thus his protector and helper, had already begun his work of protection from the present peril, and he had perfect confidence in him for the future. אֲנִי, the pronoun, when not necessary to perspicuity, is always emphatic, § 243. 1, *even I,* whose case men regard as desperate, have been thus marvellously preserved. שָׁכַבְתִּי *have lain down and slept,* indicating his sense of security as well as his safety. הֱקִיצוֹתִי *I have awaked :* some understand this of the past generally, God has always protected me in the darkness and perils of the night, and granted me slumber and safety, I can therefore trust him now. But it seems better to explain it from existing circumstances and of a definite time, the night after his flight. The culmination of his danger and hour of his most extreme peril was, when Ahithophel counselled, 2 Sam. 17 : 1, to pursue David with a large force that night and cut him off at once. The failure of Absalom to adopt that advice, which was an answer (one of those referred to in ver. 5) to David's prayer, 2 Sam 15 : 31, and the consequent salvation of that night, was really the beginning of deliverance from the entire danger. יְהוָה יִסְמְכֵנִי *Jehovah will* ever *sustain me,* fut. in habitual sense, § 263. 4, *sustains me,* is my protector then, now and always. The meaning is either, I was protected that night because God is always my protector ; or, I had this sense of security because of my consciousness that God always will sustain me.

7. Cheered not only by his knowledge that God is his protector in the general, but by this particular instance of marked and surprising deliverance, he would not be afraid, however great his perils. אִירָא, here and Ps. 27 : 1, followed by מִן, commonly with a direct object. רְבָבוֹת, with allusion to רַבִּים, רַבּוּ, vs. 2. 3. עָם *people* in a collective sense, persons ; or *nation,* the people, viz., Israel, the article omitted as it often is in poetry. שָׁתוּ, not *who have set themselves,* since this verb is never used in a reflexive or intransitive sense, but *whom they,* indef., referring to his enemies, § 243. 2, *have set* against me. This is the language of calm and quiet confidence rather than loud triumph ; hence there is no Selah to dwell upon and celebrate it in jubilant strains of instrumental melody. That this is the temper in which it is spoken is further shown by the following prayer for the granting of a deliverance not yet accomplished.

8. Having such a helper and such confidence, he does not intermit or discontinue prayer, but is enabled to pray with earnestness and hope.

קוּמָה *arise* from seeming inaction and inattention to the case of the suppliant; assume an attitude of action, address thyself to my case. אֱלֹהַי *my God*, expressive of a personal relation. הוֹשִׁיעֵנִי, save me now by shaming and destroying my enemies, *for* thou hast been my deliverer in previous perils. הִכִּיתָ *thou hast smitten all my enemies as to the cheek*, § 273. 2, treated them with deserved contumely, and by an anticipation of the following figure of beasts of prey, rendered them powerless by destroying their weapon of attack. כָל. Some interpreters have needlessly stumbled at the fact that he says *all*, though enemies were now surrounding him. It is all his enemies on the former occasions to which he refers. רְשָׁעִים, both the persecution of David by Saul and this revolt of Absalom were characterized by opposition against the legitimate and divinely constituted king. They were attempts to overthrow a divine ordinance, and defeat what was of divine appointment. Accordingly, the godly among the people were for David, and the ungodly against him. שִׁבַּרְתָּ, *broken the teeth*, as of wild beasts, destroyed their power of offence, thus rendering them harmless. Marg., see on 1 Sam. 17 : 43.

9. לַיהוָה, belongs to him as its author and source; see on ver. 3. הַיְשׁוּעָה § 245. 5. עַל עַמְּךָ, not a declaration, *is upon thy people*, but a prayer, *be upon thy people*. Their special relation to God is indicated by the use of the pronoun, and is the ground upon which the petition rests. David here, as often elsewhere, solicits not only individual blessings for himself, but rises from these to embrace in his petitions the whole people of God, of whom he was the head, in whose behalf he was so deeply interested, and whose welfare was so intimately connected with his own. His petition, it has been suggested, embraces even that misguided portion of the people, who were then in revolt.

PSALM IV.

This Psalm bears an external resemblance to Psalm 3 ; in length, 9 verses, in Selah at the end of the third and fifth verses, and in some of its expressions, viz.: רַבִּים אֹמְרִים ver. 7, comp. 3 : 3 ; רַבִּים קָמִים עָלָי ver. 9, comp. 3 : 6. With this corresponds an inward resemblance in the identity of situation. The Psalmist is surrounded by foes who would rob him of his official dignity which he had by God's gracious choice, vs. 3. 4. So that it is probably to be referred to the same occasion, the revolt of Absalom. The absence of distinct mention of Absalom interposes no objection any more than in the preceding psalm : that his adversaries are addressed by the general term " sons of men," is readily ac-

counted for, if Absalom is regarded as a tool in the hands of more designing men rather than himself the leading spirit in the rebellion.

1. This title has relation to the musical performance of the Psalm
and its authorship. נַצֵּחַ֫לַ occurs 55 times in the Psalms, and once in
Hab. 3 : 19. In this last instance it stands at the end of a metrical
composition, but with that exception always at the beginning, and it is
invariably the first word of the title in which it occurs, except in Ps. 88 ;
belonging to the leader or chief musician, i. e. committed to him as the
one charged with its musical performance. נְגִינוֹת not dependent on the
preceding participle, *to the leader in the music of stringed instruments*,
but a distinct direction respecting the mode of the performance of the
Psalm, *with stringed instruments*.

The Psalmist utters,

1. ver. 2, a prayer to God for deliverance.

2. vs. 3–6, a warning to his enemies to desist from their vain and
wicked course, and to return to the true service of God, whom they were
opposing.

3. vs. 7–9, his own joy and confidence in God.

2. אֱלֹהֵי צִדְקִי, either, *my righteous God*, an appeal to God as the
possessor and source of righteousness, and righteous in his dealings, and
as standing in an intimate relation to the Psalmist ; or, *God of my righteousness*, vindicator of my righteous cause, as 'God of my life' means,
not *my living God*, but the author and preserver of my life. צֶדֶק never
means simply 'salvation.' The first argument of his prayer is found in
the title applied to God, who, as a righteous Being, could not but favour
his servant and his righteous cause ; the next is found in God's past deliverances. בַצָּר, the article is equivalent to an unemphatic possessive,
§ 245. 3. *a, in my distress*, or is generic, § 245. 5, *in distress*. הִרְחַבְתָּ,
not to be rendered as an imperative, which would require ׃ conversive,
but as a preterite, and not probably as referring to some single definite
fact, but to the past generally ; not 'thou deliveredst' at some well-
remembered time, but *thou hast delivered* in every previous trouble. It
mars the simplicity of the Hebrew style to supply the relative, 'thou,
who hast delivered, etc.' חָנֵּנִי. Though he appeals to God's righteousness as the vindicator of his just cause, it is still only for grace or unde-
served favour that he sues.

3. בְּנֵי־אִישׁ *sons of men*, i. e. *men*, to whom he now turns from speaking to God. God was his helper, his enemies were only men. Or, if
אִישׁ involves a tacit opposition to אָדָם *nobles*, *men of high station*, many
of whom were engaged on the side of Absalom in this revolt. עַד־מֶה,
of time, *how long*, or degree, *how far, to what extent*. כְבוֹדִי official

dignity, not merely personal honour: it was the former of which the conspirators sought to rob him, and which they aimed to bring to disgrace. The question extends through the verse, and is not confined to its first clause.   רִיק ... כָּזָב may either characterize their design as vain and deceptive, one which could not be accomplished, but would disappoint their expectations ; or their measures and course of policy: they sought to advance their aims by falsehood and unworthy deeds.

4. וּדְעוּ, Vav is adversative, § 287. 1, *yet* know ; you are attempting the overthrow of my royal authority, *but* know that it is of divine origin, and cannot be overthrown.   Or it may be copulative ; the previous verse is dissuasive, as though he said, ‘cease from your vain attempt *and* know,’ or recognize the truth of the divine right of David to rule.   הִפְלָה, the roots פָּלָא and פָּלָה, though cognate, are not to be confounded. Some would give this word the sense of פָּלָא, ‘to treat in a marvellous manner,’ and apply it to the great benefits granted to David, but its proper meaning is *to separate, select, distinguish.*   חָסִיד § 185. 2, adj. derived from חֶסֶד, which denotes, see on Isa. 40 : 6, the love of God to man, or of man to God, or to one another. It may have the passive sense of *an object of divine regard,* or the active sense *of pious ;* both may here be combined, with special prominence to the former, though without excluding the latter. That God had selected him and made him the recipient of so great a benefit, ought to convince his foes that they cannot wrest it from him.

5. רִגְזוּ (1) *be angry,* so the LXX cited Eph. 4 : 26, ‘be angry and sin not :’ be angry if you can do so without sin, but this, especially in this case, in which it is directed against the Lord’s anointed, being impossible, see to it that you do not sin by anger. (2) *tremble* before God my protector and avenger, and in consequence avoid sinning longer by your hostility to me.   אִמְרוּ, not merely *speak,* but *say,* viz. : that you will discontinue your sinful course, *in your heart,* in private meditation and reflection.   עַל־מִשְׁכַּבְכֶם, not upon couches used as seats, or divans, i. e. in their meeting for consultation, but *upon your beds,* in the night, which upon the supposition of this being an evening psalm, was at hand, a time favourable to still reflection and reconsideration of their course.   וְדֹמּוּ *be still,* quietly reflect, ponder, or *desist* from your undertaking.

6. צֶדֶק *sacrifices of righteousness,* not merely externally right, agreeing in number and character with the legal prescriptions, but offered in a righteous spirit, which alone could make them acceptable. However profuse their sacrifices, while they continued in their present godless undertaking, they were sacrifices of wickedness. An allusion possibly to Absalom’s pretext, 2 Sam. 15 : 7, etc.   וּבִטְחוּ *and trust,* a second ex-

hortation, trust in God, not in yourselves and your own powers ; or, after the analogy of 'do this and live,' the second verb may denote a sequence of the first. Your present trust is presumptuous ; but offer the sacrifices of righteousness, then you may trust in the Lord. The Psalmist, in this address to his enemies, which, though in form directed to them, was really designed for himself, reviews the two leading grounds of his confidence that God would interfere on his behalf, (1) that the royal dignity of which they would deprive him was God's gift to him ; (2) that they were ungodly men, while he feared and trusted God.

7. רַבִּים, men in general, or David's desponding followers. מִי־יַרְאֵנוּ, regarded by some as an idiomatic optative, like מִי יִתֵּן, O that we might see. More probably it is the language of despondency, the question implying a negative answer ; no one can show us good. To 'see good' is to experience it ; comp. Luke 2 : 26, 'see death.' נְשָׂא = נְסָה־, the unusual orthography is perhaps designed to suggest an allusion to נֵס, comp. Ex. 17 : 15 lift up as a banner, display conspicuously, that we may rally beneath it. There is here a combined allusion to two parts of the sacerdotal blessing, 'the Lord lift up his face upon thee,' and 'the Lord cause his face to shine.' The light of the countenance is a token of favour. It was not outward good, but the Lord's favour, which the Psalmist desired.

8. This light of God's countenance, in fact, the Psalmist already possessed in the midst of his troubles, to such an extent that it gave him more joy than others found in the greatest outward prosperity. מֵעֵת, prep. in comparative sense. דְּגָנָם, suf. might refer to men in general, as Ps. 65 : 10, and then the proverbial joy of harvest is intended. More probably it relates to his foes in their times of abundance, which is tacitly contrasted with David's own destitution. Corn and wine are often combined to express agricultural products generally. רָבּוּ may agree directly with the preceding nouns, or a relative may be supplied, time of their corn and wine which abounded, or in which they abounded.

9. בְּשָׁלוֹם, state of perfect safety or security, nothing to injure or awaken apprehension. יַחְדָּו, one act coincident in time with the other ; no protracted wakefulness from anxiety, but fall asleep immediately on lying down. לְבָדָד thou alone or dwell alone, not only separated from all foes, but, as it was Israel's distinction, Num. 23 : 9, Deut. 33 : 28, separated from other nations, enjoying special protection and peculiar privileges.

15

PSALM V.

1. This Psalm presents another phase of the same great conflict between the righteous and the wicked. The hostility which in Psalm 2 was directed against Messiah, and in Psalms 3 and 4 against the king of the theocracy, his type and representative, is here in Psalm 5 expressed in terms applicable even to its humblest members, when the objects of wicked persecution by deed or word. An external point of connection with the two preceding Psalms is, that this is a morning Psalm, ver. 4, following morning and evening Psalms; also כִּי אַתָּה יְהֹוָה, last verses of 4th and 5th Psalms. אֶל־הַנְּחִילוֹת, a doubtful expression, variously explained as denoting the musical instrument, *unto*, i. e. to be sung as an accompaniment to, *the pipes* or flutes; the tune *to* the air or tune of *Nehiloth*, which must then be the name of some well-known melody, or a leading word in some composition associated with such a melody; or the subject *in reference to inheritances*, i. e. the respective lots or fortunes of the righteous and the wicked. LXX. ὑπὲρ τῆς κληρονομούσης. Vulg. *pro ea quae hereditatem consequitur*. The Psalm consists of two parts or stanzas, vs. 2–8 and vs. 9–13, each containing a prayer, an argument, and an expression of confident assurance. These divisions, though counterparts, are not, however, exactly equivalent; the second being an advance upon the first in every respect, and not a mere repetition of it. The supplication uttered in general terms in the first stanza, vs. 2–4, becomes in the second a specific prayer for protection from enemies and for the removal of difficulties. The wicked, who are spoken of generally in the first stanza, are seen in the second to be the foes of the Psalmist, and their wickedness is described with more exactness and detail. In the first stanza he anticipates protection and favour for himself; in the second all the righteous are sharers in the benefit.

2. The ideas of this verse are very simple, but the words are all poetic. אֲמָרַי from אָמַר or אָמֵר, the equivalent of which in prose is דָּבָר; הֲגִיגִי, most frequently found in poetry, answers to שֵׂיחַ; הָגִיג occurs only here and in Ps. 39 : 4; from the context there, and from an Arabic analogy, Gesenius explains it to mean *fervour*, applied to the heat of inward excitement or intense emotion; more probably, however, הָגָה = הָגַג, which is used both of speech, and thought as inward speech addressed to one's self; most frequently the latter, so here. Then אֲמָרַי, as the more general term, describing all he said to God in prayer, is divided into inaudible, *my thoughts*, known to God only, and audible, *the voice of my cry*, ver. 3. בִּינָה, both *attend to* and *understand*. The two imperatives

of this verse and that in the next verse have the paragogic הּ, § 98. 1,
converting them into earnest requests.

3. הַקְשִׁיבָה, properly *make attentive;* its proper object is 'the ear,'
which is often expressed, and is here understood. לְקֹל שַׁוְעִי *voice of my
cry,* i. e. my loud cry. The noun in every other place but this has a
feminine form, שַׁוְעָה, whence some have explained שַׁוְעִי as a Piel infin.:
it is more usual, however, to assume the existence of a noun with the
corresponding masculine form שֶׁוַע. מַלְכִּי. The titles by which God is
addressed contain a plea for his being heard, expressing as they do the
character under which the Psalmist looked to him in this emergency.
My king, not only as the great providential and moral governor of the
world, who would redress'wrong and vindicate the right, but specially as
the immediate ruler of Israel, whose king he was in a peculiar sense. It
was one of his own people, one of his immediate subjects, who appealed
to him for protection and redress, which he surely would not withhold.
וֵאלֹהָי *my God,* expressing an intimate personal relation.   כִּי— *for,* not
causal, as though the hearing must necessarily follow *because* he prayed,
but explanatory of the circumstances under which the request is made.
I ask to be heard, *for* there is something to hear, I will pray. אֵלֶיךָ אֶתְפַּלָּל :
to thee I will, perhaps also inclusive of the present, *I do pray,* as opposed
to brooding sullenly over his grief, and to seeking relief from other
sources.

4. בֹּקֶר, time when, § 274. 2. *a, in the morning,* as the first thing
in the day, showing his zeal and earnestness in it.   This is a natural
and appropriate time for prayer, and has been employed for this purpose
among all nations.   That it was so among the Jews appears from many
passages in the Psalms.   It was specially recommended in their case as
the time of the morning sacrifice, which the people accompanied by the
spiritual oblation of praise.   In later times it was stereotyped among the
canonical hours of prayer, of which mention is made in the New Testament, Acts 3 : 1.   Perhaps it is here to be taken in a collective sense,
every morning.   תִּשְׁמַע, God would hear his voice, i. e. he would pray to
God, his voice would be directed to him.   Others, with less probability,
take 'hear' in the sense of hear favourably, i. e. accept my prayer, grant
my petition.   It is then an expression, not of his own determination to
persevere in prayer, but of his confidence that his prayer would be speedily answered; Thou wilt, I trust, hear my prayer in the morning, as in
the morning I will arrange my prayer to thee; as I pray early, so I confidently hope thou wilt early grant my petition.   אֶעֱרָךְ, not *direct,* but
arrange, set in order, something consisting of various parts; its object
here is the words of his prayer.   It contains also an allusion to the

ritual service. This is the word technically used for several offices of the sanctuary, e. g. arranging the lamps or providing them with wick and oil, setting the shew-bread upon the table, and especially arranging the wood upon the altar of burnt-offering, and arranging the parts of the sacrifice upon it. This last was the first morning duty of the priest; and corresponding to that is the spiritual oblation which the Psalmist here pledges, and which could only be acceptable in connection with the atonement which the morning lamb procured or typified. אֲצַפֶּה, not *I will look up*, as a gesture of prayer, but *will watch*, as the attitude of expectation. The figure is that of a watchman stationed upon a look-out to descry objects in the distance; thus he would watch, expecting an answer to his prayer. It would be the prayer of faith, not of indifference or criminal unbelief. He has solicited gracious audience, declared his determination to pray, and expressed the hope and expectation of a favourable answer; but has not explicitly stated what his petition is. This is reserved until he comes to the beginning of the second stanza, where it appears that he desired deliverance from the persecutions of wicked enemies; that this was already in his mind appears, however, from the reason immediately assigned why he should be heard.

5. כִּי. He argues from God's holiness. I look confidently for an answer, אַתָּה, *for* thou art not a God that hast pleasure in wickedness. He has not yet said what his petition was, he does not say in the verses immediately succeeding that the wicked men whom he describes are his foes; he explains all this more fully in the next stanza. Now he only urges that his prayer is of such a nature, that a God who hates sin and will punish sinners, will surely grant it. חָפֵץ, verbal adjective with a direct object, see on Gen. 42: 18, Nah. 3: 1; the corresponding verb 's sometimes followed by בְּ, and sometimes by a direct object. יְגֻרְךָ § 102. 2, in the brief language of poetry this verb takes a suffix, though the relation is indirect, *lodge with thee*, be found in thy company, share that regard which the according of hospitality, particularly in the east, involved. רָע masc. *an evil person*, or neut. *evil;* the latter affords a more exact parallel to רֶשַׁע. God would seem to harbour sin if he tolerated it, or did not punish it.

6. יִתְיַצְּבוּ *stand* before thee as judge, endure the test of thy tribunal, or be suffered to *continue* in thy presence. אָוֶן, nonentity, emptiness, barren of all that is virtuous and good, and since this negative state implies what is positively bad, *iniquity.*

7. תְּאַבֵּד, since Jehovah hates sin, he will punish the sinner with destruction. דֹּבְרֵי § 254. 9. *b.* דָּמִים, see on Nah. 3: 1.

8. וַאֲנִי. The connection indicated by Vav will depend upon the

sense put upon this verse. According to one view it is adversative : evil shall not dwell with thee, and thou wilt destroy the wicked, *but* I shall in thy great mercy be permitted to enter thy house, to be thy guest, to be on terms of friendship and familiarity with God.   According to another view it is copulative : thou wilt destroy my wicked foes, *and* I in consequence will enter thy house to praise thee for this deliverance. To enter God's house may be spoken of as a token of familiarity and friendship, or as intimating that new matter of praise and thanksgiving would be afforded by granting him the deliverance for which he prays. חֵיכָל § 189. *b*.   The tabernacle erected by David on Mount Zion, 2 Sam. 6 : 17, is the one particularly intended.   The word strictly denotes the sacred edifice as distinguished from the court; the house of God includes the court; hence he speaks of entering God's house, but worshipping toward the palace or temple.   The temple or tabernacle proper none but the priests could enter.   The same distinction is preserved between ἱερόν and ναός in the New Testament.   בְּיִרְאָ § 254. 9.

9. Beginning of the second stanza.   נְחֵנִי *lead me*, the word is prevailingly used of divine guidance.   בְּצִדְקָתְךָ has been understood to describe that course or way in which he prays to be led; *thy righteousness*, i. e. that righteousness which thou requirest, or which thou givest, comp. δικαιοσύνη 9εοῦ, Rom. 1 : 17.   But why pray to be thus led ' on account of his enemies ?'   Various answers have been returned to this question ; as lest without this divine guidance my enemies should seduce or terrify me into sin, or lest I should give them occasion to scoff by my inconsistencies, or to rejoice at the calamities which would befall me in consequence of my transgressions, or lest I should be punished by being delivered into their hands.   But the context shows that the prayer is not so much for spiritual steadfastness as for deliverance from hostile machinations.   'Righteousness' is here the attribute of God.   *Lead me in* the exercise of *thy righteousness*, i. e. protect me from my wicked foes.   This appeal to God's *righteousness* rather than his *mercy*, looks at first sight like a claim to justification on the ground of his own merits. But it is to be observed, (1) that it is not a justification in the sight of God, which is in question, but in this controversy with his wicked enemies, whose hostility was groundless and sinful.   (2) The righteousness of God, when spoken of in relation to his true people, always in the Old Testament includes his mercy.   His righteousness is his rectitude in dealing with all according to their characters and relations.   With the wicked he stands simply upon a footing of law, and his righteousness demands their punishment as their sins deserve.   But the sins of the pious are atoned for, and he has made to them rich promises of grace.

so that his rectitude now requires the fulfilment of these promises. It is to this righteousness, of which his covenant faithfulness is an essential part, that the Psalmist here, and the people of God generally under the Old Testament, so confidently make their appeal. שׁוֹרְרָי. Gesenius assumes a root שָׁרַר, and makes this a Kal part. Others make it a Pi. part. with מ omitted from שׁוּר, to *watch, lie in wait*, comp. § 93. *e.* הַנִּשְׁאָר § 46, K'thibh הוֹשֵׁר, K'ri חַיְשֵׁר § 150. 1 (p. 181), as fut. in Prov. 4 : 25, יְיַשְּׁרוּ. That the Hiphil form with ו was not admitted by the Masorites in this verb appears from their removing it in the only other passage in which it occurs, Isa. 45 : 2 אושר (אוֹשֵׁר), K'ri אֲיַשֵּׁר. דַּרְכֶּךָ. The Vulgate transposes the suffixes and reads, 'make my way straight before thee.' *Thy way* is in this passage not the way which thou prescribest, the path of duty: make this level before me, or easy to walk in. It is rather the way in which thou leadest me ; the path of my life, not of duty, but of destiny: make that providential course in which thou leadest me a smooth and easy one, by removing obstructions, sufferings, and trials.

10. כִּי. The reason of this appeal to God's righteousness against his enemies ; *for* they are wicked and malignant. אֵין § 258. *b*, see on Gen. 40 : 8. בְּפִיהוּ § 220. 1. *c.* The *mouth, throat*, Ps. 115 : 7, and *tongue*, are spoken of as organs of speech, and *their inward part* or *heart* as the spring of what is outward. The singular suffix is distributive, 'mouth of each,' § 275. 6, or collective. קֶבֶר—, the *grave* is spoken of, not as a pit endangering passers by, but as yawning to receive the dead, destructive and insatiable, Prov. 30 : 16. יַחֲלִיקוּן *they make smooth their tongue*, use fair and flattering speeches, to cloak their mischievous designs.

11. הַאֲשִׁימֵם, not in the sense of שׁמם or שׁמד *destroy ;* אֲשֵׁם means, *to be guilty*, Hi. *make guilty*, cause them to be recognized as such, treat them as such by inflicting deserved punishment: יִפְּלוּ, some render, *let them fall*, or *they shall* certainly *fall from their counsels*, as in Lat. *spe excidere*, fail in their counsels, or their plans be frustrated ; but there is no proof that נָפַל מִן can be used in this sense. Better, *let them fall*, i. e. perish, מִן in causal sense, *in consequence of, by means of.* בְּרֹב, prep. may have its local sense *in*, or its instrumental sense *by*.

12. חוֹסֵי § 255. 1. בָּךְ *rejoice in thee*, in their relation to thee and in the blessings consequent upon it. שְׁמֶךָ. The name of God expresses that which is known of him ; it is the sum of his manifested attributes.

13. כִּי—. The reason of their exultation. צַדִּיק, indef. It may be taken individually or collectively. כַּצִּנָּה, the large shield, covering the entire person, different from מָגֵן ; § 245. 5. *d, as a shield* protects, or *as with a shield.* תַּעְטְרֶנּוּ § 274 2.

PSALM VI.

The idea is still that of the righteous persecuted by wicked enemies. Some suppose that the condition depicted is that of sore and dangerous disease; others, that what is said of bodily suffering, ver. 3, is a figure for inward distress occasioned by foes; the correct view appears to be, that the Psalmist is persecuted by foes, ver. 8, etc., which he regards as an evidence of the divine displeasure and rebuke for sin, ver. 2, and this is the occasion of physical exhaustion and undermined health. This is the first of the seven penitential Psalms, viz., 6, 32, 38, 51, 102, 130, 143. The period in David's life when it was written cannot be determined.

1. עַל־הַשְּׁמִינִית *the eighth* or *octave*, a musical term of doubtful meaning; it has been conjectured to mean an instrument of eight strings, or to denote the tone or key of performance, perhaps the bass.

The Psalm consists of two parts:

(1) vs. 2–8, a prayer enforced by the misery of his condition.

(2) vs. 9–11, confidence in the divine protection and deliverance.

2. אַל־בְּאַפְּךָ, the prayer is not merely for mitigation, comp. Jer. 10: 24, as though the meaning were, rebuke not with the severity of anger, but with the gentleness of love. He seeks the removal of the chastisement which always proceeds from displeasure against sin. תוֹכִיחֵנִי, the rebuke of God, not uttered in words, but shown by his dealings, the inflictions of his providence.

3. חָנֵּנִי § 141. 3. אֻמְלַל אָנִי, 3 pers. Pual pret., *I am one who has drooped*, § 279. *a*, or abbreviated from אֻמְלָל, either a verbal adj. or a Pual part. with מ omitted, § 93. *e*. The double accent being partly on one word and partly on the other, connects them as if they were joined by Makkeph. נִבְהֲלוּ *are terrified*, affected by my terror, lose their strength and elasticity: 'bones' are spoken of as the solid frame on which the body rests.

4. נִבְהֲלָה. Both body (נַפְשִׁי) and soul were affected by this terror.

7. *I am* already *weary*, and if matters continue so, *I will make my bed swim.* בְּכָל־לַיְלָה *all night*, or *every night.* In Baer's edition of the Psalms, from which the text is taken, Daghesh-forte is inserted in the initial letter of a word, whenever the preceding word ends in the same letter.

8. עָשְׁשָׁה refers to the dimness of the eye produced by physical exhaustion or mental suffering. בְּכַעַס, grief or indignation at treatment so unjust.

9. Upon the utterance of his prayer the Psalmist receives an inward assurance of divine protection and deliverance. פֹּעֲלֵי, their plans for his

destruction would be abortive, and might as well be abandoned. ‏רַע‎, for God had heard and would save. ‏קוֹל‎ *voice of my weeping*, i. e. my loud weeping.

11. ‏יֵבֹשׁוּ‎, they shall be brought to shame by the frustration of their plans. ‏וְיִבָּהֲלוּ‎, by a divine retaliation they shall suffer the very thing which they have inflicted upon him, vs. 3. 4. ‏יָשֻׁבוּ‎, not in adverbial sense, § 269. *a*, *they shall be ashamed again*, nor of an inward change, *they shall repent*, but, *they shall return*, retreat, be driven back, their assault repelled, or they obliged to desist from it.

PSALM VII.

This completes the first series of Psalms relating to the hostility of the wicked against the righteous, by an impressive appeal to the future and certain judgment of God.

1. ‏שִׁגָּיוֹן‎ § 193. 2, is supposed by some to characterize the style of composition. ‏שָׁגָה‎ = ‏שָׁגַג‎ *to celebrate*, hence 'a song,' or ‏שָׁגָה‎ *to stagger*, hence a song of intoxication or strong excitement, a wild and irregular verse or measure, 'a dithyramb.' Or it may describe the subject ; ‏שָׁגָה‎ *to err*, hence 'error,' either in a physical sense, i. e. relating to David's wanderings, or, in a moral sense, transgression, i. e. relating to sin. ‏עַל־דִּבְרֵי‎, not = ‏עַל־דְּבַר‎ *concerning the affair of*, i. e. concerning, but *concerning the words of*. In vs. 4–6 the Psalmist clears himself of a slanderous charge. ‏כּוּשׁ‎, perhaps the real name of some adversary of David, otherwise unknown, one of those, it may be, who were perpetually afresh poisoning the mind of Saul towards him. Some have suspected that it is an enigmatical name of Saul himself, who might be called *an Ethiopian*, from the blackness of his heart. The Psalm may be divided as follows, viz.:

(1) vs. 2–6, supplication and appeal to God.

(2) vs. 7–18, God's judgment on transgressors.

Each part is capable of subdivision : thus the first part,

vs. 2. 3, prayer for deliverance from extreme peril.

vs. 4–6, fortified by an asseveration of his innocence of what has been falsely imputed to him.

The second part into three portions of four verses each :

vs. 7–10, prayer for God's judgment.

vs. 11–14, confident assurance of it.

vs. 15–18, its actual infliction.

2. He pleads from his relation to God, and from his having in time

past put his *trust* in him, that he may not be disappointed now. הוֹשִׁיעַ denotes enlargement, positive salvation, הִצִּיל is negative, extrication from peril : they are used interchangeably as poetic equivalents.

3. Argument from the extremity of his peril. The plural of the preceding verse is here exchanged for the singular, which may be understood collectively or distributively, or may be an individualization, referring to the most prominent and dangerous of his foes, viz. : Saul, whose hostility alone made others formidable. יִטְרֹף *rend as a lion*, the most formidable and savage beast of prey, *my soul*, because the life was the object of attack. פֹּרֵק *crushing*, breaking bones.

4. vs. 4. 5 are conditional, and the apodosis is contained in ver. 6. He is willing to abjure the divine aid, if he is as guilty as he is charged with being. זֹאת may refer back to the title, 'the words of Cush,' or to what follows, and is more fully explained in the next verse. בְּכַפָּי *in my hands*, as the instruments of action, if they are soiled by contact with the pollution of crime ; as the hands of a murderer are said to be stained with blood. Others suppose the hands to be regarded as instruments of seizure ; if there be plunder iniquitously taken in my hands as evidence of robbery and injustice.

5. Connect רָע with גְּמַלְתִּי, not with שׁוֹלְמִי 'him who treated me ill.' וָאֲחַלְּצָה, Eng. Ver. makes Vav adversative and the clause parenthetic. More recent interpreters regard Vav as copulative, and render חָלַץ *to spoil*, a sense which nowhere else occurs in the verb, but is justified by its derivative חֲלִיצָה *spoils*. There seems to be an allusion to the opportunities which David had of injuring Saul in the cave at Engedi and wilderness of Ziph, but which he forbore to use ; and where, in exculpating himself to Saul, he referred to false accusations of this description, 1 Sam. 24 : 9, 26 : 19.

6. יִרְדֹּף § 60. 2. *a*. The future has a jussive sense, as is shown by the following יַשֵּׂג and יִשְׁכֹּן. If guilty of these charges, he was willing to renounce all claim upon the divine interposition, and to have permission given to the enemy to pursue his soul, i. e. his life, with deadly intent, and not only pursue, but overtake and trample it to the earth. וְיִרְמֹס, complete, helpless, and contemptuous destruction, as of something vile and worthless. וּכְבוֹדִי *honour*, personal, official, or both ; to bring this to the dust is to degrade him by the loss of it. Or it may denote the more honourable and exalted part of his nature, and thus be equivalent to 'life' and 'soul :' and to bring it to the dust will then be to sink him to the grave.

7. Having stated his case, he now appeals to God, the judge of all, for his judgment. He prays that God's judgment on the world may be-

gin, and that this particular portion of it, his own case, may be decided without further delay. קוּמָה, see on 3 : 8. הִנָּשֵׂא, either, *lift up thy- self,* parallel to the preceding verb, or *ascend* the seat of judgment. בְּעַבְרוֹת, prep. *in* the midst of, and so *because of* or *against.* וְעוּרָה *awake,* as if from sleep and previous inattention or neglect. אֵלַי *unto me,* for my advantage, or a pregnant construction, § 272. 3, *awake* and turn *to me.* מִשְׁפָּט, not accusative of direction, 'unto the judgment which thou hast commanded,' but the object of the verb, *thou hast com- manded judgment,* either justice which God has required to be practised, whence he is appealed to that he would now exercise the same, or rather a judicial process which he has resolved upon and appointed a time for executing.

8. The judgment scene is depicted. וַעֲדַת *congregation of nations,* i. e. all nations, either as spectators, or themselves to be judged. וְעָלֶיהָ, either, after the judgment is complete ascend again triumphantly to heaven, or preparatory to the judgment resume the elevated judgment- seat, here called the high place ; resume or return to it, because in suf- fering iniquity to be unpunished, he appeared for a season to have for- saken it.

9. He pleads from the necessary connection of God's universal work of judgment with the dispensing of justice in his own case. God is to judge, or judges, is the judge of nations ; judge me, do me justice. עָלָי, supply the relative, which is *upon me,* rests upon me, is possessed by me. Others render, which is *over* me as a protection and defence, or supply the substantive verb, 'let it be upon me according to my righteousness.' This desire to be treated according to his righteousness is not inconsistent with his supplications for divine mercy in the previous Psalm and elsewhere. He was guiltless as regarded man, and especially as regarded these existing charges and his existing foes, but not as re- garded God.

10. The object of this judgment for which he prays, is the destruc- tion of sin, rather than of the persons of the wicked, except so far as this is necessary to it, and the establishment and security of the righteous. יִגְמָר־, trans. or intrans. and רַע, subject or object ; hence three con- structions are possible. (1) may evil (i. e. their sin) destroy the wicked ; (2) may he put an end to the evil of the wicked ; (3) may the evil of the wicked cease. Since God is addressed both before and after, the last is to be preferred. וּבֹחֵן *a righteous God tries,* or is *a trier of hearts and reins.* Or if the language of direct address is preserved in this clause, 'thou, O righteous God, art a trier, etc.' or ' thou art a trier of hearts and reins, a righteous God.' 'Hearts and reins' denote the inte-

nor nature and state of men, their inward character as well as their
inward acts or exercises.   This is an assertion not only of God's omnis
cience, that he is acquainted with what passes within men, but also of
his justice, that he will deal with them accordingly, like a trier of metals
who discriminates dross from gold.

11.   The petition is followed by a confident expectation founded on
the divine justice.   ·ְָ, God, who is elsewhere called a shield, i. e.
protection or defence, is here represented as sustaining the shield, providing for the defence of the Psalmist.   *My shield is upon God*, rests
upon him, is furnished or supported by him.   The attribute ascribed to
God in the following words is the ground of the confidence just expressed.

12.   שֹׁפֵט *God judges*, does justice to *the righteous*, or, *God is a
righteous judge*.   שֹׁפֵט predicate, and אֵל subject, *God is angry every
day*, or the former might qualify אֵל, if the prose usage of this word be
insisted on, see on Nah. 1 : 2, and אֱלֹהִים be the subject, *God is a God
who is angry every day*.

13.   אִם־לֹא יָשׁוּב *if he*, the wicked, *shall not return*, either inwardly
repent or turn back from his assault and persecution.   As God is the
subject both before and after, some make it so in this clause by converting אִם לֹא into an asseveration.   In an oath, see on Gen. 42 : 15, אִם has
a negative sense, and אִם לֹא an opposite or positive sense ; *surely he will
return, sharpen his sword*, will again sharpen it, § 269. *a*.

14.   לַדֹּלְקִים. not *ardent* in pursuit, persecutors, but *he will make his ar-
rows to be burning*, with allusion to the practice of hurling blazing darts.

15.   He conceives mischief or harm to others and brings forth falsehood, that which disappoints his expectations ; he ruins himself instead
of those against whom he is plotting.

16.   Figure from pits dug to entrap animals.   וַיַּפְעָל *he was making
or was about to make*, fut. relative to the preceding preterite, § 263. 1.

17.   Comp. Obad. ver. 15.

18.   Praise for God's just judgment on the wicked and his vindication of his servants.   עֶלְיוֹן when used as a divine name does not receive
the article, § 246. 1.

PSALM VIII.

A devout meditation upon God's condescending grace to man as
shown in the rank assigned to him in the creation, and the dominion
granted to him over the world.   The divine goodness to man, which it
is the aim of this Psalm to celebrate, is not to be estimated by his present fallen condition, which is the fruit of his own sin, but by the gifts

and honours with which he was crowned in his primitive estate. It is man as God made him and designed him to be, who is here described, primeval man, ideal man. This ideal, imperfectly exhibited in man as he now is, finds full realization in Christ, of whom Adam was a type, and to whom the terms of the Psalm are therefore applicable in a more exalted sense than they were to him, Heb. 2 : 6–9, 1 Cor. 15 : 27. It shall hereafter be realized in all the people of God, who are to be restored in the image of Christ, and made partakers of his dignity and glory, and thus raised to a condition of which the primitive estate of man was but the image and the type.

1. הַגִּתִּית, by some derived from גַּת *a wine-press*, and thought to denote a style of music connected with the vintage ; by others from the city of *Gath*, whence the instrument or tune so designated may have been borrowed ; and by others still from נָגַן, in the sense of *the music of stringed instruments.*

The Psalm recounts,

(1) vs. 2–4, the evidences of God's greatness, as preliminary to the consideration of,

(2) vs. 5–10, his wonderful grace to man.

2. אֲדֹנֵינוּ § 201. 2, plur. suf., the Psalmist speaks not merely for himself as an individual, but for all the people of God, or for all men. שֶׁמְךָ, the name of God, i. e. that which is known of him, the revelation which he has made of himself, see on 1 Sam. 17 : 45, Ps. 5 : 11. תְּנָה § 132. 1. This word has greatly embarrassed interpreters. Some make it 3 f. pret. for נָתְנָה, as מַתָּה 2 Sam. 22 : 41 for נָתַתָּה, *which*, viz. the earth, *has given thy glory above the heavens*, i. e. has caused thy praises to reach the skies. Others, as in all the other passages in which this form occurs, imper. with ה paragogic, *which give even thy glory above the heavens*, make it still more conspicuous. But the connection seems to demand, not a prayer for enhancing God's glory, but a declaration of its conspicuity and greatness. It seems better, therefore, to regard it as a Kal infin. תֵּנָה for תֵּת or תֵּן, as רְדָה Gen. 46 : 3 for רְדָה § 148. 2, *whose glory is given*, put *upon the heavens*, lit. *the giving of whose glory* is, etc. The glory of God is displayed in the heavens, and his name is thus made resplendent in all the earth.

3. This glory is so self-evidencing that babes may be trusted to defend it against blaspheming foes. עוֹלְלִים, not babes in the spiritual sense, as opposed to the wise and prudent, Matt. 11 : 25, but young children ; enough is palpable to them to constitute an irrefragable argument of God's greatness and glory. עֹז, out of the utterances of these feeble advocates God *has founded strength*, constructed a power to still

the proudest foes. In such a cause a child can confute the most learned
and subtle infidel. For 'strength' the LXX substitute 'praise;' this
rendering is retained in Matt. 12 : 16 as substantially equivalent to the
original, inasmuch as the strength referred to consists in the conscious
or unconscious praises of infancy and childhood. The word עֹז, however, does not properly mean 'praise,' though Gesenius incorrectly attributes this meaning to it here and in a few other passages.

4. אֶצְבְּעֹתֶיךָ § 183. c, figure from human organs of construction.
יָרֵחַ § 247. :תְּכוֹנֵנָה § 86. b (2 m. s.).

5. :תִּפְקְדֶנּוּ, God is said to visit men when he manifests himself to
them either in mercy or in judgment; the former is here particularly
referred to. The future in this and the following verbs has its habitual sense, § 263. 4, describing what God is constantly doing. The
sentence begun in the preceding verse extends through the first clause
of ver. 7.

6. וַתְּחַסְּרֵהוּ § 265. a. מְעַט denotes degree, a little; in the ideal
application of this Psalm to Christ it might also have its temporal sense,
a little while, Heb. 2 : 7. 9. מֵאֱלֹהִים, for 'God' the LXX substitute
'angels,' which is retained Heb. 2 : 7, since the main idea is expressed
with sufficient accuracy. The Psalmist alludes to the fact that man was
made in the image of God.

7. כֹּל, man was constituted the head of the material and animal
creation. But as applied to Christ, the ideal man, in whom and by
whom our lapsed nature is restored, these words obtain a higher than
their original sense, and 'all' may be pressed to the widest possible extent of meaning, and embrace, as the apostle in commenting upon it explains, absolutely all things but God himself, 1 Cor. 15 : 27, Eph. 1 : 22,
Heb. 2 : 8.

8. This verse contains two poetic forms, צֹנֶה for צֹאן, or as it is once
written, צֹנֶא, and :שָׂדָי for שָׂדֶה; also one word of rare occurrence, אֲלָפִים,
equivalent in sense to the more usual and prosaic בָּקָר. The enumeration begins with the domestic animals as the most useful and the most
completely under human control, proceeds thence to wild beasts, and
thence to the inhabitants of the other elements, the birds of the air
above, the fish in the waters beneath.

9. עֹבֵר cannot agree with דְּגֵי, but is a parallel and more comprehen-
sive expression.

10. This verse repeats the sentiment with which the Psalm began,
and of which a fresh proof has now been exhibited. God's name rendered glorious by the frame of material nature is still more exalted and
ennobled by his condescending grace to man.

PSALM XXII.

The basis of this Psalm is to be sought in the typical experience of the Psalmist, the prophetic significance of which is herein developed. David, though a true servant of God, was exposed to severe suffering from the persecution of wicked men, was finally delivered, and in consequence of this deliverance grateful homage was paid to God by him and by others to whom this act of grace was made known. This was not an anomalous experience, but a law of the kingdom of God, destined to be verified not only in other instances like his own, but on a vastly greater scale in One who should be the righteous sufferer *par excellence*, and whose sufferings, coupled with his final extrication out of them, should result in the offering of grateful praise to God from all mankind in every age. The extremity of the sufferings described, and especially the consequences to follow upon their termination, are such as David could not, by the most strained exaggeration, have imputed to his own case. It is evident that he is speaking in the name of the Messiah, considered as the ideal of righteous sufferers. The same thing appears from the adoption of the first words of this Psalm by our Lord upon the cross, and the application of its language to him in repeated instances in the New Testament.

1. בְּיֶלֶת־הַשַּׁחַר. Some suppose *the hind of the dawn* to be the name of a tune or of a song whose melody was to be used in singing this Psalm; others think it to be an enigmatical description of the subject, 'the hind' perhaps a figure for persecuted innocence, with the 'dawn' of a happier morning after a night of suffering and sorrow; or, 'the hind of the dawn' may be a fanciful description of the breaking day, the first branching beams as they struggle into view being compared to antlers.

The Psalm consists of three parts, viz.:

vs. 2–11, prayer for deliverance enforced by the speaker's relation to God.

vs. 12–22, by the greatness of the peril.

vs. 23–32, praise for deliverance and its blessed results.

2. אֵלִי, see on Nah. 1:2. That God was *his God* was itself a plea why he should be heard. עָזַב § 231. 4. *a.* עֲזַבְתָּנִי, for which σαβαχθανί, שְׁבַקְתָּנִי Matt. 27:46 is the Chaldee equivalent. רָחוֹק may agree directly with the subject of the preceding verb, or the interrogation may be repeated, 'why art thou *far*, etc.' דִּבְרֵי, coördinate with the preceding noun and governed by the same preposition, מִן; though others read, *the words of my roaring* are *far* § 275. 1 *from my salvation*, i. e. far from effecting it; and others still, ' *my God, etc. etc.*' are *the words of my roaring.*

4. ‮קדוש‬. The God whom the sufferer addresses is *holy*, that is according to the proper sense of the original expression, see on Isa. 40 : 25, 41 : 14, infinitely exalted and perfectly pure. He might, therefore, be expected to possess both the ability and the disposition to save his oppressed servant. ‮יושב‬ *inhabiting*, i. e. either dwelling among so as to be surrounded by, or sitting enthroned upon *the praises of Israel*. These praises imply attributes, to which he makes his urgent appeal.

5. Argument from God's past covenant faithfulness as shown to those who were Messiah's fathers according to the flesh.

7. ‮חרפה‬, despicable and helpless, liable to be crushed. Comp. Isa. 41 : 14, 49 : 7, 53 : 3.

8. ‮יפטירו‬, these gestures of derision are expressly mentioned in the narrative of the crucifixion, Mat. 27 : 39, Mark 15 : 29.

9. ‮גל‬, not the infin. for the pret. *he rolled*, § 268. 1, as it is rendered by the LXX, but the imper. *roll*, devolve thy cause upon Jehovah, commit it to him, comp. Ps. 37 : 5, Prov. 16 : 3. A taunting and ironical suggestion made to the sufferer by the unfeeling beholders before described, who then proceed to speak of him in the third person, § 279. The evangelist records the utterance at the cross of these identical expressions and others like them, Mat. 27 : 43. ‮חפץ‬, the subject is Jehovah, not the sufferer, since this verb is used to describe the feelings of God toward men, but never those of men toward God.

10. ‮כי‬. The taunt was just. They may well say, God has delighted in me, *for* thy kind care was bestowed upon me from my birth. ‮גחי‬ § 157. 1, *thou* art *my breaking forth*, i. e. the one who brought me forth. ‮מבטיחי‬, giving me ground for trust, before I was capable of its conscious exercise, by thy gracious dealings with me.

11. ‮אל‬, this section of the Psalm closes, as it began, with the argument which has thus far been persistently pressed.

12. The second argument on which his petition is based, the proximity of the danger, and his destitution of any other source of help. The second ‮כי‬ is coördinate with the first, and both are dependent on ‮אל־תרחק‬.

13–16. His enemies, who have him completely in their power, are compared to bulls reared on the rich but solitary pastures of Bashan, and to lions. The weakness verging on dissolution, to which they have reduced him, is set forth under the emblems of water, and melted wax, and dislocated bones. The vigour and moisture of his frame is dried out, it is dry as a potsherd, and his parched tongue cleaves to his jaws. It has been suggested that the physical effects of crucifixion are here precisely described, the violent wrenching of the body, the extreme debility and exhaustion, and the raging thirst, John 19 : 28. ‮הקיפוני‬, what was accomplished by his murderous enemies was nevertheless, under another aspect, the act of God. The persecution has reached its last stage; *thou wilt*, if this murderous treatment is allowed to proceed further, *place me to the dust of death*, i. e. the grave, bring me down to it and place me there.

17. —כִּי, the proof that he is, as he has just declared, at the very point of death. חִצְפֵּרִי § 275. 2 or § 277. כָּאֲרִי *like a lion* they have encircled or beset me *as to my hands and my feet*, § 271. 4, or as we might say, 'hand and foot,' so that I can neither resist nor flee. Dr. Alexander suggests as a point of comparison, "the infliction of sharp wounds in those parts of the body, an idea common to the habits of the lion and the usages of crucifixion." The explanation of כָּאֲרִי as a plur. part. from כּוּר, which, though it does not occur elsewhere, might easily mean *to pierce*, see Gesenius Lexicon, involves the double anomaly of the insertion of א § 156. 3, and the omission of ם from the plural ending, § 199. *b*. An inconsiderable number of manuscripts read כָּאֲרוּ or כָּרוּ *they pierced*. They appear to be confirmed by the LXX, Aquila, the Syriac Peshito, and Jerome, who render this word as a verb, though with some variety in the signification which they assign to it. The Masora (according to Jacob ben Chayim, the learned editor of the Venetian Rabbinical Bible, 1525) remarks that כָּאֲרִי occurs twice in different senses, viz.: in Isa. 38 : 13, where it undoubtedly means *as a lion*, and Ps. 22 : 17, where the K'ri has כָּאֲרִי, and the K'thibh כָּאֲרוּ. De Rossi (Variae Lectiones, vol. iv.), however, confesses that he could find no such remark in any of the numerous copies which he possessed of the Masora. On the whole, the reading with ו, though adopted into the text, or at least put on a par with the received reading by several able critics, seems to have the overwhelming preponderance of critical authorities against it.

18. הֵמָּה, not his bones but his foes. יִרְאוּ־בִי, see on Gen. 44 : 34, *gaze at me*, feast themselves with the spectacle of my misery.

19. יְחַלְּקוּ, in the sense of the unfinished present, § 263. 2, *are dividing*, or proximate future, *are about to divide*, on the point of dividing. They are so sure of the death of their victim as to be already apportioning his garments amongst themselves. The exactness of its fulfilment is testified by all four of the evangelists, Mat. 27 : 35, Mark 15 : 24, Luke 23 : 34, John 19 : 23. 24. יַפִּילוּ־גוֹרָל, for Daghesh-forte conjunctive, see on 6 : 7.

20. וְאַתָּה § 243. 1, the pronoun expressed on account of the emphasis of the opposition. They are acting thus, *and* therefore do not *thou* refuse or delay thine aid.

21. מַחְרֵב, poetic individualization of deadly hostile weapons. וְנַפְשִׁי, not merely *me* but *my soul*, i. e. my life, see on 3 : 2. מִיַד־ *from the hand*, i. e. from the power of, see on Gen. 37 : 21. In this derived sense of the phrase it is here joined with 'dog,' as in 1 Sam. 17 : 37 with 'lion' and 'bear.' Others think it to be an indication that under the figure of 'dogs' men are intended. יְחִידָתִי, shown by the parallel expression נַפְשִׁי to be an epithet of his life ; *my only one*, either as possessing singular value, my darling, my most highly prized, or more strictly the only life he possessed or could have ; or it may be *my lonely one*, my life deserted as it seems to be by God as well as men.

22. רֵמִים for רְאֵמִים, by § 53. 3 ; *and from the horns of the buffaloes thou hast answered me*, i. e. answered my prayer proceeding from between their horns, or answered by delivering me from their horns, § 272. 3. Others, contrary to the accents, put a full stop after 'buffaloes,' connecting all that precedes with הוֹשִׁיעֵנִי. עֲנִיתָנִי, the deliverance prayed for is granted. This sudden transition prepares the way for the third and last division of the Psalm. The Psalmist sets forth the severity of Messiah's sufferings, but makes no explicit mention of his death. The vicarious nature of these sufferings is not declared, nor the direct connection which they have with the salvation of the world ; while stress is chiefly laid upon the results effected by his exaltation from this extremity of woe. The view presented is of course a partial one, being limited by the character of the type, which it is the province of the Psalm to unfold. In the respects referred to it is supplemented by Isa. 53.

23. אֲסַפְּרָה *declare thy name*, i. e. recount the manifestations which God has made of his glorious perfections, see on 5 : 11. It is here said with special reference to the exhibition of his power and grace just made. Quoted as the language of Messiah, Heb. 2 : 12.

25. שִׁוְעוֹ § 92. *c*.

26. מֵאִתְּךָ *from with thee*, not merely respecting thee, but derived from thee. יְרֵאָיו, change of person, § 279.

27. יֹאכְלוּ, partake of the sacrificial or eucharistic festival implied or referred to in the last clause of the preceding verse, symbolizing communion with God and all spiritual blessings. יְחִי, by some supposed to be the customary formula of benediction pronounced by the offerer of the sacrifice upon those who partook with him of the festival ; which might account for the change of person.

28. יִזְכְּרוּ *remember* the evidence now afforded of Jehovah's grace to his suffering servant, or remember God himself, whom the heathen have forgotten, 9 : 18. אַפְסֵי־אָרֶץ, see on 2 : 8. כָּל־מִשְׁפְּחוֹת, the blessing thus

16

wrought shall be co-extensive with that which it was promised Abraham should be effected through his seed, Gen. 12 : 3.

29. All nations shall thus worship Jehovah, *for* they are rightfully his. Comp. Obad. ver. 21. ישׁתחוו, the pronoun is often omitted even before participles, when the subject can be readily supplied from the context, § 243. 1.

30. אכלו, the figure of the sacrificial festival is continued. This salvation shall not only extend to all nations, but to all classes ; *the fat ones of the earth*, they who have a prosperous abundance, as well as those who are perishing in abject destitution, *going down to the dust*, the grave, and he who, § 285. 3, *has not kept his soul alive*, though dying or actually dead, he shall partake of this soul-reviving food, and shall live.

31. These benefits shall further be shared by every age. זרע *seed*, the descendants of those just spoken of, or posterity in general. יספר *it shall be related of the Lord to the* next *generation* ; the LXX connect the following יבאו with this verse, γενεὰ ἡ ἐρχομένη, but this is unnecessary. This rendering gives to the verb the same sense as in ver. 23, and is to be preferred to *it*, posterity, *shall be reckoned* (a figure from the census or enrollment, as Ps. 87 : 6) *unto* or *by the Lord to the generation*, comp. Ps. 24 : 6, i. e. to the number of his true people.

32. יבאו, the participle denotes a time contemporaneous with the action of the preceding verb, § 266. 3, *a people* not now in existence, but who shall then be *born*.

PSALM XLV.

Messiah is here presented as the ideal bridegroom. The typical basis was probably afforded by the marriage of Solomon to a foreign princess, perhaps, as many have conjectured, to the daughter of Pharaoh, king of Egypt. It cannot, however, be an ode composed in honour of that marriage. This is forbidden by its position in the book of Psalms, and its reception into the canon. A secular poem could find no place there, and would be entirely without analogy. The royal bridegroom is a divine person, ver. 7, to whom a universal reign, ver. 17, and endless homage, ver. 18, are promised. Tyre, which was never subject to any king of Israel, makes her submission to him, ver. 13. In addition to one who is designated the queen, other virgins and kings' daughters, her fellows, are upon the same occasion wedded to the king, vs. 9. 14. 15, which is contrary to the usages of real life, though significant as an allegory. Martial qualities are imputed to the king, vs. 3–5, and a line of royal ancestors, ver. 16 ; neither of which could be attributed to Solomon. Hence this Psalm has, from the earliest times, been regarded as a mystic epithalamium, representing under a figure frequently employed in both the Old and the New Testaments the union of the Lord and his people, of Christ and his church. Its admission into the canon, it is now generally confessed, proves that it was so understood at the time the canon was formed. The Targum so expounds it. The application of it to Christ, Heb. 1 : 8. 9, both implies that this view was then prevalent, and sets the seal of inspired authority upon it. Its messianic character has been almost universally recognized by Christian interpreters, and though denied by the unbelief of modern times in its repugnance to admit predictions of Christ, no other satisfactory solution has been or can be proposed.

1. עַל־שֹׁשַׁנִּים *upon lilies*, which some explain to mean, lily-shaped instruments ; others, a tune bearing that name, or associated with a song so called ; others, an enigmatical description of the subject, 'lilies' being a figure for beautiful women, Sol. Song, 2 : 2. לִבְנֵי־קֹרַח belonging *to the sons of Korah*, a Levitical family, employed with others by the appointment of David ' in the service of song in the house of the Lord,' 1 Chron. 6 : 16. 22 (Eng. Ver. vs. 31. 37), 2 Chron. 20 : 19. It belonged to them, probably, in the sense of being committed to them for musical performance, though others think that it was composed by them. מַשְׂכִּיל, an *instructive* or *didactic* Psalm ; this title would only be appropriate upon the allegorical interpretation, and may have been prefixed with the view of suggesting at the outset that this is not a mere marriage ode, and of leading the reader to seek for a deeper meaning. יְדִידֹת *lovely* women, though some give to the fem. plur. a neuter sense, *lovely* things, or an abstract, § 201. 1. *a*, *love*.

After an introduction, ver. 2, declaring the Psalmist's interest in his exalted theme, follow,

(1) vs. 3–10, the praises of the king.

(2) vs. 11–16, the queen and the wedding festivities.

(3) vs. 17. 18, conclusion.

In (1) and (3) the king is addressed ; in (2) the queen.

2. דָּבָר is governed by רֹחֵשׁ, not by אֹמֵר, which is forbidden by the accents. אֹמֵר may govern מַעֲשַׂי, or it may stand absolutely, *I am saying : my works* are or let them be *for the king*, or *respecting the king*, לַמֶּלֶךְ § 247. עֵט *my tongue is*, or may it be *the pen*, etc., i. e. rapidly record the language of my thoughts.

3. יָפְיָפִיתָ might appear to be formed by the reduplication of the first two radicals, and so it is in fact frequently explained. This would,

however, be entirely anomalous and without analogy. On the other hand, there are instances both in verbs, § 92. *a*, and nouns, § 188, of the reduplication of the last two radicals, e. g. סְחַרְחַר, דְּבַקְבַּק. A like formation from צָבָה = יְצַב § 168, would yield יְצַבְצַב, comp. the related adjective חֲמַרְמָר. The first Yodh then receives Kamets Hhatuph as the vowel of the passive reduplicated species, § 93. *a*, and the second Yodh a pretonic Kamets, § 64. 2, lest in its weakness its sound might be entirely lost. The ascription of superhuman beauty to an earthly monarch would be gross flattery. חֵן בְּשִׂפְתוֹתֶיךָ § 199. *d*, grace, which has the same two-fold sense in Hebrew as in English of favour and beauty, is predicated of the lips not as a feature of the face but as an organ of speech. The reference is to ' the gracious words which proceeded out of his mouth,' Luke 4 : 22. עַל־כֵּן cannot mean *because, propterea quod*, but must mean *therefore*. This is by some attenuated to the declaration that his more than human beauty and his grace of speech indicate that God has blessed him, and that forever; a slender basis, it must be confessed, for so grand a conclusion, if external form and the charms of eloquence are intended. But even thus the everlasting blessing implies the unending life of its recipient; he must consequently be more than mortal man. If, however, the particle be allowed its proper force, 'therefore' denotes not an index merely, but the ground. And as physical beauty and persuasive speech can be no ground for the bestowment of the divine blessing, this is an evidence of the allegorical character of the description. They must represent spiritual qualities, the beauty of holiness and words of heavenly grace and truth.

4. The conquests by which his empire is extended, are set forth not in a bald, prosaic description, but more poetically, by summoning him to do what he actually will perform. He is bidden to gird his sword upon his thigh, i. e. to prepare for martial deeds, and at the same time to gird on, as though constituting the garment with which he is invested, his glory and his majesty, terms which are repeatedly combined elsewhere to denote the divine dignity, Ps. 96 : 6, as well as the splendour of a divinely bestowed royalty, Ps. 21 : 6.

5. וַהֲדָרְךָ § 274. 2. *e*, in the royal dignity thus securely girt about him he should press on to valiant deeds and victories. צְלַח, either *pass on, press through*, or *prosper;* if the latter, it will qualify the following verb, § 269. *a*. רְכַב, either in the military chariot or on the war horse, Hab. 3 : 8, Rev. 19 : 11. אֱמֶת § 205. *b*, *for the sake of truth and meek-ness* and *righteousness*, i. e. in vindication of those who possess these qualities or represent these principles, or else on account of his own pos-session of these attributes. וְתוֹרְךָ, the right hand is personified and

represented as planning and achieving what is accomplished by means of it : let it show thee what it can do. נוֹרָאוֹת § 266. 1.

6. כִּסֵּא depends on שׁוֹנְאֶיךָ, the intervening words forming a parenthesis. וּמֶלֶךְ, the same who is addressed, but here reverentially spoken of in the third person, see on Gen. 41 : 13.

7. כִּסְאֲךָ § 221. 3. a.   The natural and obvious rendering of these words, found in all the ancient versions, and sanctioned by the authority of the New Test., Heb. 1 : 8, is, *thy throne, O God, is forever and ever.* As the divine nature of Messiah is either taught or implied in other passages both of the Psalms and of the prophets, it can create no difficulty that he is here addressed as God.   At any rate, this evident sense of the words cannot be set aside by such forced and rare, if not impossible constructions as, *thy throne of God,* i. e. divinely bestowed or established, § 256. b, or *thy throne* is the throne of *God.*

8. שֶׁמֶן, an allusion to the practice of anointing the body, particularly on festive occasions.   To anoint with the oil of gladness is to make superlatively glad.   אֱלֹהִים might be a vocative, as in ver. 7, but it seems better to make it the subject of the preceding verb. : מֵחֲבֵרֶךָ *thy fellows* in regal dignity, i. e. other kings.   The peculiar joy granted to him above others is in part, at least, that which belongs to the imposing nuptials about to be described.

9. מֹר *all thy garments* are *myrrh,* etc., so filled with these perfumes that they appear to consist of them. שֵׁן, palaces of ivory, the rooms of which were wainscoted or adorned with ivory, comp. 1 Kin. 22 : 39, Am. 3 : 15. מִנִּי § 199. b, is by some thought to be an abbreviated plural for מִנִּים *stringed instruments have gladdened thee ;* but as the existence of such a form of the plural is, to say the least, extremely doubtful, it is better to regard it as a prolonged form of the prep. מִן emphatically repeated after the noun, comp. Isa. 59 : 18, *from ivory palaces, from them,* I say.   The subject of the following verb will then be indefinite, § 243. 2. All kinds of delights were provided in these sumptuous palaces for this festive occasion.

10. The queen is in the allegory the church or chosen people ; the kings' daughters are representatives of their several nations. בִּיקְּרוֹתֶיךָ § 14. a, § 24. b. נִצְּבָה, not merely *stands* but *is placed* at thy right hand, this being the post of honour.

11. The Psalmist has thus far been occupied with the king, his character and greatness, and his part in these grand festivities.   He now turns to the queen, and reverting to the time immediately preceding the marriage which is already presupposed, ver. 10, finds her still in her father's house, awaiting the nuptial procession, and directs to her some

preliminary counsels, vs. 10–13. בַּת, a familiar form of address adopted by seniors, Ruth 2 : 8, or by teachers and advisers, Mat. 9 : 22.

12. וְיִתְאָו and *let the king desire*, equivalent to, so that he may desire. אָוָה § 201. 2, comp. Gen. 39 : 2. —וְהִשְׁתַּחֲוִי § 176. 1, denotes prostration, either in token of respect or of religious worship, and is hence particularly appropriate in describing the homage to be paid to this divine bridegroom.

13. וּבַת־צֹר, not a vocative, *O daughter of Tyre*, as some have rendered it, on the hypothesis that the Psalm celebrates the marriage of Solomon with a Tyrian princess, or still more extravagant and incredible, that of Ahab with Jezebel, who was of the royal house of Zidon, 1 Kin. 16 : 31. Daughter of Tyre, like daughter of Zion, daughter of Babylon, daughter of Egypt, is a personification of its inhabitants, and is here the subject of the following verb which agrees with it as a collective in the plural, § 275. 2 ; the same verb is to be supplied to עֲשִׁירֵי. Tyre is singled out on account of its wealth and commercial prosperity, with allusion to which 'the rich of the people,' i. e. the richest § 254. 2. *a* of every nation, עָם, in the same wide, indefinite sense as Isa. 42 : 6.

14. פְּנִימָה *within*, i. e. in her father's palace, and ready for the procession which is to convey her to the house of the bridegroom.

15. To add to the significance of the allegory the usages of real life are here departed from, and the virgin companions of the bride, identical with the kings' daughters, ver. 10, are themselves also conducted to the king precisely as the bride was. They too are wedded to him, signifying that Gentile nations shall be with Israel, and like Israel espoused to Messiah, and share the blessings of his love and favour. לְרִקְמָה, for sense of prep. see on Gen. 2 : 18. לֶךְ § 65. *a*, suf. is masc. referring to the king.

17. His sons shall replace or eclipse his ancestors, be kings as they had been, and more illustrious, inasmuch as he would partition his wide empire among them, comp. 2 Sam. 8 : 18, 1 Kin. 4 : 7, 2 Chron. 11 : 28. בְּכָל־הָאָרֶץ, not *in all the land*, but *in all the earth*, as appears from the subjugation, ver. 6, and homage, ver. 18, of the nations, and the submission of Tyre, ver. 13.

18. The church, in whose name the Psalmist speaks, shall render everlasting praise to the king, in which the nations shall join. עַל־כֵּן *therefore*, stimulated by the praise of the church, or referring back to the previous contents of the Psalm, which are also the ground of the pledge given in the preceding clause.

PSALM LXXII.

Messiah as the ideal Solomon. The reign of the former is depicted in features drawn from the latter, but freed from all imperfection and limitation, extended over all the earth and reaching through all time. Its universality and unending duration absolutely preclude any other subject. It could not, by the most strained exaggeration, be applied to Solomon himself, either in the way of description or of hopes indulged and supplications offered on his behalf. He neither ruled the whole world, nor cherished any expectation of doing so. This kingdom is described in its equity, vs. 1–4, perpetuity and everlasting consequences, vs. 5–7, universality, vs. 8–11, protection of the needy and defenceless, vs. 12–15, prosperity and renown, vs. 16. 17. The Psalm is concluded or followed by a doxology, vs. 18. 19, and a subscription, ver. 20.

1. לִשְׁלֹמֹה, prep. as in לְדָוִד 3 : 1, *by Solomon*, lit. 'belonging to Solomon' as its author. מִשְׁפָּטֶיךָ, not thy rights or prerogatives, but *thy judgments*, judicial decisions, and this not merely as precedents for his guidance, but make thy infallible decisions his, give to his administration the perfection of thine. תֵּן is in form a prayer; but as the Psalmist asks for that which he knows will certainly be granted, it is equivalent to a prediction with the added force of an earnest desire for its accomplishment. לְבֶן־מֶלֶךְ § 247, *the king's son*, is the same as the king of the first clause, who is thus declared to be of royal descent.

2. יָדִין, the form of petition is exchanged for that of confident assertion. עֲנִיֶּיךָ *thy afflicted* ones, either equivalent to thy people, who are characteristically sufferers, or distinguishing those amongst them who are in a peculiarly suffering condition, inasmuch as God is the especial patron of such, and under a less beneficent and impartial government they would be exposed to injustice and oppression. בְמִשְׁפָּט *in* the exercise of *justice*.

3. This equal government shall be productive of peace, which is represented as springing up from the soil, borne by the mountains and hills, which fitly represent the country as its prominent features and constituting so considerable a portion of the whole. The fertility of the hills of ancient Palestine, which were terraced and cultivated to their summits, adds to the beauty and appositeness of the figure. יִשְׂאוּ belongs to both clauses of the verse, and is qualified by בִּצְדָקָה § 22. *a* (5), which shows the mode of the production; this harvest of peace, in its wide sense of welfare and prosperity as well as freedom from strife and war, is brought forth by righteousness.

4. יִשְׁפֹּט *judge*, do justice to. לִבְנֵי אֶבְיוֹן *sons of the needy*, not merely poor, but born in poverty, and therefore without rich and influential friends.

5. יִרָאוּךָ, suf. refers to God, who is addressed ver. 1, while the king is spoken of throughout in the third person. The unending prevalence of piety shall be the result of this righteous reign, of course implying the perpetuity of the reign itself. עִם־שָׁמֶשׁ *with the sun*, as long as it exists, comp. Dan. 3 : 33. וְלִפְנֵי *before the moon*, as long as it is present and shines upon them. דּוֹר דּוֹרִים. an idiomatic phrase, which occurs likewise 102 : 25, Is. 51 : 8, denoting perpetual duration, whether it is to be explained as an emphatic repetition, like דּוֹר דּוֹר Ex. 3 : 15, Prov. 27 : 24, or the more usual דּוֹר וָדוֹר § 280. 2 and *a*, *generation* upon *generations*, or as in the construct relation, *generation of generations*, a superlative combination, § 254. 2. *a*, like *king of kings*, *servant of servants*, a period embracing all generations within itself, or beside which ordinary generations are insignificant.

6. Figure denoting beneficent influence.

8. The extent of his dominion. It is the kingdom of Solomon expanded to the dimensions of the earth itself. The language here used takes its shape from the bounds assigned to the promised land, Ex. 23 : 31, omitting its limitations. 'From the Red sea even unto the sea of the Philistines' becomes 'from sea to sea,' i. e. from ocean to ocean, from side to side of the sea-surrounded continents. 'From the desert unto the river' becomes 'from the river unto the ends of the earth,' i. e. from the Euphrates in both directions to the utmost limits of the world. וְיֵרְדְּ § 172. 4, *let him have dominion*, or *may he* have dominion, either an authoritative proclamation or a return to the form of petition with which the Psalm began, see on ver. 1.

9. To this universal submission there shall be no exception. Even צִיִּים, rude and barbarous tribes, shall own his sway. עָפָר יְלַחֵכוּ, figure of complete prostration, suggesting too, perhaps, that in them is realized the doom of the serpent and his seed, Gen. 3 : 14.

10. He shall receive tribute from the most distant and wealthy monarchs. וְרָאִים, see on Isa. 40 : 15. יָשִׁיבוּ, the same phrase is used of the payment of tribute, 2 Kin. 17 : 3; the same verb with אֶשְׁכָּר, which here stands in the parallel clause, in Ezek. 27 : 15. Some have thought that the verb suggests the notion of the repeated payments exacted from vassals, who are required to *return* with it again and again; more probably it implies a *return* or compensation for benefits received. אֶשְׁכָּר 1 Kin. 10 : 1.

11. וְיִתְחַזְּקוּ־. see on 45 : 12.

12. כִּי־. The homage thus yielded to him by every nation, is due

to his character as a ruler. *They shall serve him because,* etc. יַאְרִ־
§ 285. 3.

14. וְיֵיקַר־ § 147. 4, *their blood shall be precious,* he sets a high value
upon their life and will not suffer it to be destroyed, comp. 116 : 15,
1 Sam. 26 : 21, 2 Kin. 1 : 13. 14.

15. וִיחִי־, the subject of this and of the following verbs is the ran-
somed poor of the preceding verses taken distributively, § 275. 6 ; *and
let him live and he will give to him,* his Redeemer and King, *of the gold
of Sheba* in acknowledgment of the favour shown him, and in token of
subjection to his sway, *and he shall pray for him* for the increase of his
glory and the advancement of his cause and kingdom. The jussive
form has here a conditional force, as surely as he lives he will do this.
Others make Messiah the subject of some or all the verbs in this verse.

16. Its prosperity set forth under the figure of the unexampled multiplication of the products of the earth. *Let there be a handful of grain
in the earth* or land, *on the top of mountains* even, in spots least favourable for its cultivation and growth, and it shall produce a harvest that
shall wave and rustle in the breeze like the cedars of Lebanon. יְהִי־, the
jussive, as in ver. 15, is conditional. ־פִּסַּת, some render *abundance.*
A like rapid increase of its inhabitants. מֵעִיר־ *the city,* the abode of
men, comp. Num. 24 : 19.

17. וִיהִי, apoc. fut. see on ver. 8. לִפְנֵי־. see on ver. 5. יָנִין K'ri,
יָנוֹן K'thibh. ־וְיִתְבָּרְכוּ § 35. 1, *bless themselves by him,* the richest blessings shall be his, so that men can desire nothing higher for themselves
or others than to be like him, Gen. 48 : 20, or *be blessed in him,* i. e. in
virtue of their union to him or connection with him.

18. According to the prevalent opinion this doxology, however appropriate after so enraptured a prospect of the glorious future, is not a
part of the Psalm itself, but marks the close of the second division or
book of Psalms, each of which ends in like manner, 41 : 14, 89 : 53,
106 : 48 ; Ps. 150, the conclusion of the whole, is itself an extended
doxology.

19. אֶת־כָּל־הָאָרֶץ § 271. *a,* the sentence is taken from Num. 14 : 21.

20. כָּלּוּ § 93. *a.* Appended to this Psalm these words might mean,
' This sums up all that my father David desired and prayed for.' But such
a subscription sounds strangely at the end of a Psalm written by another
than David himself ; and particularly as it follows instead of preceding
the doxology, it may more naturally be thought to refer in like manner to
the books or divisions of the Psalter. *The Psalms* (תְּפִלּוֹת *prayers,* hence
psalms which consist largely of supplications, comp. 17 : 1, 86 : 1, 102 : 1,
Hab 3 : 1) *of David the son of Jesse are ended.* The Psalms of the

two preceding books, Ps. 1–41, 42–72, are with few exceptions those of David; the three books that follow, Ps. 73–89, 90–106, 107–150, contain few that are ascribed to him. In a general sense, therefore, this is the point of transition from the Psalms of David to those of other inspired singers. Some have doubtfully conjectured that this marks the end of an original collection of the Psalms, to which the name of 'the Psalms of David' was given, because they were mainly written by him, just as the entire book in its present compass is frequently so denominated for the same reason; and that the remaining portion of the collection was incorporated with it at a subsequent period. The book of Proverbs affords an instance of such an enlargement, see Prov. 25:1, as this hypothesis supposes in the Psalter.

PSALM CX.

Messiah, the ideal Melchizedek, at once king and priest by express divine appointment; his sway is resistless and his priesthood perpetual. That the subject can be no other than the Messiah is evident, since by the established regulations of the Jewish economy the regal and sacerdotal offices were preserved distinct, the one being hereditary in the family of David, and the other in that of Aaron. Saul lost the kingdom for presuming to offer sacrifice, 1 Sam. 13:9 ff, and Uzziah was smitten with leprosy for venturing into the temple to burn incense, 2 Chron. 26: 16 ff. Only he, in whom all the types centre, could be a priest upon his throne, Zech. 6:13. The messianic character of this Psalm is abundantly declared in the New Testament. Our Lord, in argument with the Pharisees, Mat. 22:43. 44, Mark 12:36, Luke 20:42. 43, sanctions this exposition of it, as well as its composition by David, and implies that these were universally acknowledged. Ver. 1 is quoted of Christ, Acts 2:34. 35, 1 Cor. 15:25, Heb. 1:13, 10:12. 13, and is the basis of all those passages which speak of his sitting at the right hand of God, Mat. 26:64, Mark 16:19, Acts 7:55, Rom. 8:34, Eph. 1:20, Col. 3:1, Heb. 1:3, 8:1, 12:2, 1 Pet. 3:22. Ver. 4 is quoted of him Heb. 5:6, 7:17. 21, and is explained at large in ch. 7 of this Epistle.

1. נְאֻם, David's calling Christ his Lord implies the mysterious constitution of his person, Mat. 22:45. שֵׁב, session at the right hand of God is equivalent to sitting with him on his throne, Rev. 3:21, and implies association with God in supreme dominion. עַד. From this passage taken singly it might be doubtful whether this particle is to be understood exclusively or inclusively, as Gen. 28:15, Ps. 112:8, that

is to say, whether the session at God's right hand, which is to continue *until* the subjugation of all foes, shall then cease, or shall be perpetual, being thenceforward freed even from the semblance of opposition. From the exposition of the apostle, 1 Cor. 15 : 24–28, however, we learn that while the Messiah is to have an everlasting kingdom, as the prophets unanimously testify, his session at the right hand of God is subject to the limitation here affixed to it. The delegation of universal authority to the Messiah is to last until the purposes of his administration are complete, but no longer. After his people are all redeemed, and his foes all subdued, he shall, in his capacity as Messiah, have no further occasion to retain the control of the universe, but shall deliver it up unto his Father. Thenceforward he shall hold simply his headship over his own people, and God shall be all in all as before the mediatorial reign began. הֲדֹם, figure of complete subjugation, comp. 1 Kin. 5 : 17 (Eng. Ver. 3), Josh. 10 : 24.

2. מַטֵּה *the rod*, as an instrument of chastisement, or as others suppose, in the sense of שֵׁבֶט 'sceptre,' though מַטֵּה has this meaning nowhere else, *of thy strength*, not thy strong rod, but the rod or sceptre of thy strength, the symbol of it, or that by which thy strength is displayed. יִשְׁלַח *send forth* on its errand of judgment from Zion the centre and seat of the theocracy; others, *stretch forth*, as 1 Sam. 14 : 27. רְדֵה, the command implies that there is nothing to prevent his doing as he is enjoined.

3. The instruments of his victories. עַמְּךָ *thy people* are *free-will offerings*, voluntarily offer themselves to the service of their king in his conflict with his foes, comp. the use of the cognate verb, Judg. 5 : 2. 9. חֵילֶךָ *day of thy power*, when it is exerted, or *of thy host*, the marshalling of thy forces. בְּהַדְרֵי־קֹדֶשׁ *in ornaments of holiness*, adorned with sacred vestments; not equipped as ordinary warriors, but in sacerdotal robes, since they are a kingdom of priests, Ex. 19 : 6, and it is not by carnal weapons that they prevail, comp. 2 Chron. 20 : 21. 22, where לְהַדְרַת־קֹדֶשׁ has the same sense as the phrase here used (לְ as in לִרְקָמוֹת Ps. 45 : 15). מֵרֶחֶם *from the womb of morning*, from which the dew is poetically represented as born; others take the prep. in its comparative sense, § 260, *more than the womb*. יַלְדֻתֶיךָ, in the only other passage in which this word occurs, Eccles. 11 : 9. 10, it denotes the early period of life; taken in this sense here, *the dew of thy youth* would mean, thy fresh and vigorous youth, which is perpetually renewed, like dew from the womb of morning. But it agrees better with the connection to understand 'youth' as a collective for young men, and thus as equivalent to 'thy people' in the first clause. These are as numerous

and universally diffused as the drops of dew, 2 Sam. 17:12, with allusion likewise, perhaps, to their sudden and noiseless appearance, and the mysterious agency by which they are produced, Mic. 5:6 (7).

4. נִשְׁבַּע, the solemnity of such an oath implies not only its inviolable truth, but the superlative importance of the subject. וְלֹא יִנָּחֵם, it is an oath that he never will recall. דִּבְרָתִי § 218, *after the manner,* character, or order, not of Aaron, who was purely a priest, but *of Melchizedek*, § 195. 3, § 218. *a,* who was both priest and king, Gen. 14:18.

5, 6. אֲדֹנָי § 199. *c,* a form used only of God as the supreme Lord. *The Lord at thy right hand* is not Messiah here designated by a divine title, but Jehovah, since Messiah is throughout the person addressed. That Jehovah is here spoken of as at the right hand of the Messiah, whereas the converse is the case in ver. 1, only shows that both expressions are figurative. He is at his right hand to aid and support him, 16:8, 109:31. מָחַץ, the alternation of tenses here and in the next verse shows that the ideal position of the Psalmist is in the midst of what he is describing, § 263. 5. *a.* He has already smitten kings; but not content with this he is going on still to judge יָדִין the nations; and now, as this majestic and fearful process has been proceeding even while the Psalmist speaks, *he has filled* the arena of the conflict, or מָלֵא intrans. *it is full of corpses,* § 271, *he has smitten the head over much land,* either collectively, as in the Eng. Ver., or some one of the more prominent and powerful of his foes, possibly the head and leader of the entire rebellious opposition, elsewhere denominated ' the prince of this world,' John 12:31, a passage which might on this view be regarded as parallel to the one now under examination ; אֶרֶץ רַבָּה might then be rendered *the wide earth,* as תְּהוֹם רַבָּה, Gen. 7:11, ' the great deep.' This blow, upon this latter understanding of it, would end the strife.

7. The refreshing draughts partaken of during or after the conflict with their reviving effect, comp. Judg. 15:18, 19. He shall not be so fatigued that he cannot prosecute the contest with vigour, nor so exhausted at its close that he cannot enjoy the fruits of victory. Others think that ' drinking of the brook in the way' denotes the unrelaxing ardour of the pursuit. He turns not aside to rest or to refresh himself, only partakes hastily of what he finds in his way, and presses without ceasing on. The subject in this verse is the Messiah, who by a change of person is here spoken of.

PROVERBS. CHAPTER VIII.

vs. 1–5. The publicity and universality of Wisdom's call.

vs. 6–21. The excellence and value of her instructions.

vs. 22–31. Her association with God himself in the production of his works.

vs. 32–36. Appeal to men to secure their own welfare by embracing her.

1. תִקְרָא § 263. 2, action already begun but to be continued in the future, *is she not crying?*

2. Wisdom occupies the most conspicuous positions, near the great thoroughfares, addressing the multitudes of passers by. עֲלֵי־דָרֶךְ § 238. 1. *o*, see on Ps. 1:3, Gen. 41:1; we speak in the same sense of houses being *on* the street. בֵּית place of *paths*, where they meet or cross; others, *within the paths*, not only on eminences by the roadside, but in the very road itself.

3. תָּרֹנָּה: § 97. 1, § 136. 1.   4. אִישִׁים § 207. 2. *e.*

5. פְּתָאיִם § 208. 3. *d.* לֵב may denote the intellectual faculty, *cause* your *heart to understand*, or better, as parallel to עָרְמָה, *intelligence*, that which is rational and sensible, which men are exhorted to *perceive* or *attend to.*

10. וְאַל § 264, qualifies the verb understood.   13. לִפְאֵת § 166. 2.

17. אֹהֲבֶיהָ, K'thibh has the 3 fem. suf., the indirect mode of speaking, for which the K'ri substitutes the first person. See a like instance, Judg. 16:18. אֵהָב § 111. 2. *b.* וּמְשַׁחֲרַי § 105. *c.* אֵתָן, the old rendering, *solid, durable,* is still preferred by many critics, and is most directly deducible from the signification of the root: others adopt the sense of *splendid.*

21. יֵשׁ is by some regarded as a noun meaning *substance, wealth,* lit. that which is or exists. There is no necessity, however, for departing from its usual sense, *there is* wherewith *to give inheritance to those who love me.*

24. נִכְבַּדְּתִּי– § 207. 2. *b.*   25. בְּטֶרֶם § 263. 1. *b.*

35. מֹצְאַי, K'thibh plur., inasmuch as the preceding singular is to be taken distributively, § 275. 6; the K'ri substitutes מֹצְאִי.

JOB. CHAPTER III.

2. וַיַּעַן, though nothing had as yet been said by his friends, there was a tacit demand in the circumstances of the case to which he makes reply. So Deut. 26:5, Isa. 14:10, where, as in this place, the Eng.

Ver. gratuitously substitutes 'speak' for 'answer;' comp. a like use of ἀποκρίνομαι in the New Testament, e. g. Mat. 11:25.

Job complains of three things:

(1) vs. 3–10, that he was ever born.

(2) vs. 11–19, that he was not suffered to die as soon as born.

(3) vs. 20–26, that he is still compelled to live in his incessant and intolerable anguish.

3. By a bold personification Job conceives of the day of his birth and the night of his conception as actual beings, which have inflicted a wanton and irreparable injury upon him, and he wishes them blotted from existence. His wish is not that their anniversaries may have no place in the calendar, or may be regarded as unlucky and inauspicious, but that the identical day and night may be non-existent. If they had never existed, he would not have been born. Job transfers himself in thought to the period before his birth, and the tenses are regulated by this ideal position. יוֹם, without the article because it is in the construct before a relative clause with the relative omitted, § 255. 2. אֲשֶׁר יֵ § 35. 1. אָמַר § 285. 3, it is a more natural construction. as well as more poetical, to read 'which *said*,' than 'in which one said.' גֶּבֶר, not *a man-child*, Eng. Ver., but *a man*, the name proper to the mature state being applied by anticipation to the infant or embryo. The emphasis is not upon the sex, implying greater joy at the birth of a son than a daughter; Job says 'a man' because he is speaking of himself. The two clauses of this verse are then separately expanded, the first in vs. 4. 5, the second in vs. 6–10. The poetic accents begin with ver. 3, and extend through the poetical portion of the book, § 31.

4. חֹשֶׁךְ *be darkness*, i. e. be no day at all. יִדְרְשֵׁהוּ *seek it*, to bring it out of this darkness into which he had wished it converted. אֱלוֹהַּ is used throughout the poetry of this book almost to the exclusion of the customary plural. It is found besides in a few other poetical passages, and but rarely in prose. נְהָרָה occurs only in this place, though common in Arabic.

5. יִגְאָלֻהוּ, not *stain*, Eng. Ver., but *redeem* or *reclaim*, bring back into their possession, as he who had parted with his property through stress of circumstances might redeem it. צַלְמָוֶת, compounded of צֵל and מָוֶת, § 195. 3; others derive it from צלם. supposing that it was prolonged from צַלְמָה, as רְבִישְׁלֵם from יְרִשָׁלַם. עֲנָנָה, in the judgment of many interpreters, not merely a single cloud, as עָנָן, but a mass or body of clouds covering the sky, § 198; though Gesenius thinks the relation of these words to be precisely the reverse, § 198. *b*. כִּמְרִירֵי, some make כ the prefixed prep., *as the bitternesses of a day*, like whatever can make

a day bitter and dreadful. It is better, however, to regard it as a radical, and to derive the word from נמר to be burned, then to be black,
§ 187. 2. e, hence obscurations. Let it suffer preternatural and alarm-
ing eclipse.

6. יחַדְ § 109. 2, § 172. 4, Kal apoc. fut. of יחֲדָה let it not rejoice
among the days of the year, Marg. Eng. Ver., not that it should be a
dismal, sorrowful day, but that it should not have the joy of belonging
to the days of the year. The days pass along, a merry, joyous band,
let it not be one of them. Of course not natural days, as in vs. 3. 4,
but civil days, embracing the entire diurnal period, in which sense they
include the night. The text of the Eng. Ver. renders it as though it
were יַחַד from יָחַד. בְּמִסְפַּר number of the months, i. e. of the days and
nights included in the months.

8. He wishes everything dire and dreadful to be heaped upon it or
employed against it, not only all real evils, but even such as are imaginary and fictitious. He, therefore, invokes the aid of sorcerers, who curse
the day, who claim the power of inflicting curses upon it, who are ready
to rouse leviathan, who, armed with their incantations, do not fear to
disturb the crocodile, as some understand it, while others suppose an allusion to serpent-charmers, and others still to the celestial serpent, whom
they instigated to swallow the sun and moon, thus producing eclipses.

9. Let it be black throughout, its twilight darkened and no dawn
succeeding it. תֵרְאֶה gaze with pleasure, see on Ps. 22 : 18, on the eye-
lids of the dawn, the first tremulous and struggling beams proceeding
from the sun, the eye of day.

10. The reason why he uttered these imprecations. בִטְנִי my womb,
that which bare me. וַיַּסְתֵּר, Vav Conv. implies a close connection of
this act with the preceding, it did not shut up, etc., and so hide. The
negative belongs to both clauses.

11. The ideal position of the speaker is shifted to the time immediately after birth. Hence the futures אָמוּת, :אֶגְוָע, and the preterite
יָצָאתִי.

13. כִּי for depends on the implied wish that he had been suffered
to perish uncared for. עַתָּה now, i. e. in the case supposed, I would have
lain down and would be quiet. Mark the change of tenses in the verbs,
all of which are affected by the preceding condition.

14. חֳרָבוֹת who built desolations, not tombs or mausoleums, nor, as
in Isa. 58 : 12, rebuilt ancient ruins, thus showing their power and greatness, but built stately edifices which are now, or soon will be, in ruins.

15. בָּתִּים, not their tombs, which some have imagined to be referred
to in this and the preceding verse, but their palaces and treasuries. The

reference is not to sums of money buried with the dead, but to the wealth possessed by them when living. : נֶכֶס § 271. 1, § 273. 1.

16. בְּפֶלֶ. By a bitter irony on worldly prosperity, kings, princes, and an abortion are all put into the same category; their condition is ultimately the same.

17. שָׁם *there*, i. e. where kings, counsellors, etc. are, the place or state of the dead. Mark the change of tenses.

18. שַׁאֲנַן § 122. 1.

19. הוּא, not predicate, *the same*, which is not the meaning of the pronoun, but copula, § 258. 2. : מְאַדֹּנָיו § 201. 2.

20. יִתֵּן, indef. § 243. 2, *why give*, or rather, as the future implies, *why continue to give*, equivalent to the passive construction, *why shall light*, i. e. life, comp. ver. 16, *be given*, not only why has it been and is it given, but why must it be given yet longer. Some supply 'God' as the subject, but this is unnecessary, and gives an uncalled for appearance of open and conscious murmuring to these moanings of uncontrollable anguish.

21. וַתְּבֹאֵנִי, change from participle to future with Vav Conversive, § 282. *c*.

23. לְגֶבֶר, construction resumed from ver. 20. Although he still speaks in general terms, the expressions show that he has his own case particularly in mind: the way is thus prepared for the next verse, in which he speaks directly of himself. וַיָּסֶךְ, pret., not part., as shown by the position of the accent, § 34; *whose way is hid*, who can discover no method of escape from these dreadful evils. יָסֶךְ, not as 1 : 10, to secure him from harm, but to shut him up to the endurance of suffering beyond the possibility of extrication.

24. כִּי, confirmatory; life is continued to those who are in this condition, *for such is my case*. לִפְנֵי *before*, sooner than; perpetually repeated, with greater frequency than his regular food. תָּבֹא, fut. in its frequentative sense, § 263. 4, so וַיִּתְּכוּ § 265. *a*.

25. The meaning is not that he had apprehensions in his former prosperity, which have now been fulfilled; but all that is dreadful in his esteem has been already, or is likely soon to be (יָבֹא fut.) realized in his experience. He endures all that he has ever conceived that is frightful. יִרֵאתִי § 172. 3, § 271. 2. יֶאֱתָיְנִי § 82. 1. *a* (3).

26. His sufferings are without intermission. There are no intervals of repose before fresh pains and troubles come. The triple repetition is emphatic. שָׁלַוְתִּי § 168. *a*.

CHAPTER XIX.

This chapter occupies a central position in the discussion, since it belongs to the second of the three series of discourses, and is uttered in reply to the second of the three friends. It is also the acme of Job's inward struggle. His greatest anguish arose from the thought which the tempter perpetually suggested, that God was cruelly pursuing him as an enemy. He here reaches the triumphant assurance, that in spite of all contrary appearances God is his redeemer, and will ultimately manifest himself as such. His bodily anguish remains. The mystery of God's dealings is still unsolved. But his personal relation to God is settled, and this gives him comparative peace. Whatever perplexity still clouds his mind, we hear no more the accents of unrelieved despair such as he has uttered hitherto.

vs. 2–22. Job entreats his friends not to aggravate the misery which God has sent upon him.

vs. 23–29. His confidence in God as his Redeemer.

2. תּוֹגְיוּן § 150. 2 (p. 181), § 172. 1. וּתְדַכְּאוּנַנִי § 105. *a* and *c*.

3. זֶה § 235. 3 (4). עֶשֶׂר, definite for a large indefinite number. תַּהְכְּרוּ־לִי § 263. 2, as their disposition is unchanged, he anticipates a continuance of the same treatment, see on Gen. 44 : 7. תַּהְכְּרוּ־, word of doubtful meaning. The Eng. Ver. renders it 'make yourselves strange,' comp. נֵכָר. From Arabic analogies some explain it to mean *stun, astonish,* and others, *treat unjustly, injure.*

4. Even if he was the guilty man that they suspected or alleged, this did not justify their treatment of him. He was himself the only sufferer by these imaginary misdeeds. He had not harmed them, and they ought not to treat him as if he had done so.

5. The condition may extend through the first clause, 'If ye will, etc., then § 287. 2 prove against me my reproach,' establish the charges with which you reproach me. Or it may extend through the entire verse, and the apodosis be found in that which follows.

6. עִוְּתָנִי. The mystery which so perplexed Job and misled his friends, was, that God appeared to be doing him a serious wrong; the sufferings inflicted upon him seemed like a declaration of his guilt, and was so understood and charged by his friends, when he was in fact innocent. This divine *perversion* of his case, this inequality in the divine proceedings, must not be urged in proof of his criminality. Others take the verb in the physical sense, *bent me down, overthrown me.*

7. אֶצְעַק *cry* at present with every prospect of continuing to do so in

17

the future, § 263. 2. חָמָס, governed directly by the verb; this was the cry that he uttered. Comp. in English, to cry murder!

8. The preterite עָשָׂה describes what God has already done; the future יָשִׂים what he is going on still further to do. These are not mutually exclusive, but supplementary, and are only poetically distinguished. Both the past, which is predicated of one act, and the future, predicated of the other, belong in fact to both.   15. מִפְּשָׁעַי § 105. e.

16. יַעֲנֵם, אֶקְרָא § 263. 1, futures relative to the preceding pret. קְרָאתִי, I called, he would not answer, I had to supplicate.

17. רוּחִי my breath, others, my spirit, as excited and querulous. זָרָה, pret. § 34, has become strange, offensive; there is no need of assuming a new root, or that the word is used in another than its proper Hebrew sense. וְחַנֹּתִי might be Kal pret. of חָנַן with Vav Conv. § 100. 2, which some render, I have to supplicate, a sense which the verb has in Hithpael but not in Kal, § 80. 1 (2), others, from an Arabic analogy, I am loathsome, but such a departure from the ordinary Hebrew usage in regard to a word of frequent occurrence is inadmissible, unless in cases of absolute necessity. Gesenius regards it as a plur. noun from חִנָּה with a suf. proper to sing. nouns. § 220. 2. a, then assuming a convenient sense and supplying the verb from the preceding clause, my entreaties are strange to, etc. It seems best to regard it as a Kal infin. with the fem. ending נִי, a few other examples of which occur, § 139. 2 ; not my supplicating, a sense which the Kal cannot have, but my caressing (lit. being gracious) is strange, repulsive to the sons of my womb, that from which I was born, as 3 : 10, my uterine brothers, not 'sons of my body,' my own children, none of whom were living. 1 : 19, though some have sought to escape this difficulty by assuming that the children of concubines or else grandchildren are intended.

18. אָקוּמָה, parag. fut. in a conditional sense, see on Ps. 72 : 15. 16, let me rise up, i. e. whenever I rise, they speak against me, ridiculing my painful and laboured movements ; or it may mean, when I rise to leave they slander me behind my back.

19. וַיְדַבְּרוּ, the plur. verb shows that the sing. subject must be understood as a collective.

20. בְּעוֹרִי, not an infin. from עָרָה with the baring of my teeth, i. e. denuded of the gums, which were wasted by disease, but as in the previous part of this same verse a noun, with the skin of my teeth, the insignificant membrane which covers the gums, a proverbial expression for a bare escape, though its origin is obscure and doubtful.

22. וּמִבְּשָׂרִי, figure from insatiable beasts of prey.

23. The second part of the chapter consists of an introduction.

showing Job's sense of the importance of what he was about to utter,
vs. 23. 24; his triumphant testimony, vs. 25–27; and a deduction from
it in the form of a warning to his friends, vs. 28. 29. מִי־יִתֵּן *who will
give*, an idiomatic mode of expressing a wish, *O that*, see on Ps. 4 : 7.
מִלָּי, the words, which he would have written, not on a fugitive leaf
merely, but recorded in a book for permanent preservation, are manifestly those which follow, not what he has said hitherto.

24. Not merely written, but cut in stone, and the letters filled with
molten lead, so that they might endure for all time.

25. וַאֲנִי, pron. emphatic, § 243. 1; Vav connects it with ver. 22,
the intervening verses being parenthetic, 'You persecute me relentlessly,
as though I were a friendless, heaven-forsaken man, *and yet I know*, if
you do not, that *my Avenger lives.'* גֹּאֵל § 35. 1, not merely *my Deliverer*, but *my Redeemer* or *Avenger*, see on Isa. 41 : 14. It belonged
to the Goel, who was the nearest kinsman, to espouse the cause of his
suffering or injured relative, to redeem his property if he had been forced
to part with it, to avenge his death if he had been unjustly slain. Such
a friend and protector Job had in God. אַחֲרוֹן *last*, not merely after
we are dead, nor generally at some future time, but in its absolute sense,
at the latest period of time. Possibly this word may here be used as an
attribute of God, Isa. 41 : 4, 44 : 6, 48 : 12, and be made the subject
of the verb. He who is *the Last shall arise* from his seeming inaction
and indifference, comp. Ps. 3 : 8, or *stand*, make his appearance. עַל־עָפָר,
not in the sense of the Latin *pulvis*, or *arena*, the scene of this contest,
but either *over the dust*, i. e. over my grave, as Ps. 22 : 16. 30, or better, *upon the earth*, as 41 : 25.

26. נִקְּפוּ, 3 pl. indef. § 243. 2, pret. relative to the following future,
§ 262. 1, *after my skin* or body, which *they shall have destroyed*, i. e.
which shall have been destroyed. זֹאת, adverbially *thus*, in the manner
in which it is now perishing; others regard the fem. as standing for the
neuter, and refer it to עוֹרִי *my skin*, viz. *this* which you here behold, or
to the declaration which he had just made, *this* shall take place, viz.,
the appearance of my Redeemer. וּמִבְּשָׂרִי *and out of my flesh*, disem-
bodied; others render, *from my flesh*, which, as his present body has
already been spoken of as destroyed, must then denote his resurrection
body. The terms of this and of the preceding verse show that Job could
not have meant that God would appear on his behalf in the present life,
and restore him again after his great emaciation. That he refers not to
recovery from disease, but to a divine vindication in the future state,
further appears from (1) the solemnity with which these words are introduced. The idea of graving upon the rock to endure forever a state-

ment which was to have an open and manifest fulfilment in a few days
at the furthest, is grandiloquent, if not absurd. (2) The condition of
Job, who is on the verge of the grave, 17 : 1. 11–16, and always repels
the idea of any earthly expectation whenever it is presented to him.
(3) The position maintained by Job in opposition to his friends. They
assert that men are rewarded in this life according to their characters.
Job denies it. If now the confidence which he here expresses is that of
an earthly reward, he comes over to their ground. (4) This is the oldest, as it has always been the most prevalent interpretation.

27. אֲנִי § 243. 1, I, the very person whom you think abandoned of
God. לִי *for me*, on my side. חָזָה, pret. relative to preceding future,
shall have beheld. זָר, some make the subject, *I, and not a stranger* in
my stead, shall behold him ; but better as the object, *behold* him *and
not estranged*, not inimical to me. כִּלְיֹ *my reins are consumed* with eager
longing for this glorious anticipation, comp. Ps. 119 : 123, or, according
to others, by this wasting disease, comp. Ps. 73 : 26.

28. Conditional sentence, the apodosis being found in the next
verse. *When ye say, How shall we persecute him*, what new assaults
shall we make upon him, *and the root of the matter*, the cause of all my
sufferings, *is found in me*, in sins of which you allege that I am guilty,—
when you treat me in this hard-hearted and unjust manner, then you
may well be afraid of the avenging sword of my great Redeemer.

29. חֵמָה *wrath*, the divine wrath awaits *transgressions of the sword*,
such transgressions as call for the sword of God's vengeance. Others,
wrath, such as you display in your harsh treatment of me, is *transgressions of the sword*. שָׁדוּן K'ri, שְׁדִין K'thibh, with the abbreviated relative, § 74 ; others, with less probability, think it to be a modified form
of the word שַׁדַּי *the Almighty*.

SONG OF SOLOMON.　CHAPTER I.

1. שִׁיר הַשִּׁירִים § 254. 2. *a*.　Marg. see on בְּרֵאשִׁית Gen. 1 : 1.

3. לְרֵיחַ *in respect to odour thy ointments are good; thy name is
ointment*, etc.

4. מֵישָׁרִים, abstr. for concrete, *the upright;* others take it adverbially, *they love thee uprightly*, sincerely.

6. שֶׁאֲנִי, the abbreviated relative, § 74, here used as a conjunction,
§ 239. 1. שָׁחֹרֶת § 188.

7. שַׁלָּמָה § 209. 1. *a*.　　　8. הַצֹּאן § 245. 2, § 260. 2 (2).

9. בְּסֻסָתִי § 218, the fem. has a collective sense, § 198.

15. יוֹנִים *thy eyes are doves*.　　17. Marg. see on Judg. 13 : 18.

CHAPTER II.

1. הַשָּׁרוֹן § 246. 1. *a.*   4. Marg. see on Gen. 44 : 10

5. חוֹלַּת, const. of source, § 254. 7.

7. אִם־ in an oath has a negative sense, see on Gen. 42 : 15.

12. הַזָּמִיר, the majority of modern interpreters render *singing,* i. e. of birds : Gesenius follows the LXX and Vulgate in giving it the sense of *pruning.*

13. סְמָדַר § 195. 1, are *blossoms,* i. e. in blossom.   לְכִי K'ri, לְכִי־ K'thibh, § 220. 1. *b* (2 per.).

14. Marg. see on Judg. 13 : 17.

THE END.